MW00388502

OF THE

Quarto.com

First Published in 2024 by Motorbooks, an imprint of The Quarto Group,
100 Cummings Center, Suite 265-D, Beverly, MA 01915, USA.
T (978) 282-9590 F (978) 283-2742

28 27 26 25 24 1 2 3 4 5

ISBN: 978-0-7603-8903-4

Digital edition published in 2024
eISBN: 978-0-7603-8904-1

Library of Congress Cataloging-in-Publication Data

Names: Graff, Gary, editor.
Title: 501 essential albums of the '90s / edited by Gary Graff.
Other titles: Five hundred and one essential albums of the '90s
Description: Beverly, MA : Motorbooks, 2024. | Includes index. | Summary: "501 Essential Albums of '90s is the ultimate curated list detailing dozens of the decade's most influential releases across all genres, featuring descriptions of the releases, album art, and artist imagery"– Provided by publisher.
Identifiers: LCCN 2024013356 | ISBN 9780760389034 (hardcover) | ISBN 9780760389041 (ebook)
Subjects: LCSH: Popular music–1991-2000–Discography.
Classification: LCC ML156.4.P6 A15 2024 | DDC 016.78164026/6–dc23/eng/20240326
LC record available at https://lccn.loc.gov/2024013356

Design & Page Layout: Justin Page
Cover Design: Justin Page

FSC
www.fsc.org
MIX
Paper | Supporting responsible forestry
FSC® C007207

Printed in Malaysia

501 ESSENTIAL ALBUMS OF THE '90s

THE MUSIC FAN'S DEFINITIVE GUIDE

EDITED BY GARY GRAFF

m

C O N T E N T S

For Arielle Ruth: This is the "old fogey" music your mom and dad listened to while they were growing up and that Grandpa wrote about while there was still a little bit of brown in his hair.

Introduction

This is a book that's designed to start arguments.

The very idea of choosing 501 essential albums from the tens, even hundreds of thousands released during a given decade is preposterous. Hell, even picking that many from a single year is a tall task. It's triage of the highest order. It goes beyond separating wheat from chaff; we're talking about determining the very highest yield in a judgment that's entirely subjective, though occasionally supported by consensus.

And yet, as music fans, we love to make these lists. They come out at the end of every year, and anymore there are half-year tallies in July, even monthly and weekly surveys of the X number of things you must hear in that period of time. It's great sport and fodder for discussion and disagreement, and when it works best, it becomes one music fan, or entity, turning another on to something they may not have heard or considered before.

It means we care—and that we care to find more than what we're fed on tight radio playlists or even random online playlists.

With this book, our goal is to encapsulate ten years of music into a collection of the best and most representative albums of that era. "Essential" is the guidepost; these are the albums you must hear to have an understanding and appreciation for all that happened between, in this case, 1990 and when we partied like it was 1999. Our contributors—a corps of music journalists, historians, musicians, and music enthusiasts—sought to balance terminally hip alternative and mainstream pop, the lowest common denominators, and the most far-flung experiments. The aim is to be comprehensive and encompass all genres without being precious and, if we did our job right, be able to hand you a book that says, "This is what you need to listen to to truly understand the decade."

Rest assured, it's no easy task, and there was a Gettysburg-worthy bloodletting that went on during the selection process. Many personal favorites were cast aside as we winnowed a significantly longer list down to these 501 entries, but there's also a passionate belief that each one belongs here and that these albums, taken in total, capture the complicated essence of what was music during the '90s.

The '90s was filled with dramatic changes in all aspects of music and the music business. Consider that as the decade began, CDs ruled, vinyl was gone, cassettes were going, and new media such as Digital Audio Tape (DAT) and MiniDisc (MD) were trying (but failing) to gain traction. Music sales were setting records, too, and it was not unusual for each week's No. 1 album to sell several hundred thousand and, in some cases, even a million copies during that first week of release. It was a bear market of the highest magnitude.

But it was also the decade that introduced us to MP3s and peer-to-peer (P2P) file sharing that would turn the industry upside down. That the music industry fought rather than embraced and enfolded the likes of Napster, BitTorrent, Freenet, Fastrack, and other services was shortsighted and became its undoing. The proverbial Pandora's box was opened, and fans chafed by overpriced CDs were more than willing to side with the pirates and get their music for free, regardless of the havoc it wreaked on the industry and, more importantly, the artists. The impact was increasingly felt as we entered the twenty-first century, but a storm was rising as the twentieth came to an end.

The music itself, meanwhile, was all over the place. The global taste consensus built by MTV began to crack early as mainstream rock and "hair metal" was plowed under in short order by an alternative rock scene led by what we'd come to call grunge out of the Pacific Northwest. After having nothing but a good time during much of the '80s, the '90s ushered in more angst and anger, whether it was from Nirvana and Pearl Jam or the new generation of gangsta rappers keeping it real in vivid, cinematic verbal detail. Even among acts signed to major labels, there was a refreshed indie spirit, a punk ethic (even if they weren't truly punk) that raged against the machine from within—and communicated a new sense of empowerment both for the bands and the listeners.

That was a prevailing theme, but the '90s offered even more than that, in every genre. Electronic music of all styles flourished, and Pop with a capital P made a comeback with new boy bands (Backstreet Boys, *NSYNC) and star singers (Britney Spears). Stalwarts held their own and, in some cases (U2's *Achtung Baby*, say, or Tom Petty's *Wildflowers*), reached new peaks. There were reunions and one-off collaborations, a surge in West Coast rap and resurgence from the East Coast, a fresh generation of country artists taking that scene into the multiplatinum orbit while a fertile alt-country/Americana scene emerged alongside, and a wealth of film soundtracks that provided new avenues for exposure. It was by all measures the most prolific and the most profitable decade for music and music sales to date—and since.

And perhaps most importantly, the exponentially increased access to the internet gave music fans vehicles to find all of these things (and more) and assume more active control over their listening habits. Monolithic media gave way to individual and compartmentalized experiences, which made the world a little smaller but the musical landscape significantly larger. Because of that, the '90s was not so arguably the last of the "great" decades when music had a chance to land, stick, and cement itself into the cultural zeitgeist. In other words, we'll be celebrating and listening to *Nevermind*, Metallica's "The Black Album," *No Fences*, *The Chronic*, and *Doggystyle* for decades, more so than so much of what came after.

With *501 Essential Albums of the '90s*, we've captured all that drama as a context, but our primary concern is the music. There was a lot of it, and a lot of it was so damn good. So dive in; we hope the book jogs some memories, causes you to pull out something you haven't listened to for a while, and hopefully find some new things to check out that you haven't heard before. It's quite possible your very favorite album is not here, but we're confident that these 501 indeed represent the very best of a pinnacle decade in music history.

Gary Graff, *editor*

Contributors

Gary Graff (GG) (editor) is an award-winning music journalist based in Detroit. He is a regular contributor to *Guitar Player*, the Cleveland *Plain Dealer*, Media News Group, *Ultimate Classic Rock*, United Stations Radio Networks, *Music Connection*, *Classic Rock*, *VenuesNow*, and other publications and has a featured weekly music news report on WHQG-FM in Milwaukee. He is the author of *Alice Cooper @ 75* and the co-author of *Neil Young: Long May You Run* and *Rock 'n' Roll Myths: The True Stories Behind the Most Infamous Legends* (both with Daniel Durchholz), and of *Travelin' Man: On the Road and Behind the Scenes with Bob Seger* (with Thomas Weschler), a Michigan Notable Book honoree. Graff also edited *The Ties That Bind: Bruce Springsteen A to E to Z* and was the series editor of the *MusicHound Essential Album Guide* series. He's contributed to other books such as *Whole Lotta Led Zeppelin*; *AC/DC: High-Voltage Rock 'n' Roll, The Ultimate Illustrated History*; *4 Way Street: The Crosby, Stills, Nash & Young Reader*; *Heaven Was Detroit: From Jazz to Hip-Hop and Beyond*; and *Fleetwood Mac: The Complete Illustrated History*, among others. Graff is also co-founder and co-producer of the Emmy Award–winning Detroit Music Awards.

Cary Baker (CB) is a writer and music historian based in the Palm Springs, California, area. The Chicago native and longtime Los Angeles resident headed publicity departments for six record companies (including Capitol and I.R.S.) and operated his own music PR firm, Conqueroo, from 2004 to 2022. He worked with such artists as R.E.M., Bonnie Raitt, Smithereens, James McMurtry, the Mavericks, Bobby Rush, Willie Nile, Marshall Crenshaw, Big Star, Colin Hay, Delbert McClinton, and Billy Joe Shaver. He's contributed to publications such as *Trouser Press*, *Hit Parader*, *Bomp!*, *Creem*, *No Depression*, *HITS*, *Best Classic Bands*, and *Blues & Rhythm* in the UK and written album and box-set liner notes for several record labels. He's also co-produced reissues, including a Blues Music Award–winning box set for Bobby Rush. Cary has served on the Recording Academy Board of Governors in Los Angeles and Chicago.

Zach Clark (ZC) grew up in metro Detroit and graduated from the University of Arizona with a degree in journalism. He spent a decade doing sports/talk radio and then transitioned to work as a news radio anchor. Today, Clark is an award-winning Detroit-based podcaster.

Jeff Corey (JC) was responsible for publicizing more than four thousand concerts and events during his nineteen years working for Palace Sports & Entertainment based out of The Palace of Auburn Hills in Michigan. In addition to events at The Palace, he also publicized shows at the company's other Michigan venues, including the Pine Knob Music Theatre, the Meadow Brook Music Festival, and Freedom Hill Amphitheater.

Ann Delisi (AD) has been a staple in Detroit's media landscape for more than forty years, working at a number of radio stations as an award-winning music director and on-air host. She is an accomplished voice-over talent, emcee, interviewer, producer, and podcaster. Presently, she hosts *Essential Music* on WDET-FM, which she launched in 2009, and since 2021 co-hosts and produces the *Don Was Motor City Playlist* with record producer and Blue Note Records President Don Was. She is a member of the Executive Committee and is the marketing chair for the Greening of Detroit and co-owns the Sprout House Natural Market, serving the Grosse Pointe Park, Michigan, community for forty years.

Marc Dorian (MD) holds a bachelor of arts in music from St. F.X. University in his native Nova Scotia. He's been entertaining audiences across the US and Canada since 1995 as a full-time piano player, keyboardist, and vocalist. A Detroit Music Award nominee, his songwriting has earned an Honorable Mention in the Billboard Song Contest and a Semi-Finalist slot in the International Songwriting Competition.

Whether as a DJ, music journalist, marketer, or author, **Helene Dunbar** (HD) has done her best to incorporate music in every aspect of her life. As a decades-long contributor to *Irish Music* magazine, she covered traditional music in the US, later working in marketing for a Nashville-based roots music label. As a writer of fiction for young adults, particularly 2019's award-winning *We Are Lost and Found*, set in the mid-'80s, she's aimed to pay homage to the music and artists who shaped her worldview.

Veteran music journalist **Daniel Durchholz** (DD) is the co-author of *Neil Young: Long May You Run* and *Rock and Roll Myths: The True Stories Behind the Most Infamous Legends* and co-editor of *MusicHound Rock: The Essential Album Guide* (all with Gary Graff). A former editor at *Request* and *Replay* magazines, STLtoday.com, and the *Riverfront Times*, he has written for numerous national and local publications. He lives in Wildwood, Missouri.

Bryan Frink (BF) is a Detroit-based musician, attorney, and woodworker. He's been performing and releasing albums on the Detroit music scene since the mid-'90s. He is currently a member of the Americana band the Steve Taylor Three, who won a 2023 Detroit Music Award for its single "Raining on Christmas," which was recorded and engineered by Bryan at Frink Studios, Inc., located at his home in Beverly Hills, Michigan. He is a graduate of Albion College and has a Juris Doctorate from Wayne State University Law School.

Michael Gallucci (MG) is the managing editor at *Ultimate Classic Rock*. His previous gigs include editor-of-chief at Diffuser.fm, managing editor of *Cleveland Scene*, and writing about music and movies for *All Music Guide*, *American Songwriter*, the A.V. Club, *Paste*, *Spin*, the *Village Voice*, and other publications and websites.

Adam Graham (AG) is a reporter covering music and entertainment in Detroit, Michigan. A native of Rochester Hills, Michigan, he studied journalism at Central Michigan University and started his career in Palm Springs, California. He has worked at the *Detroit News* since 2002. He was a teenager for most of the '90s.

Howard Handler (HH) is the president of 313 Presents, Detroit's premier live entertainment company spanning seven venues. His career included stops at Lorne Michaels's Broadway Video, MTV, NFL, Virgin Mobile, EMI Music, Madison Square Garden, and Major League Soccer. A lifelong music fan and student of pop culture, he was born and raised in Detroit.

Mike Himes (MH) has been in the music industry since 1979, primarily in the retail sector of the industry. In 1983, he opened Record Time, an independent record store in the Detroit area that grew into a world-renowned music outlet until its closing in 2011. During the twenty-eight years it was open, Record Time became the largest independent record store in the Midwest and was known for its importance in helping to develop and promote the electronic music and rap scene in the Detroit area and beyond. He has contributed to many Detroit-area magazines over the years and has served on the Detroit Music Awards steering committee. He is still active in selling music online and still works at the local record store in his hometown.

Margy Holland (MH2) is a Nashville-based writer. She served as the Country Editor for United Stations Radio Networks for more than twenty years, providing daily music news to more than nine million radio listeners per week. She has also written entertainment news for Yahoo! and Launch Radio Networks.

Brad Hundt (BH) is a veteran journalist whose career has included everything from covering municipal meetings to meeting a Beatle. The winner of several statewide and regional awards for feature, entertainment, and opinion writing, he is the editor of the opinion pages for the *Observer-Reporter* and *Herald-Standard* newspapers in Pennsylvania.

Charlie Hunt (CH) has covered jazz and adventurous music for the *Oakland Press*, the *Detroit Free Press*, and *Billboard*. He's an inveterate musicaholic who started listening to classic British rock bands, then swerved to jazz/rock and fusion pioneers such as Santana, Mahavishnu Orchestra, Chick Corea, Herbie Hancock, Steely Dan, Frank Zappa, and Bill Bruford's Earthworks. His musical interests range from Miles Davis and Joni Mitchell to Carla Bley, Laurie Anderson, Philip Glass, Jazzrausch Big Band, and the entire ECM Records catalog. He lives in Royal Oak, Michigan.

Fred Jacobs (FJ) is a veteran audience researcher and consultant from Detroit. Credited with inventing the Classic Rock radio format, he is a frequent speaker at industry events throughout the world. His company, Jacobs Media, celebrated its fortieth year in business during 2023, representing commercial, public, and Christian stations. He was inducted into the Radio Hall of Fame in 2018.

Howard Kramer (HK) is a writer, freelance museum consultant, and the former curatorial director of the Rock & Roll Hall of Fame.

Monte Mallin (MM) has been rabidly enjoying music for decades. He loves hard rocking bands like The Rolling Stones, AC/DC, Cheap Trick, . . . and Sparks? Yes, Sparks. He's been enjoying, and thinking hard about, their music since 1974 and is still obsessing over them today. He writes about them on his blog (montesnewblog.blogspot.com) and hosts a YouTube show entitled *Sparks: Entertainment and Art.* Someday, he'll figure out what it is that makes them so great. He's five decades into that project now.

Toby Mamis (TM) started out writing for underground papers and rock magazines in 1968 at the age of fifteen, including *Creem* and *Zoo World.* He moved on to doing publicity for, among others, John Lennon & Yoko Ono, the Hollies, Suzi Quatro, the New York Dolls, Lynyrd Skynyrd, and Blondie, then moved into management with Blondie, the Runaways, Joan Jett, and, currently, Alice Cooper, with whom he's worked since 1986. He appears in documentaries about Joan Jett, *Creem*, the Runaways, and Suzi Quatro.

Lynne Margolis (LM) published her first album review in Penn State University's *Daily Collegian* before MP3s, CDs, or even cassettes existed. She's since contributed to print, broadcast, and online media, including the *Christian Science Monitor*, *American Songwriter*, and *Paste* magazines; Rollingstone.com; Grammy.com; the Bluegrass Situation; NPR and various affiliates; newspapers nationwide; and dozens of regional and local magazines. She's collected inductee oral histories for the Rock & Roll Hall of Fame and Museum and contributed to the *MusicHound Essential Album Guide* series and *The Ties That Bind: Bruce Springsteen A to E to Z.* She's also toked with Willie Nelson.

Scott Mervis (SM) is an award-winning writer for the *Pittsburgh Post-Gazette*, where he's been covering music since the mid-'80s. It was a Kiss concert in 1977 that set him in motion.

Dennis Pernu (DP) is an editor and writer whose words have appeared in the *Minneapolis Star Tribune*, *Vintage Guitar*, and *No Depression.* He is credited as co-author, with Jim Walsh, of *The Replacements: Waxed-Up Hair and Painted Shoes.* Dennis lives in Minneapolis, six and thirteen blocks, respectively, from Prince's and Paul Westerberg's middle schools.

Edward Pevos (EP) is a statewide features, entertainment, travel, trending, and breaking news reporter with MLive.com, for which he covers many of the biggest events all over Michigan, interviews some of the most famous celebrities and their respective fields, and spotlights amazing things around the state that few know exist. He's spent more than two decades in journalism, as a television news producer prior to MLive—most recently in one of the largest TV news markets in the country in southeast Michigan. He is a graduate of Oakland University in metro Detroit and was born and raised in Michigan.

Carl B. Phillips (CP) is an award-winning international gospel recording artist, songwriter, producer, and actor. He's the owner of Prove Me Gospel Radio, a twenty-four-hour internet gospel radio station, and the host of *The Carl B. Phillips Show Podcast.* A fifty-year gospel music veteran, his history includes being on-air announcer for Detroit Gospel Radio and local booking coordinator for the Motor City Praise Fest, and he's been serving in his local church music department since 1976.

Gary Plochinski (GP) spent thirty-five years as a copywriter/associate creative director at various advertising agencies, including BBDO and J. Walter Thompson. He's also taught writing at the College for Creative Studies in Detroit and was a founding member of Detroit-area polka rockers band the Polish Muslims.

Mike Rankin (MR) is a retired media sales executive specializing in music and concert clients at Detroit's alternative weekly *Metro Times* during the '90s and later at alternative radio stations 89X, The River, and public radio WDET. His music tastes have been influenced by decades of guest list privileges, complimentary CDs, concert tickets (he paid for many, too), and attending South by Southwest and other festivals. Programming types often said what he liked "doesn't test well in the demo."

Tim Roberts (TR) is vice president/brand manager and Audacy Country format captain with more than four decades of on-air and radio programming background across the US. He currently oversees twenty Audacy Country stations and Audacy Country Network as well as Audacy Exclusive channels, while also actively programming WYCD-FM and WOMC-FM in Detroit and KMNB-FM Minneapolis. In 2016, he was elected to the National Country Radio Hall of Fame and is a multiple Academy of Country Music (ACM),

Country Music Association (CMA), and Marconi Award winner. He serves on the board of directors for the ACM, CMA, and the Country Radio Broadcasters Central Michigan and Cabrini, as well as the St. Jude Advisory Board. He was voted Radio Ink's No. 1 Country Programmer in 2021 and named to Radio Ink's Best PDs in America list then and during 2023. He currently resides between Farmington Hills, Michigan, and Nashville.

Starting with Xerox fanzine journalism in high school, **Rob St. Mary** (RSM) worked as a reporter/producer in commercial and public radio and podcasts for more than twenty years with stints at WWJ (Detroit), WOOD (Grand Rapids), WDET (Detroit), KAJX (Aspen), the *Detroit Free Press*, and *The Projection Booth Podcast*. He has produced two feature films, received Michigan Notable Book Award honors for his book *The Orbit Magazine Anthology*, and is a Knight Arts challenge grant awardee for documenting Detroit's late-'70s punk rock scene.

Christopher Scapelliti (CS) is editor-in-chief of *Guitar Player*, the world's longest-running guitar magazine, founded in 1967. He has authored in-depth interviews with such guitarists as Pete Townshend, Slash, Billy Corgan, Jack White, Elvis Costello, and Todd Rundgren, and audio professionals including Beatles engineers Geoff Emerick, Ken Scott, and Alan Parsons. He is the co-author of *Guitar Aficionado: The Most Famous, Rare, and Valuable Guitars in the World* and a former editor with *Guitar Aficionado* and *Guitar World* magazines.

Jenny Sherman (JS) is the digital editor for WDET-FM, Detroit's NPR station. She received her bachelor's in journalism from Michigan State University and has worked as a reporter and editor in metro Detroit for more than a decade. When she's not behind a desk, you might find her at the park with her husband and two boys, Milo and Theodore, or perusing the vinyl at her local record store.

Stacey Sherman (SS) is a veteran of the entertainment industry with more than twenty-five years of experience in radio, recording, publicity, and marketing. As a music journalist, she has contributed to numerous publications and podcasts, including *Billboard*, Media News Group, *Guitar Girl Magazine*, *The Brassy Broadcast*, *MusicBizCast*, and *We Spin*. She has shared her knowledge as a consultant for the CD Baby Music Convention, the Female Musician Academy, and the Grammy Indie Collaborative and has handled press appearances on tours with Lionel Richie and the Bacon Brothers. She is also part of the Emmy Award–winning production team for the 2021 Detroit Music Awards.

Steve Taylor (ST) is a Detroit-based singer-songwriter, teacher, and performer. He has released four solo albums and four albums with his Americana band the Steve Taylor Three, which won a 2023 Detroit Music Award for its single "Raining on Christmas." He is a graduate of Boston's prestigious Berklee College of Music and holds a master's degree in music theory from Wayne State University. In 2023, he was named "Teacher of the Year" at the Everest Collegiate High School & Academy in Clarkston, Michigan.

Ron Wade (RW) is a Detroit-area music aficionado and writer. Even though he spent much the '90s hanging outside St. Andrew's Hall, he found time during the decade to write for both *Orbit* magazine and the *Detroit Metro Times*. After *Orbit* folded, he went back to school to earn a master's degree in sport administration from Wayne State University. He spent the next fifteen years working in professional baseball with the St. Paul Saints and Detroit Tigers but never lost his love for music, finding unique ways to combine his passion for both. He is currently a clinical assistant professor of sport management at the University of Michigan.

Clark Warner (CW) is a music industry veteran, consultant, DJ, and occasional radio contributor specializing in electronic music. Based in Detroit, he is a co-founder of the Minus label with Richie Hawtin, helped grow the DJ digital store Beatport, and has contributed to events, technologies, and techniques that enhance connections between artists and fans.

Matthew Wilkening (MW) is the founding editor in chief of UltimateClassicRock.com and UltimatePrince.com. He is based in Akron, Ohio; his parents probably still regret giving him a copy of Kiss's *Hotter Than Hell* for Christmas in 1979.

Willy Wilson (WW) is a music lifer, a former record store manager, one-time radio host (WDET, WEMU, CJAM), and former scribe (*Metro Times*, *Real Detroit Weekly*, etc.) who likes nothing more than listening to records and talking about bands. Willy is currently the director of marketing at The Magic Bag Theatre in Ferndale, Michigan.

EN
90
1990
NETY

Depeche Mode

VIOLATOR

SIRE | Producers: Depeche Mode, Flood

RELEASED: MARCH 19, 1990

● Depeche Mode ended the 1980s on a high note with its massively successful *Music for the Masses* show at the Pasadena Rose Bowl. Where the band would go next was anyone's guess, but it wasn't long before we'd find out.

Personal Jesus, released six months before *Violator*, had become one of Depeche Mode's biggest sellers in the UK, reaching No. 13 on the charts. In it, songwriter Martin Gore addressed both Elvis Presley's cult-like legacy and the band's perspective on its growing fanbase. "We play these god-like parts for people," Gore told *Spin* magazine in 1990, "but no one is perfect, and that's not a very balanced view of someone."

But if Gore and bandmates Dave Gahan, Andy Fletcher, and Alan Wilder thought *Violator*, named because they thought it sounded "heavy metal" and ridiculous, would temper their fans' adoration, they were sorely mistaken. By the time the album dropped—following another hit in **Enjoy the Silence**, which won the Brit Award for Single of the Year—listeners were primed and frantic. Notably a record store signing in Los Angeles went off the rails when about 20,000 fans tried to enter a space meant to hold 150, resulting in a riot. Two more singles, **Policy of Truth** and **World in My Eyes**, followed, and *Violator* became the first Depeche Mode album to enter the Top 10 on the Billboard 200 (peaking at No. 7). It remained on the charts for seventy-four weeks and was certified triple-platinum in the US.

Producer Flood's influence and the band's willingness to try new recording approaches while maintaining—you might even say returning to—its original sound coalesced in this nine-track masterpiece. The ensuing world tour was attended by an astounding 1.2 million people, thereby guaranteeing Depeche Mode's stature as rock deity, however unwanted. *—HD*

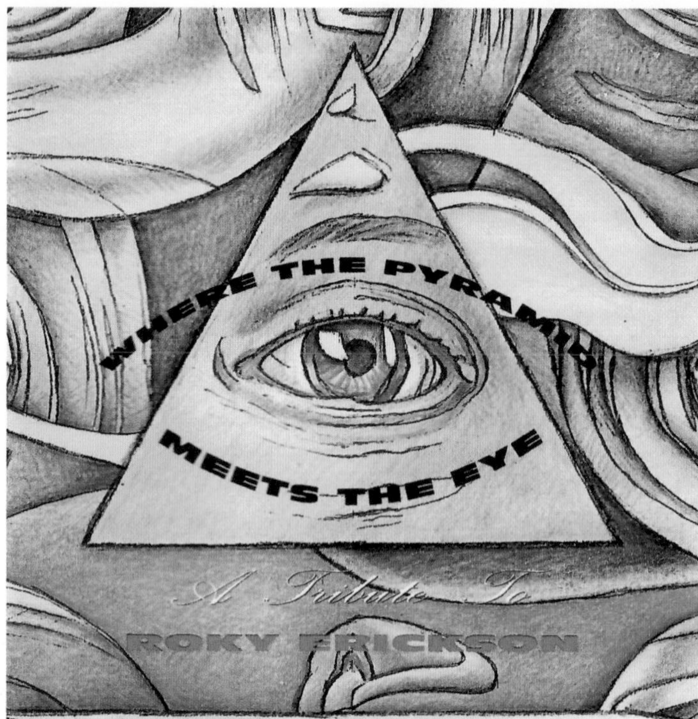

Various Artists

WHERE THE PYRAMID MEETS THE EYE: A TRIBUTE TO ROKY ERICKSON

SIRE | Producer: Bill Bentley

RELEASED: OCTOBER 13, 1990

● For far too long Roky Erickson was more a legend than a legitimate musical force, better known for his mental illness and unjust treatment at the hands of the legal system and draconian drug laws than for his music. It took a diligent and lucky record collector just to encounter his inspired work.

Erickson's songs comprise two key elements. The first is the world as observed by Roky Erickson. These observations are Technicolor, and here they unfold in the hands of performers as diverse as Primal Scream, Bongwater, and Southern Pacific. The interpretations are clear but retain lingering darkness. There is no shortage of the worrisome thoughts that tortured Erickson, particularly in Thin White Rope's **Burn the Flames**, both ZZ Top's and the Jesus and Mary Chain's **Reverberation (Doubt)**, and Sister Double Happiness's **Red Temple Prayer (Two Headed Dog)**.

The artists assembled for this tribute compilation are spot-on. While a product of its times, the roster of performers was built on Texas artists who knew Erickson (Doug Sahm, ZZ Top) and those who bore his influence (e.g., Butthole Surfers, Lyres, Lou Ann Barton, R.E.M.). Two Texas artists notably captured that second key element of Erickson's songs: the personal. T Bone Burnett, an extraordinary performer and mega producer, delivered a delicate interpretation of the unrequited love song **Nothing in Return**, while Poi Dog Pondering took on **I Had to Tell You**, the most introspective and autobiographical of Erickson's songs. Both delivered Erickson as fully human, not some sad myth.

Of all the tribute compilations that came out during the late twentieth century, this one probably achieved more for its subject than any other. Under the care of his brother Sumner, Erickson received the medical attention he needed and even returned to performing. He was met with a newly energized and devoted following before passing away in 2019. *–HK*

Jane's Addiction

RITUAL DE LO HABITUAL

WARNER BROS. | Producers: Dave Jerden, Perry Farrell

RELEASED: AUGUST 21, 1990

● The punk explosion of the '70s sent a lot of music fans to the used record stores to trade in their Led Zeppelin albums. Jane's Addiction came along and said, "Go get them back!" The Rush ones, too.

The Los Angeles quartet's injection of riff-heavy metal and prog back into present-day rock on 1988's *Nothing's Shocking* helped set the stage for a new, decadent decade of what would be called alternative rock, while also paving the way for Lollapalooza. By the release of Jane's second album, Guns N' Roses had blown up the hair metal scene and Nirvana was a year away from dropping *Nevermind*. Jane's established a middle ground with its exhilarating, arty, and aggressive new attack led by blossoming guitar hero Dave Navarro and frontman Perry Farrell, a singer with an otherworldly cry and wail.

As much as any album of its era, *Ritual de lo Habitual* was a journey—through sex, drugs, rock 'n' roll, and death—starting with **Stop**, a chaotic rocker that lurched you around like an old wooden rollercoaster. That rough ride continued through side 1 with **No One's Leaving**, **Ain't No Right**, and **Been Caught Stealing**, an anthem of sorts that featured vocal support from Farrell's dog Annie.

Side 2 plunged into dark, majestic waters with the pairing of **Three Days** and **Then She Did**, a remembrance of Farrell's ex-girlfriend Xiola Blue that, across twenty minutes, unleashed the full fury of Navarro and the rhythm section of Eric Avery and Stephen Perkins. *Ritual de lo Habitual* was peak Jane's on one of the most jarring and creative albums of the '90s—and, for a time, a final statement from the band. It would be thirteen years and detours into Porno for Pyros and the Red Hot Chili Peppers before we'd hear from the group again. *–SM*

MC Hammer

PLEASE HAMMER DON'T HURT 'EM

CAPITOL/EMI | Producers: MC Hammer, Big Louis Burrell, Felton Pilate, James Early

RELEASED: FEBRUARY 12, 1990

● Although it wasn't the first rap album to top the pop charts (the Beastie Boys and Tone Loc got there first), MC Hammer's *Please Hammer Don't Hurt 'Em* was the first hip-hop record to sell more than ten million copies, offering the first big hint of just how dominant a force the genre was about to become.

To put it kindly, there was nothing artistically remarkable about the rapping or music on this album. The rhymes were rudimentary at best, with the same simplistic lyrics repeated over and over on top of obvious and most often uncreatively rearranged samples of hits from other artists. If there was any innovation to be found here, it was the sheer audacity of how much Hammer (Stanley Burrell) borrowed from other artists and how relentlessly and repeatedly he (forgive me) hammered the hooks into the listener's ears.

The album's biggest hit and Hammer's signature song, **U Can't Touch This**, took almost every bit of its music from Rick James's "Super Freak," which resulted in a copyright infringement lawsuit and James getting songwriting credit (and millions of deserved dollars) from the rapper. Still, as fellow rapper Kool Moe Dee once pointed out, if you played "Super Freak" instead of **U Can't Touch This**, kids at the time would immediately demand that you put MC Hammer back on—clearly, something new and unique had been created, at least to their ears. *Please Hammer . . .* was also the perfect album if you needed to explain rap to your grandparents.

It's hard to disrespect the fact that MC Hammer achieved this amazing commercial success through hard work and determination, recording the now seventeen-times platinum album in a DIY recording studio on the back of his tour bus in between shows for a reported cost of just $10,000. *–MW*

Living Colour

TIME'S UP

EPIC | Producer: Ed Stasium

RELEASED: AUGUST 28, 1990

● After bursting onto the scene with 1988's *Vivid* and its eternally ubiquitous hit, "Cult of Personality," Living Colour could have easily chosen to solidify its foothold in the marketplace with a second album that simply delivered more of the same excellence. Instead, the quartet decided to dig deeper with *Time's Up*, an impressively diverse and often complex album that expanded its claims further into punk, funk, jazz, soul, and hip-hop. The sophisticated, six-and-a-half-minute riff-fest **Type** was a decidedly defiant choice of first single, a clear sign that artistic evolution, not airplay, was the band's main priority. The simmering, seductive **Under Cover of Darkness** found lead singer Corey Glover teaming with Queen Latifah to particularly stunning effect. Little Richard turned up on the frantic **Elvis Is Dead**, helping throw more gasoline on the fire Public Enemy sent in Elvis Presley's direction the previous summer with "Fight the Power." Even in these relatively lighthearted moments, the group kept its focus squarely on serious subject matter such as teenage pregnancy and cultural appropriation. With *Time's Up*, Living Colour wasn't looking to stick around or fit in. It was daring its audience to keep up. *–MW*

The Flatlanders

MORE A LEGEND THAN A BAND

ROUNDER | Producer: Royce Clark

RELEASED: 1990

● Seldom has an album title rung more true than this one. The Flatlanders' legend was established circa 1972, when Texas singer/songwriters Jimmie Dale Gilmore, Joe Ely, and Butch Hancock originally grouped for one album (and little success). But their individual work after that made fans salivate over the prospect of them working together again, which happened during the late '80s and eventually brought us *More a Legend Than a Band*, a thirteen-song set that resurrected and polished those initial recordings and lived up to the lofty anticipation.

The originals—four by Hancock, three from Gilmore (whose **Dallas** is one of his best ever)—capably fit the trio's ensemble vocal sensibility. And the covers, including Willie Nelson's **One Day at a Time** and the Cajun traditional **Jole Blon**, spoke to its roots in the fertile musical landscape of west Texas. You can hear how alien the Flatlanders must have seemed to the Nashville of nearly two decades prior, but to more open Americana ears of the '90s, this was a document of enormous importance and impact that, best of all, brought the group back to (still) active duty. *–GG*

LL Cool J

MAMA SAID KNOCK YOU OUT

DEF JAM | Producer: Marley Marl

RELEASED: SEPTEMBER 14, 1990

● "Don't call it a comeback," LL Cool J announced at the start of the title track of his fourth album. But that's exactly what it was. After ushering in a new era of hip-hop on his 1985 debut, *Radio* (the first album released by soon-to-be genre giant Def Jam), 1987's *Bigger and Deffer* was more of the same. But his third album, 1989's *Walking with a Panther*, drew heavily on ballads to play up LL's romantic side and left the rapper deflecting critics who claimed he'd gone soft.

So, *Mama Said Knock You Out* was a comeback, and a grand one at that, as the twenty-two-year-old rapper came out swinging with his toughest and most consistent set of songs. He sounded like he had something to prove, and with producer Marley Marl supplying sturdy assistance throughout, LL Cool J hit back hard. Four hit singles were released from the album—**The Boomin' System**, **Around the Way Girl**, **6 Minutes of Pleasure**, and the title track—and a breathtaking performance on *MTV Unplugged* confirmed his return. The rest of the hip-hop community spent the next few years catching up. *–MG*

George Michael

LISTEN WITHOUT PREJUDICE VOL.1

COLUMBIA | Producer: George Michael

RELEASED: SEPTEMBER 3, 1990

● George Michael's second solo album was not at all what the world anticipated. In the wake of Wham! and 1987's undeniably mature but still hit-focused *Faith*, *Listen Without Prejudice Vol. 1* was more serious, sober (even somber), and socially conscious than anything that came before, a clear bid by Michael to elevate himself beyond the pop-icon status he'd achieved to that point. That made *Listen*'s upbeat tracks (**Freedom '90** and **Soul Free**) feel like throwing bones, albeit good ones, to the punters, while the album's heart was in austere, introspective fare such as **Praying for Time**, **Something to Save**, **Heal the Pain**, **Mother's Pride**, and The Rolling Stones–quoting **Waiting for the Day** (which also sampled James Brown's "Funky Drummer").

The album's lone cover—**They Won't Go When I Go**, a deep dig from Stevie Wonder's *Fulfillingness' First Finale*—also spoke to Michael's intent on *Listen*, veering from the obvious and expected and, in its spare arrangement and aching vocals, staking an ambitious new stature. It did well at the time (high chart positions and a Brit Award for Best British Album), and time has viewed the album as Michael's moment of genuine artistic ascension, one that rendered a never-released *Vol. 2* superfluous. *–GG*

PUBLIC ENEMY
FEAR OF A BLACK PLANET
K ON WORLD SUPREMACY...THE COUNTERATTACK ON WORLD SUPREMACY...THE COUNTERATTACK ON WORL

Public Enemy

FEAR OF A BLACK PLANET

DEF JAM | Producers: The Bomb Squad

RELEASED: APRIL 10, 1990

● Public Enemy's 1988 album *It Takes a Nation of Millions to Hold Us Back* put the group in the spotlight, often to a more detrimental effect than its members anticipated. Under the microscope and hammered over its support of controversial Black leaders, the groundbreaking hip-hop troupe doubled down when it came time to make new music. **Fight the Power**, which echoed throughout the soundtrack to Spike Lee's incendiary summer 1989 film *Do the Right Thing*, and the late-1989 single **Welcome to the Terrordome**—in part addressing the media circus following the racially instigated dismissal of group member Professor Griff—targeted critics and rallied supporters.

If *It Takes a Nation of Millions* was a political cauldron of late-'80s Black concerns, *Fear of a Black Planet* was a full-on call to action. Its key songs, including those two first singles, addressed race, community, stereotypes, and pride. **Brothers Gonna Work It Out**, **911 Is a Joke**, **Burn Hollywood Burn**, and the title track only began to chip away at a movement. As Chuck D rapped on **Fight the Power**, "Now that you've realized the pride's arrived/We've got to pump the stuff to make us tough/From the heart/It's a start, a work of art/to revolutionize."

The message-board offense of *Fear of a Black Planet* was matched by its nonstop sonic assault, an overload of samples, squeals, and room-shaking effects by the production team The Bomb Squad. The musical landscape of *It Takes a Nation of Millions* sounds positively thin against the monumental sound collages assembled here. Few albums in the history of hip-hop have the lasting impact of Public Enemy's third LP; point to any pivotal moment in the genre, and this unquestionably rivals it. *–MG*

Technics

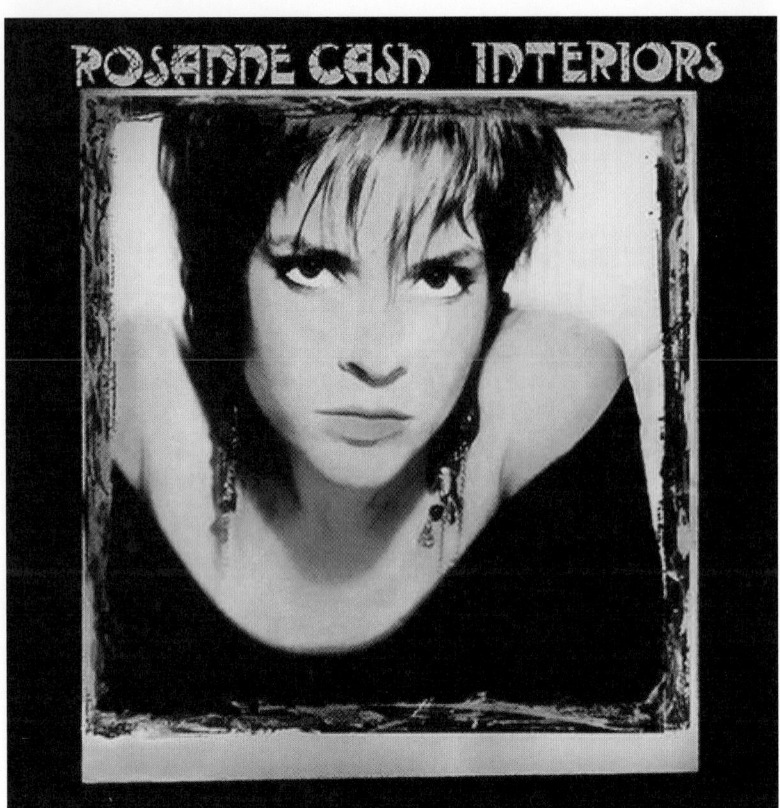

Rosanne Cash

INTERIORS

COLUMBIA | Producer: Rosanne Cash

RELEASED: OCTOBER 5, 1990

● Randy Lewis of the *Los Angeles Times* nailed it when he said *Interiors* "seems aimed less at Cash's core country audience than at pop fans who find Leonard Cohen too lighthearted."

Interiors was indeed a dark, introspective album that tracked the turmoil attendant upon her crumbling marriage to singer/songwriter (and Cash's former producer) Rodney Crowell (they would divorce in 1992). "The things that we believe in, we just throw them away/But on the surface, everything's ok," Cash sang in **On the Surface**, with—yikes!—Crowell joining in on backing vocals. It takes a singer and songwriter of extraordinary strength to be that open and forthright, and Cash was (and still is) exactly that. (For that matter, so is Crowell.) Cash wrote or co-wrote all of *Interiors'* ten songs, a first for her. And while the titles themselves are telling—**What We Really Want**, **Land of Nightmares**, **I Want a Cure**, **Paralyzed**—the songs plumbed those depths to the fullest. She produced the album herself as well, yet another achievement unlocked.

As noted above, *Interiors* broke Cash free from country music's formal constraints, landing more as a folk/pop album that retained just a nominal twang. It also cut her loose from the country singles chart, scoring just two minor hits in **What We Really Want** and **On the Surface**. No matter: The creative space she carved out for herself on *Interiors* has proven to be far better suited for a songwriter with Cash's eye for detail and emotional undercurrents. The album's honesty, nuance, and—with a nod to her skills as both songwriter and producer—tunefulness, all made *Interiors* a classic. ***–DD***

The Winans

RETURN

QWEST | Producers: Barry Hankerson, Bernard Bell, Michael J. Powell, Teddy Riley

RELEASED: JANUARY 9, 1990

● The sixth album by the Detroit gospel group comprising brothers Marvin, Carvin, Ronald, and Michael meshed gospel, Motown, and New Jack Swing to create a riveting collection of songs that put a fresh spin on a traditional form. With production by hitmakers Teddy Riley (Guy, Backstreet) and Michael J. Powell (Anita Baker, Patti LaBelle), along with featured guest artists such as Aaron Hall, Kenny G, and Stevie Wonder, *Return* sold more than half a million copies and stayed at No. 1 on the Billboard Gospel charts for two weeks, winning a *Soul Train* Music Award for Best Gospel Album and a Grammy Award nomination for Best Contemporary Soul Gospel Album.

The first single from the project, **It's Time**, opened with Riley rapping that "It's time to make that change/People of the world today are fading," followed by the impeccable vocals and harmonies from the Winans. Showing the evolution of gospel, **It's Time** delivered the timeless message that "He's coming back" with an updated, hip-hop flavor. The follow-up single, **A Friend**, also boasted the Riley writing and production touch, with his Guy mate Hall backing Marvin Winans's soulful, passionate leads. Paying homage to the church hymn "What a Friend We Have in Jesus," the Winans created a New Jack counterpart with lyrics like "All you got to do is call Him/He's just a friend."

The song **When You Cry** showcased the writing and vocal talents of Carvin Winans; produced by Michael J. Powell and featuring Kenny G on saxophone, the track brought his smooth falsetto lead vocals to the forefront with comforting lyrics. Other outstanding tracks included **Don't Leave Me** and **Everyday the Same**, which featured Wonder on harmonica. *–CP*

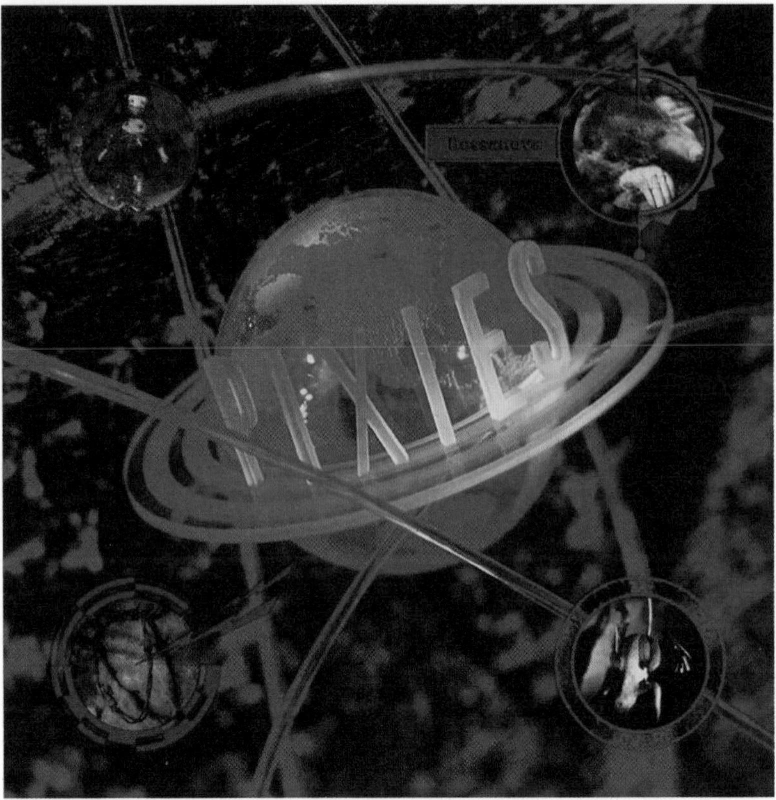

Pixies

BOSSANOVA

4AD/ELEKTRA | Producer: Gil Norton

RELEASED: AUGUST 13, 1990

● The third and penultimate album of Pixies' brief early run (eight years) came amid heightened tensions between frontman Black Francis and bassist Kim Deal over the latter's hit debut with her twin sister Kelley in the Breeders as a needed outlet for her own songs. For this recording, the Boston indie sensations relocated to Los Angeles and again set up shop with Gil Norton, the British producer behind their 1989 sophomore album *Doolittle*, which marked a sonic upgrade over its predecessor, *Surfer Rosa*.

There were certainly challenges this time out in light of Deal's distractions and a rush-job timeline that compelled Francis to scribble lyrics on napkins in the studio (not that we looked to him for the meaning of life, relationship advice, or even something coherent half the time). That may help explain why just three of *Bossanova*'s songs turned up on the 2004 compilation *Wave of Mutilation: Best of Pixies*, compared to seven from *Doolittle* and five from *Surfer Rosa*.

Nevertheless, *Bossanova* was yet another killer Pixies album, with more of the quartet's endearing, off-kilter vocals and guitarist Joey Santiago's machine-like riff factory. The album came out of the gate with a souped-up cover of the Surftones' instrumental **Cecilia Ann** and proceeded through a steady stream of thrashy screamers (**Rock Music** and **Down to the Well**) and big bangers (**Velouria** and **Dig for Fire**), employing the quiet-to-loud dynamic that Pixies did better than any of the bands that came along to copy them—often with much more lucrative financial results. *–SM*

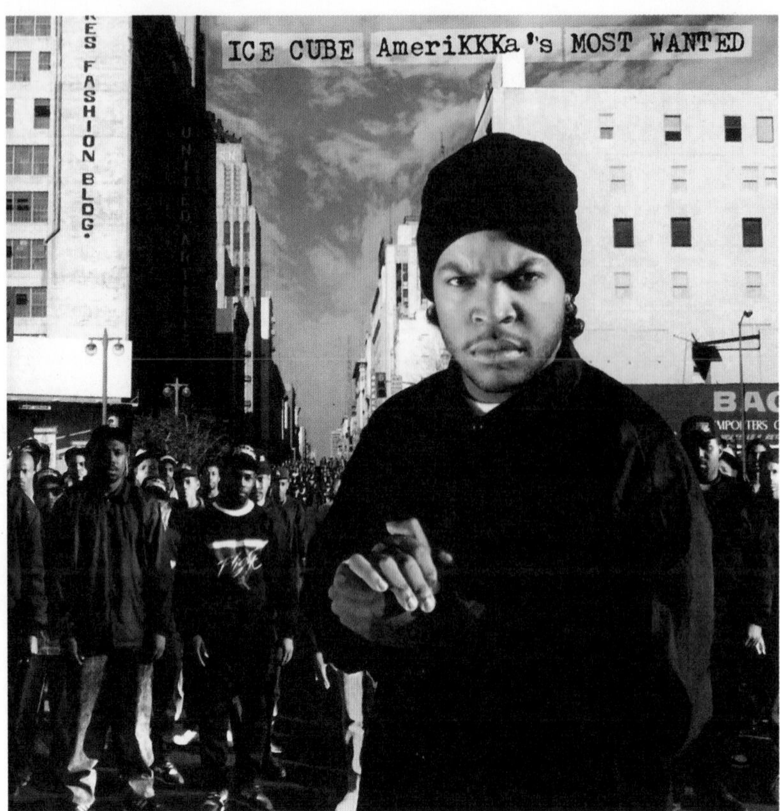

Ice Cube

AMERIKKKA'S MOST WANTED

LENCH MOB/PRIORITY | Producers: The Bomb Squad, Da Lench Mob

RELEASED: MAY 18, 1990

● Ice Cube was hailed as one of hip-hop's most promising artists when he left N.W.A, the group that made him a star, in late 1989. The troupe's *Straight Outta Compton* revolutionized the still-growing genre, helping popularize gangsta rap while launching the individual careers of Cube and mates Eazy-E, MC Ren, Dr. Dre, and DJ Yella. Royalty issues prompted Cube's departure, which the group addressed in a brief interlude on its second album, *Efil4zaggin*, referring to the rapper as a traitorous "Benedict Arnold" (Ice Cube later fired back on 1991's relentless "No Vaseline").

But the twenty-year-old rapper had moved on by then, and his debut solo album, *AmeriKKKa's Most Wanted*, didn't bother to look back. Enlisting powerhouse Public Enemy producers The Bomb Squad to help out on some tracks, Ice Cube—who penned *Straight Outta Compton*'s most memorable songs—displayed a greater social consciousness, pushing the targeted political commentary of *Compton* and "F*ck tha Police" into more expanded territories. **The Nigga You Love to Hate**, **AmeriKKKa's Most Wanted**, and **Endangered Species (Tales from the Darkside)**, a duet with Public Enemy's Chuck D, balanced anger, righteousness, and even shades of knowing mischievousness as Cube staked out his claim as the world's greatest rapper.

Few hip-hop stylists of the era possessed Ice Cube's bullhorn flow; his explosive rhymes and booming delivery were endlessly imitated during the first half of the '90s. *AmeriKKKa's Most Wanted* remains his most essential solo album and a significant part of the music's history, despite occasional throwaway tracks such as **I'm Only Out for One Thang** and **Get Off My Dick and Tell Yo Bitch to Come Here**. Follow-up LPs sold more and charted higher, but none matched the impact of his debut. *–MG*

Cocteau Twins

HEAVEN OR LAS VEGAS

4 A D | Producer: Cocteau Twins

RELEASED: SEPTEMBER 17, 1990

● Saying that the sixth and most commercially successful studio album by the pioneering Scottish dreampop trio was critically acclaimed would be a gross understatement. *Pitchfork* and *Paste*, in fact, put it atop their Greatest Dreampop Albums of all-time lists, while *Brooklyn Vegan* dubbed it the top album of 1990. But its real success came thanks to the nurture of college radio and specialty shows and club DJs who made *Heaven or Las Vegas* a *cause célèbre* on the post-punk, pre-internet alternative music scene that would soon be dominated by grunge bands.

Cocteau Twins—Elizabeth Fraser, Robin Guthrie, and Simon Raymonde—recorded *Heaven or Las Vegas* at the group's own September Sound studio in London. The songs would reflect a tumultuous time: Fraser was pregnant with her first child with Guthrie, while Raymonde and his wife were also expecting, and the bassist lost his father during the recording process. Guthrie, meanwhile, was battling a debilitating cocaine habit; and financial issues led the band to hire its first-ever manager, a relationship that didn't take long to sour. The result was a birth-and-death mix of lightness and dark that gave *Heaven or Las Vegas* great emotional heft, from the blissful first single **Iceblink Luck** and **Pitch the Baby** to more dour tracks such as Raymonde's **Frou-Frou Foxes in Midsummer Fires** and the enigmatic title track.

Throughout the album the group stripped away some of the gauzy artifice of its predecessors, without sacrificing the ethereal melodies and atmospheric textures that *were* Cocteau Twins' calling cards. Fraser's phrasing, in particular, was clearer and more readily intelligible, and Guthrie employed a hip-hop, dance club influence in the beats that gave the set a subtly different attitude and a staying power that makes it Cocteau Twins' definitive statement. *–MR/GG*

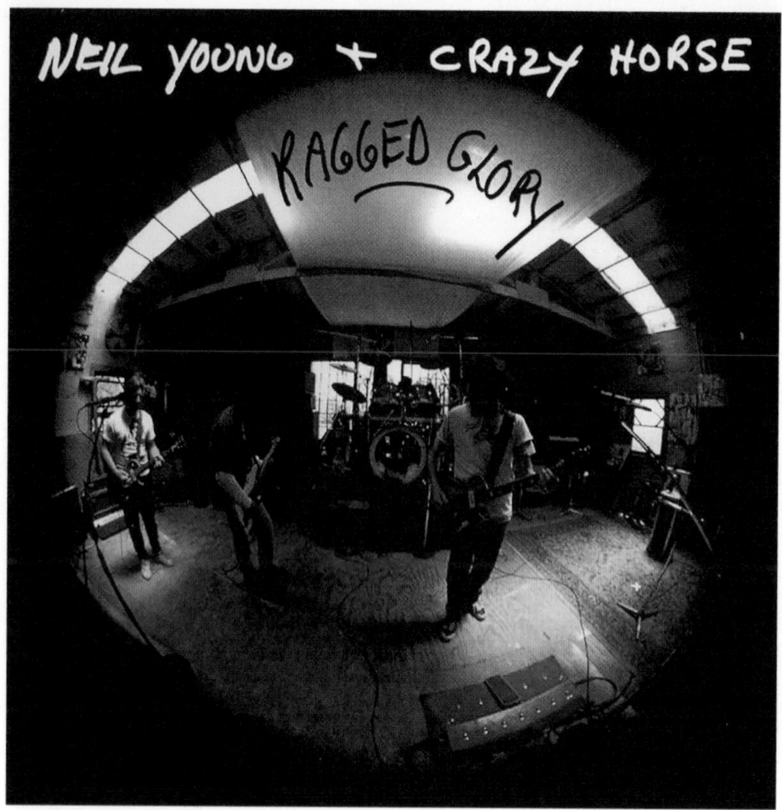

Neil Young & Crazy Horse

RAGGED GLORY

REPRISE | Producers: Neil Young, David Briggs

RELEASED: SEPTEMBER 10, 1990

● Emerging from his famously eclectic and challenging '80s, Neil Young began what would be a productive decade (five studio albums, three live sets, and an *MTV Unplugged* session) with the kind of album fans had been wanting (even clamoring for) for a couple decades.

Trade ads for *Ragged Glory* declared "Feedback Is Back," and that was no lie. Despite having sworn off Crazy Horse (again) following 1987's *Life*, Young summoned his most favorite of backing bands to his Broken Arrow Ranch in Northern California, turned up the amps, and let rip in a way that was truly (to coin his phrase from the previous year's *Freedom*) rockin' in the free world. "I had these songs and I heard them played with guitars, really loud, and [Crazy Horse] was the group to play them with," Young explained at the time. And the troupe (guitarist Frank "Poncho" Sampedro, bassist Billy Talbot, and drummer Ralph Molina) played with a hard-rocking, jammy abandon that Young hadn't tried in this concentrated a form since *Everybody Knows This Is Nowhere* in 1969.

Two of the ten tracks, **Love to Burn** and **Love and Only Love**, careened along for ten minutes or more apiece and didn't waste a note. Another, **Over and Over**, clocked in at eight and a half minutes, with the same effect. **Country Home** and **White Line** recast songs Young had played in concert over the years, while the Horse's take on **Farmer John** probably came as a shock to Don & Dewey, who originally released it in 1959. Young waxed '60s sentimental on **Mansion on the Hill** and **Days That Used to Be**, but on *Ragged Glory*, he revived Crazy Horse as a potent and decidedly present creative force, not rusty and certainly *not* sleeping. *–GG*

World Party

GOODBYE JUMBO

ENSIGN | Producer: Karl Wallinger

RELEASED: APRIL 24, 1990

● Karl Wallinger enjoyed a sweet gig during the mid-'80s, spending three years and two albums as part of the Waterboys, including 1985's high, er, water mark, *This Is the Sea*. The singer, songwriter, and multi-instrumentalist had other creative ambitions, however, which led him to leave that band in 1986 and create his own musical endeavor, which would, not unlike the Waterboys, take the form of a collective executing Wallinger's vision. Wallinger demonstrated the merits of that move with 1987's solid *Private Revolution*, but it was the successor, *Goodbye Jumbo*, that really hammered the point home.

Solid and fat-free from start to finish, the thirteen-song set benefited from nearly two years of production, steeped in the sonic influences of predecessors such as The Beatles and The Rolling Stones, but as sources rather than slavish copies. **Way Down Now**, **Put the Message in the Box**, **Is It Too Late?**, and **Thank You World** were just the top of a spirit-lifting tune stack that let the world party hearty. Listen closely to **Sweet Soul Dream**, meanwhile, and you'll hear Sinéad O'Connor on backing vocals, joining Wallinger's most potent core of Partygoers. A Grammy nomination for Best Alternative Music Performance was well-deserved for an outing that's never lost its appeal. *–GG*

They Might Be Giants

FLOOD

ELEKTRA | Producer: They Might Be Giants

RELEASED: JANUARY 15, 1990

● They Might Be Giants (TMBG) bandmates John Linnell and John Flansburgh met as Massachusetts teenagers and reunited in—where else for hipsters?—Brooklyn, quickly gaining a local following for their quirky wordplay and unusual instrumentation, which supplemented the usual rock band format with accordion, saxophone, clarinet, vacuum cleaner, xylophone, glasses, and whatever else was lying around. While their first two albums found a home on college radio and on the duo's Dial-A-Song project, TMBG's third release upped their standing.

A major label deal and access to more high-profile producers and recording studios paid off when *Flood*'s lead single, **Birdhouse in Your Soul**, reached No. 3 on Billboard's Modern Rock chart and charted in Ireland and the UK. The album also included fan favorites **Istanbul (Not Constantinople)** (originally recorded by the Four Lads) and **Particle Man**. Never ones to follow a conventional line, TMBG incorporated samples of everything from mallets and drumsticks hitting objects around Flansburgh's kitchen to the snap of a wet towel on tracks that flirted with punk, jazz, country, and alt-rock to create a uniquely recognizable sound unlike anything else you're likely to hear—then or even now. *–HD*

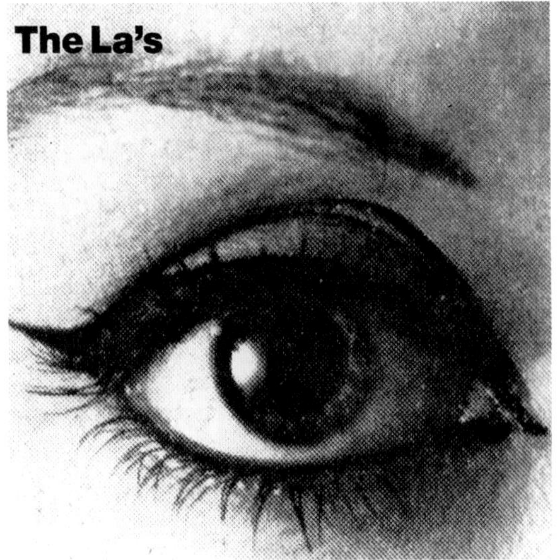

The La's

THE LA'S

POLYDOR/GO!/LONDON | Producers: Steve Lillywhite, Bob Andrews

RELEASED: OCTOBER 1, 1990

● Oasis and the '90s Britpop explosion were a few years away when this Liverpool quartet released its self-titled debut, a jangly gem produced primarily by Steve Lillywhite. Guitarist Mike Badger formed the La's in 1983 (the name is Scouse for "lads"), but Lee Mavers, who joined the following year, became its driving force, steering it through a number of lineup changes before settling into the quartet—including brother Neil Mavers on drums—that would make this landmark self-titled set. Melodically rich and hooky as all get-out, the full-length was in some ways overshadowed by its familiar-but-still-fresh single, **There She Goes**. But *The La's* offers even more instantly infectious pop songs, including **Way Out**, **Timeless Melody**, **Son of a Gun**, **Feelin'**, and **Doledrum**.

Oasis guitarist Noel Gallagher cited it as one of his favorite albums, and by all rights the group and Lee Mavers should have achieved legendary status, but the La's went on an open-ended hiatus in 1992. There have been compilations of early demos, outtakes, and performances; a 2008 deluxe edition added two discs of bonus material, including a version of the album re-produced by Mike Hedges (Siouxsie and the Banshees, Manic Street Preachers, Travis). The La's have also reformed on occasion but never released another new album. *–GG*

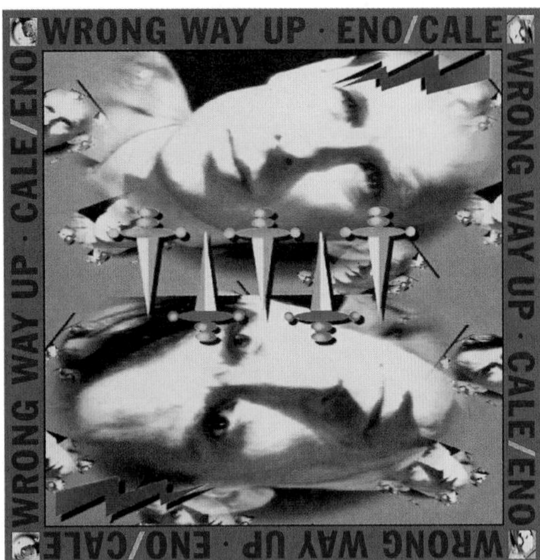

Brian Eno and John Cale

WRONG WAY UP

OPAL/WARNER BROS. | Producers: Brian Eno, John Cale

RELEASED: OCTOBER 5, 1990

● The collaboration of Brian Eno and John Cale seemed so logical that it might lead you think it had to have happened earlier in their storied careers. Oddly, no. This is the one and only time the English producer/keyboard innovator worked with the Welsh violist/bassist on a project. The result was straight from Rate-A-Record: it had a nice beat, and you could dance to it. **Been There, Done That** is a hook-laden track that defied the notion that these were artists who relied on the dark or marginal. It also featured perhaps the most striking recurring element of this record: the seamless and captivating vocals of Eno and Cale combined. Harmonies on **The River**, **One Word**, and **Spinning Away** elevate to near–Beach Boys levels. Eno has a vocal quality akin to David Crosby; if his voice was removed, the song would fall apart. That's not to say that Cale doesn't carry his weight. He's a supreme composer, and his sensibilities dovetail perfectly with Eno's to create a thoroughly enjoyable record. *–HK*

Was (Not Was)
ARE YOU OKAY?

CHRYSALIS | Producers: Don Was, David Was

RELEASED: JULY 1990

● After 1988's *What Up, Dog?* elevated this Detroit collective from wizards of weird to mainstream success with "Walk the Dinosaur," Was (Not Was) returned with more of the same. Like its predecessor, *Are You Okay?* was stocked with marquee guest vocalists, from Leonard Cohen and Iggy Pop to Syd Straw and the Roches. A big-cajones cover of the Temptations' **Papa Was a Rollin' Stone** showcased the group's three lead vocalists but threw a curveball with G Love E's rap, still a daring addition in 1990. The album didn't reap the commercial success of its predecessor and had to hold fans over for the eighteen years until Was (Not Was)'s next recorded statement. *–GG*

Slayer
SEASONS IN THE ABYSS

DEF JAM | Producers: Rick Rubin, Andy Wallas, Slayer

RELEASED: OCTOBER 9, 1990

● After the sludge-fest that was *South of Heaven*, the thrash metal quartet got back to speed and aggression (for the most part) on the last of the first five albums that Slayer fans cherish. With Rick Rubin at the helm for the third time, Slayer bashed through a set that's not for the faint of heart, from the bloody opener **War Ensemble** to the dark, tempo-shifting title track and the brutal encounter with serial killer and body snatcher Ed Gein on **Dead Skin Mask**. As bassist/vocalist Tom Araya declared in a frightening summation, "In the depths of a mind insane, fantasy and reality are the same." *–SM*

Sonic Youth
GOO

DGC | Producers: Nick Sansano, Ron Saint Germain, Sonic Youth

RELEASED: JUNE 26, 1990

● If this is what selling out sounds like, more bands should do it. The New York underground darlings jumped to a major label for this sixth album, a follow-up to its lauded 1988 release *Daydream Nation* that was more accessible while maintaining the band's trademark alternate tunings and required level of loud, noisy abrasiveness. The riffs hit like monsoons, starting with Thurston Moore's album-opening **Dirty Boots**. From there, Kim Gordon all but stole the show with **Tunic (Song for Karen)**, her stormy tribute to Karen Carpenter, and the LL Cool J–inspired **Kool Thing** with Public Enemy's Chuck D guesting. It was the first salvo of a new era for a band peaking at just the right time. *–SM*

Extreme
EXTREME II—PORNOGRAFFITTI

A & M | Producers: Michael Wagener, Nuno Bettencourt

RELEASED: AUGUST 7, 1990

● Extreme's popularity skyrocketed exponentially with its sophomore album, a twelve-song set that challenged hair metal conventions of the time. Gary Cherone's charismatic vocals, combined with Nuno Bettencourt's guitar virtuosity and the pair's boundary-pushing songwriting, came just before the grunge takeover to stake a territory all its own. **Get the Funk Out**, enhanced by six-piece horn section, pushed in one direction, while two acoustic gems, **More Than Words** and **Hole Hearted**, further showcased Extreme's versatility. The former hit No. 1 on the Billboard 200, vaulting *Pornograffitti* to double-platinum status and the band, briefly, to the top of the rock echelon. *—MD*

Michael W. Smith
GO WEST YOUNG MAN

REUNION | Producers: Wayne Kirkpatrick, Bryan Lenox, Michael W. Smith

RELEASED: OCTOBER 1, 1990

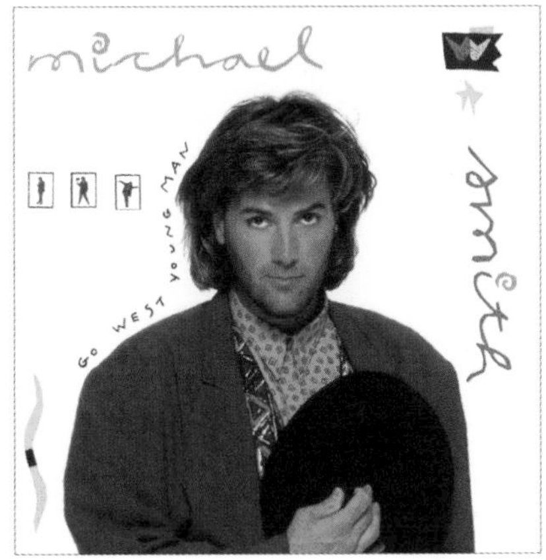

● Michael W. Smith was five albums in and a Grammy Award–winning contemporary gospel/Christian star when he decided to bust a mainstream pop move on *Go West Young Man*. The heavy drum tattoo, slick synthesizers, urgent guitar stabs, anthemic na-na's, and rapped bridge of the opening title track planted Smith's new flag while still praising Jesus. The album, sporting two songs co-written with good pal and frequent touring partner Amy Grant, was Smith's first platinum effort and gave him his first bona fide pop hit with the power ballad **Place in This World**, his only Top 10 visit on the Billboard Hot 100. *—GG*

John Zorn
NAKED CITY

ELECTRA/NONESUCH | Producer: John Zorn

RELEASED: FEBRUARY 16, 1990

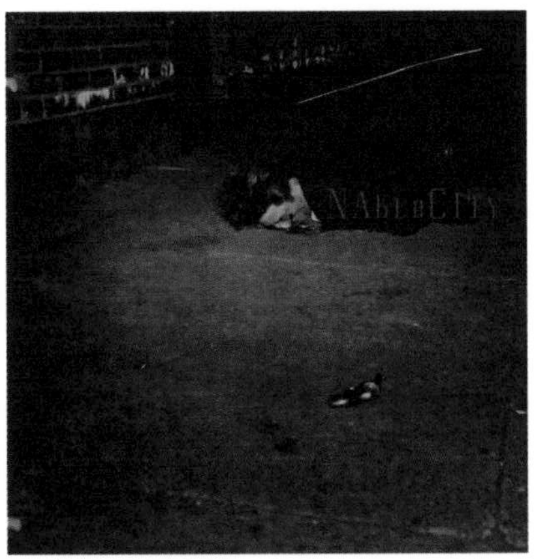

● At times jarring and impenetrable, at times beguiling, alto saxophonist John Zorn's epochal avant-garde jazz on his first project of the 1990s was a wild ride. Taken as a metaphoric soundtrack to the Big City that never sleeps, the listener needed to be prepared for anything as the twenty-six short tracks unfolded across its fifty-five minutes. Zorn unleashed searing solos with incendiary blitzes of notes, as jolting as crossing live electric wires. His rambunctious bandmates (guitarist Bill Frisell, bassist Fred Frith, and drummer Joey Baron), who would become known as Naked City, maintained the furious pace. Intermixed were compositions of unexpected allure, including stellar interpretations of cult-classic film themes. *—CH*

Mariah Carey

MARIAH CAREY

COLUMBIA | Producers: Walter Afanasieff, Mariah Carey, Rhett Lawrence, Ben Margulies, Ric Wake, Narada Michael Walden

RELEASED: JUNE 12, 1990

● There was a sound of collective jaws dropping when Mariah Carey emerged in 1990, first with the single **Vision of Love** and then with her self-titled debut album. Five years after Whitney Houston established a new benchmark for pop divadom, Carey came along as a fully formed (it seemed at the time) challenger to that throne, bypassing lady-in-waiting status with a debut worthy of somebody well beyond her years (twenty-one at the time).

Mariah Carey was certainly the product of a great deal of work—by Carey herself, as a struggling young artist from Long Island and most recently a backup singer for Brenda K. Starr, and by those around her. For Columbia Records and its chief (and Carey's future husband) Tommy Mottola, she was the label's answer to Houston, Madonna, and even Anita Baker. Carey and writing partner Ben Margulies had the goods on their demo, but Mottola took no chances, bringing in handpicked hitmakers such as Narada Michael Walden, Walter Afanasieff, and Ric Wake to tweak and polish the eleven tracks—from torchy bookends **Vision of Love** and **Love Takes Time** to guitar-rocking **You Need Me** and New Jack Swing–aping **Prisoner**—to sonic perfection.

The strategy worked to the tune of more than fifteen million copies sold worldwide, a No. 1 placement on the Billboard 200, and four No. 1 singles. But as The Who sang, it's the singer not the song, and *Mariah Carey*'s calling card was the singer herself, blowing away critics and fans alike with her range, nimble vocal runs, and that soaring, impossibly high-pitched whistle register that became a trademark. Carey fortified that technique with genuine emotional integrity, creating a performing model for aspirants who came in her wake and which Carey would build on with her subsequent releases. *–GG*

Bell Biv DeVoe

POISON

M C A | Producer: Louil Silas Jr.

RELEASED: MARCH 20, 1990

● New Jack Swing was a few years into its ascent, and New Edition's Bobby Brown had already latched on (with his *Ghostbusters II* theme, "On Our Own") by the time groupmates Ricky Bell, Michael Bivins, and Ronnie DeVoe launched their splinter group in 1989. Bell Biv DeVoe (BBD) had vocal chops (singing and rapping) to spare and plenty of creative imagination, all evident on the trio's quadruple-platinum debut.

Poison is best known for its sinewy, rat-a-tat title track, which, like the album, landed at No. 1 on the Billboard R&B charts and in the Top 5 of the Billboard 200. But that was just one of many delights on the ten-song set (including an extended club version of **Poison**), a collection laden with high-octane, dancefloor-filling bangers that weren't necessarily subtle (**Do Me!** anyone?) but hung with the best of what was going on in the subgenre and have stood up well during the intervening years.

Credit BBD's choice of writer-producers for the album's durability, particularly the likes of Elliot "Dr. Freeze" Straite and Public Enemy Bomb Squad brothers Hank and Keith Shocklee. They and *Poison*'s other collaborators kept BBD's groove tight and aggressive and gave the song arrangements plenty of space to ensure the trio was the star of the show as it tore through **Dope!**, **Let Me Know Something**, **Ain't Nut'in Changed**, and **B.B.D. (I Thought It Was Me)?** BBD gave props to its mothership, too, with the New Edition tribute track **Ronnie, Bobby, Ricky, Mike, Ralph and Johnny (Word to the Mutha)** and a couple of soulful vocal showcases (**When Will I See You Again?** and **I Do Need You**) straight out of the group's playbook.

New Edition would regroup in 1996, but BBD released three more albums and remains active on the road, the *Poison* songs reminding all of the set's defining glory. *—GG*

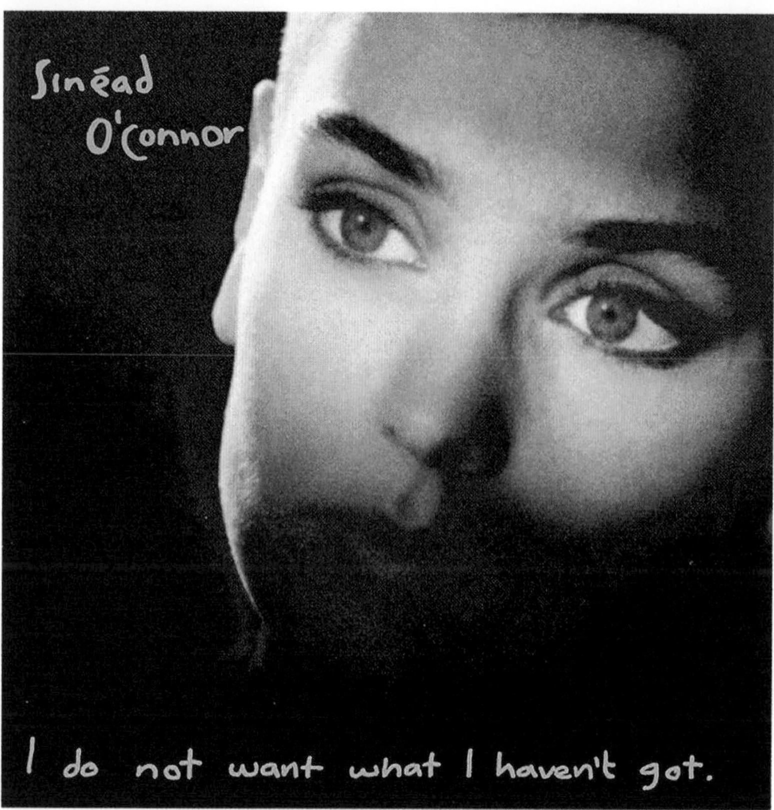

Sinéad O'Connor

I DO NOT WANT WHAT I HAVEN'T GOT

ENSIGN/CHRYSALIS | Producers: Nellee Hooper, Sinéad O'Connor

RELEASED: MARCH 12, 1990

● Unlike many artists who fell victim to the sophomore slump, Sinéad O'Connor delivered a powerful, confessional (and commercially successful) set unlike anything else released in 1990. *She* wasn't like anyone else, either: a single mother who shaved her head to thwart anyone who would promote her as a pop star, delivering songs that laid bare her anger and pain. The lengthy cover of Prince's **Nothing Compares to U** was an unlikely chart-topper fueled by a stunning video that basically framed O'Connor's mesmerizing face for its entirety.

The album opened with her speaking the Serenity Prayer as the intro to **Feels So Different**, a seven-minute song of realization that not only she but the people around her have changed. In place of a traditional rhythm section, listeners found a pulsing string arrangement that never overpowered the earnest vocal performance. Although there are other numbers that adopted that approach—the achingly beautiful **Three Babies**, **Black Boys on Mopeds**, and the heartbreak of all heartbreak songs, **The Last Day of Our Acquaintance**—there were some upbeat surprises as well. O'Connor used a sample of James Brown's "Funky Drummer" as the foundation for **I Am Stretched on Your Grave**, a hypnotic translation of a seventeenth-century Irish poem. She also offered up a bona fide rocker with **The Emperor's New Clothes**, featuring a lyric that summed up her attitude at the time: "I will live by my own policies/I will sleep with a clear conscience."

After taking the listener on an undeniable emotional journey, O'Connor closed with the title track, which begins with her taking in a deep breath before giving us the resolution, and maybe comfort, we are hoping our heroine finds: "I have all that I requested and I do not want what I haven't got." We think she might. *—AD*

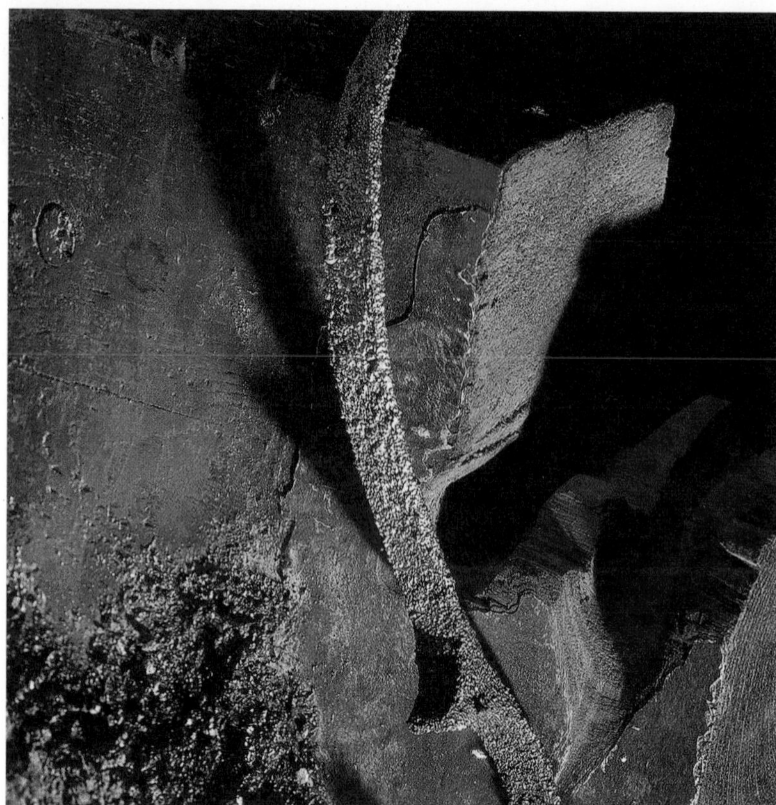

Nusrat Fateh Ali Khan

MUSTT MUSTT

REAL WORLD | Producer: Michael Brook

RELEASED: NOVEMBER 1990

● If there is a list of musical styles most unlikely to appeal to Western ears, much less produce a UK club hit, somewhere near the top must be Qawwali, a trance-inducing form of Sufi devotional music from the Indian subcontinent sung in Urdu, Hindi, Persian, and Punjabi.

Upon hearing Nusrat Fateh Ali Khan, Peter Gabriel thought otherwise.

Gabriel first worked with Khan on his album *Passion*, music originally composed for Martin Scorsese's 1988 film *The Last Temptation of Christ*, an ambient/world music mix that earned the 1990 Grammy Award for Best New Age Album. Gabriel suggested Khan team with Michael Brook, a Canadian producer, guitarist, and film music composer who had previously worked with Brian Eno, Daniel Lanois, and Jon Hassell.

Khan himself was not exclusively a Qawwali traditionalist but was, in fact, an eager experimentalist. The astonishingly prolific singer had released literally hundreds of cassettes that hewed to traditional standards but also broke taboos by addressing topics such as romantic love. Sometimes his music contained no lyrics at all, consisting of classical vocal exercises which, to unfamiliar ears, sound like wordless scatting.

It is the latter approach that comprises the lion's share of *Mustt Mustt*. Only two songs—the title track, which addresses a Sufi saint, and **Nothing Without You (Tery Bina)**, a love song—contain lyrics. The others find Khan's astonishingly dexterous, stratospheric vocals gliding high over Brook's ambient soundscapes made by musicians and instruments from all over the world. British trip-hoppers Massive Attack remixed the title track, resulting in a hypnotic East/West fusion that UK clubbers found irresistible. The album itself climbed to No. 14 on Billboard's World Music chart in 1991.

Khan continued to sing traditional Qawwali and collaborate with Brook, resulting in 1997's Grammy-nominated *Night Song* and the remix album *Star Rise*. He also teamed with Pearl Jam's Eddie Vedder on two songs for the *Dead Man Walking* soundtrack. *–DD*

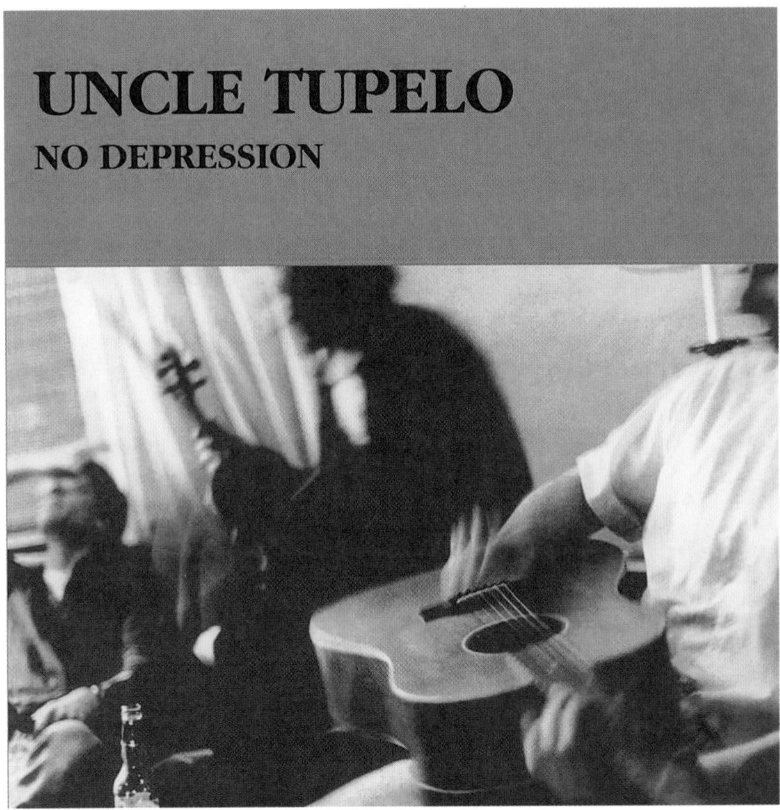

Uncle Tupelo

NO DEPRESSION

ROCKVILLE | Producers: Paul Kolderie, Sean Slade

RELEASED: JUNE 21, 1990

● It's not every band that can express its essential aesthetic in the first line of the first song on its first album, but Uncle Tupelo did exactly that on *No Depression*: "Hometown, same-town blues," guitarist/vocalist Jay Farrar intoned, "same old walls closin' in."

From there, the trio—Farrar, bassist/vocalist Jeff Tweedy, and drummer Mike Heidorn—fired off a baker's dozen of songs that expressed the deep-seated grievances and barroom plaints of small-town life as the 1980s shut down and the '90s beckoned, looking bleaker still: ennui, despair, and disaffection fueled by monotony, conformity, mind-numbing factory work (when there's work to be had), and mind-obliterating alcohol. "Whiskey bottle over Jesus/Not forever, just for now," went another essential lyric.

The suppressed frustration erupted musically as well: furious bursts of punk (check out the sonic mayhem at the conclusion of **Factory Belt**) crossbred with a country twang that pulled back just long enough to let the album's title track, a knowing yet hopeful acoustic cover of a Carter Family favorite, shine through. The song didn't just launch the album and Uncle Tupelo's brief but brilliant career; it also gave name to a music magazine that borrowed the title and ultimately to an entire musical genre (at least until it was rechristened alt-country and/or Americana).

No Depression is looked upon by some as more or less the Ur document of that whole scene. That is a gross exaggeration, given that the music draws on influences dating back generations. But the album distilled those elements in a way that informed not just Farrar and Tweedy's subsequent respective bands, Son Volt and Wilco, but so many bands and fans that even today trod a path that Uncle Tupelo blazed. *—DD*

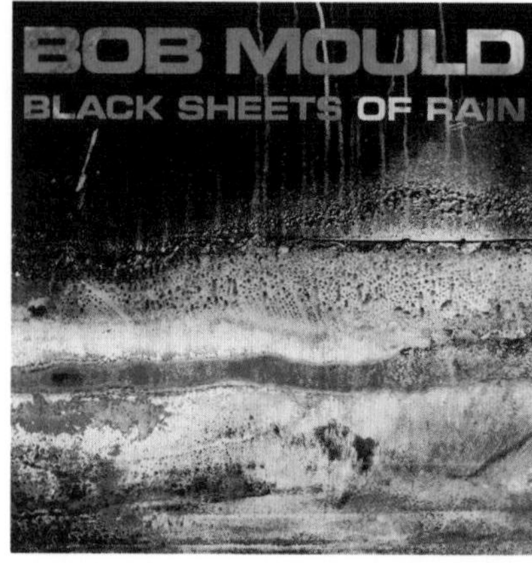

Bob Mould

BLACK SHEETS OF RAIN

VIRGIN | Producer: Bob Mould

RELEASED: MAY 1990

● After the acrimonious 1988 breakup of alternative rock legend Hüsker Dü, guitarist and co-songwriter Bob Mould shocked fans with the clean and often upbeat sounds of his 1989 solo debut, *Workbook*. The title of his sophomore album, *Black Sheets of Rain*, offered clear indication that this brief moment of sunlight had passed. With only occasional respites, namely the impossibly catchy **It's Too Late**, Mould raged over a stormy dark-gray landscape of churning guitars. "Man, tough about that timing, huh?" Mould later recalled a radio promoter telling him after *Black Sheets of Rain* failed to sell well. "If *Black Sheets* had been nine months later, you'd be Pearl Jam." *–MW*

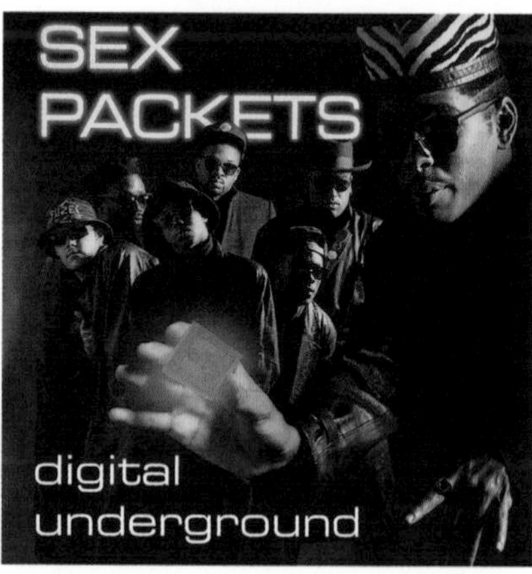

Digital Underground

SEX PACKETS

TOMMY BOY/WARNER BROS. | Producer: Digital Underground

RELEASED: MARCH 20, 1990

● Two years before Dr. Dre sent the Parliament-Funkadelic-sampling G-funk rap subgenre into the stratosphere with *The Chronic*, Digital Underground leader Shock G (Gregory Jacobs) staked claim as an even more loyal disciple of P-Funk mastermind George Clinton. He didn't just sample Clinton's music; he channeled the funk legend's sense of humor and sci-fi fascinations on Digital Underground's debut. It's also the home of the irresistible single **The Humpty Dance**, performed by Shock G's comedic alter-ego Humpty Hump and featuring a drum track that has been sampled by over a hundred of rap's biggest names. Free your mind and your ass will follow, indeed! *–MW*

The Vaughan Brothers

FAMILY STYLE

EPIC | Producer: Nile Rodgers

RELEASED: SEPTEMBER 25, 1990

● By the late 1980s, having emerged from a period of hard-won sobriety, Stevie Ray and Jimmie Vaughan were in peak form. Stepping away from their iconic and respective bands, Double Trouble and the Fabulous Thunderbirds, the brothers united for their lone studio album. Produced by Nile Rodgers (who had previously worked with Stevie Ray on David Bowie's *Let's Dance*) and fueled by the single **Tick Tock**, *Family Style* won two Grammy Awards, including Best Contemporary Blues Album. This tribute to their shared dream of a brother collaboration also served as Stevie Ray's final studio performance. Released just one month after his untimely death in a helicopter crash, it leaves behind a sentimental legacy. *–MD*

Prefab Sprout
JORDAN: THE COMEBACK

KITCHENWARE/CBS | Producer: Thomas Dolby

RELEASED: AUGUST 28, 1990

● When a band's frontman (Paddy McAloon in this case) compares an album to the K-tel compilations of yore, it sets off alarm bells. But for *Jordan: The Comeback*, it was apt in the best possible way. The British troupe's fifth studio album was a sweeping, ambitious song cycle, its nineteen Thomas Dolby–produced tracks moving from rock to disco, funk to country, and even touches of bolero, with a four-song mid-album segment connecting Jesse James and Elvis Presley as outlaw kindred spirits. Comparisons made at the time to the masterworks of Phil Spector, Brian Wilson, and The Beatles more than hold up three decades later. *–GG*

Texas Tornados
TEXAS TORNADOS

REPRISE | Producers: Bill Halverson, Texas Tornados

RELEASED: AUGUST 1990

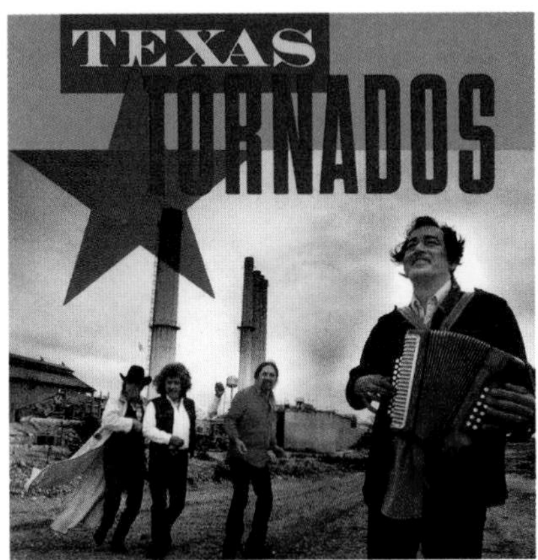

● This record is one of those "if you know, you know" sort of things. There is no mystery or pretense: Texas Tornados was pure Texas music and everything that implies—rhythm and blues, conjunto, old-school rock 'n' roll, waltzes, tear-jerking ballads, and deep, deep soul. Doug Sahm coined the band's name during the early '70s, but it came to full fruition with the addition of country star Freddy Fender, revered accordionist Flaco Jiménez, and Sahm's longtime keyboard compatriot Augie Myers. This record is best listened to in a darkened room, hazy with cigarette smoke, and a longneck beer bottle in hand. *–HK*

Midnight Oil
BLUE SKY MINING

COLUMBIA | Producers: Warne Livesey, Midnight Oil

RELEASED: FEBRUARY 9, 1990

● The seventh full-length album by Midnight Oil marked its arrival as a world-renowned rock band and a prominent voice for progressive causes, including global warming, indigenous rights, and social justice. The group was born from the punk ethos but didn't limit itself to the perceived rigors of the genre. More than any of the band's preceding records, *Blue Sky Mining* was full of infectious melody and vocal harmony with blazing guitars and pulsing drums. The fact that it was massively successful only emphasized that the voices it intended to amplify were being heard. *–HK*

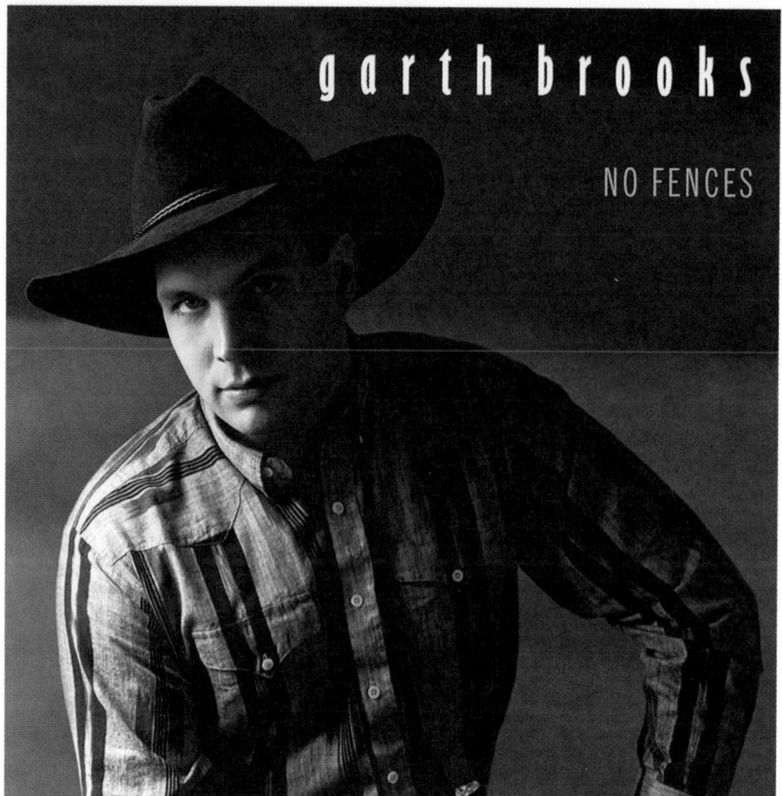

Garth Brooks

NO FENCES

CAPITOL NASHVILLE | Producer: Allen Reynolds

RELEASED: AUGUST 27, 1990

● Garth Brooks's self-titled debut album, released in 1989, put him on the map, but it was its follow-up, *No Fences*, that officially launched the Oklahoma singer and songwriter (on four tracks here) toward global superstardom. It was his first project to be released in Europe, in fact, while stateside, *No Fences* was Brooks's first No. 1 on the Billboard Country Albums chart—where it would spend 126 weeks in the Top 40—and reached No. 3 on the Billboard 200. All four of its singles hit No. 1 on the Hot Country Songs chart, too, and did the same in Canada. To date, it's been certified eighteen-times platinum, the best-seller of Brooks's robust catalog.

Continuing his association with producer Allen Reynolds, *No Fences* is the home of some of Brooks's most beloved and enduring hits: the party anthem **Friends in Low Places** (previously recorded by David Chamberlain and Mark Chesnutt); **The Thunder Rolls**, an ode to marital discord; the sentimental **Unanswered Prayers**; and the lively, celebratory **Two of a Kind, Workin' on a Full House**, originally recorded by co-writer Dennis Robbins, formerly of the rock band the Rockets. **Wild Horses**, meanwhile, provided the requisite cowboy content and scored another Top 10 hit from the album.

No Fences was named Album of the Year by the Country Music Association (CMA) and the Academy of Country Music (ACM). Brooks also walked away with wins at both award shows that year for Single of the Year (**Friends in Low Places**) as well as the prestigious Entertainer of the Year. Brooks went on to sell more than 160 million albums (and counting), earning the distinction of being the top-selling solo artist in US history according to the Recording Industry Association of America (RIAA). He is also the only act to have nine albums certified by the RIAA for sales of more than ten million copies each. *—MH2*

Fugazi
REPEATER

DISCHORD | Producers: Fugazi, Ted Niceley

RELEASED: APRIL 19, 1990

● Incubated over three previous EPs, Fugazi was well honed by the time the defiantly iconoclastic Washington, DC, quartet hit the studio to make its first full album. Ian MacKaye and company do a lot of righteous raging against the machine throughout these eleven tracks, putting capitalism and gun violence in their crosshairs, but it's Fugazi's musical attack that made *Repeater* a classic. It was the birth of a new kind of "alternative" rock, with all four members, particularly the rhythm section of bassist Joe Lally and drummer Brendan Canty, locked in tight enough to let the songs careen with an anarchic and inventive power. *–GG*

A Guy Called Gerald
AUTOMANIKK

COLUMBIA/CBS | Producer: Ricky Rouge (aka Gerald Simpson)

RELEASED: 1990

● The early emotive rhythms that Gerald Simpson (aka A Guy Called Gerald) created in his Manchester, England, home studio shared the relationships captured in a late-night club. His massive 1989 track "Voodoo Ray" romanticized subculture beats and melody that connected futuristic funk intimately to house, acid, and techno. The production cues on *Automanikk* leaned from technically elegant to inventive and adventurous, uniquely translating a personal and patient story of man and machine. The album's single, **FX**, featured pulsing remix duties from Detroit techno pioneers Derrick May and Carl Craig. Simpson's ability to design and direct new genres by harnessing technology deserves higher praise and deeper listening. *–CW*

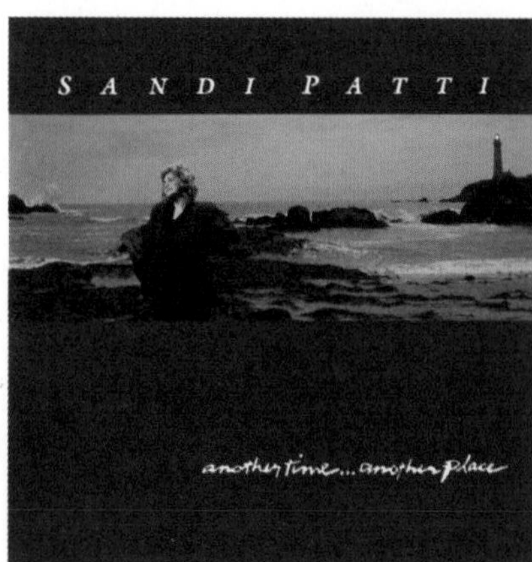

Sandi Patti
ANOTHER TIME . . . ANOTHER PLACE

WORD | Producers: Greg Nelson, Sandi Patti

RELEASED: SEPTEMBER 17, 1990

● During the '80s and early '90s, Sandi Patti reigned as a leading voice of contemporary Christian music, dressing up her testimony with pop-friendly melodic savvy to hover near the fringes of the pop mainstream. This, Patti's twelfth studio album, was a defining effort that scored her fifth and final Grammy Award (Best Pop/Contemporary Gospel Album) and was certified gold. It featured duets with fellow Christian stars Amy Grant (**Unexpected Friends**) and Wayne Watson (the title track) among its eleven songs, as well as players such as Toto's Jeff Porcaro and all-star bassist Nathan East. *–GG*

Jack DeJohnette
PARALLEL REALITIES

MCA | Producers: Jack DeJohnette, Pat Metheny

RELEASED: 1990

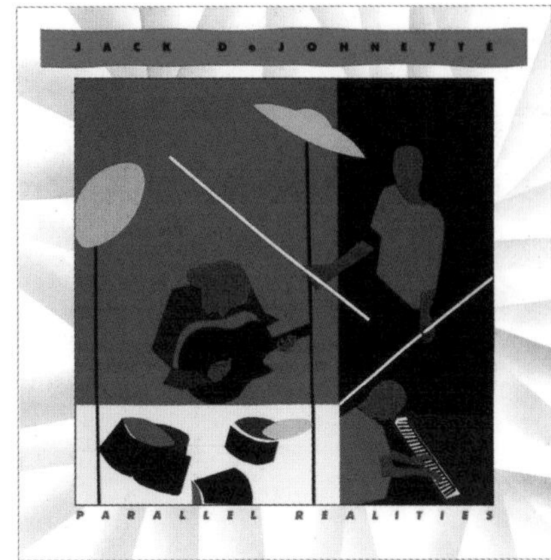

● The beauty behind this elite trio of jazz veterans—Jack DeJohnette on drums and keyboard bass, Pat Metheny on guitars, and piano legend Herbie Hancock—is how apt the composition and connection of the performance fits this album's title. All three brilliant musicians made their mark, entry, or loudest bang amid the jazz fusion scene of the 1970s. *Parallel Realities* displayed their masterful craft as they bridged jazz styles of different decades with force and grace. Collectively they also forged a recording polish and song structure reflecting where contemporary jazz had traversed a decade before the new millennium arrived. *—CW*

Happy Mondays
PILLS 'N' THRILLS AND BELLYACHES

FACTORY | Producers: Paul Oakenfold, Steve Osborne

RELEASED: NOVEMBER 5, 1990

● England's druggy, dance-inducing Madchester scene was well established by the time mainstay Happy Mondays issued its third album. *Pills 'n' Thrills and Bellyaches* was a defining moment, however, when all the trippy ingredients were knitted together into a joyous forty-four-minute party helmed by ace remixers Paul Oakenfold and Steve Osborne. Oakenfold's loops gave the ten songs a deep, grooving exuberance that allowed the band, and particularly guitarist Mark Day, a wide creative berth. Shaun Ryder's opium-fueled lyrics fit those sonic surroundings perfectly, and tracks such as **Kinky Afro**, **Donovan**, and a cover of John Kongos's **Step On** rank as enduring classics. *—GG*

Judas Priest
PAINKILLER

COLUMBIA | Producer: Chris Tsangarides

RELEASED: SEPTEMBER 14, 1990

● Having already been at the forefront of two revolutions in heavy metal, Judas Priest's legacy was secure long before the '90s. Its attempt to fit in with the poppier mainstream hair metal movement of the late '80s seemed to signify the end of its days as a pioneer. So nobody was prepared for the fury the band unleashed on *Painkiller* by embracing and sometimes improving on the music made by a new wave of Priest-loving thrash and speed metal acts. Pairing new levels of speed and intensity with the band's hard-earned sense of songcraft, the album helped Judas Priest connect to a new generation of metal maniacs. *—MW*

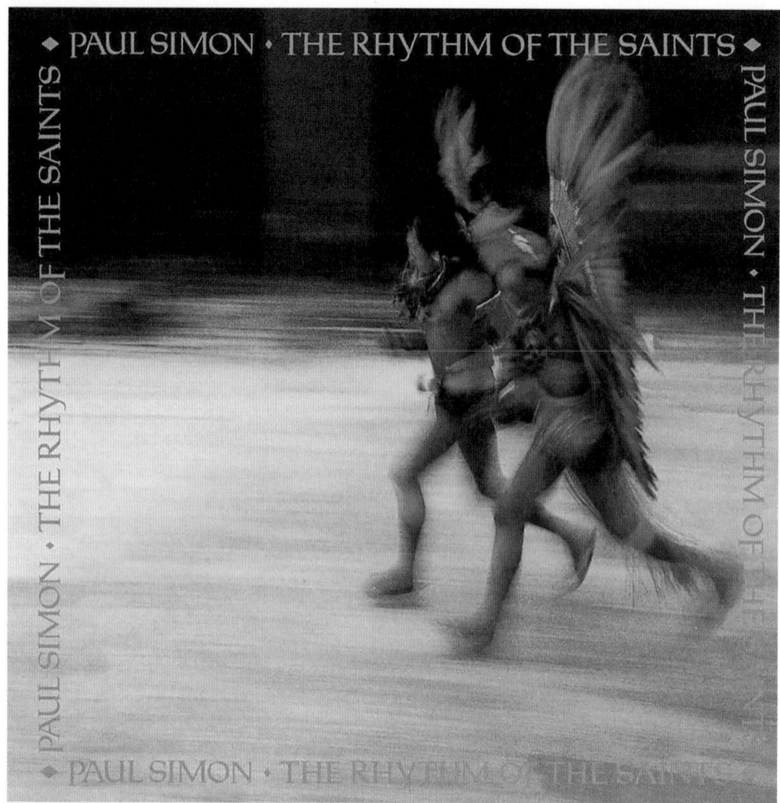

Paul Simon

THE RHYTHM OF THE SAINTS

WARNER BROS. | Producer: Paul Simon

RELEASED: OCTOBER 16, 1990

● After you've taken the pop world to a foreign place (Africa), and in the process won the Grammy Award for Album of the Year, what do you do for an encore? If you're Paul Simon, you throw another dart at the map and find another locale rife with musical inspiration.

Coming after one of Simon & Garfunkel's periodic reunions, 1986's *Graceland* reminded the world of Simon's creative daring and fearless acumen—to the tune of five-times platinum sales. This was not new. Simon had explored international styles with Garfunkel and on his own, with hit-making results, but *Graceland* was his most intensive immersion to date and a career high point.

For its follow-up, Simon headed to the Southern Hemisphere again, this time to South America (primarily Brazil) and its many rhythms, some of them with their own African roots, of course. Over the set's ten songs, Simon and his corps of indigenous and American musicians drew on forró and gaucho, sertanejo, and pagode, with great appreciation for subtlety and nuance and weaving them together with Western motifs so completely that it's impossible to separate the elements. That, in turn, made each song a unique adventure and the album as a whole an aural travelogue that truly evoked **The Coast**, **The Cool**, **Cool River**, and the **Spirit Voices** he was writing about.

The Obvious Child was illustrative as the album opener, its polyrhythmic percussive assault a cultural counterweight to the lyrics' reference to Simon's beloved Yankee Stadium. There were moments of beautiful, deceptive simplicity in something like **Born at the Right Time**, but on tracks such as **Can't Run But**, **The Cool, Cool River**, and the engrossing **Proof**, Simon took listeners on evocative journeys that engage a range of senses beyond the ears. *The Rhythm of the Saints* was not the monolith that *Graceland* was, but it was another gutsy (and Grammy-nominated) outing emboldened by its predecessor's success. *–GG*

1991

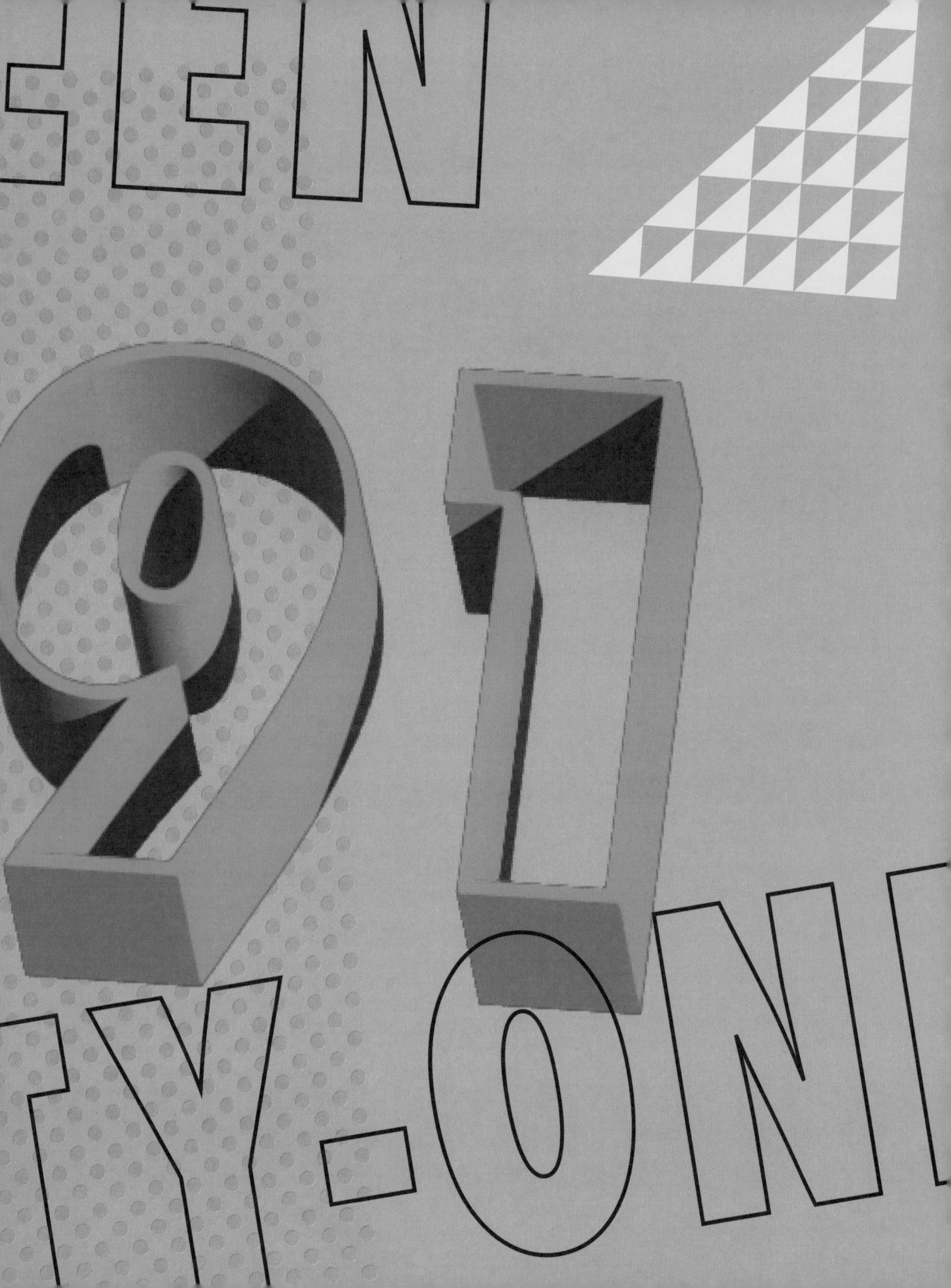
91

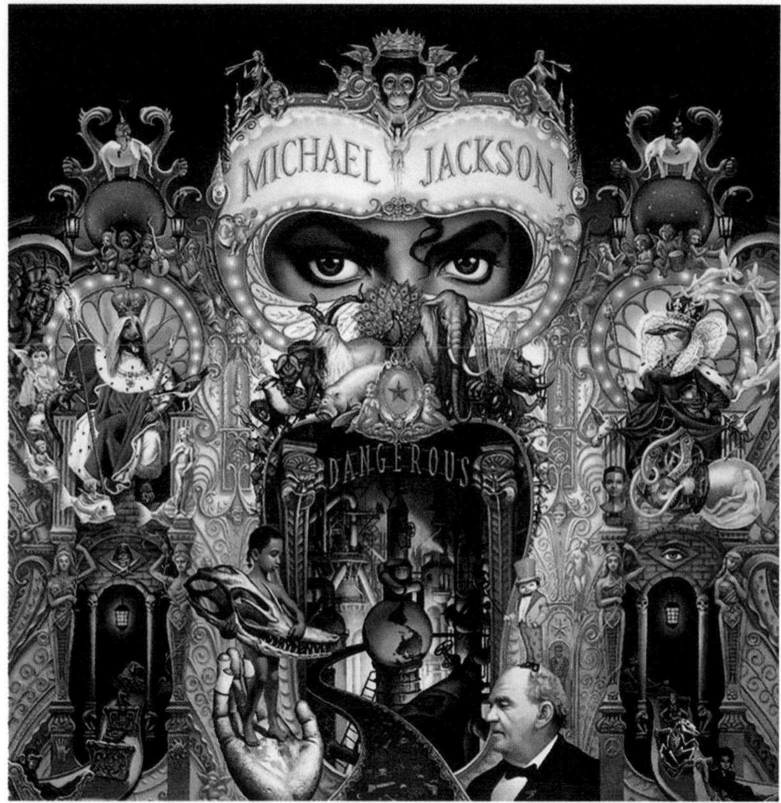

Michael Jackson

DANGEROUS

EPIC | Producers: Michael Jackson, Bill Bottrell, Bruce Swedien, Teddy Riley

RELEASED: NOVEMBER 26, 1991

● After spending the previous decade-plus riding the careful—and history-making—production auspices of Quincy Jones, Michael Jackson was due for a change. Hell, the tabloid morass of his extra-musical life pretty much demanded he give people something to talk about other than his . . . idiosyncrasies, to use a polite term.

Dangerous did it. Coming four years after *Bad*, the fourteen-song set found Jackson exploring fresh directions with a cadre of new collaborators, including New Jack Swing architect Teddy Riley and avant rock producer Bill Bottrell, along with longtime engineer Bruce Swedien, whose presence ensured things didn't get too, well, dangerous. But they were risky from the get-go, as tracks like **Jam** (with a Heavy D rap), the angry **Why You Wanna Trip on Me**, and even the poppier **In the Closet** launched *Dangerous* with edgy rhythmic and sonic experiments that applied Jackson's take to sounds his sister Janet and Prince were mining in their own works that were leaving him in the dust.

Dangerous has some of the Jackson requisites, of course: the celebrity rock guitarist cameo (Slash on **Give In to Me**); a gospel nod (**Keep the Faith** with Andraé Crouch); well-intentioned but hokey commentary (the "We Are the World" rewrite **Heal the World** is no "Man in the Mirror"), and some pop schmaltz (**Will You Be There**). But most of the album is expansive and experimental, not merely more in touch with contemporary trends but finding ways to make them his own. Riley laid some New Jack groundwork for Jackson to manipulate, while Wreckx-n-Effect (**She Drives Me Wild**) and L.T.B. (**Black or White**) brought more rap to the mix.

Despite its No. 1 debut, *Dangerous* wasn't universally embraced at the time, but in hindsight, it stands as a brave step and the last truly important album Jackson would release. *—GG*

Pearl Jam

TEN

EPIC | Producers: Rick Parashar, Pearl Jam

RELEASED: AUGUST 27, 1991

● *Ten* is not only one of the greatest debuts from a rock band, but it might be the seminal album of the so-called grunge movement. While some fans point to Nirvana's *Nevermind*, late summer and early fall of 1991 saw *Ten*, released one month before *Nevermind*, helping to open the floodgates for other new bands of the era, including Stone Temple Pilots, Bush, Live, and more.

Ten showcased the vocal prowess and writing of Eddie Vedder, whose signature sound helped elevate Pearl Jam beyond just a key player in the Seattle music scene. Guitarists Stone Gossard and Mike McCready, bassist Jeff Ament, and drummer Matt Cameron recorded the initial five-song core of *Ten* as an instrumental demo with roots in Gossard's and Ament's previous band, Mother Love Bone. When the tape made its way to Vedder in San Diego, it was a match made in musical heaven.

Ten is one of those rare albums that is highly enjoyable front to back. Unlike many grunge-labeled artists, Pearl Jam defied easy classification. Its sound and songs appealed to modern and classic rock fans alike—alternative in attitude but timeless in execution, power chords and hooks included.

Ten took its time moving up the charts, finally hitting No. 2 on the Billboard 200 in late 1992, as well as scoring two Grammy Award nominations. **Alive**, **Even Flow**, and **Jeremy** became rock radio staples, the latter's shocking video winning four trophies, including Video of the Year at the 1993 MTV Video Music Awards.

The success of the alternative format during the early '90s was highly attributable to the power, majesty, and enduring quality of *Ten*, which has aged well and sounds every bit as contemporary and powerful as it did when it was released. *–FJ*

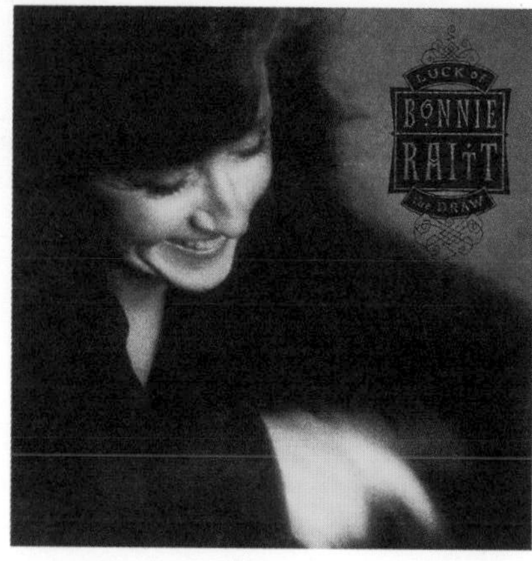

Bonnie Raitt
LUCK OF THE DRAW

CAPITOL | Producers: Bonnie Raitt, Don Was

RELEASED: JUNE 1991

● *Luck of the Draw* was definitive proof that *Nick of Time*, Bonnie Raitt's career-reviving Grammy-winning album, was no fluke. Featuring many of the same names (co-producer Don Was, writer/duet partner John Hiatt), plus Bruce Hornsby, Richard Thompson, Delbert McClinton, and other luminaries, it captured the seductive singer/songwriter and slide guitarist at a confident peak, starting with the sassy **Something to Talk About**. Dropping R&B, gospel, soul, blues, and reggae grooves with a beguiling mix of playfulness and restraint, she also revealed aching vulnerability on **I Can't Make You Love Me**, the exquisite Allen Shamblin–Mike Reid ballad that became another signature song. *–LM*

The Orb
THE ORB'S ADVENTURES BEYOND THE ULTRAWORLD

BIG LIFE | Producers: Alex Paterson, Andy Falconer, Kris Weston, Jimmy Cauty

RELEASED: APRIL 2, 1991

● As '90s electronic music and club culture evolved and expanded, the sonic tapestry behind The Orb's *Adventures Beyond the Ultraworld* captured the stars and space to create a longer, stranger trip. This off-world soundtrack was designed from a unique blend of influences: house music, dub reggae, classical minimalism, and DJ and sample techniques born in the underground chill-out club culture of late-'80s London. Featuring the single **Little Fluffy Clouds**, the album's hyper-original style helped usher in the popularity of trip-hop, ambient, and electronica by elegantly looping inventive samples, dub bass lines, and studio-punched soundclash. *–CW*

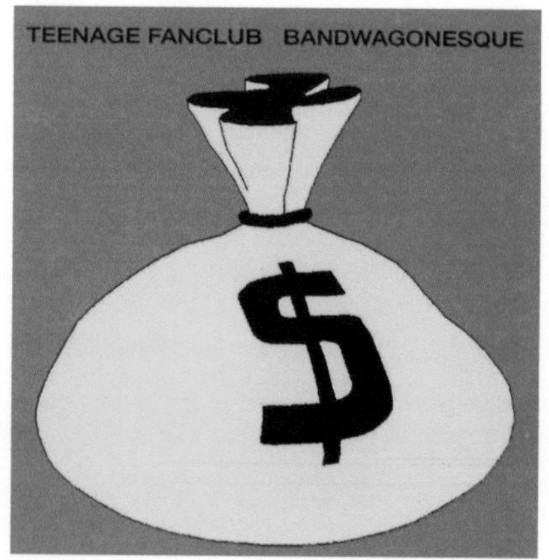

Teenage Fanclub
BANDWAGONESQUE

CREATION/DGC | Producers: Don Fleming, Paul Chisholm, Teenage Fanclub

RELEASED: NOVEMBER 19, 1991

● Indebted to Big Star and gifted with spectacular power-pop hooks reminiscent of the genre's '80s heyday, Teenage Fanclub's *Bandwagonesque* came out of nowhere, at least in the US, where three of its songs landed on the Alternative Rock chart. Boasting a trio of strong singers and songwriters (Norman Blake, Gerald Love, and Raymond McGinley), the Scottish band had no shortage of talent or material when assembling the twelve tracks for its third album. Subsequent records contained a similar surfeit of consistency, but *Bandwagonesque* remains an unquestionable masterpiece. *–MG*

Dolly Parton
EAGLE WHEN SHE FLIES

COLUMBIA NASHVILLE | Producers: Dolly Parton, Steve Buckingham, Gary Smith

RELEASED: MARCH 7, 1991

● Fans welcomed Dolly Parton's return to her country roots after her pop releases of the '80s, particularly the triple-platinum soundtrack hit "9 to 5." This was her thirty-first album release, and it spawned several hit country singles: the chart-topping **Rockin' Years** (a duet with Ricky Van Shelton), **Silver and Gold**, and the title track helped make the album No. 1 on Billboard's Country Album chart and her first platinum-selling solo studio album in fourteen years. *Eagle When She Flies* also featured collaborations with Lorrie Morgan on **Best Woman Wins**, while Emmylou Harris (**Country Road**), Alison Krauss (**If You Need Me**), and Vince Gill and Patty Loveless (**Silver and Gold**) are among those contributing background and harmony vocals. –*TR*

Joe Jackson
LAUGHTER & LUST

VIRGIN | Producers: Joe Jackson, Ed Roynesdal

RELEASED: APRIL 29, 1991

● After a decade of increasingly eclectic genre and recording experimentations, Joe Jackson began to re-explore pop music with 1989's excellent *Blaze of Glory* and narrowed his focus even tighter on *Laughter & Lust*. The result was the most straight-ahead display of his songwriting skills and pop instincts in more than a decade, featuring shoulda-been hit singles such as **Obvious Song** and **Stranger Than Fiction**, as well as a powerful cover of Fleetwood Mac's **Oh Well**. *Laughter & Lust*'s lack of commercial success sent Jackson back down his experimental path, and it would be nearly a decade before he returned to the pop world. –*MW*

Saint Etienne
FOXBASE ALPHA

HEAVENLY | Producer: Saint Etienne

RELEASED: SEPTEMBER 16, 1991

● With *Foxbase Alpha*, Saint Etienne reshaped '90s Britpop with the grooves of Swingin' London and the beats of house music, reanimating the analog past for the digital age. Founders Bob Stanley and Pete Wiggs demonstrated talent for sampling incidental magic on a minor-key hip-hop cover of Neil Young's **Only Love Can Break Your Heart** and on **Spring**, which used Bobby Reed's "The Time Is Right for Love" as a supple bed for Sarah Cracknell's liquid purr. Best of all was the anthem **Nothing Can Stop Us Now**, where a throwaway intro from a Dusty Springfield record became a heart-fluttering hook. –*CS*

Ice-T

O.G. ORIGINAL GANGSTER

SIRE | Producers: Ice-T, DJ Aladdin, Shafiq Husayn

RELEASED: MAY 14, 1991

● Ice-T had plenty to say on his fourth studio album, and he saved his most incendiary remarks for the set's spoken word outro. "F*ck the police, f*ck the FBI, f*ck the DEA, f*ck the CIA, f*ck Tipper Gore, Bush and his crippled bitch," the MC said, or bellowed in a plainspoken, matter-of-fact cadence. "This is Ice-T, I'm outta here. Told ya: you shoulda killed me last year."

No mincing words there. This was the West Coast gangsta rap pioneer's most pointed and sprawling work yet, a massive twenty-four-track effort that found him extolling street-life tales (**Midnight**, a prequel to his 1986 classic "6 in the Mornin'"), missives about the pratfalls of fame (**Lifestyles of the Rich and Infamous**), prison stories (**The Tower**, built around a sample of John Carpenter's *Halloween* theme), songs about writing songs (**Mind Over Matter** and **Pulse of the Rhyme**), and even hard rock headbangers (**Body Count**, a precursor to the following year's debut of Ice-T's metal outfit of the same name).

O.G. Original Gangster was also Ice-T's commercial peak, topping out at No. 15 on Billboard's Top 200 on the strength of a pair of crossover singles: **New Jack Hustler (Nino's Theme)**, a propulsive anthem told from the perspective of Wesley Snipes's *New Jack City* character Nino Brown, and the album's title track, which brought a street term meaning "originator" to the masses. The song is the reason the term "O.G." would veer wildly from its initial intended meaning and enter the everyday lexicon for decades to come, used to describe everyone from athletes to actors.

Ice-T would go on to a lucrative acting career himself, appearing on *Law & Order: Special Victims Unit* for more than twenty seasons. When it comes to rapper/actors, you could say he's an O.G., and no one ever doubted his credentials. *—AG*

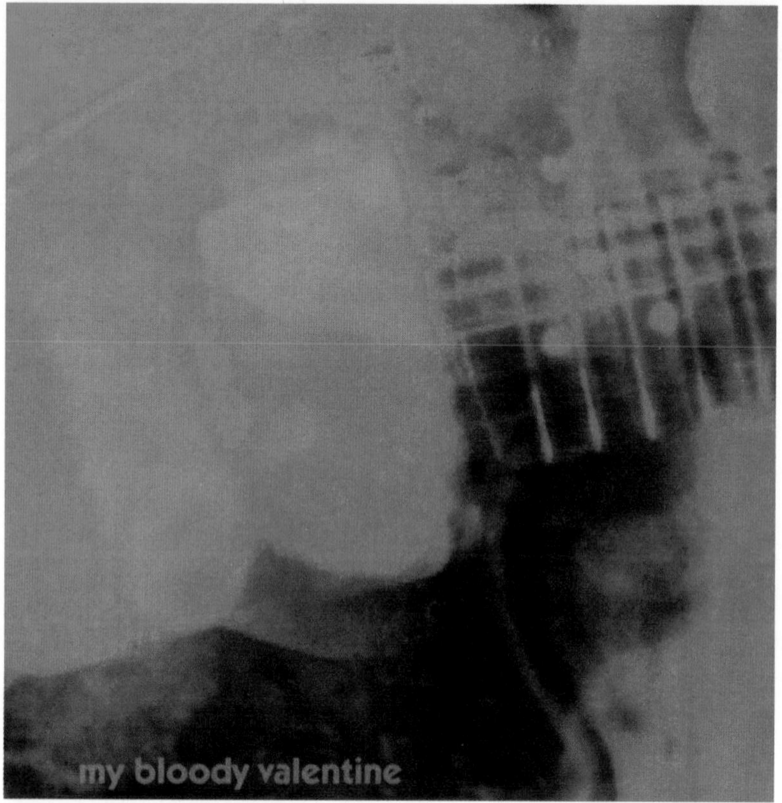

My Bloody Valentine

LOVELESS

CREATION | Producers: Kevin Shields, Colm O'Ciosoig

RELEASED: NOVEMBER 4, 1991

● Sessions for My Bloody Valentine's second album began four months after the release of its 1988 debut, *Isn't Anything*. The label expected the recording to last five months, but it took more than two and a half years. *Loveless* was a labor of love for My Bloody Valentine leader Kevin Shields but a thorn in the side for everyone else involved. The frustrating process reportedly led to the bankruptcy of London-based Creation Records and the band's disintegration in the wake of Shields's increasingly erratic behavior.

But few albums from the era have had the lasting impact of *Loveless*. It sounded out of place and time then, and it still does now. A milestone record in the history of several '90s genres—shoegaze, dream-pop, noise rock, and indie—the album's use of the studio as a key component of its sound remains unmatched, as does Shields's tremolo-enhanced guitar vibrato. A wall of noise ran through *Loveless*'s best songs—**Only Shallow**, **When You Sleep**, **I Only Said**, and **Soon**—that rarely interfered with melody. Shields and guitarist Bilinda Butcher shared vocals, often burying them as sensual pillows beneath blankets of guitars, keyboards, and drums.

There are moments where *Loveless* sounded like a rock 'n' roll orchestra, with layered guitars giving the false impression that dozens of instruments were used during recording. (My Bloody Valentine's tour in support of the album has been called one of the loudest in history.) Shields was like a '90s version of Phil Spector, even recording in mono as he developed a sound and style all his own. While the implications of Shields's fastidious working process reverberated for years, the quartet responsible for *Loveless* ultimately managed to release a follow-up—a mere twenty-two years later. *—MG*

Red Hot Chili Peppers

BLOOD SUGAR SEX MAGIK

WARNER BROS. | Producer: Rick Rubin

RELEASED: SEPTEMBER 24, 1991

● Red Hot Chili Peppers were five albums in when everything came together.

The quartet had a new label and a new producer in Rick Rubin, as well as some momentum from the platinum showing of 1989's *Mother's Milk*, which brought guitarist John Frusciante and drummer Chad Smith on board. Hunkering down in The Mansion, a reputedly haunted Los Angeles enclave that had reportedly hosted Harry Houdini, the Chili Peppers made its best album to date amid the friendly ghosts, inspired by residential bonhomie that gave the band a focused sense of purpose.

The results were in the proverbial grooves: seventeen hot tracks that started with a count-off into the frenetic funk of **The Power of Equality** and rode an evocative ebb and flow over the course of its seventy-four minutes. The group homed in on songs this time, shedding the gratuitous excesses that had limited its previous albums and drawing strength from Frusciante's melodic sensibilities and Smith's granite pocket that gave Flea's bass and Anthony Kiedis's lyrics room to dance and carom around the arrangements. *Blood Sugar Sex Magik* had plenty of texture, but this time, the band (probably via Rubin) knew how to use it to more transcendent effect.

The Chili Peppers party raged on tracks such as **If You Have to Ask**, **Suck My Kiss**, and the Grammy-winning **Give It Away**. But **Breaking the Girl** took the band in a fresh psychedelic direction (Mellotron included) that was every bit as exciting. **I Could Have Lied** was a gentle delight, but the soaring **Under the Bridge** was the breakthrough pop hit, six-times platinum and reaching No. 2 on the Billboard Hot 100.

Blood Sugar Sex Magik put the Chili Peppers atop the following year's Lollapalooza tour bill, though Frusciante left shortly before the run, ending the first of his three tenures in the band. *—GG*

Guns N' Roses

USE YOUR ILLUSION I/ USE YOUR ILLUSION II

GEFFEN | Producers: Mike Clink, Guns N' Roses

RELEASED: SEPTEMBER 17, 1991

● It's hard to deny that Guns N' Roses (GNR) *Use Your Illusion* albums could use some editing. The twin double albums' thirty tracks clock in at a more than two-and-a-half-hour run time. But watch the disagreements that start when fans start picking *which Use Your Illusion* songs to cut. It soon becomes clear that there was at least some method to GNR's indulgent madness. Or maybe the band was just inspired and talented enough to get away with it. Your call.

It's important to remember that Guns N' Roses had exactly one full-length album under its belt before the quintet started recording what became the *Use Your Illusion* opus. The 1987 debut album, *Appetite for Destruction*, made GNR a superstar act, almost universally hailed as a savior of "real" rock music. But the resulting pressures, addictions, and conflicts fractured the group. As a result, the *Use Your Illusion* albums found Guns N' Roses simultaneously expanding its range in very impressive ways and utterly falling apart from within.

Drummer Steven Adler was fired early in what ballooned into the more than a year-and-a-half-long recording process. His replacement, Matt Sorum, noticeably shifted the band's sound away from rock and toward metal. Elsewhere, you can hear the individual band members' tastes and ambitions veering off in wildly divergent directions. While guitarist Izzy Stradlin continued to successfully mine *Appetite*-era territory, singer Axl Rose set his sights on grandiose, ornate epics like **November Rain**, **Coma**, and **Estranged**.

Although Rose and Stradlin teamed up on some of the album's most thrilling tracks, including **You Could Be Mine** and **Don't Cry**, their differing approaches and, more importantly, the band's combustible interpersonal dynamics couldn't hold together for much longer, and by 1997, Rose was the only founding member left in the band. *–MW*

R.E.M.

OUT OF TIME

WARNER BROS. | Producers: Scott Litt, R.E.M.

RELEASED: MARCH 12, 1991

● R.E.M. had surprised fans to varying degrees over the course of its first ten years and six albums. But *Out of Time*, its second in a reported multimillion-dollar deal with Warner Bros., was a shock—albeit a very pleasant one.

The Athens, Georgia, quartet—the toast of the alt-rock world during the '80s—brought the fresh right out of the box here, too. A familiar shimmering guitar pattern introduced **Radio Song** but quickly gave way to a taut semi-funk groove accented by strings and brass honks and an industry-skewering rap by Boogie Down Productions' KRS-One. Then came **Losing My Religion**, an elegiac acoustic guitar- and mandolin-driven ode that gave R.E.M. its first Top 5 hit on the Billboard 200 and won two Grammy Awards.

Message delivered, the group spent the rest of the quadruple-platinum set (which took home the Grammy for Best Alternative Music Album) doing whatever it damn well pleased. There are references to the Byrds (**Near Wild Heaven**) and The Velvet Underground (**Low**). Michael Stipe's wordless vocals floated alongside flute and strings during **Endgame**. **Belong** offered spoken-word art-pop. If the dense, moody **Country Feedback** lacked twang, that was found in **Texarkana**, amid a familiar, surging guitar attack. The closing **Half a World Away** and **Me in Honey**—the latter one of three tracks featuring Kate Pierson of the B-52's—could have fit on any of the band's preceding albums but demonstrated how much clarity Scott Litt's production brought to the party.

And while there was grousing about the frothiness of **Shiny Happy People**, a duet with Pierson, we're betting a fair share of those folks actually sang along in secret.

Out of Time was R.E.M. at its boldest, both to date and perhaps ever, and an album that in its own way telegraphed the sonic openness that would play out during the rest of the decade. *—GG*

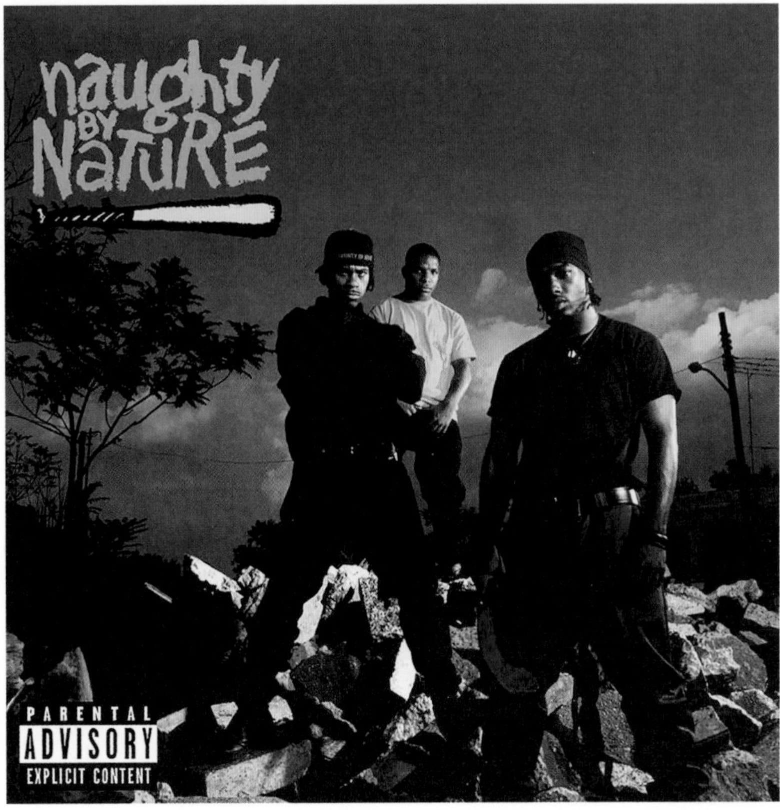

Naughty by Nature

NAUGHTY BY NATURE

TOMMY BOY | Producers: Naughty by Nature, Louie Vega

RELEASED: SEPTEMBER 3, 1991

● In the summer of 1991, everybody was down with **O.P.P.** How can we explain it? That was the question (and subsequent explanation) that made this Grammy-nominated cheater's anthem (O.P.P. is code for [o]ther [p]eople's, well, significant other is a polite way of putting it) ring out from car stereos in New York and Los Angeles and everywhere in between. The bouncy, singsong-y party jam, built around a playful sample of The Jackson 5's "ABC," became a crossover smash, reaching No. 6 on Billboard's Hot 100 at a time when rap songs typically didn't crack the Top 10. In the process, it teed up the East Orange, New Jersey, trio's self-titled sophomore album for success.

Prior to Naughty by Nature, Anthony "Treach" Criss, Vincent "Vin Rock" Brown, and Keir "DJ Kay Gee" Gist released *Independent Leaders* under the moniker The New Style in 1989. That set caught the ear of Queen Latifah, a native of neighboring Newark, who took the group under her wing and repackaged it as Naughty by Nature. Latifah appears on **Wickedest Man Alive**, a Caribbean-flavored reggae-rap song that showcases Treach's dexterous style and flow, which is as sharp as the machete he wields on the album's cover. Treach's lyrics are so tongue-twisting that Eminem once said **Yoke the Joker**, the album's opener, nearly made him hang up his pen.

Everything's Gonna Be Alright, the second single, followed **O.P.P.**'s successful pop-rap formula, flipping a sample of Bob Marley's "No Woman No Cry" underneath a gritty tale of absentee fathers. It's an example of what Naughty by Nature does best: straddling the worlds of pop and rap and showing the two could peacefully coexist. And if there's a problem, that machete is never far from reach. *–AG*

Prince and the New Power Generation

DIAMONDS AND PEARLS

PAISLEY PARK/WARNER BROS. | Producer: Prince

RELEASED: OCTOBER 1, 1991

● After spending the entirety of the '80s forcing his peers to scramble to keep up with his relentless innovation and productivity, Prince took a minute to get his bearings straight for the next decade. There's nothing particularly wrong with either 1989's *Batman* or 1990's *Graffiti Bridge* soundtracks, but for the first time, even loyal fans were forced to admit there were high *and* low points on a Prince album. It was also clear that Prince had lost his hold on mainstream fans, as the latter album failed to sell a million copies—something that hadn't happened to Prince since 1980's *Dirty Mind*. Hip-hop and New Jack Swing artists and producers, including Prince's former Time cohorts Jimmy Jam and Terry Lewis, had supplanted him on the airwaves.

Realizing it was a time for multiple changes, Prince formed a new backing band that he made an important part of the marketing campaign for 1991's *Diamonds and Pearls*, wisely representing himself as a bandleader for the first time since the days of The Revolution.

He also totally overhauled his sonic palette, trading the icy synths and drum machines of the '80s for real drums and warmer, more traditional instrumentation. More importantly, he delivered some of his most undeniable singles in years, from the sultry T-Rex groove of **Cream** to the elegant title track and the wonderfully horny **Gett Off**. Not everything clicked; in particular, the contributions from in-house rapper Tony M. made parts of the album sound almost immediately dated.

Prince did far better when following his own idiosyncratic nature on album cuts such as the propulsive **Willing and Able** and the jazzy **Strollin'**. In short, Prince was right to seek change but fared better when walking his own path instead of chasing trends. *–MW*

Dinosaur Jr

GREEN MIND

BLANCO Y NEGRO/SIRE | Producer: J Mascis

RELEASED: FEBRUARY 19, 1991

● Amherst, Massachusetts–based Dinosaur Jr first piqued interest in the late '80s with a pair of LPs on revered indie label SST. With roots in hardcore punk, the band became notorious for punishing volume but also the soaring guitar flights of J Mascis.

By 1991, Mascis essentially *was* Dinosaur Jr. Bassist Lou Barlow had bolted to form the lo-fi standard bearer Sebadoh, and drummer Murph appeared on just three songs from this fourth album, leaving Mascis playing virtually everything. Opener **The Wagon** was nearly five glorious minutes of Mascis's pedalboard peregrinations and Murph percussion that (here as elsewhere) was as melodic as it was rhythmic. Murph later noted that Mascis, a former drummer, always conceived the drum tracks before teaching them to him. That lack of autonomy would see Murph following Barlow out the door, though the original trio re-formed in 2005.

Blowing It and **I Live for That Look** also delivered on the promise of **The Wagon**, with Mascis's trademark slack vocal style providing a compelling counterpoint to the urgent drumming and perfectly reflecting the prevailing Gen X ennui. Mascis provided a reprieve with the acoustically driven **Flying Cloud** before pivoting back with the pounding post-punk urgency of **How'd You Pin That One on Me**, whose layered guitars complement a dyspeptic lyric that was difficult not to read as a Barlow diss track.

On side two, **Muck** served up quasi-funk, and the closing title track was notable for its hooky chorus. But the highlights here were **Water** and **Thumb**, with engineer Sean Slade's Mellotron underpinning the Mascis guitar passages that continued to serve as the album's statement of purpose—particularly **Thumb**, on which Mascis seemed to channel Funkadelic's Eddie Hazel.

Given a major-label budget, *Green Mind* found Mascis, intentionally or not, challenging the ossified concept of guitar hero. *–DP*

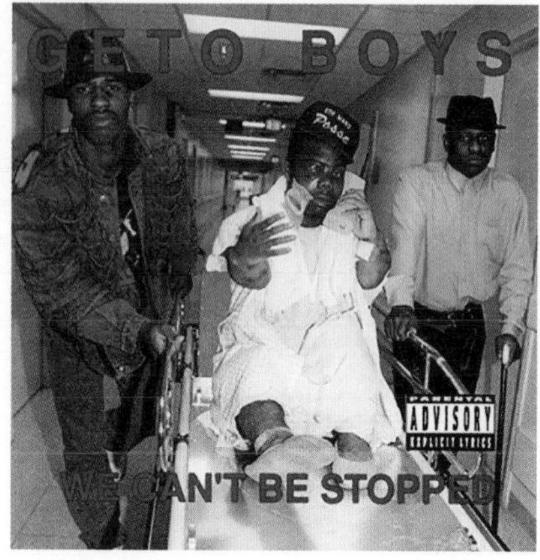

Geto Boys

WE CAN'T BE STOPPED

RAP-A-LOT | Producers: Bushwick Bill, James Smith, John Bido, Johnny C, Roland Scarface, Simon, Willie D

RELEASED: JULY 9, 1991

● You can't judge a book by its cover, but you can judge the Geto Boys' third album by *its* cover featuring the Houston group's Bushwick Bill in a hospital bed after being shot in the eye. Funk samples propel lyrics glorifying violence and misogyny, an approach that's as bright as it is devastating. The album is defined by the seminal **Mind Playing Tricks on Me**, which plays like a gangster's journal entry. *We Can't Be Stopped*, while fighting off endless calls for censorship, helped define Southern rap and pioneered the horrorcore form on its way to going platinum. *–ZC*

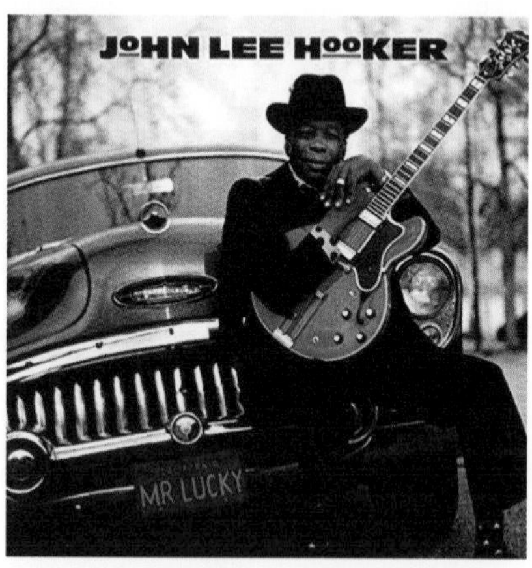

John Lee Hooker

MR. LUCKY

CHARISMA/VIRGIN | Producers: Roy Rogers, Ry Cooder, Carlos Santana

RELEASED: SEPTEMBER 1991

● Entering his sixth decade as a recording artist, John Lee Hooker was not merely hot again; he was at a career zenith. A singular artist, his music frequently had a rawer edge than his contemporaries, and he didn't need to reinvent anything. On *Mr. Lucky*, the seventy-seven-year-old bluesman was surrounded by friends and admirers, and because of the way Hooker worked, much of the record was cut live. One can hear each collaborator light up when the tape rolled: Carlos Santana is set free playing alongside his hero, but no one makes everything work better than Ry Cooder and his ensemble on **This Is Hip**. *–HK*

Various Artists

JUICE (ORIGINAL MOTION PICTURE SOUNDTRACK)

MCA/SOUL | Producers: Assorted

RELEASED: DECEMBER 31, 1991

● Ernest R. Dickerson's urban crime drama was set in Harlem and co-starred Tupac before his move to the wild, wild West, but the soundtrack represented both coasts—albeit with a leaning toward the East Coast. The consistently strong fourteen-song set hit No. 17 on the Billboard 200 and No. 3 on the Top R&B/Hip-Hop Albums chart, while original tracks from Naughty by Nature (**Uptown Anthem**) and Eric B. & Rakim (**Juice [Know the Ledge]**) had robust lives of their own. The UK got some representation, too, thanks to Brand New Heavies and N'Dea Davenport's brassy funk jam **People Get Ready**. *–GG*

The Mekons
THE CURSE OF THE MEKONS

BLAST FIRST/A&M | Producers: The Mekons, Ian Caple

RELEASED: 1991

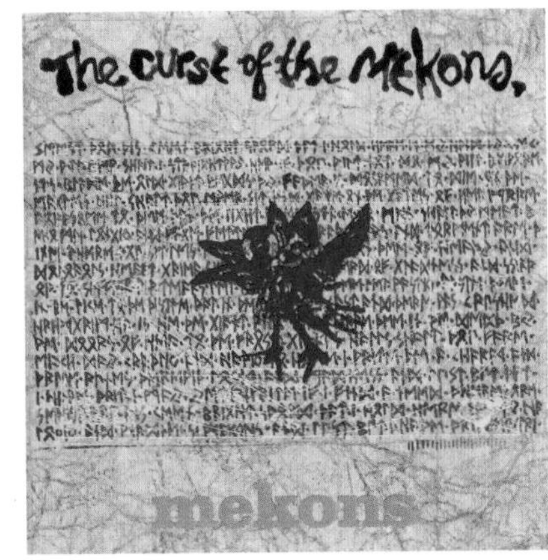

● After eight albums, you'd figure the Mekons would know what they were doing—which was absolutely the case on *The Curse of the Mekons*. After setting a high bar two years earlier with *The Mekons Rock 'n Roll*, the British troupe maintained its sonic standards but shot stylistically wider. It still cranked on tracks such as **The Curse** and **Funeral** but explored a more eclectic path that included a folky cover of country singer John Anderson's **Wild and Blue**. Other tracks pursued trippy ambience, New Wave-y grooves, and plenty of Celtic and American roots flavors, along with sharp lyrical looks at the sociopolitical climate. *–GG*

Marc Cohn
MARC COHN

ATLANTIC | Producers: Marc Cohn, Ben Wisch

RELEASED: FEBRUARY 12, 1991

● Marc Cohn's self-titled debut led to his 1992 Grammy Award for Best New Artist, but it also did wonders for the City of Memphis Tourism Board after **Walking in Memphis**, the first single, reached No. 13 on the Billboard Hot 100. Cohn's almost smoky voice vividly recounted his journey of self-discovery from Beale Street to Graceland. The autobiographical songwriting and poignant piano continued throughout the album, allowing Cohn's storytelling to shine on **Silver Thunderbird** and address his own mortality with **True Companion**. The songs were simple narratives that encouraged the listener to connect on their own spiritual level. *–SS*

Primal Scream
SCREAMADELICA

SIRE | Producers: Andrew Weatherall, Hugo Nicolson, The Orb, Hypnotone, Jimmy Miller

RELEASED: 1991

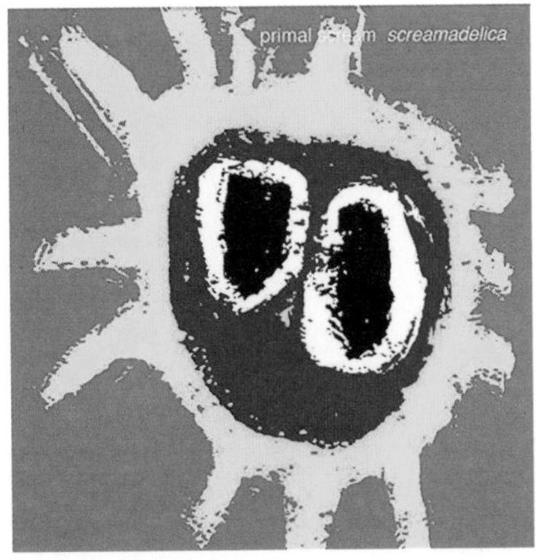

● Before the group took guitars to the foreground, Bobby Gillespie's Primal Scream collected the players, producers, DJs, and remixers (sometimes all the above) who defined the UK's post-rave, pre-shoegaze sound and style. In hiring Andrew Weatherall for the producer's chair and featuring vocals by Gillespie and Denise Johnson (A Certain Ratio), Jah Wobble, and The Orb, among others, Primal Scream crafted a timeless tapestry of modern soul, house, ambient, and space rock. Standout songs such as **Movin' on Up**, **Come Together**, and **Loaded** rocked everything from clubs and festival tents to chill-out rooms and live stages. *–CW*

Matthew Sweet

GIRLFRIEND

ZOO ENTERTAINMENT/BMG | Producers: Fred Maher, Matthew Sweet

RELEASED: OCTOBER 22, 1991

● *Girlfriend* is a classic album that almost wasn't. When he made the album, Matthew Sweet was signed to A&M Records. But before the ink was dry, all the people interested in promoting Sweet had left the label. He asked for (and miraculously received) his release, moving on to Zoo Entertainment, which signed Sweet, quickly dropped him, and—persuaded by music journalist Bud Scoppa, then working for Zoo—reeled him back in.

Good thing, too, because *Girlfriend* was a power-pop masterpiece. But unlike most records of that subgenre, it wasn't a perfectly produced, every-hair-in-place kind of record. "*Girlfriend* is a more non-production style record," Sweet said at the time of its release. "We just stripped everything away, and what you hear is real basic, just a few simple instruments."

The instruments that stood out most, of course, were the serrated-edged guitars of Richard Lloyd and Robert Quine. While Sweet's tightly constructed songs and stacked harmonies gave away his Big Star and Beatles influences, the raw, raucous soloing of Lloyd and Quine (think electric-Neil Young-meets-Television) perfectly conveyed the roiling emotions of the lyrics.

And regarding those lyrics, Sweet wrote the album in the wake of the dissolution of his marriage and the beginning of a new relationship. Thus, he mixed the ups and downs of songs such as the hopeful rockers **I've Been Waiting** and the title track on one hand and, on the other, breakup songs that hurt so good, like **Divine Intervention**, **Looking at the Sun**, **You Don't Know Me**, and **Nothing Lasts**. The latter, incidentally, was supposed to be the album's title but was quashed when Tuesday Weld, whose teenaged visage graces the cover, didn't want her photo associated with such a negative phrase. Sweet changed it, and a classic was ready to be unleashed. *–DD*

Massive Attack

BLUE LINES

WILD BUNCH/VIRGIN | Producers: Massive Attack, Jonny Dollar

RELEASED: APRIL 8, 1991

● *Blue Lines*, the debut album by English collective Massive Attack, is widely considered the first trip-hop album, although the term was not made popular until later. With its music blending American hip-hop, soul, and reggae into an electronic British club sound, the album firmly established the group as one of the decade's most ingenious and influential British bands.

Formed during 1988, Massive Attack's core included Grantley "Daddy G" Marshall, Robert "3D" Del Naja, Adrian "Tricky" Thaws, and Andrew "Mushroom" Vowles. Their talents and key contributions from other musicians, along with strategic sampling, created a rarely heard (or seen) combination of originality, heaviness, beauty, and cool atmosphere, becoming what many feel is one of the best dance albums of all time. Although she was not credited as a band member, singer and rapper Neneh Cherry's contributions were also significant, as she provided musical arrangements, studio space, and financing for the upstart band.

Of *Blue Line*'s nine tracks, a highlight (and its highest-charting single) was **Unfinished Symphony**, which rose to No. 3 on the UK Dance Chart. The lush chill-out anthem featured soulful vocals from English singer Shara Nelson and a sinister, whispered rap from producer Jonny Dollar. The album's opener, **Safe from Harm**, also featured Nelson's sultry vocals with poppy percussion, grooving guitars laying the bed, and Del Naja's chopped-up rhyming. *Blue Line*'s first released single, **Daydreaming**, again showcased Nelson, with the group's Thaws providing the rap this time.

The diverse collection of songs also included strong dub influences with vocals from Jamaican roots-reggae singer Horace Andy on three tracks, including the horn-heavy **Five Man Army**. The only song on the album not penned by Massive Attack was a cover of William DeVaughn's 1974 US R&B hit, **Be Thankful for What You've Got**, reimagined in the group's tripped-out style. *–JC*

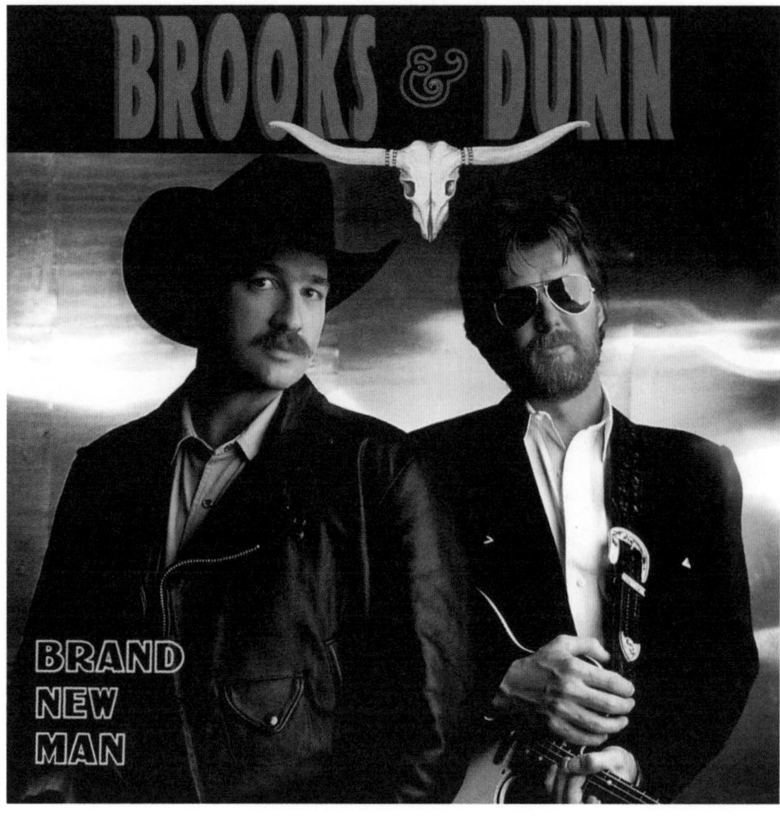

Brooks & Dunn

BRAND NEW MAN

ARISTA | Producers: Don Cook, Scott Hendricks

RELEASED: AUGUST 13, 1991

● Brooks & Dunn earned their place as country music's dynamite duo with the release of this debut album that gave '90s country fans a brand-new sound to line dance to with its spirited, honky-tonk flair.

Kix Brooks and Ronnie Dunn had been solo artists when then–Arista label executive Tim DuBois introduced the singer/songwriters over lunch and proposed that they join forces. He ultimately gave the duo a record deal. Its first offering, *Brand New Man*'s title track, was co-written by Brooks and Dunn alongside producer Don Cook; it quickly caught the attention of radio and fans alike, giving the duo its first No. 1 on the Billboard Hot Country Songs chart in June 1991. At the time, it was incredibly rare for a debut act to hit that mark out of the box; in fact, it had only happened once before in country music.

It was followed immediately by three more chart-toppers: **Boot Scootin' Boogie**, **My Next Broken Heart**, and **Neon Moon**. **Boot Scootin' Boogie** alone could arguably be credited as the catalyst for the country line dancing craze of the '90s. Another single from *Brand New Man*, **Lost and Found**, peaked at No. 6, while the album was certified six-times platinum.

Since their *Brand New Man* debut, Brooks & Dunn have released nearly a dozen studio albums, charting almost two dozen No. 1 country hits and more recently appearing on tracks with younger hitmakers such as Kane Brown and Kacey Musgraves. They firmly earned their spot as both the best-selling and most awarded duo in country music history. *—MH2*

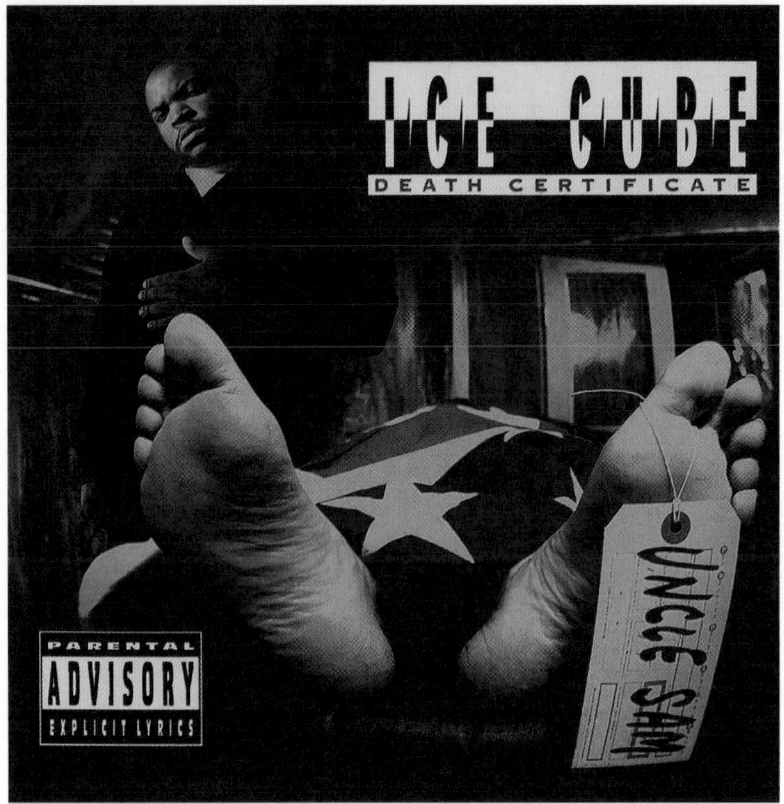

Ice Cube

DEATH CERTIFICATE

LENCH MOB/PRIORITY | Producers: Ice Cube, Sir Jinx, the Boogie Men

RELEASED: OCTOBER 29, 1991

● Between August 1988 and October 1991, Ice Cube released three classic and impressively different hip-hop albums. After serving as the primary lyricist and standout rapper on N.W.A's unflinchingly raw masterpiece *Straight Outta Compton*, he launched his solo career with 1990's *AmeriKKKa's Most Wanted*. With production help from Public Enemy's The Bomb Squad, that album found Ice Cube successfully adapting his charismatic rapping style to fit over edgy, dense soundscapes.

The following year he delivered what just might be his masterpiece: *Death Certificate*. The sophomore solo album featured a fuller, slightly more relaxed production style that drew heavily on '70s funk and soul samples, perfect to emphasize the cinematic nature of Ice Cube's storytelling style. **My Summer Vacation** is a perfect example; as Ice Cube rode a deep groove built off George Clinton's "Atomic Dog," he told the tale of Los Angeles drug dealers who relocate to St. Louis in hopes of becoming bigger fish in a smaller pond, only to encounter new and inevitably tragic consequences. It contained enough detail and nuance to fill an entire season of *The Wire*, but Ice Cube wrapped it all up in just under four minutes.

The album was rightfully criticized for containing homophobic, racist, and anti-Semitic lyrics; Ice Cube's UK label stripped two tracks from its release over such concerns. These sentiments tainted the otherwise masterful closing N.W.A diss track, **No Vaseline**, which made it quite clear Ice Cube didn't consider his former bandmates to be in his league, lyrically.

With the notable exception of his 1992 single "It Was a Good Day," *Death Certificate* marked the apex of Ice Cube's recording career, as he increasingly shifted his focus to film. But if his ticket to rap's eventual Hall of Fame wasn't already punched, this album made it nothing more than a formality. *—MW*

Chris Whitley

LIVING WITH THE LAW

COLUMBIA | Producer: Malcolm Burn

RELEASED: JULY 2, 1991

● Houston, Texas–born singer/songwriter Chris Whitley's debut album was a bluesy, swampy entry during a year in which grunge would take a foothold on the charts with Nirvana's *Nevermind*, Pearl Jam's *Ten*, and Soundgarden's *Badmotorfinger*.

Living with the Law was recorded in New Orleans in producer Daniel Lanois's home studio, although the album was helmed by Lanois associate Malcolm Burn. The songs were written for Whitley's solo gigs on the Lower East Side of New York City while he was working in a factory; he intended for the compositions to remain in their simplest form instead of the full band and production treatment they received here. Nevertheless, the result was a hypnotic and moody collection fueled by the Delta blues and pulls the listener into a dusty world of isolation, drug abuse, and the dark side of the human condition. The standout tracks were **Big Sky Country** and **Dirt Radio**, with an intimate, focused sound and feel that Whitley would abandon on future recordings. Luckily for us, Burn's vision delivered one of the most captivating albums of the decade. Whitley would pass away fourteen years later at the age of forty-five. *–AD*

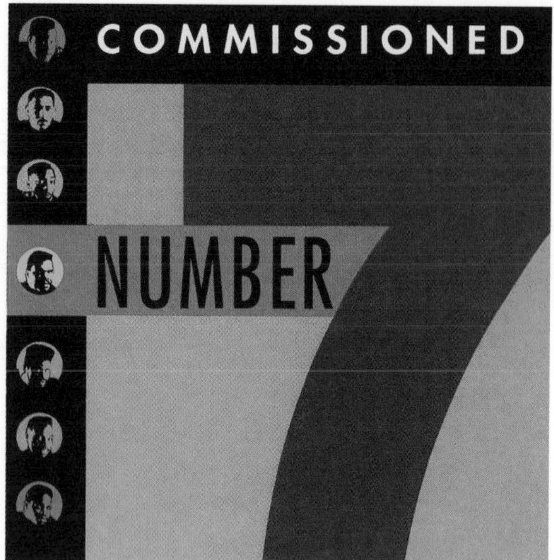

Commissioned

NUMBER 7

BENSON | Producers: Fred Hammond, Mitchell Jones, Bernard Wright, Maxx Frank

RELEASED: MARCH 19, 1991

● Commissioned's seventh album was its first release after the departure of founding members Michael Brooks and Keith Staten, and it marked the arrival of Marvin Sapp, Maxx Frank, and Eddie Howard. That coincided with a change of label and, more importantly, in musical direction, transforming and updating its sound to reflect New Jack Swing and hip-hop while still delivering a gospel message. With original member Fred Hammond taking over production along with Mitchell Jones, Maxx Frank, and R&B producer Bernard Wright, Commissioned's smooth harmonies remained intact over contemporary beats and melodies. Hammond's **King of Glory**, written with Wright, featured a synth bass line, a guest appearance by gospel rap group Transformation Crusade, and Hammond's and Sapp's intense vocals, becoming an instant fan favorite. Stylistically, tracks such as **Second Chance**, **Love U with the Rest of My Life**, **We Are Overcoming**, **Hold Me**, and **I Was Thinking of You** (written by original member Jones along with Parkes Stewart) could groove alongside anything on the mainstream Urban and R&B charts. *Number 7* reached, appropriately, No. 7 on Billboard's Top Gospel Albums chart and No. 22 on top Contemporary Christian, establishing a template Commissioned would use to even greater effect for the rest of the decade. *–CP*

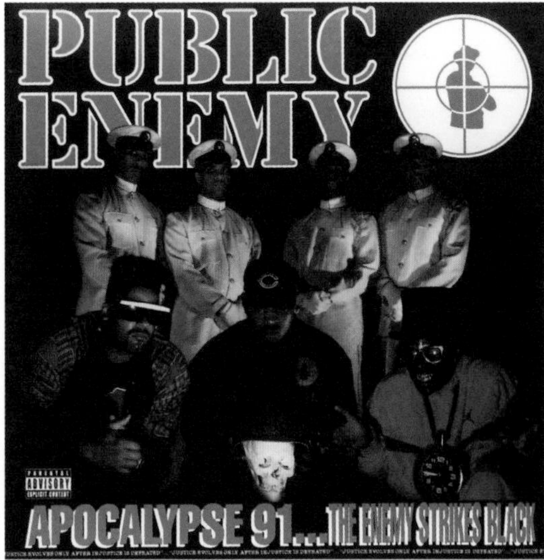

Public Enemy

APOCALYPSE 91 . . . THE ENEMY STRIKES BLACK

DEF JAM/COLUMBIA | Producers: Gary G-Wiz, The Bomb Squad, The Imperial Grand Ministers of Funk

RELEASED: OCTOBER 1, 1991

● Public Enemy's fourth album is often and wrongly considered a step down from its acknowledged twin masterpieces, *It Takes a Nation of Millions to Hold Us Back* (1988) and *Fear of a Black Planet* (1990). Leaner, meaner, and more direct in every way, *Apocalypse 91 . . . The Enemy Strikes Black* found Chuck D, Flavor Flav, Terminator X, and their production partners trimming back the sprawling cinematic approach of previous Public Enemy albums but still offering plenty to make your head spin.

While some may miss the dizzying, dense sound collages and kettle whistles from earlier efforts like "Don't Believe the Hype" or the original "Bring the Noise," *Apocalypse 91*'s slightly sparer sound allowed more of the spotlight to shine on Chuck D's incredible voice and lyrics, which is always a good thing. The self-professed "rhyme animal" identified and addressed a litany of social ills here with unblinking fury and new levels of clarity. He was particularly effective on the gospel-tinged, slow-burning epic **By the Time I Get to Arizona**, in which he blasts the state for refusing to honor Martin Luther King Jr.'s birthday as an official holiday. *–MW*

Bryan Adams

WAKING UP THE NEIGHBOURS

A & M | Producers: Bryan Adams, Robert John "Mutt" Lange

RELEASED: SEPTEMBER 24, 1991

● Bryan Adams caused a bit of a ruckus with his sixth studio album. It marked the Canadian singer/songwriter's first collaboration with Robert John "Mutt" Lange, a producer and songwriting partner known for his Midas touch with artists such as AC/DC and Def Leppard. Lange put his signature polish and punch on the record, and the creative pairing resulted in a carefully crafted, guitar-based pop collection, bucking the grunge and metal trends of the time. Straight-up rock tunes like the singles **Can't Stop This Thing We Started** and **There Will Never Be Another Tonight** emphasized Adams's gravelly voice and some memorable guitar hooks, balanced by mid-tempo ballads such as **Do I Have to Say the Words?** and **Thought I'd Died and Gone to Heaven**. The combination succeeded in putting Adams back on commercial radio; even some controversy surrounding existing Canadian content laws didn't stop the momentum of the international hit single **(Everything I Do) I Do It for You** from the film *Robin Hood: Prince of Thieves*. Released ahead of the album, the song topped the charts in nineteen countries, won a Grammy Award, and scored an Academy Award nomination. In un–Canadian Nice fashion, *Waking Up the Neighbours* generated plenty of noise. *–SS*

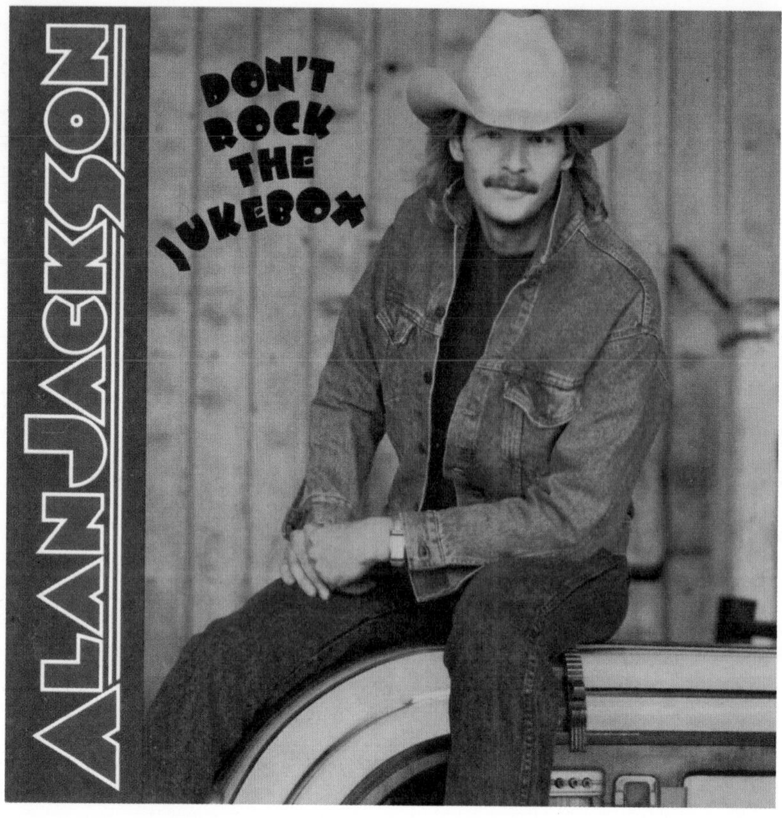

Alan Jackson

DON'T ROCK THE JUKEBOX

ARISTA | Producers: Scott Hendricks, Keith Stegall

RELEASED: MAY 14, 1991

● Alan Jackson's third album solidified his spot as one of the hottest new acts in country music. Four of its five singles climbed to No. 1 on the Billboard Hot County Singles Tracks chart, including the title track, **Someday**, **Dallas**, and **Love's Got a Hold on You**. Another single, **Midnight in Montgomery**, a tribute to Hank Williams, peaked at No. 3.

Jackson co-wrote all but one of the ten songs, showcasing his talent as a tunesmith in collaboration with co-producer Keith Stegall and Don Sampson. He and Randy Travis, meanwhile, teamed up on the album's **From a Distance**. *Don't Rock the Jukebox* also featured notable Nashville players such as Paul Franklin on steel guitar, Mark McClurg on fiddle, Roy Huskey Jr. on upright bass, and Hargus "Pig" Robbins on piano.

Coming from a hardcore country traditionalist, *Don't Rock the Jukebox*'s title track finds Jackson pleading to hear some true country music instead of rock 'n' roll, explaining that "I wanna hear some Jones, 'cause my heart ain't ready for the Rolling Stones." In addition to referencing the iconic George Jones there, Jackson tapped the legendary singer (aka The Possum) to make a guest appearance on another track, **Just Playin' Possum**.

Don't Rock the Jukebox climbed to No. 17 on the all-genre Billboard 200 and No. 2 on the Top Country Albums charts, higher than either of its predecessors. The project has been certified four-times platinum and was named the Academy of Country Music's Album of the Year in 1991. The title track won the Academy of Country Music's Single Record of the Year trophy, and **Midnight in Montgomery** won Music Video of the Year honors at the 1992 Country Music Association Awards. *–MH2*

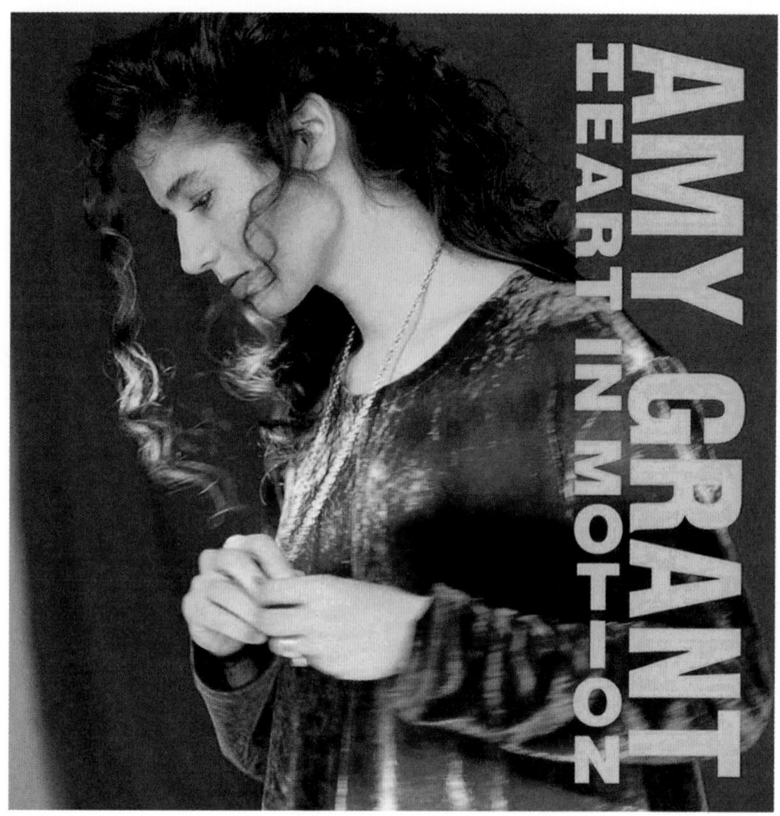

Amy Grant

HEART IN MOTION

A&M/MYRRH | Producers: Brown Bannister, Michael Omartian, Keith Thomas

RELEASED: MARCH 5, 1991

● *Heart in Motion* was Amy Grant's ninth studio album, but for many music lovers this was, for all intents and purposes, the Christian singer/songwriter's first. The crossover album made Grant a household name in the world of pop music, playing like a greatest hits compilation, peaking at No. 10 on the Billboard 200 and hitting the top of the Christian chart. And it doesn't get any bigger than the album's first single, **Baby Baby**, which reached No. 1 on the Billboard Hot 100. The song also earned Grant three Grammy Award nominations, including Song of the Year.

Baby Baby was just the first of a string of hits from *Heart in Motion*, which was also nominated for the Album of the Year Grammy (losing to Quincy Jones's *Back on the Block*). The next single, **Hope Set High**, wasn't released to the pop market, but it maintained Grant's position atop the Christian chart. The crossover momentum from **Baby Baby** continued as **Every Heartbeat** made its way to No. 2 on the Hot 100. Additional singles **That's What Love Is For** and **Good for Me** followed it into the Top 10. **I Will Remember You** gave Grant one more Top 20—the only time she'd enjoy that kind of mainstream pop success.

Heart in Motion ran deeper than the hits. **Ask Me** and **Galileo**, while not singles, were two of the album's catchiest tunes, making for a filler-free set that packed a significant punch. It's been certified six-times platinum and introduced Grant to a wider audience that had minimal exposure to her previous releases. It also ushered in a brief few years of other pop successes, which Grant managed to enjoy without alienating her core Christian audience and to which she returned in earnest more than a decade later. *–EP*

Metallica

METALLICA

ELEKTRA | Producers: James Hetfield, Bob Rock, Lars Ulrich

RELEASED: AUGUST 12, 1991

● Metallica was certainly teed up for something special as it rolled into its fifth studio album.

Already established at the top of the thrash metal mountaintop, the San Francisco quartet was coming off an attention-getting slot on Van Halen's Monsters of Rock tour and its first Top 10 multiplatinum album in 1988's . . . *And Justice for All*. But the group still pushed out of its comfort zone this time around. "The challenge before was to fit every riff in the universe into one song and make it work," frontman James Hetfield, who co-produced the album with drummer Lars Ulrich and hard rock hitmaker Bob Rock, explained when *Metallica* (aka "The Black Album") was released. "This time it was to have one riff and fit other things around it and make it just as exciting. It was a completely opposite style, and it was definitely challenging. But it came out alright."

No kidding.

The focused, streamlined approach of *Metallica* proved to be exactly what the mainstream rock world was waiting for. The set sold 2.2 million copies during its first week out and stayed at No. 1 on the Billboard 200 for four weeks. The opening **Enter Sandman** entered the pantheon of generational rock anthems. **Wherever I May Roam** and **Sad but True** were close behind it, while tracks such as **Nothing Else Matters** and **The Unforgiven** offered textbooks on how to incorporate true power into ballads and make them as heavy as any of the album's rock tracks. The set also nabbed Metallica its third Grammy Award, and first for an album, in the Best Metal Performance category in 1992—a vindication after infamously losing two years earlier to Jethro Tull.

All these years later, more than thirty million copies sold worldwide don't lie. Not bad for coming out "alright." *—GG*

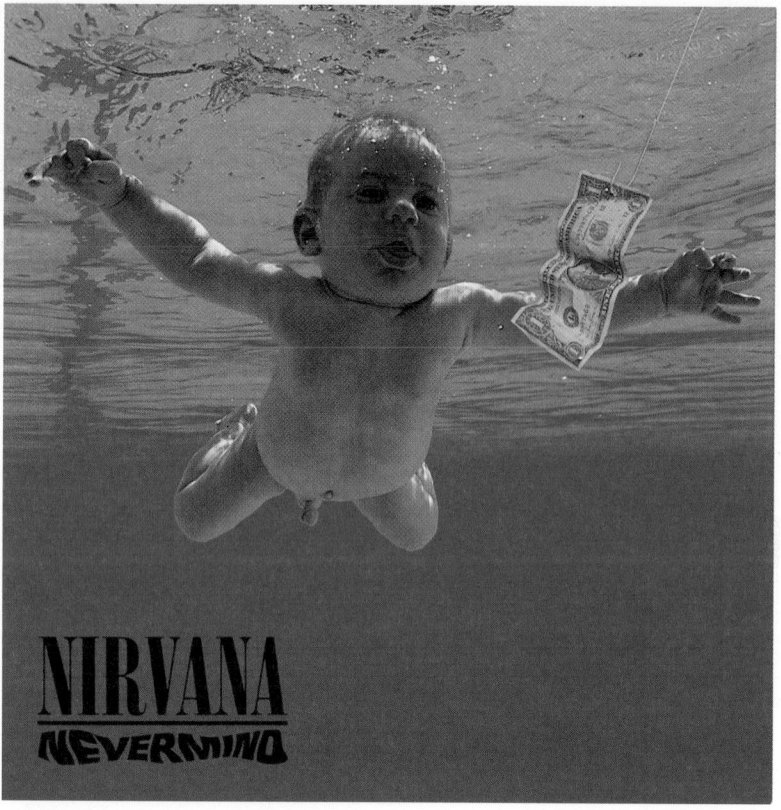

Nirvana

NEVERMIND

DGC | Producer: Butch Vig

RELEASED: SEPTEMBER 24, 1991

● Few albums are as consequential to rock music as Nirvana's *Nevermind*. Iconic to many for its indelible cover and ubiquitous platinum single, **Smells Like Teen Spirit**, the Seattle trio's seminal sophomore album set in motion a musical sea change that put alternative rock in a dominant position on the mainstream map.

A distinct reproach to the glam metal that ruled the airwaves at the time, not even the band members could have predicted *Nevermind*'s diamond-certified success and the commercial juggernaut it would become, earning an eternal place in the GOAT level of the rock canon. *Nevermind* would sell more than thirty million copies worldwide, hitting No. 1 on the Billboard 200 by January 1992 and becoming the second best-selling album released in 1991, just behind Metallica's fifth studio album (aka *The Black Album*).

It's hard to pinpoint the exact source of the magic that made *Nevermind* so relentlessly successful. Many of its tracks, such as **Breed**, **Territorial Pissings**, and the hidden **Endless, Nameless** retained the raw and distorted sound that dominated Nirvana's debut album, *Bleach*, released just two years prior and with far less fanfare on the independent Seattle label Sub Pop. Other tracks like **In Bloom**, **Lithium**, and the almost whisper-quiet **Something in the Way** highlighted the progression of Nirvana's sound, with more soft-to-loud dynamics to showcase Kurt Cobain's aching vocals and haunting melodies. Combined with Dave Grohl's fluid, flexible drumming style (on his first recording with the group) and producer Butch Vig's inspired, high-fidelity mixing, *Nevermind* was much more commercially viable than its predecessor, an ambivalent experience for Cobain in particular as he grappled with the success it brought.

Though Cobain later criticized *Nevermind* for sounding too polished (blaming Vig), there is little debate among fans and music critics about the album's lasting legacy and its profound effect on popular music at the time. *–JS*

crown
Power Base-2

American Music Club
EVERCLEAR

ALIAS | Producers: American Music Club, Bruce Kaphan, Norman Kerner

RELEASED: OCTOBER 5, 1991

● Listening to American Music Club was never what you'd call a fun experience. Mark Eitzel, the San Francisco group's frontman and songwriter, cut through to the deepest sources of pain and frustration without any pretense of beauty in those sorrowful emotions. He could make you feel not only his hurt but also his inability to find any redemption—for himself or his listener. That certainly made the group's songs more compelling, however, and never more so than on *Everclear*. The eleven-track set was Eitzel and company's most focused and fully realized to date and perhaps ever. The songs—whether the mournful **Why Won't You Stay**, the unusually anthemic **Rise**, or the actually playful **Crabwalk**—maintained Eitzel's strong point of view but were delivered with more authority thanks to muscled-up production that gave guitarist Mark "Vudi" Pankler room for sonic embellishment. Multi-instrumentalist Bruce Kaphan, boosted to full-time membership and co-production, brought an array of new tones, too. Eitzel's melancholy had never received that much musical dressing before, and on *Everclear*, more was better and impactful, helping to make Eitzel *Rolling Stone*'s Songwriter of the Year. *–GG*

Soundgarden
BADMOTORFINGER

A & M | Producers: Terry Date, Soundgarden

RELEASED: OCTOBER 8, 1991

● Following releases with respected indie labels Sub Pop and SST, Soundgarden was a test case for the majors, proving there were gold and platinum records to be pulled from the great Pacific Northwest flannel mine when *Louder Than Love* was released by A&M in 1989. That opened the door for Pearl Jam and Nirvana to release *Ten* and *Nevermind*, respectively, on major labels just a few weeks ahead of *Badmotorfinger*, kick-starting rock's so-called grunge era in earnest.

Soundgarden's third full-length featured better production and more focused songs that cut a different path through an era dominated by hair metal. Soundgarden was metal without being mystical, prog without being pedantic, and blues without being bitter—a sonic stew with main ingredients like the Stooges and Led Zeppelin but often served up with odd tunings and spicy time signatures. Chris Cornell brought a novelistic approach to his lyrics, making them more descriptive than prescriptive and delving into topics from religious hypocrisy (**Jesus Christ Pose**) and repression (**Rusty Cage**) to social alienation (**A Room a Thousand Years Wide**). Cornell's frame of "looking California and feeling Minnesota" (**Outshined**) made *Badmotorfinger* a compelling ride even for those otherwise disinterested in the burgeoning alternative scene. *–RSM*

Mudhoney

EVERY GOOD BOY DESERVES FUDGE

SUB POP | Producer: Conrad Uno

RELEASED: JULY 26, 1991

● Convinced early twenty-four-track efforts were too polished, Seattle's godfathers of grunge regrouped in an eight-track basement studio and birthed the album that guitarist Steve Turner still cites as his band favorite.

Every Good Boy Deserves Fudge began with the walk-on instrumental dirge **Generation Genocide** before properly launching with **Let It Slide**, showcasing the trademark interplay between Turner's fuzzed-out leads and frontman Mark Arm's slide guitar. Mudhoney always leaned more heavily on Sonics-style garage/psych than grunge's nominal Big Four (Nirvana, Pearl Jam, Soundgarden, and Alice in Chains), and while there were nods to the old reductive argument that Grunge = Black Flag + Black Sabbath (**Thorn** and **Broken Hands**, respectively), Mudhoney was at its best when it got off on the thirteenth floor with nuggets like **Into the Drink** and **Who You Drivin' Now?** Dig, for example, Turner's period-perfect double-tracked electric and acoustic leads on the former.

This embrace of broader influences often made Mudhoney more compelling than the grunge cash cows who followed. And with a respectable seventy-five thousand units out the door, *Every Good Boy* even saved the group's label, Sub Pop, from dissolution. *—DP*

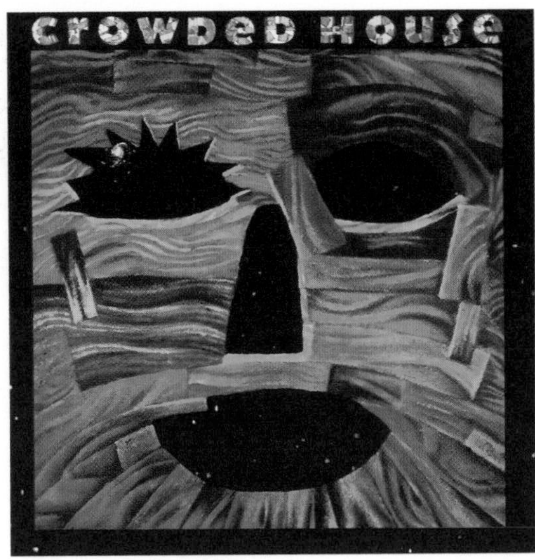

Crowded House

WOODFACE

CAPITOL | Producers: Mitchell Froom, Neil Finn

RELEASED: JULY 1, 1991

● New Zealand's Crowded House had already dented the American charts and consciousness with its namesake 1986 debut album (and the singles "Don't Dream It's Over" and "Something So Strong"), which reached an impressive No. 12 on the Billboard 200—better than frontman Neil Finn had done with his previous band, Split Enz. The group's 1988 follow-up, *Temple of Low Men*, was a disappointment, however, so stakes were high for *Woodface*, released three years later. It actually was intended to be released under the moniker the Finn Brothers, with Neil joined by older sibling and Split Enz mate Tim Finn. Capitol Records, however, reportedly liked the Finn Brothers' songs better than what Crowded House had submitted and asked the band to include a few of them on its third album. Tim agreed under the condition he could *join* Crowded House, and the brothers wound up co-writing seven of *Woodface*'s fourteen tracks. **Chocolate Cake** was perhaps a bit too satirical and quirky to succeed in the US, but *Woodface* is nevertheless a gem. **Weather with You** provided a breakthrough for the band in the UK, and **Four Seasons in One Day** evoked Beatles comparisons that were spot-on. *—CB*

BeBe and CeCe Winans

DIFFERENT LIFESTYLES

CAPITOL | Producers: BeBe Winans, Keith Thomas, Rhett Lawrence

RELEASED: JUNE 24, 1991

● The fourth album by brother-and-sister duo Benjamin "BeBe" and Priscilla "CeCe" Winans launched the pair (children of gospel pioneer David "Pop" Winans) into the R&B stratosphere. *Different Lifestyles* featured background vocals by leading gospel and R&B stars of that day, including Whitney Houston, Luther Vandross, Take 6, and the duo's older brothers in the Winans (Marvin, Carvin, Ronald, and Michael).

Different Lifestyles spent seven weeks at No. 1 on the Billboard Top Gospel Albums chart and crossed over to the top spot on the Top R&B/Hip-Hop Albums chart. It also won the 1992 Grammy for Best Contemporary Soul Gospel album, as well as Best Gospel Album at the *Soul Train* Music Awards.

The first single, **Addictive Love** (co-written with Keith Thomas), spearheaded the crossover, spending two weeks at No. 1 on the R&B Singles chart. The follow-up single, a remake of the Staple Singers' 1972 hit **I'll Take You There**, also topped the R&B charts. Featuring Mavis Staples, the remake updated the classic song with a relaxing groove as the three vocalists indeed took listeners somewhere else entirely.

MC Hammer, then at the height of his own "Can't Touch This" fame, showed up on the fifth single, **The Blood**, sharing his spiritual side as he rapped, "I got what I need/I got the blood/And it's the power." With other lyrics similar to the church hymn "God Lead Us," the Winans and Hammer bridged traditional gospel, R&B, and hip-hop to create a song that worked for multiple generations of listeners. Other tracks, including **It's OK**, **Supposed to Be**, and **Depend on You**, fortified the album's spiritual depth, and noted musicians such as guitarist Paul Jackson Jr., drummer Ricky Lawson, and trumpeter/arranger Jerry Hey ensured a state-of-the-art standard for this breakthrough. *—CP*

Garth Brooks

ROPIN' THE WIND

CAPITOL NASHVILLE | Producer: Alan Reynolds

RELEASED: SEPTEMBER 2, 1991

● Garth Brooks was well on his way to conquering the country music world—the whole music world, really—by the time he released his third album. This ten-song set was the quintessential Garth as fans had come to know him: tributes to the working man, reflective ballads on lost love, and rockin' country cuts that connected listeners to the arena-sized energy of his live shows and spoke to his taste in choosing top-rate material.

The album launched five Top 5 Country chart hits, three of which went No. 1. Beyond chart positions and radio play, however, these were songs—particularly **Rodeo**, **Papa Loved Mama**, and his emotive rendition of Billy Joel's **Shameless**—that became staples in Brooks's catalog and tentpoles for country's rapid ascent into the pop mainstream. **The River**, meanwhile, was a life-journey anthem that Brooks wrote with Victoria Shaw and described in the liner notes of *The Hits* as "a song of inspiration . . . a song that I will be proud of a hundred years from now."

When half an album is hits, it's easy to view the rest as filler, but that was hardly the case on *Ropin' the Wind*. It would be hard to find another artist who wouldn't kill to have tracks such as **Against the Grain**, **Burning Bridges**, **Cold Shoulder**, **We Bury the Hatchet**, and **In Lonesome Dove** in their repertoires, but for Brooks, it was just part of a consistent embarrassment of riches that would be the calling card for his first seven solo albums.

With this album, Brooks cemented his position as a dominant force in country music and beyond, a whopping fourteen-times platinum success that also gave him his first No. 1 on the all-genre Billboard 200. *—TR/GG*

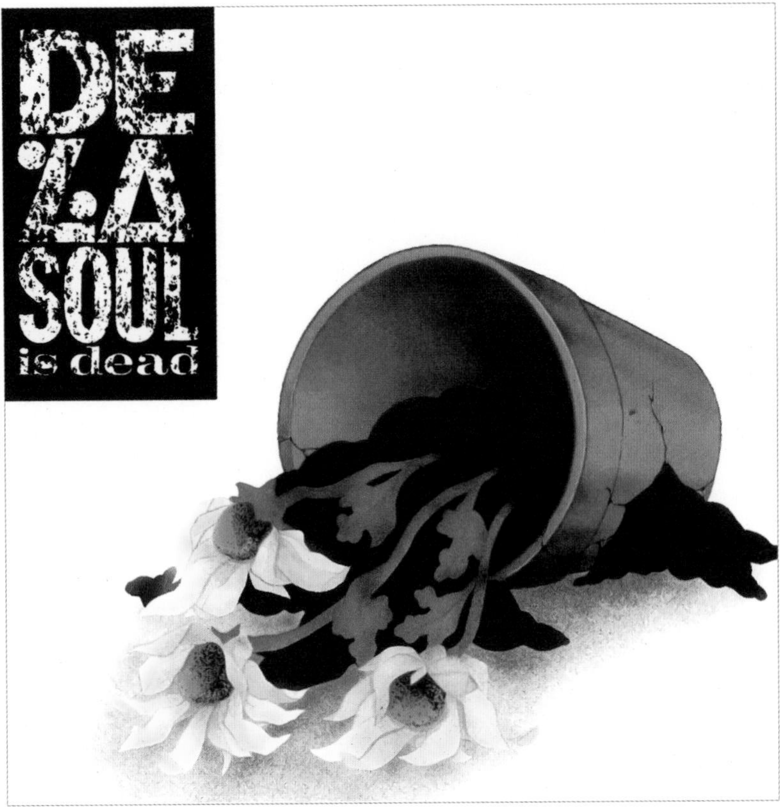

De La Soul

DE LA SOUL IS DEAD

TOMMY BOY | Producers: De La Soul, Prince Paul

RELEASED: MAY 13, 1991

● De La Soul's 1989 album *3 Feet High and Rising* was a landmark hip-hop record that positioned the Long Island, New York, trio and its producer Prince Paul as alternative-rap pioneers and the greatest defenders of the genre's "Daisy Age." Armed with a seemingly endless supply of samples (which later resulted in a load of legal trouble), De La Soul found comfort and camaraderie in its mix of bedroom jokes, suburban psychedelia, and skewering of hip-hop's increasing commercialism. So, where to go from there?

On its second album, De La Soul tore down the template it had erected for *3 Feet High and Rising* and shredded any expectations. It's spelled out right there in the title: *De La Soul Is Dead*. The samples, properly credited this time, weren't as obvious, and the rhymes were not as playful. The conceptual threads that tied together *3 Feet High and Rising* aren't completely abandoned but used sparingly here, opening the group to more musical possibilities. The result is a darker, more burdened album but also a more focused one in the end.

The songs on *De La Soul Is Dead* push against the group's reputation as peace-loving hippies. Drug addiction (**My Brother's a Basehead**), sexual abuse (**Millie Pulled a Pistol on Santa**), and the weight of fame (**Ring Ring Ring [Ha Ha Hey]**) are covered in unflinching terms. The music—once again overseen by Prince Paul with assistance from the group's Posdnuos, Trugoy the Dove, and Maseo—is appropriately more aggressive and deeper than it was on its predecessor.

Dismissed upon its release by some expecting another *3 Feet High and Rising*, *De La Soul Is Dead*'s stature has grown considerably over the years. *–MG*

A Tribe Called Quest

THE LOW END THEORY

JIVE | Producers: A Tribe Called Quest, Skeff Anselm

RELEASED: SEPTEMBER 24, 1991

● A Tribe Called Quest (ATCQ) is one of rap's powerhouse quartets, a legendary group. But its second release and defining album, *The Low End Theory*, was a dance between a pair: group members Q-Tip and Phife Dawg. The album represents Phife's breakout lyrical performance, standing confidently alongside Q-Tip at the mic.

ATCQ got a group producing credit for *The Low End Theory*, with Q-Tip leading that effort. But unlike its 1990 debut album, *People's Instinctive Travels and the Paths of Rhythm*, ATCQ was assisted this time by Skeff Anselm, who worked with other heavy-hitting acts of the early '90s such as De La Soul and Heavy D. Anselm assisted in pioneering a fresh fusion of hip-hop and jazz, which elevated both genres and, along with Gang Starr, Digable Planets, and others, helped pave the way for an exciting musical synthesis. The bass lines on **Buggin' Out** and **Excursion** took the listener for a walk through a smoky New Orleans club, and the second single, **Jazz (We've Got)**, sampled organist Jimmy McGriff's "Green Dolphin Street." It was a more adventurous and sophisticated counter to the gangsta rap getting the headlines and radio spins.

But *The Low End Theory*'s true gift was that lyrical interplay between Q-Tip and Phife Dawg. The tone leans toward the positive throughout these fourteen tracks, but *The Low End Theory* still addresses critical issues of the day, particularly on **The Infamous Date Rape**. The album-closing **Scenario**, meanwhile, features members of Leaders of the New School, including Busta Rhymes, whose verse was a breakout moment often credited for helping to launch his solo career.

The Low End Theory made its mark at No. 13 on Billboard's Top R&B/Hip-Hop albums chart and ultimately went platinum, while **Check the Rhyme** hit No. 1 on the Hot Rap Songs survey. It's also remained a fixture on lists of the best albums not only of its year or decade but of all time. *–ZC*

Primus
SAILING THE SEAS OF CHEESE

INTERSCOPE | Producer: Primus

RELEASED: MAY 14, 1991

● This second album was the breakout for the California noise-funk-metal trio that fell from the Zappa tree and became the weirdest outlier in the alt-rock scene. This gooey voyage began with frontman Les Claypool beckoning us with a bowed bass and sideways vocal before moving on to some of the decades-long staples of Primus's explosive concert sets, including **Jerry Was a Race Car Driver**, **Those Damn Blue Collar Tweakers**, and **Tommy the Cat** (featuring a guest vocal from Tom Waits as the title character). Embrace the absurdity while you pass the time (signatures) with this purposefully and unapologetically bizarre set. *–SM*

Robbie Robertson
STORYVILLE

GEFFEN | Producers: Robbie Robertson, Gary Gersh, Stephen Hague, Martin Page

RELEASED: SEPTEMBER 30, 1991

● Robbie Robertson's second solo album is an ode to The Band alumnus's love of New Orleans and its music. Robertson's deep, almost sultry voice evoked the city's famed redlight district for which the album is named. The record is steeped in the history and heart of the area, with Crescent City stalwarts Aaron and Ivan Neville featured on the first single, **What About Now**, while the Rebirth Brass Band lends a traditional jazz backline feel to **Go Back to Your Woods**. Robertson's writing weaves a story that reaches out and settles into the listener's soul like a damp draft from the nearby swamps. *–SS*

Various Artists
UNTIL THE END OF THE WORLD
(MUSIC FROM THE MOTION PICTURE SOUNDTRACK)

WARNER BROS. | Producer: Sharon Boyle

RELEASED: DECEMBER 10, 1991

● When film director Wim Wenders solicited contributions for the *Until the End of the World* soundtrack, he asked artists to predict the types of music they'd create a decade later. The resulting tracks by Talking Heads (**Sax and Violins**), R.E.M. (**Fretless**), Depeche Mode (**Death's Door**), Julee Cruise (**Summer Kisses, Winter Tears**), Elvis Costello (**Days**), Jane Siberry and k. d. lang (**Calling All Angels**), U2's title track, and others were both futuristic and timeless. Bookended by Graeme Revell's evocative score, every song was a clear standout while creating a whole greater than the sum of its stellar parts. *–HD*

Temple of the Dog
TEMPLE OF THE DOG

A & M | Producers: Rick Parashar, Temple of the Dog

RELEASED: APRIL 15, 1991

● Temple of the Dog was a one-off Seattle supergroup, basically the then-unknown Pearl Jam (*Ten* came out months later) plus Chris Cornell of Soundgarden, also just a few months before *Badmotorfinger* vaulted his band's status. The mission was to pay tribute to Andrew Wood, the Mother Love Bone and Malfunkshun frontman who died from a heroin overdose thirteen months before *Temple of the Dog* came out. The tone is simultaneously mournful and celebratory and the playing as hot as it would be on *Ten*, with Cornell and Eddie Vedder coexisting nicely—and in exciting tandem on the single **Hunger Strike**. *–GG*

Various Artists
BRINGING IT ALL BACK HOME
(MUSIC FROM THE BBC TV SERIES)

B B C | Producers: Donal Lunny, Bruce Talbot

RELEASED: MAY 1991

● This is a soundtrack so strong it can stand without a film. Accompanying a five-part BBC TV series about the connections between traditional music of the British Isles and the music that emerged from American Appalachia, *Bringing It All Back Home* is an encyclopedia of stellar performances. Producer Donal Lunny pulls the musical thread through a constellation of roots performers musically traveling through Ireland, Scotland, and England. Standouts include **Rose Connolly** by the Everly Brothers; **Sonny** by Emmylou Harris, Dolores Keane, and Mary Black; and the gut-wrenching **Kilkelly** by Mick Moloney, Jimmy Keane, and Robbie O'Connell. So many songs of leaving, but so good we're happy to stay. *–HK*

Talk Talk
LAUGHING STOCK

VERVE/POLYDOR | Producer: Tim Friese-Greene

RELEASED: SEPTEMBER 15, 1991

● Talk Talk began speaking a new language with 1991's *Laughing Stock*. Having shed bassist Paul Webb and the band's previous label, singer Mark Hollis and drummer Lee Harris moved on from 1988's *Spirit of Eden* by torching their New Wave roots and exploring an atmospheric soundscape that ended up being the British band's final recording. *Laughing Stock* was created in literal darkness, celebrated silence over sound, and left most guest contributors on the cutting-room floor. More impressive in retrospect than upon release, *Laughing Stock* is often credited with kicking off the post-rock genre. For those fortunate enough to understand Talk Talk's new approach, *Laughing Stock* was poetry. *–HD*

Fishbone

THE REALITY OF MY SURROUNDINGS

COLUMBIA | Producers: Fishbone, David Kahne

RELEASED: APRIL 23, 1991

● Experiencing whiplash while motionless is virtually impossible—unless you're listening to *The Reality of My Surroundings*, the third album from Fishbone. While the band was labeled as an alternative rock act, this eighteen-track album grabs from punk, ska, soul, funk, reggae, and hard rock. There is a manic attitude to the theme- and genre-blending as interspersed skits and mini-songs knit together full-length fare overflowing with energy. While the album has some bright vibes, there is also social commentary on racism (**So Many Millions**) and the crack epidemic (**Junkies Prayer**, **Prayer to the Junkiemaker**) that gripped Fishbone's home base of Los Angeles at the time.

Fishbone started garnering a cult following during the late '70s, but *The Reality of My Surroundings* was the group's most commercially successful release, selling more than 200,000 copies. In what is considered one of the best musical performances in *Saturday Night Live*'s storied history, Fishbone played two singles from the album (**Sunless Sunday** and **Everyday Sunshine**) that gave the masses a taste of the band's particular madness. Broad commercial success has criminally eluded Fishbone over the years, but *The Reality of My Surroundings*, perhaps ahead of its time, has achieved the rare feat of growing in popularity and regard. *–ZC*

Various Artists

BOYZ N THE HOOD (MUSIC FROM THE COLUMBIA MOTION PICTURE)

QWEST/WARNER BROS. | Producer: John Singleton

RELEASED: JULY 9, 1991

● If you had to hand somebody just one album as a chronicle of early-'90s hip-hop, well, there are a few titles that fit the bill. But the companion to *Boyz N the Hood*, the directorial debut by John Singleton (who also executive-produced its soundtrack), should be in the discussion. There was no shortage of gritty urban dramas at the time (or albums to go with them), but *Boyz N the Hood* is top of the heap, populated by a mix of ace rap and R&B tracks, some specifically for the film and some previously unreleased, that represents a strong measure of the musical landscape at the time. That includes essential fare such as Ice Cube's **How to Survive South Central**, Tevin Campbell and Chubb Rock's **Just Ask Me**, Compton's Most Wanted's **Growin' Up in the Hood**, Tony! Toni! Toné!'s **Me and You**, and Too $hort's **It's Your Life**. The aces in the hole, however, are samples from the jazz score by Quincy Jones (**Setembro [Brazilian Wedding Song]**) and Stanley Clarke (**Black on Black Crime**) that give this soundtrack breadth and depth lacking from similar collections. *–GG*

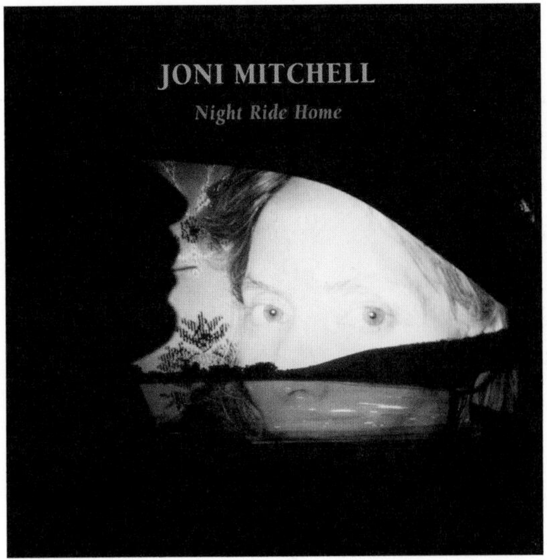

Joni Mitchell

NIGHT RIDE HOME

GEFFEN | Producers: Joni Mitchell, Larry Klein

RELEASED: FEBRUARY 19, 1991

● After mixing it up with Peter Gabriel, Willie Nelson, Don Henley, Billy Idol, Tom Petty, and Wendy & Lisa on her last album of the '80s, *Chalk Mark in a Rain Storm*, Joni Mitchell greeted the '90s by narrowing the sessions to a core band of bassist and then-husband Larry Klein and drummer Vinnie Colaiuta, with some accents from saxophonist Wayne Shorter and guitarists Bill Dillon and Michael Landau. Her fourteenth album had a melancholy air far removed from Mitchell's effervescent work of the late '60s through the mid-'70s. Nearing her fifties, she applied jazz-pop textures to sober songs about divorce settlements (**The Windfall**), child molestation (**Cherokee Louise**), and loneliness (**Two Grey Rooms**). The core song—and only *Night Ride Home* track on Mitchell's 1996 *Hits* anthology (it charted in her native Canada only)—was **Come In from the Cold**, in which she looked back at the innocence of the '50s and idealism of the '60s, singing, "When I thought life had some meaning/When I thought I'd had some choice/I was running blind and I made some value judgments/In a self-important voice." It's another step toward this hippie-era icon coming to terms with a less idealistic age. *–SM*

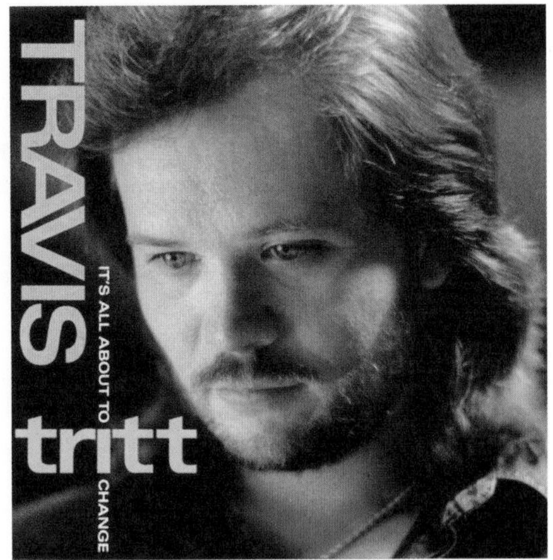

Travis Tritt

IT'S ALL ABOUT TO CHANGE

WARNER BROS. NASHVILLE | Producer: Gregg Brown

RELEASED: MAY 28, 1991

● After achieving double-platinum status in 1990, Travis Tritt's follow-up third album sealed the deal for him as a bona fide country superstar. The ten-song set—triple-platinum and the highest chart showing of his career (No. 2 on Billboard Top Country Albums)—continued Tritt's productive association with producer Gregg Brown and was also a testament to his songwriting skills (he penned seven of its tracks).

The monster first single, **Here's a Quarter (Call Someone Who Cares)**, was a huge radio and stadium smash (resulting in quarters flying everywhere when it was played), but Tritt ran the full spectrum of his vocal prowess on heartfelt ballads such as **Anymore** (with an incredibly moving video alongside) and showed off his honky-tonk chops on **The Whiskey Ain't Workin'**, co-written by and recorded with buddy Marty Stuart. **Bible Belt**, meanwhile, was another tasty treat featuring the band Little Feat, while Tritt's version of Jimmie Skinner's **Don't Give Your Heart to a Rambler** was pure country gold.

Anymore gave Tritt his first No. 1 country hit and was one of five Top 5 singles to come from the album. If this country gem isn't in your collection, that's something that definitely should change. *–TR/GG*

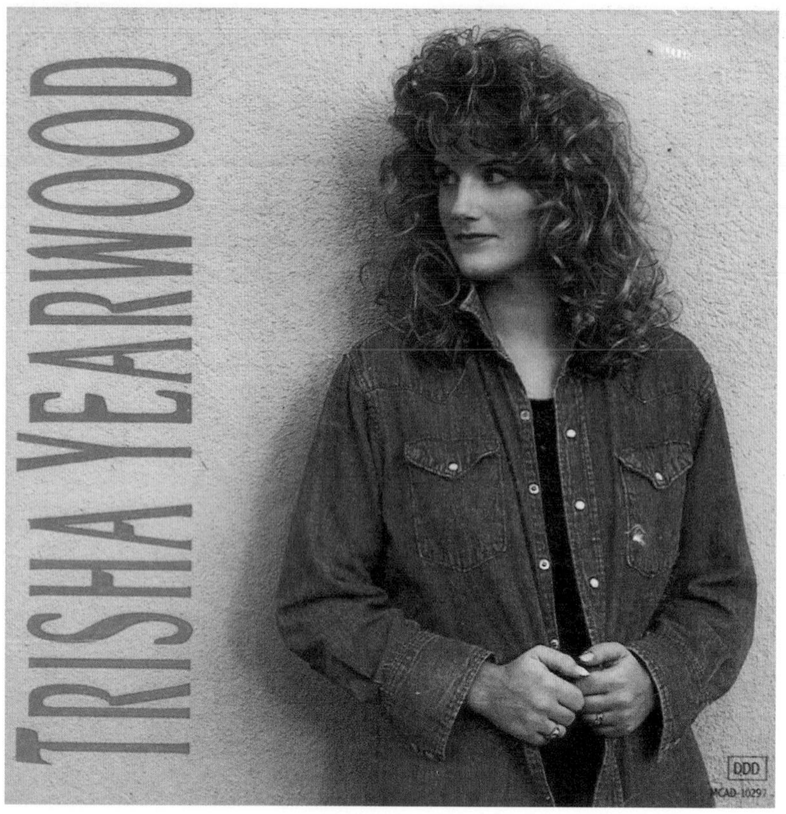

Trisha Yearwood

TRISHA YEARWOOD

MCA | Producer: Garth Fundis

RELEASED: JULY 2, 1991

● Her name is well known now for more than just music in a lot of households, but it was Trisha Yearwood's eponymous debut that helped usher in a new era of female country music and launch her decades-long career.

Yearwood was on the leading edge of a '90s movement that saw female artists building on trailblazers such as Dolly Parton, Loretta Lynn, Reba McEntire, and K. T. Oslin. Women were beginning to rule the country airwaves with bold declarations and an everywoman relatability. Unlike some of her female peers, Yearwood did not present herself as a sex symbol, instead using her strong, versatile voice as a remarkable asset perfectly suited to both ballads and up-tempo selections.

The lead single, **She's in Love with the Boy**, peaked at No. 1 on the Billboard Hot Country chart, helping make this the first debut album by a female country artist to sell a million copies. The album was produced by Garth Fundis, using top-notch session players and choice Nashville songwriters such as Carl Jackson, Hal Ketchum, and an up-and-coming Garth Brooks. It was Brooks, two years into his own recording career, who helped facilitate Yearwood's introduction to Fundis, and the second single, **Like We Never Had a Broken Heart**, was a Yearwood/Brooks duet that landed in the Top 5 on the country charts. **The Woman Before Me** was another Top 5 single, and its traditional country sound allowed Yearwood to squeeze every last bit of feeling into her lyrical interpretation.

Her ability to select songs and mold her voice around them to convey exactly the right emotion was apparent and would remain essential to Yearwood's career as mainstream country gained crossover appeal. *Trisha Yearwood* captured the artist and the genre, with all the ingredients coming together at the right time to create a recipe for long-lasting success. *–SS*

Van Halen

FOR UNLAWFUL CARNAL KNOWLEDGE

WARNER BROS. | Producers: Andy Johns, Ted Templeman, Van Halen

RELEASED: JUNE 17, 1991

● After exploring a range of styles with the help of a healthy dose of keyboards on its first two Sammy Hagar–fronted albums, Van Halen went back to basics with *For Unlawful Carnal Knowledge*. Except for the ubiquitous piano-based hit single **Right Now**, the focus here was squarely on Eddie Van Halen's guitar prowess. By this time, he was past the point of unveiling jaw-dropping new techniques on every album, but he remained impressive, inventive, and utterly unique on tracks such as **Poundcake**, **Judgement Day**, and the bluesy **In 'n' Out**.

The sophomorically titled set (F.U.C.K., get it?) was also possibly the best-sounding Van Halen record ever, with Led Zeppelin and Rolling Stones engineering legend Andy Johns giving the rhythm section of Alex Van Halen and Michael Anthony a massive, full body. Hagar also might have been at the peak of his vocal powers, although his more conventional songwriting approach had stripped the band of a bit of its David Lee Roth–era daring. Apart from the trippy prog rock of **Pleasure Dome**, things got a tad monolithic on side 2, but the quality of each track remained top notch, even if they didn't combine to form as cohesive of an album as previous Van Hagar efforts. *–MW*

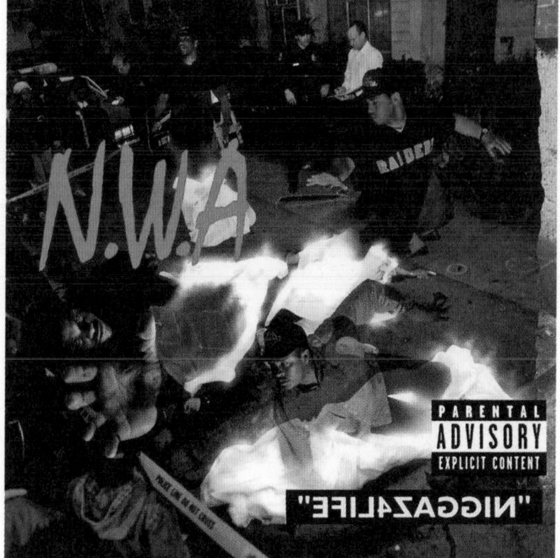

N.W.A

NIGGAZ4LIFE

RUTHLESS/PRIORITY | Producers: Eazy-E, Dr. Dre, DJ Yella

RELEASED: MAY 28, 1991

● There's a lot *not* to like about N.W.A's second and final studio album. There's no question the group lost a lot with the departures of Ice Cube and The D.O.C. from its ranks. And the unrepentant misogyny in the eighteen-track set's second half is shameful and even embarrassing for a troupe that was such a potent and provocative voice of the street on *Straight Outta Compton* just three years before. What raises *Niggaz4Life* (aka *Efil4zaggin* when the title was printed backward on the cover) out of that gutter is sound. Dr. Dre and DJ Yella were hitting peak powers as producers, using samples, turntable techniques, and more to turn the songs into sonic symphonies, bolstering Eazy-E and MC Ren in a swirl of moving audio parts that was daring and, at times, audacious—for example, even trying on country with **Automobile**. Even its objectionable parts were undeniably "real" reflections of the culture they were operating in, and, truth be told, it would not have been true to N.W.A to pull any punches. It's not for the faint of heart or politically correct, but *Niggaz4Life* shows growth that Dre in particular would build on after N.W.A's breakup in this album's wake. *–GG*

P.M. Dawn

OF THE HEART, OF THE SOUL AND OF THE CROSS: THE UTOPIAN EXPERIENCE

GEE STREET/ISLAND | Producer: P.M. Dawn

RELEASED: AUGUST 6, 1991

● During its tragically short career, P.M. Dawn often achieved musical utopia, fearlessly blending pop and R&B into its hip-hop base through unexpected samples and its own songwriting smarts. The New Jersey duo's first and only chart-topping hit, **Set Adrift on Memory Bliss**, brilliantly sampled Spandau Ballet's "True," and similar genre-melding invention can be found elsewhere on the album with highlights such as **Paper Doll** and **Reality Used to Be a Friend of Mine**. Although the group was criticized by some as too soft, P.M. Dawn unapologetically continued further down its own unique path on subsequent releases. A lack of commercial success and other issues caused the group to become largely inactive at the turn of the century, and frontman Prince Be's 2016 death from diabetes complications robbed the music world of a brilliant and sadly all-but-forgotten genius. Do yourself a favor and listen to each of those first three records all the way through at least once in your life. *–MW*

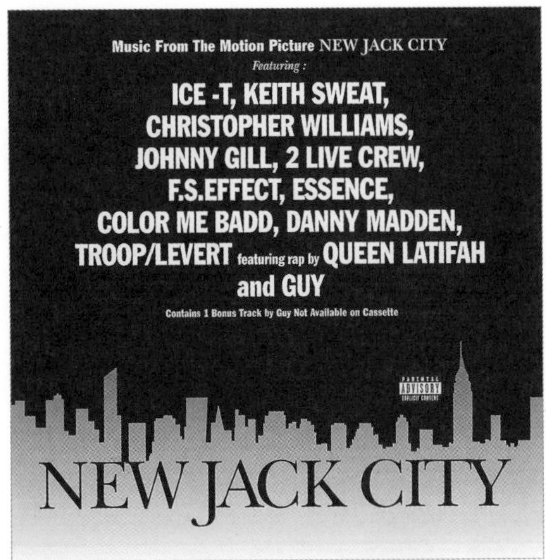

Various Artists

NEW JACK CITY

(MUSIC FROM THE MOTION PICTURE SOUNDTRACK)

GIANT/REPRISE/WARNER BROS. | Producers: Al B. Sure!, Bobby Wooten, Carl McIntosh, Danny Madden, DJ Aladdin, Dr. Freeze, Ellis Jay, Grandmaster Flash, Guy, Ice-T, Keith Sweat, Mike "Mike Fresh" McCray, Randy Ran, Rodney "Kool Collie" Terry, Stanley Brown, Teddy Riley, Bernard Belle, Vassal Benford

RELEASED: MARCH 5, 1991

● Eleven original tracks featured on this companion to Mario Van Peebles's crime film about Nino Brown, a drug kingpin played by Wesley Snipes. The album opened hard with Ice-T, who also stars in the film, rapping about the social cycle that creates predators like Nino in **New Jack Hustler (Nino's Theme)**. Queen Latifah, Troop, and LeVert blend rap's main ingredients with R&B, working over beds mashing up the O'Jays' "For the Love of Money" and Stevie Wonder's "Living for the City." Soulful sensuality is delivered by Keith Sweat (**[There You Go] Tellin' Me No Again**), Johnny Gill (**I'm Still Waiting**), and Color Me Badd (**I Wanna Sex You Up**). The film's title alludes to the genre dubbed New Jack Swing, an amalgamation of R&B and hip-hop crafted by producer Teddy Riley, who appeared on the title track with his group Guy and would go on to create chart-topping hits for Michael Jackson and Bobby Brown. If you were looking for a single record to showcase where these two genres were headed, this soundtrack was a perfect choice. *–RSM*

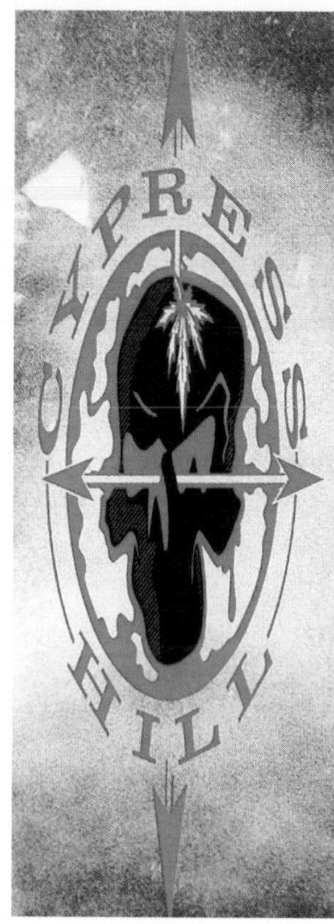

Cypress Hill

CYPRESS HILL

RUFFHOUSE/COLUMBIA | Producer: DJ Muggs

RELEASED: AUGUST 31, 1991

● Cypress Hill entered the rap scene with this self-titled masterpiece, a sixteen-track set that was unmistakably original and distinctive. Even lesser-known tracks such as **Psychobetabuckdown** were immediately recognized as something that could only be the products of the trio from South Gate, California.

Vocally, the contrast between the group's Louis "B-Real" Freese and Senen "Sen Dog" Reyes was as sharp as it was creative. B-Real's aggressive tones contrasted and complemented Sen Dog's more bass-driven and deliberate attack. Staying true to its roots, Cypress Hill also broke ground as a pioneering Latin rap group, interspersing Spanish and south-of-the-border polyrhythms. Oddly enough, the producer and sonic architect was co-founder Lawrence "DJ Muggs" Muggerud, who was Italian. But fusing a wide range of influences—also including rock, jazz, and blues—he created a dynamic sound. The beats were chaotic, but Muggs ensured that they made sense.

The subject matter on *Cypress Hill* was scooped right out of life in South Central Los Angeles: raw, violent, and unforgiving. Cannabis has since become mainstream, but Cypress Hill was ahead of the game, weeding out nuances for tracks such as **Stoned Is the Way of the Walk** and **Something for the Blunted**.

How I Could Just Kill a Man and **The Phuncky Feel One** both hit No. 1 on the Billboard Hot Rap Songs chart, and **Hand on the Pump/Real Estate (No. 2)** helped push *Cypress Hill* to Top 5 on the Top R&B/Hip-Hop Albums survey as well as double-platinum status. The success also helped Cypress Hill land on the Lollapalooza tour in 1992, exposing the group to an even broader mainstream audience and giving its unmistakably hardcore sound a crossover appeal. *–ZC*

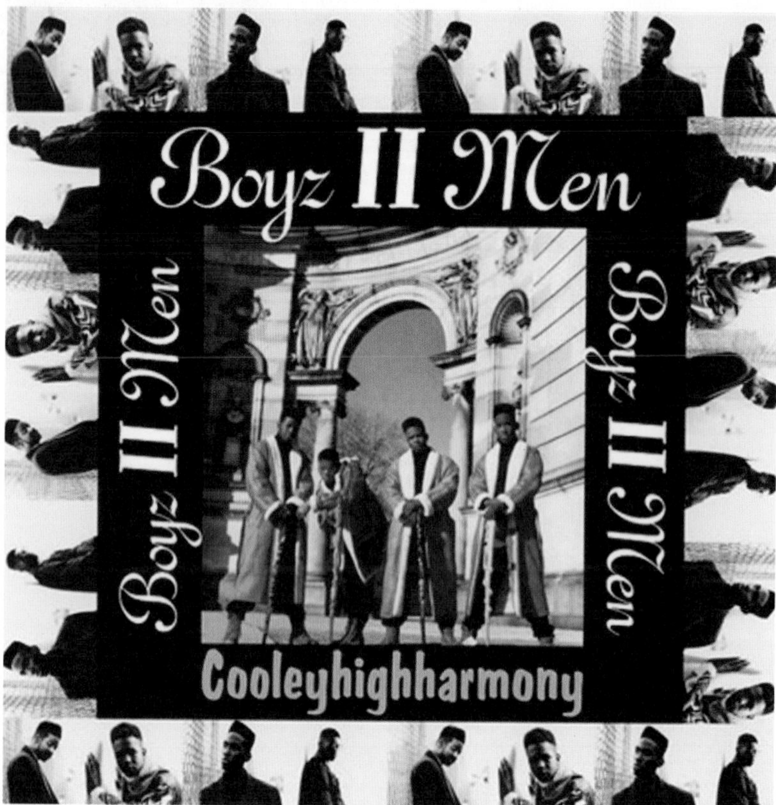

Boyz II Men

COOLEYHIGH-HARMONY

MOTOWN | Producers: Dallas Austin, The Characters

RELEASED: APRIL 30, 1991

● If New Edition and New Kids on the Block made the pop world safe again for boy bands in the '80s, Boyz II Men benefited from their respective hiatuses during the early '90s—the former's in particular, as it was New Edition's Michael Bivins who signed on to manage the upstart Philadelphia quartet that was named after New Edition's hit "Boys to Men."

It's easy to see why the light bulb (and cash register) went off for Bivins. Boyz II Men was (and remains, albeit as a trio since 2003) a classic vocal group in every sense, with multiple lead singers, smooth harmonies, and a vintage, soulful tonality that spanned doo-wop to New Jack. They were solid songwriters as well, fully formed by the time they got their shot with Bivins and a deal with Motown Records.

Cooleyhighharmony was produced primarily by urban hitmaker Dallas Austin with two songs by the Characters, and it divided its ten tracks evenly between upbeat and ballads, interestingly starting with the latter to show off the group's vocal prowess. In other words, it eased the listener in with the silky-smooth likes of **Please Don't Go** and **It's So Hard to Say Goodbye to Yesterday** (originally from the 1975 film *Cooley High*), giving way to the energetic explosion of the introductory single **Motownphilly**. The gambit worked; it was a platinum Top 5 smash that launched *Cooleyhighharmony* to No. 1 on the Billboard R&B chart (and No. 3 on the all-genre Billboard 200 and nine-times-platinum sales).

Even bigger things were ahead for Boyz II Men, as it topped the charts with "End of the Road" from the *Boomerang* film soundtrack and "In the Still of the Nite (I'll Remember)" from *The Jacksons: An American Dream* TV miniseries, both of which were added to a re-release that gave *Cooleyhighharmony* new life the following year. *–GG*

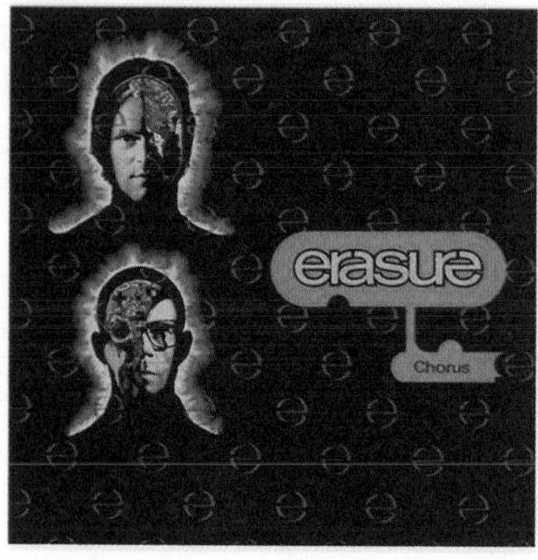

Erasure
CHORUS

SIRE/REPRISE | Producer: Martyn Phillips

RELEASED: OCTOBER 15, 1991

● Already established as masters of electronic anthems, the fifth studio album from Erasure (singer/songwriter Andy Bell and composer/keyboardist Vince Clarke, founder of Depeche Mode and Yazoo) begged listeners to pay attention to the lyrics as much as the high-energy dance beats. The album's four singles—**Chorus**, **Breath of Life**, **Am I Right?**, and **Love to Hate You** (an obvious homage to Gloria Gaynor's "I Will Survive")—deftly tackled topics such as the environment, aging, and self-acceptance even as they became worldwide club favorites and radio hits. The result was a jewel in the band's catalog. *–HD*

Bruce Cockburn
NOTHING BUT A BURNING LIGHT

TRUE NORTH/COLUMBIA | Producer: T Bone Burnett

RELEASED: NOVEMBER 5, 1991

● Impeccably produced by T Bone Burnett and assisted by Joe Henry, *Nothing but a Burning Light* conveyed Bruce Cockburn's considerable social conscience and spirituality, vocal and guitar playing prowess, and thoughtful lyrics that were never strident or preachy. Evoking big-sky country, it balanced the bite of **Mighty Trucks at Midnight** with the introspective beauty of **One of the Best Ones**. Instrumental surprises include the surf rock–leaning **Actions Speak Louder** and a commanding cover of Blind Willie Johnson's **Soul of a Man**. With guest contributors such as Jackson Browne, Booker T. Jones, Sam Phillips, Larry Klein, and Jim Keltner, it was an ideal marriage of melody, lyrics, instrumentation, and arrangement. *–LM*

Sam Phillips
CRUEL INVENTIONS

VIRGIN | Producer: T Bone Burnett

RELEASED: MAY 28, 1991

● Few made a better transition from contemporary Christian artist to pop music than Sam Phillips, let alone to progressive, forward-thinking, roots-indebted pop music. Phillips laid down a significant marker with her 1989 secular debut, *The Indescribable Wow*. On *Cruel Inventions* two years later, she continued her pop explorations with a stellar supporting cast including bassist Jerry Scheff, guitarist Marc Ribot, and then-husband T Bone Burnett producing. Like her friend Elvis Costello, Phillips's lyrics convey darkness that hews to melodic earworms. You'll find yourself effortlessly singing along until you realize exactly what you're singing about. *–HK*

Drivin' N' Cryin'
FLY ME COURAGEOUS

ISLAND | Producer: Geoff Workman

RELEASED: JANUARY 8, 1991

● There was more drivin' than cryin' on this ballsy fourth album by the Southern-flavored rockers from Atlanta, who were fresh off touring with R.E.M. when they recorded it. The hard-rocking title track and first single sounded like a rallying cry for the Gulf War, and it was embraced as such by some in the military, including pilots who listened to it before takeoff. Frontman Kevin Kinney, who was then reading John F. Kennedy's *Profiles in Courage*, quickly dismissed that interpretation as "total nonsense," and the band pushed beyond with muscular rockers such as **Chain Reaction**, **Build a Fire**, and **Rush Hour**. *–SM*

Buddy Guy
DAMN RIGHT, I'VE GOT THE BLUES

SILVERTONE | Producer: John Porter

RELEASED: JULY 1, 1991

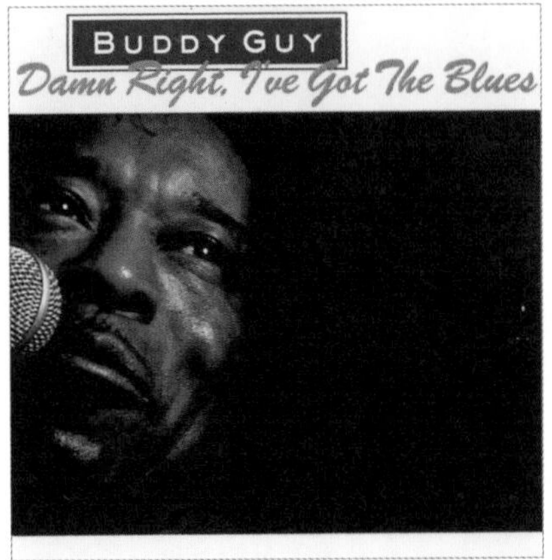

● At the start of the '90s, Buddy Guy was criminally under-recognized but a legend to acolytes of his Chess records and session work with Jimi Hendrix, Eric Clapton, and Jeff Beck. Guy grabbed the spotlight with *Damn Right, I've Got the Blues*, his first new album in a decade. The Grammy Award–winning comeback included contributions from Clapton, Beck, and Mark Knopfler, but Guy was the real star, at the top of his game—vocally, too—from the title track through hot covers of **Mustang Sally** and Willie Dixon's **Let Me Love You Baby**, as well as the album-closing instrumental **Rememberin' Stevie** (as in Ray Vaughan). We were damn glad to have him back. *–GG*

Elvis Costello
MIGHTY LIKE A ROSE

WARNER BROS. | Producers: Elvis Costello, Mitchell Froom, Kevin Killen

RELEASED: MAY 14, 1991

● Elvis Costello wanted to reclaim his birth name, Declan MacManus, for his thirteenth studio album but lost that battle with his still-new label Warner Bros. But in the "a rose by any other name" department, this is arguably one of Costello's best albums, filled with well-crafted and sometimes-idiosyncratic (of course) delights. It includes two writing collaborations with Paul McCartney (**So Like Candy** and **Playboy to a Man**), a trumpet solo by his father Ross MacManus (**Invasion Hit Parade**), and a track written by Costello's then-wife Caitlin O'Riordan (**Broken**). Mitchell Froom's production adds just the right amount of avant ambience. *–GG*

U2

ACHTUNG BABY

ISLAND | Producers: Daniel Lanois, Brian Eno

RELEASED: NOVEMBER 18, 1991

● In October 1990, U2 headed to Berlin to record in the neglected Hansa Studios on the site of a former SS ballroom—which worked out as well as one might guess. Directionless, the famously united band fractured along musical lines. Electronic dance music? Heartfelt rock anthems? Arguments escalated.

Then, cinematically, the stirring song **One** arose from a jam session, the clouds parted, and the band high-tailed it home. Back in Dublin, Ireland, the quartet got to work "chopping down *The Joshua Tree*," in reference to its multiplatinum 1987 album.

And what a sound it made when it fell.

"I'm ready for the laughing gas . . . I'm ready for what's next," Bono sang on **Zoo Station**, *Achtung Baby*'s wall-of-noise opener. "Next," in this case, meant a painful snapshot of guitarist The Edge's divorce and a lyrical pivot from the messy and dirty world of politics into the messier and dirtier world of relationships. Here, U2's core religious imagery was augmented, though mired in at once elegant and unmistakably sexual innuendo; but nowhere is there a love song, not even to God (if you think **One** qualifies, re-read the lyrics). Ultimately, *Achtung Baby* was an album in which everyone can see themselves, even if they don't like the view.

Five singles (**The Fly**, **Mysterious Ways**, **One**, **Even Better Than the Real Thing**, and **Who's Gonna Ride Your Wild Horses**) propelled *Achtung Baby* to No. 1 on charts around the world, including the Billboard 200, and diamond-certified sales in the US. The band's two-year tour in support of the album also broke new ground with its 130-foot (39.6-m) video wall, flying East German Trabant cars, live calls to world leaders, and a second stage out on the stadium floors. The album was also celebrated, deservedly, during U2's 2023–2024 residency opening Sphere in Las Vegas. *—HD*

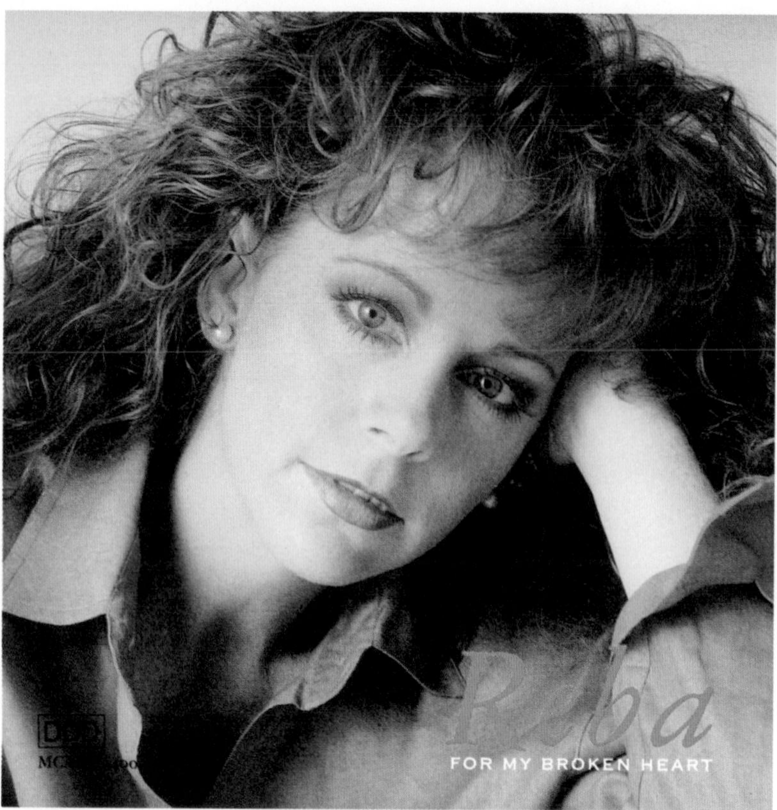

Reba McEntire

FOR MY BROKEN HEART

MCA | Producers: Tony Brown, Reba McEntire

RELEASED: OCTOBER 1, 1991

● The best-selling project of Reba McEntire's nearly fifty-year career happened to be her seventeenth studio album. To date it has sold more than four million copies and produced two No. 1 country hits: the title track and **Is There Life Out There**. Two other singles, **The Greatest Man I Ever Knew** and her cover of Vicki Lawrence's 1973 hit **The Night the Lights Went Out in Georgia**, gave McEntire two more hits; at the time, *For My Broken Heart* became her highest-charting album on the Billboard 200, peaking at No. 13 (it would be surpassed by her next three releases).

The project's title took on special meaning, as it was McEntire's first studio recording since losing eight members of her touring band in a plane crash following a concert in March 1991; a bout with bronchitis had kept McEntire away from that fateful flight. She began the recording process just two months after the tragedy and dedicated the album to those lost band members. In the liner notes, McEntire wrote, "It seems your current emotional status determines what music you'd like to hear. That's what happened on the song selection for this album. If for any reason you can relate to the emotion packed inside these songs, I hope it's a form of healing for all our broken hearts."

McEntire co-wrote one song for the album, **Bobby**, and was supported by noted musicians such as Mark O'Connor on fiddle and mandolin, Larrie Londin on drums, Matt Rollings and John Barlow Jarvis on keyboards, and Leland Sklar on bass. Vince Gill, Linda Davis, and Harry Stinson provided backing vocals.

In addition to being the top seller of McEntire's career, *For My Broken Heart* earned the distinction of being the first album by a female country artist to be certified double platinum. *—MH2*

1992

92
TWO

Alice in Chains

DIRT

COLUMBIA | Producers: Dave Jerden, Alice in Chains

RELEASED: SEPTEMBER 29, 1992

● If 1990's *Facelift* was an album by a hard rock band from Seattle, the sophomore full-length of Alice in Chains (AiC) was a time-specific masterpiece from a Seattle rock band. The debut had landed AiC comfortably in the album-rock world of its time, even snagging an opening spot for Van Halen. But much changed during the next couple of years: Nirvana and Pearl Jam released their landmarks *Nevermind* and *Ten*, respectively, in 1991, and the film *Singles*, which came out eleven days before *Dirt*, further defined Seattle's "grunge" scene. There was greater context and sense of place for AiC and its brutally dark and honest new release.

Jerry Cantrell was still AiC's main songwriter, but frontman Layne Staley co-wrote four tracks with the guitarist and two on his own, while Slayer's Tom Araya added to the heaviness with his contributions to **Iron Gland**. With Staley fresh out of rehab and other band members dealing with addictions, *Dirt* has been wrongly typecast as a concept album about drug use, specifically heroin. That was certainly an explicit theme on tracks such as **Junkhead**, **God Smack**, and **Sickman**. But there was much more to the thirteen songs. Explorations into mortality, romance, and family relationships (notably **Rooster** about Cantrell's Vietnam vet father) made *Dirt* more of a treatise about the grim resolve of finding a way to navigate and endure life's dirtiest circumstances—and to kick some ass while doing it, blending dirgey angst with explosive, face-melting heavy-rock dynamics.

Dirt reached No. 6 on the Billboard 200 and has been certified five-times platinum. Its singles **Would?** (also on the *Singles* soundtrack), **Them Bones**, **Rooster**, and **Down in a Hole** have remained staples not just in AiC's catalog but for rock (mainstream *and* alternative) in general. If anyone ever asks, "What was grunge?" this is an album that best represents it. *–GG*

T Bone Burnett

THE CRIMINAL UNDER MY OWN HAT

COLUMBIA | Producers: T Bone Burnett, Bob Neuwirth

RELEASED: JULY 14, 1992

● By the time of his eighth solo album, T Bone Burnett was more famous as a producer (Los Lobos and Elvis Costello, notably) than an artist, even though '80s entries such as *Proof through the Night* and *The Talking Animals* received some attention. *The Criminal Under My Own Hat* came after a five-year break from his own work. During that interim, Burnett developed a creative vocabulary that fused angular rock and acoustic singer/songwriter introspection, separated on his previous releases, into a spirited mélange in which one complemented the other. Recording in Los Angeles and Nashville, Burnett had plenty of stellar help, a formidable corps that included Jerry Douglas on dobro, Mark O'Connor on violin and mandolin, Marc Ribot on guitar, Jim Keltner on drums, Van Dyke Parks on accordion, and bassists Jerry Scheff and Edgar Meyer, among others. It gave Burnett a welcome new artistic identity, even as a social commentator on the scathing **I Can't Explain Everything**. We'd have to wait fourteen years before he'd exercise that music again, though, mostly owing to outside duties that earned him two Grammy Awards as Producer of the Year, Non-Classical during the interim. *–GG*

Lyle Lovett

JOSHUA JUDGES RUTH

CURB/MCA | Producers: George Massenberg, Billy Williams, Lyle Lovett

RELEASED: MARCH 31, 1992

● By 1992, Lyle Lovett had already provided irrefutable evidence that country was a wildly inaccurate label for his sophisticated gospel-, blues-, and jazz-steeped arrangements and erudite lyrics that were alternately heart-tugging and devilishly sly. This time out, the tall Texan toned down the humor of 1989's *Lyle Lovett and His Large Band,* instead shaping the musical syllables of Memphis, North Dakota, and Baltimore into a travelogue of moody, richly detailed landscapes, drawing road maps of emotion with each crag in his deeply nuanced voice. Supported by Matt Rollings's elegant piano, Lovett rendered ballads, including **She's Already Made Up Her Mind** and **North Dakota**, the latter featuring Rickie Lee Jones, with beautiful understatement. Willis Alan Ramsey's and Arnold McCuller's vocal interplay on **She Makes Me Feel Good** enhanced its great groove, and McCuller, Francine Reed, Sweet Pea Atkinson, and other top gospel vocalists turned **Church** and **Since the Last Time** into tour-de-force roof-raisers. Only one song, **She's Leaving Me Because She Really Wants To**, truly enters country territory, with hurtin' harmonies by Emmylou Harris and weepy steel from Jay Dee Maness. Another fine example of Lovett's ability to craft singular music with impeccable taste. *–LM*

Eric Clapton
UNPLUGGED

DUCK/REPRISE/MTV | Producer: Russ Titelman

RELEASED: AUGUST 25, 1992

● *MTV Unplugged* was one of the most adventurous music programs ever created by the channel—or any outlet for that matter. A showcase for rock bands that typically played amplified, *Unplugged* provided great players the opportunity to show off their acoustic chops, often creating fresh interpretations of their biggest hits. For Eric Clapton, long considered one of rock's all-time great guitarists, *Unplugged* captured an artist at his most mature, sober prime. The rebooted **Layla** in particular—a jazzy, loping, and brilliant counterpoint to the ferocious angst of Derek and the Dominos' original—continues to be heard on Classic Rock radio. Importantly, Clapton used the acoustic format to show off his bluesy roots, going back to his early days with the Yardbirds and John Mayall's Bluesbreakers on renditions of Muddy Waters's **Rollin' and Tumblin'**, Son House's **Walkin' Blues**, and more. But it was **Tears in Heaven**, a new Clapton track written with lyricist Will Jennings, that emotionally connected him to untold millions of old and new fans. The song was a moving tribute to his four-year-old son, Conor, victim of a tragic domestic accident. Amid the many amazing acoustic revelations here, it's the song that seared the album into our memories. *–FJ*

Soul Asylum
GRAVE DANCERS UNION

COLUMBIA | Producer: Michael Beinhorn

RELEASED: OCTOBER 6, 1992

● Soul Asylum's sixth studio album rocketed the band from college radio obscurity to mainstream stardom. While the album marked the band's evolution to a more polished sound, it did not compromise its raw, emotive energy. The production provided a brighter spotlight for frontman Dave Pirner's distinctive gravelly vocals and showcased the band's aptitude for crafting catchy hooks with introspective lyrics. The album's success was driven by three Top 10 Mainstream Rock chart singles: **Somebody to Shove**, **Black Gold**, and **Runaway Train**, the latter of which gave Soul Asylum its first Billboard Hot 100 hit (peaking at No. 5) and won a Grammy for Best Rock Song. Its video also featured images of missing teenagers and led to twenty-six of them being found. **Somebody to Shove** epitomized Pirner's ability to twist a phrase, and during the breakdown in **Black Gold**, you can hear live news coverage of the Rodney King beating that occurred during the recording of the album. *Grave Dancers Union*'s impact was so complete that Soul Asylum was invited to perform at Bill Clinton's inauguration the following year after Chelsea turned her parents onto the band. The album spent seventy-six weeks on the Billboard 200 and was certified double platinum. *–BF*

Little Earthquakes

Tori Amos

LITTLE EARTHQUAKES

ATLANTIC | Producers: Tori Amos, Eric Rosse, Davitt Sigerson, Ian Stanley

RELEASED: JANUARY 6, 1992

● Tori Amos's recording career started in 1988 as the leader of the synth-pop band Y Kant Tori Read. Its self-titled debut bombed, and the group broke up not long after its release. But Atlantic Records heard something in the group's singer, songwriter, and piano player. Four years later, Amos debuted as a solo act with *Little Earthquakes*, a defining record of the era that went on to sell more than two million copies.

The alternative music revolution was just getting started when the album was released in early 1992, and Amos's intimate and personal songs fell right in with the changing tide. Although the music relied heavily on her classically trained piano playing, *Little Earthquakes* quickly gained a fanbase due to Amos's emotional singing and confessional songwriting. **Me and a Gun** resonated in particular; it detailed her rape at the age of twenty-one with a stark, a cappella performance that was as chilling as it was cleansing.

The unorthodox nature of *Little Earthquakes* has distinguished it as one of the most influential albums of the decade. Scores of artists, especially women, found inspiration in Amos's simultaneously tough and delicate songs and skewed arrangements: **Crucify**, **Silent All These Years**, **Winter**, and **China** certainly helped set a new singer/songwriter standard. "So you found a girl who thinks really deep thoughts/What's so amazing about really deep thoughts?/Boy, you best pray that I bleed real soon/How's that thought for you?" she asked in **Silent All These Years**, a declaration of independence from years of hurt and neglect.

Amos pushed her work even further from the mainstream on subsequent records. She's at the center of a rising storm here. *–MG*

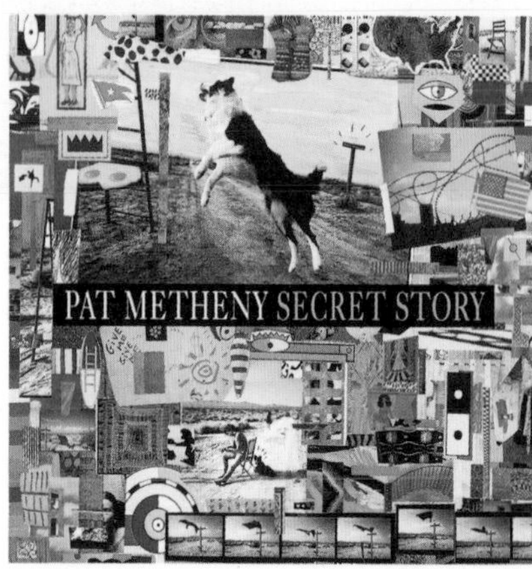

Pat Metheny
SECRET STORY

GEFFEN | Producer: Pat Metheny

RELEASED: JULY 8, 1992

● *Secret Story* found thirty-eight-year-old Pat Metheny at a personal crossroads. Reflecting on the breakup of a five-year romantic relationship, the guitarist sculpted an escapist, multitextured, and transcendental thrill ride that won the Grammy for Best Contemporary Jazz Album. Not exactly jazz, the episodic songs were injected with Asian chants, complex rhythms, hints of minimalism, and even art rock. And, in a first for Metheny, nearly each of the eleven tracks was enhanced by his own orchestrations that added a grandiose majesty. The album's delicate closing song sequence is tender and heart-wrenching, and Metheny's guitar and synth solos were among his best—fluid, enterprising, piercing, and dramatic, all with a positive vibe. *–CH*

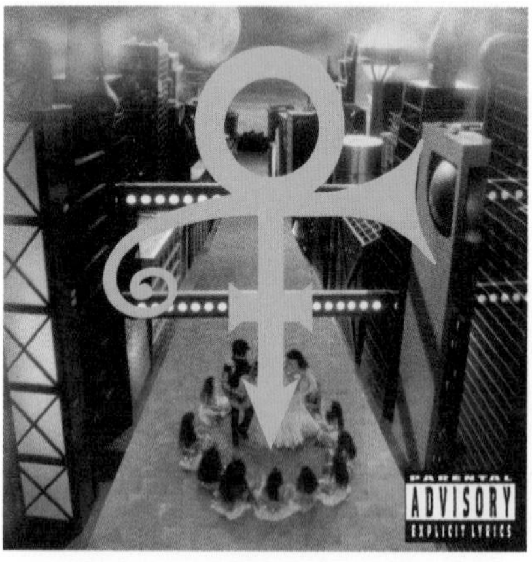

Prince
(LOVE SYMBOL)

PAISLEY PARK/WARNER BROS. | Producers: Prince and the New Power Generation

RELEASED: OCTOBER 13, 1992

● Prince closed out his hitmaking era in 1992. After *(Love Symbol)*—coined for his unpronounceable melding of the men's and women's astrological symbols, to which he'd change his own name—he'd chart just one more song in Billboard's Top 10. *(Love Symbol)* is an altogether funky saga, beginning with the in-your-face **My Name Is Prince** and the R-rated **Sexy MF**. An inscrutable storyline, with Kirstie Alley as a frustrated reporter, runs through the seventy-five-minute opus, but its pop highs remain intact, including the majestic **7**, the strikingly soulful **The Morning Papers**, and the dizzying **3 Chains O' Gold**, a rock opera in and of itself. *–AG*

L7
BRICKS ARE HEAVY

SLASH | Producers: Butch Vig, L7

RELEASED: APRIL 14, 1992

● It wasn't pretty, this third album from the band that gave us the famed used-tampon-throwing incident at that year's Reading Festival. *Bricks Are Heavy* was ugly, dirty, angry grunge from four Los Angeles women under the helm of Butch Vig, who had just produced *Nevermind* for L7's touring partners, Nirvana. On its tightest, most consistent set, L7 lashed out at Reagan/Bush militarism with the metal grind of **Wargasm** ("Tie a yellow ribbon 'round the amputee") and roared out a call to action with their signature song **Pretend That We're Dead**, declaring, "They're neither moral nor majority." *–SM*

Pantera
VULGAR DISPLAY OF POWER

ATCO | Producer: Terry Date

RELEASED: FEBRUARY 25, 1992

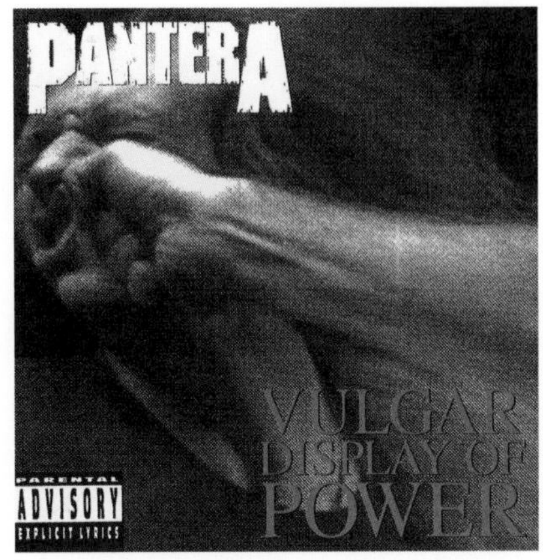

● Pantera's second major-label release found the band going further into the creation of what the Texans dubbed "groove metal," an alloy of thrash and hardcore punk but with swagger. That bounce is most evident on **Walk**, an ode to respect, and **A New Level**, a ditty about rising above haters. What Pantera captured here would influence so-called "nu metal" bands such as Korn and Slipknot later in the decade—a neat trick given Pantera's earlier indie incarnation as glam metal. But some of that old style sneaks in on the mutilated ballads **This Love** and **Hollow**. *–RSM*

House of Pain
HOUSE OF PAIN

TOMMY BOY | Producers: DJ Lethal, DJ Muggs, Ralph Tha Funky Mexican, Pete Rock

RELEASED: JULY 21, 1992

● "Pack it up, pack it in, I came to win," the Los Angeles trio declared on its breakthrough hit, **Jump Around**. And House of Pain certainly scored a victory with its debut album. The Irish heritage card was a good hook, but they didn't take it over the top, focusing on an aggressive attack and working-class swagger that was no gimmick. DJ Lethal (Leor Demant, later of Limp Bizkit) was the not-so-secret weapon throughout, fortifying Danny Boy O'Connor's and Everlast's (Eric Schrody) rhymes with an arsenal of sound. **Jump Around** is still heard at sports events worldwide, but there's plenty more pleasing *Pain* in these seventeen tracks. *–GG*

Straight Ahead
LOOK STRAIGHT AHEAD

ATLANTIC | Producer: Sylvia May

RELEASED: APRIL 1992

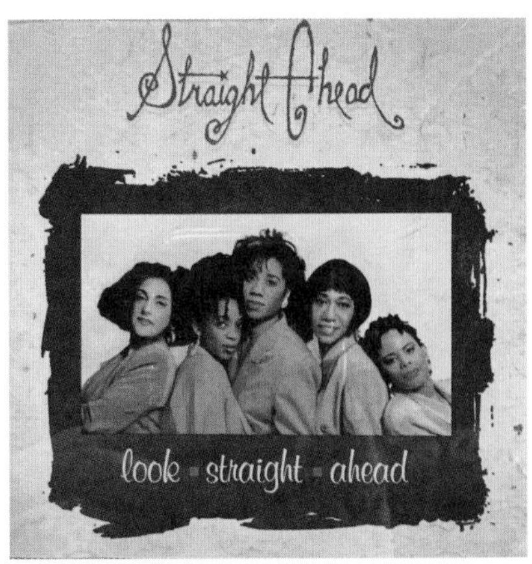

● This debut by a Detroit quintet of twenty-something women, all superb jazz instrumentalists, was a delight from beginning to end. Straight Ahead's cohesive energy echoed the musical terrain of Chick Corea's *Return to Forever* and Jean Luc Ponty's fusion bands, yet its overall sound was original and homegrown. The group struck pop-jazz gold on violinist Regina Carter's **You Touch Me**, a gospel-infused gem. Carter stood out carrying melodic lines, rendering captivating solos and artfully blending her instrument with her bandmates. The ensemble also recast several jazz standards that rival the originals, including John Coltrane's **Impressions** and Stanley Clarke's **Light as a Feather**. *–CH*

1992

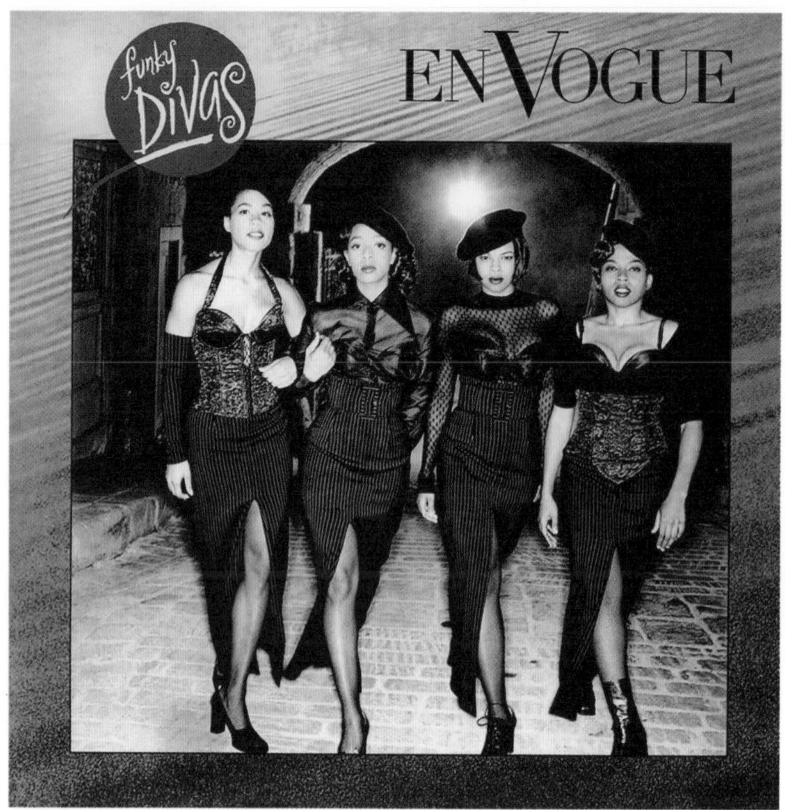

En Vogue

FUNKY DIVAS

EASTWEST | Producers: Denzil Foster, Thomas McElroy

RELEASED: MARCH 24, 1992

● The '90s became the new '60s, of a sort, with the release of En Vogue's *Funky Divas*. The Oakland, California, quartet's second album carried Supremes and Martha and the Vandellas vibes, utilizing the sweet and powerful voices of Terry Ellis, Dawn Robinson, Cindy Herron, and Maxine Jones. Together their vocals were sweet and sassy, with plenty of power. You didn't have to look any further than the second and fourth singles, **Giving Him Something He Can Feel** and **Give It Up, Turn It Loose**—written, like most of the material, by producers Denzil Foster and Thomas McElroy—to feel the sources En Vogue was drawing from. While both songs sound like they could have been recorded at Studio A in Motown's Hitsville USA headquarters, at the same time, they're fresh, cool, and current.

Then there were *Funky Divas'* lead and third singles, **My Lovin' (You're Never Gonna Get It)** and **Free Your Mind**. Both were anthemic hits that make you want to turn your radio dial all the way up and belt out the songs. Other *Funky Divas* tracks, such as the jovial **This Is Your Life**, the sultry **Desire**, the rap-flavored **It Ain't Over Till the Fat Lady Sings**, a colorful remake of The Beatles' **Yesterday**, and the smooth, jazzy **Love Don't Love You** provided further showcases for the quartet's vocal skills.

Funky Divas peaked at No. 8 on the Billboard 200 and No. 1 on the R&B/Hip-Hop chart on its way to triple-platinum sales. It also received four Grammy nominations and several *Soul Train* Music Award nods, plus the latter's Sammy Davis Jr. Entertainer of the Year Prize. Decades later, nothing sounds like *Funky Divas* and its powerful combination of individual voices and harmonies. *—EP*

Annie Lennox
DIVA

RCA | Producer: Stephen Lipson

RELEASED: APRIL 6, 1992

● Annie Lennox put her wings to the test with her first solo effort apart from Eurythmics. Each of the twelve tracks on *Diva* was written or co-written by Lennox and delivered in her rich voice, showcasing a range of tones and vocal styles. The resonant piano chords on the airy **Why**, the plucked strings of the upbeat **Walking on Broken Glass**, and the dramatic downbeat of **Little Bird** all made for a bold statement of individuality and occasional social commentary. With *Diva*, Lennox looked in the mirror and found an artist with distinctive style and attitude but none of the pretentious ego the title implies. *–SS*

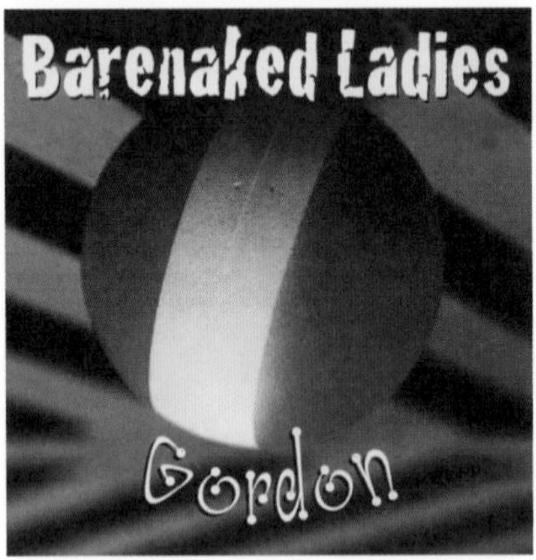

Barenaked Ladies
GORDON

REPRISE/SIRE | Producer: Michael Phillip Wojewoda

RELEASED: JULY 28, 1992

● Barenaked Ladies' name was enough to snag some attention for a brand-new band, and the music on the Toronto quintet's full-length debut was more than enough to keep it. Barenaked Ladies' approach—witty, irreverent, instrumentally sophisticated, and vocally harmonic—was well honed on several previous EPs and demos. *Gordon* had everything we'd come to know and love about Barenaked Ladies, including a musical dexterity that flowed between styles and one track (**The King of Bedside Manner**) recorded with everyone in the studio literally bare naked. **Brian Wilson** and **If I Had $1000000** became beloved Barenaked Ladies tentpoles, but the whole of *Gordon* displayed a fully formed band that balanced offbeat, *Kids in the Hall*–like humor with deeply affecting lyrics whose nuances still reward repeated listens. *–GG*

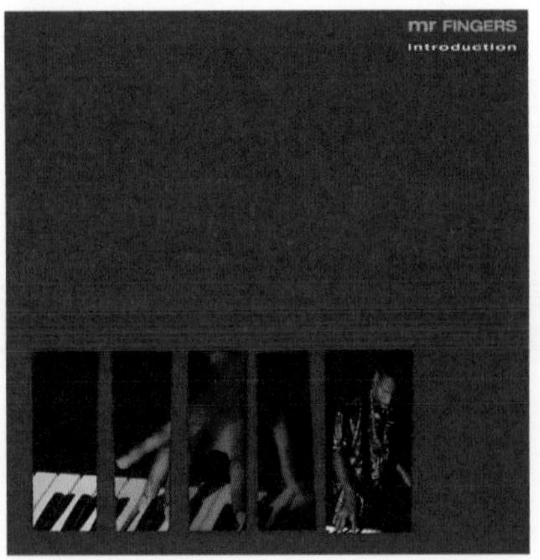

Mr. Fingers
INTRODUCTION

MCA | PRODUCER: MATT HEARD

RELEASED: JUNE 23, 1992

● Chicago DJ, musician, and producer Matt Heard was a well-established force in the international house music scene by the time he made his "solo" debut under the moniker Mr. Fingers, adopted from the name of his band, Fingers, Inc. *Introduction* was a somewhat surprisingly chilled-out affair, grooving smoothly through its thirteen tracks in hypnotic and even soothing, but still danceable, fashion. **Closer**, **What About This Love**, and **On My Way** became club classics, and jams such as **Empty** and **On a Corner Called Jazz** displayed the considerable depth and sophisticated vision of Heard's musical well. *–GG*

Inner City
PRAISE

VIRGIN | Producers: Kevin Saunderson, Juan Atkins ("One Nation"), Altern 8 ("Let It Reign")

RELEASED: JUNE 2, 1992

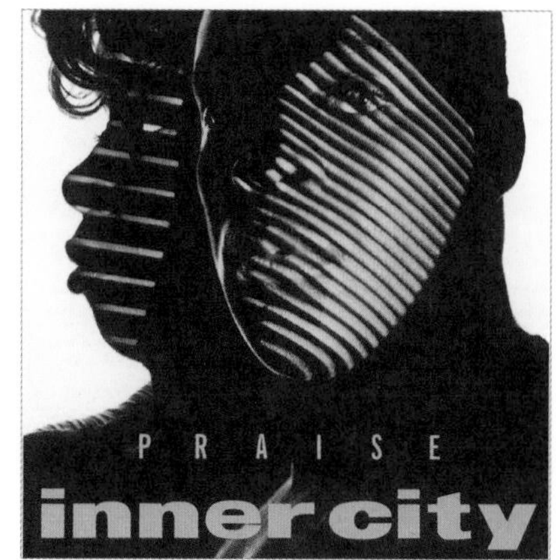

● Following the universal affection for the sound of Motown, Detroit Techno—championed by Inner City—pushed yet another genre to a global profile, mixing soul and style through technology. Led by Kevin Saunderson and featuring vocalist Paris Grey, the project followed up its back-to-back late-'80s hits "Good Life" and "Big Fun" with this powerful album. Standout tracks such as **Pennies From Heaven**, **Follow Your Heart**, and **Hallelujah** reflected the troupe's popularity in the UK and abroad, taking cues from breakbeat and rave while staying faithful to the uplifting songwriting, vocals, keyboards, and driving bass that made the Inner City sound a signature few could mimic. *—CW*

---

k. d. lang
INGÉNUE

SIRE/WARNER BROS. | Producers: Greg Penny, Ben Mink, k. d. lang

RELEASED: MARCH 17, 1992

● Canadian k. d. lang burst into 1992 by pivoting from the country music in which she had become an award-winning mainstay. Perhaps that move was prescient, as many country stations rejected her later that year when she came out as gay. The left turn to lush, sophisticated pop worked to her benefit, and the torchy *Ingénue* birthed two successful singles, the bouncy **Miss Chatelaine** and the career-defining **Constant Craving**. "Even through the darkest phase/Be it thick or thin/Always someone marches brave/Here beneath my skin," she observed in the latter. And lang has lived up to that assessment over the years, moving in and out of retirement but continuing to advocate for numerous causes. *—HD*

Don Byron
TUSKEGEE EXPERIMENTS

NONESUCH | Producer: Arthur Moorhead

RELEASED: FEBRUARY 11, 1992

● On Don Byron's avant debut, the virtuoso clarinetist tapped the notorious medical experiments perpetrated against unsuspecting Black men from 1932 to 1972. The resulting musical creation spanned cerebral, bucolic, and foreboding ground. On **Waltz for Ellen,** Byron's solo clarinet opened the set with spry notes that tiptoed, ballet-like, through the piece. Subsequent tracks with fuzz-tone guitar by Bill Frisell and dense interplay by bassist Lonnie Plaxico and drummer Ralph Peterson Jr. pushed the album into another dimension. The title track, sung by poet Sadiq, told the Tuskegee story and memorialized the plight of the men who suffered through the ignoble experiment, while the clarinet/piano duet **Auf einer Burg** provided a haunting conclusion. *—CH*

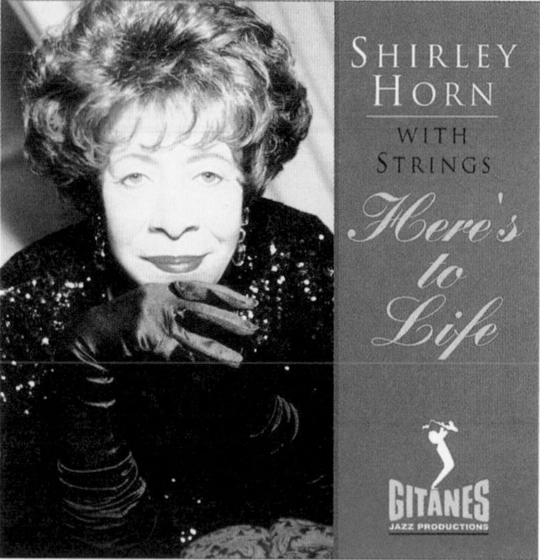

Shirley Horn

HERE'S TO LIFE

VERVE MUSIC GROUP/GITANES JAZZ
Producer: Johnny Mandel

RELEASED: 1992

● Shirley Horn's peerless originality was honed as a singer and pianist in jazz trios during the '50s and '60s. When Miles Davis heard Horn's 1960 album *Embers and Ashes*, he invited her to play sets at the Village Vanguard in New York City. Thus, the first phase of her career accelerated, though it was paused for most of the late '60s and '70s to raise her daughter.

Horn's career reignited in the late '80s. Rarely did she deviate from her trio format with longtime bassist Charles Ables and drummer Steve Williams—until *Here's to Life*, which partnered her with Johnny Mandell, the masterful TV/movie composer/arranger who had worked with Frank Sinatra, Peggy Lee, and Barbra Streisand. Mandell's deft orchestrations enriched Horn's music, and she rarely sounded better.

For the title track and **Where Do You Start**, Horn sang near the forty-nine-piece orchestra, leaving the piano accompaniment to Alan Broadbent. Her controlled singing was cushioned by the strings and brass, the orchestra accentuating her sensitive articulation and allowing space and silence to forge suspense. **Here's to Life** became her signature song, and Mandell won a Grammy for Best Instrumental Arrangement Accompanying Vocals. *–CH*

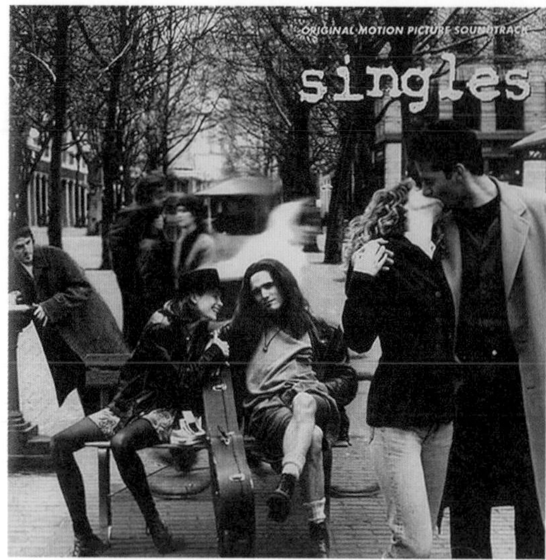

Various Artists

SINGLES (ORIGINAL MOTION PICTURE SOUNDTRACK)

EPIC SOUNDTRAX | Producers: Cameron Crowe, Danny Bramson

RELEASED: JUNE 30, 1992

● The *Singles* soundtrack generated buzz for the rom-com written and directed by Cameron Crowe and featured songs by bands on the forefront of the grunge revolution, including Soundgarden, Pearl Jam, Alice in Chains, Screaming Trees, and Mudhoney. The standout track on the album, Mother Love Bone's **Chloe Dancer/Crown of Thorns**, showcased the emotional angst and power at the heart of the sound. For context, the set also included tracks from legacy Seattle artists such as Jimi Hendrix and the Lovemongers (featuring Heart sisters Ann and Nancy Wilson). **Dyslexic Heart** and **Waiting for Somebody**, meanwhile, were the first solo releases by Paul Westerberg after the breakup of the Replacements (from Minneapolis, but certainly kindred spirits and forebears for its neighbors to the west). The album's sequencing was brilliant, crafting an emotional arc that mirrored the roller-coaster Gen X romantic relationships at the center of the film, an artfully curated experience that elevated the impact of each song within the narrative of the movie. The album was certified double platinum and held the No. 19 spot on *Rolling Stone* magazine's 2019 list of the 50 Greatest Grunge Albums. *–BF*

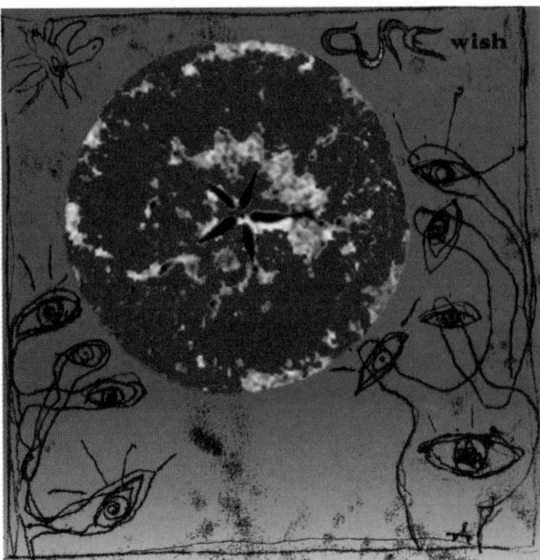

The Cure

WISH

FICTION/ELEKTRA | Producers: David Allen, Robert Smith

RELEASED: APRIL 21, 1992

● Longtime darlings of goth kids everywhere, The Cure made the world fall in love with them—and not just on Friday—with its ninth studio album. Released on the heels of 1989's double-platinum *Disintegration*, a highly successful world tour, and numerous interband lawsuits, *Wish* debuted a new lineup behind founding members Robert Smith, Simon Gallup, and Porl Thompson, adding drummer Boris Williams and the band's roadie, Perry Bamonte, on guitar and keyboards.

Debuting at No. 1 on the UK albums chart (the only Cure album to date to do so) and No. 2 on the Billboard 200 on the strength of the effervescent lead single **High**, *Wish* was really boosted by its second single, the buoyant **Friday I'm In Love**, which Smith considered a very naive, happy type of pop song largely foreign to the band's catalog. It was that combination of unexpected joy filtered through a band known for its dark chords and bleak lyrics that provided the magic. Truer to form, *Wish*'s third single, the Franz Kafka–inspired **A Letter to Elise**, ended with the love interest hanging herself. *–HD*

INXS

WELCOME TO WHEREVER YOU ARE

ELEKTRA | Producers: Mark Opitz, INXS

RELEASED: AUGUST 3, 1992

● "If I could just be everything and everyone to you/ This life would just be so easy," Michael Hutchence sang in **Not Enough Time**, one of the five singles from INXS's eighth studio album. Coming off the massively successful X-Factor Tour and the Australian band's first concert album, *Live Baby Live*, INXS hadn't anticipated the wall of grunge that was overtaking the music industry in 1992. The band needed to pivot to stay relevant, and it answered the challenge by pushing in fresh directions of its own with an album that opened with sitars before incorporating a full orchestra and a heap of vocal distortion. *Welcome To Wherever You Are* debuted at No. 1 in the UK and No. 2 in INXS's homeland, but American sales didn't come close to its predecessors, *X* and the multi-platinum *Kick*. Still, **Heaven Sent**, **Not Enough Time**, and **Beautiful Girl** deservedly hit the Top 10 on Billboard's Alternative chart. As band members navigated personal issues, their efforts to expand INXS's sound, however successful, also felt overly obvious. The band's decision to wait until its next album (1993's *Full Moon, Dirty Hearts*) to tour again was a misstep that further hampered exposure for this sadly underappreciated set. *–HD*

1992

Beastie Boys

CHECK YOUR HEAD

GRAND ROYAL/CAPITOL
Producer: Mario "Mario C." Caldato Jr.

RELEASED: APRIL 21, 1992

● It took some years before *Paul's Boutique*, the Beastie Boys' sample-heavy follow-up to its blockbuster 1986 debut *Licensed to Ill*, was embraced by critics and audiences. By the time 1992 rolled around, Michael "Mike D" Diamond, Adam "MCA" Yauch, and Adam "Ad-Rock" Horovitz were very much in need of a comeback.

They got one with *Check Your Head*, a back-to-basics gut check that found the three picking up their instruments, re-embracing their pre–*Licensed to Ill* punk roots, and rapping like they had something to lose, which they did. It was their reinvention, and it was so successful that people went back and reevaluated *Paul's Boutique* to find that they'd overlooked a gem all along.

A Cheap Trick sample (from *Live at Budokan*) opened *Check Your Head*, which saw the Beastie Boys—joined by keyboardist Mark "Money Mark" Nishita—alternating between hip-hop throwdowns (**Jimmy James** and **Pass the Mic**), funk grooves (**Funky Boss** and **Something's Got to Give**), punk rock dispatches (**Time for Livin'**), and '70s-style instrumental jams (**Groove Holmes** and **In 3's**). It was several worlds removed from the frat-boy bacchanalia of *Licensed to Ill*, from which the group also took great pains to distance itself. Out was the casual misogyny and juvenile humor; in was a focus on instrumentation and maturity, while still making room for fun like **Professor Booty**. And **So What'cha Want**, three and a half romping, stomping minutes of playful hip-hop boasts (MCA says he's "Sweeter than a cherry pie with Reddi-Whip topping") earned the Beastie Boys a home on alt-rock radio, which embraced the group for the remainder of its career.

Check Your Head went on to sell more than two million copies and put the Beastie Boys on a path to a 2012 Rock Hall induction. Comeback fully achieved. *—AG*

U.N.C.
Stüssy

Screaming Trees
SWEET OBLIVION

EPIC | Producer: Don Fleming

RELEASED: SEPTEMBER 8, 1992

● The Great Grunge Sweepstakes left many stellar bands not exactly in the dust heap of history but, shall we say, criminally overlooked. *Sweet Oblivion* was Screaming Trees' third major-label release. Its minor hit **Nearly Lost You** was, full stop, a standout rock track of the period, but the entire album crackled with Mark Lanegan's singular vocals and the force of nature that was the band's new drummer, Barrett Martin (check **The Secret Kind**). Too frequently reduced to accounts of their onstage skirmishes, brothers Gary Lee and Van Conner held down guitar and bass, respectively, and gave Screaming Trees a bit more psychedelic flavor than most of its peers. *–DP*

Dream Theater
IMAGES AND WORDS

ATCO | Producer: Dave Prater

RELEASED: JULY 7, 1992

● This was Dream Theater's second album but the one where the prog-metal quintet's legend really began. With new vocalist James LaBrie emerging from an extensive audition process, Dream Theater forged its dynamic ensemble footing, so much so that the group planned on (and recorded enough material for) a double album that was ultimately scuttled by the record company. That may have been a wise decision in the end, as *Images and Words* remains the group's greatest commercial success and only gold-certified album, while the lead track **Pull Me Under** was its only Top 10 hit on any chart. *–GG*

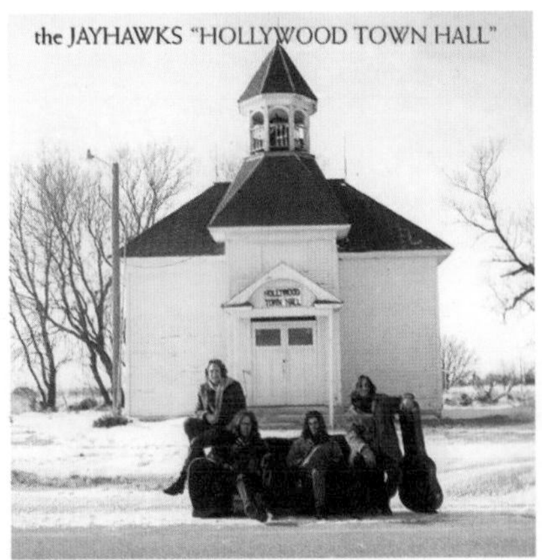

The Jayhawks
HOLLYWOOD TOWN HALL

AMERICAN RECORDINGS | Producer: George Drakoulias

RELEASED: SEPTEMBER 12, 1992

● From the opening chords of **Waiting For the Sun**, one could have thought they'd discovered a great lost Tom Petty record—that is, until the soaring tenor of Gary Louris delivered you to another place. This album got even better when Mark Olson, whose world-weary voice was a perfect counterpoint to Louris, chimed in. The Jayhawks were not reinventing anything here but adding a collection of thoughtful and beautifully recorded American rock 'n' roll songs to an established tradition. On *Hollywood Town Hall*, the Jayhawks laid down the template for a highly respectable career and discography. *–HK*

Stone Temple Pilots
CORE

ATLANTIC | Producer: Brendan O'Brien

RELEASED: SEPTEMBER 29, 1992

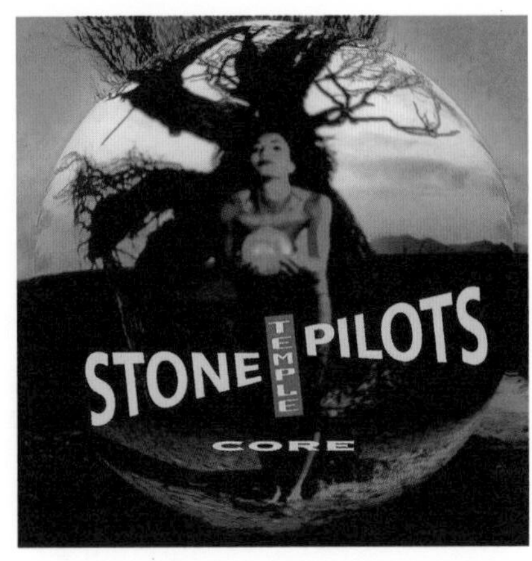

● Blending grunge and hard rock, Stone Temple Pilots' eight-times platinum debut was a pillar of '90s rock. With tracks such as **Plush** and **Creep**, *Core* showcased the band's knack for potent, angst-filled narratives with catchy melodies and abundant hooks. The album, which reached No. 3 on the Billboard 200, was an emotional roller coaster of dark themes that ranged from the controversial (**Sex Type Thing**) to the psychedelic (**Wicked Garden**). Robert DeLeo's Motown-inspired bass lines, his brother Dean's chorus pedal–infused guitar tones, and Scott Weiland's raw and impassioned vocals placed Stone Temple Pilots between mainstream hard rock and alternative while establishing a solid base for the band to build upon. *–BF*

Ministry
PSALM 69: THE WAY TO SUCCEED AND THE WAY TO SUCK EGGS

SIRE | Producers: Hypo Luxa (Al Jourgensen), Hermes Pan (Paul Barker)

RELEASED: JULY 1992

● Ministry and the industrial metal movement were primed for a breakthrough at the start of the '90s, so Sire Records happily coughed up big bucks for Ministry's follow-up to 1989's brilliant *The Mind Is a Terrible Thing to Taste*. By his own admission, frontman Al Jourgensen spent much of that money on drugs and made his label wait nearly a year for *Psalm 69*. While the album wasn't quite as strong overall as its predecessor, the primal power of tracks like the President George H. W. Bush–baiting **N.W.O.** or the harrowing addiction howl of **Just One Fix** remain among the band's all-time highlights. *–MW*

Joe Henry
SHORT MAN'S ROOM

MAMMOTH | Producer: Joe Henry

RELEASED: JUNE 16, 1992

● Joe Henry could have been eclipsed by marital lineage—he's Madonna's brother-in-law, after all (and co-wrote her 2000 hit "Don't Tell Me," among others). But Henry, raised mostly in Detroit's northern suburbs, has long been a literate and artful singer/songwriter (and all-star producer), and with the self-produced *Short Man's Room*, his fourth release, he found his own voice. Backed by the Jayhawks and Soul Asylum guitarist Dan Murphy, Henry was comfortable in early alt-country/Americana, shining especially on the waltz-time **A Friend in You** and the mortality rumination **One Shoe On**, while **King's Highway** found fans in Joan Baez and Gov't Mule, who both covered it. *–GG*

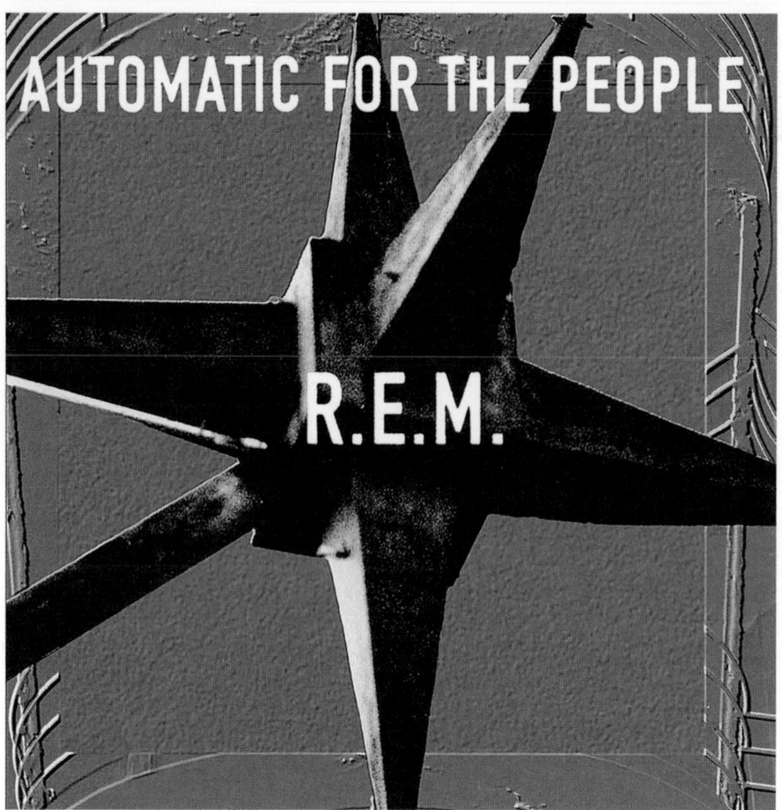

R.E.M.

AUTOMATIC FOR THE PEOPLE

WARNER BROS. | Producers: Scott Litt, R.E.M.

RELEASED: OCTOBER 5, 1992

● There's a moment at the very beginning of **Everybody Hurts** where Michael Stipe hummed a single note. He's finding the key to the song, like someone standing at the base of a mountain, ready to hike to the top but knowing it's a challenging climb. Stipe stepped into the song gingerly. He tempered his volume but never let off the momentum. As the track built—firm guitars, swirling strings, tasteful percussion—Stipe unleashed his vocals like he never had before. The song was an emotional climax of understanding and compassion and a defining moment for R.E.M. on its eighth studio album.

R.E.M. released five full-length titles during the '90s. Almost any of them could merit an entry in this book. But the quadruple-platinum *Automatic for the People*, which spawned additional hits in **Drive** and **Man on the Moon**, represented a musical high point in a career that had only trended up. Perhaps it was that fact that R.E.M. didn't tour behind 1991's *Out of Time*, a massive hit album, and the world was hungry for the band. No matter how it set the table, with *Automatic for the People*, R.E.M. delivered a clear-eyed, full-throated masterpiece.

Stipe's lead vocals, so often mixed down and deliberately obscured on R.E.M.'s early releases, took center stage again on *Automatic for the People*. His confidence as a performer and musical entity had grown in strides; now he was a storyteller, a narrator, a conduit for a range of emotions. Peter Buck, not a traditional guitar hero, found new contrasting contours in his playing. Mike Mills's biggest trick was hiding in plain sight: he anchored everything with a level of bass guitar proficiency that rivaled Paul McCartney and Chris Squire, not to mention his prolific ability on keyboards. And like Mills, drummer Bill Berry was a unicorn, but behind a trap kit. *—HK*

DESPERATION
ANGELS

Neil Young

HARVEST MOON

REPRISE | Producers: Neil Young, Ben Keith

RELEASED: OCTOBER 27, 1992

● Until he started digging around in his archives, Neil Young seemed like the sort that didn't much care to look back. By turns a folk-rock icon, punk godfather, hippie technocrat, rockabilly hep cat, wannabe bluesman, and flannel rocker emeritus, Young circled back on himself with the release of *Harvest Moon*.

The long-awaited sequel to *Harvest*, his 1972 ready-for-the-country blockbuster, *Harvest Moon* was for fans of the earlier album as familiar as a comfy old chair. Weeping steel guitars, loping rhythms, luxuriant vocal choruses, and songs about hearth and home dominated. Young even reassembled much of *Harvest*'s cast, including Ben Keith, Tim Drummond, Kenny Buttrey, arranger Jack Nitzsche, and background vocalists Linda Ronstadt and James Taylor.

The album contained some of Young's most heartfelt love songs: **Unknown Legend**, **Such a Woman**, and the title track were presumably addressed to his then-wife Pegi. There was even a love song (of sorts) to Young's favorite (albeit demised) dog, **Old King**. **From Hank to Hendrix**, ostensibly about a couple "headed for divorce/California style," seemed to encompass so much more—a rip in the social fabric of post–Los Angeles riots America and the disappearance of a shared culture.

Two of Young's perennial subjects, our self-destructive tendencies and the fragility of the ecology, are addressed in **War of Man** and the extended cut **Natural Beauty**, respectively. And in **Dreamin' Man**, he sings, "I've always been a dreamin' man, yes, that's my problem."

Well, hardly.

Unlike most sequels, which merely revisit the triumphs of the original, *Harvest Moon* was a measure of the time and distance traversed by Young and his audience between the two albums and a reckoning of what they've gained (love and kids, mainly) and lost (a lot, it seems, personally and politically) during the interim. ***–DD***

Rage Against the Machine

RAGE AGAINST THE MACHINE

EPIC | Producers: GGGarth, Rage Against the Machine

RELEASED: NOVEMBER 3, 1992

● Rap-rock was around before Rage Against the Machine (RATM), but with the arrival of its self-titled debut, the Los Angeles quartet took the subgenre to a new level. RATM came out swinging as a political powerhouse, releasing the LP on Election Day and featuring controversial cover artwork depicting a Buddhist monk who immolated himself in public in 1963 as a protest against US involvement in Vietnam. The music inside was equally brutal.

With a focus on Zach de la Rocha's abrasive voice and the guitar pyrotechnics of Tom Morello, RATM didn't so much set a new standard as steamroll the era's musical landscape and make almost everyone else seem pale in comparison. RATM's conviction to the material made it real, and that authenticity made the group and its music frightening. Nobody sounded like *Rage Against the Machine* in 1992, and few artists ever tried to replicate its sound. It was that original.

The album's most intense moments gained support from Morello, the most innovative rock guitarist since Eddie Van Halen. Armed with his instrument and a wah-wah pedal, he made his guitar cry, sing, shout, and sound like a DJ working a pair of turntables. It gave the band's music a bed to spring from and thrilling layers of sound to complement de la Rocha's uncompromising rhymes. "F*ck you, I won't do what you tell me," he repeated on the highlight track, **Killing in the Name**, setting a stage for the band's statement of purpose.

Rap-rock was dismissed as the worst of both worlds even before Rage Against the Machine. But with its debut album, RATM temporarily turned that tide, shooting down doubters with music that transcended all expectations. *—MG*

Sugar
COPPER BLUE

RYKODISC | Producers: Bob Mould, Lou Giordano

RELEASED: SEPTEMBER 4, 1992

● After a two-album detour as a singer/songwriter solo artist following the breakup of college radio favorites Hüsker Dü in 1988, Bob Mould returned to his old band's post-punk-meets-proto-alternative textbook as part of Sugar, another trio built on a basic guitar-bass-drums setup. Leaning more heavily on his pop sensibilities, Mould crafted the first of only two albums by the short-lived band, a record of scarred love songs informed by the new musical landscape forged by Nirvana's model-shifting *Nevermind* a year earlier. It marked a new start for one of the most talented songwriters of the '80s. *–MG*

Underground Resistance
REVOLUTION FOR CHANGE

NETWORK | Producers: Various

RELEASED: 1992

● Underground Resistance (UR) is techno's Wu-Tang Clan, a collective working under an umbrella that's at once a group, a record label, an aesthetic, and a school of thought. Coming out of a Detroit plowed under by Reaganomics, UR (formed by Jeff Mills and "Mad" Mike Banks with a cast of, well, a bunch) channeled its anger and angst into relentless, hard-hitting, and determinedly lo-fi grooves drawn from Motown, Chicago house, industrial, acid, and electro. This first title under the UR moniker gathers key early tracks such as **Riot**, **Punisher**, **Predator**, and **Quadrasonic**. UR continues in various forms, but this is the enduring aural mission statement. *–GG*

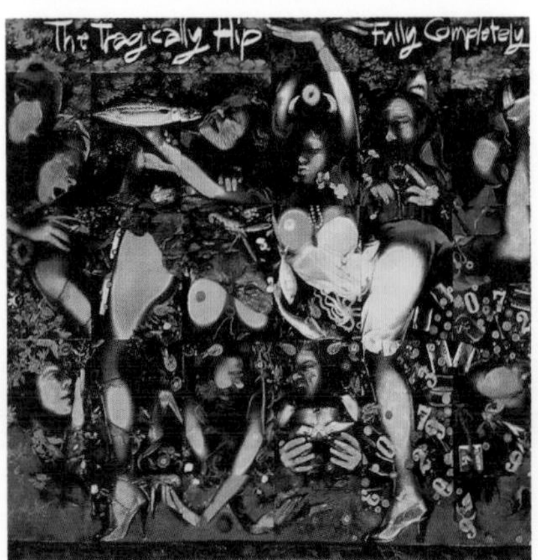

The Tragically Hip
FULLY COMPLETELY

MCA | Producer: Chris Tsangarides

RELEASED: OCTOBER 6, 1992

● The Tragically Hip solidified its legacy in Canadian rock with this third album. Featuring three Top 20 Canadian singles, *Fully Completely* showcased frontman Gord Downie's poetic storytelling, exploring Canada's cultural identity on **Fifty Mission Cap**, which recounted Toronto Maple Leaf star Bill Barilko's mysterious disappearance, and The Tragically Hip's first Billboard chart entry, **Courage**, dedicated to author Hugh MacLennan. While the album missed the international limelight, it reigned supreme on home soil, topping Canada's RPM albums chart and selling more than a million copies. Downie's passing in 2017 brought The Tragically Hip to an end, but *Fully Completely* remains the quintessential representation of the band. *–MD*

George Strait

PURE COUNTRY (ORIGINAL MOTION PICTURE SOUNDTRACK)

MCA | Producers: Tony Brown, George Strait, Steve Dorff

RELEASED: SEPTEMBER 15, 1992

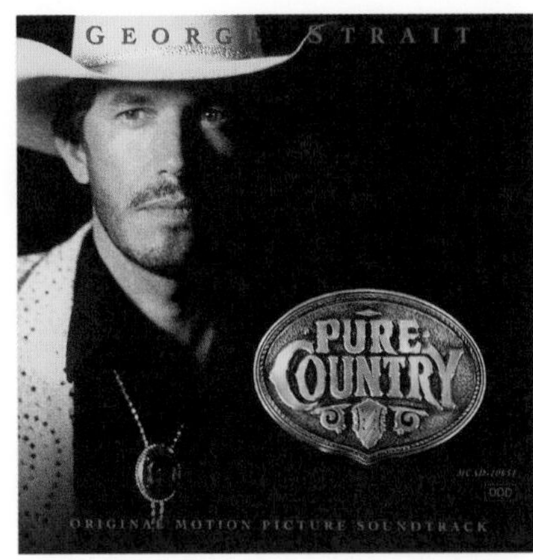

● Twelve albums and thirty-four Top 10 hits into his career, George Strait was wearing the King of Country crown. A movie and its accompanying soundtrack seemed like an inevitable next step. Directed by Christopher McGee, *Pure Country* featured Strait as fictional country singer Dusty Chandler and was a modest box office success. The soundtrack, comprising songs Strait sang (as Chandler) in the film, did even better. Strait's second release of 1992, five months after *Holdin' My Own*, hit No. 1 on Billboard's Top Country Albums chart and No. 6 on the Billboard 200, its six-times platinum sales giving Strait his most successful album and further cementing a legend Dusty Chandler could only dream about. –***TR/GG***

1992

Lucinda Williams

SWEET OLD WORLD

CHAMELEON | Producers: Gurf Morlix, Dusty Wakeman, Lucinda Williams

RELEASED: AUGUST 25, 1992

● Sensual and elegiac are such divergent descriptors that it would seem unlikely to fit songs from each category on a single album. But that's what Lucinda Williams did on her fourth album. Few songwriters decorate their material with such exacting, writerly detail. The title track's catalog of temporal pleasures a late friend left behind was palpable. **Little Angel, Little Brother**, and **Pineola** mined much the same territory with equally devastating impact. But then Williams expressed a carnal longing on **Something About What Happens When We Talk** and **Lines Around Your Eyes** and just plain horniness on the smoldering **Hot Blood**, balancing, or at least briefly allaying, the pain expressed in those other songs. –***DD***

10,000 Maniacs

OUR TIME IN EDEN

ELEKTRA | Producer: Paul Fox

RELEASED: SEPTEMBER 29, 1992

● *Our Time in Eden* was singer/songwriter Natalie Merchant's studio swan song with the band she joined at age seventeen. But Merchant clearly telegraphed she was ready to leave the band's protective garden when, on the lead single **These Are Days**, she sang, "It's true that you are touched by something that will grow and bloom in you." The song reached No. 1 on Billboard's Modern Rock chart, and while the double-platinum album also included the Top 5 **Candy Everybody Wants**, it was gems like the haunting **I'm Not the Man** and the heartbreaking confessional **Jezebel** that really made the album bloom. –***HD***

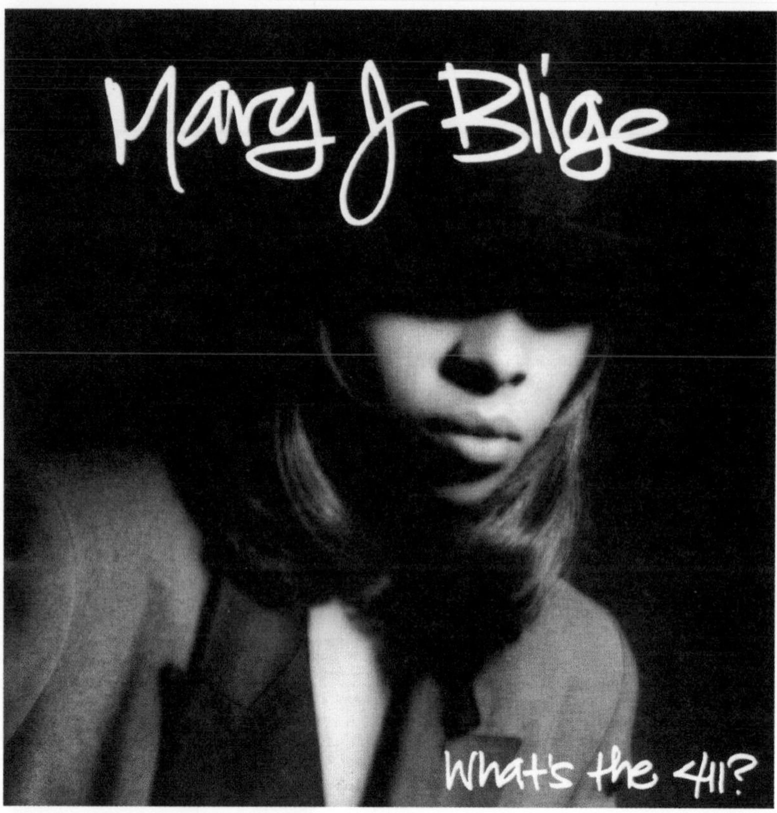

Mary J. Blige

WHAT'S THE 411?

UPTOWN/MCA | Executive Producer: Sean "Puffy" Combs

RELEASED: JULY 28, 1992

● Mary J. Blige's coronation as the Queen of Hip-Hop Soul came quickly in the wake of this career-making debut. The triple-platinum set hit No. 6 on the Billboard 200 and topped the R&B Album charts. It launched four Top 10 R&B/Hip-Hop Songs and won two *Soul Train* Music Awards. Most importantly, it established a beachhead for female performers in the pop/soul/rap hybrid of New Jack, making it clear she could hang with the guys and bring a fresh level of emotional resonance to the mix, as well as some Pentecostal church-bred chops.

Born in the Bronx and raised in Georgia and Yonkers, Blige was still a teenager when she signed her recording deal, after Uptown Records' Andre Harrell heard her mall recording-booth version of Anita Baker's "Caught Up in the Rapture." But Blige had already lived a life. Some of those details—about childhood molestation, sexual harassment, and drug and alcohol abuse—would surface on later revealing recordings. *What's the 411?*, with Sean "Puffy" Combs in the executive producer's chair, revealed Blige as a strong woman with a voice to match, fearless enough to make Rufus and Chaka Khan's **Sweet Thing** her own (as well as a hit) and make the promises to her mate in **My Love** and **Love No Limit** sound more like commands than submissions. Blige also held her own alongside boyfriend K-Ci Halley of Jodeci on **I Don't Want to Do Anything**, while **You Remind Me** and **Reminisce**, both written and produced by Dave "Jam" Hall, were prototypes for the "New Jill" corps, Blige's commanding performances riding confidently along the beds of urgent beats.

It's to Blige's credit that she would grow and evolve from this point. But *What's the 411?* was a fully formed arrival that opened a portal that remains fertile today. *–GG*

P-93
RALPH LAUREN
Established '67
POLO
POLO

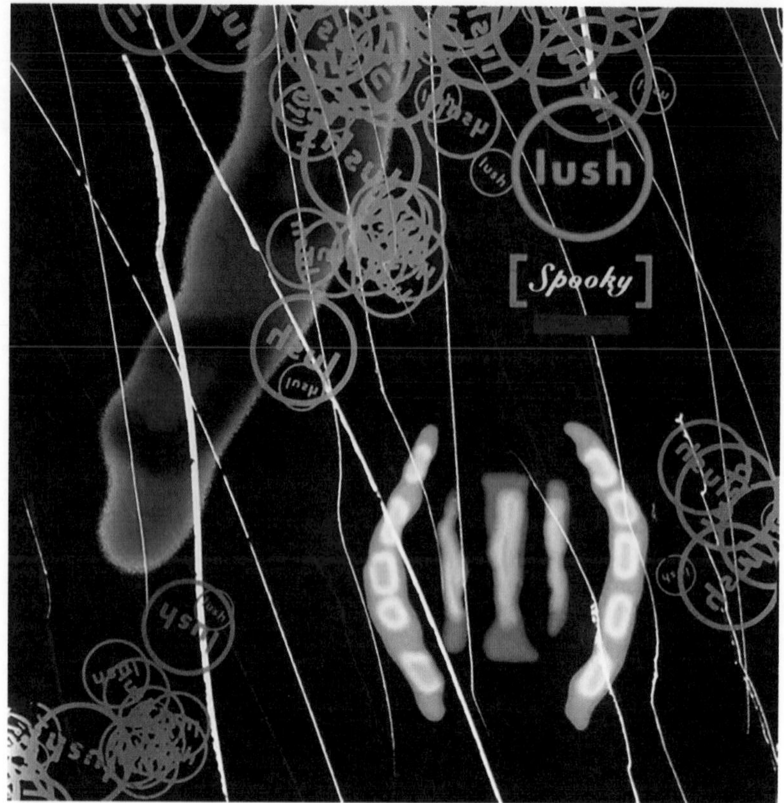

Lush

SPOOKY

4AD | Producer: Robin Guthrie

RELEASED: JANUARY 27, 1992

● The fortunate people who strayed from monochrome radio during the early '90s were treated to the rise of shoegaze, a genre with an ocean of variation but characterized mainly by walls of guitars, vocals, and pedal effects. In January 1992, grunge was dominating the airwaves four months after the release of Nirvana's *Nevermind*, but a lot of people, including Perry Farrell of Jane's Addiction, had been turned on to a group out of England on the trusted 4AD label, led by two women who would influence many others. Farrell invited Lush on the 1992 Lollapalooza tour, and a covert genre became part of the rock mainstream.

The reason *Spooky* stood out from others was the brilliant songwriting of Lush's founding members, Miki Berenyi and Emma Anderson. Listening to it today, it's not hard to imagine people at parties or in college dorms hearing the bass introduction to **Laura** or **For Love** and asking, "Who is *this*?!" Fans adored Lush's haunting harmonies, but Berenyi's 2022 memoir *Fingers Crossed: How Music Saved Me from Success* revealed that this was not the result of a smooth relationship between the creative forces in the band. In fact, the book made clear that it was a miracle Lush even lasted as long as it did. The band broke up after drummer Chris Acland's suicide in 1996 but managed to re-form in 2016 before coming apart again.

Do yourself a favor: Listen to *Spooky* and get lost in it. By the time you get to **Nothing Natural**, the Anderson-penned second track, you will have been transported to another world. It may be cliché to say listening to *Spooky* is a **Superblast**, like its third single, but it's the most appropriate adjective to describe the experience. *–RW*

Aphex Twin

SELECTED AMBIENT WORKS 85-92

APOLLO | Producer: Richard James

RELEASED: NOVEMBER 9, 1992

● The electronic music world was forever reprogrammed when Aphex Twin (Richard James) unleashed this unprecedented masterpiece. *Selected Ambient Works 85–92* proved that electronica could be more than just a DJ's tool. At the time, electronic music was primarily released as singles and made just for fans and satisfied those who were hungry for something more, something different, and something special, which James delivered in abundance

Using mostly equipment he made in his home studio, James worked diligently on his craft; *Selected Ambient Works 85–92* was the result of a very young man's output over a seven-year period, some of which he had recorded at the age of fourteen. The name of the album would lead one to believe the record is all ambient music, but that's far from the fact. It covered a wide variety of electronic styles, including, of course, the sort of melodic and atmospheric tracks the title suggested, but mixed with simple, lush, and innovative techno melodies as well as complex and quirky soundscapes. The result was a perfect musical tapestry from start to finish.

Xtal, the album's opening track, set the tone with its ethereal, ambient vibe. **We Are the Music Makers** had a catchy mid-tempo pace and a *Willy Wonka and the Chocolate Factory* movie sample featuring Gene Wilder. **Delphium** was reminiscent of early Detroit techno, and **Heliosphan** had a deep, driving beat and haunting feel. *Selected Ambient Works 85–92* is rightly considered one of the best electronic records ever produced and was a keystone in the history of music in general, launching James's career and inspiring legions of artists in the process. *—MH*

Leonard Cohen

THE FUTURE

COLUMBIA | Producers: Leonard Cohen, Steve Lindsey, Bill Ginn, Leanne Ungar, Rebecca De Mornay, Yoav Goren

RELEASED: NOVEMBER 24, 1992

● Leonard Cohen was not a revolutionary folkie in the '60s. In fact, his earlier songs gained popularity via covers by commercial-sounding artists such as Judy Collins ("Suzanne") and Jeff Buckley ("Hallelujah"), since his vocals, like those of Bob Dylan and Neil Young, have always been an acquired taste.

But political darkness found Cohen in the early '90s. *The Future* is a mid-career milestone pointing to where all of Cohen's future albums would go lyrically and sonically until his death in 2016.

Apocalyptic in vision, *The Future* appears to find Cohen processing American life after the fall of the Berlin Wall, the Los Angeles riots, the AIDS crisis, and even the ubiquity of advertising slogans. Building on the sinister vibes found on 1988's *I'm Your Man*, Cohen ventures past his usual stories of spiritual tumult inside the romantically thwarted.

While dark, *The Future* was far from a dirge. Cinematic production, female backing vocals, and a full choir created compelling scenes like the mid-tempo, fiddle-inflected **Closing Time**, correlating the end of the night at a whiskey-soaked bar with the end of the world. The martial gallop of **Democracy** asked if Americans had become too hopeful now that the Cold War was over. **Light as the Breeze**, with its airy keyboard and slide guitar, returned Cohen to the guise of romantic seeker finding spiritual benediction on his knees before his woman.

While the album's forceful opening title track found him invoking biblical and Jewish prophetic visions—nothing new for this grandson of a Montreal rabbi—Cohen's embrace of Buddhism cut through the darkness as he resolutely reminded us on **Anthem** that there is "a crack in everything/That's how the light gets in." Not long after the album was released, Cohen went to live in a Zen monastery for five years. As a musical kōan, *The Future* still gives us much to contemplate. ***–RSM***

Los Lobos
KIKO

SLASH/WARNER BROS. | Producers: Mitchell Froom, Los Lobos

RELEASED: MAY 26, 1992

● Los Lobos spent the early part of its career establishing itself as the ultimate bar band. There's nothing wrong with that, certainly, but *Kiko* took the East Los Angeles quintet to an entirely different creative place. That was due, in part, to the band's fully mature songwriting, mostly by guitarist David Hidalgo and drummer/guitarist Louie Perez (guitarist Cesar Rosas contributes only a pair of songs). But the real secret sauce came from co-producer Mitchell Froom. Textured and looped, the album's sound ranges from gauzy and atmospheric to dense and downright quirky. Led by **Kiko and the Lavender Moon**, **Angels With Dirty Faces**, and **Wicked Rain**, *Kiko* was a daring, creative left turn that paid off handsomely. *–DD*

Phish
A PICTURE OF NECTAR

ELEKTRA | Producers: Phish, Kevin Halpin

RELEASED: FEBRUARY 18, 1992

● The Phish legend began but hardly ended on the Vermont jam band's third album. After two developmental works, the quartet entered a "real" studio with a co-producer, celebrated its roots with the title (a nod to early supporter Nectar Rorris), and found a fresh way forward with just over an hour of music that was all over the place. Songs ran from twenty seconds to nearly nine minutes, and tracks such as **Tweezer**, **Chalk Dust Torture**, and **Guelah Papyrus** became live staples. This is where Phish truly found itself and learned how to be exciting in the studio as well as onstage. *–GG*

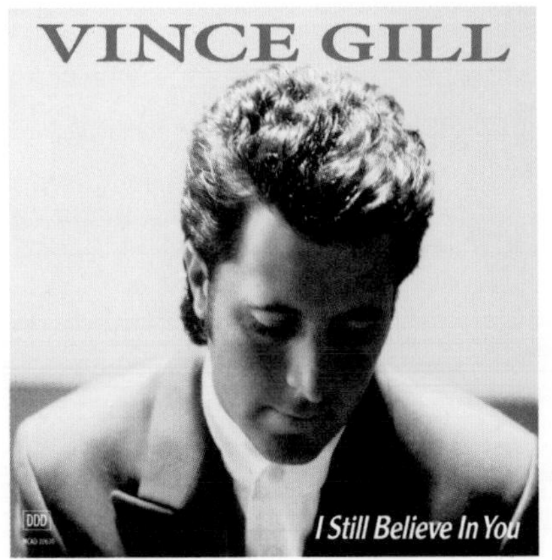

Vince Gill
I STILL BELIEVE IN YOU

MCA | Producer: Tony Brown

RELEASED: SEPTEMBER 1, 1992

● Vince Gill's fifth studio album produced five Top 5 singles, four of which went to No. 1 on the Billboard Hot Country Songs chart. The title track was Gill's first career chart-topper, in fact, followed at the summit by **Don't Let Your Love Start Slippin' Away**, **One More Last Chance**, and **Tryin' to Get Over You**. The title track also scored Grammy Awards for Best Country Song and Best Country Vocal Performance, while Gill, who wrote or co-wrote all ten tracks, took home Album of the Year at the Country Music Association Awards, in addition to Vocalist of the Year, Song of the Year, and Entertainer of the Year. *–MH2*

The Pharcyde
BIZARRE RIDE II THE PHARCYDE

DELICIOUS VINYL/EASTWEST | Producers: J-Swift, L. A. Jay, SlimKid 3

RELEASED: NOVEMBER 24, 1992

● It was easy to consider, even dismiss, hip-hop collective The Pharcyde as a "pack of class clowns set loose in a studio," as *Rolling Stone* described the Los Angeles quartet when its debut album was released. Reassessment came quickly, however, along with a deeper recognition and appreciation for The Pharcyde's nimble vocal skills and humor-filled lyricism, as well as J-Swift's sophisticated soundscaping, filled with textures and old-school funk and jazz samples. The group could be topical (**Officer**), but at a time gangsta rap was all the rage, The Pharcyde brought the "alternative" to the West Coast and made an album that's bona fide classic. *–GG*

1992

Stan Getz & Kenny Barron
PEOPLE TIME

VERVE/GITANES JAZZ | Producer: Jean-Philippe Allard

RELEASED: 1992

● Recorded live March 3–6, 1991, at the Café Montmartre jazz club in Copenhagen, Denmark, *People Time* distilled the essence and sheer brilliance of the stellar piano/tenor sax duet performances by Stan Getz and Kenny Barron. As it turned out, these were also Getz's last concerts; he died of liver cancer three months later. Over fourteen savory ballads, their interplay created its own charisma. Getz's mellifluous tenor was graceful and rich in tone; he lingered over notes, unfurling the melodies to perfection. Barron complemented that with deft chording sequences and rippling waves of intricate notes, best heard on **East of the Sun (and West of the Moon)**. *–CH*

Jimmy Scott
ALL THE WAY

SIRE/WARNER BROS./BLUE HORIZON | Producer: Tommy LiPuma

RELEASED: 1992

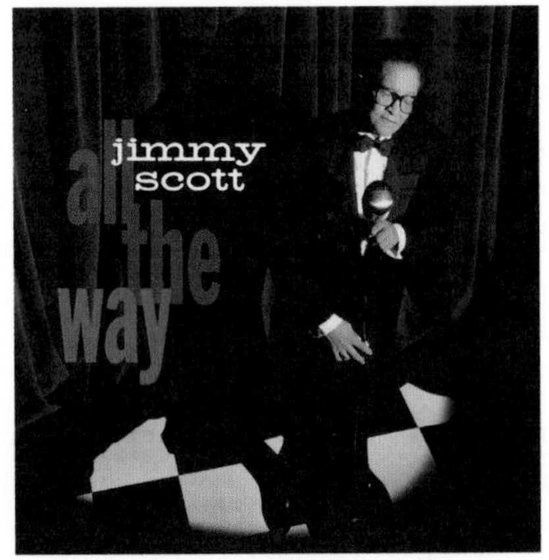

● For the most part, jazz vocalist "Little" Jimmy Scott flew under the radar of public acclaim—and that's not a crack about his diminutive physical stature. Chronically underappreciated, he was a singer's singer whose career was beset by bad luck, dirty dealing, and personal demons, resulting in long absences from music. This late-career revival came complete with ace material (**All the Way**, **Embraceable You**, and **Someone to Watch Over Me**) and high-profile musicians (Kenny Barron, Ron Carter, and David "Fathead" Newman). Scott's high, otherworldly voice was haunting and his phrasing deeply emotional. He inhabited a song as few others could. It was impossible not to hang on every word. *–DD*

Peter Gabriel

US

REAL WORLD | Producers: Peter Gabriel, Daniel Lanois

RELEASED: SEPTEMBER 28, 1992

● There are myriad ways to interpret the pronoun "us," and the same can be said for the sixth solo studio album by Peter Gabriel. Putting aside the social consciousness of his previous releases, Gabriel turned things around on an incredibly introspective record that explored his personal relationships at the time. The autobiographical songs touch on love, self-esteem, division, and unity, drawing heavily on a biblical Garden of Eden theme; the lush, sometimes dark melodies allowed the listener space for their own self-reflection.

The album-opening **Come Talk to Me** set the tone with wailing bagpipes over a somber drumbeat and served almost as an invitation, featuring the plaintive voice of Sinéad O'Connor, who also guests on the symbolism-laden **Blood of Eden**. World beats featured throughout the record, notably via Manu Katché on percussion, pairing with longtime Gabriel bassist Tony Levin for memorable grooves on **Steam** and **Digging in the Dirt**. The multicultural rhythms helped make the album a worldwide chart success, briefly peaking at No. 2 on the Billboard 200. Gabriel's "album as art" approach was on full display, beautifully rendered by a husky-voiced singer working his way through his own emotional strife with all-encompassing strokes that vividly captured the shared humanity of us all. *–SS*

Wynonna

WYNONNA

CURB/MCA | Producers: Tony Brown, Paul Kennerley

RELEASED: MARCH 31, 1992

● During the early '90s, Wynonna Judd was best known as half of one of the most successful acts in country music, the Judds. Beginning in 1983 Wynonna and her mother, Naomi, racked up nearly two dozen hit songs, five Grammys, and numerous other awards before the duo was forced to call it quits in 1991 after Naomi was diagnosed with hepatitis C and could no longer tour.

Wynonna wasted little time in launching a solo career the very next year with this ten-song project that produced three consecutive No. 1 hits on the Billboard Hot Country Singles & Tracks chart, starting with **She Is His Only Need**. **I Saw the Light** and **No One Else on Earth** followed, while the album's final single, **My Strongest Weakness**, which was co-written by mother Naomi and Mike Reid, peaked at No. 4. The *Wynonna* album was certified five-times platinum and set her up as one of the most celebrated female country voices throughout the '90s, one that *Rolling Stone* magazine, in fact, later dubbed "the voice of her generation." *–MH2*

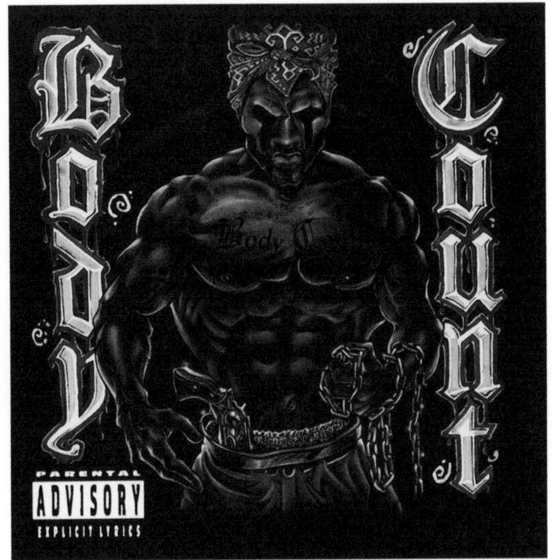

Body Count

BODY COUNT

SIRE | Producers: Ice-T, Ernie C

RELEASED: MARCH 30, 1992

● To say that **Cop Killer**, Ice-T's Molotov cocktail of a protest song on the debut from his Los Angeles thrash metal outfit Body Count, "hit the fan" would be an understatement. The stink reached the highest office in the land, with President George H. W. Bush condemning Sire Records' parent company Warner Bros. for releasing the album and Vice President Dan Quayle labeling the song "obscene" (it was an election year, after all). Four months after *Body Count*'s release, Ice-T, who later would ironically portray a cop on TV's *Law & Order* franchise, bowed to the pressure and pulled **Cop Killer** from the album; it remained commercially unavailable in any official capacity for decades. The rest of *Body Count* is just as inflammatory but in a cartoonish way: **KKK Bitch** concerns, er, relations with a Klansman's daughter, while **Momma's Gotta Die Tonight** finds the narrator burning his mother alive and chopping her to bits. It wasn't meant to be taken any more seriously than a horror movie, but it struck a chord in the culture wars, leading Ice-T to re-record 1989's "Freedom of Speech" for re-released versions of the album as a not-so-subtle commentary. Its chorus: "Freedom of speech, just watch what you say." *–AG*

Pavement

SLANTED AND ENCHANTED

MATADOR | Producer: Pavement

RELEASED: APRIL 20, 1992

● If there's a ground zero for '90s indie rock—as opposed to '80s college rock and the more commercial modern rock that created a stir at the top of the decade—it's Pavement's debut album, *Slanted and Enchanted*. Made by two Stockton, California, friends and an older drummer who owned the studio where the band had recorded a handful of earlier EPs, the LP shifted the underground's perceptions of art rock, lo-fi, and noise upon its release.

Some songs sounded like fragments—**Zurich Is Stained** and **Chesley's Little Wrists** didn't even make it to two minutes—while others (**Summer Babe** and **Trigger Cut** particularly) skimmed the edges of pop music. Stephen Malkmus and Scott Kannberg constructed lyrics that sounded stitched together from random notes left around the studio. Guitars were occasionally out of tune; Malkmus's strained vocals even more so. It's not a simple album to ease into. Its accessibility depends on the listener's tolerance for a band staking out a claim on musical terrain rarely explored before.

Like a '90s version of The Velvet Underground, Pavement's curiosity and penchant for lo-fi noise came naturally. The band later expanded its lineup and sound palette. Its next album, 1994's *Crooked Rain, Crooked Rain*, got close enough to mainstream alt-rock that it even had a Top 10 hit on Billboard's Modern Rock chart. But Pavement soon returned to the deconstructed studio experiments of *Slanted and Enchanted* before making one final album in 1999.

Over the years, the band's reunions have sparked renewed interest and expanded reissues of its five albums, but this debut remains Pavement's powder-keg moment, an influential record by a band whose casual approach defined its entire career and, eventually, a new generation of indie artists. *—MG*

Dr. Dre

THE CHRONIC

DEATH ROW/INTERSCOPE | Producer: Dr. Dre

RELEASED: DECEMBER 15, 1992

● "Welcome to Death Row." That's Dr. Dre's greeting at the top of *The Chronic*, his solo debut which arrived during 1992's closing days to redefine the sound of West Coast rap. Its effect was seismic. Its legend is just as large.

The album came after the dissolution of N.W.A and found Dre directing an assortment of MCs dubbed the Death Row Inmates: The Lady of Rage, Daz, Kurupt, Jewell, RBX, and Geto Boy's Bushwick Bill all popped in and out of tracks, creating a loose family feel. But it was Snoop Doggy Dogg (who debuted with Dre earlier that year on the soundtrack cut "Deep Cover") who became Dre's copilot, the Scottie Pippen to his Michael Jordan, and the pair established themselves as rap's platinum duo.

The Chronic's first single, **Nuthin' But a "G" Thang**, announced the duo's arrival, its laid-back atmospherics built on a loop from Leon Haywood's 1974 track "I Want'a Do Something Freaky to You" and its sound evoking images of palm trees, backyard barbecues, lowriders, and Los Angeles sunsets. It was the blueprint for G-Funk, the synth-heavy, '70s-inspired blend of George Clinton samples, speaker-shaking drums, and heavy bass grooves that took over rap and made everywhere feel like So-Cal.

Dre came baring grudges. His take-no-prisoners attitude was embodied by **F*ck Wit Dre Day** (shortened to **Dre Day** for radio and MTV), which took aim at Dre's ex-N.W.A bandmate Eazy-E (who released his *5150: Home 4 Tha Sick* EP the same day as *The Chronic*) while also dissing Tim Dog, 2 Live Crew's Uncle Luke, and Ice Cube.

The Chronic was a resounding success, cementing Dre as his generation's greatest hip-hop producer. Death Row would crumble amid co-founder Marion "Suge" Knight's legal troubles just a few years later, but *The Chronic* remains a towering achievement that resonates beyond rap music. *—AG*

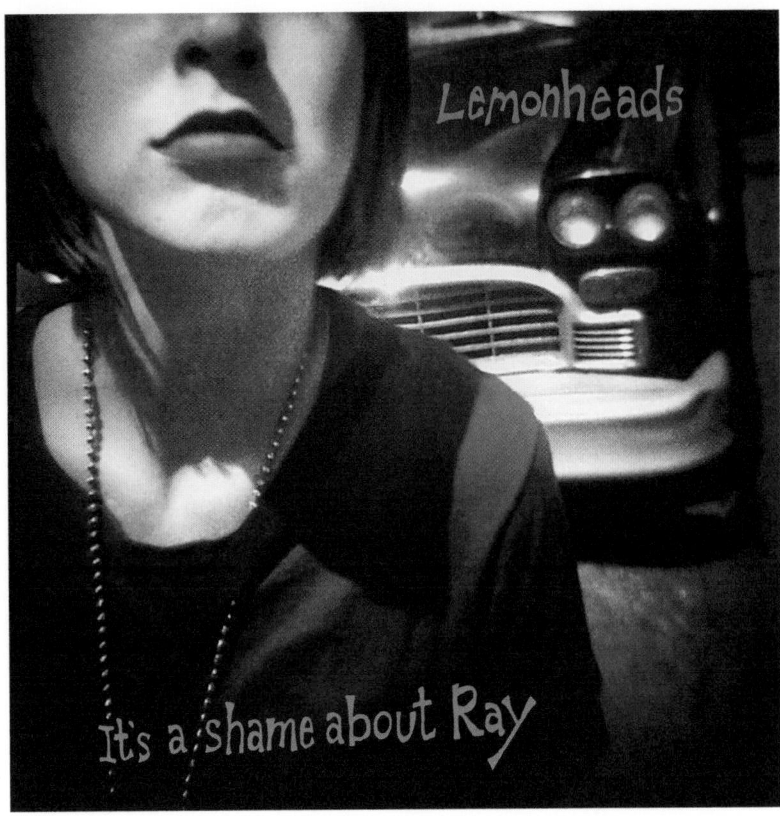

The Lemonheads

IT'S A SHAME ABOUT RAY

ATLANTIC | Producers: The Robb Brothers

RELEASED: JUNE 2, 1992

● The Lemonheads' fifth album marked the band's explosion into mainstream '90s pop culture. While prior albums offered glimpses of Evan Dando's grunge-pop sensibilities, *It's a Shame about Ray* showcased those songwriting talents to much better effect, especially in highlighting the clever lyrical expressions in songs like **Alison's Starting to Happen** and **Bit Part**.

The Lemonheads was formed by three Boston-area suburbanites, but by 1992 the group was primarily a vehicle for Dando and initially only a hit with college and underground radio stations. Tighter songwriting and more polished production changed all that on *It's a Shame about Ray*, whose title track, co-written by Dando and Tom Morgan, reached No. 5 on the Billboard Modern Rock chart; a video featuring Johnny Depp ensured hot rotation.

Much of the album is fortified with pop hooks over loud, grungy guitars, while **Hannah & Gabi** (featuring guest slide guitar by Steely Dan/Doobie Brothers veteran Jeff "Skunk" Baxter) and **My Drug Buddy** (or **My Buddy** if you bought your CD after the record company got concerned about the original title) showcased Dando's Americana and country influences. Juliana Hatfield's backing vocals added a layer of depth to many tracks as well. *Ray*'s genius, however, lay in its brevity—most of the songs are under three minutes, with the original release clocking in under thirty minutes total (quite a counter in the CD era, when albums were routinely seventy minutes or longer).

A cover of Simon & Garfunkel's "Mrs. Robinson," recorded for the twenty-fifth anniversary of *The Graduate* a few months after the album's release, boosted *Ray* even further. The album's No. 36 position on the Billboard 200, along with a gold certification, was the Lemonheads' high-water mark. *Ray* remains a legacy cornerstone of the '90s alt-rock landscape. *—BF*

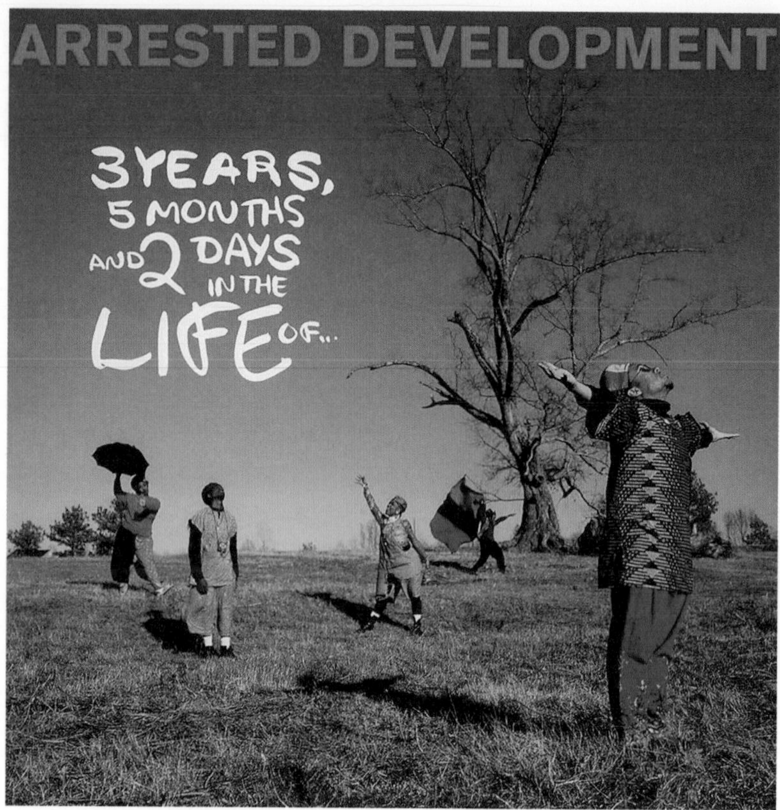

Arrested Development

3 YEARS, 5 MONTHS AND 2 DAYS IN THE LIFE OF . . .

CHRYSALIS/EMI | Producer: Speech

RELEASED: MARCH 24, 1992

● For a brief time during the early '90s, Arrested Development looked like it was on its way to becoming rap music's next big thing. The Atlanta collective's debut album—a mix of hip-hop spirituality and pop radio–ready songs—spawned three hit singles, topped *The Village Voice*'s prestigious Pazz & Jop Critics Poll, and eventually sold more than four million copies. Despite all this *and* winning the Best New Artist Grammy for 1992, Arrested Development fizzled out, albeit temporarily, after just one more album.

But for a year or so, **Tennessee**, **People Everyday**, and **Mr. Wendal** (all Top 10 hits on the Billboard 100 and the R&B/Hip-Hop charts) were inescapable. Arrested Development put a counter spin on hip-hop, which was increasingly dominated by the sounds and themes explored by acts like N.W.A, Ice Cube, Ice-T, and Public Enemy. *3 Years, 5 Months and 2 Days in the Life of . . .* wasn't part of the Native Tongues alternative rap movement that included such luminaries as De La Soul, Jungle Brothers, and A Tribe Called Quest but, rather, an extension of it, sprouting new branches of influences. With samples covering Sly & the Family Stone, Prince, and Earth, Wind & Fire, the music was familiar and exhilarating, the words smart and encouraging.

3 Years, 5 Months and 2 Days in the Life of . . . was also a key release in the rise of Southern hip-hop, but more importantly, it established a place on the charts for inclusive rap music that promoted individualism over a gang mentality. Group leader Speech went on to a solo career with middling success; singer Dionne Farris, however, had a No. 4 hit in 1995 with "I Know," a year before Arrested Development's first breakup. The group reunited in 2000 and has released several more albums. *–MG*

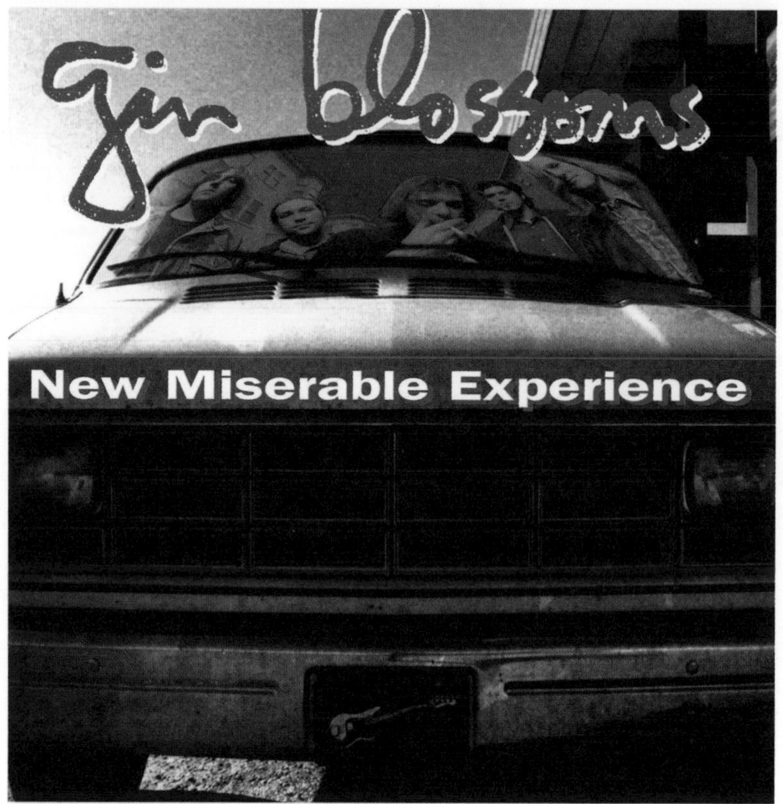

Gin Blossoms

NEW MISERABLE EXPERIENCE

A & M | Producers: Gin Blossoms, John Hampton

RELEASED: AUGUST 4, 1992

● Gin Blossoms' major-label debut was a tuneful antidote to the excesses of grunge that dominated the early '90s. Hailing from Tempe, Arizona, the band plied an alt-rock groove that bore the influence of jangle-pop acts such as the Byrds and R.E.M. Yet, just as those groups sat comfortably amid the hard rock styles of their respective eras, Gin Blossoms' introspective complaint-rock fit easily into the landscape defined by the angst-ridden Seattle acts.

The group's tunes were driven by crunchy guitar hooks and solid beats, while Robin Wilson's strong but vulnerable vocals had an appealing frailty in an era when gruff-voiced belters were dominating airwaves. Behind the music, the group had its fair share of drama. Guitarist and songwriter Doug Hopkins suffered from alcoholism and mental health issues, leading to his expulsion from the band in early 1992 as recording was wrapping up. He watched from the sidelines as *New Miserable Experience* climbed the charts, thanks in large part to his tunes. Hopkins's suicide in December 1993 amid the Gin Blossoms' success gave the group an air of tragedy to underscore the downcast nature of its songs.

Among the best here were Hopkins's **Hey Jealousy** (Gin Blossoms' biggest hit), **Found Out About You**, and **Lost Horizons**, all of which had first appeared in different versions on *Dusted*, the band's largely ignored 1989 independent debut. Equally strong were Wilson's own **Allison Road** and **Until I Fall Away**, a co-write with guitarist Jesse Valenzuela.

Ironically, although it never achieved fame on par with its Seattle counterparts, Gin Blossoms may have one-upped them with *New Miserable Experience*, an album that continues to sound fresh and timeless long after the grunge party called it a night. *—CS*

Sade

LOVE DELUXE

EPIC | Producer: Sade Adu

RELEASED: NOVEMBER 3, 1992

● Sade is both the name of the band and the abbreviated first name of Nigerian-born British singer/songwriter/producer Helen Folasade Adu, who fronted this crack group of musicians that laid the bed for her sumptuous, smoky vocals. During the smooth-jazz era of the early '90s, Sade expanded her sound, adding a sophisticated blend of soul, funk, and Afro-Cuban rhythms. After keeping fans waiting five years, the group released its fourth album, *Love Deluxe*. The LP went on to become a worldwide success, hitting the Top 10 in several countries while peaking at No. 3 on the Billboard 200 chart and achieving quadruple-platinum status in the US. Among its nine songs, the first released single, **No Ordinary Love**—with its soft, hypnotic bass and yearning vocals—scored a Grammy for Best R&B Performance by a Duo or Group with Vocal. The album's subsequent singles included **Feel No Pain**, with plucky, jazzy guitar work; **Kiss of Life**, featuring a glorious piano intro and luscious vocals which might be the best moment of the collection; and **Cherish the Day**, highlighted by a haunting guitar intro worth a listen on its own. *–JC*

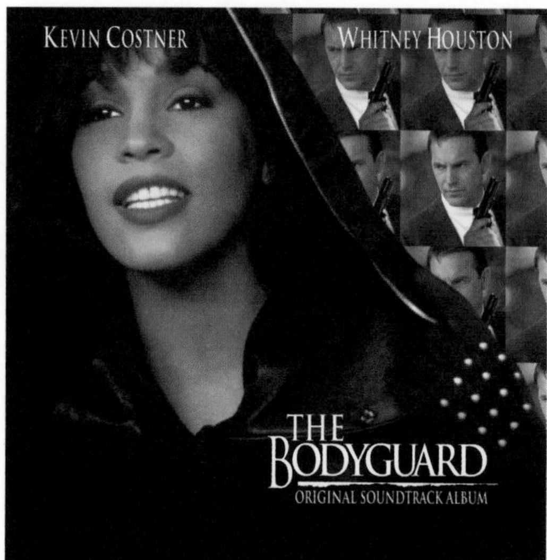

Various Artists

THE BODYGUARD (ORIGINAL SOUNDTRACK)

ARISTA/BMG ENTERTAINMENT

Producers: Whitney Houston, David Foster, Narada Michael Walden, et al.

RELEASED: NOVEMBER 17, 1992

● People will always love this soundtrack for one reason: **I Will Always Love You**, Whitney Houston's remake of the 1974 Dolly Parton song that served as the film's love ballad and signature piece. Like the movie ($411 million worldwide box office), the song was a blockbuster, becoming the best-selling single of 1992 with a then-record fourteen-week stay at No. 1 on the Billboard 100. It won two Grammy Awards, including Record of the Year, and ranks as the biggest of Houston's many hits. It certainly brought a great many ears to the eighteen-times platinum album (worldwide sales of more than forty-five million) to hear a few more songs by Houston as well as tracks by Kenny G (on his own and with Aaron Neville), Lisa Stansfield, Joe Cocker and Sass Jordan, and Alan Silvestri's instrumental title theme. Indicative of the soundtrack's impact was the fact that Curtis Stigers's cover of **(What's So Funny 'Bout) Peace, Love, and Understanding** netted a seven-figure royalty check for Nick Lowe, who had written it eighteen years earlier. And rest assured, no one was surprised by the 2017 appearance of *I Wish You Love: More from the Bodyguard*, a cash-in that was roundly and deservedly ignored. *–GG*

1992

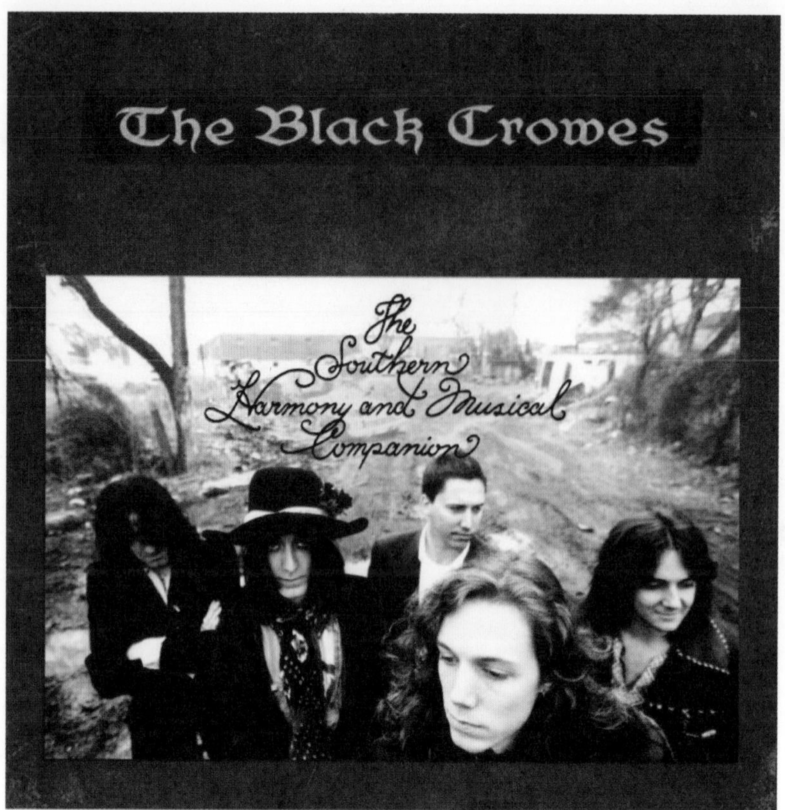

The Black Crowes

THE SOUTHERN HARMONY AND MUSICAL COMPANION

DEF AMERICAN | Producers: George Drakoulias, The Black Crowes

RELEASED: MAY 12, 1992

● The Black Crowes, by their own account, went into the recording of their second album brimming with confidence—and they should have. The Atlanta group's 1990 debut album, *Shake Your Money Maker*, was a multiplatinum breakthrough that launched a slew of rock radio hits and positioned the band as saviors of a sort for the genre as hair metal gave way to grunge.

The band's creative ambitions had grown over nearly two years of touring, and *The Southern Harmony and Musical Companion*—taking its name from an 1835 Baptist hymnal—followed suit. The ten-song set, co-produced with *Shake Your Money Maker*'s George Drakoulias, was more nuanced, with more expansive arrangements and a greater range of dynamics and textures. After the dense and more direct sonic attack of the first album, the Crowes created more space for subtleties and clearly benefited from the advanced musicianship of new members Marc Ford on guitar and Eddie Harsch on keyboards. Frontman Chris Robinson's lyrics grew more poetically evocative, exploring emotional complexities with echoes from American Southern literature.

The Black Crowes could still rock up a storm, mind you. **Sting Me** and **Remedy** launched the album with enough guitar-shredding oomph to power a small town, and **No Speak No Slave** grooved hard enough to break through concrete. But tracks such as **Thorn in My Pride**, **Bad Luck Blue Eyes Goodbye**, **Sometimes Salvation**, and the wistful **My Morning Song** dug deep on all fronts, demonstrating just how much the group had grown.

And fans embraced the changes. The album debuted at No. 1 on the Billboard 200 on its way to double-platinum sales and launched four No. 1 Rock chart singles, giving a characteristic middle finger to those who predicted the Crowes' flight would be short. *–GG*

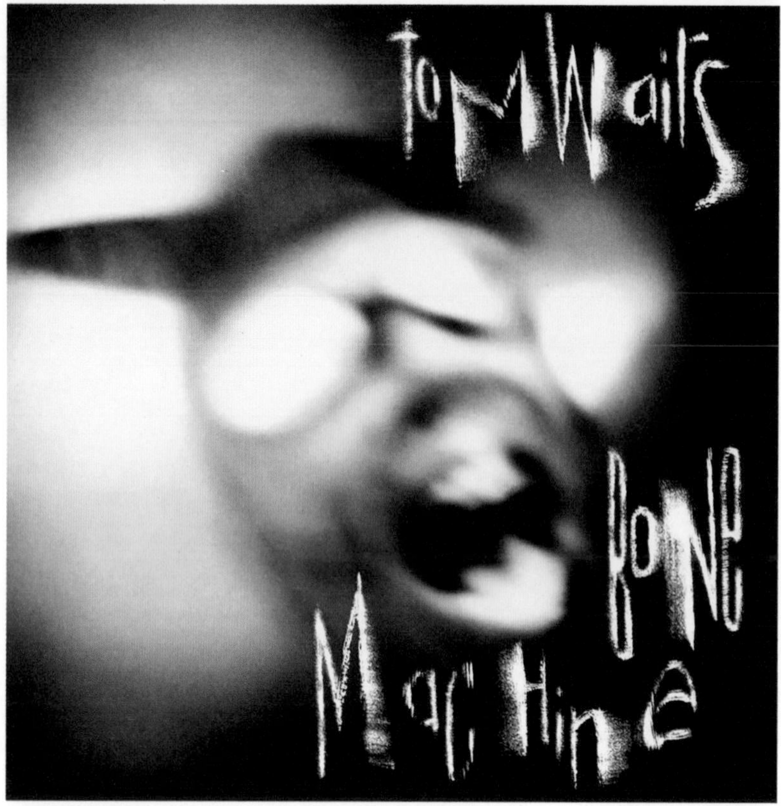

Tom Waits

BONE MACHINE

ISLAND | Producers: Tom Waits, Kathleen Brennan

RELEASED: SEPTEMBER 8, 1992

● Just in case we needed a reminder of our mortality, Waits sets us straight on the second track of his eleventh studio album, pushing his gravelly voice to its highest register to sing, "We're all gonna be/Just dirt in the ground."

Needless to say, this is not a party album.

Bone Machine was so named for its raw, stripped-to-the-bones minimalism—from the get-go with the nightmare vision of the opening **Earth Died Screaming**. It was recorded in a room with just a water heater and cement floor in the basement of Prairie Sun Recording studios in Cotati, California, and it half sounds like Waits is chained up down there.

Four albums into his conversion from offbeat but traditional jazz-blues growler into red-pilled Captain Beefheart believer, *Bone Machine* found Waits obsessing over murder, death, and whatever horror was next. He made most of the unearthly noise himself (much of it banging on things), with guest contributions from the likes of Primus bassist Les Claypool, drummer Brain, Los Lobos' David Hidalgo, saxophonist Ralph Carney, and hired-gun guitarist Waddy Wachtel.

Although most of *Bone Machine* reveled in a primal, lo-fi maelstrom, there were moments when Waits reverted back to more traditional song form, such as on the gospel-blues of **Jesus Gonna Be Here**, the pair of pretty piano ballads **Little Rain** and **Whistle Down the Wind**, and the grungy guitar rocker **I Don't Wanna Grow Up** (later covered by the Ramones).

Fifty minutes and sixteen tracks in, Waits seemed to emerge from the basement and into the pub for something of a peaceful resolution on **That Feel**, a boozy singalong with his Rolling Stones pal Keith Richards, on which the two legends assured us "There's one thing you can't lose/And it's that feel." *–SM*

Mary Chapin Carpenter

COME ON COME ON

COLUMBIA NASHVILLE/TRISTAR | Producers: Mary Chapin Carpenter, John Jennings, Steve Buckingham

RELEASED: JUNE 30, 1992

● While the '90s launched boy bands and bubblegum pop, it also gave us a generation of independent women who were more than crop tops and platform boots. Singer/songwriter Mary Chapin Carpenter was the thirty-something thinking woman's voice in a world where "pickup lines" referred to school carpools, not bars.

Come On Come On was defined by the Ivy League–educated Carpenter's perfect combination of intellect and ability to cut to the heart of the contemporary country music audience—and beyond. Whether dueting with Joe Diffie on **Not Too Much to Ask** or delivering a cover of Dire Straits' **The Bug**, Carpenter's rich, dusky voice and some jangly electric guitar arrangements reminiscent of the British Invasion gave the album a fuller sound that tiptoed around the edges of crossover.

Come On Come On was her most commercially successful release and charted a whopping seven singles between 1992 and 1994. **I Feel Lucky** won a Grammy in 1993, and her cover of Lucinda Williams' **Passionate Kisses** took home trophies for both women at the 1994 ceremony. The music video for **He Thinks He'll Keep Her** was a live performance of the song with backing vocals by Emmylou Harris, Trisha Yearwood, Patty Loveless, Pam Tillis, Kathy Mattea, and Suzy Bogguss taken from the 1993 CBS television special *Women of Country*. The single, which became a signature song for Carpenter, was her first No. 1 on the Radio & Records charts and served as a solid example of the album's recurring theme: conflicted women who must rely on their own inner strength for a solution.

Carpenter made a statement about identity and independence by simultaneously being wry, sassy, witty, intelligent, introspective, and vulnerable. *Come On Come On* said we've all been there, and that sometimes it's okay to wear pajamas to school drop-off. *–SS*

79

1993

Wu-Tang Clan

ENTER THE WU-TANG (36 CHAMBERS)

LOUD | Producer: RZA

RELEASED: NOVEMBER 9, 1993

● Widely considered one of the most significant hip-hop albums of all time, let alone the '90s, Wu-Tang Clan's multiplatinum debut still resonates strongly. Released during the golden era of New York hip-hop, *Enter the Wu-Tang (36 Chambers)* had a raw authenticity and cinematic yet gritty production style that set the group apart from the East Coast turn toward jazz rap and West Coast's burgeoning G-funk scene.

The ten-strong Wu-Tang collective quickly established itself with the release of the single **Protect Ya Neck** eleven months before *Enter . . .* came out. With two additional singles preceding release, anticipation ensured a high debut (No. 8 on Billboard's Top R&B/Hip-Hop Albums) for the full-length. Laden with obscure samples from classic kung fu films—a genre beloved by Wu-Tang's de facto leader and mastermind producer Robert "RZA" Diggs—the twelve-track album was anchored by a deeply rooted ethos in Five Percent Nation teachings and eastern philosophy, drawing parallels between the films' lethal martial arts masters and Wu-Tang's MCs, whom RZA called "lyrical assassins." The group's ten original members—RZA, GZA (aka Genius), Ol' Dirty Bastard, Method Man, Ghostface Killah, Raekwon the Chef, Inspectah Deck, U-God, Masta Killa, and DJ 4th Disciple—each had their own distinctive style and flow, with a palpable hunger for success that seeped into every verse.

Songs such as **Tearz** and **Can It Be All So Simple** explored heavy themes like loss, gun violence, and drug use, realities of the members' upbringings in the housing projects of Staten Island. **C.R.E.A.M.**, with its menacing melody and infectious hook, was the album's most commercially successful track, delivering gut-wrenching verses from Raekwon and Inspectah Deck about life on the streets of Shaolin. The mythology behind this iconic album went on to fundamentally shape Wu-Tang and pave the way for a more experimental era of hip-hop. *—JS*

Sting
TEN SUMMONER'S TALES

A & M | Producers: Sting, Hugh Padgham

RELEASED: MARCH 9, 1993

● Sting took on the role of troubadour for his fourth solo release, a play on both his given name (Sumner) and a character in Chaucer's classic *The Canterbury Tales*. The Englishman sang about romance throughout the narrative in his distinctive, grainy voice, whether it was the slow, sensuous balladry of **Fields of Gold**, the bright scatting of **She's Too Good for Me**, or the swingy pop of the Grammy Award–winning **Prologue (If I Ever Lose My Faith in You)**. A master of genres, Sting created another auditory journey with elements of jazz, reggae, and rock, turning these *Tales* into more than just the sum of their parts. *–SS*

Urge Overkill
SATURATION

GEFFEN | Producers: Butcher Bros., Andy Kravitz

RELEASED: JUNE 8, 1993

● In one of the decade's genius moves, velvet-clad and medallioned Chicago alt-rockers Urge Overkill enlisted the Butcher Bros.—until then best known for producing hip-hop breakthroughs Cypress Hill and Kris Kross—to helm its major-league debut. The result was arguably the most riff-a-licious album of the '90s. An M.O. that Urge Overkill began probing on three prior indie releases achieves apex-predator status on tracks like **Sister Havana**, **Positive Bleeding**, and **Stalker** (the best song Kiss never wrote). Nash Kato, King Roeser, and Blackie Onassis would reach even greater heights with their *Pulp Fiction* soundtrack entry before imploding in an elegant mess a few years later. *–DP*

Henry Threadgill
TOO MUCH SUGAR FOR A DIME

AXIOM | Producers: Henry Threadgill, Bill Laswell

RELEASED: JANUARY 26, 1993

● Saxophonist, flutist, and composer Henry Threadgill—a jazz innovator integral to world music and avant-garde—spearheaded bands that evolved from the '70s free-jazz Air to his '80s seven-piece Sextett to the eccentric '90s amalgamation Very Very Circus. Outrageous and playful, *Too Much Sugar for a Dime* let loose two and sometimes three tubas to lead an ensemble also fitted with two electric guitarists, violins, and drums that hashed out nonlinear melodies, chords, and themes. Drummer Gene Lake's brilliantly topsy-turvy backbeats and splashy cymbals kept the band on its feet, while Threadgill's gritty alto sax allowed all the intense flavors to flourish and tantalize. *–CH*

Paul Westerberg
14 SONGS

SIRE/REPRISE | Producers: Paul Westerberg, Matt Wallace

RELEASED: JUNE 15, 1993

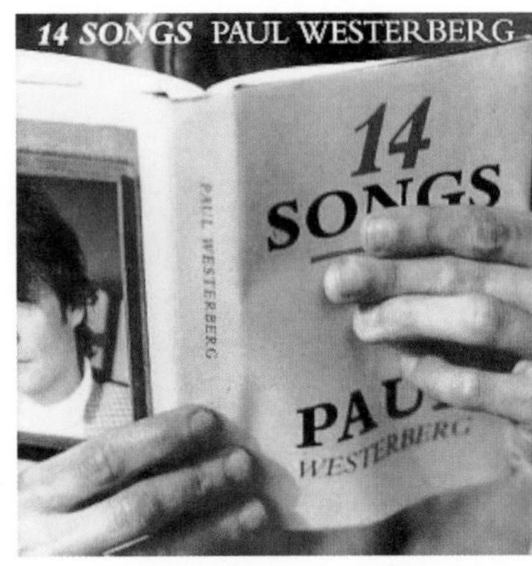

● As frontman of the Replacements, a debaucherous quartet of larkers if ever there was one, Paul Westerberg rose above the shenanigans to emerge as one of the most literate songwriters of the '80s. His first official solo release played on the literary conceit with a title riffing on J. D. Salinger's *Nine Stories*. While the Minneapolitan offered Faces-style rockers such as **World Class Fad** and **Silver Naked Ladies** (Faces keyboardist Ian MacLagan appeared on the latter), **First Glimmer** and **Black Eyed Susan** hinted at Westerberg's future (and even more compelling) basement recordings under both his given name and the Grandpaboy moniker. *–DP*

Mazzy Star
SO TONIGHT THAT I MIGHT SEE

CAPITOL | Producer: Dave Roback

RELEASED: OCTOBER 5, 1993

● There were albums in 1993 that sold more than Mazzy Star's sophomore release, but few songs were as ever-present in dark college dorm rooms or smoky bars than **Fade Into You**. Hope Sandovol's honeyed and instantly recognizable voice cut through the heavy distortion of the grunge era while journalists tried to figure out how to categorize the band she fronted. Country-goth? Dream pop? Alt-rock? Did it matter? No other single was widely released from the album, although **Into Dust** has been used in myriad TV shows. Mazzy Star's lone platinum release is a stunner best paired with a hearty cabernet and an existential crisis. *–HD*

Cassandra Wilson
BLUE LIGHT 'TIL DAWN

BLUE NOTE | Producer: Craig Street

RELEASED: NOVEMBER 2, 1993

● Cassandra Wilson's maiden Blue Note album was pivotal for her career and for the entire jazz vocal oeuvre. Few sounds are more sublime than her silky, languorous alto or the African gospel harmony trio she split herself into on **Sankofa**, one of *Blue Light*'s three originals. But what made this work so influential is how Wilson sculpted songs we thought we knew into revelatory new versions. Witness her two Robert Johnson covers: **Come On in My Kitchen** beckons with siren-like allure; **Hellhound on My Trail** sends the hound's hot breath right down your neck. With innovative instrumentation and arrangements, *Blue Light* set a new template for jazz singers. *–LM*

Janet Jackson

JANET.

VIRGIN | Producers: Jimmy Jam, Terry Lewis, Janet Jackson

RELEASED: MAY 18, 1993

● She grew up in the public eye, took *Control* of her career in 1986, and led a *Rhythm Nation* in 1989. For her fifth studio album, Janet Jackson stripped down her persona and was just plain *janet.*

Linking with her familiar Minneapolis producers Jimmy Jam and Terry Lewis, Jackson used the album—the first release under her reported $40 million deal with Virgin Records, which made her pop's highest paid performer at the time—to explore her sexuality in ways she hadn't previously. Issued two days after her twenty-seventh birthday, *janet.* was slinky and romantic and signaled a newfound freedom for the singer. The fresh direction was laid bare on a *Rolling Stone* cover that September, a full version of the cropped album cover that featured a topless Jackson, arms above her head, a pair of hands cupping her breasts from behind.

The first single, **That's the Way Love Goes**, a cool slice of funky bedroom R&B backed by a down-tempo hip-hop beat, was a window into the album, and it camped out at No. 1 on Billboard's Hot 100 for eight weeks, her longest-running No. 1. The horny club banger **Throb** and the yearning PDA anthem **Any Time, Any Place** fell into the same lustful groove, while **Again**, the album's second No. 1 hit, was a tender, almost whisper-quiet piano ballad, an alternative side of the album's stark intimacy

Elsewhere there was a grab bag of sounds: **If**, an industrial dancefloor rocker; **Whoops Now**, a playful Motown-style number; and **New Agenda**, political pop with an assist from Chuck D of Public Enemy. Cementing Jackson as a sex symbol and furthering her standing as one of the era's preeminent hitmakers, *janet.* sold more than fourteen million copies, becoming the best-selling album of her career. ***–AG***

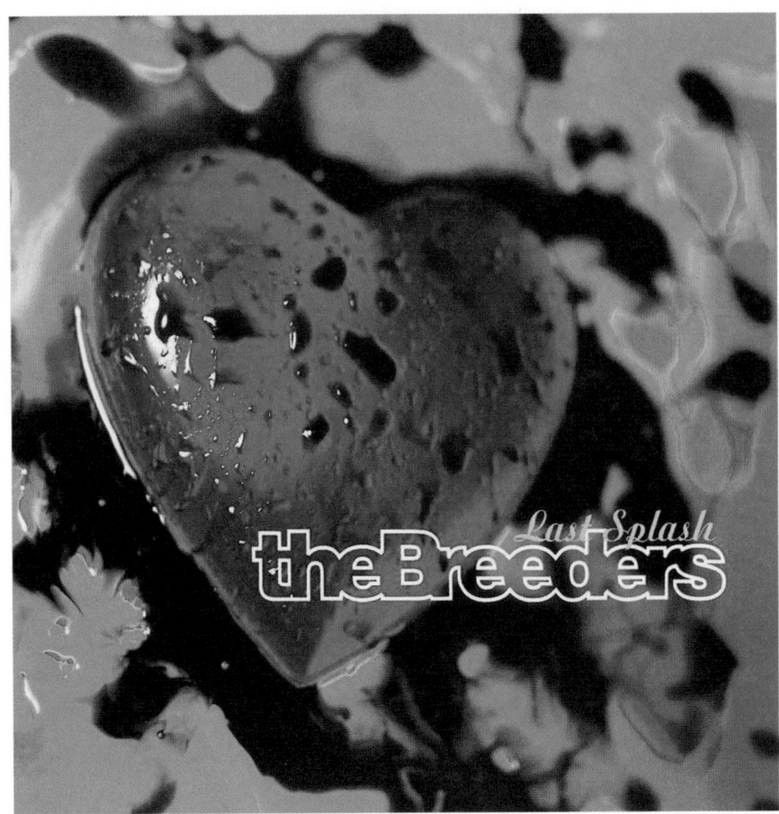

The Breeders

LAST SPLASH

4AD/ELEKTRA | Producers: Kim Deal, Mark Freegard

RELEASED: AUGUST 30, 1993

● On August 9, 1993, an alert went out across the airwaves: *Ahooh! Ahooh! Ahooh! Ahooh! Ahooh! Ahooh!* A few seconds later, the bass line to **Cannonball** kicked in—and a generation would sing about being "the bong in this reggae song."

When the Breeders' *Last Splash* was released later that month, it housed much more than just early-'90s alt-rock. It was a complex mix of styles from twangy (**No Aloha** and **Flipside**) to crunchy (**Saints**) to country (**Drivin' on 9**, an Ed's Redeeming Qualities cover that would not have been out of place at the Grand Ole Opry). *Last Splash* propelled the Breeders into the spotlight, landing the band on the Lollapalooza tour in 1994 and lead singer and songwriter Kim Deal on the cover of *Spin* magazine.

With Deal front and center on guitar (alongside twin sister Kelley), comparisons to her other band, Pixies, were inevitable, especially when *Last Splash*'s opening track, **New Year**, aped the quiet/loud/quiet structure which that group had perfected. But listening to *Last Splash* felt like you were at a party with the coolest musicians taking turns onstage, playing whatever fit their mood. Plus, if you were into alternative music during the '90s, there were few things more reliable than a new release from 4AD Records; the UK label had a distinct style and a reputation for beautiful artwork. Walking into any record store, people saw 4AD covers and wanted to know, "What does *that* record sound like?"

Last Splash's impact has only grown over time, with many artists citing both the album and the Breeders as influences. Testament to that resonance has been provided by not one but two reissues, one each for its twentieth and thirtieth anniversaries, both expanded to include demos, live recordings, and other extras. That first splash is still making ripples today. *–RW*

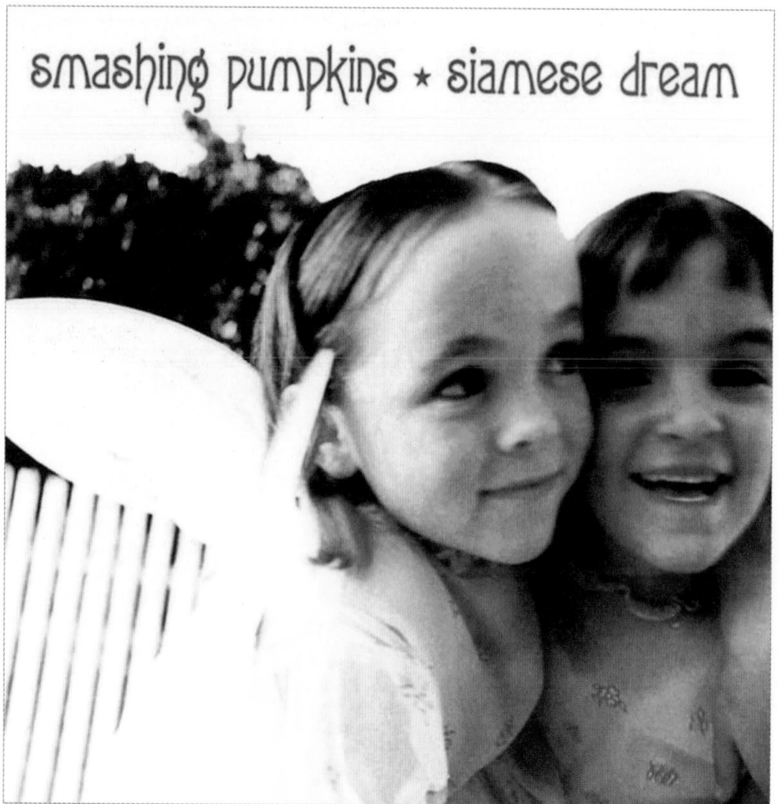

1993

The Smashing Pumpkins

SIAMESE DREAM

VIRGIN | Producer: Butch Vig

RELEASED: JULY 27, 1993

● The anticipation for The Smashing Pumpkins' second studio album grew after the critical success of its debut, *Gish*. When it was confirmed that Butch Vig (producer of *Gish* and Nirvana's *Nevermind*) would be back behind the board, expectations soared. *Siamese Dream* exceeded those expectations, but recording was extremely difficult and exacerbated interband tensions.

Frontman Billy Corgan ended up playing most of the instruments himself, much to the displeasure of bandmates James Iha (guitar), D'Arcy Wretzky (bass), and Jimmy Chamberlain (drums). But the result was undeniably brilliant—a dense rock album full of power, angst, melancholy, rage, and release. In 1993, there was still a stigma of weakness around mental health issues when Corgan told *Spin*, "If you really listen to the record, you would know that I'm a real wimp. And a hopeless romantic." Corgan was not a wimp; in fact, he was a perfectionist in the studio who used everything at his disposal to bring his vision to life. As a result, *Siamese Dream* pushed the band to new levels: No. 10 on the Billboard 200, multiplatinum sales, and a headlining spot on the 1994 Lollapalooza tour.

One main reason *Siamese Dream* resonated with listeners is that when Corgan screamed "The killer in me is the killer in you!" during **Disarm**, "Let me out!" in **Cherub Rock**, or "I shall be free" in **Rocket**, they related to it. Like the best artists, Corgan put to words and music emotions that are extremely difficult to verbalize. People who couldn't articulate their feelings could just immerse themselves in these songs because *Siamese Dream* was an album made by an adult who, like so many others, was still processing the turmoil of adolescence. Playing it loud wasn't a replacement for good therapy, but it came damn close. *–RW*

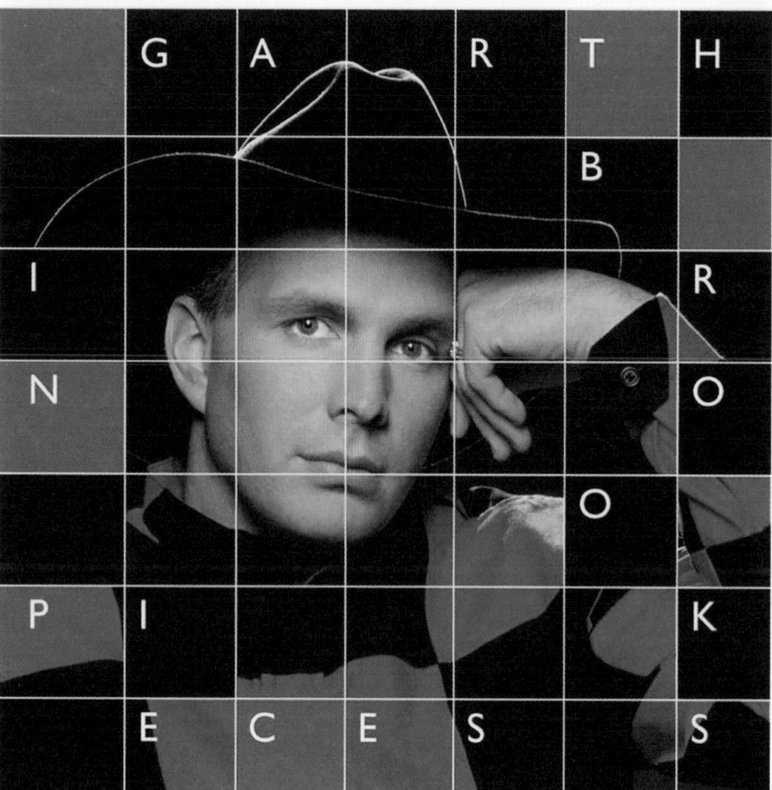

Garth Brooks

IN PIECES

LIBERTY | Producer: Allen Reynolds

RELEASED: AUGUST 31, 1993

● Garth Brooks had announced a goal "to be known as the artist of the decade for the '90s," and by the time of his sixth studio album (counting the 1992 holiday set *Beyond the Season*), he was well on his way to accomplishing that.

Those releases had reached No. 1 or 2 on Billboard charts and were all multiplatinum. In 1992, however, he started talking about retiring, about "just staying home and being dad" to then-newborn first daughter, Taylor. Given his landmark success, it caused a seismic shock not just in Nashville but in the wider music industry. The golden egg goose was about to leave the nest—though Brooks began walking back and qualifying his plans in short order.

In Pieces came along to prove it was much ado about nothing. The ten-song set did, however, have a kind of free-spirited swing that could be credited to Brooks's joy at home and to at least broaching the idea of taking time off—though it should be noted that his first full-scale world tour began in 1993. Brooks described the recording process as looser and more live in the studio, with the players who had been on the road with him gelling into a more cohesive and formidable outfit in the studio.

Good songs—never a problem in Brooks's world—also helped. He co-wrote six of the ten tracks, including the rip-roaring first single **Ain't Going Down ('Til the Sun Comes Up)** and the anthemic **Standing Outside the Fire**. Brooks and company also cooked up a definitive rendition of Dennis Linde's **Callin' Baton Rouge**, which was first recorded by the Oak Ridge Boys, while **The Red Strokes**, bolstered by an award-winning video, became a much-loved deep cut. All that made *In Pieces* another, you guessed it, No. 1, diamond-certified smash. *–GG*

Salt 'N' Pepa

VERY NECESSARY

NEXT PLATEAU | Producers: Herby "Luvbug" Azor, Steve Azor, Sandra "Pepa" Denton, DJ Wynn, Cheryl "Salt" James, De De "Spinderella" Roper, Tommy "D.J. Grand" Shannon, WEATOC, Inc

RELEASED: OCTOBER 12, 1993

● The misogyny sadly prevalent in rap met its match with Salt 'N' Pepa's fourth album. On *Very Necessary*, the New York trio of Cheryl "Salt" James, Sandra "Pepa" Denton, and Deidra "DJ Spinderella" Roper pushed back as strong women demanding—hell, commanding—respect and propers. Alongside a growing list of like-minded artists, including recording partners En Vogue and Mary J. Blige, Salt 'N' Pepa fought the chauvinistic power with wit, wiles, and muscle to match the men.

The group, formed in 1985, had displayed significant growth on its previous album, *Blacks' Magic* (1990). *Very Necessary* was another step forward, its thirteen tracks produced and written mostly by Herby "Luvbug" Azor, Salt 'N' Pepa's guiding force since the beginning. The group sounded even more assured and, in appropriate spots, cocky over the course of the album, confidently knitting together R&B, rap, pop, and, in the opening **Groove Me**, dancehall. The sisters were doing more of it themselves this time, too, with Salt and Pepa producing and co-writing the first single, **Shoop**, and **Sexy Noises Turn Me On**. Spinderella, meanwhile, had her hands all over **Step**. They would, in fact, be ready to step away from Luvbug after this, although that parting would be acrimonious.

Very Necessary was triumphant, however. The album gave the group its only Top 5 appearance (No. 4) on the Billboard 200 and was certified five-times platinum. **Shoop** and the platinum **Whatta Man** (with En Vogue) were the group's only Top 5 hits on the Billboard Hot 100 and also topped the Hot Rap Songs chart. The track **None of Your Business**, meanwhile, brought Salt 'N' Pepa its only Grammy for Best Rap Performance by a Duo or Group. (The group would receive a Grammy Lifetime Achievement Award in 2021.) In a long career with not a lot of output, *Very Necessary* was a definitive moment. *—GG*

Lenny Kravitz

ARE YOU GONNA GO MY WAY

VIRGIN | Producer: Lenny Kravitz

RELEASED: MARCH 9, 1993

● When Lenny Kravitz burst onto the scene with *Let Love Rule* in 1989, it was obvious he had immense talent. Like one of his chief musical influences, Prince, Kravitz played every instrument on his debut. By 1993, he had released two studio albums filled with moments of analog brilliance that distinctly stood out from other early-'90s offerings.

But Kravitz was just warming up. The most apt metaphor to describe his effort on *Are You Gonna Go My Way* is to compare him to a professional athlete fully unlocking their potential. Instead of using vintage equipment to create songs that sounded like they were from two decades earlier, Kravitz recorded modern songs that nodded to the past but weren't overpowered by nostalgia. He still leaned into his influences unapologetically: **Come On and Love Me** could be a lost Curtis Mayfield track, **Believe** had a guitar solo worthy of Paisley Park, and **Eleutheria** was Kravitz as Bob Marley. The reason it worked better on *Are You Gonna Go My Way* than on his previous albums is that he figured out how to take those influences and turn them into a sound more distinctly his own. *—RW*

Us3

HAND ON THE TORCH

BLUE NOTE | Producers: Mel Simpson, Geoff Wilkinson

RELEASED: NOVEMBER 16, 1993

● Britain's Us3 cut a deal with Blue Note Records to allow the jazz rap troupe to use samples from the label's vaunted catalog, a surefire source of inspiration that connected Blue Note's illustrious past to a bold and promising future. And, just like that, *Hand on the Torch* made jazz cool again. In fact, *Hand on the Torch* was Blue Note's first platinum-certified album. **Cantaloop (Flip Fantasia)**, a funky, freewheeling jaunt built on the melodic line from pianist Herbie Hancock's "Cantaloupe Island," led the way. Its grooving bass line, rap/scat lyrics, and warbling trumpet sounded simultaneously new and vintage—as well as funky, heady, and danceable. Across all thirteen tracks of the Grammy-nominated album, the rapping is poetic, artful, and smart. The sampled source material is freshly reinvented by the inspired production team of Geoff Wilkinson and Mel Simpson. **Just Another Brother** was enlivened by soprano sax, sampled trumpet echoes of Freddie Hubbard, and lyrics sung and rapped in a reggae parlance. Horace Silver, Thelonious Monk, Sonny Rollins, Reuben Wilson, and Joe Sample were also some of those Blue Note legends whose material is heard in a new light via this *Torch*. *—CH*

Cypress Hill
BLACK SUNDAY

RUFFHOUSE/COLUMBIA | Producers: DJ Muggs, T-Ray

RELEASED: JULY 20, 1993

● Cypress Hill delivered a near-perfect blend of the familiar and the innovative on its sophomore album. The woozy, off-kilter beats and samples of the trio's star-making 1991 debut returned in a slightly deeper and darker form on *Black Sunday*. The spiritually perfect sample of Black Sabbath's "The Wizard" on **I Ain't Goin' Out Like That** exemplifies the group's increasingly rock-friendly vibe. Cypress Hill had toured with the Beastie Boys and as part of Lollapalooza following the release of its first album, building a diverse fanbase drawing equally from rap, alternative, and rock fans. To paraphrase Grace from *Ferris Bueller's Day Off*, the sportos, the motorheads, geeks, sluts, bloods, wasteoids, dweebies, and dickheads all adored Cypress Hill. Upon *Black Sunday*'s release, Cypress Hill became the first rap act to have two albums in the Top 10 of the Billboard 200 at the same time, and the set's lead single, **Insane in the Brain**, even cracked the Top 20 of the Hot 100. Special praise must be handed out for the genius sampling of Dusty Springfield's "Son of a Preacher Man" on the deep track **Hits from the Bong**. *–MW*

Uncle Tupelo
ANODYNE

SIRE/REPRISE | Producer: Brian Paulson

RELEASED: OCTOBER 5, 1993

● This should have been an exciting new chapter for Uncle Tupelo—a major-label debut that found principals Jay Farrar and Jeff Tweedy joined by new drummer Ken Coomer, bassist John Stirratt, and multi-instrumentalist Max Johnston. Instead, it became the alt-country pioneers' swan song.

The signs of disaffection were everywhere on *Anodyne*, especially on the fierce, Farrar-led **Chickamauga**. Named for a bloody Civil War battle, the song's lyrical content is pure interband venom ("Fighting fire with unlit matches/From our respective trenches"). **Anodyne**, **Steal the Crumbs**, and **Fifteen Keys** all brim with similar loathing and resentment.

Tweedy's **The Long Cut** seems more conciliatory yet resigned to what by then must have seemed inevitable. Elsewhere the band, having gathered plenty of hard-won music business experience, vented that knowledge on **We've Been Had**, which posited that all your favorite bands are showbiz phonies.

That said, the music was fantastic. The quieter numbers—**Slate**, **New Madrid**, **High Water**, and **Acuff-Rose**—were fleshed out by Johnston's banjo, fiddle, and lap steel, and by the steady thwack of Coomer's drumming. The rockers, meanwhile, matched their raging sonics to the lyrics' roiling emotions. Few bands breaking up acrimoniously end on such a musical high note. *–DD*

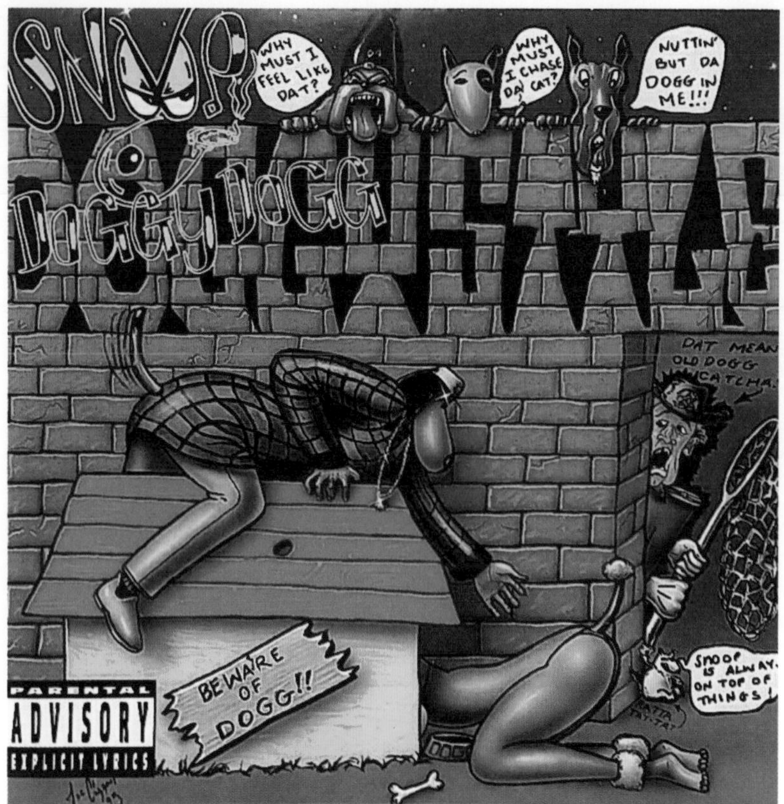

Snoop Doggy Dogg

DOGGYSTYLE

DEATH ROW/INTERSCOPE | Producer: Dr. Dre

RELEASED: NOVEMBER 23, 1993

● By fall 1993, listeners didn't need an introduction to Snoop Doggy Dogg. But he offered one anyway with **Who Am I? (What's My Name?)**, a G-funk-laden trunk-rattler that served as the official christening of Snoop Doggy Dogg, solo star.

The lanky, laid back, irresistibly charismatic MC was already a known entity, debuting with Dr. Dre on 1992's "Deep Cover" and riding shotgun with the producer through the rap-redefining *The Chronic* album later that year. When it came time to go on his own, Snoop was ready. But it wasn't all smooth sailing for the twenty-two-year-old Long Beach, California, native, born Calvin Broadus. The summer before *Doggystyle*'s arrival, Snoop (still Snoop Doggy Dogg, before later shortening to just Snoop Dogg) was arrested in connection with the death of Philip Woldemariam, an alleged rival gang member who was killed in Los Angeles in August 1993. That landed Snoop on *Newsweek*'s cover, snarling underneath the headline "When Is Rap 2 Violent?" just as *Doggystyle* was hitting stores.

You couldn't buy better promotion (Snoop was later cleared of all charges). *Doggystyle* debuted at No. 1 on the Billboard 200—higher than *The Chronic*'s peak at No. 3—and sold 806,000 copies during its first week. Dre handled production, lacing it with towering George Clinton samples, soul loops, and lowriders-full of West Coast swagger. Snoop managed the rest with his effortless charm on party anthems such as **Gin and Juice** and **Lodi Dodi**, his update of Doug E. Fresh's and Slick Rick's "La Di Da Di." And he was liberal with his spotlight, sharing it with his cohorts—Lady of Rage, the Dogg Pound, Warren G, and Nate Dogg—just as Dre had previously done with him. Snoop would be a fixture for decades, but in terms of his solo output, *Doggystyle* was his finest day. *—AG*

Aerosmith

GET A GRIP

GEFFEN | Producer: Bruce Fairbairn

RELEASED: APRIL 20, 1993

● Aerosmith's eleventh studio album was a commercial powerhouse, keeping a firm grip on a triumphant streak that began with the multiplatinum success of 1987's *Permanent Vacation* and continued with *Pump* two years later. *Get a Grip* flaunted the quintet's hard rock swagger and showcased compelling power ballads that dominated radio and MTV. After Geffen's initial rejection, Steven Tyler, Joe Perry, and company rallied to craft more radio-friendly material in collaboration with acclaimed hitmakers such as Desmond Child, Jim Vallance, and Mark Hudson, among others—a move that paid off handsomely.

The album spawned four Top 30 hits, spearheaded by **Livin' on the Edge**, which held an impressive nine-week reign atop the Billboard rock chart and earned a Grammy for Best Rock Performance by a Duo or Group with Vocal in 1994—a feat repeated the following year with the album's harmonica-infused ballad **Crazy**. Bolstered by iconic music videos featuring a teenage Alicia Silverstone, the power ballad trifecta of **Crazy**, **Amazing** (with Don Henley on backing vocals), and the colossal hit **Cryin'** became MTV fixtures. This fourteen-song collection marked Aerosmith's first album to top the Billboard 200, selling more than twenty million globally and becoming the group's top-selling album worldwide. *–MD*

Morphine

CURE FOR PAIN

RYKODISC | Producers: Paul Q. Kolderie, Mark Sandman

RELEASED: SEPTEMBER 14, 1993

● Two-string bass. Baritone sax. Drums. Guitar? Not necessary. Singer/bassist Mark Sandman, sax player Dana Colley, and drummers Jerome Deupree and (on three tracks) Billy Conway created a unique sound that Sandman referred to as "low rock." They introduced their unorthodox instrumentation on the group's 1992 debut album *Good*, but it was this follow-up, *Cure for Pain*, that secured the band's standing in the alternative rock music world. The songs **Mary Won't You Call My Name?**, **Sheila**, **Let's Take a Trip Together**, **In Spite of Me**, and **Thursday** soundtracked David O'Russell's indie film *Spanking the Monkey*, opening the door for the album's commercial success. *The Sopranos* and *Beavis and Butt-Head* would also feature songs from *Cure for Pain*, helping prompt sales of more than three hundred thousand copies.

This sophomore album demonstrated a more sophisticated approach in both lyrics and instrumentation, elevating the sparse sound of *Good*. **All Wrong** and **Thursday**, among others, created a wall of that "low rock" sound, making it hard to believe there were only three instruments in the mix. **Buena** is the standout track; the title translates to the word *good* and, boy, is it. You never even find yourself longing for a guitar solo. *–AD*

A Tribe Called Quest

MIDNIGHT MARAUDERS

JIVE | Producers: Q-Tip, Large Professor, Skeff Anselm, Ali Shaheed Muhammad

RELEASED: NOVEMBER 9, 1993

● A who's-who of hip-hop players features in the artwork of *Midnight Marauders*, the third album from Queens, New York, hip-hop trio A Tribe Called Quest. Dozens of luminaries, from Chuck D to Heavy D to Kool Moe Dee, are pictured with headphones on, grooving to the group's savvy fusion of rap, jazz, and pop sensibilities.

By the time it was released, listeners everywhere had caught on to Tribe's quest. *Midnight Marauders* became its first Top 10 album, debuting at No. 8 on the Billboard 200, and the first single, **Award Tour**, was granted Buzz Clip status on MTV. **Award Tour** also showed off the album's expanded sound, bigger and hookier than Tribe's previous work but just as impeccably cool.

Tribe's heart lay in the interplay between Q-Tip and Phife Dawg. The MCs—one smooth, one gruff—completed each other in ways told and untold. "When's the last time you heard a funky diabetic?" Phife asks on the Busta Rhymes–assisted **Oh My God**. Q-Tip's response: "I don't know, man . . . ." They came from different schools: Q-Tip spit conscious raps; Phife was obsessed with sports references. But together, Tribe made sense, and *Midnight* is its finest hour. *—AG*

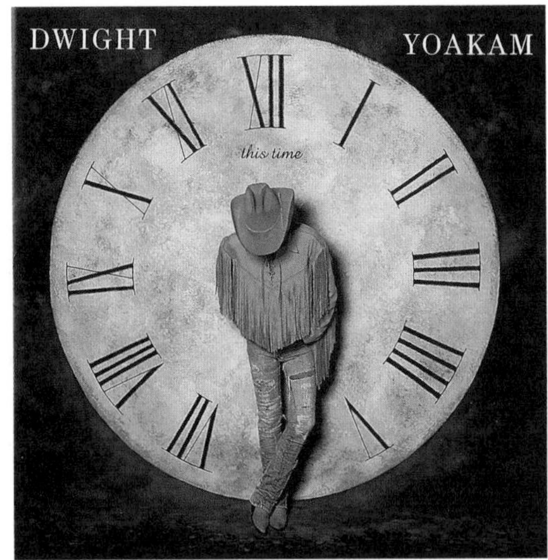

Dwight Yoakam

THIS TIME

REPRISE | Producer: Pete Anderson

RELEASED: MARCH 23, 1993

● Dwight Yoakam and producer/guitarist Pete Anderson always had contemporary ambitions for the music they were making, which was audible on Yoakam's albums but sublimated by the romance of hat-wearing singer/guitarist/songwriters as a second coming of yesteryear—particularly Buck Owens' Bakersfield sound.

On *This Time* Yoakam and Anderson kept one boot firmly in the familiar but continued to stretch, getting closer to Anderson's goal of making "Dwight Yoakam music" that wasn't easily consigned to any one corner of the country world. This was most fully realized in **A Thousand Miles from Nowhere**, the second single and a lush sonic adventure unlike anything Yoakam had released (it was so evocative it ended up in two films, *Red Rock West* and *Chasers*). Yoakam was still honky-tonkin' on *This Time*, especially on the title track, but fans clearly didn't mind him pushing the envelope. The album reached No. 4 on the Billboard Top Country Albums chart and was certified triple-platinum, his first and only multimillion seller. Three singles (**Ain't That Lovely Yet**, **A Thousand Miles . . .**, and **Fast as You**) peaked at No. 2 on the Hot Country Songs chart—not too shabby, but the latter was undeservedly Yoakam's last Top 10 single. *—GG*

Frank Sinatra

DUETS

CAPITOL | Producers: Phil Ramone, Hank Cattaneo

RELEASED: NOVEMBER 2, 1993

● To bring Frank Sinatra's music to a new generation, Capitol Records reunited the crooner with a fifty-four-piece orchestra and classic Nelson Riddle arrangements of his standards, then added a corps of younger hit-makers to duet on them. It was an eyebrow-raising concept, and while Sinatra was no stranger in the night to controversy, for once it wasn't his personal life drawing attention. When he requested that his singing partners submit their contributions electronically rather than being together for the recordings, many feared the album would simply be a stunt of engineering.

Sinatra won out. His partners—including Tony Bennett, Natalie Cole, Aretha Franklin, Julio Iglesias, Liza Minnelli, Carly Simon, Barbra Streisand, and Luther Vandross—contributed performances that were creatively uneven but commercially successful: *Duets* debuted at No. 2 on the Billboard 200—Sinatra's first Top 10 showing since 1966—and sold more than three million copies in the US, his first album to do so. It also launched an accompanying TV special and a sequel (which won Sinatra a final Grammy) and made similar projects part of the music industry's quiver.

Sinatra's often shaky baritone showed his age on many of the tracks, while some of his partners, such as Gloria Estefan, seemed out of their depths. Some pairings that looked good on paper (Sinatra and Anita Baker singing **Witchcraft**, for instance) paled in execution. The most interesting track was **I've Got You Under My Skin**; Bono, straight off U2's *Achtung Baby*, was all falsetto and growling purr. It at least sounded like the two artists were genuinely playing off each other. Appropriately, Sinatra got the last word on the closing track, **One for My Baby**. Kenny G's sax was fittingly nonintrusive as Sinatra poured a lifetime of reflection and yearning into his vocals. One last time for the long, long road. ***–HD***

Big Chief

MACK AVENUE SKULL GAME

SUB POP | Producers: Big Chief, Al Sutton

RELEASED: 1993

● Influenced by old-school Detroit funk, the MC5's two-guitar attack, and punk rock, Big Chief crafted its musical masterpiece as a soundtrack to a Blaxploitation film that existed only in the group members' collective mind. Bassist Matt O'Brien and drummer Mike Danner laid down the tight grooves while Mark Dancey and Phil Durr propelled the tunes with their twin guitars, all driving underneath former Necros singer Berry Henssler's rough 'n' tough vocals. The aces in the hole were Detroit blues diva Thornetta Davis's pleading vocals and Was (Not Was)'s trumpeter Rayse Biggs and saxophonist Dave McMurray. Aside from the Beastie Boys, no one pulled off anything like this better. *–WW*

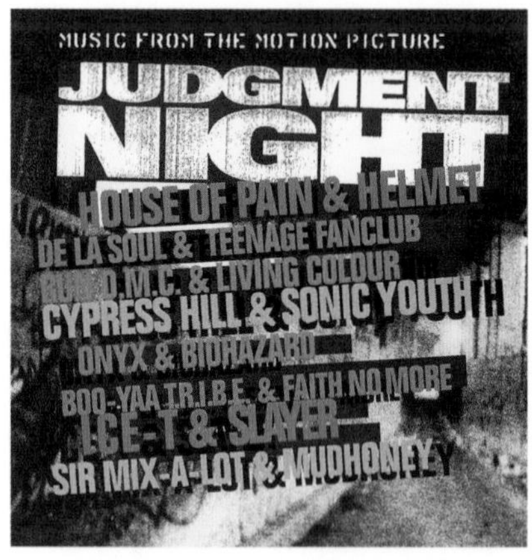

Various Artists

JUDGMENT NIGHT
(MUSIC FROM THE MOTION PICTURE)

IMMORTAL/EPIC SOUNDTRAX | Producer: Happy Walters

RELEASED: SEPTEMBER 14, 1993

● Rap-and-rock pairings weren't anything new by 1993, seven years after Aerosmith and Run-D.M.C. walked that way. But this soundtrack to the Emilio Estevez–starring thriller went a step further, throwing a house party for rappers and rockers and watching them mingle. The result was some heavy thrashing between Helmet and House of Pain, Biohazard and Onyx, and Slayer and Ice-T, while Sir Mix-A-Lot and Mudhoney and Pearl Jam and Cypress Hill locked into steady rock grooves. The gem was De La Soul and Teenage Fanclub's **Fallin'**, a breezy ego check built from a Tom Petty loop that showed how rap-rock could extend past the parameters of either genre. *–AG*

F.U.S.E.

DIMENSION INTRUSION

PLUS 8/WARP | Producer: Richie Hawtin

RELEASED: JUNE 7, 1993

● F.U.S.E. stands for Futuristic Underground Subsonic Experiments, which pretty much summed up the first studio album from techno pioneer Richie Hawtin. An energetic and driven twenty-two-year-old, the British-born Hawtin put together a thirteen-song set that is widely considered one of the greatest electronic albums ever in his studio in Windsor, Ontario. Hawtin set out to create something in between the futurism of Detroit techno and the hypnosis of Chicago house music. The result was a variety of thumping, acid-tinged floor stompers; hypnotic songs; and minimal techno gems for the ages. *–MH*

Melissa Etheridge
YES I AM

ISLAND | Producers: Melissa Etheridge, Hugh Padgham

RELEASED: SEPTEMBER 21, 1993

● Melissa Etheridge's fourth studio album came out nearly nine months after *she* came out, though she claimed that's not what the title meant. *Yes I Am* was driven by bluesy rock guitar rhythms and Etheridge's powerful, Joplin-esque voice on tracks such as **I'm the Only One** and the Grammy-winning **Come to My Window**. The soul-searching ballad **I Will Never Be the Same** lent itself to the authenticity Etheridge embraced in her songwriting. Her combination of storytelling folk roots, blustery rock grooves, and passionate, arena-sized delivery not only led to six-times platinum success but served as a touchstone for a generation struggling to find its voice. *–SS*

Anthrax
SOUND OF WHITE NOISE

ELEKTRA | Producers: Dave Jerden, Anthrax

RELEASED: MAY 25, 1993

● Maybe Anthrax was inspired (or threatened) by the sudden emergence of grunge. Perhaps the unbelievable success its labelmates Metallica achieved after simplifying its sound on 1991's *Metallica* (aka "The Black Album") opened the quintet's eyes. Or maybe Anthrax was just sick of being typecast as jokesters in jam shorts. Whatever the reasons, Anthrax made big changes for *Sound of White Noise*, replacing longtime frontman Joey Belladonna with the gruffer John Bush, moving away from its thrash roots and tackling more serious subject matter. It all worked shockingly well, with Anthrax reborn as a more diverse band without sacrificing any intensity. *–MW*

Plastikman
SHEET ONE

ANOVAMUTE | Producer: Richie Hawtin

RELEASED: NOVEMBER 6, 1993

● "An analogy of a trip" is how Richie Hawtin described *Sheet One*, the debut album under his moniker Plastikman. With this album, his music portrayed a man made of plastic melting into the dancefloor in the wee hours of the morning. A masterpiece of minimal acid techno was born from this vision, a simplistic and captivating journey combining haunting melodies with sci-fi samples. *Sheet One* evokes an almost druggy state of mind with its layers of beauty and quirky rhythms, taking listeners on a journey that pleased the mind and the soul—a trip well worth taking. *–MH*

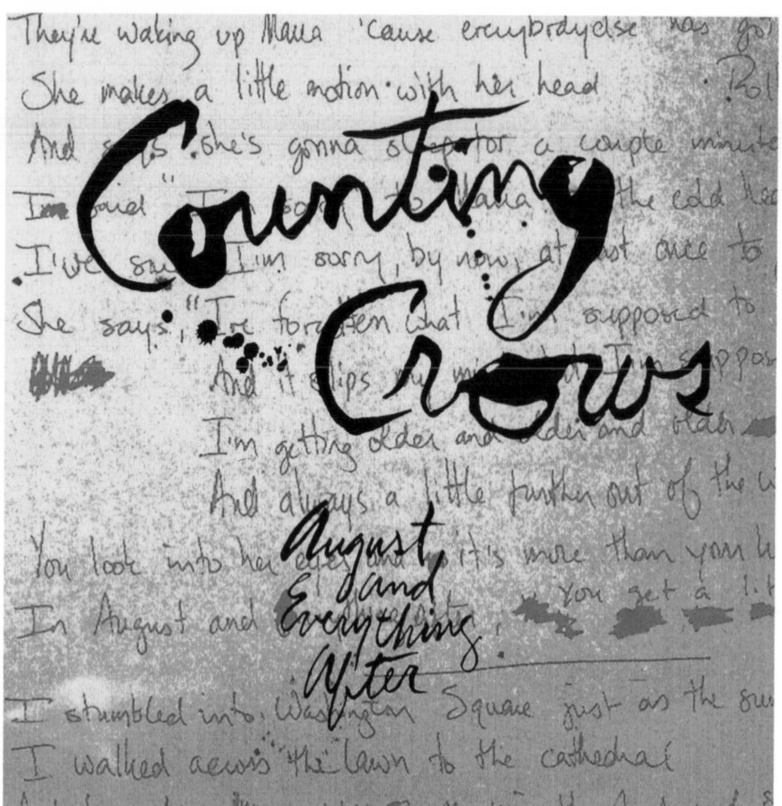

Counting Crows

AUGUST AND EVERYTHING AFTER

GEFFEN | Producer: T Bone Burnett

RELEASED: SEPTEMBER 14, 1993

● Successful bands tend to develop slowly, taking a few records before delivering a classic; artists such as Bruce Springsteen (*Born to Run*) and Tom Petty (*Damn the Torpedoes*), for example, were three albums in before their breakthroughs. Counting Crows, on the other hand, offered a career-defining work right out of the gate.

Coming at the height of grunge and gangsta rap, *August and Everything After* was full of catchy, well-crafted songs driven by acoustic guitars, accordion, mandolin, and other instruments that were not the status quo, at least in the rock mainstream. The album broke through on Billboard's Alternative and Mainstream Rock charts thanks to the singles **Mr. Jones** and **Round Here** and reached No. 4 on the Billboard 200. It established the band—which had played in Van Morrison's honor at his Rock & Roll Hall of Fame induction nine months before the album's release—as a force in roots-based rock, drawing comparisons to The Band and, yes, Morrison himself. Frontman and chief songwriter Adam Duritz's distinctive voice and sophisticated lyrics distinguished all eleven songs.

August . . . began with the stunning, moody, and introspective **Round Here**. From the opening lyric ("Step out the front door like a ghost into the fog/Where no one notices the contrast of white on white") the listener was drawn into Duritz's world of shadow and light. His lyrics were poetic, meaningful, and literate throughout. Up-tempo tracks such as **Mr. Jones**, **A Murder of One**, and **Rain King**, the album's third single (based on the book *Henderson the Rain King* by Saul Bellow), sat next to exquisite ballads like **Sullivan Street** and **Raining in Baltimore**. Counting Crows has not repeated this album's breakthrough, seven-times platinum success, but it firmly established a band whose success lies in timeless songwriting, lyricism, and musicianship. *–ST*

1993

Clint Black

NO TIME TO KILL

RCA | Producers: James Stroud, Clint Black

RELEASED: JULY 13, 1993

● Clint Black returned to the control board for a second time, co-producing his fourth studio album—and to good effect. *No Time to Kill* yielded five Top 5 hits on the Billboard Hot Country Singles & Tracks chart: The lead single, **A Bad Goodbye**, featuring Wynonna Judd, peaked at No. 2, followed by the title track (No. 3), **State of Mind** (No. 2), and **Half the Man** (No. 4). The album's sole No. 1 hit, **A Good Run of Bad Luck**, was subsequently featured on the soundtrack to the 1994 movie *Maverick*, starring Mel Gibson, Jodie Foster, and James Garner.

Black may have been one of the many "hat acts" to emerge during the late '80s—he was part of the class of '89 with Garth Brooks and Travis Tritt—but his success was due in no small part to his modern take on the sounds of classic country music, which set him apart from the others. His songwriting was as important to the process as his singing and performing, with Black refusing to record any song he didn't have a hand in writing. *No Time to Kill* was no exception, as he wrote or co-wrote all ten songs.

The project included a songwriting collaboration with Jimmy Buffett on the track **Happiness Alone**, while the album's title, *No Time to Kill*, was a play on the title of Black's debut album, *Killin' Time*, and was his fourth consecutive album to be certified at least platinum. It reached No. 2 on Billboard's Top Country Albums charts and No. 14 on the Billboard 200—the last time to date that he hit the Top 20 there with an album of all-new material. ***–MH2***

Pearl Jam

VS.

EPIC | Producers: Brendan O'Brien, Pearl Jam

RELEASED: OCTOBER 19, 1993

● Though Pearl Jam's debut album, *Ten*, preceded Nirvana's *Nevermind* by a month in 1991, it was the latter band that became the standard bearer for the Northwest grunge rock movement both were lumped into. That both albums were successful created a perceived rivalry between the two, and even though Nirvana was in front of Pearl Jam with its follow-up, *In Utero*, *Vs.* gave Pearl Jam its own foothold and identity within what was becoming one of rock's most rapidly crowded communities.

A palpable sense of purpose can be heard throughout *Vs.*'s twelve tracks. Pearl Jam and producer Brendan O'Brien channeled the pressure of expectations and came up with forty-six minutes of music that was galvanizing from front to back—roaring out of the gate with the jet-propulsion grooves of **Go** and **Animal** and slamming hard on **Glorified G**, **Dissident**, **Leash**, and **Rearviewmirror**. Frontman Eddie Vedder shoveled even deeper into his angst than he did on *Ten*, and he most effectively channeled it toward the narrative on **Daughter**, where the instrumentalists' acoustic-electric blend forged a stunning new dynamic path for the band. *Vs.* also furthered the notion that the Mike McCready and Stone Gossard pairing was a new guitar hero tandem, which played a big part in making Pearl Jam mainstream radio–accessible and arena-ready less than three years after its formation.

The audience was primed, too. *Vs.*'s first-week sales of more than 950,000 copies not only put it at No. 1 on the Billboard 200 but set a record that stood for five years on its way to seven-times platinum status. **Go** and **Dissident** were Top 5 Mainstream Rock chart singles, while **Daughter** hit No. 1 there and on the Alternative Airplay chart and went platinum. All of that combined to make Pearl Jam the reluctant but unquestioned leader of its particular movement. *—GG*

Nirvana

IN UTERO

DGC | Producer: Steve Albini

RELEASED: SEPTEMBER 21, 1993

● Kurt Cobain introduced *In Utero*, the follow-up to Nirvana's world-shaking 1991 breakthrough album *Nevermind*, with a wry, hilarious, and self-deprecating kiss-off: "Teenage angst has paid off well/Now I'm bored and old." The reference is to "Smells Like Teen Spirit," the single that changed everything for Nirvana and for the alt-rock movement and which catapulted Cobain to unwitting generational spokesperson status. *In Utero* was very much a reaction to (and, specifically, against) *Nevermind*'s success, and Cobain, all of twenty-six, declared himself over it the very first chance he got.

In Utero's sound is also a rebuttal to *Nevermind*'s polished sonic perfection, with producer Steve Albini—known for his work on Pixies' *Surfer Rosa*, a Cobain favorite—mixing the album like it was covered in mud. Concessions were eventually made for its anti-commerciality, and **Heart-Shaped Box** and **All Apologies** were touched up for radio consumption. Cobain may not have loved the game, but he was willing to play it; his relationship with fame was nothing if not fraught.

In Utero was twelve tracks of raw and abrasive rock. Cobain's guitars squeal and hiss, Krist Novoselic's bass is so low it scrapes the ground, and Dave Grohl sounds like he's trying to pound his drums through the floor. But there was beauty in the sludge, inside the pained moans of **Pennyroyal Tea**, the naked pleas of **Frances Farmer Will Have Her Revenge on Seattle** ("I miss the comfort in being sad," Cobain wails), and in the pure brute force of **Scentless Apprentice** and **Milk It**. It became Nirvana's final studio album (Cobain would commit suicide just six months after its release), and there was messy poetry in the album's finality. "All in all is all we are," Cobain repeats at the end of album-closing **All Apologies**. It's a gutting but lovely goodbye. *–AG*

1993

Meat Loaf

BAT OUT OF HELL II: BACK INTO HELL

MCA | Producer: Jim Steinman

RELEASED: SEPTEMBER 14, 1993

● Meat Loat went through his own kind of hell during the sixteen years between the first entries in his *Bat Out of Hell* series. Unprepared for the megaplatinum success of the first *Bat* in 1977, the man the *New York Times* called Mr. Loaf (né Marvin Lee Aday) lost his voice (psychosomatically), had a falling out with *Bat* composer Jim Steinman while first trying to make *Bat II*, and declared personal bankruptcy, the result of twenty-two lawsuits waged against former managers and other handlers. He did manage to release four more albums, most of which fell quickly into obscurity.

Making up with Steinman gave wing to *Bat II*, and the result made a lot of **Rock and Roll Dreams Come Through** for the duo and for dedicated *Bat* fans. The best news was it was more of the same: *Bat II* was as bombastic and grandiose as its predecessor. The opening track and first single, **I'd Do Anything for Love (But I Won't Do That)** weighed in at twelve minutes, **Objects in the Rear View Mirror May Appear Closer Than They Are** at more than ten, and four others at seven minutes or more. There was another dramatic spoken-word piece (**Wasted Youth**). Orchestral layers of instruments collided with operatic choirs of backup vocals, with Loaf roaring Steinman's expressions of teen lust and buoyant idealism atop it all, with a modicum—but only a modicum—of maturity gleaned from the intervening years.

It may have seemed like an odd release when grunge was ruling the rock world, but *Bat II* made its way to No. 1 on the Billboard 200 on its way to five-times platinum sales. **I'd Do Anything for Love . . .** was a platinum chart-topper as well. It would be thirteen years before *Bat III* took flight, but at this moment, two out of an eventual three definitely wasn't bad. *—GG*

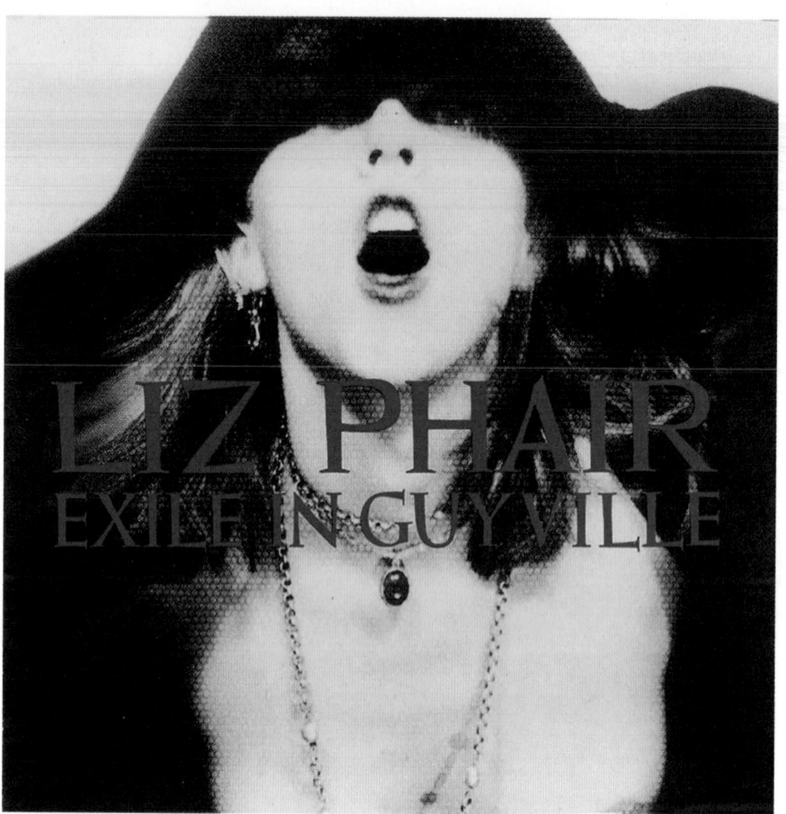

1993

Liz Phair

EXILE IN GUYVILLE

MATADOR | Producers: Liz Phair, Brad Wood

RELEASED: JUNE 22, 1993

● Liz Phair was a relative unknown when her debut album became one of the most celebrated records of the lo-fi indie-rock boom during the early and mid-'90s. The Chicago singer/songwriter had earlier sketched out songs in a series of cassette tapes under the name Girly-Sound. Initial attempts to turn those home-recorded demos into something more skidded off course a few times before local producer Brad Wood stepped in and helped Phair shape what eventually became *Exile in Guyville* into a stirring expression of female independence.

Although Phair has claimed the album was a song-by-song reply to The Rolling Stones' *Exile on Main St.*, evidence hasn't always backed that up. No matter. With *Exile in Guyville* Phair created a loose concept album about a woman's view of the scene around her, which just happened to include men not exactly comfortable with the notion of strong women. From the opening **6'1"** to the closing **Strange Loop**, the record unravels as a fifty-five-minute tour of awakenings—social, sexual, and otherwise.

The lo-fi sound of *Guyville* (Phair and Wood perform almost everything themselves) proved the perfect complement to Phair's emotional bloodletting. Whether sidestepping responsibility on the album's most commercial song, the single **Never Said**, or looking for commitment on the cult favorite **F*ck and Run**, Phair ran a gamut of feelings, sparing nobody in the process—including herself.

Guyville's influence was felt almost immediately; while not a commercial hit, peaking at No. 196 on the Billboard 200, the album found legions of supporters in the growing indie scene. Within a few years, more women with guitars and notebooks filled with confessional songs started to surface across the planet. They all have Liz Phair to thank. *–MG*

Sheryl Crow

TUESDAY NIGHT MUSIC CLUB

A & M | Producer: Bill Bottrell

RELEASED: AUGUST 3, 1993

● It's hard to remember now, but **All I Wanna Do**, the breezy, beer-buzzy tune that broke Sheryl Crow's career wide open, was not the first single from her debut album, *Tuesday Night Music Club*, but rather the third. A&M Records' continued promotion of Crow was evidence of a lot of faith, especially considering the singer/songwriter had already scrapped an album that she felt was unrepresentative of her talents.

The album's backstory is legend. Crow joined a weekly jam session frequented by Bill Bottrell, David Baerwald, and Kevin Gilbert. Co-writes began to emerge, and Bottrell refocused the sessions toward developing a Crow-fronted album. The resulting release's runaway success led to acrimony and accusations, and a lot of hate was heaped on Crow. But the album's greatest legacy is not Crow's perseverance, though that is certainly a major part of it. Rather, *Tuesday Night Music Club* spoke frankly about sexual harassment in the music industry decades before the #MeToo movement caught fire. **What I Could Do for You** was about a groping music executive promising a young female artist the moon if only she'd play along. **The Na-Na Song** went even further, naming Michael Jackson manager Frank DiLeo as the perpetrator (Crow was a backup singer on Jackson's *Bad* tour).

The album had other worthy yet more conventional achievements, songs that played out like well-wrought short stories—**Run Baby Run** and **Leaving Las Vegas**—and others about strained relationships, including **Strong Enough**, another Top 5 hit. And then there's the aforementioned **All I Wanna Do**. Crow had pulled a book of poems off a shelf and began reading aloud Wyn Cooper's "Fun," and the song developed from there—to the tune of Grammy Awards for Record of the Year and Best Female Pop Vocal Performance, as well as Best New Artist. *—DD*

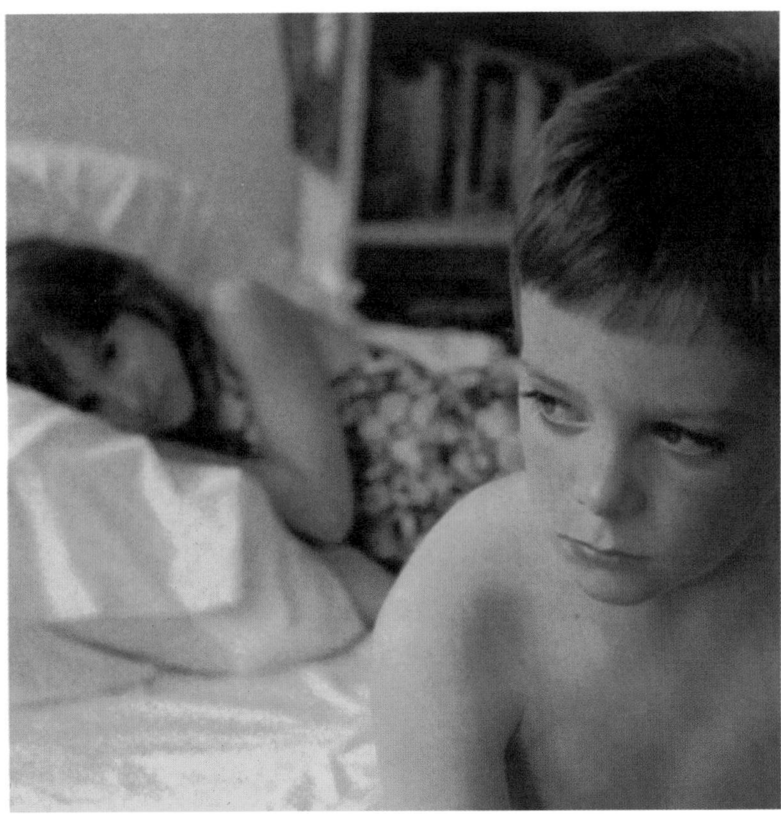

The Afghan Whigs

GENTLEMEN

ELEKTRA | Producer: Greg Dulli

RELEASED: OCTOBER 5, 1993

● Even though the Afghan Whigs were often lumped with other grunge-era acts, and indeed released two albums on Seattle-based Sub Pop before making the major-label leap for its fourth, *Gentlemen*, the Cincinnati band approached guitar-based alternative music from a different direction. Frontman Greg Dulli was enamored with soul music: he included Motown covers on the band's records and in its setlists, and the Afghan Whigs recorded parts of *Gentlemen* at Memphis's Ardent Studios, where some of Stax's classic songs were created.

For this dark, soulful song cycle about the end of a relationship, Dulli turned to piano, cello, and Mellotron to help tell his story. There are still plenty of guitars and alt-rock trappings, underlining songs such as **Debonair**, **What Jail Is Like**, and the title track. But it's Dulli's words and impassioned delivery that made *Gentlemen* a masterpiece of the period.

He didn't hold back: "Ladies, let me tell you about myself/I got a dick for a brain/And my brain is gonna sell my ass to you," he sang on **Be Sweet**, one of several songs that painted a sinister portrait of a man who's shed both decorum and dignity during the final stages before a breakup. Dulli claimed the album wasn't autobiographical, but it was hard not to read some of the author in these scarred, personal songs. By the end of *Gentlemen*'s forty-nine minutes, there was a sense of relief for having survived the tormented soul-cleansing. Dulli would take the Afghan Whigs even further into soul music on its next record, 1996's *Black Love*, but *Gentlemen* is the centerpiece of its catalog and one of the most under-celebrated works of the '90s—a conceptual piece about the darkest, most harrowing aspects of love. *–MG*

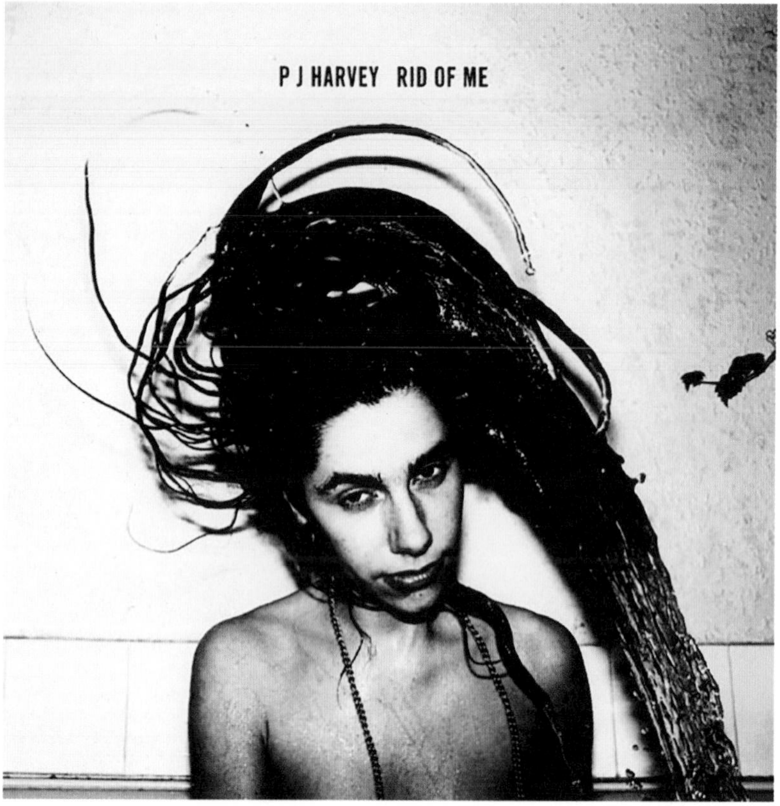

PJ Harvey

RID OF ME

ISLAND | Producer: Steve Albini

RELEASED: APRIL 26, 1993

● Few artists of the '90s elicited more consensus praise from music critics than Polly Jean Harvey, and it was well deserved. Throughout her career she has radically reinvented her musical persona with each album. After her successful debut, *Dry*, Harvey went into the studio with producer Steve Albini, drummer Robert Ellis, and bassist Steven Vaughan to record the follow-up, *Rid of Me*, the apex of PJ Harvey's post-punk/lo-fi era.

A gifted songwriter, Harvey packed *Rid of Me* with a ferocious minimalism that added weight to every word and chord. Vocally, Harvey veered all over the place, from a soothing quiet to feminine rage, but never out of control. *Rid of Me* starts with Harvey singing as a jilted lover in a dark conversation with the target of her affections: "Tie yourself to me/No one else, no/You're not rid of me." The quiet verse/loud chorus formula of the title track was worked to perfection on multiple other songs, with **Me-Jane** standing out among them. The first single, **50ft Queenie**, was an absolute blast of power from beginning to end; the fact that it's one of the few songs that Harvey has consistently played live ever since is a testament to its brilliance. **Man-Size Sextet** puts the listener in an uneasy space with strings straight out of a horror movie; it makes the string-free **Man-Size** that comes later in the album even more impactful.

Harvey's brilliant cover of Bob Dylan's **Highway 61 Revisited** made the listener wish she did more of those, but when an artist like Harvey has so much to say, it's probably hard to let someone else's words do the talking. *Rid of Me* closed with a tornado of electric guitar on **Ecstasy**, which was an apt description of what you should feel after listening to this brilliant album. *–RW*

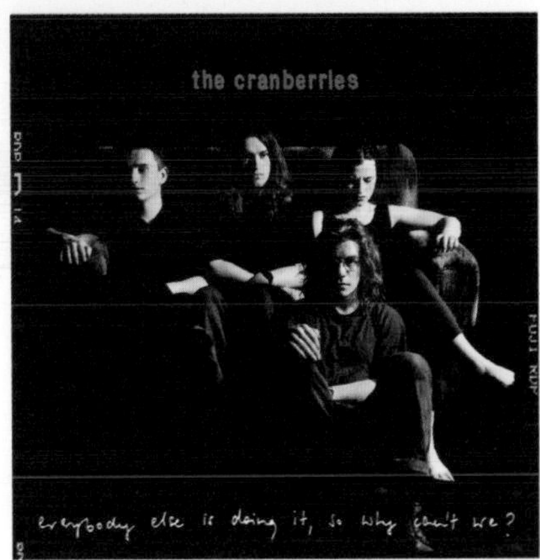

The Cranberries

EVERYBODY ELSE IS DOING IT, SO WHY CAN'T WE?

ISLAND | Producer: Stephen Street

RELEASED: MARCH 1, 1993

● It made sense that Dolores O'Riordan got the lead vocal gig in the Cranberries at nineteen by showing up to the audition with a Sinéad O'Connor song. Three years later, she was revealed to the world as a similarly enchanting young Irish singer, with a yodel in her delivery, on this debut album that took off with the stunning hits **Dreams** and **Linger**. Sonic connections to the Smiths, meanwhile, came from guitarist/songwriter Noel Hogan (an acknowledged Johnny Marr disciple) and producer Stephen Street, who had engineered that band's *Meat Is Murder*. *–SM*

Run-D.M.C.

DOWN WITH THE KING

PROFILE | Producers: Pete Rock, Q-Tip, EPMD, KayGee, Jam Master Jay, The Bomb Squad, Daniel Shulman, Run-D.M.C., Chyskills, Jermaine Dupri, Clifton "Specialist" Dillon

RELEASED: MAY 4, 1993

● *Back from Hell*, Run-D.M.C.'s first attempt at changing its style to keep up with hip-hop's quickly evolving trends, missed the mark pretty badly. The trio came up with a much better plan on *Down with the King*, teaming on each track with a like-minded roster of next-gen producers such as A Tribe Called Quest's Q-Tip, EPMD, and Public Enemy's The Bomb Squad. Nearly every collaboration proved to be an inspired one, and the obvious mutual love and respect on display across the entire album made a powerful statement about the impact of Run-D.M.C. and the longevity of hip-hop. *–MW*

Terence Trent D'Arby

SYMPHONY OR DAMN

COLUMBIA | Producer: Terence Trent D'Arby

RELEASED: MAY 3, 1993

● Oh, what could have been. After delivering a chart-topping, crowd-pleasing debut with 1987's *Introducing the Hardline* and then alienating most mainstream fans with 1989's deliberately challenging but half-excellent *Neither Fish nor Flesh*, Terence Trent D'Arby achieved a near-perfect balance with the ambitious but more accessible *Symphony or Damn*. The one-man writing/performing/producing dynamo blended genres in dazzlingly inventive new ways, from the funked-up hard rock of **She Kissed Me** to the throbbing, seductive soul of **Succumb to Me**. Although the album hit No. 4 and spawned four Top 20 singles in the UK, it was largely ignored elsewhere, ending D'Arby's days as a hitmaker. *–MW*

Me'Shell NdegéOcello
PLANTATION LULLABIES

MAVERICK | Producers: David Gamson, Andrew Betts, Bob Power, Me'Shell NdegéOcello

RELEASED: OCTOBER 19, 1993

● The music world was as unprepared for Me'Shell NdegéOcello as it was to describe her music. Hailing from the world of Washington, DC, go-go music, and following an unsuccessful audition for Living Colour, NdegéOcello's thirteen-track debut was a barrier breaker that required a dictionary's worth of hyphens to categorize a swaggering blend of R&B, funk, hip-hop, and psychedelia that some considered the birth of neo-soul. Her lyrics about race and gender inequities cut no quarter, and the impact of these *Lullabies*—including a pair of Grammy nominations—was nothing short of immense. *–GG*

1993

Various Artists
COMMON THREAD: THE SONGS OF THE EAGLES

GIANT | Producer: James Stroud

RELEASED: OCTOBER 12, 1993

● This tribute album started as a charity project for Eagles co-founder Don Henley's Walden Woods Project. The thirteen songs were mostly faithful to the originals, though some added slight twang or Nashville-style instrumentation. Country stars such as Tanya Tucker, Alan Jackson, Vince Gill, and Trisha Yearwood recorded Eagles hits ranging from **Already Gone** to **Tequila Sunrise** and helped propel *Common Thread* to triple-platinum and a Country Music Association Album of the Year award. Travis Tritt's cover of **Take It Easy** was the big winner—its video reunited Eagles for the first time since 1980 and led to hell freezing over as the band reunited the following year. *–SS*

New Order
REPUBLIC

QUEST/WARNER BROS. | Producers: Stephen Hague, New Order

RELEASED: MAY 11, 1993

● Barely speaking to each other and rarely sober, New Order recorded *Republic* to assist its financially beleaguered former label Factory Records and Manchester's famed Hacienda Club, both of which the band had a financial stake in. Four singles dropped from the album, including the infectious club favorite **World (The Price of Love)**. But it was the lead single **Regret** that pushed *Republic* to the top of the UK Albums Chart and No. 11 on the Billboard 200. Sadly, this was the quartet's only album of the '90s, and it would be eight years before New Order recorded again. *–HD*

1993

The Muffs
THE MUFFS

WARNER BROS. | Producers: Rob Cavallo, David Katznelson, The Muffs

RELEASED: MAY 11, 1993

● Seemingly coming out of nowhere (following a few indie singles), the Muffs sprang from Kim Shattuck's fertile imagination while she was still in the Los Angeles girl garage group the Pandoras. Joining her were Pandoras bandmate Melanie Vammen, bassist Ronnie Barnett, and drummer Chris Crass. The result was powerful songs—short blasts of emotion-wrought, often sarcastic lyrics sung loudly and without filter by Shattuck over guitar-driven, punk-yet-pop rock. Think Sex Pistols with a hoarse Joan Jett singing outtakes from The Beatles' *A Hard Day's Night*.

While there were similarities to the subsequent Rob Cavallo–produced *Dookie* by Green Day, *The Muffs* was rougher around the edges. Starting with **Lucky Guy**, it didn't let up through sixteen short songs, most sporting '60s-ish melodies. Highlights included **Big Mouth** and **Everywhere I Go** (later used in a Fruitopia TV commercial), and the Beatlesque **Another Day**, plus the fifty-one-second **Stupid Jerk**, written by "Metal" Mike Saunders of Angry Samoans. *The Muffs* rocked unflinchingly from start to finish, even when the pace slowed for the contemplative **All for Nothing**. There's a reason why artists as prominent as The Who and Elvis Costello publicly mourned Shattuck's passing in 2019 from ALS. The songs. The passion. The *songs*. *—TM*

Sarah McLachlan
FUMBLING TOWARDS ECSTASY

ARISTA | Producer: Pierre Marchand

RELEASED: OCTOBER 22, 1993

● Sarah McLachlan was two albums in before *Fumbling Towards Ecstasy* made its triple-platinum breakthrough impact outside her native Canada. The twelve-song set was a dark, deeply reflective exploration for the Nova Scotia–born singer/songwriter, and her soul-baring intensity was evident throughout. Most notably, **Possession** was a true account of her personal experience with stalkers. The songs remained pure and simple without being simplistic in their message or arrangements, and McLachlan's clear soprano soared to even greater, almost angelic, heights whether accompanied by solitary piano or layered against the backdrops of Pierre Marchand's lush, ethereal production. *–SS*

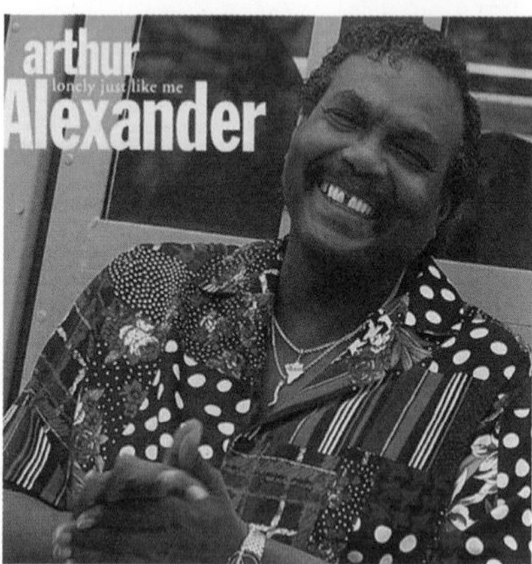

Arthur Alexander
LONELY JUST LIKE ME

ELEKTRA/NONESUCH | Producers: Ben Vaughn, Thomas Cain

RELEASED: MAY 1993

● Why is Arthur Alexander the only songwriter covered by The Beatles, The Rolling Stones, and Bob Dylan? A listen to this lovingly assembled comeback should provide more than adequate insight. Alexander was the living embodiment of Southern soul. An entirely instinctive musician with a delicate sense for words and melody, his songs connected the Black experience with country music like no other. Three chords and the truth were the backbone of **Every Day I Have to Cry** and the title cut. Alexander had quit music and was a school bus driver in Cleveland prior to cutting this record. Sadly, he died shortly after its release. *–HK*

Frank Zappa
THE YELLOW SHARK

BARKING PUMPKIN | Producer: Frank Zappa

RELEASED: NOVEMBER 2, 1993

● The last Frank Zappa album released during his lifetime was commissioned by Ensemble Modern. Zappa rearranged some of his classic works (**Dog Breath Variations**, **Uncle Meat**, and **Be Bop Tango**) and wrote new compositions, including string quartets, a piano duet, and ensemble pieces that were by turns provocative, challenging, and whimsical. The finished tracks were stitched together from several live performances (as was often Zappa's wont). Highlights include **Ruth Is Sleeping**, the multipart **Times Beach**, the avant-comical **Welcome to the United States**, and a breakneck version of **G Spot Tornado**. Zappa regarded this collaboration as one of the most satisfying of his career. In terms of his classical output, it may also be his best. *–DD*

James
LAID

FONTANA | Producer: Brian Eno

RELEASED: NOVEMBER 1, 1993

● Any song with the lyrics "This bed is on fire with passionate love/ The neighbours complain about the noises above/But she only comes when she's on top" was bound to get attention, which is exactly what happened with the title track from this Manchester, England, band's fifth studio album. The song gave the group its first appearance on the Billboard Hot 100 (No. 61) and hit No. 3 on the Alternative Airplay chart. Produced by Brian Eno, *Laid* had equally enduring (and endearing) tracks such as **Sometimes (Lester Piggott)** (inspired by a horse-racing jockey) and **Say Something**. *Laid* was James's first and only gold-certified release in the US and second in its homeland. *–HD*

1993

Tony! Toni! Toné!
SONS OF SOUL

WING/MERCURY | Producers: Tony! Toni! Toné!

RELEASED: JUNE 22, 1993

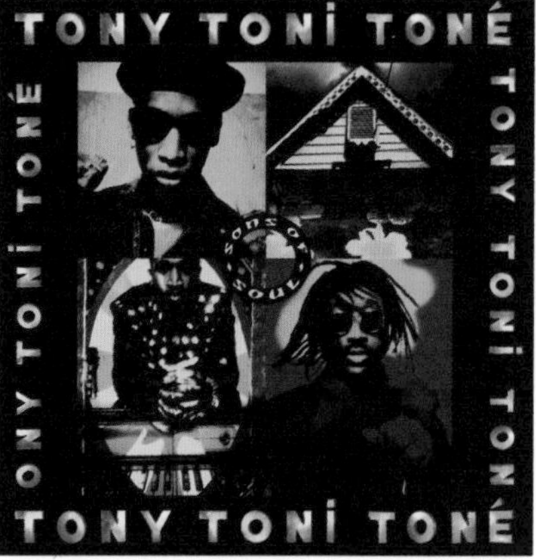

● Burned a bit by the retro tag placed on 1990's *The Revival*, Tony! Toni! Toné! fused old-school and new sensibilities on its follow-up—to phenomenal effect. The Oakland, California, trio invoked New Jack Swing in the lyric of the opening **If I Had No Loot**, but *Sons of Soul* was much more than that. Its fifteen tracks were classic soul and funk at their core, spiced up with raps, samples, and turntable tricks. Some recording in Trinidad yielded jams like **What Goes Around Comes Around** and **Dance Hall**, so funky they make the speakers (or earbuds) sweat. *–GG*

Slowdive
SOUVLAKI

CREATION | Producer: Slowdive

RELEASED: JUNE 1, 1993

● Slowdive's second album positioned the sound and soft power of shoegaze well beyond the '90s. The balance of heavy guitar washes, ethereal vocal ease, and production warmth influenced a genre and generation. Slowdive on record and on stage held extreme duality, revealing how a studio can enhance and support such songs of beauty and bliss. As a unit that has outlasted many of its peers, this era of the band brought heavy touring and a growing fanbase. Songs such as **When the Sun Hits**, **Alison**, and **Sing** (a collaboration with Brian Eno) made *Souvlaki* a spark that fueled even stronger expansions from frontman Neil Halstead and the group. *–CW*

1994

94

1994

Soundgarden

SUPER-UNKNOWN

A & M | Producers: Michael Beinhorn, Soundgarden

RELEASED: MARCH 8, 1994

● With *Superunknown*, Soundgarden hit the mainstream and hit it hard. The Seattle band's fourth album debuted at No. 1 on the Billboard 200, went six-times platinum, and spawned five singles that went on to dominate the US Alternative Airplay and Mainstream Rock charts. Most notable among those, of course, was **Black Hole Sun**, a trippy yet heavy-hitting track with an even trippier video that became an MTV staple back when that still meant something.

Perhaps *Superunknown* was simply the right album at the right time. Pearl Jam's *Ten* and Nirvana's *Nevermind* had softened the ground that later nurtured hit albums such as Alice in Chains' *Dirt*, Stone Temple Pilots' *Purple*, and Hole's *Live through This*. Trends aside, by the time of *Superunknown*, Soundgarden had reached a level of musical maturity that made its songwriting simultaneously more sophisticated (check some of those crazy time signatures), more melodic, and more accessible. The quartet's obvious classic rock antecedents, including The Beatles and Led Zeppelin, were plainly evident in songs such as **Head Down**, **Half**, **Black Hole Sun**, and others, though the Zep comparison especially was anathema to frontman Chris Cornell, who abhorred hard rock's toxic machismo.

But while the album's radio-ready sound struck a chord with the masses, *Superunknown* hardly presented a kinder, gentler Soundgarden. Themes of apocalypse, alienation (a grunge given), and suicide—chilling, given Cornell's eventual self-determined demise—dominate the lyrics. At the time, Cornell dismissed the latter reading as too literal; **Let Me Drown**, he admitted, was "one of the most disturbing songs I've ever written. It made me question whether it was a song that was alright to play." But others, he maintained, were "like watching a horror movie; it makes you feel better after feeling worse." *–DD*

1994

Weezer

WEEZER

DGC | Producer: Ric Ocasek

RELEASED: MAY 10, 1994

● By the time Weezer distinguished itself as a tour de force in the alt-rock scene with its self-titled debut (aka "The Blue Album"), grunge had been mortally wounded by the death of Kurt Cobain. Released less than a month after Cobain's death (and on Nirvana's label), *Weezer* dripped with distortion in the manner of most grunge records of the year yet didn't really fit the grunge mold. Instead, it fully embraced the heavy metal glam sound that frontman Rivers Cuomo grew up idolizing. With those roots, combined with an endearingly nerdy aesthetic, hooky power-pop melodies, and seriously overdriven guitars, Weezer achieved a category all its own—and with much commercial appeal, reaching gold status in just under seven months and certified triple platinum by 1995.

Though the quartet originally planned to record the album in its garage rehearsal space in Los Angeles (the inspiration for the track **In the Garage**), the label insisted they record at Electric Lady Studios in New York City with producer Ric Ocasek, former lead singer and chief songwriter for the Cars. The pairing turned out to be a smashing success, as the finished product was polished and radio-friendly but still retained the garage rock feel the group wanted. Cuomo's autobiographical lyrics ran the gamut of emotions (and seriousness) from the fragile ego on display in **No One Else** and **The World Has Turned and Left Me Here** to the ethereal freedom of **Surf Wax America** and the crushing disappointment of **Say It Ain't So**, making the album feel earnest and raw and, perhaps most importantly, relatable.

Undone—The Sweater Song, **Buddy Holly** (boosted by its clever *Happy Days* video), and **Say It Ain't So** were Top 10 Alternative Airplay hits, ensuring a foothold that allowed Weezer to explore and experiment on subsequent albums—though none have equaled Weezer's first success. *–JS*

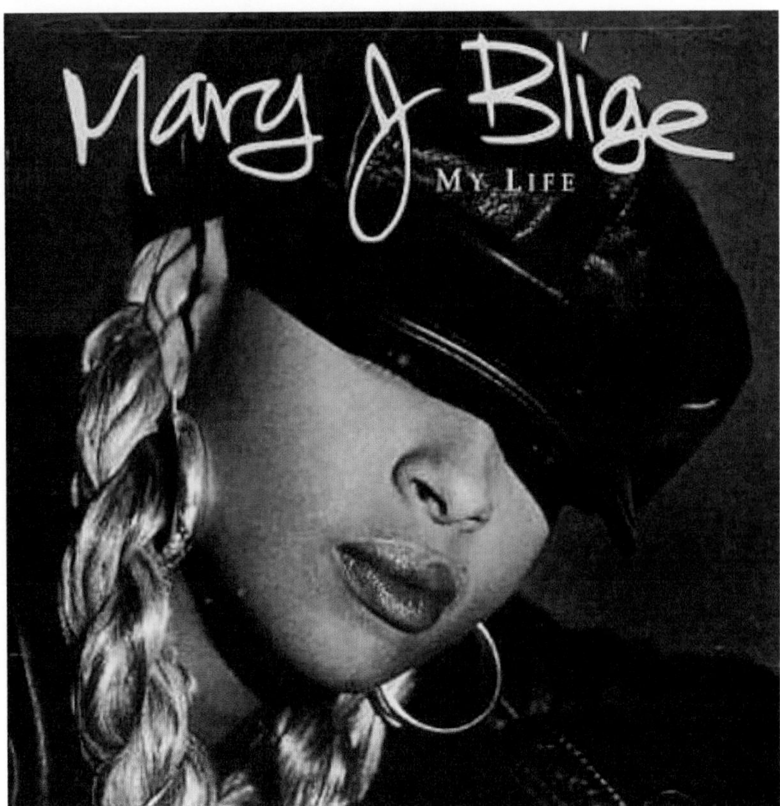

Mary J. Blige

MY LIFE

UPTOWN/MCA | Producers: Sean "Puffy" Combs, Chucky Thompson, Nashiem Myrick, Dalvin DeGrate, Herb Middleton, Prince Charles Alexander, Poke

RELEASED: NOVEMBER 29, 1994

● At the start of her career, Mary J. Blige demonstrated a knack for titles that told you exactly what her albums were about—essentially, the 411. Her debut, 1992's *What's the 411?*, was indeed an introduction to the New Yorker's skill and psyche. The follow-up *My Life* went even further, its seventeen tracks (songs and skits) as confessional as any Laurel Canyon singer/songwriter of the early '70s and revealing a great deal about what made the twenty-three-year-old Blige the damaged but unbreakable force we heard on this outing.

There was drama all over the project, starting in the studio where some of the production team was jettisoned after demanding more money from Blige's primary majordomo, Sean "Puffy" Combs. Others stepped into the breach, but Combs also had issues with chief recording engineer Prince Charles Alexander over credits. Then there was Blige's life, which, as *My Life*'s principal lyricist, she poured into the album. She was in a dark place, mired in an abusive relationship with Jodeci/K-Ci & JoJo singer K-Ci Hailey (who co-wrote two of the album's tracks) and battling clinical depression and substance addictions. Heavy stuff, in other words; there's a reason the lone cover here is **I'm Going Down**, the Norman Whitfield–penned Rose Royce single from 1976.

But Blige is cheering herself on as well. Songs such as **I'm the Only Woman**, **You Gotta Believe**, and **Be Happy** are statements of purpose and of an intent to push beyond that which was dragging her down and build something better. The soulful pathos clicked as *My Life* spent eight weeks at No. 1 on Billboard's Hot R&B/Hip-Hop Albums chart and peaked at No. 7 on the Billboard 200. It was certified triple platinum and nominated for a Grammy Award for Best R&B album. *–GG*

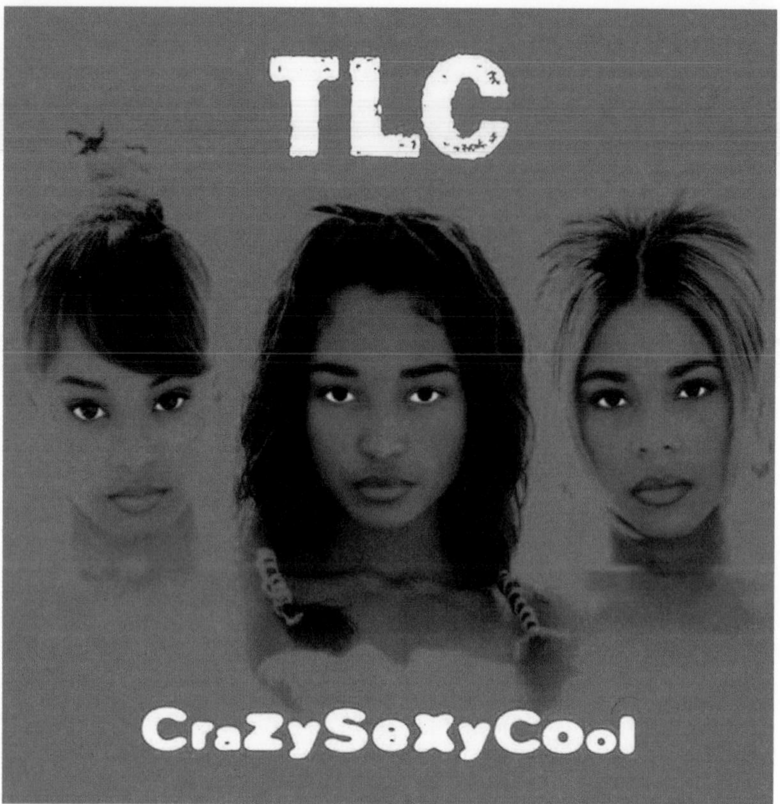

TLC

CRAZYSEXYCOOL

LAFACE/ARISTA | Producers: Dallas Austin, Babyface, Chucky Thompson, Jermaine Dupri, Organized Noize, Sean "Puffy" Combs, Jon-John

RELEASED: NOVEMBER 15, 1994

● TLC started well. *Ooooooohhh . . . On the TLC Tip* was a four-times platinum debut with three Top 10 Billboard Hot 100 hits. But the sophomore effort *CrazySexyCool* was the real groundbreaker for the Atlanta trio of Tionne "T-Boz" Watkins (Cool), Rozonda "Chilli" Thomas (Sexy), and Lisa "Left Eye" Lopes (Crazy).

With *CrazySexyCool*, TLC became the first all-female group to achieve diamond status, with more than ten million copies sold. Less rap-oriented than the group's debut but hardly conventional R&B, *CrazySexyCool* offered a fresh hybrid, at once sensual and swaggering, with a strong sense of self, purpose, and empowerment coming from the group members. The album's first single, **Creep**, earned TLC its first No. 1 on the Billboard Hot 100 for a four-week stay, but that wasn't even its biggest hit. That distinction went to **Waterfalls**, the third single, which logged seven weeks atop the chart and, like **Creep**, went platinum. **Red Light Special** and **Diggin' in You** also reached the Top 5, and all four went Top 10 on the Hot R&B/Hip-Hop Songs chart. The set was bookended by rap features—Phife Dawg of A Tribe Called Quest on **Intro-lude** and OutKast's André 3000 on **Something Wicked This Way Comes**—while Prince's **If I Was Your Girlfriend** received a more feminist perspective in TLC's hands.

CrazySexyCool netted four Grammy nominations, too, winning Best R&B Album and, for **Creep**, Best R&B Performance by a Duo or Group with Vocals. **Waterfalls**, meanwhile, brought home four MTV Video Music Awards. It would be five years before TLC's next album, *FanMail* in 1999, but *CrazySexyCool* (also the title of a 2013 VH1 biopic about the group) maintained its stature during the interim while some of the group members' personal dramas kept them in the headlines. ***–EP/GG***

1994

Digable Planets

BLOWOUT COMB

PENDULUM | Producers: Digable Planets, Dave Darlington

RELEASED: OCTOBER 18, 1994

● Fresh off the gold-status success of their 1993 breakout album, *Reachin' (A New Refutation of Time and Space)*, Digable Planet's second (and final) studio record reaffirmed the Brooklyn-based trio as one of the premier players in New York's burgeoning jazz rap scene. More overtly political in its messaging than its predecessor, *Blowout Comb* was injected with references to the Black Panther movement, Marxism, and Five Percent Nation ideologies that were prevalent within Black culture at the time in response to intensifying racial unrest. Even the album's liner notes were modeled after the official Black Panther community newspapers of the '70s. The track **Dial 7 (Axioms of Creamy Spies)** took a particularly provocative tone, encouraging Black people to "steal your mind back" and join against "imperial fascists," referencing political activists such as Che Guevara and Mumia Abu-Jamal.

But there was much more to *Blowout Comb* than its social commentary. The album's obscure jazz and funk samples, blended with live instrumentation, gave each track a satisfying sonic richness seldom heard before. Though lauded by fans and tempered by the group's signature laid-back coolness and quintessential '90s boom bap style, the album didn't have the commercial appeal of the debut, which had nabbed Digable Planets a Grammy for Best Rap Performance by a Duo or Group for the crossover hit single "Rebirth of Slick (Cool Like Dat)." Receiving less label support, *Blowout Comb* peaked at No. 32 on the Billboard 200 and No. 13 on Billboard's Top R&B/Hip-Hop Albums chart, several spots lower on each.

With time, however, the album gained the regard it deserved, becoming a defining work of the jazz rap subgenre that still resonates with fans today. Digable Planets disbanded a few months after the record's release, reuniting and releasing a compilation album a decade later. *—JS*

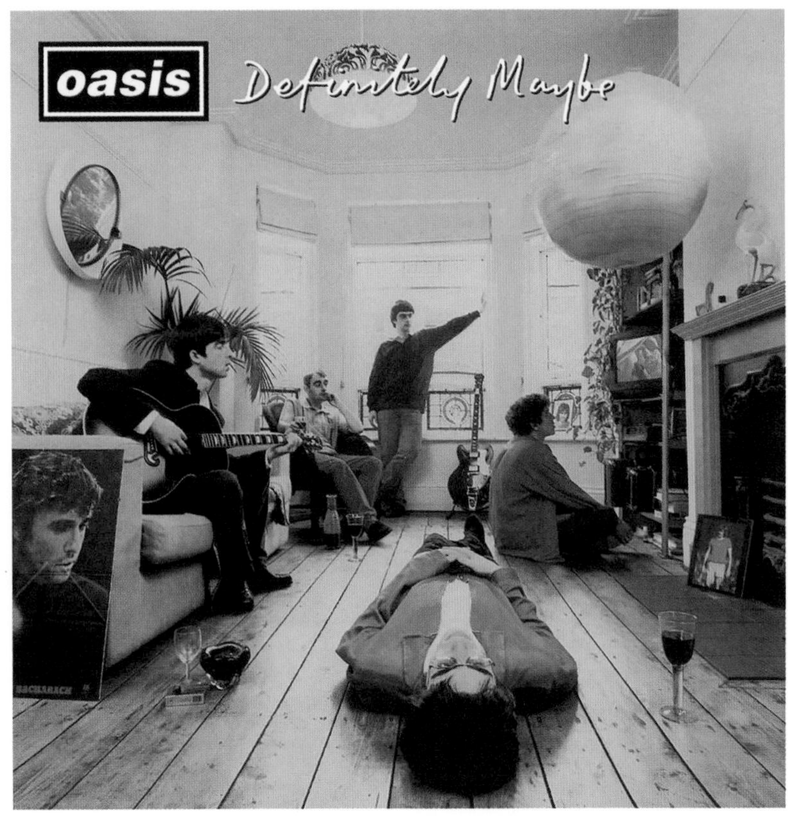

Oasis

DEFINITELY MAYBE

CREATION | Producers: Owen Morris, Mark Coyle, Noel Gallagher

RELEASED: AUGUST 29, 1994

● Technically, the members of Oasis weren't yet rock stars when *Definitely Maybe* was released. But the album is a declaration, the sound of the group willing itself into the spotlight. "Toniiiiiiiiight, I'm a rock 'n' roll star," Liam Gallagher wails on the opening track. You gonna tell him he's not?

Definitely Maybe introduced the world to the forever feuding Gallagher brothers—Liam and songwriter/guitarist Noel, his big brother—a pair of working-class lads from Manchester, England, who took on the globe even as they warred with each other. Guitarist Paul "Bonehead" Arthurs, bassist Paul "Guigsy" McGuigan, and drummer Tony McCarroll rounded out the lineup, though the non-Gallagher personnel would shift throughout the band's existence.

Definitely Maybe was full of loud guitars, sneering attitude, and several metric tons of swagger. Forget introspection—Oasis was chasing immortality, and the group found it in **Live Forever**, a bulletproof rocker for the ages about not being beholden to the limits of time or space. "You and I are gonna live forever," the chorus goes, and it makes you think that band just might. Everything is mega and anything is possible on *Definitely Maybe;* the trick is the nuggets of encouragement baked into the booze-soaked psalms. "I'm feeling supersonic, give me gin & tonic," Liam sang on **Supersonic**. Later, on the squealing, hedonistic **Cigarettes & Alcohol**, he comes on like a motivational speaker, turning a song about overindulgence into an anthem for self-starters.

As the Britpop movement it helped usher in took flight, the band's dreams of superstardom were made whole when Oasis headlined Britain's Glastonbury Festival the year after *Definitely Maybe*'s release. Then again, was there ever a doubt it would? Then and forever more, Oasis's members *are* rock 'n' roll stars. *—AG*

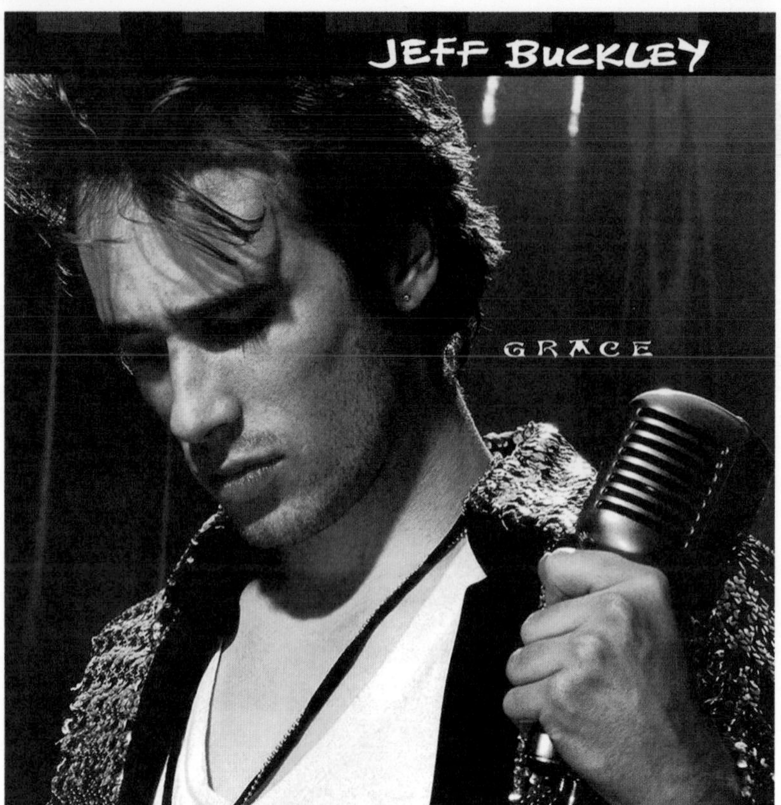

Jeff Buckley

GRACE

COLUMBIA | Producers: Andy Wallace, Jeff Buckley

RELEASED: AUGUST 23, 1994

● Many artists' lives have been cut short after they left a body of work that seems to sustain us as the years tick by. But in the case of Jeff Buckley, just one singular studio album, *Grace*, was released during his life. The night before he was to begin working on his follow-up, *My Sweetheart the Drunk*, he drowned in the Mississippi River in Memphis, Tennessee. He was thirty. Unlike his father (folk singer Tim Buckley, who died of a heroin overdose), Jeff Buckley's death was ruled accidental. No drugs were found in his system. It was a tragic end to a mysterious and charismatic artist, whose success with the *Grace* album came years after he passed away.

Grace followed the stage-setting four-song EP *Live at Sin-E*, which sampled the breadth of the California-born Buckley's musical scope during residencies at the New York club that gave the set its name. Under the direction of producer Andy Wallace, Buckley assembled seven original songs and three covers. His soaring four-octave vocal range (sounding eerily like his father) and uncategorizable musical approach were lauded by critics, but *Grace* struggled to make a commercial mark. Buckley's haunting rendition of **Hallelujah** would become the definitive version of Leonard Cohen's masterpiece and Buckley's signature track; eleven years after his death, it took No. 1 on the Billboard Digital Songs chart and was later added to the Library of Congress's National Recording Registry.

Grace is not an immediate experience, but after repeated listens, it seeps into your psyche with songs such as **So Real**, **Last Goodbye**, and **Lover, You Should've Come Over**. And each listen undoubtedly prompts the question, "What kind of music would this extraordinary artist be creating today?" *–AD*

Dave Alvin
KING OF CALIFORNIA

HIGHTONE | Producer: Greg Leisz

RELEASED: MAY 1, 1994

● With the rootsy *King of California*, Dave Alvin found his voice. He had been touring solo or with just a couple of side musicians, forcing him to rethink his material. The result mostly features stripped-down versions of songs by the Blasters (**Little Honey**, **Border Radio**, and **Barn Burning**) and X (**Fourth of July**), songs from his earlier solo albums (**Every Night About This Time**), plus some new songs (including the terrific title track) and covers. Alvin's guitar work is as fine as ever, but his singing is the real story. "It's not that I've become Pavarotti," he said, "but at least I know now what to do with my voice." *–DD*

The Bottle Rockets
THE BROOKLYN SIDE

EAST SIDE DIGITAL | Producer: Eric "Roscoe" Ambel

RELEASED: NOVEMBER 1994

● Bottle Rockets (BoRox) frontman Brian Henneman should have been our go-to explainer of the rural American underclass rather than, say, J. D. Vance. He did it more honestly and a generation sooner. Hailing from the fringes of the St. Louis exurbs, the BoRox understood the adrenaline rush of the big city but offered both genuine insight and sharp-witted criticism of twang talkers, trailer mamas, and NASCAR obsessives. **Welfare Music** is perhaps alt-country's most knowing political anthem and **Sunday Sports** one of its most explosive rockers, while **1000 Dollar Car** is simply solid automotive advice. These guys knew their way around a love song (**I'll Be Comin' Around** and **Pot of Gold**), too. *–DD*

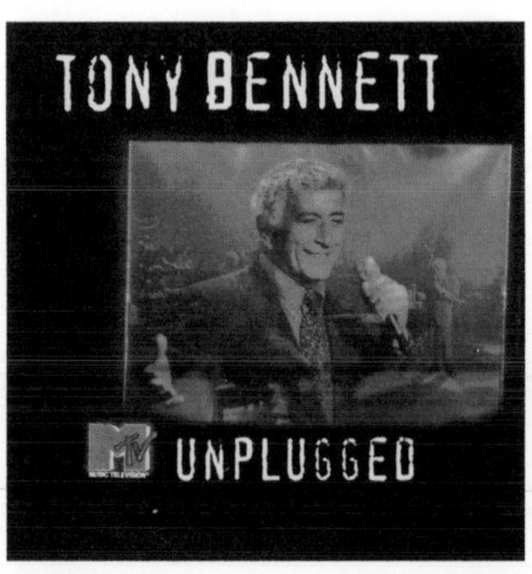

Tony Bennett
MTV UNPLUGGED

COLUMBIA | Producers: David Kahne, Danny Bennett

RELEASED: JUNE 28, 1994

● By the 1990s, Tony Bennett's son Danny had become his manager and hatched a plan to introduce his father to a generation unfamiliar with him, culminating with an appearance on *MTV Unplugged*. Backed by the Ralph Sharon Trio, Bennett, still in excellent voice and performing with renewed vigor, ran through classics of the Great American Songbook as well as his signature song, **I Left My Heart in San Francisco**. Younger fans/acolytes k. d. lang and Elvis Costello also stopped by to further solidify Bennett's hip bona fides. It worked; the album went platinum and won Grammys for Album of the Year and Best Traditional Pop Vocal Performance. *–DD*

Various Artists

CLERKS (MUSIC FROM THE MOTION PICTURE)

CHAOS/COLUMBIA | Producers: Various

RELEASED: OCTOBER 11, 1994

● Kevin Smith's comedy about Gen X slackers working retail and hating every minute of it comes with a soundtrack that was likely more expensive than the film's $27,575 budget. Miramax put money behind mostly indie and post-hardcore needle drops (The Jesus Lizard, Girls Against Boys, Bash & Pop [post-Replacements Tommy Stinson], Bad Religion), with a few major-label acts such as Alice in Chains and Soul Asylum. Two tracks by Smith's friends from New Jersey, Love Among Freaks, were enjoyable fun, as was the film dialogue peppered between the tracks throughout the disc, including the indelible "I'm not even supposed to be here today!" *–RSM*

Tori Amos

UNDER THE PINK

ATLANTIC | Producers: Tori Amos, Eric Rosse

RELEASED: JANUARY 31, 1994

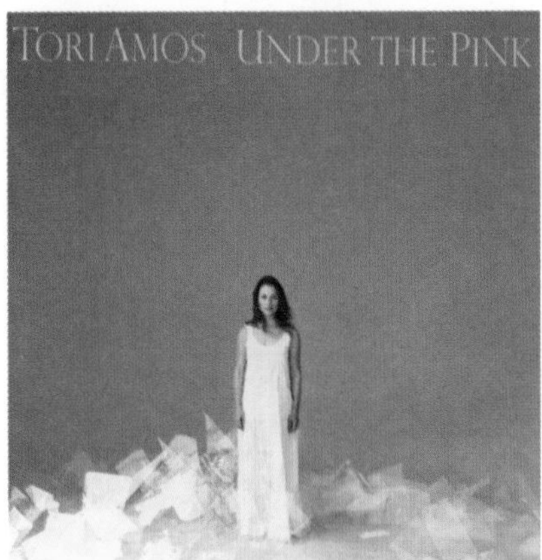

● Tori Amos's 1992 solo debut, *Little Earthquakes*, was such a seismic arrival that it was hard to imagine what the piano-playing singer/songwriter would do next. With *Under the Pink* Amos showed there was more where that came from. The double-platinum, twelve-song set was even more adventurous and ambitious than its predecessor, building on the idiosyncrasies that already fascinated fans while also maintaining an engrossing if sometimes skewed melodicism that was more than just gratuitously quirky, including the poppy **Cornflake Girl** and **God**, an eyebrow-raising chronicle of grievances against a higher power. *–GG*

The Future Sound of London

LIFEFORMS

VIRGIN | Producer: The Future Sound of London

RELEASED: MAY 23, 1994

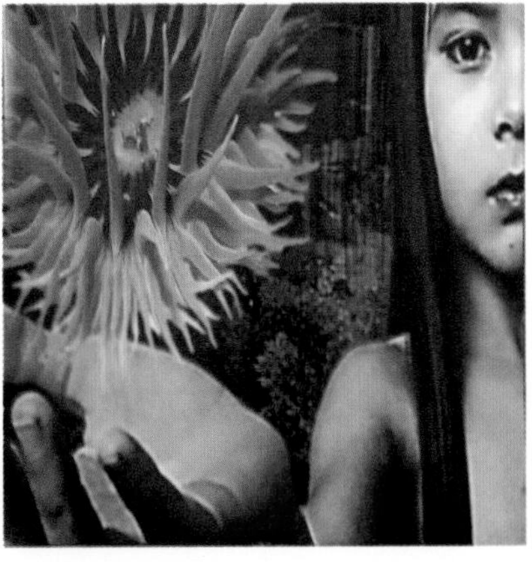

● Just as *Sgt. Pepper's Lonely Hearts Club Band* showed pop music could be a richly rewarding listening experience, *Lifeforms* demonstrated that techno could be engrossing without an emphasis on the beat. Garry Cobain and Brian Dougans were given carte blanche after their 1991 debut, *Papua New Guinea*, became a club smash. The result was *Lifeforms*, on which the duo wove a trippy aural tapestry using varied strains of electronica, from down-tempo to ambient. **Cascade** and the title track became hits in their own rights, while the album proved that techno could exist independently of the dancefloor. *–CS*

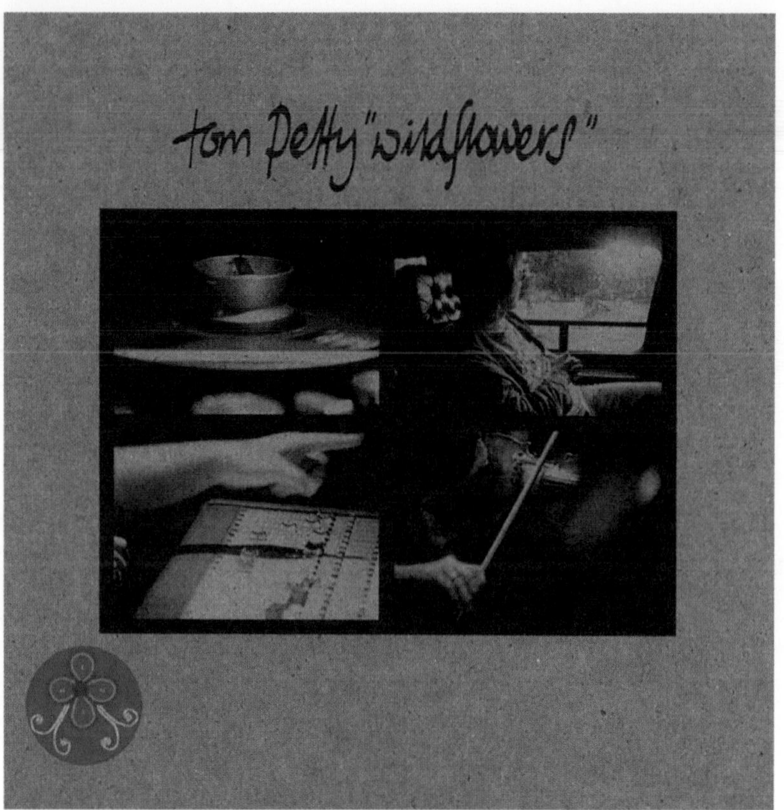

1994

Tom Petty

WILDFLOWERS

WARNER BROS. | Producers: Rick Rubin, Tom Petty, Mike Campbell

RELEASED: NOVEMBER 1, 1994

● Tom Petty stepped outside of the Heartbreakers to make a solo album with 1989's *Full Moon Fever* and, in the process, scored one of the most successful albums of his career. He repeated that feat five years later with *Wildflowers*, a fifteen-song collection that shows Petty at the peak of his songwriting powers.

The album's enduring legacy—some justifiably consider it Petty's all-time best—owes much to the diversity of the songs. It was originally conceived as a double album, but by winnowing it to a single disc (albeit a CD-size sixty-three minutes, the remainder of which would surface on a 2021 box set), it displayed a range of winsome acoustic ballads, up-tempo rockers, moody diversions, and points in between. The title track and album opener, for instance, is classic Petty, strumming an acoustic guitar and perhaps telegraphing his own emotions as he declares, "You belong somewhere you feel free." The rocking **You Wreck Me**, one of two tracks co-written with Heartbreakers guitarist and *Wildflowers* co-producer Mike Campbell, became a concert staple for the band, as did the single **You Don't Know How It Feels**, which raised eyebrows with the controversial (for 1994, at least) chorus line about rolling another joint. The dueling finger-picked acoustic guitars on **Don't Fade on Me** showcase how instinctually synced Petty and Campbell were musically. **It's Good to Be King**, meanwhile, features excellent keyboard work from the Heartbreakers' Benmont Tench, and the album-closing **Wake Up Time** offers a rare moment of Petty on piano.

All of the Heartbreakers play on the album, along with an assortment of guests, including Ringo Starr and the Beach Boys' Carl Wilson, but *Wildflowers* is unquestionably one man's deep and heartfelt expression, rendered with an exquisite sincerity that holds its own alongside any of the legendary singer/songwriter classics that came before it. *—ST*

1994

Portishead

DUMMY

GO! BEAT/LONDON | Producers: Portishead, Adrian Utley

RELEASED: AUGUST 22, 1994

● By 1994, trip-hop was well-established, thanks to acts such as Wild Bunch, Massive Attack, Neneh Cherry, and even Björk. But nobody did it quite like (or with as much impact as) Portishead on its debut.

Hailing from Bristol, England, the trio of Beth Gibbons, Geoff Barrow, and Adrian Utley formed during recording for Cherry's second album, *Homebrew*, in 1992 and forged its own kind of soundscape, incorporating scratching, looping, sampling, and other techniques (engineer Dave McDonald, sometimes thought of as Portishead's fourth member, is even credited with nose flute on **Pedestal**). The experimental collisions brought together hip-hop, jazz, and bluesy melancholy, along with elements of dub, ambient, and cinematic scores, all topped by Gibbons's languid vocals. The arsenal of samples included songs by Isaac Hayes, Weather Report, War, and Lalo Schifrin, among others. Britain's *Select* magazine nailed it when it described *Dummy* as "lounge music for arty schizos." The companion remix set *Glory Times* in 1995, which also included the theme from Portishead's short film *To Kill a Dead Man*, displayed how flexible and open-ended *Dummy*'s songs were.

Universally acclaimed, *Dummy* was arguably the easiest and most captivating front-to-back listen of any trip-hop album—ever. It topped the UK Dance and R&B Albums charts with two singles, **Sour Times** and **Glory Box**, hitting the Top 20; the former even made it to No. 53 on the Billboard Hot 100 in the US, where *Dummy* was certified gold. Most importantly, *Dummy* won the coveted Mercury Music Prize in 1995. But the trip-hop label became something of an albatross for Portishead. In the wake of *Dummy*'s success, the group distanced itself from the descriptor, although not the music, as its self-titled 1997 follow-up stayed in the same lane. And why not, since it's one Portishead paved so well? *—GG*

Eagles

HELL FREEZES OVER

EAGLES RECORDING COMPANY/GEFFEN
Producers: Eagles, Elliot Scheiner, Rob Jacobs, Stan Lynch

RELEASED: NOVEMBER 8, 1994

● With a title inspired by Don Henley's prediction about what it would take for Eagles to get back together amid their nearly fifteen-year breakup, this live/studio hybrid may not have made hell actually freeze over, but it made the band a hotter commodity than ever. The quintet was reunited by a 1993 tribute album, *Common Thread: The Songs of the Eagles*, and a video for Travis Tritt's version of "Take It Easy" that featured the group members. Everybody kissed and made up, or close enough to work together again, resulting in the first brand-new Eagles songs since *The Long Run* in 1979.

Most of *Hell Freezes Over* hailed from the reunion's launch, a pair of April 1994 live performances at Warner Burbank Studios that were filmed and recorded and particularly highlighted by a new Flamenco-style acoustic guitar intro Don Felder created for the set's acoustic take of **Hotel California**. The vocal harmonies sounded a bit weathered, but not in an unpleasant way, while everyone's instrumental chops were intact. And though the song selection had plenty of hits, it also dug deep for a few nicely rendered surprises, such as Joe Walsh's **Pretty Maids All in a Row** from *Hotel California* and Henley's solo track **New York Minute**.

The new material may not have ranked with Eagles' formidable arsenal of greatest hits, but it did show the band still had gas in the creative tank. **Get Over It** was a solid Henley–Glenn Frey rocker, while Timothy B. Schmit's honey-sweet **Love Will Keep Us Alive** (by outside writers including Paul Carrack and Traffic's Jim Capaldi) was Adult Contemporary gold.

Hell . . . led to a full-blown tour that was heaven for fans and the band members' coffers, and Eagles have remained in flight ever since. **–GG**

Nas

ILLMATIC

COLUMBIA | Producers: DJ Premiere, Faith N, Large Professor, L.E.S., Nas, Pete Rock, Q-Tip

RELEASED: APRIL 19, 1994

● Exceeding or even meeting the hype of expectation is a tricky thing. For Nas, the hype started in 1991 at the age of seventeen with a showcase introduction on Main Source's *Live at The Barbeque*. It took Nasty Nas three years to follow that up, but it was worth the wait. *Illmatic* was a smash debut, helping to set a new tone for East Coast hip-hop.

When *Illmatic* dropped, Nas was a seasoned twenty-year-old. During the album's forty minutes—compact by CD-age standards—he painted vivid pictures of what it was like to come up in New York's Queensbridge neighborhood. The city serves as a vivid backdrop for a violent romp through the drug game in **New York State of Mind**, with its legendary beat by Gang Starr DJ Premiere. With A Tribe Called Quest's Q-Tip also helping produce, *Illmatic* drew a line back to that group's style of alternative rap, particularly on **One Love**, a spoken-word letter from Nas to his friends in prison. Throughout *Illmatic*, Nas vaults himself into the conversation about rap's most articulate and lyrical poets, drawing comparisons to legends such as Tupac Shakur. His rhymes and rhythms expand what we think of as rap music, exploring new directions and stylistic terrains.

The accolades for *Illmatic* are as innumerable as they are deserved. It was certified double platinum and logged spots at No. 12 on the Billboard 200 and No. 2 on the Top R&B/Hip-Hop Albums chart. In 2020, *Illmatic* was added to the Library of Congress's National Recording Registry, where it was described as "one of rap's most vital pieces of work."

In the aforementioned **New York State of Mind**, Nas boasts "I never sleep, 'cause sleep is the cousin of death." He was on to something because *Illmatic* has had the eyes of hip-hop fans wide open for decades. *–ZC*

Jann Arden
LIVING UNDER JUNE

A & M | Producers: Jann Arden, Ed Cherney

RELEASED: JUNE 1994

● "Could I be your girl?" With that question, Jann Arden politely found her way into the corps of strong, female artists making noteworthy music amid the grunge-laden rock music scene of the '90s. *Living Under June*, Arden's second studio album, showcased the Canadian artist's introspective singing and songwriting, touching on universal feelings of love, loss, loneliness, and self-discovery. The second single **Insensitive** reached No. 12 on the Billboard Hot 100, and **Unloved** was a duet with Jackson Browne. The album remains a musical benchmark for taking a soul-searching journey, then boldly expressing the raw emotions felt along the way. *—SS*

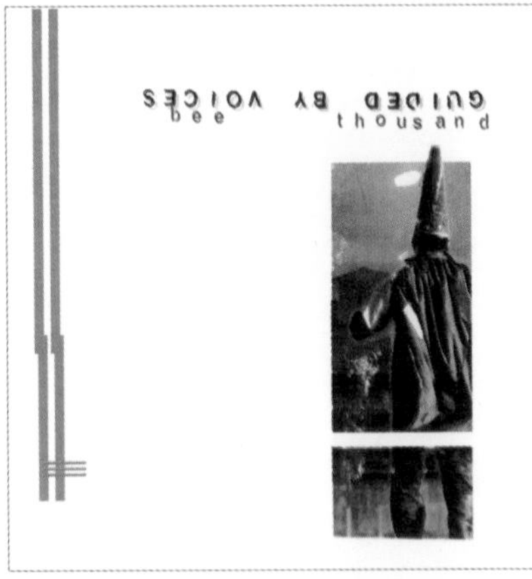

Guided by Voices
BEE THOUSAND

SCAT | Producer: Unlisted

RELEASED: JUNE 21, 1994

● Guided by Voices' (GBV) discography stretches to dozens of records beginning with its mid-'80s formation, so finding the one recorded work that best represents the band's ragtag but charming brand of lo-fi indie rock can be daunting. *Bee Thousand*, GBV's seventh album, was the Dayton, Ohio, group at its most scrappy and enigmatic. Robert Pollard led the most durable lineup of GBV through a twenty-song, thirty-six-minute whirlwind of demos, basement sketches, and literate garage rockers that ranged from Beatlesque pop to half-formed punk fragments. The result? A genre-defining LP and a national deal with Matador Records. *—MG*

Alice Cooper
THE LAST TEMPTATION

EPIC | Producers: Don Fleming, Duane Baron, John Purdell, Andy Wallace

RELEASED: JULY 12, 1994

● After regaining some commercial punch with his *Trash* and *Hey Stoopid* albums, the king of shock rock found something even more shocking: the real world. *The Last Temptation*, his thirteenth "solo" set, is a potent and hard-rocking commentary about a landscape even more dire than any of the macabre fantasies the evil Alice character had conjured (try not to have your heart absolutely shattered by the sentiments expressed in **Lost in America**). *The Last Temptation* was the start of a trilogy and a comic book series, an artistic high point if not the best-selling entry in Cooper's lengthy career. *—GG*

Various Artists

THE CROW (ORIGINAL MOTION PICTURE SOUNDTRACK)

ATLANTIC | Producers: Various

RELEASED: MARCH 29, 1994

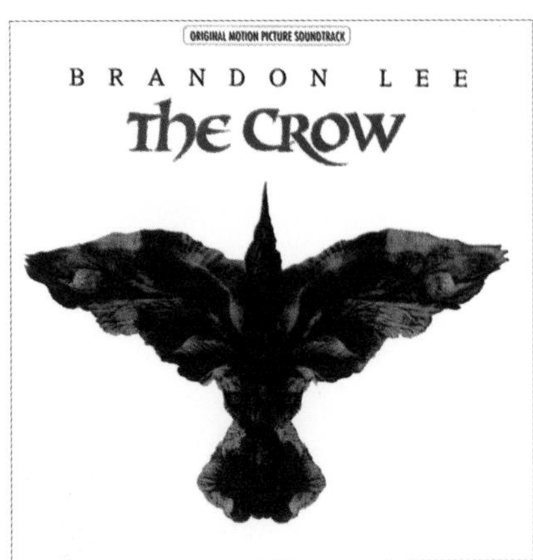

● It's impossible to tell the story of Eric Craven, the main character in *The Crow*, without a soundtrack as dark as the titular corvid. This collection of songs demanded to be heard in full without interruption. The opening strains of The Cure's **Burn** slithered into your ear and transported you to Devil's Night in the fictional version of Detroit created by graphic novelist James O'Barr. Through covers from Nine Inch Nails (Joy Division's **Dead Souls**), Pantera (Poison Idea's **The Badge**), and Rollins Band (Suicide's **Ghost Rider**), the darkness did not end until **It Can't Rain All the Time**, when Jane Siberry promised, "Your tears won't fall forever." *–RW*

Autechre

AMBER

WARP | Producer: Autechre

RELEASED: NOVEMBER 7, 1994

● Autechre had few off-world rhythm rivals when the duo's second full-length was released by powerhouse UK indie label Warp. The longtime production duo of Sean Booth and Rob Brown fueled an underground electronic music blueprint with their influential synthetic, raw, and submerged programming, and with their mixing finesse. On tracks such as **Foil**, **Yulquen**, and **Montrea**, Autechre channeled a sci-fi soundtrack that expertly slipped volume, repetition, and ambience between the notes. *Amber* both punished with percussion and calmed the senses, letting us inhale and exhale without knowing what waited, or lay around the corner. *–CW*

Various Artists

NATURAL BORN KILLERS (A SOUNDTRACK FOR AN OLIVER STONE FILM)

NOTHING/INTERSCOPE/ATLANTIC | Producer: Trent Reznor

RELEASED: AUGUST 23, 1994

● When director Oliver Stone decided Quentin Tarantino's script about young serial killers in love and on the (very violent) run was the perfect way to vivisect America's societal heart of darkness, he called upon Nine Inch Nails' (NIN) Trent Reznor to assist him with musical direction. Using the film's cut-up style, Reznor brought in a new NIN track (**Burn**) along with needle drops ranging from Bob Dylan and Patti Smith to L7 and Nusrat Fateh Ali Khan to Dr. Dre and Leonard Cohen, all stitched together with dialogue. Not a traditional soundtrack album, it's more like an arresting seventy-five-minute radio drama. *–RSM*

1994

Beastie Boys

ILL COMMUNICATION

GRAND ROYAL/CAPITOL | Producers: Beastie Boys, Mario Caldato Jr.

RELEASED: MAY 31, 1994

● After dramatically changing up the sound on each of its first three albums—smashing together spare 808 drumbeats and Led Zeppelin guitar riffs on 1986's *Licensed to Ill*, creating the *Sgt. Pepper's* of rap with the densely layered samples of 1989's *Paul's Boutique*, and playing their own instruments on 1992's *Check Your Head*—the Beastie Boys aimed for refinement rather than reinvention on *Ill Communication*.

Don't get that twisted—this is far from a retread. *Ill Communication* found Ad-Rock, MCA, and Mike D experimenting more boldly than ever before, blending influences from a wider array of genres and making sure their own contributions were always the most important part of the formula.

The lead single, **Sabotage**, just might be the Beastie Boys' masterpiece, pairing punkish fuzz bass with funk guitar, dramatic drum breaks, and turntable scratches to create something that was both completely new and also instantly "favorite couch" familiar. (It's hard to talk about the Beastie Boys' music without also mentioning the trio's highly curated accompanying visual elements, and the Spike Jonze–directed, '70s cop show–parodying video for **Sabotage** ranks among their greatest achievements in this field.)

While the funk and jazz instrumentals on the back half of the album were hit-and-miss, the group's hip-hop powers remained fully intact. Each time Keith Richards starts going on (and on) about how he and Ronnie Wood practice "the ancient art of weaving" with their guitars, it would be nice to tie him to a chair and make him listen to the way the Beastie Boys took turns going solo, teaming up in different combinations and finishing each other's sentences on the dazzling, Jimmy Smith–sampling **Root Down** and then see if he still really thinks that rap is just people yelling at him and telling him it's music. *–MW*

OutKast

SOUTHERNPLAY-ALISTICADILLAC-MUZIK

ARISTA LAFACE | Producer: Organized Noize

RELEASED: APRIL 26, 1994

● "The South got something to say." That's what Andre 3000 told the audience at 1995's Source Awards as his Atlanta duo, OutKast, accepted the award for New Artist of the Year. It was booed by the New York crowd uninterested in those Southern pronouncements, but the speech became a clarion call for a new wave of hip-hop artists who weren't from the East or West Coasts but were ready to be heard.

It was OutKast's debut album, the sprawling Southern rap opus *Southernplayalisticadillacmuzik*, that brought André Benjamin and his partner-in-rhyme Antwan "Big Boi" Patton to the stage that night. A peach cobbler of funk grooves, soul rhythms, streetwise rhymes, and Southern slang, the album is a slow ride through the Atlanta neighborhoods of East Point, College Park, Decatur, and da 'Briar, which encompassed OutKast's entire worldview. This was their musical postcard, as vivid as anything that had come from the Bronx or Compton before it.

Player's Ball serves as the introduction into OutKast's universe, with Big Boi and André trading rhymes about a holiday odyssey through their city and with Sleepy Brown, part of production trio Organized Noize, singing the chorus. The song was originally included on LaFace's Christmas album, which accounts for its references to silent nights and spiked eggnog. **Git Up, Git Out** is a motivational anthem about making something of oneself and is one of two tracks on the album featuring fellow Atlantans Goodie Mob, while **Funky Ride** is a blunted near-instrumental with a wailing Prince-like guitar solo that stretches well past the six-minute mark.

OutKast's musical journey would only get deeper, richer, and stranger from here, and it paved the road for an eventual regional takeover of rap. The South, and hip-hop, would never be the same. *—AG*

1994

Massive Attack

PROTECTION

WILD BUNCH/CIRCA | Producers: Massive Attack, Nellee Hooper

RELEASED: SEPTEMBER 26, 1994

● The second album by the English trip-hop collective Massive Attack, formed in 1988, solidified its status as a driving force in the electronic music scene. *Protection* featured founding members Robert "3D" Del Naja, Adrian "Tricky" Thaws, and Grant "Daddy G" Marshall, along with a host of contributing instrumentalists and vocalists. Although labeled an electronic music album, *Protection* defied description by incorporating a range of styles, including R&B on the title track and **Sly**, rap on **Karmacoma** and **Eurochild**, reggae-tinged synth pop on **Spying Glass**, and classical-influenced electronic instruments on **Weather Storm** and **Heat Miser**.

The album was a hit in the UK, reaching two-times platinum status, but a more modest success in the US, peaking at No. 19 on Billboard's Heatseekers chart. *Protection*'s best-selling single was its title track and opening song, which peaked at No. 14 on the UK Singles chart. The song's plush, slow groove and torchy sensuality showcased soulful vocals by Tracey Thorn from the English duo Everything but the Girl, who also penned its lyrics. Thorn also contributed impassioned vocals to the reggae-influenced **Better Things**. **Sly**, featuring vocals by Scottish singer Nicolette over a musical bed of poppy percussion and flowing orchestral synths, was the first single released from the album and charted at No. 24 in the UK, while **Karmacoma** was a minor UK hit with its rollicking percussion, flute-like synthesizers, and rapped vocals by Tricky and 3D.

One of the charms of *Protection* was that no song sounded like the others, and one of its most memorable tracks was the gorgeous instrumental **Weather Storm**, featuring Craig Armstrong's exquisite piano work. *Protection*'s finale, however, was a forgettable live version of the Doors' classic **Light My Fire**, an odd choice that didn't really fit the standard established by the other nine tracks. *–JC*

TEXMEX

Pavement

CROOKED RAIN, CROOKED RAIN

MATADOR | Producer: Pavement

RELEASED: FEBRUARY 14, 1994

● Who says the indie-rock universe can't have diss tracks? In the most infamous verse on this sophomore album from Stockton, California's Pavement, Stephen Malkmus took a direct shot at two of the reigning bands of the day, The Smashing Pumpkins and Stone Temple Pilots, those "elegant bachelors." It's tucked into **Range Life**, a languid country-rock song reminiscent of The Rolling Stones from twenty years prior. Later, on the cacophonous outro track **Fillmore Jive**, Malkmus declared, "See those rockers with their long curly locks?/Good night to the rock 'n' roll era."

If you're going to sling those arrows, even if it's just in character, you'd better back it up, and Pavement did on this staggeringly good self-produced album that had way too much fun effing around with the conventions of indie rock. The quintet sounded positively drunk with excitement in making a grand entrance with the heavy riff and cowbell of **Silence Kid** before noisily twisting the song into knots. New drummer Steve West helped contribute to the ruckus with the Keith Moon clatter he brought to the song and continued to command right into the unhinged **Elevate Me Later**.

Throughout *Crooked Rain, Crooked Rain*, Pavement turned on a dime, taking listeners through punk, jazz, prog, psychedelic, and country, and teetering on the edge of chaos while also delivering flashes of lush, shimmering melody. That's exemplified by the breakout single **Cut Your Hair**, the group's *The Tonight Show with Jay Leno* moment that found Malkmus in top form, declaring, "Songs mean a lot when songs are bought/ And so are you" before screaming, "Attention and fame's a career, career, career!"

Pavement rewrote the indie-rock book on this one—while pissing off a lot of people in the process. ***–SM***

Boyz II Men

MOTOWN | Producers: Dallas Austin, Babyface, Boyz II Men, Tim & Bob, The Characters, Jimmy Jam & Terry Lewis, Brian McKnight, L. A. Reid, Tony Rich

RELEASED: AUGUST 30, 1994

● Talk about star power: Boyz II Men's sophomore album had one hitmaker after another behind it, including Babyface, Rock & Roll Hall of Fame producers Jimmy Jam and Terry Lewis, L. A. Reid, Brian McKnight, and the legendary writer/producer team of Tim Kelley and Bob Robinson—among others. There was no shortage of Grammy Awards and No. 1 hits in the pedigree. To say they knew what to do with the powerful harmonies of this quartet (Nathan Morris, Shawn Stockman, Michael McCary, and Wanya Morris) is an understatement, as *II* showcased those flawless vocals to their fullest potential.

And that potential was already sky-high thanks to the band's first album, *Cooleyhighharmony*, a nine-times platinum smash whose hit "End of the Road" was featured in the *Boomerang* film soundtrack and set a record by spending thirteen weeks at No. 1 on the Billboard 100.

All Boyz II Men did with *II* was top that. Babyface's **I'll Make Love to You** stayed at the top of the Hot 100 for a whopping fourteen weeks. The Boyz then dethroned themselves with the album's second single, **On Bended Knee**, another soulful, harmonic masterpiece. Those led *II*'s variety of delicious flavors, from the doo-wop/rap-blending single **Thank You** to the dance-club sound of **Vibin'**, the passionate **Water Runs Dry**, the romantic **50 Candles**, and the sweet a cappella remake of The Beatles' **Yesterday**.

In addition to giving Boyz II Men its first No. 1 album on the Billboard 200 and twelve-times platinum sales, *II* took home Grammy Awards for Best R&B Album and Best R&B Performance by a Duo or Group (**I'll Make Love to You**). And while the Boyz didn't have nearly the same success after this album, they set the bar higher for any R&B and pop vocal groups that came in its wake. *—EP*

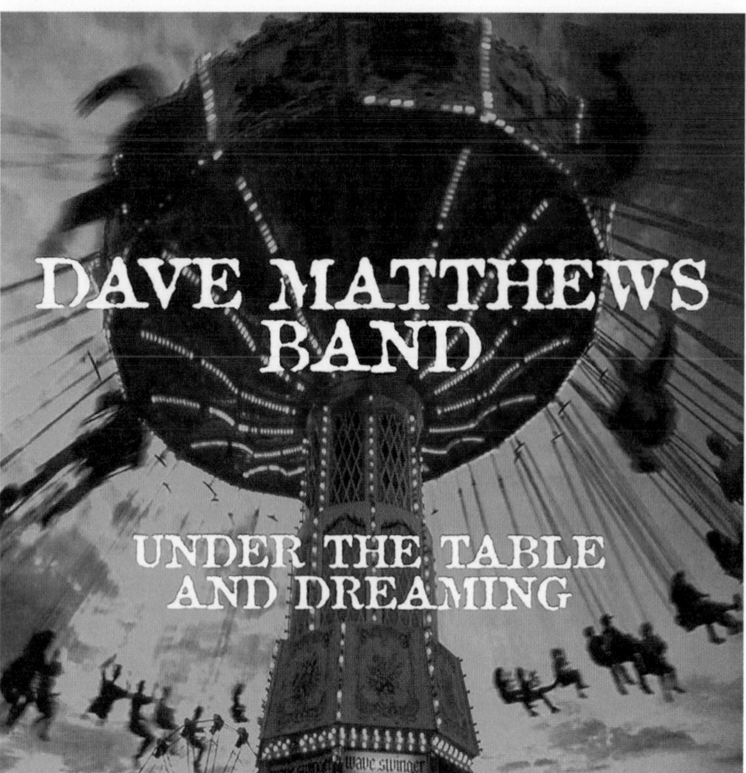

1994

Dave Matthews Band

UNDER THE TABLE AND DREAMING

RCA | Producer: Steve Lillywhite

RELEASED: SEPTEMBER 27, 1994

● Eager for something to dig besides grunge's kill-me-now nihilism and gangsta rap's kill-you-now violence, Phish- and Grateful Dead–loving college kids were ecstatic when the Dave Matthews Band's major-label debut punched their ears with an exuberant blend of Afropop and jazz- and funk-infused rock. The Charlottesville, Virginia–based band's infectious melodies provided the perfect outlet for noodle dancers ready to follow a next-gen Captain Trips, especially one who constructed extraordinarily tight grooves featuring fiddle, saxophone, and no electric guitar—a setup almost unheard of in rock. South African–born Matthews also enticed listeners with metaphor-heavy, stream-of-consciousness lyrical musings that hinted at deep meanings.

What Would You Say, the deceptively bouncy first single, contemplated the ephemeral nature of life and the need to live fully. **Typical Situation** obliquely alluded to apartheid. **Ants Marching** lamented conformity and our tendency to live automaton lives. But Matthews' convoluted phrasing and word combinations, sometimes sounding like nursery rhymes written in a *very* altered state, left vast room for interpretation. He even referred to such states in **Jimi Thing** and **Rhyme & Reason**, the latter a study of addiction, though it would be a mistake to assume he was the junkie. As he sang in **Warehouse**, "You can read in whatever you're needing to."

With Steve Lillywhite's crisp production, the album ebbed and flowed like tides, alternating contemplative moments of gentle resonance with bursts of energy. Delightful twists such as **Warehouse**'s mid-song shift toward Tropicália and the soprano sax-and-fiddle call-and-response in **Ants Marching** (which became the band's most-performed anthem) helped send the album to No. 11 on the Billboard 200 and sextuple platinum sales despite mixed reviews from critics. **What Would You Say**, featuring Blues Traveler's John Popper on harmonica, scored a Grammy nomination for Best Rock Performance and became the catalyst for decades of fan adoration. *–LM*

Various Artists

REALITY BITES (ORIGINAL MOTION PICTURE SOUNDTRACK)

RCA | Producers: Various

RELEASED: FEBRUARY 1, 1994

● Amplifying the era's disaffected-youth zeitgeist with co-star Ethan Hawke's **I'm Nuthin'**, the *Reality Bites* soundtrack also mingled eras by placing World Party's **When You Come Back to Me** (an homage to David Bowie's "Young Americans"), Big Mountain's reggaefied cover of Peter Frampton's **Baby, I Love Your Way**, The Knack's late-'70s power-pop staple **My Sharona**, and Squeeze's '80s pop gem **Tempted** alongside contemporaneous entries from the Posies, Crowded House, Me Phi Me, Julianna Hatfield, and U2. Singer/songwriter Lisa Loeb's impassioned **Stay (I Missed You)** made her the first artist without a recording contract to top the Billboard Hot 100. The soundtrack itself went double platinum. *–LM*

Freedy Johnston

THIS PERFECT WORLD

ELEKTRA | Producer: Butch Vig

RELEASED: JUNE 28, 1994

● Freedy Johnston's major-label debut was a gift that's kept on giving. It felt ostensibly happy (you could dance a jig to **Delores**) until you listened more closely to the songs' forlorn lyrics couched in minor keys. At least half the tracks (including **Bad Reputation**, **Edie's Tears**, and the title track) sounded like they could have been singles. *This Perfect World* found a welcome at the then-prevalent commercial Triple A radio format, at home alongside the likes of Crowded House and Lowen & Navarro. Critics in real time preferred Johnston's prior album *Unlucky*, but song for song, this is the better of the two—and that isn't just talk, talk, talk. *–CB*

Various Artists

KEITH WHITLEY: A TRIBUTE ALBUM

BNA | Producers: Blake Mervis, Randy Scruggs

RELEASED: SEPTEMBER 27, 1994

● Keith Whitley released just two full-length studio albums before his death in 1989 at the age of thirty-four from alcohol poisoning. He was held in high regard by his peers, eleven of whom joined forces for this gold-certified tribute that helped affirm his legend. Alison Krauss and Union Station's rendition of **When You Say Nothing at All** was a breakthrough that gave the band its first Top 10 single. The real hooks here, however, are demo versions of four previously unreleased songs. One of them, **I Just Want You**, was a duet with Lorrie Morgan, with whom Whitley had been nominated for Grammy and Academy of Country Music Awards four years prior. *–GG*

Live
THROWING COPPER

RADIOACTIVE | Producer: Jerry Harrison

RELEASED: APRIL 26, 1994

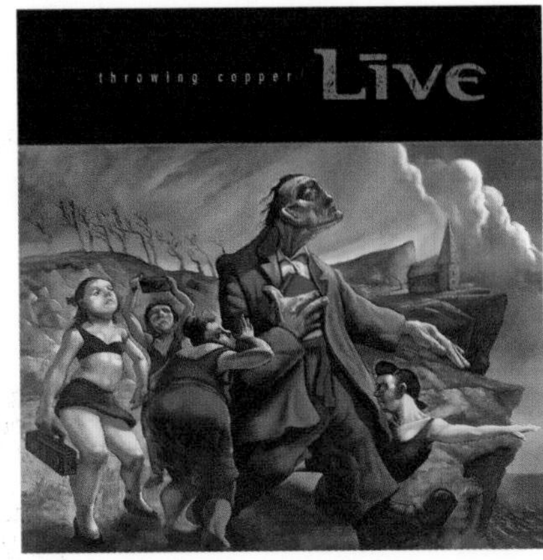

● Live's third studio album was also the band's most popular. Produced by Jerry Harrison of Talking Heads, the combination of rock and grunge gave the album the sound of its time but with a commercial sensibility that would put it at the top of the Billboard 200 with eight-times platinum sales. It launched a parade of hits, including **Selling the Drama** and **Lightning Crashes**, which both hit No. 1 on the Alternative Airplay chart, and **I Alone** and **All Over You**, which were Top 10 hits. Strong tracks such as **The Dam at Otter Creek**, **Top**, and **Waitress**, meanwhile, displayed depth beyond the singles. *–EP*

The Mavericks
WHAT A CRYING SHAME

MCA NASHVILLE | Producer: Don Cook

RELEASED: FEBRUARY 1, 1994

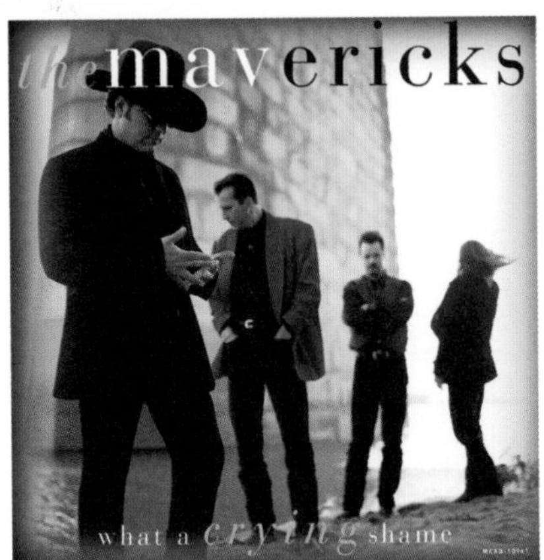

● This album will get the party started. In addition to putting the Mavericks on the map with its largest audience yet, it garnered some well-deserved industry recognition. Raul Malo, with his soaring lead vocals, and the band were in top form, melding their distinctive, border-straddling country sound with touches of Roy Orbison, Elvis Presley, and Johnny Cash—and covering Bruce Springsteen's **All That Heaven Will Allow**. Other standout moments were **There Goes My Heart**, **O What a Thrill**, and the title track—the Mavericks' biggest hits up to that point. It was also the group's first album to chart, reaching No. 6 on the Top Country Albums chart and certified platinum. *–HH*

Reba McEntire
READ MY MIND

MCA NASHVILLE | Producers: Tony Brown, Reba McEntire

RELEASED: APRIL 26, 1994

● Reba McEntire and producer Tony Brown delivered a gem for her nineteenth studio album, which continued a winning stream with triple-platinum sales and a No. 2 position on both the Billboard 200 and Top Country Albums charts. The set showcases all McEntire's vocal and emotional power, evident in its string of Top 5 country hits: **Why Haven't I Heard from You**, **Till You Love Me**, **And Still**, and the No. 1 **The Heart Is a Lonely Hunter**. **She Thinks His Name Is John** was country's first song to address AIDS, which led to some airplay resistance but did not slow the album's momentum. *–TR*

The Notorious B.I.G.

READY TO DIE

BAD BOY | Producers: Sean "Puffy" Combs, Mister Cee, Bluez Brothers, DJ Premier, Easy Mo Bee, Rashad Smith, Lord Finesse, Poke, Darnell Scott, Chucky Thompson

RELEASED: SEPTEMBER 13, 1994

● Christopher Wallace's debut album was notorious and big—not only in commercial terms. *Ready to Die* was nothing less than an artistic and conceptual triumph whose impact is nearly impossible to overstate. It changed the course of hip-hop and music in general and was made all the more powerful by the Notorious B.I.G.'s murder just two and a half years later.

Ready to Die—whose seventeen songs and skits took "Biggie" from birth to a death (fading heartbeat and all, in the closing track **Suicidal Thoughts**)—was a pivotal moment in rap. West Coast gangsta was the genre's dominant force by the early '90s, and Wallace, assisted in no small part by Sean "Puffy" Combs's patronage and production, succeeded in bringing the spotlight back east with his casual but intense flow and vivid storytelling, putting us right inside the drug deals, the homicides, and the sheer grit of his reality. But Biggie really scored by conveying the emotions (and not just the dark ones) that came with all that; keeping it "real" was not just a cliché but the real deal on *Ready to Die*. You can even find the lyrics to **Things Done Changed** in *The Norton Anthology of African American Literature*.

There were legal issues with several of the samples Combs employed, but nothing could diminish the achievement of Biggie's performance and pen. *Ready to Die* peaked at No. 3 on Billboard's Hot R&B/Hip-Hop Albums chart and was certified six-times platinum, while **Big Poppa**, a six-million-selling No. 1 hit on the Rap chart, was nominated for a Best Rap Solo Performance at the 1996 Grammy Awards. You'll also find it, deservedly, on myriad lists of best albums of all time, rap or otherwise. *—GG*

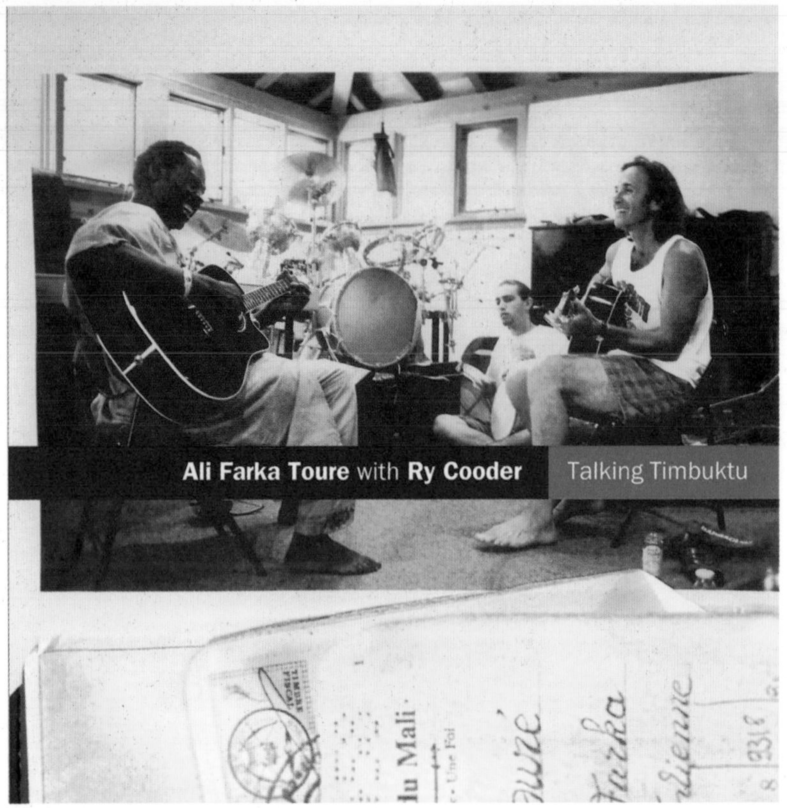

1994

Ali Farka Touré and Ry Cooder

TALKING TIMBUKTU

WORLD CIRCUIT/HANNIBAL | Producer: Ry Cooder

RELEASED: MARCH 1994

● For an album that presented as a potentially complicated collaboration—American roots guitarist Ry Cooder and Malian guitarist Ali Farka Touré getting together to find some kind of musical middle ground—*Talking Timbuktu*'s origin story was remarkably simple. "My friend Nick Gold at the record company said, 'You wanna do this?'" Cooder recalled. "I said, 'Sure.' I had a vague idea of who Ali Farka was. He played some interesting guitar, and Nick said, 'Make a record together,' so we did. It took three days. It was interesting and fun."

Touré was performing in the States, and Cooder joined in on a couple of dates before they went into the studio. Both played a host of stringed instruments while the multilingual Touré sang in Songhai, Bambara, Peul, and Tamasheck. The material ranged from love songs to others espousing hard work, evoking a river spirit, protesting military recruitment, and so on. The music was a sublime combination of Touré's arid, hypnotic desert blues and Cooder's brilliant instrumental interjections, perhaps best displayed on the closing track, **Diaraby**.

Both before and after *Talking Timbuktu*, Cooder recorded other hands-across-the-water projects with V. M. Bhatt, Manuel Galbán, and more (most famously, of course, with the Buena Vista Social Club). His theory of how to approach those projects was simple: "Make something happen," he said. "Musicians play together and the way the mind works is, 'Let's seek something together.' Not to replicate or copy or just keep repeating the past, but to make something interesting out of it. Otherwise, we'd just be a bunch of uncles singing the same song over and over again." *–DD*

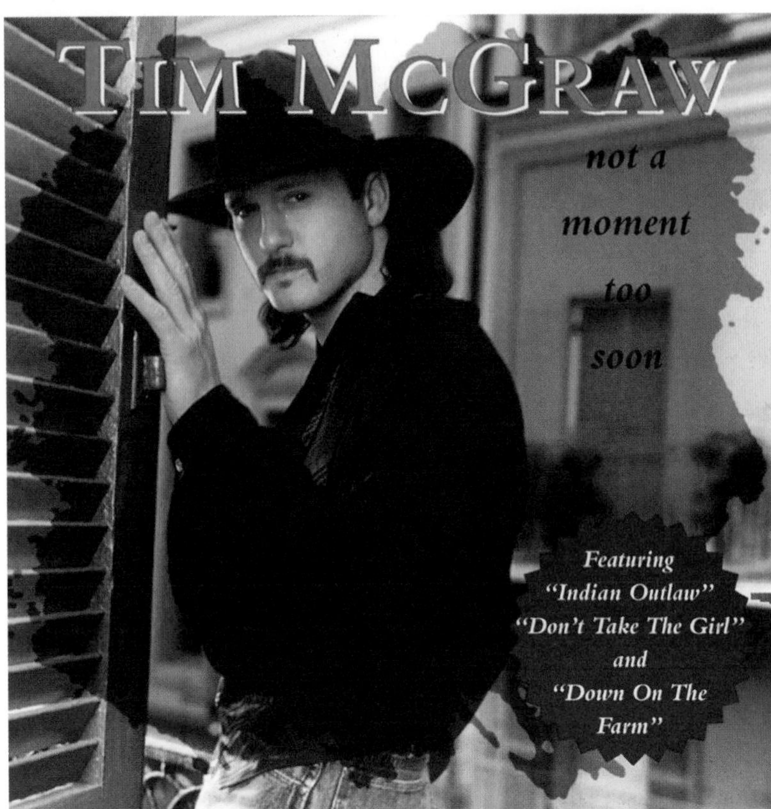

Tim McGraw

NOT A MOMENT TOO SOON

CURB | Producers: Byron Gallimore, James Stroud

RELEASED: MARCH 22, 1994

● Tim McGraw has released a full discography of albums, but it's his second effort, *Not a Moment Too Soon*, that stands as his top-selling studio album to date at six-times platinum—equaled only by his first *Greatest Hits* compilation six years later. *Not a Moment Too Soon* topped both the Billboard 200 and the Top Country Albums charts, spending twenty-six weeks in a row at No. 1 on the latter on its way to status as the best-selling country album of 1994. It also launched five Top 10 country hits, including two No. 1's: the title track and **Don't Take the Girl**.

Its reign started on a controversial note, however. The first single, **Indian Outlaw**, was McGraw's first chart hit (Nos. 15 and 8 on the Billboard Hot 100 and Hot Country charts, respectively), but some from the Native American community and its supporters found the lyrics offensive, leading to some radio stations refusing to play the song. The success of **Don't Take the Girl** redeemed him, however, followed by **Down on the Farm**, **Not a Moment Too Soon**, and **Refried Dreams** into early 1994.

Not a Moment Too Soon was named Album of the Year at the 1994 Academy of Country Music Awards, where McGraw also took home Top New Male Vocalist honors. In addition, it was the Top New Country Album for Billboard, and the Billboard Awards named McGraw Top New Country Artist, as did the American Music Awards.

All told, it was an auspicious start from which McGraw has built a superstar career in country music and beyond, including acting turns and collaborations with his wife, Faith Hill. *–MH2*

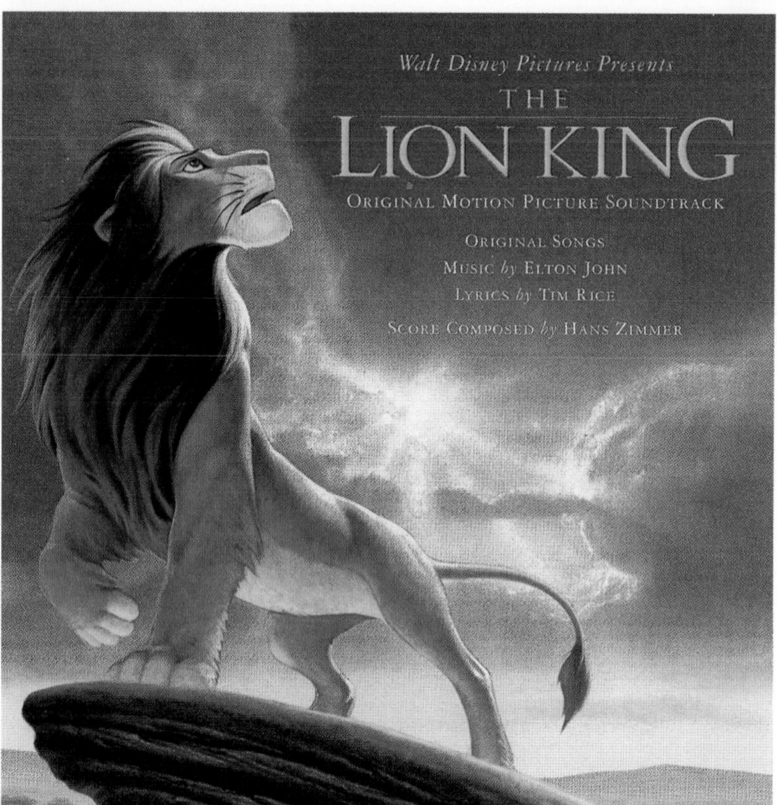

Walt Disney Pictures Presents
THE
LION KING
ORIGINAL MOTION PICTURE SOUNDTRACK
ORIGINAL SONGS
MUSIC by ELTON JOHN
LYRICS by TIM RICE
SCORE COMPOSED by HANS ZIMMER

Various Artists

THE LION KING (ORIGINAL MOTION PICTURE SOUNDTRACK)

WALT DISNEY | Producers: Hans Zimmer, Mark Mancina, Jay Rifkin, Chris Thomas

RELEASED: APRIL 27, 1994

● Disney was on a roll in the early '90s. *The Little Mermaid*, *Beauty and the Beast*, and *Aladdin* reestablished the studio as king of animated features at the box office and in merchandising. The soundtracks for all three did well, too, but *The Lion King* took things to another level.

Tim Rice, a lyricist best known for his work with Andrew Lloyd Webber, had worked on *Aladdin* and was brought back for *The Lion King*, although he insisted on recruiting his own musical partner this time. Neither new Disney mainstay Alan Menken nor ABBA's Benny Andersson were available, so Rice reached out to Elton John, who gladly accepted. They wrote six songs together, five of which made the film, and the results were stellar—both musically and commercially.

The movie-opening **Circle of Life** and the lush **Can You Feel the Love Tonight** locked themselves into the Disney canon almost immediately and became part of John's oeuvre, too. The latter, performed by John, hit No. 4 on the Billboard Hot 100 and was certified platinum; it won the Academy Award for Best Original Song, a Golden Globe for Best Song (Motion Picture), and a Grammy for Best Male Pop Vocal Performance. John's version of **Circle of Life**, meanwhile, made it to No. 18 on the Hot 100 and No. 2 on the Adult Contemporary chart and was also nominated for an Academy Award and a Grammy for Song of the Year. It, too, was certified platinum.

The songs, the movie's huge box office, and John's star power propelled the soundtrack album to No. 1 on the Billboard 200 and a spot as the No. 4 best-selling album of 1994. It's also the only animated film soundtrack to be certified diamond for sales of more than ten million copies. The Mouse, we're sure, was happy this *Lion* roared as loudly as it did. *—GG*

Bush

SIXTEEN STONE

TRAUMA/INTERSCOPE | Producers: Clive Langer, Alan Winstanley, Bush

RELEASED: DECEMBER 6, 1994

● Bush took it unnecessarily on the chin as its debut album paraded to the Top 5 of the Billboard 200 chart and multiplatinum status in the US and in the quartet's native UK. It was the first big hit album of what has been called "post-grunge," and it surfaced eight months after Kurt Cobain's suicide (though it had been recorded a few months prior), which put *Sixteen Stone*'s dark 'n' stormy attack on a pedestal for haters.

In truth, this is a polished and tightly arranged hard rock outing, drawing on some of the same sources as much of the Seattle crowd Bush was accused of aping, and scored an arena-sized following with anthems such as **Everything Zen**, **Comedown**, and **Machinehead**. The unlikely hit **Glycerine**, meanwhile, glistened within its drone-y torpor. Gavin Rossdale—just before his rock 'n' roll power coupledom with No Doubt's Gwen Stefani—was another aching male but one with enough heart to take his gender to task in **Testosterone** and give his rock star compatriots some what-for in **Monkey**. Bush is still with us, to the band's credit, and time has certainly been a friend to *Sixteen Stone*. *—GG*

Beck

MELLOW GOLD

DGC/BONG LOAD | Producers: Beck Hansen, Tom Rothrock, Rob Schnapf, Carl Stephenson

RELEASED: MARCH 1, 1994

● With one throwaway line about his supposedly terrible rapping skills, Beck Hansen created an anthem for the *Reality Bites* generation—even though he'd fought against releasing **Loser**, the DIY-recorded single that launched a major-label bidding war. That funky pastiche of droning slide guitar, sampled drumbeats, and improvised lyrics set the tone for *Mellow Gold*, Beck's big-league bow.

The album's lo-fi mashup of blues, folk, hip-hop, alt-rock, sludge metal, and surrealist, stoner-haze lyrics made Beck a poster child for slackerdom. But his matrilineal links to Andy Warhol's Factory and the Fluxus Movement and his gift for spinning pop culture and beat poetry influences into slyly astute (and tuneful) observations about power, capitalism, consumerism, and environmental destruction placed him among pop's avant-garde hipster innovators. For all their ironic, self-deprecating wit, songs such as **Soul Suckin' Jerk** exposed the vulnerability, longing, frustration, and desperation experienced by many disaffected youths.

In **Blackhole**, Beck even turned unpleasant childhood memories into a beautiful, trance-inducing tone poem. But over the crazy-cool, laid-back groove of **Beercan**, *Mellow Gold*'s other charting single, he expertly rapped what might be the album's ultimate message: "Just shake your boots and let it all get loose." *—LM*

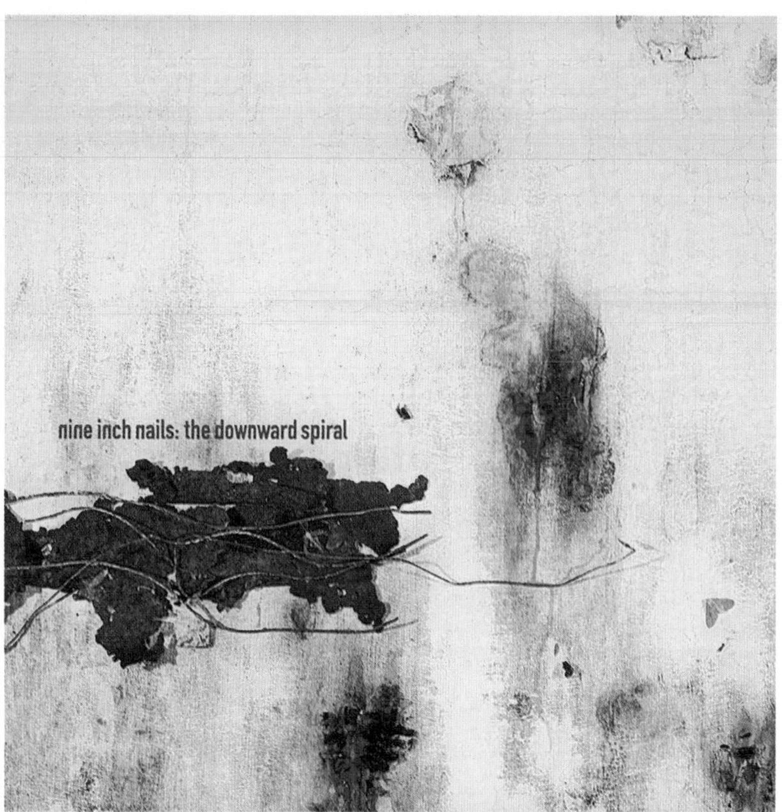

Nine Inch Nails

THE DOWNWARD SPIRAL

NOTHING/INTERSCOPE | Producers: Trent Reznor, Flood

RELEASED: MARCH 8, 1994

● With Nine Inch Nails' 1989 debut album, *Pretty Hate Machine*, Trent Reznor proved that industrial music could have a place in the mainstream if it played by some of pop's old rules. By instilling melody and traditional verse-chorus-verse structures to industrial rattles and clangs, virtual one-man band Reznor had a hit on his hands, eventually selling more than three million copies of an independently released record from a genre that rarely peeked out of the underground.

For Nine Inch Nails' follow-up LP, he aimed bigger. A sixty-five-minute concept album about one man's mental breakdown, *The Downward Spiral* perfectly captured the ethos of the flourishing alt-rock movement of the mid-'90s. Dark, despairing, and filled with loud, aggressive music that wore its bruised heart on its sleeve, the fourteen-track album was a critical work during what was arguably the biggest year for the alt-rock nation. Adding to its legend, the album was recorded in the house where the Manson Family murdered actress Sharon Tate and others during the summer of 1969. The result was an album of harrowing imagery, abrasive sounds, and lyrical themes that encompassed complete hopelessness.

The Downward Spiral, with its unflinching look at depression and suicide, somehow became a commercial juggernaut. It peaked at No. 2, went four-times platinum, and featured a handful of radio hits, including **Closer**, a widely misinterpreted song about self-hate. And then there was **Hurt**, a six-minute track that brought *The Downward Spiral* to its drawn conclusion. The slow-building ballad, whose industrial buzzes underlie an irresistible pop chorus, was covered by Johnny Cash and served as a requiem to his long career. *The Downward Spiral* had that much reach. *–MG*

Blur

PARKLIFE

FOOD | Producers: Stephen Street, Stephen Hague, John Smith, Blur

RELEASED: APRIL 25, 1994

● After becoming disillusioned with American life while touring during the early '90s, Blur frontman Damon Albarn dedicated himself to celebrating English culture. The 1994 masterpiece *Parklife* serves as a whirlwind tour through the history of British pop music, challenging the dour, serious sensibilities of grunge with something much brighter, more upbeat, and certainly no less sophisticated. Together with Oasis's *Definitely Maybe*, released a few months later, *Parklife* came to define the Britpop movement.

The two bands spent much of the '90s feuding with each other, but Oasis's Noel Gallagher couldn't deny that *Parklife*'s lyrics were "like southern England personified." With a title drawn from the country's love of greyhound racing, *Parklife*'s lyrics captured various aspects of British life, from unemployment lines to bank holidays spent at the pub to suburban disillusionment. **Magic America** finds Albarn mocking Brits who want to cross the Atlantic to live in a land of skyscrapers, fast food, shopping malls, and all-day porn channels.

An endlessly listenable record with a timely and perfectly expressed point of view, *Parklife* deservedly became a cultural touchstone in England, remaining on the UK charts for nearly two years and cementing Blur's place as one of its generation's most important bands. *–MW*

Nirvana

MTV UNPLUGGED IN NEW YORK

DGC | Producers: Alex Coletti, Scott Litt, Nirvana

RELEASED: NOVEMBER 1, 1994

● Nirvana was one of the biggest bands on the planet when it performed a set for MTV's popular *Unplugged* series during November 1993. The group had followed its landmark 1991 album *Nevermind* with the raw and uncompromising *In Utero* in 1993. Two months after the second album's release (and its debut at No. 1), Kurt Cobain, Krist Novoselic, Dave Grohl, and touring guitarist Pat Smear performed an hour-long set at New York's Sony Music Studios with help from cellist Lori Goldston and Meat Puppets members Cris and Curt Kirkwood.

Instead of playing the best-known songs from its two hit albums, Nirvana filled its setlist with deep cuts: covers of David Bowie (**The Man Who Sold the World**), the Vaselines (**Jesus Doesn't Want Me for a Sunbeam**), and Lead Belly (**Where Did You Sleep Last Night**), plus three Meat Puppets favorites. It was a revelatory performance, a stripped-down antidote to the blistering abrasion of *In Utero*. The program aired on December 16, 1993; four months later, Cobain died from a self-inflicted gunshot wound. When *MTV Unplugged in New York* arrived as an album in November 1994, it served as a requiem for the late Nirvana leader and a memorial to his legacy. *–MG*

Herbie Hancock

DIS IS DA DRUM

POLYGRAM | Producers: Herbie Hancock, Bill Summers, Mars Lasar

RELEASED: OCTOBER 26, 1994

● Downplaying the spontaneity and newness of his drum loop–based acid jazz, keyboardist Herbie Hancock called out, "This is something we've just been working on." He then fired up a full course of eleven pulsating, danceable tracks fusing drum machines with snippets of repeating melodic phrases and samples and synthesizer washes overlaid with percussion, sound effects, vocals, and jazz improv. His likely objective was to deploy trailblazing studio and technical wizardry to top the jazz-fusion success of his 1973 hit album *Headhunters*.

Dis Is da Drum's title track was a rollicking party jam loaded with generous dabs of funk, rap, and jazzy synth licks constructed from riffs, chords, and melodic lines all swirled with heavy drum and rhythm backbeats. Without a break, it was followed by **Shooz**, a quick percussive blast of sequenced polyrhythms by co-producer Bill Summers and percussionist Moreira. **The Melody (On the Deuce by 44)**, meanwhile, sported heavy hip-hop rapping. Hancock modernized **Butterfly** from the original cushy smooth-jazz version on the 1974 album *Thrust* by contrasting a pulsing Minimoog bass against rippling countermelodies played by flutist Hubert Laws. The funkified beats of **Rubber Soul** and **Bo Ba Be Da** were crowd-pleasers sure to get hips gyrating to their infectious, syncopated grooves. *–CH*

Jimmy Page and Robert Plant

NO QUARTER: JIMMY PAGE & ROBERT PLANT UNLEDDED

ATLANTIC | Producers: Jimmy Page, Robert Plant

RELEASED: OCTOBER 31, 1994

● Two Led Zeppelin reunions had been dissatisfying on many fronts, making the possibility of more seem remote. But when MTV reached out with an idea for one of its *Unplugged* episodes, Jimmy Page and Robert Plant were game. "Forgetting" Zep mate John Paul Jones's phone number, the two reunited for this ambitious troll through the Zep catalog, plus four new songs, accompanied by expanded instrumentation (mandolin, bodhran, hurdy-gurdy, banjo) and an eleven-member ensemble.

The results were revelatory, from Blind Willie Johnson's **Nobody's Fault but Mine**, slowed considerably from the slamming version on *Presence* in 1976, and peaking with an epic **Kashmir** that sounded even more in tune with the Vale of Kashmir than its 1975 original. Both men were clearly comfortable and invigorated by these new sonic surroundings (which weren't completely unplugged, of course), and the new tracks fit well enough to suggest a future was at hand. Page and Plant managed to tour and release a new studio album, 1998's *Walking into Clarksdale*, before pulling the curtain on this chapter. *–GG*

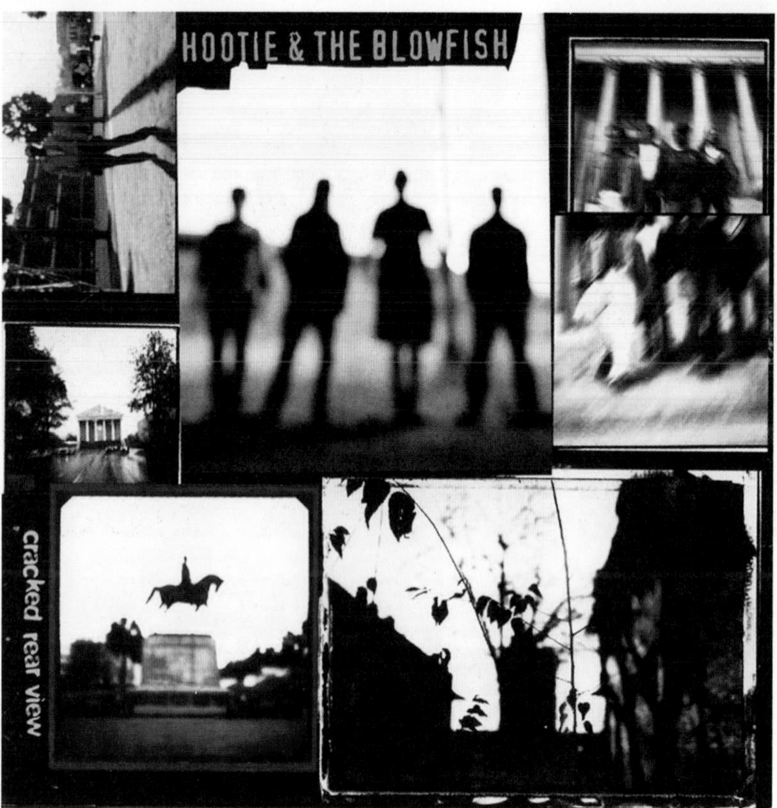

1994

Hootie & the Blowfish

CRACKED REAR VIEW

ATLANTIC | Producer: Don Gehman

RELEASED: JULY 5, 1994

● To say that Hootie & the Blowfish's debut was a success is a gross understatement. Not only did it become the top-selling album in the US in 1995 and earn a Grammy Award for Best New Artist, but at twenty-one-times platinum, it ranks as one of the best-selling albums of all time.

Following the 1993 *Kootchypop* EP, *Cracked Rear View* introduced the polished, melody-rich rock sound of the South Carolina quartet to mainstream music listeners. It was a wildly popular option at a time when the darker grunge sound dominated the rock scene. Produced by Don Gehman, who had previously worked with such established artists as John Mellencamp and R.E.M., *Cracked Rear View* featured eleven original compositions and a shortened version of the traditional spiritual **Sometimes I Feel**.

Cracked Rear View was an instant and ubiquitous hit machine throughout 1994 and 1995 beginning with its first single, **Hold My Hand**, an anthem of positivity that gave the group an immediate Top 10 berth on the Billboard Hot 100. The poignant tune showcased the soulful baritone of Darius Rucker, who, as lead singer and frontman, was often misidentified as Hootie (actually the nickname of one of the band's friends). The song also included background vocals by rock legend David Crosby. It was the first of a string of hits; the second single, **Let Her Cry**, snagged a Grammy for Best Pop Performance by a Duo or Group after reaching No. 2 on Billboard's Pop Songs chart.

Subsequent successes included the uptempo **Only Wanna Be with You**, the dynamic ebb-and-flow track **Time**, and **Drowning**, which peaked at No. 21 on Billboard's Mainstream Rock Tracks listing. All of that kept Hootie & the Blowfish front and center well into 1995 and made *Cracked Rear View* a veritable greatest hits album. *–JC*

1995
HOOTIE

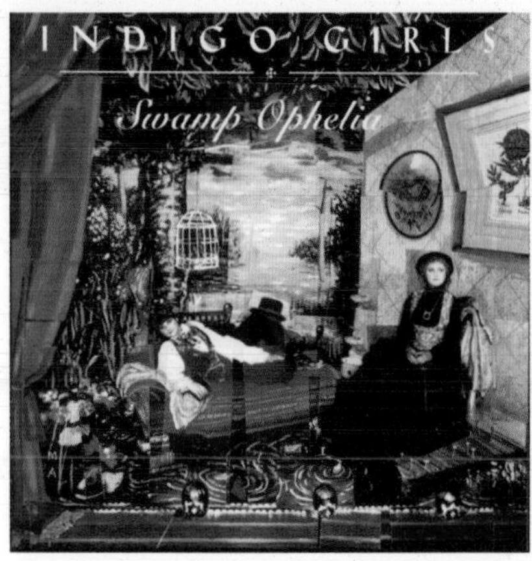

Indigo Girls
SWAMP OPHELIA

EPIC | Producers: Peter Collins, Indigo Girls

RELEASED: MAY 10, 1994

● By the time of their fifth studio album, this Atlanta-based duo had already won a Grammy Award for Best Contemporary Folk Album. *Swamp Ophelia* maintained many of the stylistic hallmarks that catapulted Indigo Girls to fame: intricate harmonies, unique songcraft, and emotionally charged lyrics that evoked the best of forebears like Joan Baez, Joni Mitchell, Bob Dylan, and Paul Simon. All eleven tracks were credited separately to Emily Sailers or Amy Ray. The range was impressive; Sailers's **Power of Two** ranks among Indigo Girls' best love songs, while the duo waltzed its way through **Reunion** and Ray leaned into her rock roots for the album-closing **This Train Revised**. *–ST*

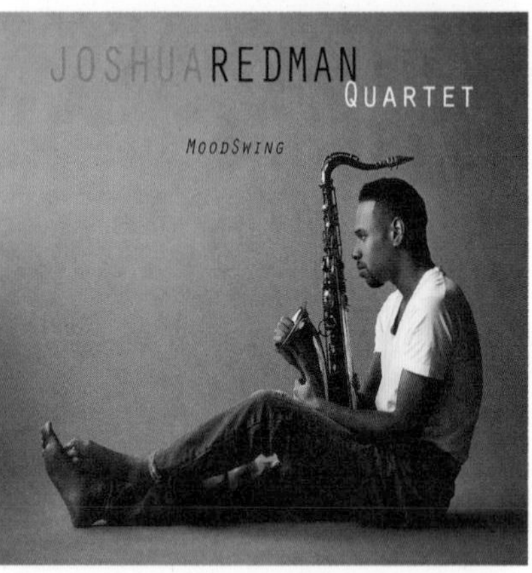

Joshua Redman Quartet
MOODSWING

WARNER BROS. | Producer: Matt Person

RELEASED: SEPTEMBER 13, 1994

● By the time he released *Moodswing*, the twenty-five-year-old son of sax legend Dewey Redman was already soaring with two 1993 recordings (his self-titled debut and *Wish*, with guest guitarist Pat Metheny) boosting his credentials. Joshua Redman penned all eleven tracks for his newly formed quartet, offering an emotional palette of introspective, well-crafted melodies. On **Sweet Sorrow**, his droll sax coos with sultry emotion. On **Chill**, his solos prance catlike. **Alone in the Morning** casts a light samba spell. And the uplifting melody of **Faith** swings, imbued by the fervent, low-register notes from Redman's tenor. *–CH*

Melvins
STONER WITCH

ATLANTIC | Producers: Melvins, GGGarth

RELEASED: OCTOBER 18, 1994

● Of all the Seattle-area bands signed to major labels during the post-Nirvana gold rush, Melvins may have been the most influential and deserving. Naturally, it also probably benefited the least. Still, we got three great records out of the trio's Atlantic Records years, and *Stoner Witch*, home to perhaps the closest thing Buzz Osbourne and Dale Crover have ever had to a hit in **Revolve**, still makes a great jumping-on point for anyone curious about the group. And let's be clear, you should hear *everything* you possibly can from these ever-inventive, constantly evolving hard rock geniuses. *–MW*

Sloan
TWICE REMOVED

GEFFEN | Producer: Jim Rondinelli

RELEASED: AUGUST 30, 1994

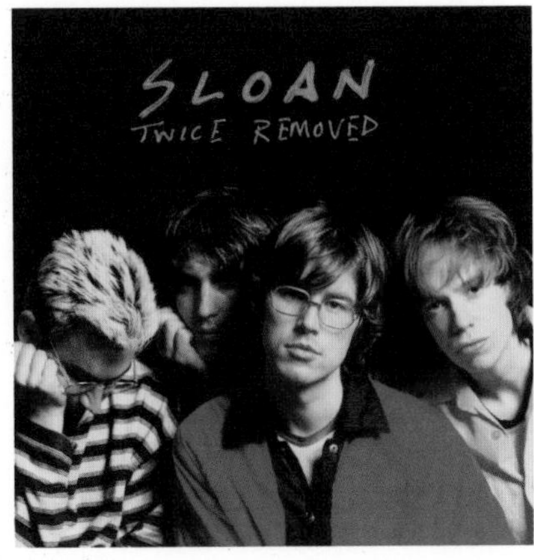

● When Sloan finished *Twice Removed*, Geffen Records asked the Halifax, Nova Scotia, quartet to re-record the album, suggesting that the band return to the grungey flavor of its 1992 debut, *Smeared*. Sloan refused, and the label's response was to pull promotional support, burying what *Spin* magazine declared "One of the Best Albums You Didn't Hear" of 1994. Since each of the band's four members took turns writing and singing the songs, *Twice Removed* served up a broad sampling of styles, from power pop to artsy opus (**Before I Do**), along with great hooks throughout. It's an album that deserves to be heard as the band intended. *–GP*

Ted Hawkins
THE NEXT HUNDRED YEARS

DGC | Producer: Tony Berg

RELEASED: MARCH 29, 1994

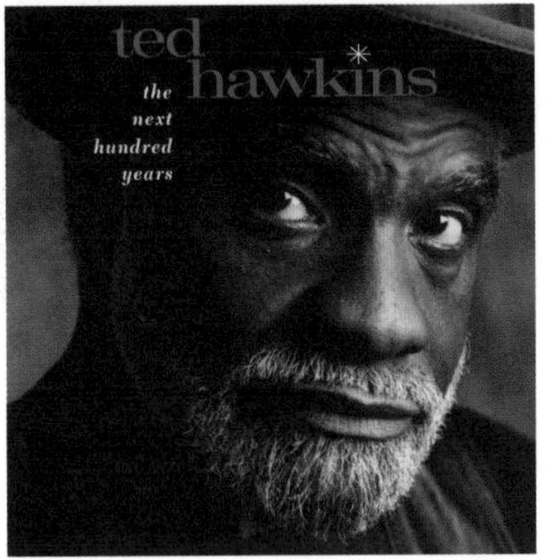

● From street performer on Venice Beach to major-label recording act was a long, hard journey for Ted Hawkins. And the results were simply remarkable. At the age of fifty-seven, Hawkins delivered one of the most authentic, soulful, and bluesy records ever. The Mississippi-born troubadour bared his soul on the album, and the pureness and honesty within its songs reflected his life's journey in a way that engulfed the listener from start to finish. It was as if he knew this would be his swan song; Hawkins passed away within a year of its release, leaving us with a true classic. *–MH*

Sponge
ROTTING PIÑATA

WORK GROUP | Producers: Tim Patalan, Sponge

RELEASED: AUGUST 2, 1994

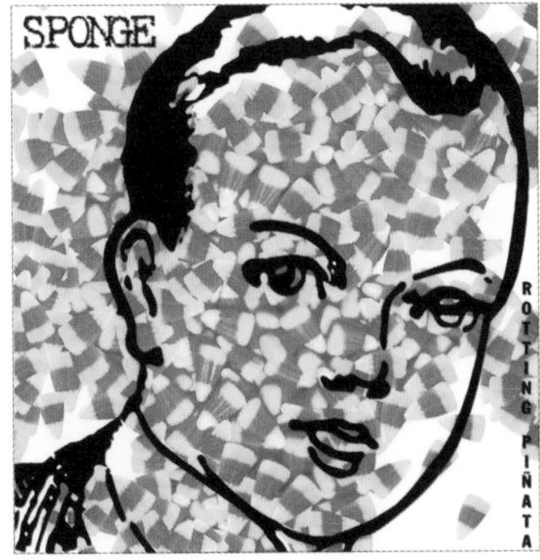

● After the dissolution of Detroit's industrial-flavored Loudhouse, four members decided to continue, moved drummer Vinnie Dombroski up front, and crafted a debut that's quintessential '90s. *Rotting Piñata* checked off lots of alt-rock boxes but distinguished itself from grunge thanks to the direct tie to the proto-punk of Michigan forebears such as the Stooges and MC5. Dombroski's lyrics were intriguingly ambiguous—angsty but not in a snowflakey way. The album produced two Top 5 Modern Rock hits in **Plowed** and **Molly (16 Candles Down the Drain)** and was certified gold. The fact that Sponge still has a healthy touring life speaks to the indelible impact made by *Rotting Piñata*. *–GG*

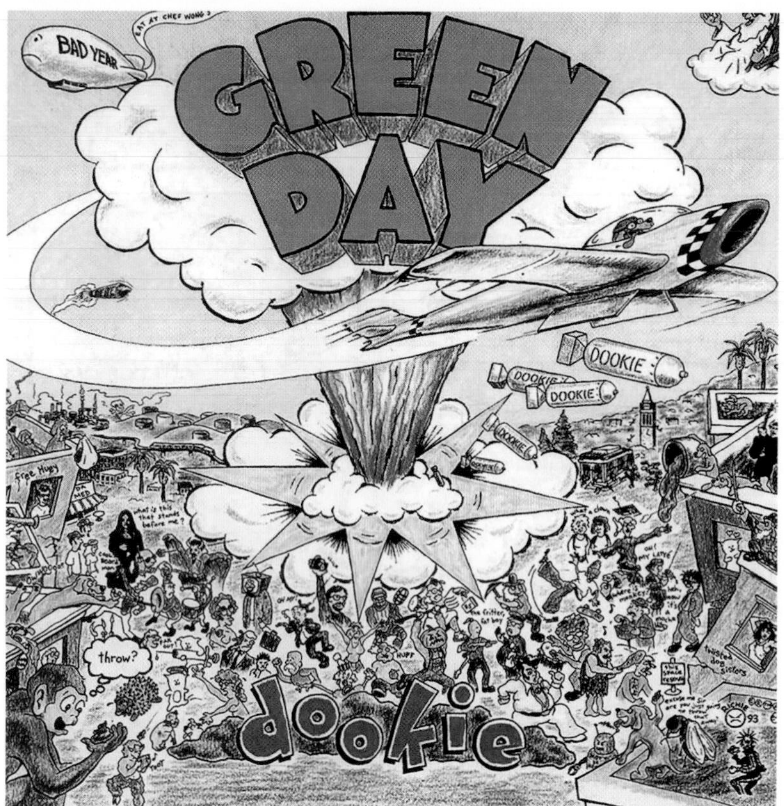

Green Day

DOOKIE

REPRISE | Producers: Rob Cavallo, Green Day

RELEASED: FEBRUARY 1, 1994

● When Green Day titled its third album and major-label debut *Dookie*, the young punks must have been pretty confident it wasn't a piece of you-know-what. They were, and it wasn't. You can just imagine the scatological reviews that would have followed otherwise.

Dookie may have seemed like a load of whiny brattiness to the old Clash fans, but for a segment of a restless Gen X it captured real, everyday life in a raw, game-changing, genre-defining pop-punk package. While Nirvana was up the coast brooding rather opaquely about boredom and apathy, the Berkeley, California, trio was laying it out there in plain English and having a blast doing it, starting with the opening line "I declare that I don't care no more!" And what kid couldn't relate to this classic verse from the breakout single **Longview**: "I sit around and watch the phone/But no one's calling/Call me pathetic, call me what you will/My mother says to get a job/But she don't like the one she's got/When masturbation's lost its fun, you're f*cking lazy."

Under the helm of producer Rob Cavallo, the pop-punk goodness is darn-near relentless on *Dookie*, which spawned four more singles: the hyper, panic-driven **Basket Case**; the more amped-up **Welcome to Paradise** (originally on 1991's *Kerplunk!*); **She**, inspired by a feminist poem an ex showed to frontman Billie Joe Armstrong; and **When I Come Around**, a lurching mid-tempo anthem about a boy who won't be tied down.

Dookie shot to No. 2 on the Billboard 200, sold more than twenty million copies worldwide, won a Grammy Award, propelled the group to Woodstock '94, topped *Rolling Stone*'s 50 Greatest Pop-Punk Albums list, and established Green Day as the premier band in a genre ready to explode. *–SM*

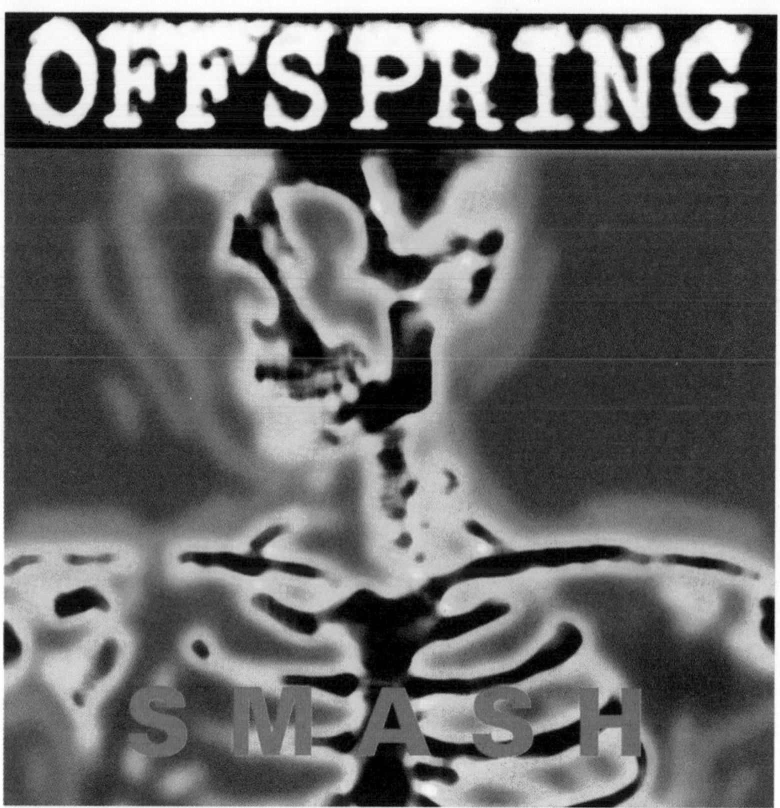

1994

The Offspring

SMASH

EPITAPH | Producer: Thom Wilson

RELEASED: APRIL 8, 1994

● The aptly named *Smash* was the second part of the one-two punch, following Green Day's *Dookie* just over two months before, that gave punk rock a beachhead in the pop mainstream, not unlike what Pearl Jam's *Ten* and Nirvana's *Nevermind* did for grunge three years prior.

Like Green Day, The Offspring had been around for a minute, forming a decade earlier in Orange County and releasing two albums and an EP before making *Smash*. That EP, *Baghdad*, had convinced Bad Religion's Brett Gurwetiz to sign The Offspring to his Epitaph label for its second album, *Ignition*, in 1992. But there was little to indicate the, well, smash success that awaited what the band did next.

Recorded on a budget of just $20,000, *Smash* was in some ways more of the same—only better. Frontman Bryan "Dexter" Holland's songwriting had grown; it was still punky and adrenalized but even more clever. The arrangements were tighter, and Thom Wilson's production was glossier and more radio-friendly. The dynamic **Come Out and Play** hit No. 1 on Billboard's Modern Rock Tracks chart, while the cheeky follow-up, **Self Esteem**, relatable to so many insecure male youths, reached No. 4 and **Gotta Get Away** made it to No. 6. All three also crossed over to the Top 20 of the Mainstream Rock Tracks chart and were certified gold.

All of that, in turn, drove *Smash* to sales of more than six million copies, as well as Top 5 album charts around the world, including Canada, Germany, Switzerland, Sweden, and Australia. It remains The Offspring's all-time best-seller. The legion of punk rock acts that got deals in the wake of *Smash*'s and *Dookie*'s breakthroughs owed those bands a fruit basket—or at least a thank-you note. *–GG*

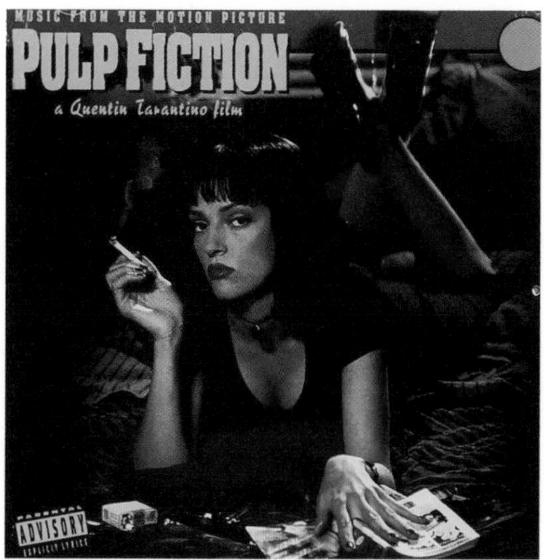

Various Artists

PULP FICTION (MUSIC FROM THE MOTION PICTURE)

M C A | Producers: Quentin Tarantino, Karyn Rachtman

RELEASED: SEPTEMBER 27, 1994

● The carefully selected mélange of songs that make up a movie soundtrack can often be redefined by the film's images. That's true to the tenth power for Quentin Tarantino's *Pulp Fiction*, one of his best both cinematically and musically. Lovingly curated by Tarantino and music supervisor Karyn Rachtman, *Pulp Fiction*'s soundtrack avoided big hits, instead seeking out more offbeat tunes that reflect the vibe of the film. The result? An energetic, fresh sound aurally matching the unpredictable, quirky nature of the film itself.

Highlights include Dusty Springfield's **Son of a Preacher Man** and the Chuck Berry classic **You Never Can Tell**, now forever linked with Uma Thurman and John Travolta's memorable characters and their dance sequence in the film, as well as Urge Overkill's cover of Neil Diamond's **Girl You'll Be a Woman Soon**. But it's Dick Dale's galloping surf rock anthem **Misirlou** that shaped the look and feel of *Pulp Fiction*, instantly searing the film's identity. In addition to the great music, the soundtrack also featured three dialogue segments, including the famous and essential "Royale with Cheese" tête-à-tête between Travolta and Samuel L. Jackson. *–FJ*

Pearl Jam

VITALOGY

E P I C | Producers: Brendan O'Brien, Pearl Jam

RELEASED: NOVEMBER 22, 1994

● Having positioned itself among the leaders of the grunge revolution, Pearl Jam got weird on its third album. The classic rock and punk influences that ran through its first two records were still present, but, firmly settled on top of the commercial mountain, the Seattle five-piece revealed its experimental side while still giving fans the gnarly guitars and Eddie Vedder's anguished howls that made *Ten* and *Vs.* such monster hits.

In some ways, *Vitalogy* was Pearl Jam's reaction to that success. The album was mostly written and recorded on tour, allowing the band to indulge in its most primal urges as it pieced together tracks that rarely sounded like they belonged on the same record. **Bugs**, for instance, was spoken-word rambling over a single repeated accordion riff. **Aye Davanita** broke things down further to a wordless chant, and **Stupid Mop**, a seven-and-a-half-minute sound collage that must have confused the hell out of "Even Flow" lovers, dispensed with the music altogether. Still, *Vitalogy* debuted at No. 1 and went five-times platinum: **Not for You**, **Corduroy**, and **Better Man** were all radio hits not too far removed from the expectations Pearl Jam was quickly shedding. *–MG*

Johnny Cash

AMERICAN RECORDINGS

AMERICAN RECORDINGS | Producer: Rick Rubin

RELEASED: APRIL 26, 1994

● Larger than life and "a walking contradiction, partly truth and partly fiction," in the words of his friend Kris Kristofferson, Johnny Cash was both a rock 'n' roll and country music legend. Yet in the early '90s, he found himself at loose ends, without a record label or an idea of what to do next.

Enter producer and American Recordings label founder Rick Rubin, who, together with Cash, decided to make a record with only voice and guitar, performing material that distilled Cash's sin-and-salvation image down to its very essence. To that end, they gathered songs: Cash originals and covers of tunes by Kristofferson, Tom Waits, Nick Lowe, Glenn Danzig, and others. On the side of salvation, there was **Why Me Lord?**, **The Beast in Me**, **Oh, Bury Me Not**, and **Down There by the Train**. Sin inhabits **Thirteen** and especially *American Recordings'* lead track, **Delia's Gone**, a murder ballad so coldly vicious it out-gangsta'd any gangsta rap you could name. Even the black-and-white album cover played into the idea of Cash as a man with a divided soul.

American Recordings was a sensation that rocketed Cash back to relevance. He and Rubin continued with *Unchained* in 1996, this time adding Tom Petty & the Heartbreakers as Cash's backing band, plus guest appearances by Marty Stuart, Flea, Lindsey Buckingham, and Mick Fleetwood. The songs on *Unchained* cast a wider net thematically and musically, the artists covered ranging from Beck, Soundgarden, and Petty himself to the Carter Sisters, Dean Martin, and Jimmie Rodgers.

Both *American Recordings* and *Unchained* won Grammy Awards, for Best Contemporary Folk Album and Best Country Album, respectively. Three more albums in the series were released after the turn of the century, two (plus the box set *Unearthed*, with even more material from the sessions) after Cash's death in 2003 at the age of seventy-one. *—DD*

3C34

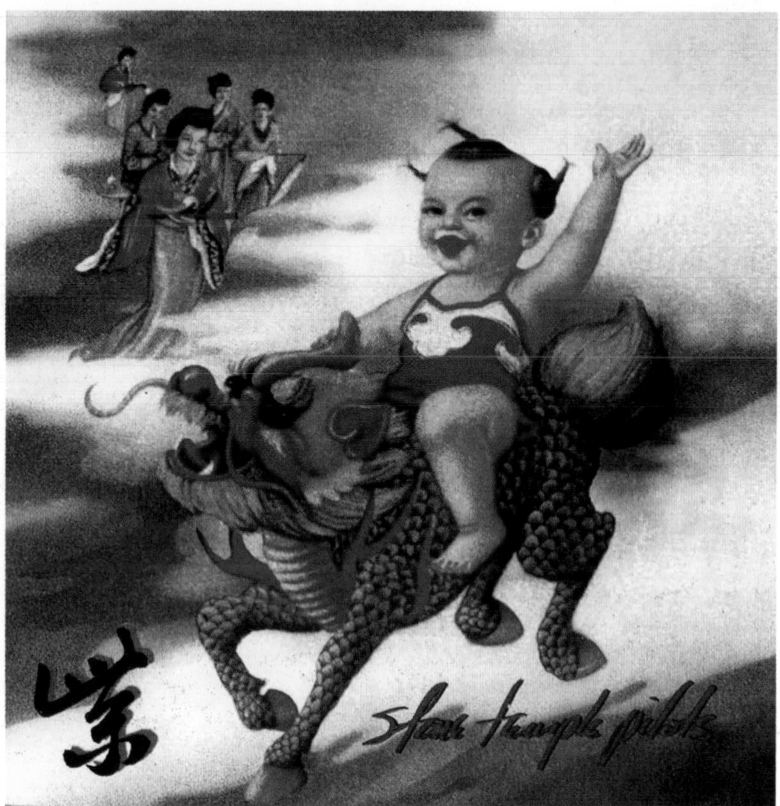

1994

Stone Temple Pilots

PURPLE

ATLANTIC | Producer: Brendan O'Brien

RELEASED: JUNE 7, 1994

● Stone Temple Pilots' (STP) first album, *Core,* was a hit with the record-buying public but trashed by most critics, the general complaint being that it was generic, copycat grunge. The quartet held the singular distinction of being named Best Band of 1994 by *Rolling Stone* readers and Worst Band of 1994 by the magazine's critics. Whether it was a desire to silence those cynics or just flex its musical muscles, STP expanded its sonic palette for its second release.

On *Purple,* the band injected elements of blues, jazz, country, funk, and folk into its songwriting and performance while staying true to the grungey rock roots of *Core.* This expanded musical direction was particularly showcased on the track **Lounge Fly**, which opened with psychedelic guitar, moved to a funky verse akin to the Red Hot Chili Peppers, then shifted to a rock anthem chorus followed by a soft acoustic guitar bridge before grinding to the finish. **Interstate Love Song** was as at home on a Texas roadhouse jukebox as it was on arena stages, and **Big Empty** started with jazzy chords and vocals before hitting its rocking, singalong chorus.

The experiment not only worked artistically but paid off big as **Purple** debuted at No. 1 on the Billboard 200 chart, where it stayed for three weeks, eventually selling more than six million copies. **Vasoline** and **Interstate Love Song** were both No. 1 Mainstream Rock chart hits and No. 2 on Alternative Airplay. *Purple* also made some of 1994's best albums lists, achieving the rare feat of converting detractors into believers while keeping its core audience happy. *–GP*

Toad the Wet Sprocket

DULCINEA

COLUMBIA | Producer: Gavin MacKillop

RELEASED: MAY 24, 1994

● Nearly three years after Toad the Wet Sprocket's first platinum success, *Dulcinea* did even better, its No. 34 showing on the Billboard 200 fifteen places higher than *Fear*'s peak. More importantly, it continued Toad's creative ascent with twelve richly layered and passionately performed songs that ruminated on love, death, and the afterlife.

Lyrically, *Dulcinea* leaned toward the heavy, opening with **Fly from Heaven**, in which lead singer and primary songwriter Glen Phillips assumed the biblical role of the Apostle James and sang about Saint Paul and Jesus. And on the album-closing **Reincarnation Song**, Phillips invoked the titular theory, singing, "I hurry back to little Earth for another life." The singles **Fall Down** and **Something's Always Wrong**, meanwhile, were minor-key jaunts with propulsive electric guitars and layered vocal harmonies (the former hit No. 1 on Billboard's Modern Rock chart). Other highlights included the whimsical **Stupid** and the country-flavored **Nanci**. Interestingly **Crowing**, the song with arguably the broadest commercial potential, was never released as a single. As on *Fear*, guitarist Todd Nichols made a strong mark, co-writing six tracks with Phillips. *Dulcinea* was a snapshot of the Santa Barbara, California, band at the peak of its commercial and creative powers. *–ST*

Sparks

GRATUITOUS SAX & SENSELESS VIOLINS

LOGIC | Producers: Ron Mael, Russell Mael

RELEASED: NOVEMBER 15, 1994

● The venerable art rock duo Sparks, led by brothers Ron and Russell Mael, was still producing excellent music as it released its sixteenth album, but things weren't looking bright during the years preceding it. The duo had become an afterthought to many by 1994, and it had been six years since Sparks' last release. But this was worth the wait. On *Gratuitous Sax & Senseless Violins*, the Maels borrowed from then-popular Eurosynth stylings, but as always, the album sounds like Sparks, from Russell's soaring, interpretative vocals to principal lyricist and older brother Ron's compelling and well-crafted compositions.

The album charted well in Germany and other territories. And why not, since the songs were steeped in well-established sonics? You could dance to it, but the provocative underlying messages in many of the songs, including the hit **When Do I Get to Sing "My Way"** (which even reached No. 9 on the Billboard Dance Club Songs chart) and **Let's Go Surfing**, kept us listening, too. *Gratuitous Sax . . .* was a gem that received near-universal acclaim and is still beloved by Sparks fans. It perhaps lacked some of the quirkiness the Maels are known for, but it's an important entry in the Sparks canon. *–MM*

Various Artists

RHYTHM, COUNTRY AND BLUES

MCA | Producers: Tony Brown, Don Was

RELEASED: MARCH 1, 1994

● The premise behind this collection was that country and R&B artists share more than one might think—particularly genuine emotion and a soulful world outlook that made them peas which rolled separate ways when the pod was cracked open. To demonstrate this, duets were match-made in sometimes-heavenly and sometimes-unlikely pairs, a concept that became commonplace in later years but was revolutionary and even consciousness-raising in the mid-'90s.

With a pair of Grammy-winning producers at the helm—Tony Brown from Nashville and Don Was from Los Angeles—*Rhythm, Country and Blues* succeeded more as a discussion than an album, which is what made it important. But it still had plenty of highlights. Al Green and Lyle Lovett locked in to each other like long-lost brothers on Willie Nelson's **Funny How Time Slips Away**, and Chet Atkins and Allen Toussaint slipped into an easy-grooving Nashville-meets-N'awlins rendition of the latter's **Southern Nights**, which Glen Campbell had made a hit in 1977. The Staple Singers and Marty Stuart were certainly kindred spirits before they crafted their take on The Band's **The Weight**, while Little Richard and Tanya Tucker shared a kind of "Are we really doing this?" attitude that enlivened Eddie Cochran's **Something Else**; Sam Moore and Conway Twitty made easy work of Tony Joe White's **Rainy Night in Georgia**.

At its worst, *Rhythm, Country and Blues* sounds forced (listen to Clint Black with the Pointer Sisters on Aretha Franklin's **Chain of Fools** and Patti LaBelle and Travis Tritt on Sam & Dave's **When Something Is Wrong with My Baby**). But everybody is professional enough to pull their songs off in competent fashion, and the project's greater contribution was that genre-blending conversation that made it a foundation, certainly, for country's eventual embrace of R&B and Black artists into its fold. *–GG*

Hole

LIVE THROUGH THIS

D G C | Producers: Sean Slade, Paul Q. Kolderie

RELEASED: APRIL 12, 1994

● It is virtually impossible to discuss *Live Through This* without mentioning the tragic details that surrounded its release. Hole—Courtney Love (vocals/guitar), Eric Erlandson (guitar), Patty Schemel (drums), and Kristen Pfaff (bass)—recorded the tracks for their second studio album during late 1993. Marketing and promotion for the release was well underway when Love's husband, Kurt Cobain, committed suicide four days before the album hit shelves. The band was still processing Cobain's death when, two months later, Pfaff died of a drug overdose. Amid these tragedies, Hole moved forward with promotion, recruiting Melissa Auf der Mar to replace Pfaff and proceeding to tour.

The surrounding drama meant a lot of media attention was focused on things other than the music, but it didn't diminish the fact that *Live through This* was a fantastic rock album. The powerful opener **Violet** started in an unusual way, with the line "And the sky was made of amethyst." It implied the listener was jumping into a story somewhere in the middle, which made Love's screaming, "Go on take everything!" a few seconds later simultaneously jarring and intriguing.

Hole continued to take the listener on a journey, with Love's voice providing the perfect delivery vessel. **Miss World**, **Plump**, and **Asking for It** all reveled in loud choruses echoed by guitars turned up to the proverbial 11. **Doll Parts** stood out even more with its sparse chords and haunting conclusion "someday you will ache like I ache." It was impossible to hear those words and not remember a grieving widow was singing them.

It was unfair that Cobain's death overshadowed *Live through This*, but the album endures as a milestone of its era, one that retains a power that pushes beyond that tragedy to stand strong on its own. *–RW*

ETEEN
95
1995
Y-FIVE

1995

Björk

POST

ONE LITTLE INDIAN/ELEKTRA | Producers: Björk, Nellee Hooper, Graham Massey

RELEASED: JUNE 7, 1995

● For the follow-up to her 1993 *Debut*, former Sugarcubes singer Björk Guðmundsdóttir turned up the volume on her sound and herself. The opening track **Army of Me** was a tank, rolling over anyone who dare come in her path: "And if you complain once more, you'll meet an army of me," the Icelandic pixie warned over a gurgling trip-hop beat. Few were willing to challenge her.

The assault of sound came as Björk expanded her musical (and physical) universe, moving from her homeland to London as her solo career took flight. *Post* boasted a darker, clubbier sound, and **Enjoy**, produced and co-written by Massive Attack alumnus Tricky, embodied the moody, electronic, primal direction of the album. That didn't mean it was all heavy, and **Isobel** was a lush sojourn through the wilderness, a spiritual quest from the forest to the big city that mirrors her own personal journey.

No matter what musical beds she's singing over, from electronic to classical, Björk's voice is her most unique instrument and sharpest weapon, ranging from powerful to delicate, from muted to a lion's roar, all within a matter of moments. Her poetry on *Post* was vivid and inquisitive, like a child's view of the world. "All the modern things, like cars and such, have always existed," she sang on **The Modern Things**, arguing they've been patiently waiting inside a mountain for their time to take over the world, and that time had arrived.

Everything came together on **It's Oh So Quiet**, a boisterous cover of Betty Hutton's 1951 original, a big band explosion that mirrored the feeling of losing yourself and falling in love. It put Björk at the center of a Busby Berkeley musical, and her scream at the end of the song was the sound of her achieving the spiritual and personal freedom she'd always sought. And it was anything but quiet. *—AG*

Robyn
ROBYN IS HERE

RICOCHET/ARIOLA/BMG | Producers: Ulf Lindström, Johan Ekhé, Denniz Pop, Max Martin

RELEASED: OCTOBER 13, 1995

● Before she was dancing on her own, Robin Carlsson was a teenage pop singer in her native Sweden, ready to take on the world. *Robyn Is Here*, her bubbly debut, evoked early-'90s R&B more than it did late-'90s teen pop, save for a pair of standout singles. **Do You Know (What It Takes)** and **Show Me Love** rode elastic grooves that bounced like rubber balls, Robyn's voice beaming like sunshine atop them. Both were produced by then up-and-coming Swedish pop mastermind Max Martin, and both became US Top 10 hits. Robyn later retooled her career as an indie-pop dynamo, lessons learned here serving as her foundation. *–AG*

Golden Smog
DOWN BY THE OLD MAINSTREAM

RYKODISC | Producers: Golden Smog, James Bunchberry Lane

RELEASED: 1995

● Golden Smog began as lark, but when some of the finest from Minneapolis (and environs) became a collective, greatness was inevitable. On its first full-length, Golden Smog—comprised of the Jayhawks' Gary Louris and Mark Perlman, Wilco's Jeff Tweedy, Run Westy Run's Kraig Johnson, Soul Asylum's Dan Murphy, and the Honeydogs' Noah Levy (fusing middle and street names into label-skirting pseudonyms)—combined sweet harmonies, fine pickin', and dollops of humor into raggedly glorious alt-country/Americana. Highlights included **V**, the jaunty **Pecan Pie**, **He's a Dick**, and the touching **Radio King**. Taking looseness cues from Faces (even covering **Glad and Sorry**), this Golden Smog incarnation clearly had way too much fun. *–LM*

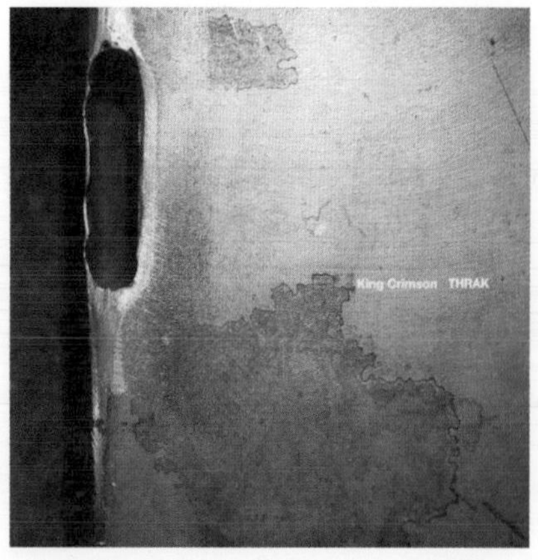

King Crimson
THRAK

VIRGIN | Producers: King Crimson, David Bottrill

RELEASED: APRIL 3, 1995

● King Crimson showed its mettle as the rare '60s prog franchise to adapt to the new wave of the '80s, and then, eleven years after *Three of a Perfect Pair*, it was back in experimental mode on its lone '90s studio album, with a "double trio" lineup. With guitarists Robert Fripp and Adrian Belew, bassists Tony Levin and Trey Gunn, and drummers Bill Bruford and Pat Mastelotto, it was by no means one of King Crimson's more easily digestible albums but still one of its most ambitious. *–SM*

Jars of Clay

JARS OF CLAY

ESSENTIAL | Producers: Jars of Clay, Adrian Belew

RELEASED: OCTOBER 24, 1995

● "Rain, rain on my face/It hasn't stopped raining for days," Dan Haseltine sang on **Flood**, the lead single from Jars of Clay's self-titled debut. Those "days" equaled forty, unsurprising given the band's Christian roots. Divine intervention and shimmering production from Adrian Belew (King Crimson, Talking Heads) catapulted the multiplatinum album into Billboard's Top 200 for all of 1996. Rich harmonies, a hard-driving beat, and one heck of a chorus resulted in the hookiest song about spiritual despair you'll ever hear and pushed the track to No. 12 on the Billboard Modern Rock chart. While less mainstream, the rest of the album was equally appealing. One listen is not nearly enough. *–HD*

Rancid

. . . AND OUT COME THE WOLVES

EPITAPH | Producers: Jerry Finn, Rancid

RELEASED: AUGUST 22, 1995

● Comparisons to The Clash abound on this third album from the Berkeley, California, band that sparked the mid-'90s punk revival alongside Green Day and The Offspring. . . . *And Out Come the Wolves* was the commercial breakout led by the success of the infectious ska-punk single **Time Bomb**, followed by **Ruby Soho** with its explosive, shout-along chorus. Running nineteen songs over forty-nine minutes, there was barely a skip thanks to the playful range of styles, the cascade of hooks, and the rough-and-tumble vocal interplay between guitarists Tim Armstrong and Lars Frederiksen. *–SM*

Jewel

PIECES OF YOU

ATLANTIC | Producer: Ben Keith

RELEASED: FEBRUARY 28, 1995

● Jewel first asked who would save her soul in her clear, lilting voice on her debut album, but *Pieces of You* barely charted until two years later, when she toured as support for Bob Dylan and gained public exposure as a folk rock artist. The collection of songs was written mostly by Jewel Kilcher as a teenager, and the lyrics—whether the plaintive yearning for love lost in **Foolish Games** or her contemplating over smiley-faced eggs on the hit **You Were Meant for Me**—reflected a high school diary-like innocence. This naïveté, delivered over catchy, sweet guitar melodies, combined to make a charming record, which went twelve-times platinum and received a pair of Grammy Award nominations. *–SS*

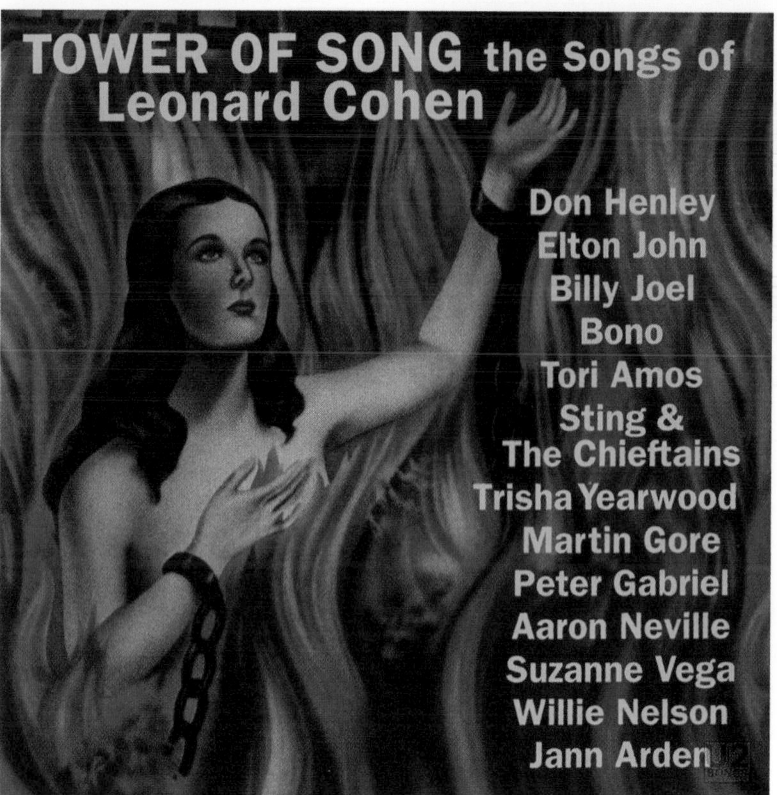

TOWER OF SONG the Songs of Leonard Cohen
Don Henley
Elton John
Billy Joel
Bono
Tori Amos
Sting &
The Chieftains
Trisha Yearwood
Martin Gore
Peter Gabriel
Aaron Neville
Suzanne Vega
Willie Nelson
Jann Arden

Various Artists

TOWER OF SONG: THE SONGS OF LEONARD COHEN

A & M | Producers: Various

RELEASED: SEPTEMBER 26, 1995

● There's something undeniably cool about Leonard Cohen. The Canadian poet moved to the US during the '60s, falling in with Andy Warhol before Judy Collins turned his poetry into music by recording "Suzanne" and then urging Cohen to perform as well. Cohen continued writing poetry, but his music achieved cult status. His best-loved song, "Hallelujah," didn't release until 1984 and has been widely covered—notably by John Cale in 1991 and Jeff Buckley in 1994—but didn't hit the charts until after Cohen's death in 2016.

Nevertheless, his songwriting was respected enough to germinate several tribute albums, including Jennifer Warnes's *Famous Blue Raincoat* (1983) and the alt-rock-oriented *I'm Your Fan: The Songs of Leonard Cohen* (1991). *Tower of Song: The Songs of Leonard Cohen* brought together more mainstream artists, including Don Henley, Billy Joel, Sting with the Chieftains, U2's Bono, Tori Amos, Elton John, Trisha Yearwood, Aaron Neville, Willie Nelson, Peter Gabriel, Jann Arden, Suzanne Vega, and Depeche Mode's Martin Gore.

Though uneven like most compilations, Cohen reportedly was satisfied—particularly with Joel's rendition of **Light as the Breeze**. Amos's **Famous Blue Raincoat** sounds like she might have written it herself, and John lightens up **I'm Your Man** with a tongue-in-cheek disco mix. It's also interesting to hear the country stalwarts give Cohen's songs that kind of treatment on their contributions. Other tracks aren't quite as satisfying: Henley's **Everybody Knows** sounds as unfortunately craggy as the original, while Gabriel's **Suzanne** feels simultaneously over-contrived and flat.

The elephant in the room is Bono's mostly spoken-word **Hallelujah**, which he once called "the most perfect song in the world." Cohen reportedly was pleased, but Bono later apologized: "The lyric explains it best," he's said. "There's the holy and the broken hallelujah, and mine was definitely the broken one." *—HD*

Foo Fighters

FOO FIGHTERS

ROSWELL/CAPITOL | Producers: Dave Grohl, Barrett Jones

RELEASED: JULY 4, 1995

● Foo Fighters put Nirvana drummer Dave Grohl back on his musical feet, literally and figuratively, just fifteen months after Kurt Cobain's suicide ended that band—and quite unexpectedly. "This wasn't supposed to be anything," Grohl mused a few years later, after a few more Foo Fighters albums. "This started out as a demo tape . . . I copied for a bunch of my friends, and it circulated and then it became an album and then it became a band and then it became a career."

This twelve-song debut certainly got that career off to a raucous and defining start. "This is a call to all my past resignations/It's been too long," he sang at the outset, and *Foo Fighters*—on which Grohl wrote, sang, and played almost everything himself (the Afghan Whigs' Greg Dulli contributed guitar on **X-Static**)—was a cathartic workout that blew past the numb of Nirvana's unexpected end with the declaration that **I'll Stick Around** and surprisingly good-humored sentiments in **Big Me**, **Weenie Beenie**, and **For All the Cows**. You can, of course, hear Nirvana but also Grohl's other roots from the Washington, DC, punk scene he came up in and the melodic pop and rock he also favored.

His return, after a stint backing underground bass hero Mike Watt, was warmly welcomed. *Foo Fighters* (a term World War II pilots used to describe UFOs) was certified platinum and launched three Top 10 Alternative Airplay and Mainstream Rock chart singles in Billboard. It was nominated for a Grammy Award for Best Alternative Music Album, ironically won by Nirvana's *MTV Unplugged in New York*. Grohl wound up turning Foo Fighters into a full-fledged band (with Nirvana touring guitarist Pat Smear on board) that continues to this day and was inducted into the Rock & Roll Hall of Fame in 2021. *–GG*

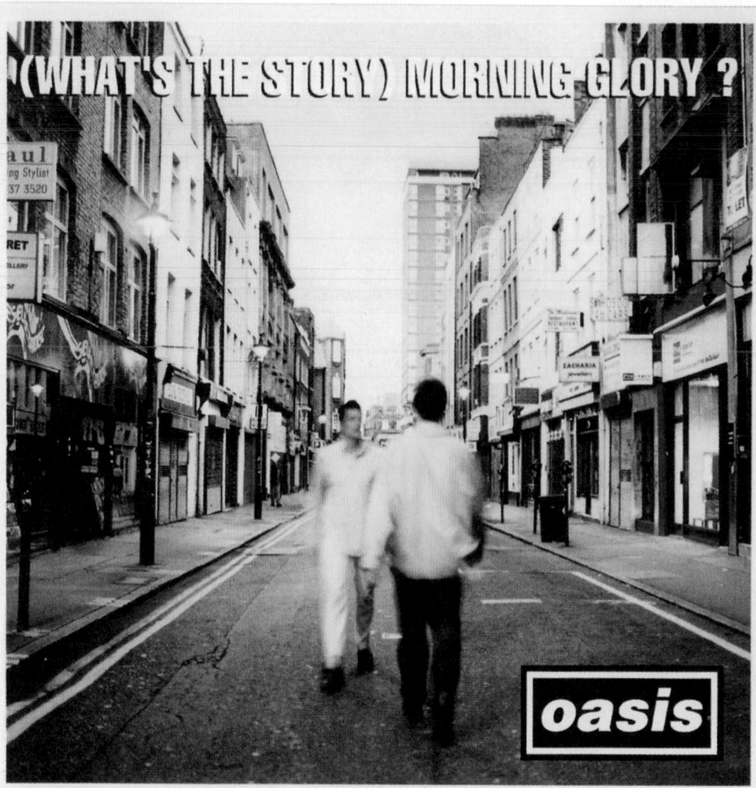

Oasis

(WHAT'S THE STORY) MORNING GLORY?

CREATION | Producers: Owen Morris, Noel Gallagher

RELEASED: OCTOBER 2, 1995

● Fourteen months after announcing its presence to the world with its debut album *Definitely Maybe*, Oasis cemented its place among the biggest acts of the decade with the release of *(What's the Story) Morning Glory?* The songs were anthems meant to be sung in the arenas and stadiums which Oasis soon would be headlining.

If there was a halfway point between the two albums, it might be the thirty-nine seconds between the title track and **Champagne Supernova**. The song **Morning Glory** was a loud, guitar-heavy anthem similar to "Rock and Roll Star" from Oasis's debut, while **Champagne Supernova** was a seven-and-a-half-minute epic fortified by Mellotron and with Paul Weller of The Jam on lead guitar. Between the two songs was an island of guitar feedback, harmonica, and ocean waves that echoed what has passed and previews what's to come.

When recording started on . . . *Morning Glory?*, Noel Gallagher's drive for perfection led to the band's decision to replace drummer Tony McCarroll with Alan White. Given additional studio toys to play with (and a larger budget), the band flexed its creative muscles. Noel Gallagher's songwriting reflected the confidence of a man who knew his songs would be sung by millions, while younger brother Liam Gallagher, whose confidence as a singer never wavered since he first set foot on a stage, showcased a voice in top form on **Cast No Shadow** and **She's Electric**. Noel also sang lead vocals for the first time on **Don't Look Back in Anger**, something he'd have to do with other songs at various times during the Gallagher brothers' tumultuous pairing.

If there's any doubt about the durability of this album, **Don't Look Back in Anger** and **Wonderwall** are still belted out by fans at concerts and football (soccer) matches. *–RW*

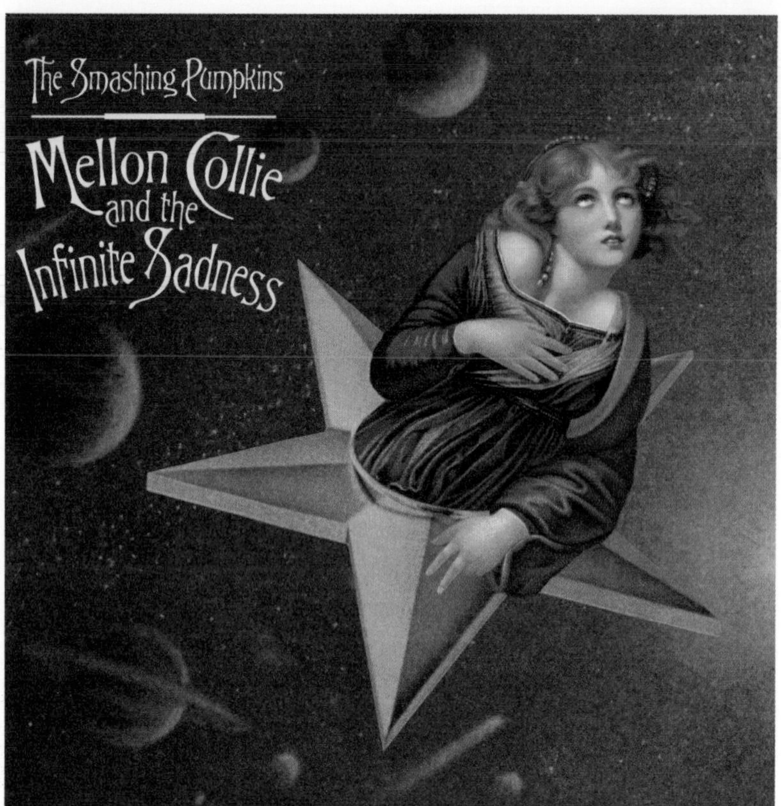

The Smashing Pumpkins

MELLON COLLIE AND THE INFINITE SADNESS

VIRGIN | Producers: Flood, Alan Moulder, Billy Corgan

RELEASED: OCTOBER 24, 1995

● Everything about the Smashing Pumpkins' third studio album was larger than life, starting with that title, a gangly, over-the-top summation of frontman Billy Corgan's ambition and worldview as he sought the mantle of World's Biggest Band, '90s edition. You want sad? They'll be the saddest, while also being the loudest, and they'd prove it over the course of a two-hour, twenty-eight-track double album, separated by themes: *Dawn to Dusk* for the first half, *Twilight to Starlight* for the second. (There was even a "The" affixed to the band's name for the album. No longer was it merely Smashing Pumpkins; it was *The* Smashing Pumpkins, with all the grandeur implied by the qualifier.)

That ambition carried over to the recording sessions: Corgan and his bandmates—guitarist James Iha, bassist D'arcy Wretzky, and drummer Jimmy Chamberlin—worked up nearly sixty songs. Many of the spillovers would wind up on *The Aeroplane Flies High*, a singles box set released thirteen months later. For the album, the hippie psychedelia of 1993's *Siamese Dream* was gone, replaced by a sonic barrage that ranged from arena rock epics (**Porcelina of the Vast Oceans**) to blistering metal tirades (**Tales of a Scorched Earth**) to whisper-soft lullabies (**Lily [My One and Only]**) to campfire singalongs (**Farewell and Goodnight**), often over the course of just a few songs. The singles were just as varied, from the angsty grunge battle cry of **Bullet with Butterfly Wings** to the moody experimental synth-pop of **1979** and the soaring, orchestra-backed **Tonight, Tonight**. All were massive, and the album went on to sell more than ten million copies.

Corgan said at the time the band set out to make *The Wall* for Generation X, and the results spoke for themselves. Smashing Pumpkins—er, *The* Smashing Pumpkins—never climbed higher. *—AG*

DC Talk

JESUS FREAK

FOREFRONT/VIRGIN | Producers: Mark Helmerman, Toby McKeehan, John Mark Painter

RELEASED: NOVEMBER 21, 1995

● More so than the vast majority of its faith-based colleagues, DC Talk is the band that pushed the Christian music envelope into contemporary credibility. The trio of Toby McKeehan, Michael Tait, and Kevin Max, with roots in the (Jerry) Falwell Singers, formed at Liberty University in Lynchburg, Virginia, and bonded over a shared love of rock and especially hip-hop. The latter informed the group's first three albums, including 1992's platinum *Free at Last*, which also gave DC Talk its first No. 1 on the Christian charts.

Jesus Freak gave the group's sizeable audience yet another surprise, however. DC Talk came out rocking this time, not quite nü metal, and certainly not singing about the nookie, but clearly influenced by the alternative guitar bands so prevalent at the time. Still rapping in spots, DC Talk kept itself lyrically pious and even covered *Godspell*'s **Day by Day**. But the title track was its own "Smells Like Teen Spirit" for the genre. Despite the stretch *Jesus Freak* found open ears, topping the Christian charts again, crossing over to the Top 20 on the Billboard 200, and winning a Grammy Award for Best Rock Gospel Album. *–GG*

Alison Krauss

NOW THAT I'VE FOUND YOU: A COLLECTION

ROUNDER | Producers: Alison Krauss, Union Station

RELEASED: FEBRUARY 7, 1995

● Though technically a compilation, as the title indicates, this album hit many fans like a new release, providing a perfect introduction to Alison Krauss (with and without Union Station) seven albums into her recording career. By that time, she and the band had barely grazed the charts and were definitely flying under the radar, but their rendition of **When You Say Nothing at All** from *Keith Whitley: A Tribute Album* in 1994 hit No. 3 on Billboard's Hot Country Singles & Tracks chart and won the Country Music Association Award for Single of the Year.

The twelve-track *Now That I've Found You* tells the rest of the story, including a new recording of the Foundations' **Baby, Now That I've Found You** that won a Grammy Award for Best Female Country Vocal Performance and a cover of Bad Company's **Oh, Atlanta**. *Now That I've Found You* hit No. 2 on Billboard's Country Albums chart and No. 13 on the Billboard 200 and went double-platinum, indications of the substantial audience that finally found Krauss and company in its wake. *–TR/GG*

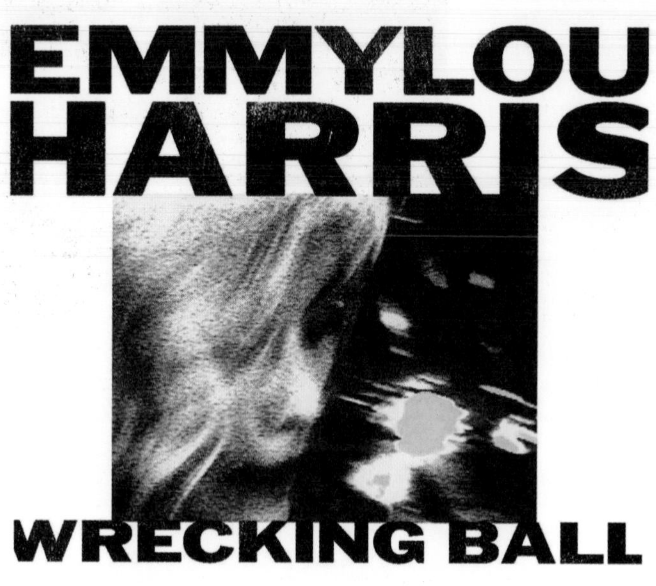

Emmylou Harris

WRECKING BALL

ELEKTRA | Producer: Daniel Lanois

RELEASED: SEPTEMBER 26, 1995

● Emmylou Harris's cracked, crystalline voice has often been described as "angelic." But until Daniel Lanois came along to produce her eighteenth studio album, *Wrecking Ball*, no one was able to achieve or even conceive of a sound so appropriately otherworldly with which to surround it.

Lanois came to the project having co-produced (along with Brian Eno) U2 albums, including *The Joshua Tree* and *Achtung Baby*. He co-produced Peter Gabriel's *So* and Robbie Robertson's self-titled album and helmed Bob Dylan's *Oh Mercy* and the Neville Brothers' *Yellow Moon*. Though Harris's music had always been forward-looking, *Wrecking Ball* was a bold and stunning departure, even for her. Early in her career, she had helped to popularize country rock through her work with Graham Parsons, and on her own albums, she'd proved that songs by The Beatles and Merle Haggard could happily coexist. Meanwhile, her devotion to country classics by Buck Owens, Dolly Parton, Patsy Cline, and others qualified her as a New Traditionalist long before there even was such a thing.

Over the years, her career waxed and waned, and country radio began to ignore her, so Harris emphatically lit out for new territory. On *Wrecking Ball*, she took on songs by an eclectic mix of artists, including Dylan (**Every Grain of Sand**), Jimi Hendrix (**May This Be Love**), Steve Earle (**Goodbye**), Neil Young (the title track), Lucinda Williams (**Sweet Old World**), and Gillian Welch (**Orphan Girl**) as well as Lanois's **Where Will I Be** and **Blackhawk**, among others. Among the band members and backing vocalists were Lanois, U2 drummer Larry Mullen Jr., Daryl Johnson, Malcolm Burn, Brian Blade, Young, Kate and Anna McGarrigle, and others.

Lanois's richly textured sonics and Harris's gossamer vocals made for a haunting, evocative mix. The album won a Grammy Award for Best Contemporary Folk Album. Given her past bona fides, Harris could have easily assumed a comfortable role as a country-music elder stateswoman. Instead, *Wrecking Ball* opened exciting new creative vistas for her. *—DD*

The Beatles

ANTHOLOGY 1-3

APPLE/CAPITOL | Producers: George Martin, Jeff Lynne, The Beatles

RELEASED: NOVEMBER 20, 1995 (1); MARCH 12, 1996 (2); OCTOBER 28, 1996 (3)

● "No, there is absolutely nothing where we are going to collaborate. So, that's the end of that." That's what Ringo Starr grumpily told an interviewer for *Goldmine* magazine during 1992. The pledge didn't hold, because within two years, Starr was back in the studio with George Harrison and Paul McCartney to record two "new" Beatles songs built around John Lennon demos for *The Beatles Anthology*, the television series recounting the group's history that spawned three double-disc sets starting in November 1995. The new songs, **Free As a Bird** and **Real Love**, were centerpieces of the first two albums (a third song, **Now and Then**, was abandoned until 2023), but the studio outtakes, demos, and live recordings spread over the six discs of *The Beatles Anthology* revealed something long known to collectors of bootlegs: there was some interesting and truly revelatory material that had been stashed in the vaults.

Anthology 1 went back to the band's prehistory, where a 1958 demonstration disc recording of **That'll Be the Day** by the pre-Beatles Quarrymen showed Lennon's budding skill as a vocalist. Other highlights included a hard-charging 1963 live recording from a Swedish tour which showed the band could rock as hard before an audience as any of its contemporaries. The group's transition away from the road and to the studio was the focus of *Anthology 2*, which spanned from 1965 to early 1968. It featured the only other take McCartney attempted of **Yesterday**, an early, pulsating version of **Tomorrow Never Knows**, and an outtake of **And Your Bird Can Sing** with Lennon and McCartney laughing uncontrollably throughout.

The tumultuous years before The Beatles' dissolution were covered on *Anthology 3*. Some of the outtakes from the sessions that later became *Let It Be* were aimless and draggy, but a polished demo of **Come and Get It**, given to Badfinger, and **The Long and Winding Road** without the orchestral overdubs more than made up for those shortcomings. *–BH*

Bruce Springsteen

THE GHOST OF TOM JOAD

COLUMBIA | Producers: Bruce Springsteen, Chuck Plotkin

RELEASED: NOVEMBER 21, 1995

● With fans hoping that his E Street Band reunion for new tracks on 1995's *Greatest Hits* album would stick, Bruce Springsteen decided on another left turn for his next effort. While comparisons to 1982's stark *Nebraska* were apt, *The Ghost of Tom Joad* was markedly different, primarily because it was intentional where its predecessor was accidental. Springsteen had a clutch of songs he heard with minimal but essential musical accompaniment, hitting the studio with a sound in mind that was different than anything he'd attempted before.

"I just wasn't sure of my rock voice," Springsteen explained at the time, "so I kind of went to where I thought I could be most useful . . . I wanted to make a record where I don't have to play by the rules, I don't have any singles and none of that kind of stuff." *Tom Joad*'s folky narratives were, in many ways, grounded in the themes he'd explored in all his work to that point and drew from a variety of sources—including *The Grapes of Wrath*, which, of course, inspired the album's title. The twelve tracks chronicled Rust Belt decay (**Youngstown**), illegal aliens and the drug trade (**Balboa Park** and **Sinaloa Cowboys**), racial prejudices (**Galveston Bay**), and a rash of lost characters trying to find their place. Bringing them to sonic life, he had help from E Street present (wife Patti Scialfa, Danny Federici, and Garry Tallent) and future (Soozie Tyrell) among a small cast of other players.

There were no hits, as expected; it was Springsteen's first album to miss the Top 5 of the Billboard 200 since *The Wild, the Innocent & the E Street Shuffle* in 1973. But *Tom Joad* still hit a nerve—including a gold album and a Grammy for Best Contemporary Folk Album. *—GG*

D'Angelo
BROWN SUGAR

E M I | Producers: D'Angelo, Bob Power, Ali Shaheed Muhammad, Raphael Saadiq

RELEASED: JULY 3, 1995

● If, like an ever-increasing number of us, you were born after The Beatles released all of its albums, it's impossible to truly comprehend how revolutionary *Please Please Me* was. Compared to *Sgt. Pepper's Lonely Hearts Club Band* or even *Help!*, The Fab Four's debut album sounds a bit simplistic. But there's a reason almost every single one of your favorite rock stars knows exactly where they were and how much their worlds changed when The Beatles first appeared on *The Ed Sullivan Show*. And that's the right way to think about D'Angelo's debut album. Of course, 2000's *Voodoo* and 2014's *Black Messiah* were more unique, fully formed musical statements, but *Brown Sugar* helped mark an important turning point in soul music. D'Angelo is the rare artist who had fully ingested the classic R&B values of legendary predecessors such as Prince and Stevie Wonder (with whom he shared the ability to write, perform, and produce as a one-man band) while also fully embodying more modern, hip-hop-influenced tastes and sensibilities. *Brown Sugar* exuded a warm, musicianship-driven sound that boldly contrasted with the cold, digital productions preferred by the genre's biggest stars at the time of its release, making D'Angelo one of the early pioneers of the Neo Soul movement. *–MW*

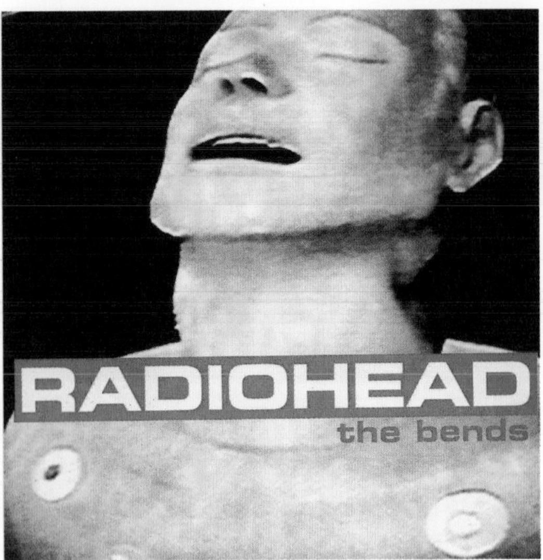

Radiohead
THE BENDS

C A P I T O L | Producers: John Lecki, Nigel Godrich, Jim Warren, Radiohead

RELEASED: MARCH 13, 1995

● The meteoric success of "Creep," Radiohead's 1992 debut single, put the British quintet on a dizzying trajectory to stardom that it was not quite prepared for. That uneasiness, combined with pressure from the label to release an equally marketable follow-up, left the band feeling painfully self-conscious, taking ten months to piece together what would eventually become this introspective sophomore album.

The quintet's insecurity stifled early recording sessions with producer John Leckie at RAK Studios in London, but it eventually found its footing as well as a kinship with Nigel Godrich, a young engineer on the project who would go on to produce every Radiohead album that followed. More confident and sonically interesting than the grungey 1993 debut *Pablo Honey*, *The Bends* was as diverse as it was moody, ranging from the guitar-heavy anthem of its title track to the melancholic **Fake Plastic Trees** and **High and Dry** to the more electronic-leaning **Planet Telex**. *The Bends* produced five charting singles and sold roughly three million copies, peaking at No. 4 on the UK albums chart. But though regarded by many fans as one of Radiohead's finest albums, it was subsequently overshadowed just two years later by *OK Computer*. *–JS*

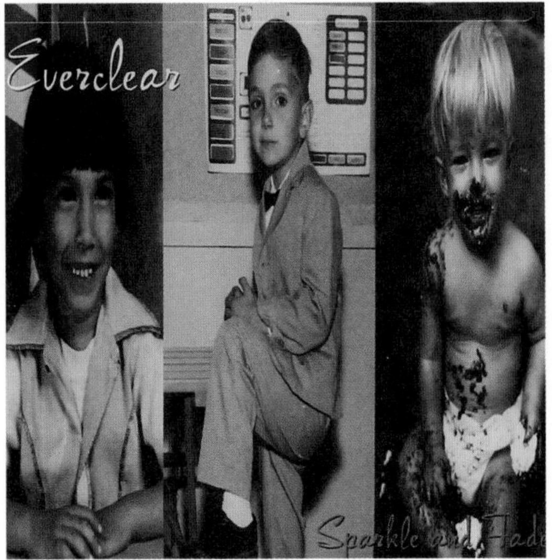

Everclear

SPARKLE AND FADE

CAPITOL | Producer: Art Alexakis

RELEASED: MAY 23, 1995

● A vehicle for the semi-autobiographical songwriting of frontman Art Alexakis, Everclear broke out in 1995 with its second LP, notable for its four impossibly tuneful singles that tweaked the eardrums of the MTV *120 Minutes* set and eventually sent the record to platinum status. To be sure, those hits—**Heroin Girl**, **Santa Monica**, **Heartspark Dollarsign**, and **You Make Me Feel Like a Whore**—traded on the prevailing loud-fast ethos of the decade's alternative rock movement, but the juxtaposition of Alexakis's bummer tales of addiction, race, and crummy relationships with catchy melodies gave Everclear a bit of a unique selling point. Which is not to say this album is a four-trick pony: **Pale Green Stars**, though of a tamer velocity, had all the pop savvy required to have made it another successful single, and **Electra Made Me Blind** gave the period's wildest noise merchants a run for their flannel. While Alexakis would further plumb his confessional style with 2000's superb *Songs From an American Movie* divorce-song cycles, Everclear's Portland, Oregon, base of operations and trio format drew inevitable comparisons to Nirvana in a post-Nirvana world. In truth, the band was more accessible both sonically and lyrically than its Pacific Northwest peers. *–DP*

Elastica

ELASTICA

DGC | Producers: Marc Waterman, Elastica

RELEASED: MARCH 13, 1995

● At the height of Britpop, Elastica dropped a thirty-eight-minute power-pop masterpiece with snaky bass lines and catchy hooks that elicited comparisons to Wire and the Stranglers. (These comparisons would be so close that they had to be settled out of court.) The songs were short—only four of the sixteen tracks exceeded three minutes in length—but they packed an irresistible punch. Fronted by Justine Frischmann after her brief stint in Suede, the songs on *Elastica* were the antithesis of the lad culture that Britpop had become synonymous with. Elastica sang about male impotence (**Stutter**), trysts in a Ford Fiesta (**Car Song**), and an ode to petroleum jelly as a lubricant (**Vaseline**, whose chorus would often be changed to "twinkle twat" when performed live). Songs from Elastica were so irresistible they were included on several movie soundtracks at the time (*Trainspotting*, *Mallrats*). There is considerable doubt about whether Pablo Picasso actually said, "Good artists borrow from their influences. Great artists steal." What is not in doubt is that Elastica may have done both on this album, and we are all the better for that. *–RW*

Moby
EVERYTHING IS WRONG

MUTE/ELEKTRA | Producer: Moby

RELEASED: MARCH 14, 1995

● Moby's major label debut album was the sound of all the genre-bending New York electronic musician's musical personalities—techno, punk, blues, classical—joining forces and shutting down the dancefloor at your favorite neighborhood watering hole. The unifying presence was Moby himself, a one-man band and an early face of '90s dance music culture. He was assisted here by dream pop vocalist Mimi Goese, who guested on the ethereal **Into the Blue** and **When It's Cold I'd Like to Die**, while the colossal **God Moving Over the Face of the Waters** was etched in stone when it soundtracked the closing moments of Michael Mann's 1995 crime saga *Heat*. *–AG*

Various Artists
WAITING TO EXHALE (ORIGINAL SOUNDTRACK ALBUM)

ARISTA | Producer: Kenneth "Babyface" Edmonds

RELEASED: NOVEMBER 14, 1995

● Released in support of the film adaptation of the Terry McMillan novel, *Waiting to Exhale* stood as an R&B album all on its own. Babyface wrote and composed fifteen of the sixteen tracks, but it was the who's-who lineup of female artists—among them Toni Braxton, TLC, Mary J. Blige, and the film's star, Whitney Houston—who took the spotlight. The record was nominated for eleven Grammy Awards, with Houston's **Exhale (Shoop, Shoop)** winning Best R&B Song. *Waiting to Exhale* was more than a star-studded compilation of songs for a film; it was a curated collection of voices, connecting to each other from one track to the next. *–SS*

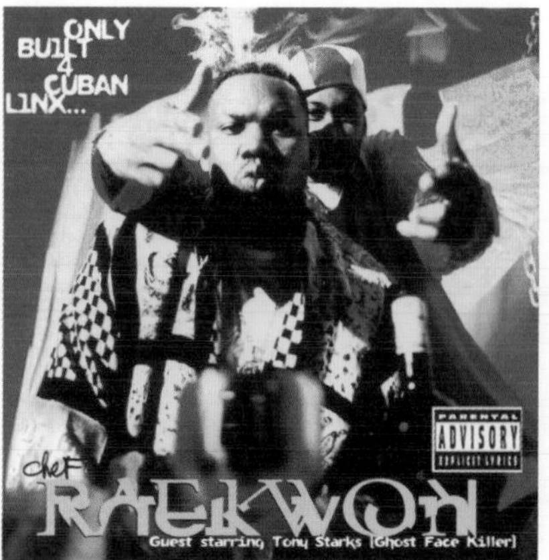

Raekwon
ONLY BUILT 4 CUBAN LINX . . .

LOUD/RCA | Producer: RZA

RELEASED: AUGUST 1, 1995

● The solo debut from Wu-Tang Clan's Raekwon, known colloquially as *The Purple Tape* because of the original cassette casing's color, was a joint effort, with Ghostface Killah appearing on two-thirds of the tracks and every Wu member eventually clocking in at some point. It's a dense and layered crime rap manifesto, with RZA's icy instrumentals laying the sonic foundation and snippets from John Woo's *The Killer* laced throughout. Rae and Ghost are lyrically dazzling, crafting head-spinning, gritty tales of street life so vivid it feels like a documentary. It became the most heralded Wu spinoff album for a reason: it's purple gold. *–AG*

Shaggy
BOOMBASTIC

VIRGIN | Producers: Tony Kelly, Bobby Digital, Robert Livingston

RELEASED: JULY 11, 1995

● *Boombastic* may not have been a real word, but there was no denying the impact the third studio album by Jamaican artist Shaggy (born Orville Richard Burrell) made on both the reggae and pop music scenes when it landed. Five singles were released, including **In the Summertime**, but it was the title track that helped propel the record to a 1996 Grammy Award for Best Reggae Album. *Boombastic* embodied the catchy beats and irresistible rhythm of the island, while Shaggy's rich, smooth voice danced over lyrics with a distinctive patois. His fantastic style and charisma created a whole new entry in the cross-cultural musical lexicon. *–SS*

Joan Osborne
RELISH

BLUE GORILLA | Producer: Rick Chertoff

RELEASED: MARCH 21, 1995

● Exuding earthy sensuality in nearly every note, *Relish* heralded the arrival of an original new voice, a grainy alto stitching blues, soul, and gospel into powerful tales of sin, salvation, troubled souls, and hot sex. With the Hooters' Eric Bazilian and Rob Hyman, Osborne crafted bewitching musings such as the slinky **Spider Web**, in which Ray Charles gains his sight but loses his sound. Ironically, its breakout hit—Bazilian's **One of Us**, which ponders God as human—contained Osborne's least-representative vocal. Still, *Relish*'s seductive, spiritual, empathic, and feminist tone drew multiple Grammy nominations and triple-platinum sales and earned Osborne prominent Lilith Fair billing. *–LM*

Pulp
DIFFERENT CLASS

ISLAND | Producer: Chris Thomas

RELEASED: OCTOBER 30, 1995

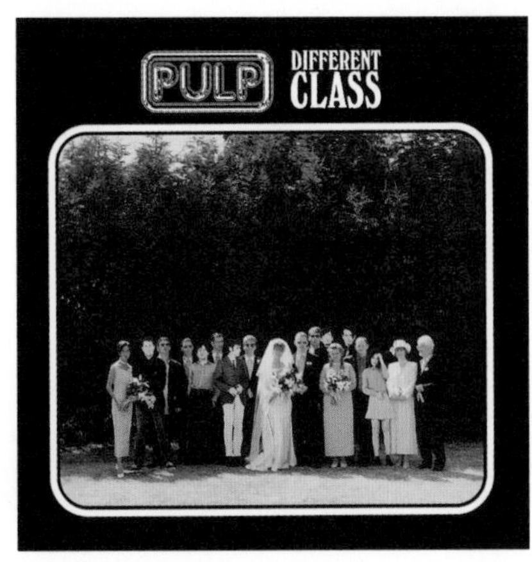

● Pulp's mainstream breakthrough was a long time coming. After forming in Sheffield, England, during the late 1970s (its debut album came out in 1983), it was during the Britpop explosion of the mid-'90s that Jarvis Cocker's cheeky art rock collective captured the zeitgeist with its class warfare anthem **Common People**, a triumphant, galvanizing screed against wealthy poseurs who glorify the struggles of the working class. It's one of four UK Top 10 hits on *Different Class*, Pulp's fifth album; **Sorted for E's & Wizz, Disco 2000**, and **Something Changed** were also windows into Cocker's sardonic eye, bittersweet soul, and restless wit. *–AG*

Alanis Morissette

JAGGED LITTLE PILL

MAVERICK/REPRISE | Producer: Glen Ballard

RELEASED: JUNE 13, 1995

● Alanis Morissette was Canada's answer to Debbie Gibson before she unleashed her raw, unapologetic third studio album, *Jagged Little Pill*. After being dropped by her label, the nineteen-year-old headed to Los Angeles. Within five minutes of arriving, she was robbed. The silver lining was that the robber took her money and left her lyrics, which would result in an album that went on to sell thirty-three million copies.

Morissette met record producer Glen Ballard, with whom she had an immediate rapport, and they quietly began working together. The songs formed quickly, with Morissette delivering vocals in one or two takes for almost every track. Morissette opted to not fix the flaws as many artists would have, and the spontaneity of those initial takes was like capturing lightning in a bottle. The finished album was rejected by a dozen labels until Guy Oseary, an executive at Madonna's Maverick Records, signed Morissette after hearing just thirty seconds of **Perfect**.

Six of the twelve songs on *Jagged Little Pill* became cross-format hits, but it was **You Oughta Know** that got everyone who heard it to do a mental double-take. It delivered in-your-face lyrics about love and betrayal; its anger and explicit lyrics provided a visceral singalong for broken hearts everywhere, with backing from Red Hot Chili Peppers members Dave Navarro on guitar and Flea on bass, and with Benmont Tench from Tom Petty's Heartbreakers on organ.

Jagged Little Pill won four Grammy Awards, including Album of the Year and Best Rock Album. It typecast Morissette as an angry young woman, but she simply reminded her critics that no one is singularly defined by one emotion. After selling that many albums, it's safe to assume that there were moments when she was quite happy. *–AD*

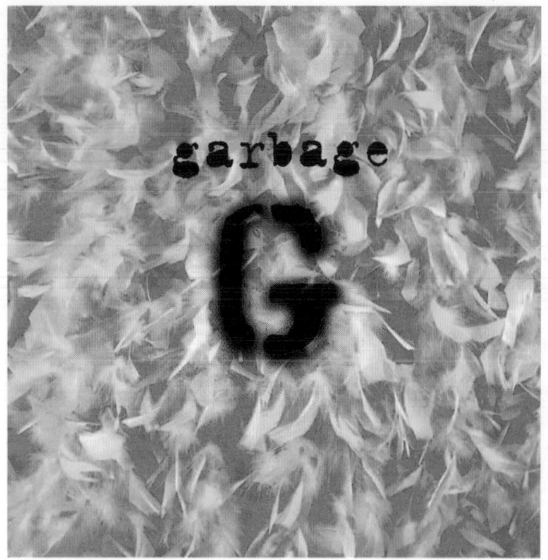

Garbage

GARBAGE

ALMO SOUNDS | Producer: Garbage

RELEASED AUGUST 15, 1995

● On *Garbage's* opening track, **Supervixen**, Shirley Manson commanded the listener to "bow down to me." By the end of the album, you were more than willing to oblige. The band Garbage was the brainchild of Butch Vig—producer of iconic albums by Nirvana, The Smashing Pumpkins, Sonic Youth, and others—who teamed with Wisconsin pals Steve Marker and Duke Erikson to create a fresh sound that blended elements of grunge, electronica, and rock. After joining forces with Scottish singer Manson, from the band Angelfish, they created an album that was completely different than anything on rock radio. *Garbage* is an expertly blended cocktail of electronic beats and razor-edged guitar mixed with Manson's vocals that ranged from purr to punky sneer to an angry roar. The biggest singles from the album displayed different areas of the band's brilliance, from the guitar-heavy defiance of **Vow** to the trip-hop grooves of **Queer**, the goth/pop straddle of **Only Happy When It Rains** to the sinewy funk bass lines of **Stupid Girl**. Even the **Vow** B-side **#1 Crush** became a hit after being featured in the film *Romeo + Juliet*. Decades later, these songs don't feel dated—just irresistible. *–RW*

Tricky

MAXINQUAYE

4TH & B'WAY | Producers: Tricky, Mark Saunders, Howie B, Kevin Petrie

RELEASED: FEBRUARY 20, 1995

● Bristol-born rapper and producer Tricky got his start in Massive Attack, the pioneering trip-hop group whose 1991 LP *Blue Lines* was a defining work of the era. But his diminished role in the group—he's barely a presence on *Blue Lines*—sent Tricky to a solo career that found him exploring similar territory while expanding its boundaries. *Maxinquaye*, his debut album, settled into an area that's part trip-hop, part experimental electronica, and part post-R&B. Its influence over the years can be heard from the first notes of the opening track, **Overcome**.

Recorded in his home studio in London with Martina Topley-Bird (among others, including Tricky) on vocals, *Maxinquaye* glided over soundscapes shaped from scratchy samples—a thick coating of dusty noise permeated each of the set's dozen songs. The album, named after Tricky's mother, quickly settled into a soulful, intimate groove. The twenty-seven-year-old Tricky drew from his life for inspiration; his insecurities, relationships, and drug use tied together many of the songs. The always-inventive music was consistently underlined by layers of dirty audio fog, a central instrument in *Maxinquaye*'s multileveled toolbox. *–MG*

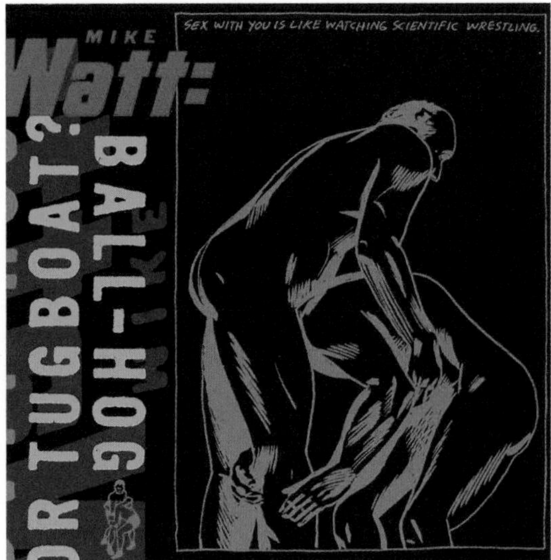

Mike Watt

BALL-HOG OR TUGBOAT?

COLUMBIA | Producer: Mike Watt

RELEASED: FEBRUARY 28, 1995

● The fifty guest musicians across the seventeen tracks presented here were testament to Mike Watt, the beloved bass man who co-founded So-Cal punk pioneers the Minutemen, and to a career bridging the second wave of US punk and the exploding alternative movement of the early '90s.

Watt, who famously and endearingly refers to himself in the third person, mobilized members of the Beastie Boys, Bikini Kill, Black Flag, Sonic Youth, Circle Jerks, Soul Asylum, Screaming Trees, Meat Puppets, Pixies, Dinosaur Jr, and Red Hot Chili Peppers, to name a few. The results were as eclectic as the roster would suggest. More accessible songs included a cover of Tony and Chip Kinman's delicious double-entendre, **Big Train** (one of just two tracks on which Watt tackled lead vocals and including the slide guitar histrionics of Nels Cline); the solid road-trip advice of **Piss-Bottle Man**, starring Lemonhead Evan Dando on vocals; and the minor Modern Rock hit **Against the 70's**, featuring Pearl Jam's Eddie Vedder and Dave Grohl during his transition from Nirvana to Foo Fighters.

Other highlights included Funkadelic's **Maggot Brain**, featuring keyboardist Bernie Worrell and Dinosaur Jr's J Mascis in the Eddie Hazel guitar chair, and the wistful **Drove Up from Pedro** (an addendum to the Minutemen classic "History Lesson—Part II"), sung by Geraldine Fibbers' Carla Bozulich. *—DP*

The Chieftains

THE LONG BLACK VEIL

RCA VICTOR | Producers: Paddy Maloney, Chris Kimsey, Ry Cooder

RELEASED: JANUARY 24, 1995

● The Chieftains did more to spread and preserve traditional Irish music than any other group or single artist from the Emerald Isle. But after thirty years of Uilleann pipes, tin whistles, harps, and bodhráns, the Paddy Maloney–led group expanded its terrain into collaborations with contemporary artists. *Irish Heartbeat*, a hit album with Belfast native Van Morrison, led to a Christmas themed long-player, and *The Bells of Dublin* teamed the group with Kate and Anna McGarrigle, Elvis Costello, and Marianne Faithful, among others. With *The Long Black Veil*, the Chieftains brought to their world a collection of sympathetic talents that flirted with rock 'n' roll while firmly anchored to Irish folk roots. The Chieftains' resident musical savant Derek Bell noted to Trouser Press at the time, "We feel we can unearth common musical ground with anyone." And they did it deftly. Moving contributions from Ry Cooder, Sinéad O'Connor, and Mark Knopfler were purely natural pairings, every note evoking the sea's mist in the Irish air. While The Rolling Stones were the marquee attraction, it's Mick Jagger's solo vocal turn on the title song that shined brightest. *—HK*

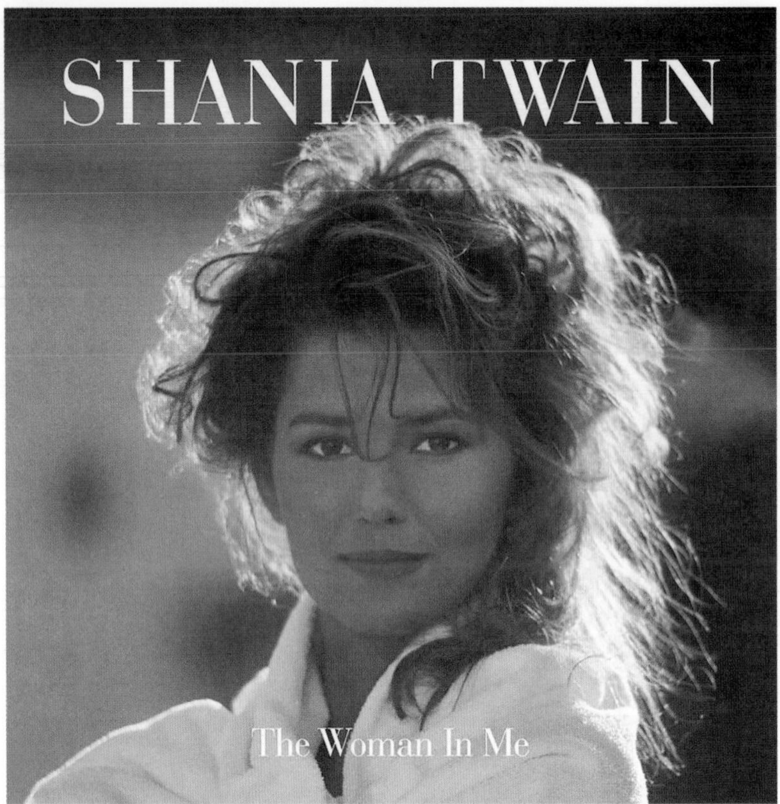

1995

Shania Twain

THE WOMAN IN ME

MERCURY | Producer: Robert John "Mutt" Lange

RELEASED: FEBRUARY 7, 1995

● They say the third time's the charm, but for Shania Twain, it only took two attempts to become a global country superstar. *The Woman in Me* followed her commercially dismal self-titled 1993 debut. It wasn't until Twain joined forces with legendary rock hitmaker Mutt Lange (AC/DC, Def Leppard) that things turned around in a major way. The two forged a long-distance friendship, discussing their fondness for one another's chosen musical genres while Lange lived in Europe and Twain in Nashville. Their first in-person meeting during the annual Fan Fair (now called CMA Fest) in Nashville in June 1993 led to songwriting together; they fell in love and were married in December.

The Woman In Me was the couple's first in-studio collaboration; they co-wrote most of its twelve tracks together. Eight singles were ultimately released to country radio, beginning with **Whose Bed Have Your Boots Been Under?**, which was Twain's first gold single. The follow-up, **Any Man of Mine**, became the first of four No. 1 country hits off the album, while **The Woman in Me (Needs the Man in You)** was Twain's first crossover hit on the Adult Contemporary chart.

The Woman in Me album went on to sell more than twenty million copies worldwide and win a boxload of awards, including Grammys for Best Country Album (and a Best New Artist nomination), a Juno for Country Female Vocalist of the Year, Album of the Year from the Academy of Country Music Awards, Country Album of the Year and Best Female Country Artist from Billboard, and the American Music Award for Favorite Country New Artist. In addition to introducing fans to a new kind of country music with its rock-influenced melodies and Lange's punchy production style, Twain's midriff-baring wardrobe choices and visually adventurous videos set her apart from the country pack. *–MH2*

Charlie Haden/Hank Jones

STEAL AWAY

VERVE | Producer: Charlie Haden

RELEASED: APRIL 4, 1995

● Pairing acoustic double bass and piano, two jazz legends delivered a heartfelt and contemporary treatment of a treasury of spirituals, folk songs, and hymns centered around slavery, racism, and civil rights. The selected material resonated with their life experiences, religious souls, and inner voices. Immediately, there was a spring in Hank Jones's piano keys touch on **It's Me Oh Lord**. The duet format allowed Charlie Haden's deep and luxurious bass sound to stand apart and to lead melodically, as on the slave song **Nobody Knows the Trouble I'm In**. Haden also contributed a respectful original, **Spiritual**, a tribute to civil rights activists Martin Luther King, Medgar Evers, and Malcolm X. *—CH*

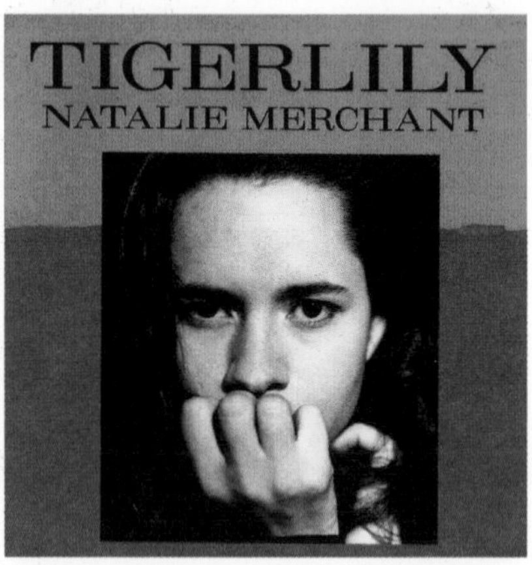

Natalie Merchant

TIGERLILY

ELEKTRA | Producer: Natalie Merchant

RELEASED JUNE 20, 1995

● A collective gasp came from college radio fans in 1993 when Natalie Merchant announced she "didn't want art by committee" and left 10,000 Maniacs, the band she'd fronted since she was seventeen. Less than two years later, her solo debut entered the Billboard charts. *Tigerlily* could never be mistaken for a 10,000 Maniacs album, however. Aside from the three singles—**Carnival**, **Wonder**, and **Jealousy**, all of which hit the Billboard Hot 100—the eleven-track album was more solemn and less catchy than the band's work. But the five-times platinum set—re-recorded by Merchant as *Paradise Is There: The New Tigerlily Recordings* in 2015—validated her instinct to go it alone. *—HD*

1995

Son Volt

TRACE

WARNER BROS. | Producers: Brian Paulson, Son Volt

RELEASED: SEPTEMBER 19, 1995

● The 1994 breakup of Uncle Tupelo spawned two great bands: Jeff Tweedy's Wilco and Jay Farrar's Son Volt. Son Volt's original lineup featured Farrar on guitar and vocals, original Tupelo drummer Mike Heidorn, and brothers Dave and Jim Boquist (a multi-instrumentalist and bassist, respectively). Their debut was a stone classic of alt-country. Four songs especially were standouts: **Windfall**, which precisely described Farrar's stoic manner and musical approach; **Tear-Stained Eye**, a shoulda-been country classic that never got the Merle Haggard cover it deserved; and two muscular rockers (**Route** and **Drown**) that proved the post-Tupelo Farrar could still blow the roof off the dump. *—DD*

Donald Lawrence and the Tri-City Singers
BIBLE STORIES

CRYSTAL ROSE/SPARROW | Producers: Donald Lawrence, Kevin Bond

RELEASED: MAY 1, 1995

● The sophomore project from Donald Lawrence and the Tri-City Singers was a groundbreaking thematic album reflecting stories of the Bible through song. Lawrence served as the vocal coach for the R&B group En Vogue and the musical director for Stephanie Mills; he used all those experiences to bring *Bible Stories* to life. Known for being the first gospel project to use looping technology, *Bible Stories* landed at No. 1 on the Billboard Gospel Album charts and received a Grammy Award nomination for Best Gospel Album by a Choir or Chorus. Its outstanding tracks included **Stranger**, **A Message for the Saints**, **Oh Peter**, **I Am God**, and **When Sunday Comes**, the latter featuring Reverend Daryl Coley. *–CP*

GZA
LIQUID SWORDS

GEFFEN | Producer: RZA

RELEASED: NOVEMBER 7, 1995

● The chill running through the debut album from GZA was as cold as the wailing winds of a Staten Island winter. The third Wu-Tang solo shot of 1995, following releases by ODB and Raekwon, it confirmed the Wu-Tang Clan's oldest member was also its most calculated, his flows resembling complex math equations or physics formulas. With Wu-Tang mastermind RZA at the helm, *Liquid Swords* was pointed in its execution; sound clips from 1980's *Shogun Assassin* appeared throughout, adding to its cinematic scope. The album finally went platinum in 2015, twenty years after its release. While its attack was swift, it left a lasting mark. *–AG*

Mobb Deep
THE INFAMOUS

LOUD | Producers: Mobb Deep, The Abstract

RELEASED: APRIL 25, 1995

● Mobb Deep had no use for niceties on its second album. The Queens duo of rappers Prodigy and Havoc painted a hostile portrait of the New York streets in their tales of hustlers, dreamers, and the hopeless trying to make it through one more day without dying. Dark and despairing, *The Infamous* helped set the tone for East Coast hip-hop during the mid-'90s, its repeating synth loops and minimal production coloring songs such as **Shook Ones (Part II)** and **Survival of the Fittest**. *–MG*

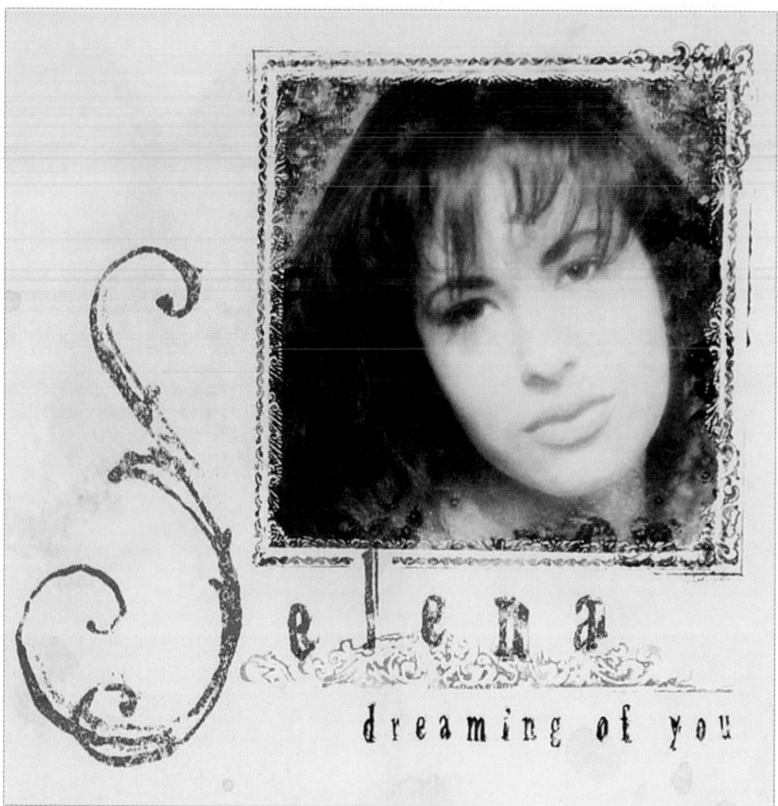

Selena

DREAMING OF YOU

EMI/EMI LATIN | Producers: Keith Thomas, Guy Roche, Rhett Lawrence, Arto Lindsay, Susan Rogers, David Byrne, A. B. Quintanilla III, José Hernández

RELEASED: JULY 18, 1995

● What was to be triumph ended in tragedy when Selena Quintanilla was murdered on March 31, 1995, at the age of twenty-three by a former business associate while she was in the midst of recording her first predominately English-language album. That *Dreaming of You* was as special as it turned out was a credit to both Selena's legacy and the work of those who picked up the pieces.

Selena was a hitmaking legend in the Latin music community by the mid-'90s, and the English-language tracks on *Dreaming of You* gave the Anglo audience its most accessible taste of her yet. The smooth, sultry **Missing My Baby** (with Full Force), the slinky **Captive Heart**, and the lush title track hit the Pop (with a capital P) target dead-on—though some would complain that they airbrushed away the fire of her previous recordings. **God's Child (Baila Conmigo)** with Talking Heads' David Byrne was certainly hipper, and the Spanish half of the rest of the album, some of it remixes of previously released songs, offered a juxtaposition to open newcomers' ears to Selena's earlier catalog.

Dreaming of You was a posthumous breakthrough. It debuted at No. 1 on the Billboard 200, a first for a predominately Spanish-language album. Its 175,000 first-day sales was a record for a female solo artist. The album was named Female Pop Album of the Year at the Billboard Latin Music Awards and Album of the Year at the 1996 Tejano Music Awards. *Dreaming of You* was her lone entry on the Billboard Hot 100 (No. 22) and was certified gold. Selena's death may have brought greater attention and driven sales, as is usually the case, but *Dreaming of You* showed many the great potential that remained. *—GG*

SONY
Professional

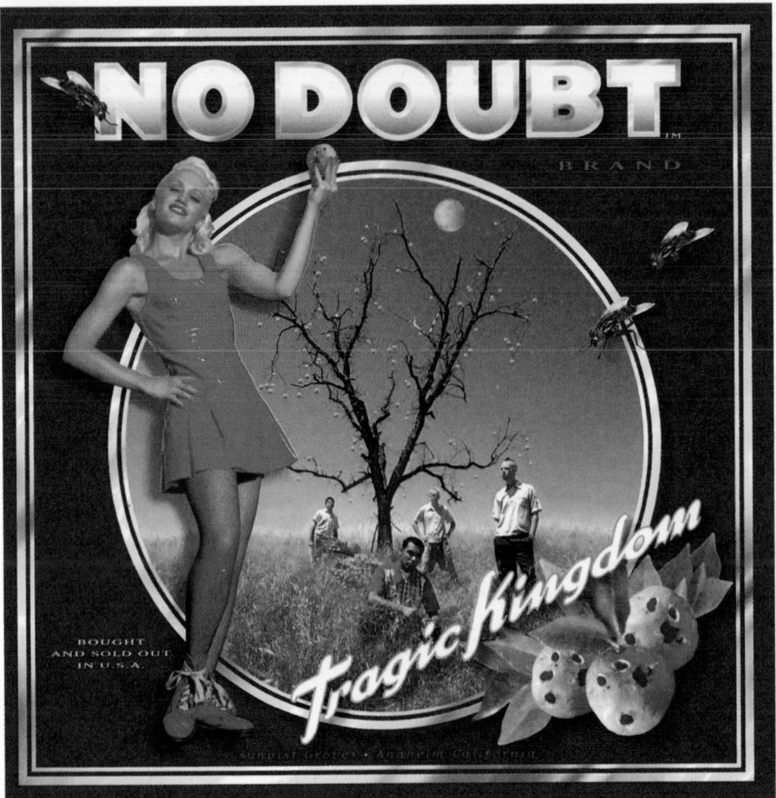

No Doubt

TRAGIC KINGDOM

TRAUMA/INTERSCOPE | Producer: Matthew Wilder

RELEASED: OCTOBER 10, 1995

● Listeners knew *Tragic Kingdom* was new territory for No Doubt at the opening notes of its first track, **Spiderwebs**, which went on to become one of the quartet's biggest hits. The song is relentless like a roller coaster that maintains its dizzying momentum until you're clapping at the end gate. You just want more of it.

The entire fourteen-track album, in fact, boasted a kind of carnival feel—bright tones and instrumental colors supporting Gwen Stefani's commanding vocals and rough-hewn attitude, which was part doe-eyed romantic and part tough-girl muscle. It's an hourlong aural thrill ride with enough musical substance to make it more than a cheap thrill. Years later, it sounds as fresh as the day the CD was unwrapped and jammed into your five-disc changer. *Tragic Kingdom* may have taken its title from a disparaging term one of guitarist Tom Dumont's seventh-grade teachers used for Disneyland, but for fans who drove it to No. 1 on the Billboard 200 and diamond-certfied sales, it felt like one of the happiest places on Earth.

This didn't mean everything was hunky-dory, though. After the commercial shortcoming of 1995's *The Beacon Street Collection*, the band was under the gun, smartly enlisting an outside producer (Matthew Wilder of "Break My Stride" fame) to serve as song doctor as well as engineer. Stefani and bassist Tony Kanal had also broken up, which accounted for some of the lyrical darkness but also gave No Doubt a generational hit in **Don't Speak**, which set a record atop the Billboard Hot 100 Airplay chart.

But it was really *Tragic Kingdom*'s eclectic array—encompassing rock, pop, reggae, and ska across tracks such as **Just a Girl**, **Happy Now?**, **Different People**, **Sunday Morning**, and **World Go 'Round**—that carried the weight and made sure the ride would stay thrilling for years to come. *–EP*

Bone Thugs-N-Harmony

E. 1999 ETERNAL

RUTHLESS | Producers: Eazy-E, DJ U-Neek, Tony C, Kenny McCloud

RELEASED: JULY 25, 1995

● Asking if Bone Thugs-N-Harmony is a one-hit wonder this long after the Cleveland rap trio released its sophomore album is crazy. The Grammy Award–winning group has sold more than fifty million albums, after all. But back in 1995—on the heels of the previous year's debut EP *Creepin on ah Come Up* and the hit "Thuggish, Ruggish Bone"—that was a fair question.

The group made clear there was more to come with *E. 1999 Eternal*. Opening with the words "welcome to the dark side," the troupe wasted no time setting the tone for the tone; its brand of G-funk, personified with dark and violent lyrics that amplified crime and drug use, illustrated what the gritty life was like on the east side of Cleveland. Across seventeen tracks, Bone Thugs-N-Harmony demonstrated why it was one of the most lyrically creative rap groups of all time, able to flow at rapid pace while harmonizing multiple voices at once. The most impressive thing about Bone Thugs-N-Harmony's career-defining album is that it remains as on point and relevant as when it was released—fitting for an album set, conceptually, in the future.

The album also served as a tribute to its executive producer, the legendary Eric "Eazy-E" Wright of N.W.A fame, who died four months before *E. 1999 Eternal* dropped. Eazy-E signed Bone Thugs to Ruthless Records in 1993 and produced its first two albums. The group offered **Tha Crossroads** as a salute to its fallen mentor as well as other departed members of its families.

E. 1999 Eternal sold more than three hundred thousand copies during its first week of release and became the group's best-selling album after going four-times platinum, and **Crossroad** spent eight weeks at No. 1 on the Billboard Hot 100. It was also nominated for Best Rap Album at the 38th Annual Grammy Awards in 1996, along with **1st of tha Month** in the Best Rap Performance by a Duo or Group category. *–ZC*

1996

96
-SIX

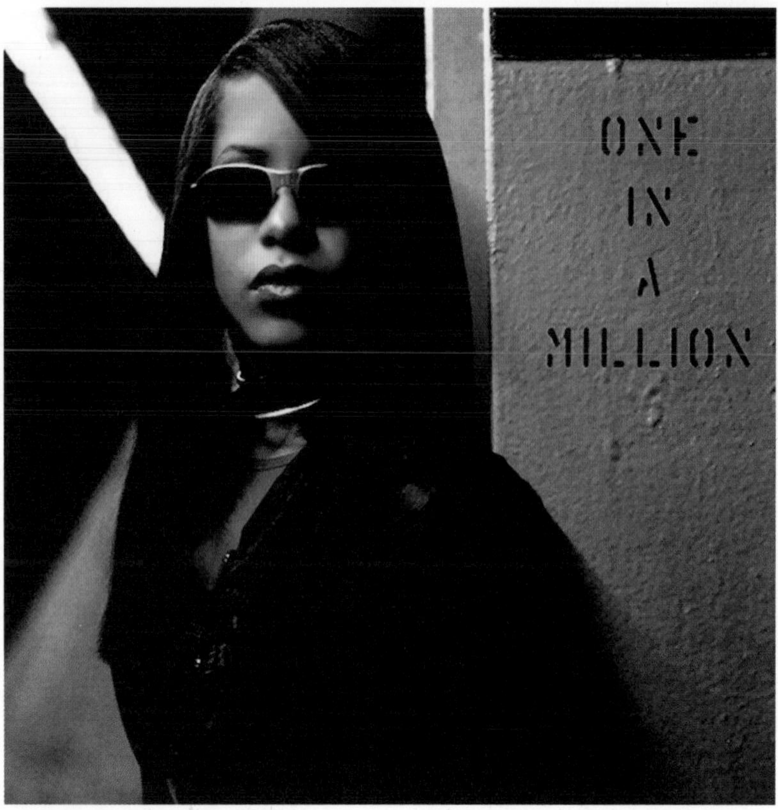

1996

Aaliyah

ONE IN A MILLION

BLACKGROUND/ATLANTIC | Producers: Timbaland, Carl-So-Lowe, J. Dibbs, Jermaine Dupri, KayGee, Vincent Herbert, Rodney Jerkins, Craig King, Darren Lighty, Daryl Simmons

RELEASED: AUGUST 13, 1996

● When a Bahamian plane crash took her life in August 2001 at the age of twenty-two, Aaliyah was already considered a generation-defining songstress thanks to 1996's *One in a Million*. The album showed stunning depth for a seventeen-year-old. Aaliyah had arrived on the scene with 1994's *Age Ain't Nothing But a Number*, but *One in a Million* made her a superstar.

The journey from first album to second was turbulent. *One in a Million* was Aaliyah's first release after her tumultuous split from R. Kelly, following an illegal marriage. Sean "Puffy" Combs was slated to produce the album but dropped out. Enter the relatively unknown Timbaland and Missy Elliott, whose fingerprints were all over this album. Hip-hop beats intertwined with Aaliyah's velvety-smooth R&B tones throughout. *One in a Million* pushed boundaries with funk and electronica samples, setting it apart from others in the genre at the time. The songs showed the range of the Aaliyah/Timbaland/Missy Elliott trio, maybe none more than the title track, with its mashup of funk and hip-hop flavors. The rest of the album ranged from covers of the Isley Brothers (**Choosey Lover**) and Marvin Gaye (**Got to Give It Up** with Slick Rick) to the more pop-inspired fare such as **Everything's Gonna Be Alright**.

One in a Million bettered its predecessor in commercial terms as well. It hit No. 10 on the Billboard 200 and No. 2 on the Top R&B/Hip-Hop Albums chart on its way to triple-platinum certification. It produced a No. 1 single in **If Your Girl Only Knew**, while **Are You That Somebody?** was nominated for a Grammy, two MTV Music Video Awards, and a pair of *Soul Train* Lady of Soul Awards. Aaliyah never got the chance to blossom into a full-blown diva, but thanks to *One in a Million*, we can be confident she would have gotten there. *–ZC*

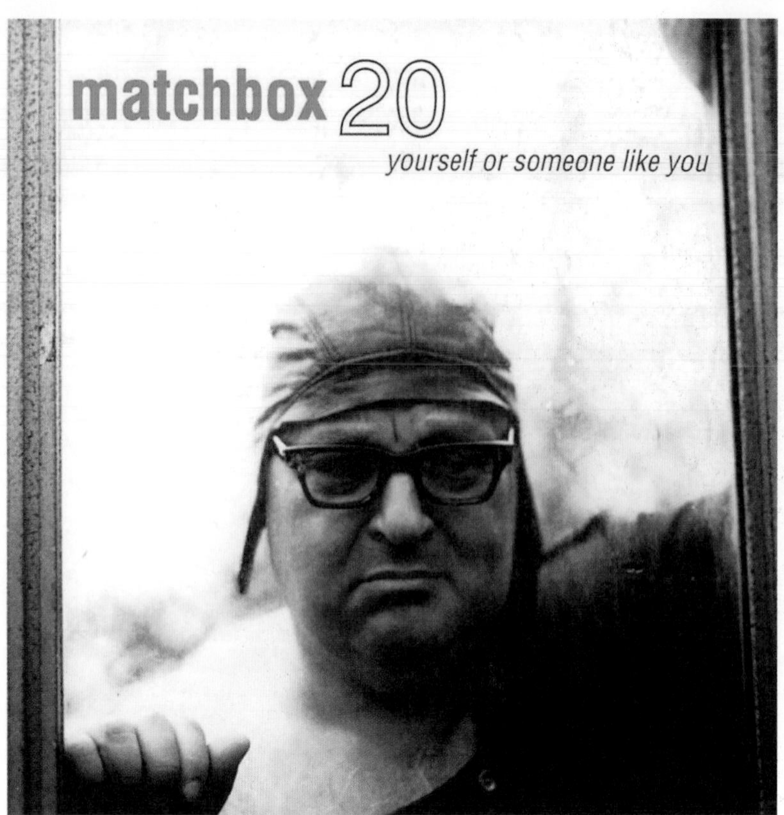

Matchbox Twenty

YOURSELF OR SOMEONE LIKE YOU

LAVA/ATLANTIC | Producer: Matt Serletic

RELEASED: OCTOBER 1, 1996

● A shift from grunge in the mid-'90s left a musical wilderness waiting to be explored, and Matchbox Twenty pushed its way in with its debut album. Merely one year after being co-founded by Rob Thomas and Paul Doucette in Orlando, Florida, the band became part of the public consciousness.

Mainstream rock was taking over, and with it came even more emphasis on commercial radio—and Matchbox Twenty was all over the airwaves from 1996 to 1998 (and beyond). *Yourself or Someone Like You* contained what are still some of the band's most well-known songs thanks to heavy rotation (some may say *too* heavy) on Top 40 radio. The lyrics may have been burned into our collective brains, but what made those hooks memorable could also be attributed to Thomas's skill as a singer and songwriter. His slightly gritty voice fit these songs perfectly because he was telling stories he knew. There was even a creep of Thomas's Southern accent in **3AM** and heard throughout the album, which lent an authenticity and vulnerability to the songs. References to anger, emotional abuse, and loneliness come up repeatedly, even on more upbeat tracks such as **Real World**.

Producer Matt Serletic, known for his work with Collective Soul, made heavy use of lead and rhythm guitars, which were especially notable when **Push** juxtaposed the gentle, elegant progressions against Thomas's fierce vocals. The album showcased a variety of arrangements, allowing each song to revel in its own personality rather than conforming to a specific genre. As such, *Yourself . . .* was one of Matchbox Twenty's edgier records, straddling the line between alternative and pop and representing a shift from the loud, disenfranchised angst expressed by grunge to the more mellow, fretful dissatisfaction that would define '90s mainstream pop and, eventually, emo rock. *–SS*

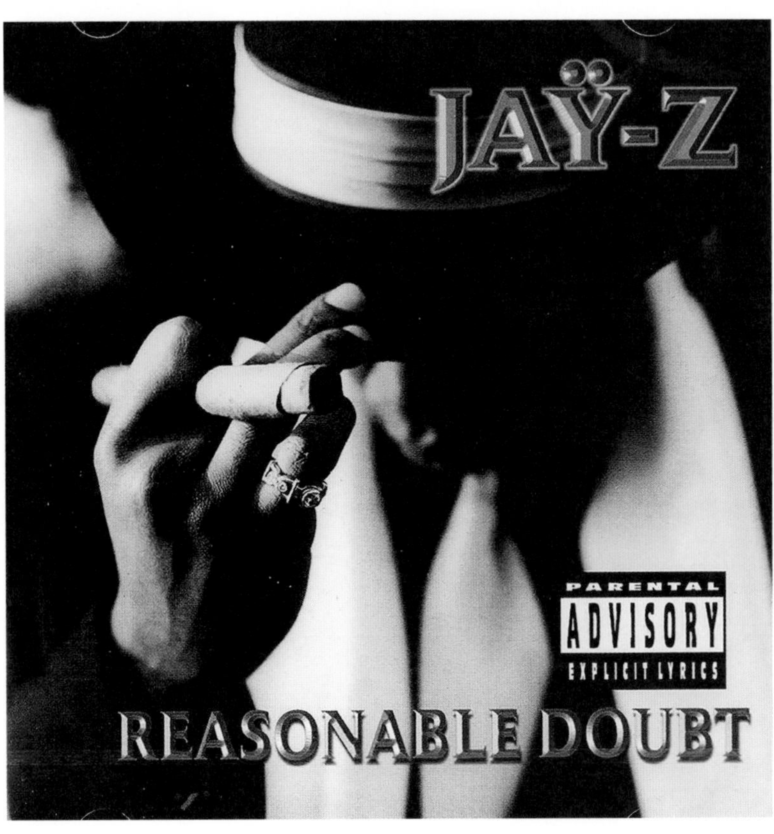

Jay-Z

REASONABLE DOUBT

ROC-A-FELLA/PRIORITY | Producers: Jay-Z, Damon Dash, Kareem "Biggs" Burke

RELEASED: JUNE 25, 1996

● Jay-Z's debut was not a hit at the time of its release. The perceived commercial failure of *Reasonable Doubt*—it peaked at No. 23 on the Billboard 200—became a key component of Shawn Carter's origin story as he developed into one of the most accomplished rappers of all time.

Reasonable Doubt was his blueprint before *The Blueprint*. It laid out Jay-Z's hustle and his street smarts as he navigated New York's streets and lived out his gangster movie fantasies, like those depicted in *Carlito's Way* (heavily referenced here) and *Scarface*. Mostly it illustrated his lyrical prowess, the way his precise, dexterous wordplay intertwined with his impeccable flow. Jay-Z was rapping for his life on *Reasonable Doubt*, but he never let you see him sweat.

Jay-Z was twenty-five years old when he released this—old enough to have been around the block, young enough to be driven by an insatiable hunger to succeed. That ambition is all over tracks such as **Politics as Usual** and **22 Two's**, the latter built around a verse where Jay-Z flips twenty-two variations on the words to, too, and two in a pure flex of his poetic muscle. Another key to Jay-Z's story was his early affiliation with the Notorious B.I.G., and he and "Biggie" traded rhymes on the enthralling **Brooklyn's Finest**, which came so early in the album (track three) it was like he couldn't wait to show it off.

Elsewhere, **Can I Live** made good on its loop of Isaac Hayes's "The Look of Love," and **Dead Presidents II** borrowed a Nas sample that would go on to become a point of contention in the pair's future feud. By that time, *Reasonable Doubt* had rightfully been etched in stone as a classic. It even eventually went platinum, so Jay-Z truly had nothing to complain about. *–AG*

Squirrel Nut Zippers

HOT

MAMMOTH | Producers: Brian Paulson, Mike Napolitano

RELEASED: JUNE 4, 1996

● Swing was the thing, again, during the mid-'90s, and Squirrel Nut Zippers (SNZ) definitely had that thing at the right time. The American roots–digging North Carolina troupe was in peak form with its second album, mining a brassy territory between the New York City ballrooms and the N'awlins speakeasies with authentic spirit, chops, and good humor. *Hot* scorched its way to No. 27 on the Billboard 200 and was certified platinum, while the single **Hell** gave SNZ a Top 20 hit on the Alternative Airplay chart. *–GG*

Rage Against the Machine

EVIL EMPIRE

EPIC | Producer: Brendan O'Brien

RELEASED: APRIL 16, 1996

● With its sophomore release, Rage Against the Machine continued what it did best: politically charged protest anthems that violently fused rock and hip-hop with angry rap verses layered over metal jams. *Evil Empire* pulled no punches. The stomping **Bulls on Parade** objected to the American military-industrial complex, while **Down Rodeo** dealt with systemic racism. *Evil Empire* debuted at No. 1 on the Billboard Hot 200 and equaled the triple-platinum sales of the band's self-titled 1992 debut. **Tire Me**, meanwhile, won a Grammy for Best Metal Performance despite getting zero radio play, and **Bulls on Parade** and **People of the Sun** were nominated for Best Hard Rock Performance. *–ZC*

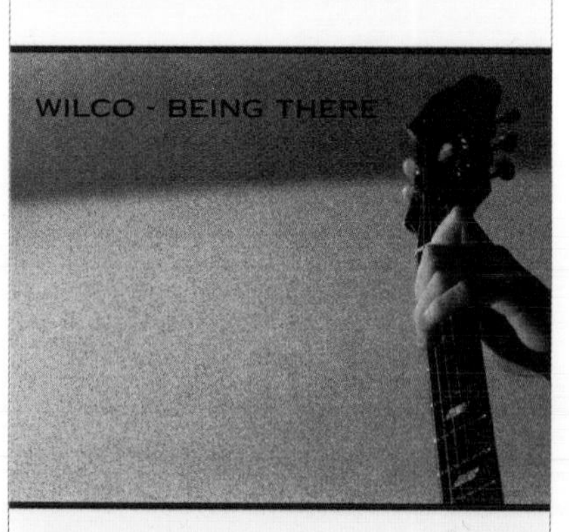

Wilco

BEING THERE

REPRISE | Producer: Wilco

RELEASED: OCTOBER 29, 1996

● As the album where Wilco began to grow out of the alt-country roots that were seeded throughout its 1995 debut, *Being There* was a double-record rock 'n' roll history lesson, from riff-driven, Rolling Stones–like pop (**Outtasite [Outta Mind]**) to stripped-down surrealism (the seven-minute **Sunken Treasure**) to quoting the co-founder of proto-punks Pere Ubu on the six-and-half-minute opener, **Misunderstood**. Newcomer and multi-instrumentalist Jay Bennett pushed leader Jeff Tweedy into more ambitious musical ground, as the band tackled everything from hazy abstraction to buoyant power pop, paving the way toward its future masterpiece, *Yankee Hotel Foxtrot*. *–MG*

R.E.M.
NEW ADVENTURES IN HI-FI

WARNER BROS. | Producers: Scott Litt, R.E.M.

RELEASED: SEPTEMBER 10, 1996

● R.E.M.'s *Monster* tour nearly killed them: multiple band members were rushed to hospitals, and drummer Bill Berry collapsed onstage after suffering a brain aneurysm. But from that tour sprang *New Adventures in Hi-Fi*, a brave and, yes, adventurous fourteen-song collection recorded on the road with no organizing principle. The band worked through stark folk-pop (**How the West Was Won and Where It Got Us** and **E-Bow the Letter**), arena rock (**The Wake-Up Bomb** and **Leave**), and even a lounge-lite instrumental (**Zither**). Its singles never ignited radio, but *New Adventures in Hi-Fi* is a solemn and sweet closing chapter for Berry, who departed R.E.M. in 1997. *–AG*

Stereolab
EMPEROR TOMATO KETCHUP

ELEKTRA | Producers: John McEntire, Paul Tipier, Stereolab

RELEASED: MARCH 18, 1996

● At the time of its release, *Emperor Tomato Ketchup* was Stereolab's most experimental album to date. The band was well known for the dissonant, lo-fi direction of its earlier works, but *Emperor Tomato Ketchup* was a 180-degree pivot from that. The British-French sextet explored a more pop-centric direction this time while also incorporating loops and soundscapes and taking cues from musical sources such as Can, Neu, Faust, and French Ya-Ya pop sounds. Unapologetically adventurous and supported by college and alternative radio stations, *Emperor Tomato Ketchup* remains one of the most influential albums of the '90s. *–WW*

Patti Smith
GONE AGAIN

ARISTA | Producers: Malcolm Burn, Lenny Keye

RELEASED: JUNE 18, 1996

● Patti Smith's first new album in eight years was the product of great trauma: the deaths of her husband and MC5 alumnus Fred "Sonic" Smith and her brother Todd, as well as former boyfriend Robert Mapplethorpe, Patti Smith Group keyboardist Richard Sohl, and Kurt Cobain. Smith processed all that with a ferocious kind of grace on *Gone Again*'s eleven intense tracks, which included a co-write with Fred (**Summer Cannibals**), contributions from Tom Verlaine and John Cale, and Jeff Buckley's last recorded studio performance. *–GG*

Weezer

PINKERTON

D G C | Producer: Weezer

RELEASED: SEPTEMBER 24, 1996

1996

● Division ran, and still runs, deep in our country, and it extends all the way down into the recesses of the pop-punk world, where Weezer's sophomore album still reigns as one of the most loved and hated records ever—even by its creators. "*Pinkerton* is a hideous record," Weezer frontman Rivers Cuomo told *Entertainment Weekly* in 2001, deeming it "a hugely painful mistake that happened in front of hundreds of thousands of people and continues to happen on a grander and grander scale and just won't go away."

What went so right—and wrong—with the record? After the breakout success of the band's self-titled 1994 debut (aka "The Blue Album"), with its three charting singles and highly played videos, Cuomo, disillusioned with the rock-star lifestyle, moved back east from Los Angeles and enrolled at Harvard University to study music history and composition and try to blend back into a normal life. *Pinkerton*, released in lieu of a planned space-rock opera and named for the *Madame Butterfly* character BF Pinkerton (not the security company), chronicled Cuomo's loneliness, social anxiety, and frustration with girls during his stint on campus. The mood was reflected in both the sex-obsessed lyrics and the heavier, more dissonant sound of the self-produced album, which spawned just two minor alt-rock hits in **El Scorcho** and **The Good Life**. It was voted the third worst album of the year by *Rolling Stone* readers.

As time passed, however, the angsty *Pinkerton* gained a cult following, in part for being, of all things, a seminal emo album. Cuomo himself re-embraced it as "brave," and the band unleashed it again on fans during a 2010 tour, playing it in its entirety. To this day, at any mention of *Pinkerton*, Weezer fan pages still light up. *–SM*

MAS

Alejandro Escovedo

WITH THESE HANDS

RYKODISC | Producer: T. S. Bruton

RELEASED: JUNE 18, 1996

● By the time Alejandro Escovedo started his solo career, he'd already lived a number of musical lives. Coming from a family of players, Escovedo played punk rock with the Nuns in San Francisco and Judy Nylon in New York before moving to Austin, Texas, and playing roots rock with Rank and File, True Believers, and the Setters, as well as glam rock with Buick MacKane. Twenty years into his career, he struck out on his own.

With These Hands was Escovedo's third solo album. It was more accomplished sonically than its predecessors and included guest appearances by niece Sheila E., Willie Nelson, Jennifer Warnes, and Charlie Sexton, among others. Thematically, Escovedo moved on somewhat from the aching autobiographical topics that dominated predecessors *Gravity* and *Thirteen Years*—or maybe he was just able to make his troubles seem somewhat more universal. Among the album's highlights were the edgy rockers **Put You Down** and **Little Bottles**; the late-night laments **Pissed Off 2AM** and **Sometimes**; **Nickel & Spoon**, which featured Nelson's distinctive voice and guitar; and, wearing a favorite influence on his sleeve, **Tugboat**, dedicated to the Velvet Underground guitarist Sterling Morrison, who passed away while Escovedo was writing the album. *—DD*

Various Artists

TRAINSPOTTING (MUSIC FROM THE MOTION PICTURE)

CAPITOL | Producers: Various

RELEASED: JULY 9, 1996

● As the mid-'90s Britpop and Cool Britannia movements were having their moments, the soundtrack to Danny Boyle's propulsive, darkly comic take on author Irvine Welsh's heroin saga gave them a center. The *Trainspotting* soundtrack rounded up some of Britpop's key movers and shakers—Blur, Pulp, Elastica, Sleeper—alongside electronic acts (Leftfield, Underworld) and key '70s and '80s forebears (Lou Reed, Brian Eno, Iggy Pop, New Order) for a collection of songs united by their zeal for life.

Or maybe their **Lust for Life**. That 1977 hell-raiser from punk godfather Iggy Pop opened the album, as well as the movie, its swinging, exhilarating drumbeat setting the tone for what followed. Sleeper turned in a driving cover of Blondie's 1980 disco-flavored rocker **Atomic**, and Pulp's **Mile End**, an ode to slumming it, captured the film's celebration of squalor, its shrugged-shoulders approach to dead-serious subject matter and just-get-by attitude.

Underworld's euphoric, pounding **Born Slippy** was *Trainspotting*'s signature song, its cavernous beat and repeated rhythms echoing the vicious doom cycle of its main characters. But for as bleak as it could be, *Trainspotting* was ultimately hopeful, and that can be attributed to those songs that became its heartbeat. *—AG*

Steve Earle

I FEEL ALRIGHT

E-SQUARED/WARNER BROS. | Producers: Ray Kennedy, Richard Bennett, Richard Dodd

RELEASED: MARCH 5, 1996

● A brash outlaw-country disciple with actual outlaw bona fides and a testosterone-tough but still-soft heart, Steve Earle used his second post-jail album to confess the errors of his ways while defiantly insisting he'll never completely reform or just go away. Musically, he traversed territory between Buddy Holly and The Beatles (with a nod to the Bobby Fuller Four) in **Hard-Core Troubadour**, **More Than I Can Do**, and **Poor Boy**, then spooned up the honey-sweet love song **Valentine's Day** with Fairfield Four harmonies before rocking with feral urgency on **The Unrepentant**. He addressed his addiction struggles with a pair of finely picked back-porch blues tunes, **South Nashville Blues** and **CCKMP**, the latter's numbing harmonium drone reinforcing his admission that cocaine cannot kill his pain but heroin can.

Earle belied once-common Bruce Springsteen comparisons with songs like his mandolin-led outlaws-on-the-run saga **Billie and Bonnie**, which owed more to Robert Earl Keen's "The Road Goes on Forever"; in fact, besides an ad-libbed "Rosalita" reference in **Hard-Core Troubadour**, Earle comes closest to invoking The Boss with his harmonica on the Lucinda Williams duet **You're Still Standin' There**. *I Feel Alright* proved Earle was the one still standing—finally clean and creatively resurrected. *–LM*

Various Artists

RENT: ORIGINAL BROADWAY CAST RECORDING

DREAMWORKS | Producers: Arif Mardin, Steve Skinner

RELEASED: AUGUST 27, 1996

● Based on Puccini's 1896 opera *La Bohème*, Jonathan Larson's *Rent* was a rock opera with a clear lineage from *Hair*. The story revolved around a group of young bohemians—diverse in gender, sexuality, socioeconomic standing, ethnicity, and HIV status—struggling to make a life, make love, and make ends meet in New York's gritty Alphabet City. The moving **Seasons of Love** became a standalone hit, and the cast recording even included an alternate version of the song with Stevie Wonder. The rest of the set is a somewhat jarring mashup of dialogue (both sung and spoken) and the kind of quippy modern rock tracks that play best onstage. The importance of the musical can't be overstated, but there's not a lot on the recording that you'll walk around singing or humming.

Larson, who wrote the lyrics and music and tragically died suddenly at the age of thirty-five the night before the show's off-Broadway premier, prophetically gifted the character of Roger Davis, an HIV-positive songwriter played by Adam Pascal, the lyric "I'm writing one great song before I go . . . one blaze of glory." *Rent* won four Tony Awards, including Best Musical, as well as a Pulitzer Prize. *–HD*

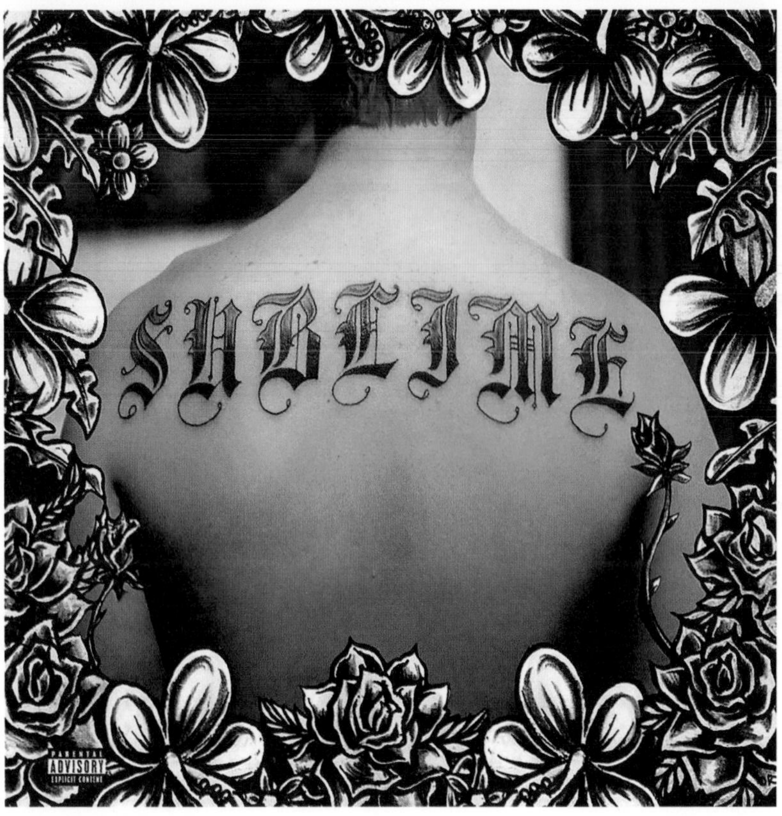

Sublime

SUBLIME

MCA | Producers: Paul Leary, David Kahne

RELEASED: JULY 30, 1996

● Ska has a quirky ability to convey dark themes disguised by an incredibly bright and bouncy sound. And that's exactly what Sublime's self-titled album did. Though considered ska, the album plays with a pan-pop music sound. Despite the brightness, *Sublime* was a collection of seventeen incredibly raw and emotionally honest tracks that flip the notion of Southern California happiness on its head.

The songs on Sublime's third album and first major label release were marked by promiscuous drug use, living in poverty, and the ramifications of violence and social injustice. Tracks such as **Santeria** and **The Ballad of Johnny Butt** offered a laid-back, island-flavored vibe verging on reggae, but **Paddle Out** and **Same in the End** were frantic to the point of almost being manic. A gentle bass line and slow drumbeat made **Garden Grove** feel light and airy, but the song lamented the financial toll wreaked by the narrator's drug addiction. **April 29, 1992 (Miami)**, meanwhile, spoke specifically about the Los Angeles riots that started on that date, turning the city upside down.

The songs were not entirely fiction, of course. Sublime frontman Bradley Nowell famously struggled with heroin addiction, providing a major through line for the album. Sadly, Nowell fatally overdosed in a San Francisco hotel room at the age of twenty-eight, just two months before *Sublime* dropped. That scotched any possibility of a major tour to support the album, but *Sublime* still debuted at No. 13 on the Billboard 200 and was certified five-times platinum. The breezy **What I Got** hit No. 1 on the Alternative Airplay chart, with **Santeria** and **Wrong Way** both reaching No. 3. It's a toss-up as to whether Sublime was the beneficiary of the rise of Third Wave ska during the mid-'90s or if the album's great commercial success is what put Third Wave on the map. *–ZC*

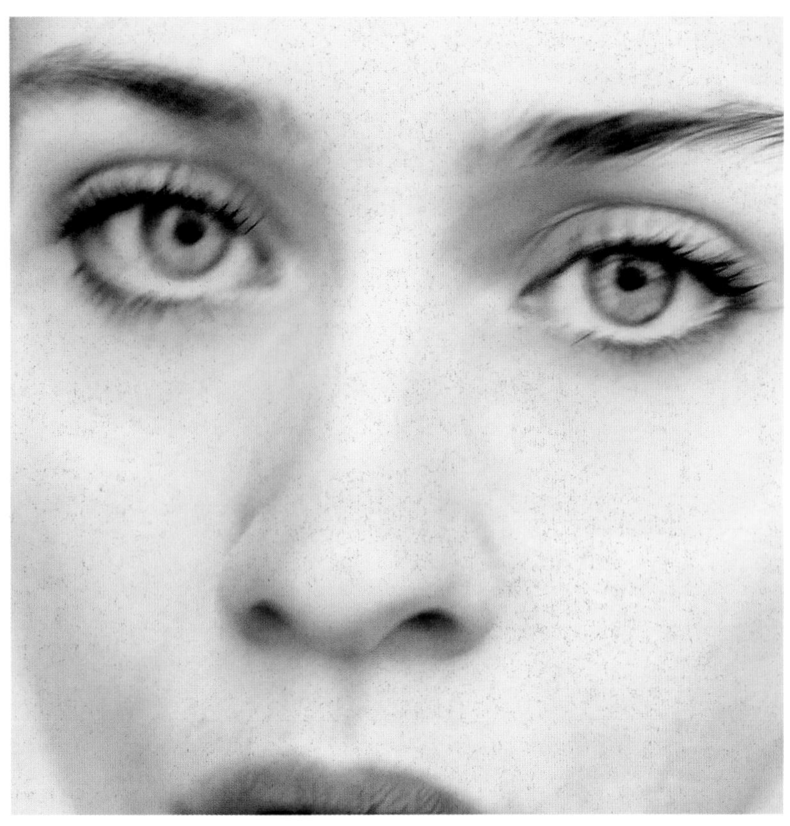

Fiona Apple

TIDAL

WORK/COLUMBIA | Producer: Andrew Slater

RELEASED: JULY 23, 1996

● *Tidal* introduced the music world to eighteen-year-old singer/songwriter Fiona Apple. The New York City native dealt with a traumatic childhood by utilizing poetry and songwriting to provide an outlet to her angst-filled upbringing; in doing so, she created one of the rare fully formed debut releases. The album eventually earned three-times platinum status, and few could believe it was written by someone so young.

With Apple's background in classical piano and her deep voice capable of handling a wide range of tone and emotion with ease, *Tidal*'s ten songs ranged in style from trip-hop to jazz to piano pop with a rich, atmospheric quality crafted from its lush production, its moodiness unspooling slowly from track to track. *Tidal* was released in an era that spawned a bumper crop of similar young female pop performers, but nobody else addressed and validated the emotional baggage held by teenagers quite like Apple did.

Of the three singles released from the album, **Criminal**, written in just forty-five minutes after the label asked Apple for something with clear-cut hit potential, became its biggest hit. With a menacing vibe and lyrics describing her guilt for using her sexuality to her advantage, it rose to No. 2 on Billboard's Adult Alternative Songs chart and was certified platinum. **Sleep to Dream** and **Shadowboxer**, the other two singles, showcased Apple's feelings of skepticism, sensitivity, and wisdom, though also expressing anger over betrayal and other injustices in the world.

Although not released as a single, **The First Taste** was another highlight. The lament about first love provided the album's most musically complex song, with a Latin-tinged beat carrying guitars, percussion, and electric synths along for a catchy ride. *Tidal* finished on a high note with **Carrion** and its showstopping piano-led chorus and a symphonic buildup to its conclusion. *–JC*

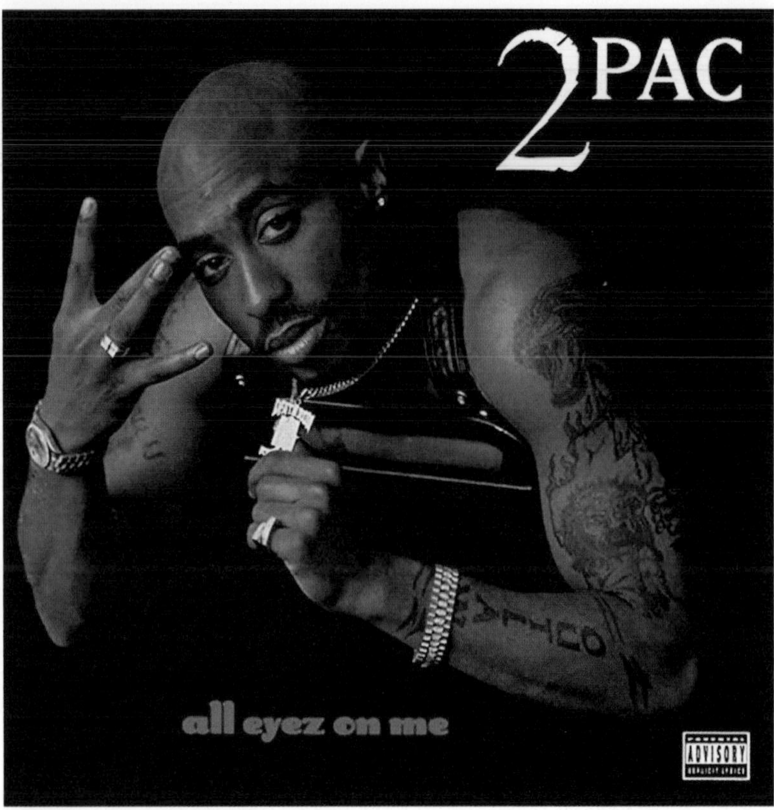

2Pac

ALL EYEZ ON ME

DEATH ROW/INTERSCOPE | Producer: Suge Knight

RELEASED: FEBRUARY 13, 1996

● What happens when a musical genius has nothing to do but read books from Niccolò Machiavelli and Sun Tzu? A seminal rap album, that's what.

In 1995, Tupac Shakur (né Lesane Crooks) was incarcerated until Death Row Records chief Suge Knight and producer Jimmy Iovine paid more than a million dollars to bail him out. The deal in return was that Shakur would release three albums on Death Row. Over the course of two months, 2Pac laid down tracks for the first double album in rap history. The pent-up aggression of being behind bars came screaming through the first track, **Ambitionz Az a Ridah**, and didn't stop for more than two hours. There was a frantic nature to the whole thing but also incredible range.

2Pac's flow was cut by an absurd list of rap A-listers, including features from Snoop Dogg, Method Man and Redman from Wu-Tang Clan, Nate Dogg, and Dr. Dre, among others. Tracks such as **I Ain't Mad at Cha**, in which Shakur envisioned his own death, not only cut deep but were prophetic—he was gunned down in Las Vegas at the age of twenty-five, just seven months after *All Eyez on Me* was released.

The album was also home to 2Pac's most famous track, **California Love**; it featured Dr. Dre, who produced it, and Roger Troutman of the band Zapp and was billed as a "Remix" that spent eight weeks at No. 1 on the Billboard Hot 100 and was nominated for a Grammy Award. *All Eyez on Me* has been certified diamond, and its reputation has only grown over the years—partly due to the tragic circumstances that followed. But the album is indeed 2Pac personified: violent and profane but authentic tales crafted by a brilliant wordsmith. *–ZC*

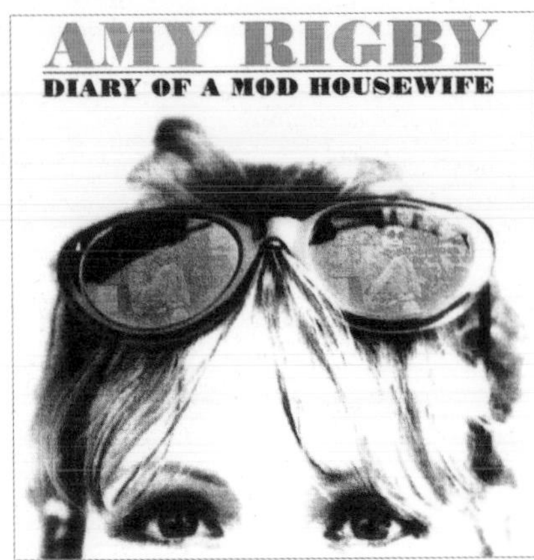

Amy Rigby

DIARY OF A MOD HOUSEWIFE

KOCH | Producer: Elliot Easton, Gene Holder

RELEASED: 1996

● With a novelist's eye for detail and a satirist's keen wit, Amy Rigby spun mundane moments into brilliantly insightful chronicles of romance versus the weight of dashed dreams and hope that clings despite life's disappointments. Drawing on '60s girl groups, twangy country, punk, folk, and rockabilly, she delivered forlorn laments with melodic charm, enhanced by production from Cars guitarist Elliot Easton and Gene Holder of the dB's, along with Greg Leisz's dobro and steel guitar. *Salon* labeled Rigby's debut "perfect." In a more just world, songs such as **Beer & Kisses** with John Wesley Harding and **The Good Girls** would have been hits. *–LM*

R. L. Burnside

A ASS POCKET OF WHISKEY

MATADOR | Producer: Matthew Johnson

RELEASED: JUNE 18, 1996

● There's a special place in heaven for young artists who make a point of bringing their roots to the spotlight. R. L. Burnside was a true Mississippi Delta juke joint musician who existed on the fringes, even to most blues fans. But in the company of the indie music trio Jon Spencer Blues Explosion, Burnside was infused with underground cred that introduced a style of music to a generation which might never have encountered it. The rhythm section kicked like Led Zeppelin's John Bonham and John Paul. The crunching guitars were more downtown New York than rural Clarksdale. Standing tall in the middle was Burnside, as authentic as red clay and twice as dirty. *–HK*

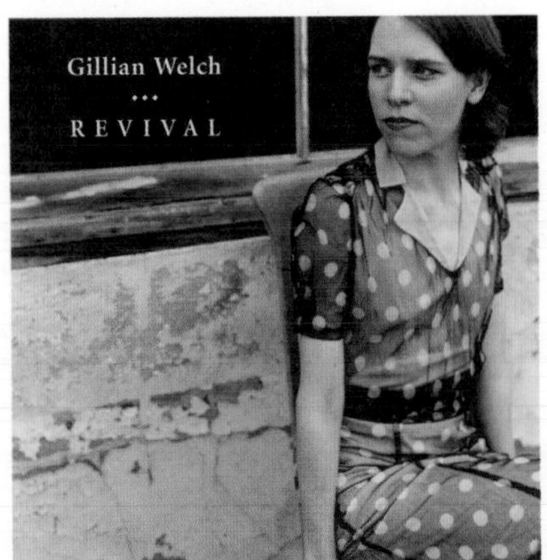

Gillian Welch

REVIVAL

ALMO SOUNDS | Producer: T Bone Burnett

RELEASED: APRIL 9, 1996

● When Gillian Welch arrived on the scene, she was disparaged by some critics as a carpetbagging Californian masquerading as a Carter Family wannabe. But did where she came from really matter? *Revival*'s ten songs, written by Welch herself and in collaboration with her musical partner, David Rawlings, were set in spare instrumental surroundings. The heartbreaking **Orphan Girl**—subsequently covered by Emmylou Harris, Ann Wilson, Patty Griffin, and Linda Ronstadt, among others—led the way, but **Annabelle**, **One More Dollar**, and **Acony Bell** were just as fine. If *Revival* doesn't contain enough Appalachian authenticity to please everyone, it'll do until the real thing comes along. *–DD*

Deana Carter

DID I SHAVE MY LEGS FOR THIS?

CAPITOL | Producers: Chris Farren, Jimmy Bowen, John Guess

RELEASED: SEPTEMBER 3, 1996

● Despite being born and raised in Nashville and the daughter of musician and singer Fred Carter Jr., Deana Carter was thirty-one when she finally opted to follow her dream of being an entertainer. Even she was surprised when her debut single, **Strawberry Wine**, a five-minute country waltz, climbed straight to No. 1 on the Billboard Hot Country Singles chart in 1996. The single was the first of four from this album released to country radio, with two of those—**We Danced Anyway** and **How Do I Get There**—also topping the charts. Carter's breakout album went on to sell more than five million copies. *–MH2*

Various Artists

THAT THING YOU DO! (ORIGINAL MOTION PICTURE SOUNDTRACK)

PLAYTONE/EPIC | Producers: Tom Hanks, Adam Schlesinger, Andy Chase, Steve Tyrell, Mark Wolfson, Uncle Bob

RELEASED: OCTOBER 1996

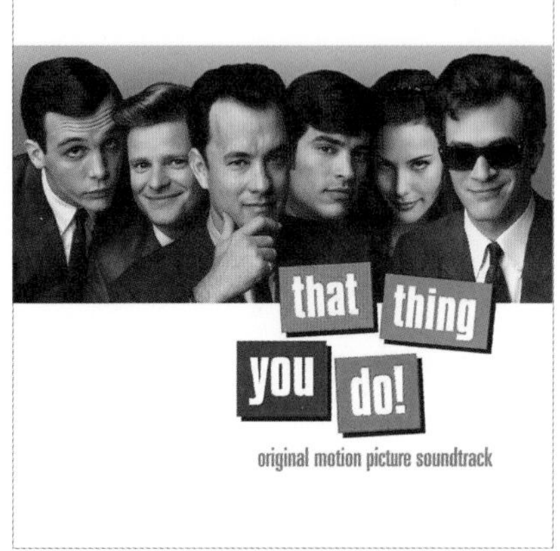

● The Tom Hanks–written and directed (his first) fable was a welcome antidote to the scores of unfulfilling movies about music that came before it. *That Thing You Do!* glibly captured the innocence of mid-'60s pop, screaming teens and all, and its soundtrack was a big part of what made it work—starting with the title track. Penned by Fountains of Wayne's Adam Schlesinger, it could have been of its time but also made sense in the lens of '90s power pop. The same could be said for the other tracks by the fictional Wonders and their compatriots, making for a period-perfect and an enjoyably retro listen independent of the movie. *–GG*

Trans-Siberian Orchestra

CHRISTMAS EVE AND OTHER STORIES

LAVA/ATLANTIC | Producers: Paul O'Neill, Robert Kinkel

RELEASED: OCTOBER 15, 1996

● Greg Lake sang about believing in Father Christmas, but the late Paul O'Neill really had the spirit. The composer-producer-musician had written **Christmas Eve/Sarajevo 12/24** for the band Savatage's 1995 album *Dead Winter Dead*, then expanded his vision into Trans-Siberian Orchestra, a prog-cum-heavy rock collective that would go on to become a seasonal touring juggernaut built on the multiplatinum success of this debut album. O'Neill and company mashed up favorite seasonal favorites with pompy hard rock in a way that certainly made Beethoven, or Tchaikovsky, roll over and Rudolph run, run—but in the happiest possible way. *–GG*

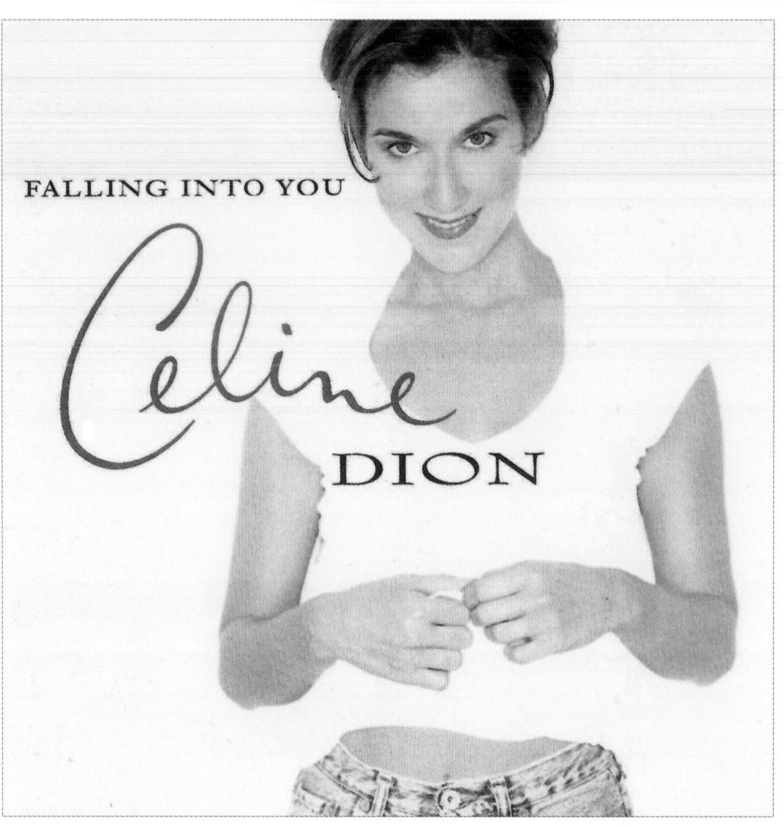

1996

Celine Dion

FALLING INTO YOU

COLUMBIA | Producers: Roy Bittan, Jeff Bova, David Foster, Humberto Gatica, Jean-Jacques Goldman, Rick Hahn, Dan Hill, John Jones, Rick Nowels, Aldo Nova, Steven Rinkoff, Billy Steinberg, Jim Steinman, Ric Wake

RELEASED: MARCH 1996

● US fans had taken notice of what their neighbors to the north already knew about Celine Dion with the release of her three previous English-language albums. But *Falling Into You* quickly put a huge stamp on the Canadian superstar's status in the States with the lead single **Because You Loved Me** (also from the *Up Close and Personal* film soundtrack). You can't get much more star power behind a power ballad than Diane Warren writing it and "hitman" David Foster producing; combine those two multi-award winners with a singer who would end up being known for having one of the most flawless voices in music history, and you had a huge hit on your hands. It topped the Billboard Hot 100 and won a Grammy, along with nominations for Academy and Golden Globe Awards.

And that was just scratching the surface of Dion's fourteenth studio album. The follow-up single, **It's All Coming Back to Me Now**, was a similar showstopper, and Dion followed that by making Eric Carmen's hit **All by Myself** her own. The rest of *Falling Into You* was packed with power and romance and one catchy song after another—the title track, **Make You Happy**, **Dreamin' of You**, **I Love You**, and **If That's What It Takes**. If that's not enough, the album had another definitive remake: Ike and Tina Turner's **River Deep, Mountain High**. Dion also took on Carole King's **(You Make Me Feel Like) A Natural Woman**, which appeared as a bonus track on the Asian edition of the album.

There's no wonder *Falling Into You* won Grammy Awards for Album of the Year and Best Pop Album and a Juno for Best Selling Album in Canada. It was the release that propelled Dion into the stratosphere as one of pop music's top voices of all-time. *—EP*

Boston

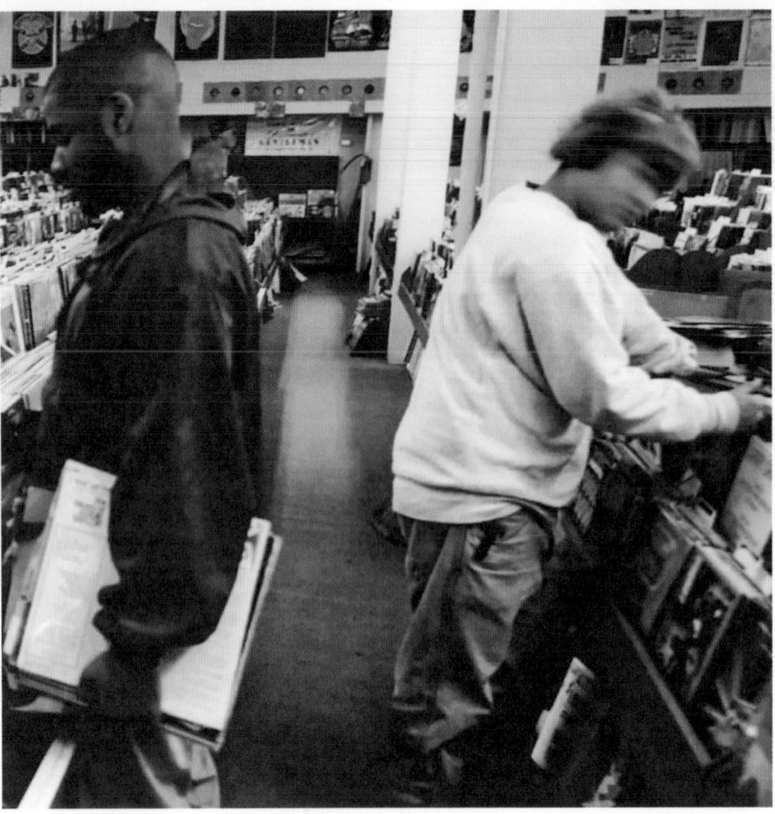

1996

DJ Shadow

ENDTRODUCING

● ● ●

M O ' W A X | Producer: DJ Shadow

RELEASED: SEPTEMBER 16, 1996

● DJ Shadow's earliest mixtapes scarcely hinted at what was to come from the California-based producer. Using the medium to showcase his edits of existing songs, with small amounts of cutting and scratching incorporated, these self-released works were not much different than other period bedroom tapes that rarely traveled outside their creators' zip codes. But the painstaking process of assembling his label debut, *Endtroducing . . .*, over two years yielded something quite special: effectively, the first album made entirely from samples.

DJ Shadow—born Josh Davis in San Jose and twenty-two at the time he started work on *Endtroducing . . .* —scoured the used bins at a local record store for cheap and mostly obscure vinyl. Working at first in his apartment and later in the home studio of fellow crate digger Dan the Automator, Shadow put together his instrumental hip-hop album using only an '80s sampler, a vintage turntable, and a digital audiotape recorder, stitching together passages from the records he had acquired. The sixty-three-minute result remains one of the most ambitious and influential records of all time.

Because of the relative obscurity of the sampled songs—Metallica, Pink Floyd, and A Tribe Called Quest are the most familiar names, but good luck trying to place them—the thirteen tracks sounded like new compositions. (Indeed, only a few of the sampled artists received co-writing credit.) The LP flowed at a single, mostly continual pace; moods shifted, needle dust settled, and the atmosphere heightened throughout. Few albums in the history of popular music sounded like *Endtroducing . . .* when it was released in 1996. Since then, it has inspired artists as diverse as J Dilla and Radiohead and helped launch the popularity of instrumental hip-hop over the years. By the time DJ Shadow released another album in 2002, his debut's legacy was secured. ***—MG***

MAXWELL'S URBAN HANG SUITE
01 THE URBAN THEME 02 WELCOME 03 SUMTHIN' SUMTHIN'
04 ASCENSION (DON'T EVER WONDER) 05 DANCEWITME 06 ...TIL THE COPS COME KNOCKIN'
07 WHENEVER WHEREVER WHATEVER 08 LONELY'S THE ONLY COMPANY (I&II) 09 REUNION
10 SUITELADY (THE PROPOSAL JAM) 11 THE SUITE THEME
COLUMBIA
0 7464-66434-2 6

Maxwell

MAXWELL'S URBAN HANG SUITE

COLUMBIA | Producers: Maxwell, Peter Mokran, Stuart Matthewman

RELEASED: APRIL 2, 1996

● Listen to Gerard Maxwell Rivera's effortlessly smooth, cohesive, and seductive debut album and it's easy to understand how it helped kick-start the neo-soul movement. You may be surprised to learn just how much hard work and struggle went into its creation and release and how close it came to failing to connect with the audience it deserved.

After spending years honing his songwriting and multi-instrumentalist skills while building a buzz with live performances in his hometown of New York City, Maxwell signed a major label record deal in 1994. In the spirit of heroes such as Stevie Wonder and Prince, he fought hard to maintain creative control of his work. He turned in the record during mid-1995 but was forced to wait nearly a year for it to be released due to upheaval at the label as well as the company's concern that this retro-leaning music and image would not fly with modern record buyers. Upon initial release, it seemed the label's fears might be realized, but the late-summer release of the sublime second single **Ascension (Don't Ever Wonder)** and a wave of positive press and fan reaction brought the album to platinum status and put Maxwell in the worldwide spotlight.

And thank goodness, because *Maxwell's Urban Hang Suite* deserved every bit of the "instant classic" praise it received. **Til the Cops Come Knockin'** might be the best slow jam since Prince's "Adore," and in retrospect, the delicate **Whenever Wherever Whatever** betrayed his love of Kate Bush well before his cover of "This Woman's Work" for *MTV Unplugged.* Although Maxwell's reverence for the R&B geniuses who came before him was constantly evident, there was nothing remotely dated about this album. Your wife, mother, sister, grandmother, and great-grandmother could all fall in love with it equally. *–MW*

Marilyn Manson
ANTICHRIST SUPERSTAR

NOTHING/INTERSCOPE | Producers: Sean Beavan, Marilyn Manson, Dave Ogilvie, Trent Reznor

RELEASED: OCTOBER 8, 1996

● After a promising debut with 1994's *Portrait of an American Family* and the following year's exquisitely disturbing cover of Eurythmics' "Sweet Dreams (Are Made of This)," Marilyn Manson took a career-defining leap forward with *Antichrist Superstar*. **The Beautiful People** announced the group's arrival as a superstar act, but make no mistake, this is a complete album, with surprising range and smart sequencing. Marilyn Manson, particularly its controversial frontman, had already proven it could command mainstream attention. With *Antichrist Superstar*'s dark, heady mix of shock metal, goth rock, and industrial soundscapes, the group proved it was well worth the attention. *–MW*

Orbital
IN SIDES

INTERNAL/FFRR | Producers: Paul and Phil Hartnoll

RELEASED: APRIL 29, 1996

● Four albums in, Orbital brothers Paul and Phil Hartnoll hit a personal peak and found entirely new parameters for electronic music. Almost two years after the celebrated sonic circus of *Snivilisation*, the duo dialed back a bit, finding magic in the comparative simplicity of these six (or eight, depending on how you count the two-parters) tracks, all of which are six minutes or longer. The arrangements are still precise and the sounds inventive, but there's a spaciousness that makes *In Sides* more accessible and easier to follow—what Vox smartly termed "soundtracks for movies which don't exist." *–GG*

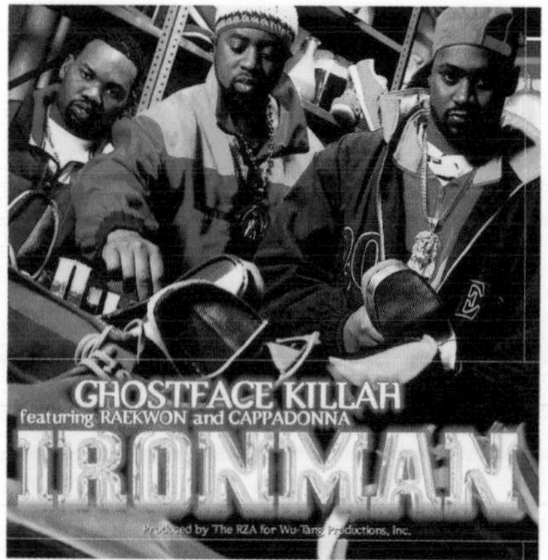

Ghostface Killah
IRONMAN

EPIC | Producer: RZA

RELEASED: OCTOBER 29, 1996

● After proving himself to be one of the most distinctive members of the groundbreaking Wu-Tang Clan collective on its 1993 debut *Enter the Wu-Tang (36 Chambers)* and serving as a vital co-star on bandmate Raekwon's 1995 solo debut, *Only Built 4 Cuban Linx*, Ghostface Killah made the most of his turn in the spotlight on *Ironman*. Wu-Tang production mastermind RZA loosened up the group's trademark claustrophobic sound just a touch with a heavier reliance on vintage soul samples, providing the perfect soundtrack for Ghostface's gritty crime stories, which found him mixing in some vulnerability with the more expected braggadocio. *–MW*

Sleeper
THE IT GIRL

INDOLENT | Producer: Stephen Street

RELEASED: MAY 6, 1996

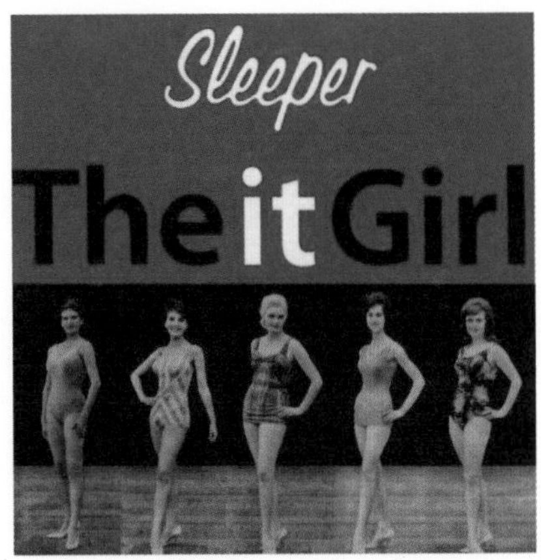

● Britpop wasn't entirely a boys' club. Along with Elastica's Justine Frischmann, Sleeper singer/songwriter Louise Wener helped put a female face on the movement, and *The It Girl*, the band's sophomore set, was full of crisp character sketches, spring-loaded guitars, and wry British wit. Blur producer Stephen Street provided the requisite Britpop bounce, as Wener sharply detailed the dissolution of a relationship (**What Do I Do Now?**) and the ill-fated connection between a young lass and her much older sugar daddy (**Nice Guy Eddie**). Sleeper split after its next album and re-formed in 2017, but Wener kept writing, going on to author a handful of well-received novels. *–AG*

Everything But the Girl
WALKING WOUNDED

ATLANTIC | Producers: Ben Watt, Spring Heel Jack, Howie B, Todd Terry, Rob Haigh

RELEASED: MAY 6, 1996

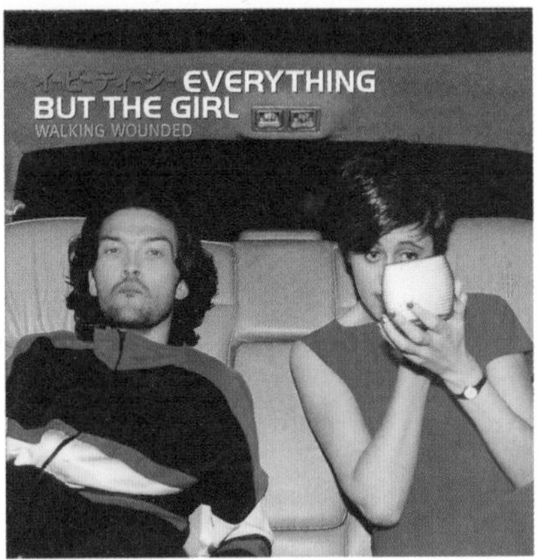

● As Everything But the Girl (Ben Watt and Tracey Thorn) was brainstorming *Walking Wounded*, DJ Todd Terry was remixing the duo's previous single, "Missing," into an international club hit. No surprise, then, that the album leaned heavily into electronica, embracing the winning juxtaposition of Thorn's torchy voice against pulsing yet spare beats. "I wanted everything for a little while," Thorn sang on **Wrong**, *Walking Wounded*'s second single and another international hit. But the couple pivoted by starting a family and launching solo careers. *Walking Wounded* reached No. 4 in the UK and No. 37 on the Billboard 200 in the US, making it Everything But the Girl's highest-charting album until it re-formed for 2023's *Fuse*. *–HD*

Lil' Kim
HARD CORE

ATLANTIC | Producers: Sean "Puffy" Combs, Jermaine Dupri, Daven "Prestige" Vanderpool, et al.

RELEASED: NOVEMBER 12, 1996

● Brooklyn-born Kimberly Jones was inspired by the female MCs who came before her, but she pioneered her own style by being just as tough—and just as sexually frank—as her male counterparts. On her debut album *Hard Core*, Lil' Kim was a mafioso dripping in luxury labels and a woman in full control of her sexuality, squeezing triggers on one song and objectifying a list of male R&B singers the next. Mentored by the Notorious B.I.G., who appeared on several tracks, Lil' Kim paved the way for the next evolution of female rap, from Nicki Minaj to Cardi B. *–AG*

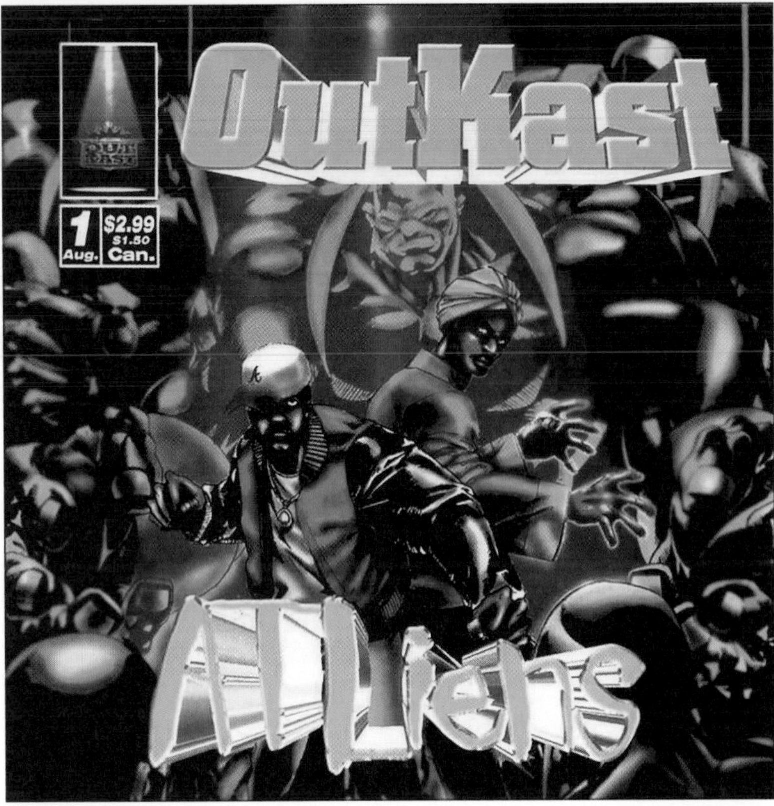

OutKast

ATLIENS

ARISTA/LAFACE | Producers: Organized Noize, OutKast

RELEASED: AUGUST 27, 1996

● There are plenty of legendary pairs: Sherlock and Watson, Shaggy and Scooby, Thelma and Louise. But none of those are real. What about Andre "3000" Benjamin and Antwan "Big Boi" Patton? On the OutKast duo's second album, *ATLiens*, the musical pair proved they were as real as it gets.

The fifteen-track *ATLiens* didn't just have a clever title. It described exactly what it was—a Southern rap album set in space. But while the album pictured an out-of-this-world future, the sounds were throwback '60s funk. Compared to the lighter and earthier approach on 1994's *Southernplayalisticadillacmuzik*, OutKast left the atmosphere on *ATLiens* for a darker sound that was not menacing but, rather, the evolving sound of maturing artists. The verbal volley between Big Boi and Andre 3000 on a track such as **Babylon** was stunning; the song gave a window into Andre's famous personal complexities, though it's Big Boi who opened the track with a face-melting rap.

ATLiens' title track has grown into one of OutKast's most popular songs, a loving ode to its Georgia roots. A track like **Jazzy Belle**, meanwhile, offered a stark contrast between OutKast and its contemporaries in the rap game; it's an anti-gangster rap track, extolling the virtues of women.

ATLiens wasn't just a defining moment for OutKast either. It helped define a soon-to-explode Southern rap scene. It also found Andre and Big Boi taking a step forward as co-producers with Organized Noize, the trio that produced *ATliens*' predecessor. Their work resulted in double-platinum sales along with a No. 1 spot on Billboard's Top R&B/Hip-Hop Albums chart and No. 2 on the Billboard 200. Three tracks hit Top 10 on the Hot Rap Songs survey, with **Elevators (Me & You)** reaching No. 1. *–ZC*

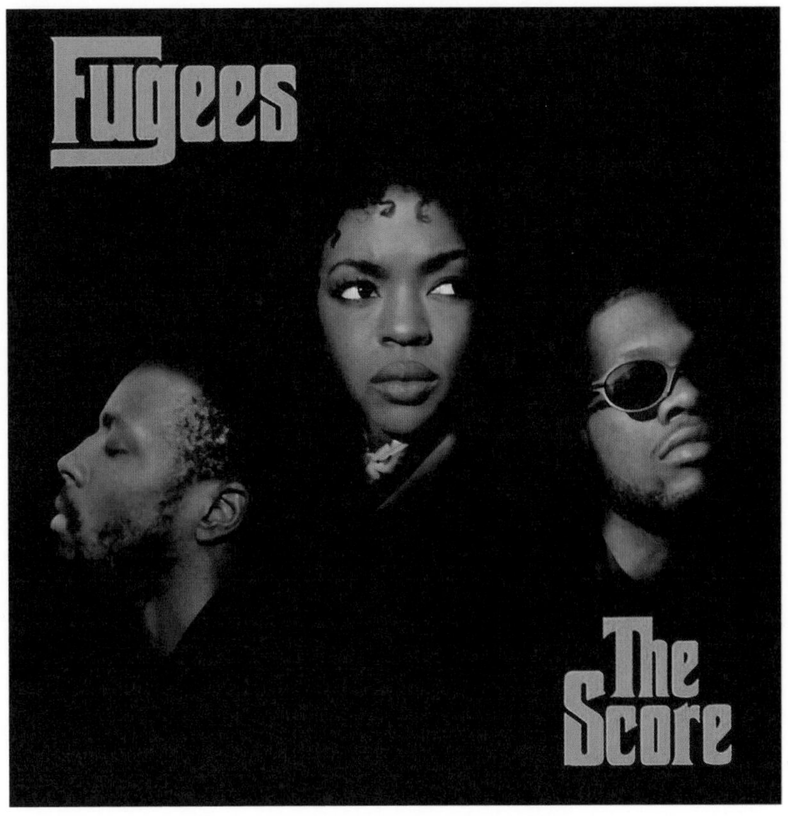

Fugees

THE SCORE

RUFFHOUSE/COLUMBIA | Producers: Pras, Wyclef, Lauryn Hill, Jerry "Te Bass" Duplessis, Diamond D, John Forte, Shawn King, Warren Riker, Salaam Remi

RELEASED: FEBRUARY 13, 1996

● Hip-hop trio Fugees' 1994 debut, *Blunted on Reality*, didn't even crack the Billboard 200. Two years later, *The Score* stayed at No. 1 for four weeks and sold more than six million copies. It remains the best-selling album ever by a rap group. Those two years—in reality, it was more like four because the label delayed its release for months after it was completed—made a big difference; Wyclef Jean, Lauryn Hill, and Pras Michel were given total control of their second LP and seized the opportunity to ease into the project without outside pressure or interference.

Jean, a Haitian native, enlisted respected reggae drummer Sly Dunbar and bassist Robbie Shakespeare as the rhythm section for much of *The Score*. Their presence gave the album the lived-in appeal of so many of the classic '70s soul records that inspired it. Covers of Roberta Flack's "Killing Me Softly With His Song" (shortened to **Killing Me Softly**) and a reworked version of Bob Marley's **No Woman, No Cry** were the most direct results, but nearly every track bears some imprint of an earlier era, including the use of a minor Delfonics hit "Ready or Not Here I Come (Can't Hide from Love)" in **Ready or Not** and Fu-Gee-La's interpolation of a Teena Marie "Ooo La La La" chorus.

While all three members contributed performances, songwriting, and production to *The Score* and were all instrumental to its success, its breakout moment belonged to Hill, twenty-one at the time and still living with her parents. Fugees were soon torn apart: a romantic relationship, among other jealousies, between Hill and Jean broke down, and the group went its separate ways after its one indisputable classic. *–MG*

1996

Belle and Sebastian

IF YOU'RE FEELING SINISTER

JEEPSTER | Producer: Tony Doogan

RELEASED: NOVEMBER 18, 1996

● When Belle and Sebastian signed with London's Jeepster Records for its second album, the Scottish septet insisted on no singles or photos or any other kinds of promotion. The music would have to sell itself—and, boy, did it.

It was the group's big move, of course. Belle and Sebastian, named from a short story by frontman Stuart Murdoch that was inspired by a television adaptation of the French novel *Belle et Sébastien*, released its independent debut *Tigermilk* earlier in 1996, which led to the deal with Jeepster. The album also welcomed singer-violinist Sarah Martin, adding more weapons to Belle and Sebastian's musical arsenal—with an immediate payoff.

Grounded in acoustic trappings of guitar, piano, strings, and Mick Cooper's occasional trumpet, *If You're Feeling Sinister* was a gem of songcraft so smart and instantly engaging that it placed Murdoch in a league with the likes of Paul Simon, Ray Davies, and Morrissey. Much of *If You're Feeling Sinister*, in fact, feels like the Kinks if they left their electric guitars behind while picnicking in the village greens of Muswell Hill. There was both intricacy *and* simplicity at work here, and genuine melodic beauty.

Drop the needle anywhere—**The Stars of Track and Field**, **Seeing Other People**, **Like Dylan in the Movies**, **Judy and the Dream of Horses**, **Me and the Major**, **Mayfly**, **Get Me Away From Here, I'm Dying**, the title track—and you found something absolutely familiar and classic but so sincere that it sounded completely fresh, especially amid the louder trappings of Britpop. Murdoch explained, in song, that "All I wanted was to sing the saddest songs/If somebody sings along/I will be happy now." Rest assured, he and his listeners had every reason to be overjoyed. *—GG*

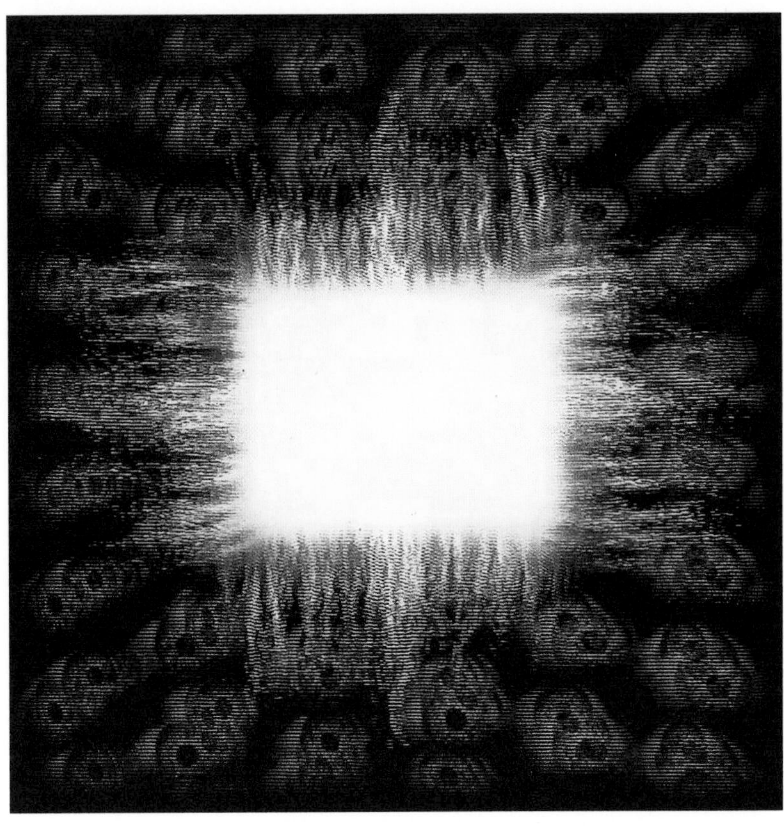

Tool

ÆNIMA

ZOO/VOLCANO | Producer: David Bottrill

RELEASED: SEPTEMBER 17, 1996

● Some of rock's great, canonical albums ran in the range of forty minutes. Tool has no flair for such brevity, however. The Los Angeles quartet's Grammy-winning sophomore album, following the aggro-metal EP *Opiate* and the debut full-length *Undertow*, weighed in at seventy-seven minutes while establishing Tool, with new bassist Justin Chancellor on board, as something unique from the rest of the Lollapalooza-era pack.

Although it looks legit, *Ænima* is not in fact a real word—rather, it's the union of *anima* (Latin for "soul") and *enema* (a certain gross process of elimination), suggesting that Tool would indeed hit you on both ends. *Ænima* consisted of nine songs and six interludes—instrumental, spoken, and ambient. Setting up the epic finale, **Third Eye**, was a clip from comedian Bill Hicks talking about reaching untapped creative potential. That theme extended into the liner notes as well, where frontman Maynard James Keenan dished on ketamine theory, Timothy Leary, and religion. "Beliefs are dangerous," Keenan concluded. "Beliefs allow the mind to stop functioning."

Musically, *Ænima* was where Tool began to perfect the architecture of its sound, patiently building songs with heavy riffs and polyrhythms, setting up loud, eargasmic explosions. The result was an album stocked with Tool staples: the aggressive lead single **Stinkfist**; the metaphysical **Forty Six & 2**; **Hooker with a Penis**, Keenan's response to fan who claimed the band had sold out; and the title track, a prayer for California to drift off the continent that won the Grammy for Best Metal Performance.

Ænima, which was also nominated for a Best Recording Package Grammy, was certified triple-platinum after debuting at No. 2 on the Billboard 200. It was a new start for the world's greatest prog-metal band, a last gasp for the '90s with even greater achievements to come. *–SM*

Sheryl Crow

SHERYL CROW

A & M | Producer: Sheryl Crow

RELEASED: SEPTEMBER 24, 1996

1996

● Sheryl Crow burst onto the scene with her debut release, *Tuesday Night Music Club* and its hit "All I Wanna Do." It won multiple Grammy Awards and vaulted her to stardom. Yet, the collaborative nature of the project, involving a team of male songwriters, invited criticism that questioned the authenticity of her achievements, compelling Crow to address skeptics head-on the next time out.

For Crow's sophomore effort, *Tuesday Night Music Club* producer Bill Bottrell withdrew, and Crow took control of the project. Collaborating with new writing partner Jeff Trott, she sculpted an album characterized by a distinct, darker tone, fusing organic rock instruments with modern percussion loops for an adventurous sonic exploration. Addressing societal issues, Crow touched on abortion in **Hard to Make a Stand** and boldly tackled gun violence with **Love Is a Good Thing**; the latter's controversial lyrics led to Walmart refusing to carry the album in its stores. Crow's firsthand experiences during a visit to war-torn Bosnia inspired **Redemption Day**, which was later covered by Johnny Cash and released posthumously in 2010.

Sheryl Crow's commercial success was undeniable, achieving triple-platinum status and reaching No. 6 on the Billboard 200. Its charting singles included the anthem **If It Makes You Happy**, the irresistibly catchy **A Change Would Do You Good**, and the emotionally charged ballad **Home**. The album continued Crow's Grammy streak with trophies for Best Rock Album and Best Female Rock Vocal Performance in 1997. Most importantly, *Sheryl Crow* established her as a singer/songwriter with staying power and remains one of the most highly regarded of her albums. *–MD*

Yo-Yo Ma/Edgar Meyer/ Mark O'Connor

APPALACHIA WALTZ

SONY CLASSICAL | Producers: Edgar Meyer, Mark O'Connor

RELEASED: SEPTEMBER 17, 1996

● Cellist Yo-Yo Ma has long been the most famous classical musician in the world, but over the years, he has defied musical boundaries and connected classical music with jazz, folk, bluegrass, and various kinds of world music. For *Appalachia Waltz*, Ma collaborated with double bassist/composer Edgar Meyer and fiddler/composer Mark O'Connor, artists whose work also defies simple categorization. At the time, Ma said of the project, "All of us, in a certain way, are very much interested in American music. I am truly interested in finding the soul of America, period, in all of its incredible richness and diversity. Can one find that?"

Appalachia Waltz was his answer. It included traditional tunes that helped to make America musically distinctive, including fiddle music drawing on Southern folk styles and the virtuosic Texas tradition, and which also point to those styles' sources in Celtic and Scandinavian heritage. Among those pieces were **Star of the County Down**, **The Green Groves of Erin/The Flowers of Red Hill,** and **College Hornpipe**. Original compositions by both Meyer and O'Connor followed those traditions and expanded upon them: O'Connor's stunningly beautiful title track and the mandolin excursion **Butterfly's Day Out**; Meyer's playful **Pickles**, and the dynamic **Druid Fluid**, co-written by the pair. *–DD*

The Wallflowers

BRINGING DOWN THE HORSE

INTERSCOPE | Producer: T Bone Burnett

RELEASED: MAY 21, 1996

● After a tepid response to its self-titled 1992 debut, the Wallflowers catapulted into the commercial spotlight with its sophomore release. Crafted by frontman Jakob Dylan (yes, Bob's son), the songs blended acoustic finesse with electric vigor, an approach that struck creative gold and propelled *Bringing Down the Horse* to quadruple-platinum status. Dylan's flair for captivating melodies and poignant Springsteen-esque storytelling shines vividly throughout. The Grammy-nominated single **6th Avenue Heartache** boasted the additional firepower of guest Mike Campbell from Tom Petty's Heartbreakers on slide guitar and Counting Crows' Adam Duritz lending his distinct voice for background vocals. **One Headlight**, marked by its driving pulse and enhanced by the warm organ accents of Rami Jaffee that were integral to the band's signature sound, became a ubiquitous hit that secured the No. 1 spot on all three of Billboard's Rock-related airplay charts and won two Grammy Awards. In total, *Bringing Down the Horse* produced four singles, including the Grammy-nominated **The Difference** and **Three Marlenas**. The album itself climbed to No. 4 on the Billboard 200. Although success at that level has evaded the Wallflowers since, *Bringing Down the Horse* firmly anchored the band in the pop culture tapestry and allowed it to keep recording and touring. *–MD*

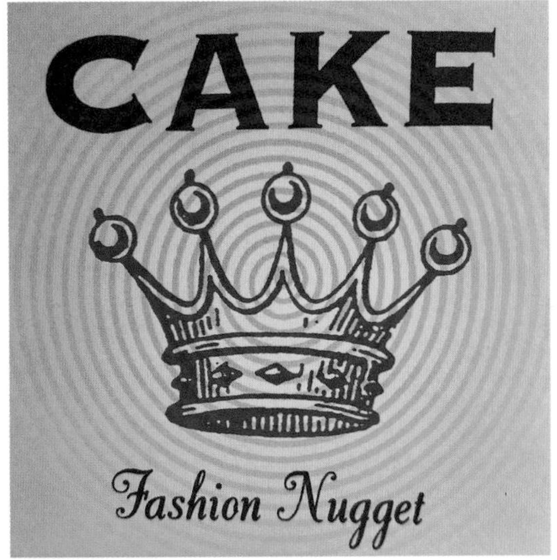

Cake

FASHION NUGGET

CAPRICORN | Producer: Cake

RELEASED: SEPTEMBER 17, 1996

● At a time when alternative music swirled with imitators, Cake offered a breath of fresh air. Not quite alternative rock, not quite country—with a trumpet player and some G-funk whistle synth thrown in for good measure—the genre-defying group from Sacramento, California, rose from near anonymity to the top of the college radio charts with its second album, *Fashion Nugget*. The first single, **The Distance**, peaked at No. 4 on Billboard's Alternative Airplay chart, helping it go platinum in less than eight months.

Recorded and produced by the band, *Fashion Nugget* offered the same wry originality that colors Cake's entire body of work, centered around frontman John McCrea's signature rubato phrasing, deadpan vocals, and sardonic lyrics. Its fourteen tracks ran the gamut from the catchy alternative riffs on **It's Coming Down** and **Nugget** to the country twang of **Stickshifts and Safetybelts**, with slower tracks such as **Friend Is a Four Letter Word** balancing the decidedly unserious **Race Car Ya-Yas** and Cake's quirky cover of Gloria Gaynor's **I Will Survive**.

Though it was not Cake's highest-charting album, *Fashion Nugget* remains one of the most beloved and is nearly impossible to listen to without cracking a smile. *–JS*

Donnie McClurkin

DONNIE MCCLURKIN

WARNER ALLIANCE | Producers: Bill Maswell, Victor and Cedric Caldwell, Mark Kibble

RELEASED: OCTOBER 29, 1996

● Donnie McClurkin's self-titled outing was his debut release, but he was certainly a known quantity already. He'd been an associate pastor at Marvin Winans's Perfecting Church in Detroit and would spend more than a decade assisting the gospel star, eventually establishing a branch of the church in Freeport, New York. McClurkin was also a featured vocalist with the Ron Winans Family and Friends Choir and sang with his own New York Restoration Choir; in fact, McClurkin re-recorded two songs previously done with those choirs, **Stand** and **Speak to My Heart**, both released as singles from *Donnie McClurkin*. Andraé Crouch, one of McClurkin's mentors and a father of contemporary gospel music, joined him for a duet on a remake of Crouch's **We Expect You**, and McClurkin put a church touch on New Orleans standard-bearer Allen Toussaint's spirit-buoying **Yes We Can Can**. The album was publicly lauded by Oprah Winfrey, which helped propel *Donnie McClurkin* to No. 4 on the Billboard Gospel chart and gold sales. It also was nominated for a Grammy Award for Best Contemporary Soul Gospel Album. Focusing on his ministry, McClurkin released several live albums in *Donnie McClurkin*'s wake, but it was eighteen years before his next studio album, *Duets*, surfaced in 2014. *–CP/GG*

Spice Girls

SPICE

VIRGIN | Producers: Absolute, Richard Stannard, Matt Rowe

RELEASED: SEPTEMBER 19, 1996

1996

● By the second half of the '90s, what listeners wanted—what they really, really wanted—was pop music. Enter the Spice Girls: five cheeky lasses from Britain who took the globe by storm with a buoyant teen pop sound and a universal message of Girl Power.

They weren't just singers; they were characters, each geared toward a different segment of the audience. Geri "Ginger Spice" Halliwell was the spitfire redhead. Melanie "Scary Spice" Brown was the brash, outspoken one. Emma "Baby Spice" Bunton was the adorable blonde. Melanie "Sporty Spice" Chisholm was the tomboy-type, and Victoria "Posh Spice" Beckham was the fashion-forward diva. (The names were coined by a journalist early on, but they stuck and became part of Spice Girls lore.)

Spice, the fivesome's debut album, was set up by the worldwide smash **Wannabe**, the group's debut single, a blast of pure pop bombast with an undeniable call-and-response hook and an elastic bass line. It was an ode to friendship, fun, and zig-a-zig-ahhing. So what if it didn't mean anything? It made people happy. The rest of the album was made up of dance-pop bops (**Say You'll Be There** and **Who Do You Think You Are**), a PG-13 ballad (**2 Become 1**), an ode to the girls' mums (**Mama**), and a song that sampled Digital Underground (**If U Can't Dance**). *Spice* sold some twenty-three million copies worldwide. Clearly, it made people happy.

Thanks to record biz entrepreneur Simon Fuller, the Spice Girls were a marketing machine as much as a musical act, and their likenesses appeared on everything from dolls to bedsheets to lunchboxes. The crass commercialism was no secret: it was the whole point, and everyone was along for the ride—most of all the Girls themselves, who made Girl Power not only a rallying cry but the standard going forward. *–AG*

1996

1996

Beck

ODELAY

DGC | Producers: Beck Hansen, the Dust Brothers, Mario Caldato Jr., Brian Paulson, Tom Rothrock, Rob Schnapf

RELEASED: JUNE 18, 1996

● "Loser," the surprise hit that anchored Beck's 1994 album *Mellow Gold*, arrived at the right time. With alternative music strengthening its foothold in the mainstream and the slacker generation defining itself with antihero anthems such as Radiohead's "Creep," the twenty-three-year-old Los Angeles singer/songwriter connected with his glassy-eyed personality and sound. Labeled a hip-hop folk artist for his combination of rap delivery and acoustic guitars, Beck lived up to the slacker tag: *Mellow Gold*, his third album overall, was unreliable and inconsistent.

By the time *Odelay* was released two years later, ambition and a dizzying sense of adventure elevated Beck and his music. Initial sessions for the record with *Mellow Gold* producers Tom Rothrock and Rob Schnapf had mostly stalled (though one song survived on the final track listing); the Dust Brothers—the L.A. duo responsible for the sample-heavy feast of Beastie Boys' 1989 triumph *Paul's Boutique*—were enlisted to complete the LP. The result was one of the most freewheeling albums of the era.

Combining pop, rock, folk, hip-hop, and psychedelia, *Odelay* bended genres to fit its needs. The first single, **Where It's At**, required a guidebook to identify all of its samples (some lifted from a sex education album). **Jack-Ass** turned a sample from Van Morrison's '60s garage band Them into a country-folk lament. Other tracks took *Mellow Gold*'s hip-hop folk template and spun them through Beck's layered, stream-of-consciousness songwriting, with the Dust Brothers' inventive and influential use of samples accenting it all. Beck went on to explore other areas of music—Tropicália, soul, and a '70s-inspired singer/songwriter breakup album followed in succession—but *Odelay* remains his one-of-a-kind masterpiece, both a product of its time and a defining statement from it. ***–MG***

LeAnn Rimes

BLUE

CURB | Producers: Wilbur C. Rimes, Chuck Howard, Johnny Mulhair

RELEASED: JULY 9, 1996

● LeAnn Rimes made history with the release of her 1996 debut album, *Blue*. For starters she was just thirteen years old at the time. The Mississippi native, raised in Texas, came out of talent shows, school musical theater productions, and an appearance on *Star Search*, where Rimes was champion for a week. She also sang the national anthem at Dallas Cowboys football games and recorded independently before being discovered by Dallas radio personality Bill Mack and signing a national recording deal.

Her work on *Blue* earned Rimes a Grammy Award for Best New Artist, making her the youngest person to win a Grammy and the first country artist to win that category. Rimes also took home Best Female Country Vocal Performance honors for the title track, which she'd first recorded for her second album, *All That*, in 1994. Mack, who wrote the song, received the Best Country Song trophy. Rimes's performance of the throwback, '50s-flavored **Blue** drew vocal comparisons to the late Patsy Cline. Released a month ahead of the album, it hit No. 10 on the Billboard Hot Country Songs chart and helped drive the *Blue* album to a No. 1 Top Country Albums debut and No. 3 on the Billboard 200.

Blue spawned other big country hits, including a rendition of **Unchained Melody**, **The Light in Your Eyes**, and a chart-topping **One Way Ticket (Because I Can)**, which made Rimes just the fourth teenaged country artist to accomplish that feat. *Blue* was certified six-times platinum, and in addition to the Grammys, Rimes also took home a haul of prizes from the American Music Awards, the Academy of Country Music Awards, the Billboard Music Awards, the CMT Music Awards, the Country Music Association Awards, and the World Music Awards. *–MH/GG*

1997

ETEEN
97
SEVEN

Foo Fighters

THE COLOUR AND THE SHAPE

ROSWELL/CAPITOL | Producer: Gil Norton

RELEASED: MAY 20, 1997

● The first Foo Fighters album was essentially a solo effort from former Nirvana drummer Dave Grohl. For its follow-up, Grohl wanted to make the Foo Fighters a real band, so while touring to promote the debut, Grohl enlisted bassist Nate Mendel and drummer William Goldsmith from Sunny Day Real Estate, along with former Nirvana touring guitarist Pat Smear. Then the fun began.

The band recorded its first sessions in late 1996, and neither Grohl nor producer Gil Norton were happy with the results. After a few months to mull things over, the band reconvened, with Grohl drumming rather than Goldsmith—who quit the band when he found out, despite Grohl's pleas to continue as the touring drummer. Adding to this angst was Grohl's recent divorce from his wife of three years, photographer Jennifer Youngblood. Despite all this drama, or possibly because of it, the end result was an album that is regarded by many as the band's finest as well as its best-seller.

Foo Fighters established its signature sound here: guitars coming at you from every direction, vocals that ranged from a whisper to a scream (mostly a scream), and Grohl's flair for injecting first-rate pop melodies into ferocious hard rock arrangements. While some songs such as **My Poor Brain**, **Up In Arms**, and **February Stars** started out as soft ballads, it wasn't long before the volume and tempo cranked up. The singles—**Monkey Wrench**, **Everlong**, and **My Hero**—became rock radio and performance staples, and *The Colour and the Shape* was nominated for a Grammy Award for Best Rock Album. Grohl has often said that the songs and the track sequence resembled a therapy session, taking listeners from despair to newfound happiness. It was a session definitely worth sitting in on. ***–GP***

1997

The Notorious B.I.G.

LIFE AFTER DEATH

BAD BOY/ARISTA | Producers: Sean "Puffy" Combs, Mark Pitts, the Notorious B.I.G., The Hitmen, Buckwild, Clark Kent, DJ Premier, Easy Mo Bee, Havoc, Daron Jones, KayGee, RZA

RELEASED: MARCH 25, 1997

● Good things come to those who wait, it's said. *Great* things came to those who waited for the Notorious B.I.G.'s second album.

There was a two-and-a-half-year gap between *Ready to Die* and *Life After Death*—an eternity, especially in the wake of the former's success. But Biggie's legend was only growing throughout that time, and the New York MC fed fans' appetite via collaborations with Michael Jackson and R. Kelly and an appearance on *The Panther* soundtrack. All the while he and his team of producers were crafting an epic work—two discs and twenty-five tracks—that took *Ready to Die*'s voluminous virtues to a next level and built a bridge between dark gangsta and more pop-oriented rap styles (particularly on the track **Mo Money Mo Problems**) that's still resonating in that community.

Assisted by a seriously who's-who guest list and exploring many of the same street-level themes as its predecessor, *Life after Death* also spotlighted Biggie's feuds with fellow rappers on tracks such as **Kick in the Door**, **Long Kiss Goodnight**, **Notorious Thugs**, **What's Beef**, and others and called out hip-hop's dangerous coastal divide on **Going Back to Cali**. Those would, of course, prove eerily prescient, as Biggie was gunned down in Los Angeles sixteen days before *Life After Death*'s release—at the time, reputedly as revenge for the killing of rival Tupac Shakur less than six months before.

There was indeed life after his death for the album. It sold nearly 690,000 copies its first week to debut at No. 1 on the Billboard 200 and has been certified eleven-times platinum. It was nominated for three Grammy Awards, and, along with *Ready to Die*, it's deservedly mentioned in any discussion of the best rap album of all time. *—GG*

Puff Daddy & The Family

NO WAY OUT

ARISTA/BAD BOY | Producers: Sean "Puffy" Combs, The Hitmen

RELEASED: JULY 22, 1997

● Sean "Puffy" Combs's moment in the sun wasn't supposed to happen like this. The Bad Boy Records founder's debut album, *No Way Out*, came just four months after the slaying of the Notorious B.I.G., his close friend and his label's biggest star. "What I'ma do now, huh?" a shook Puffy asked early in the album, as if directly addressing the heavens. The answer wasn't immediately clear.

The shadow of death loomed over *No Way Out*, and several tracks explicitly addressed Biggie's murder. On **Pain**, Puffy questioned whether he should continue and says B.I.G.'s angel visited, offering words of encouragement. "He put his hands on my head and said, 'I live through you,'" Puff rapped. "Make hits continuous, this is what we do."

Puffy understood hitmaking, so *No Way Out* came stacked with them, using Bad Boy's winning formula of constructing chart-toppers from the bones of already-massive songs: **Can't Nobody Hold Me Down**, which reworked Grandmaster Flash and the Furious Five's "The Message," spent six weeks at No. 1 on the Billboard Hot 100, and **Been Around the World**, a makeover of David Bowie's "Let's Dance," hit No. 2. Then there was **I'll Be Missing You**, Puff's grand ode to his fallen friend, built around the Police's "Every Breath You Take." The song spent the summer at No. 1, leading the Hot 100 for eleven weeks.

Puffy rapped on every track on *No Way Out*, but his strength was in producing, taking various song elements and building a coherent whole. That could mean lacing samples (the *Rocky* theme on **Victory**), placement of guest vocalists (The LOX, Lil' Kim, and Biggie on **It's All About the Benjamins**, Jay-Z on **Young G's**, Twista on **Is This the End?**), or just mood curation. Even if that mood was sometimes grim, Combs found the light and turned *No Way Out* into a hit parade. *—AG*

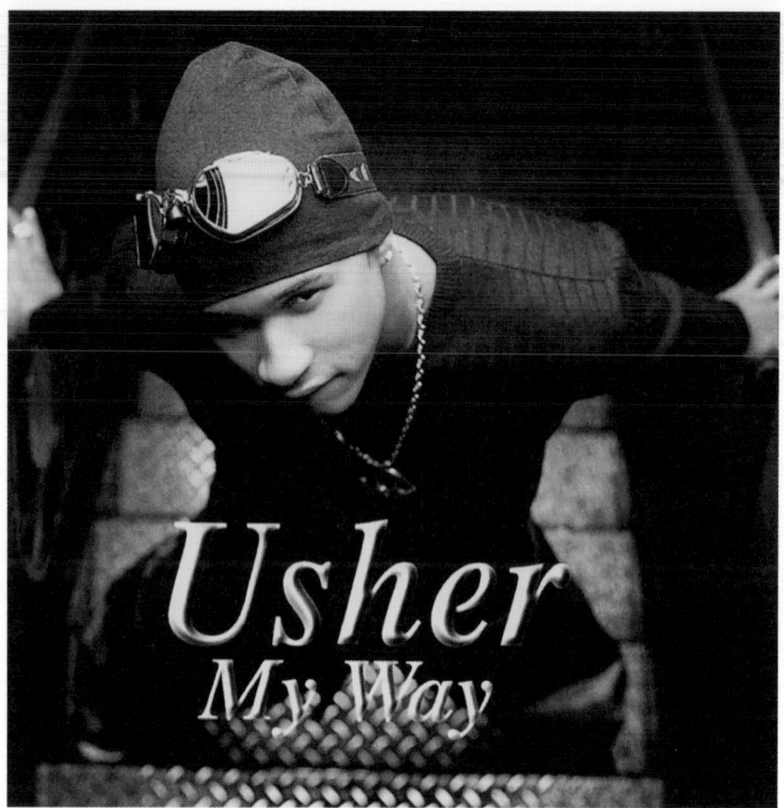

Usher

MY WAY

LAFACE/ARISTA | Producers: Babyface, Jermaine Dupri, Manuel Seal, Sprague "Doogie" Williams

RELEASED: SEPTEMBER 16, 1997

● Usher Raymond IV was not yet the King of R&B when his sophomore album was released—more like the prince. But *My Way* was the key step toward that coronation, a seven-times platinum smash that built exponentially from the modest arrival of his self-titled 1994 debut. It was smooth, silky, and soulful, his come-hithers more refined—and believable—three years later at nineteen years old, and in no small part thanks to his producers (Babyface and Jermaine Dupri in place of Puff Daddy and L. A. Reid), who had a better grasp on what kind of songs their progeny could deliver most consistently.

1997

Usher's label, LaFace, kept him visible during the interim between albums. He dueted with Monica on "Let's Straighten It Out" in 1994 (she returned the favor on *My Way*'s **Slow Jam**) and appeared on the imprint's *Rhythm of the Games* benefit album for the 1996 Summer Olympic Games and on the soundtrack of *Kazaam* that same year. By the time sessions began for *My Way*, it was clear Usher was not a banger or a New Jack, although hip-hop elements would be woven into some of the ten tracks (notably Lil' Kim's cameo on **Just Like Me**). Instead, Usher took things **Nice & Slow**, as the song says, surrounded by languid beats and carefully placed sonic details designed to enhance rather than encase his vocals.

It worked. *My Way* hit No. 4 on the Billboard 200 and No. 1 on the Top R&B/Hip-Hop Albums chart. **Nice & Slow** was No. 1 on the Hot 100, and the Grammy Award–nominated **You Make Me Wanna . . .** and **Slow Jam** each hit No. 2. **You Make Me Wanna . . .** also won a *Soul Train* Music Award, and Usher scored three Billboard Music Awards from the project, including Artist of the Year. *–GG*

Whiskeytown
STRANGERS ALMANAC

OUTPOST/GEFFEN | Producer: Jim Scott

RELEASED: JULY 29, 1997

● Alt-country barely had a name, much less the genre label "Americana," when *Strangers Almanac* turned Raleigh, North Carolina's Whiskeytown into the band most likely to take it to the mainstream as the post-grunge next big thing. Indeed, its mix of Gram Parsons, Replacements, and Rolling Stones influences (dubbed "country and Westerberg" by *Entertainment Weekly*) contained large doses of reckless charm and substantial flashes of songwriting brilliance from frontman Ryan Adams—both alone and in collaboration with bandmates Phil Wandscher and Caitlin Cary. Adams' volatility, however, steered the band toward implosion after just one more album, 2001's *Pneumonia*.–***LM***

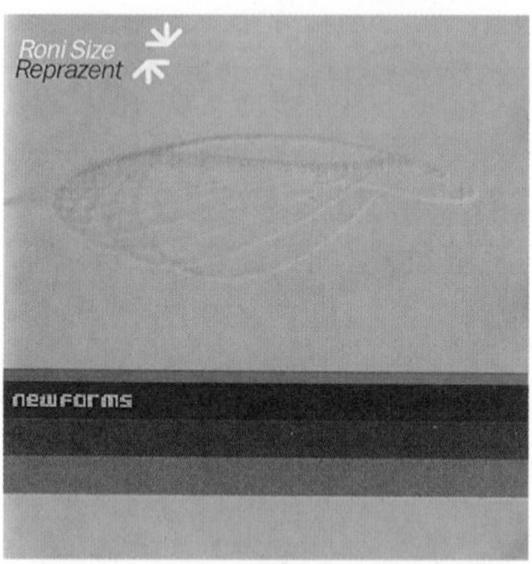

Roni Size & Reprazent
NEW FORMS

TALKIN' LOUD/MERCURY/UNIVERSAL MUSIC | Producers: Roni Size, DJ Die, Krust, DJ Suv

RELEASED: JUNE 23, 1997

● Roni Size's first artist album opens with a promise of "fresh hits from '97" and a declaration that "now we're getting into this sound/Pick it up, shake it up, turn it upside-down!" Hailing from Bristol, England, Size (né Ryan Williams) made his name first as a DJ and producer, pioneering drum 'n' bass with releases on his WTP label. Deploying his collective, Reprazent, Size delivered an opus with *New Forms*, two CD-length discs populated by twenty-two beat-crazy tracks displaying extreme versatility and adventurous dynamics, making it a worthy winner of 1997's Mercury Music Prize. –***GG***

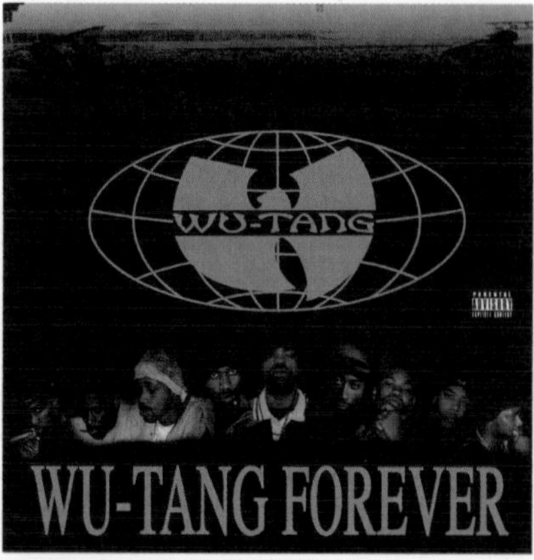

Wu-Tang Clan
WU-TANG FOREVER

LOUD/RCA | Producers: RZA, 4th Disciple

RELEASED: JUNE 3, 1997

● It probably should have been one disc, but Wu-Tang Clan's follow-up to 1993's *Enter the Wu-Tang (36 Chambers)*, which drastically altered hip-hop's landscape, was as big as a movie and even longer than that summer's top blockbuster, *Men in Black*. Getting everyone together was a feat in itself after five Wu-Tang solo projects, but the members had room to spread out over *Wu-Tang Forever*'s twenty-seven bombastic tracks. The winner here was **Triumph**, featuring all nine killer bees (plus Wu-affiliate Cappadonna), with a vivid opening rhyme from Inspectah Deck that ranks among hip-hop's all-time greatest verses. Rap as cinema: Wu got it locked. –***AG***

The New Life Community Choir featuring John P. Kee
STRENGTH

VERITY/TYSCOT | Producer: John P. Kee

RELEASED: OCTOBER 28, 1997

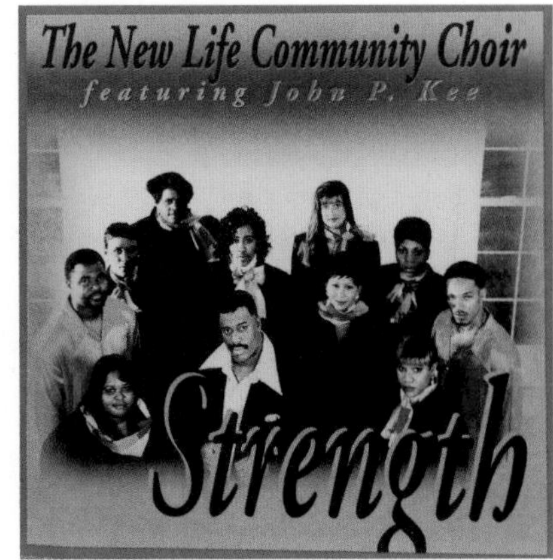

● The fourteenth release from John P. Kee and the New Life Community Choir mixed traditional and contemporary gospel with the soulful sounds Kee learned playing with R&B groups to create a hybrid. The set reached No. 2 on Billboard's Gospel Albums chart, residing there for eighty-seven weeks. Kee wrote thirteen of the fourteen tracks, and *Strength* showcased his soulful, husky voice in addition to his ability to write songs which have remained staples in African American church choir repertoires. Among *Strength*'s outstanding entries were a remake of James Cleveland's classic **Lord Help Me to Hold Out**, **Turn Around**, **I Do Worship**, **Clap Your Hands**, and the title track. *—CP*

Diana Krall
LOVE SCENES

IMPULSE | Producer: Tommy LiPuma

RELEASED: AUGUST 26, 1997

● By her fourth recording, Diana Krall had found her comfort zone in jazz trio settings. She built an uncanny rapport with bluesy guitarist Russell Malone and deep sonorous bassist Christian McBride, and her popularity rose among jazz and crossover audiences. For *Love Scenes*, Krall created a cinematic album, casting her spell on a trove of ballads. She took a different tack on each selection, displaying both originality and versatility. On **Peel Me a Grape**, she was beguiling and sassy. Then she shifted to a whisper on the George and Ira Gershwin classic **They Can't Take That Away from Me** from the film *Shall We Dance*. *—CH*

Yo La Tengo
I CAN HEAR THE HEART BEATING AS ONE

MATADOR | Producer: Roger Moutenot

RELEASED: APRIL 22, 1997

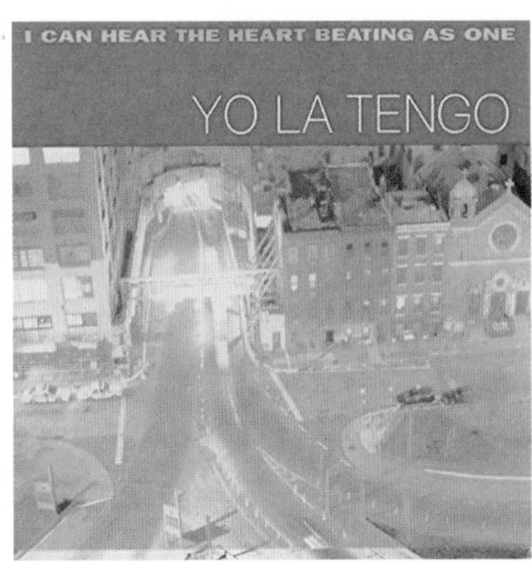

● Yo La Tengo's status as indie rock leaders was well entrenched by the time the New Jersey trio rolled into its eighth album—the one where it decided to shake things up. Recorded in Nashville and New York with producer Roger Moutenot, who'd also helmed 1995's lauded *Electr-O-Pura*, *I Can Hear the Heart Beating as One* found Yo La Tengo embracing bossa nova (**Center of Gravity**), psychedelia (**We're an American Band**, *not* Grand Funk Railroad's), trip-hop ambience (**Damage**), jazz (**Moby Octopad**), and trance (**Autumn Sweater**)—all while keeping its trademark melodic focus and melancholy lyricism intact. A definitive statement—Beach Boys and Anita Bryant covers and all. *—GG*

Janet Jackson

THE VELVET ROPE

VIRGIN | Producers: Janet Jackson, Jimmy Jam, Terry Lewis

RELEASED: OCTOBER 7, 1997

1997

● Janet Jackson was coming off three consecutive No. 1 albums when she released her most intimate work, the end product of a period that found the thirty-one-year-old superstar dealing with depression issues that led to a mental breakdown. By putting the focus on her well-being—emotional, physical, and sexual—*The Velvet Rope* was both a form of therapy and a coming out for an artist who for too long was made to feed the industry machine, the same one that eventually helped destroy her older brother Michael.

Despite its fragile origins, *The Velvet Rope* was a celebratory record that occasionally got dark and dirty but came out stronger and more confident at the other end. The twenty-two tracks (including a handful of seconds-long interludes) were designed to fit a concept album about Jackson's growth as an independent artist and putting herself first above all else. She'd worked thematically before—1989's *Janet Jackson's Rhythm Nation 1814* surveyed social issues from the perspective of a young Black woman at the end of the '80s—but *The Velvet Rope* examined its issues on more personal levels.

Once again produced by Jimmy Jam and Terry Lewis—the writing and production team whose own success was secured after their work on Jackson's 1986 breakthrough LP *Control*—Jackson's sixth album was less pop-oriented and more R&B-indebted than its predecessors. Dusty needle drops, deep bass, and silky grooves recalling early '70s soul music were all over *The Velvet Rope*. A string of similar-sounding records soon followed its release, along with an inevitable debut at No. 1 on the Billboard 200. The album even managed to bring together Q-Tip and Joni Mitchell on the highlight **Got 'til It's Gone**. Emotional recalibration has never sounded so inviting. ***–MG***

Kenny Chesney

I WILL STAND

BNA | Producers: Buddy Cannon, Norro Wilson

RELEASED: JULY 15, 1997

● When he released his fourth studio album, Kenny Chesney was still wearing a cowboy hat and staunchly in the neo-traditional world, making a name as an exciting live performer who soon would be filling some of the world's biggest venues. *I Will Stand* rode that momentum. Reaching No. 9 on Billboard's Top Country Albums chart, it was Chesney's first album certified gold and housed his first No. 1 country hit, **She's Got It All**, and another single, the reflective **That's Why I'm Here**, that reached No. 2. *I Will Stand* also featured a strong rendition of Tony Joe White's **Steamy Windows**, while Chesney co-wrote three of the album's tracks: **You Win, I Win, We Lose**; **She Always Says It First**; and **Lonely, Needin' Lovin'**.

The album closed with an acoustic version of **When I Close My Eyes**, the Keith Palmer track that appeared on Chesney's 1995 album, *Me and You*. *I Will Stand*'s "event" moment, meanwhile, was **From Hillbilly Heaven to Honky Tonk Hell**, a stone country celebration with guest appearances by George Jones and Tracy Lawrence. Chesney entered the multiplatinum ranks on his next album, *Everywhere We Go*, but *I Will Stand* was a fine farewell to the traditional lane that brought him to the party. *–TR/GG*

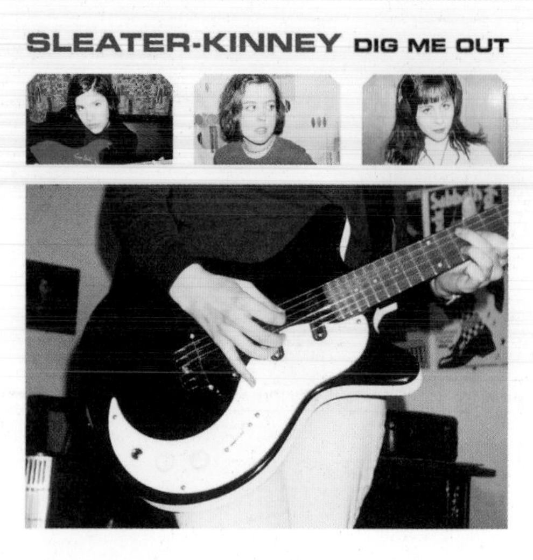

Sleater-Kinney

DIG ME OUT

KILL ROCK STARS | Producer: John Goodmanson

RELEASED: APRIL 8, 1997

● Sleater-Kinney was starting to pick up buzz in the indie-rock scene in 1996 when it entered the studio at the end of the year to begin work on its third album, *Dig Me Out*. With a new drummer, a new label, and a fresh set of songs that alternated between scarred vulnerability and stinging feminism, the Olympia, Washington, trio wiped away much of the baggage of '90s alternative rock by stripping the music to punk's essentials. It also helped that drummer Janet Weiss's swinging style was influenced as much by The Rolling Stones' Charlie Watts and the Kinks' Mick Avory (dig *The Kink Kontroversy* homage on *Dig Me Out*'s album cover) as she was by the usual punk scene suspects.

Dig Me Out's best songs—**One More Hour**, **Little Babies**, and the title track—wasted no time making their points. The thirteen songs clocked in at an economical thirty-six minutes, a nod to both the album's punk and '60s rock roots as singers and guitarists Carrie Brownstein and Corin Tucker worked out genre- and gender-specific issues. Even though the album didn't chart, it became Sleater-Kinney's best-selling record, positioning it as one of the era's best indie bands. *–MG*

Buena Vista Social Club

BUENA VISTA SOCIAL CLUB

WORLD CIRCUIT/NONESUCH | Producer: Ry Cooder

RELEASED: SEPTEMBER 16, 1997

● Ry Cooder went to Havana, and all he brought us back was a great album. Cuba was still largely off-limits for Americans, unknown and exotic in March of 1996, when the habitually curious muso hit town to rediscover a group of veterans from the country's pre-Castro showroom era and give them a fresh platform. Cooder—assisted by his son Joachim and bandleader Juan de Marcos González—unearthed obscured talents such as Eliades Ochao, Company Segundo, Ibrahim Ferrer, Rubén González, Omara Portuondo, Manuel Mirabal, and others and introduced the rest of world to the infectious styles of son cubano, bolero, trova, filin, guajira, and criolla.

The world listened, too. The album won the 1998 Grammy for Best Traditional Tropical Latin Album, and the Library of Congress installed it in the National Recording Registry in 2022. Cooder brought the Buena Vista collective to Amsterdam and New York for live performances, which provided additional footage for Wim Wenders's 1999 documentary of the same name. The endeavor peeled back the curtain on one of the world's most mysterious societies, revealing a spirit and humanity that had been subsumed by decades of political hostility. Listen to it and you'll love it—and buy the T-shirt, too. *—GG*

Ween

THE MOLLUSK

ELEKTRA | Producer: Andrew Weiss

RELEASED: JUNE 24, 1997

● After dipping a toe into more traditional recording methods for 1994's excellent *Chocolate and Cheese*, Ween took a deliberate step back to its early DIY roots by renting a New Jersey shore beach house—in the winter—to write and record its 1997 masterpiece, *The Mollusk*. The frigid nautical setting seeped into nearly every song to varying degrees, creating the quintet's most thematically consistent and musically accomplished album to date. If you don't understand how wrong the people who dismiss Ween as novelty pranksters are, this is where to dive in and get your bearings straight. Gene Ween (Aaron Freeman) and Dean Ween (Mickey Melchiondo) are exceedingly talented songwriters and performers who have absorbed a staggering range of influences and can consistently blend them into songs that hearken back to beloved touchstones but remain fully unique, exciting, and forward-thinking. A strong prog-rock streak ran through *The Mollusk*, best exemplified by epic guitar showcases such as **The Golden Eel** and **Buckingham Green**. The pain from a breakup Freeman was enduring at the time added a somber sense of loss to songs such as **It's Gonna Be (Alright)**, **Cold Blows the Wind**, and the heart-wrenching pirate-at-sea breakup closer **She Wanted to Leave**. *—MW*

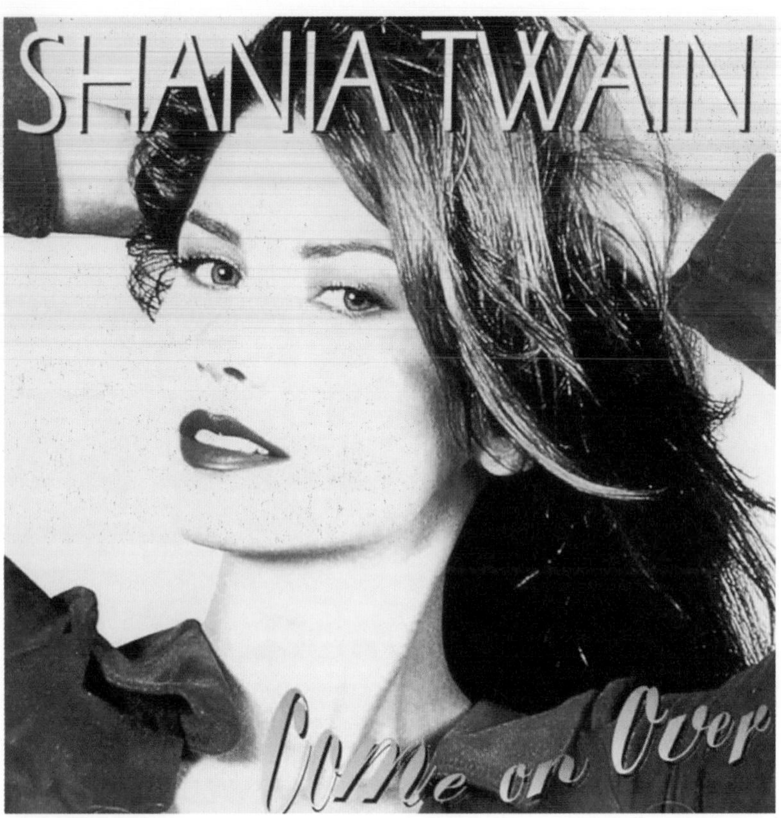

Shania Twain

COME ON OVER

MERCURY NASHVILLE | Producer: Robert John "Mutt" Lange

RELEASED: NOVEMBER 4, 1997

● With seven now-familiar opening guitar notes and a saucy "Let's go girls!," Shania Twain planted her thigh-high boot right through the conventional country music mainstream. Everything about *Come On Over*, her third studio album—from the whopping sixteen tracks (all originals by Twain and producer/husband Mutt Lange) to the glossy fashion and slick, rock 'n' roll–flavored production—went against traditional Nashville canons. In doing so, Twain and producer Lange set a new standard for pop-country crossover. The Canadian singer/songwriter had already made some noise with her award-winning sophomore release, *The Woman In Me* (also produced by Lange), but powerful hooks and sassy lyrics made *Come on Over* much more pop-forward. She started a new era in Nashville, opening the door for fans who previously said, "I don't like country, but . . ."

Lange, already well known for his hitmaking work with rockers such as AC/DC and Def Leppard, brought his arena-sized production and attention to sonic detail into the album. The resulting creation was a powerhouse, with a staggering total of twelve released singles, which only increased its crossover impact. They had all the bases covered: fiddles and pedal steel for the country-leaning **Love Gets Me Every Time** and **Honey I'm Home**, the guitar-driven pop of **Man! I Feel Like a Woman**, the gushy romance of **You're Still the One**, and even some Zydeco and accordion thrown in for good measure on **Don't Be Stupid (You Know I Love You)**.

Come on Over was an invitation to a global audience previously untapped by country music. Selling more than forty million copies worldwide and winning four Grammy Awards in both Pop and Country categories over the course of two years, Twain impressed a lot of people with her confident stance on a new, creative direction of what it meant to be country. *–SS*

Various Artists

ANTHOLOGY OF AMERICAN FOLK MUSIC

SMITHSONIAN FOLKWAYS | Producer: Harry Smith

RELEASED: AUGUST 19, 1997

● When *Anthology of American Folk Music* was first released in 1952 as three double LPs, its legality was a gray area, since none of the recordings from the '20s and '30s were formally licensed for inclusion. The set went in and out of print for decades until Smithsonian Folkways secured the rights to all eighty-three songs and reissued the album as a six-CD box set in 1997 with remastered sound, expanded liner notes, and a curator's attention to detail. The *Anthology* had become one of the most valued records of the twentieth century as folk music grew in popularity during the '60s; the reissue emphasized just how much the work endures.

Portland, Oregon–born visual artist and experimental filmmaker Harry Smith compiled *Anthology of American Folk Music* using his collection of out-of-print 78s. The folk, blues, country, and gospel tracks were sourced from both popular (the Carter Family, Charley Patton) and obscure (Bill and Belle Reed, Uncle Eck Dunford) artists who recorded for a variety of labels, including still-thriving majors such as Columbia, from 1926 through 1933. The songs spanned from seventeenth-century traditional numbers (**The House Carpenter**) to contemporary pieces (**Down on Penny's Farm**).

Divided into three thematic volumes—*Ballads, Social Music*, and *Songs*—the *Anthology* told a singular story of the roots of American music. Its initial influence was on the folk singers of the early '60s, including Bob Dylan and Joan Baez; that influence has since grown to touch artists as diverse as Elvis Costello and Sonic Youth. The 1997 Grammy-winning reissue replicated Smith's specially designed notes, a vital read in the understanding of the importance of the material, while new essays put the music in historical perspective. After all these years, *Anthology of American Folk Music* remains one of the most important albums ever released. *—MG*

Martina McBride

EVOLUTION

RCA | Producers: Paul Worley, Martina McBride, Clint Black, James Stroud, Dan Shea

RELEASED: AUGUST 26, 1997

1997

● Martina McBride already had three albums under her belt and some moderate country music success before the release of *Evolution*, an album that put her on the path to becoming a household name. The project marked a departure for McBride, as she opted to make a more pop-leaning album. Even the set's title was intentional, McBride told *Billboard*: "*Evolution* felt like the point where everything clicked. Paul Worley and I were talking about what to name the record. He said, 'You should name it *Evolution*, because it really does feel like you have turned the corner. You're solid. You've had hit songs under your belt, you've done some touring, you're a few years older.' I had a baby at that point. People really reacted to that record."

That they did. *Evolution* was McBride's highest-charting album to date—No. 4 on Billboard's Top Country Albums chart and No. 24 on the Billboard 200, with three-times platinum sales. The album produced two No. 1 hits on Billboard's Hot Country Songs chart, **A Broken Wing** and **Wrong Again**. The latter was also McBride's first crossover to the Billboard Hot 100, peaking at No. 61. Four other singles—**Happy Girl**, **Still Holding On** with Clint Black, **Valentine** with Jim Brickman, and **Whatever You Say**—also made the country charts. The Black and Brickman songs also appeared on their 1997 albums, *Nothin' but the Taillights* and *Picture This*, respectively.

The album put McBride in the awards hunt as well. **Still Holding On** received a Grammy Award nomination for Best Country Collaboration with Vocals, while both the Academy of Country Music (ACM) and the Country Music Association (CMA) nominated McBride for their top Female Vocalist honors. **A Broken Wing**, meanwhile, was nominated for Single of the Year by the CMA and Music Video of the Year by the ACM. *–MH2*

Ivy

APARTMENT LIFE

ATLANTIC | Producers: Andy Chase, Adam Schlesinger, Peter Nashel

RELEASED: OCTOBER 6, 1997

● When Adam Schlesinger died of COVID-19 in 2020 at age fifty-two, obituaries noted his prolific work, including with the band Fountains of Wayne and his writing for the soundtrack to the film *That Thing You Do!* But Ivy, the trio Schlesinger formed during the mid-'90s with Andy Chase and Dominique Durand, deserved greater mention. On its 1997 sophomore release, the group explored pop sensibilities that blended '60s West Coast sunshine, spare rhythms, and European cool. Much of the latter could be attributed to the Paris-born Durand, whose lilting voice added an exotic color not unlike Nico provided for the Velvet Underground. *–HK*

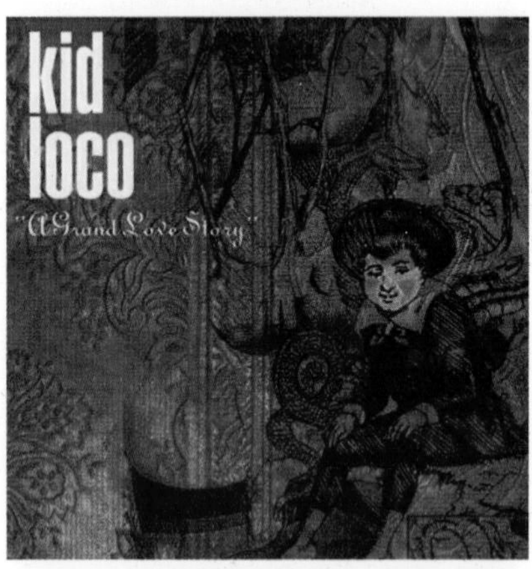

Kid Loco

A GRAND LOVE STORY

YELLOW PRODUCTIONS | Producer: Jean-Yves Prieur (Kid Loco)

RELEASED: NOVEMBER 25, 1997

● From start to finish *A Grand Love Story* sent you on a blissful sonic journey, making it the perfect chicken soup for the soul—warm, hearty, and filling in every way. The ten-track set offered a blend of lush, cinematic-styled down-tempo songs using jazzy and soulful rhythms garnished with the brilliant use of elegant samples. Cultivating bits from Three Dog Night and George Benson, among others, it provided a listening experience that was both modern yet retro-inspired. The sexiness that filled the album set it apart from the many other down-tempo releases of this era, making it a true classic. *–MH*

Various Artists

TITANIC (MUSIC FROM THE MOTION PICTURE)

SONY CLASSICAL/SONY MUSIC SOUNDTRACKS
Producers: James Horner, Simon Franglan

RELEASED: NOVEMBER 18, 1997

● Was there really no room for Jack on that floating door? No? Then you're probably humming Celine Dion's **My Heart Will Go On**. It's a safe bet you know the music, as the companion to the 1997 film *Titanic* was one of the best-selling albums of all time and the highest-selling mostly orchestral soundtrack at more than thirty million copies (the No. 5 album of the decade, according to Billboard). **My Heart Will Go On**, meanwhile, was a generational smash that topped charts in more than twenty-five countries. The swelling, romantic, Celtic-tinged soundscape composer James Horner created for the rest was perfect for the story. *–HD*

Kool Keith

SEX STYLE

FUNKY ASS RECORDS | Producers: Kut Masta Kurt, TR Love

RELEASED: FEBRUARY 3, 1997

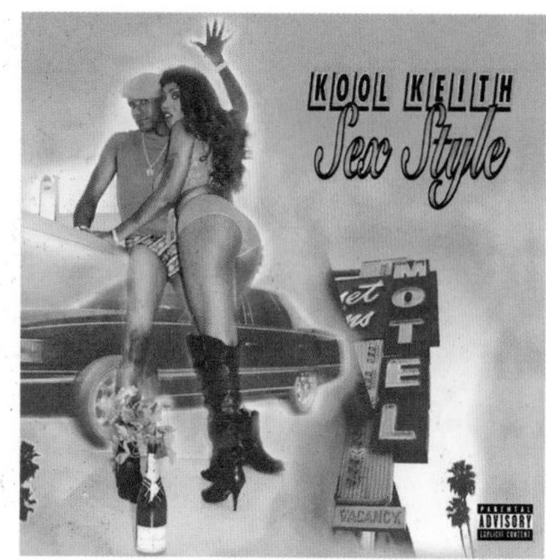

● *Sex Style* was a psychosexual pornocore romp that made 2 Live Crew look like choirboys. Kool Keith, the legendary Bronx MC and member of Ultramagnetic MCs, took listeners to outer space with his Dr. Octagon project, but *Sex Style* is like a visit to a smut shop—or a sleazy hourly motel. He rapped about masturbation, sexual fantasies, breakfast cereal, and R&B singers, often all in the same breath, while Kut Masta Kurt's beats sampled adult films and funky drum loops. Anyone can rap about eroticism, bodily fluids, and consumer products, but no one else did it as convincingly as Kool Keith. *–AG*

Ben Folds Five

WHATEVER AND EVER AMEN

550/CAROLINE/EPIC | Producers: Ben Folds, Caleb Southern

RELEASED: MARCH 18, 1997

● This Chapel Hill, North Carolina, trio stayed true to its alternative piano rock niche on its platinum second album, *Whatever and Ever Amen*, even under the arm of a mainstream label. Brimming with dynamic tracks that showcased Folds's mastery of piano—and elevated by Robert Sledge's ultra-fuzzy bass tone—the album was full of youthful exuberance and longing, offering a full-bodied sound not often heard from a three-piece. **Brick** was its biggest hit, but other tracks stood out, such as the scorching **Songs for the Dumped** and the jazzy opus **Selfless, Cold and Composed**. The group eventually disbanded, and this record remains its most successful to date. *–JS*

Spiritualized

LADIES AND GENTLEMEN WE ARE FLOATING IN SPACE

DEDICATED/ARISTA | Producers: Jason Pierce, John Coxon

RELEASED: JUNE 16, 1997

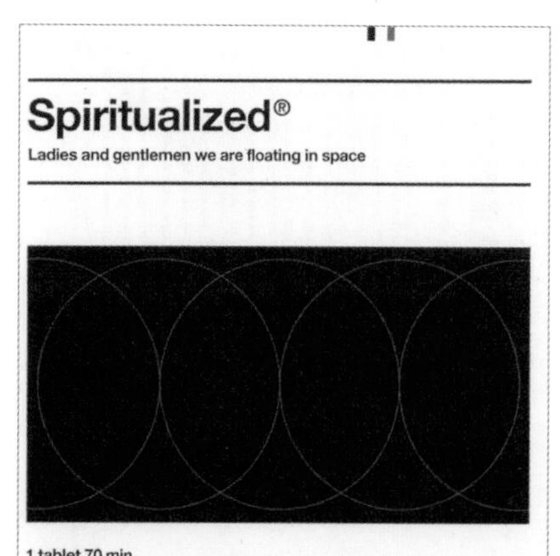

● Spiritualized's third studio album was a potent fever dream of space rock, gospel, and ambient sounds that Britain's *Melody Maker* rightly called "one mind-blowing perspective-fusing supernova of an album." It may or may not have been about the breakup of founder Jason Pierce and keyboardist Kate Radley—who secretly married The Verve's Richard Ashcroft shortly before recording (Pierce said much of the album was written prior to the split). Listeners could relate; the album beat out Radiohead's *OK Computer* and The Verve's *Urban Hymns* for *New Musical Express* Album of the Year in the UK while also giving the band its first Top 5 entry in its homeland's charts. *–HD*

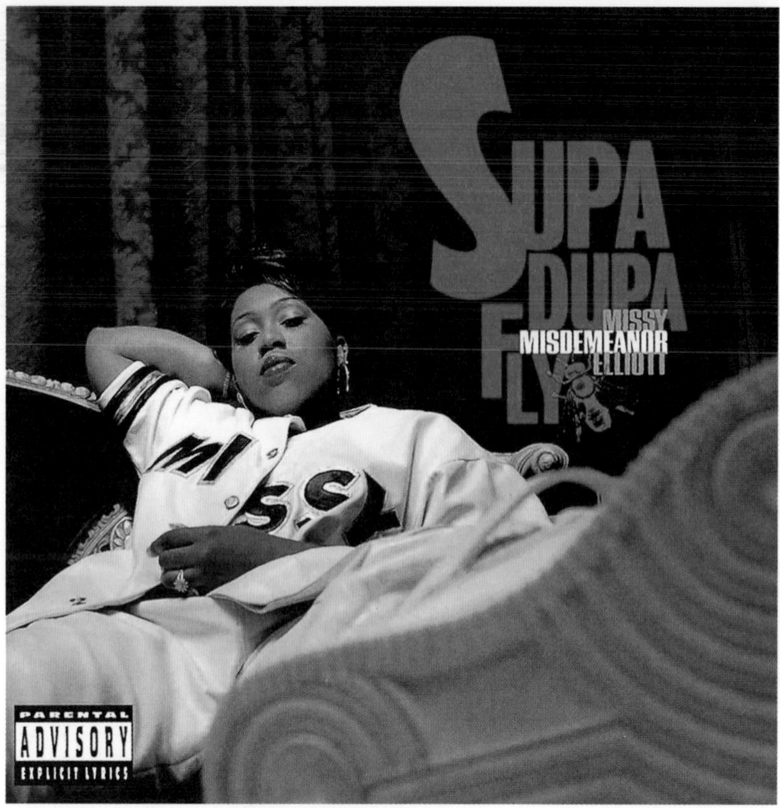

Missy "Misdemeanor" Elliott

SUPA DUPA FLY

THE GOLDMIND, INC./ELEKTRA | Producers: Missy Elliott, Timbaland

RELEASED: JULY 15, 1997

1997

● Missy Elliott got top billing on *Supa Dupa Fly*, but it presents her and producer Timbaland as a package deal. "We so tight that you get our styles tangled," Missy raps on the sparse, bottom-heavy banger **The Rain (Supa Dupa Fly)**, and it's easy to see why. As a team, they were inseparable.

Melissa Elliott met Timothy Mosley coming up in the Norfolk, Virginia, area. The pair was linked professionally as early as 1993, when they both appeared on Jodeci's *Diary of a Mad Band*, and they collaborated heavily—her as writer, him as producer on Aaliyah's 1996 album *One in a Million*. When it came time for Elliott to take center stage as an artist, she made a seismic impression in **The Rain**'s eye-popping Hype Williams–directed video. Wearing an inflated black vinyl suit and a bejeweled headpiece with built-in sunglasses, she looked like a crazed comic book character, and hip-hop had never seen anything like her. It instantly presented Elliott as a weirdo outsider to rap's mainstream, not beholden to the rules and expectations of her contemporaries. A new kind of star was born.

And Timbaland was her co-pilot. He produced the entirety of **Supa Dupa Fly** with his space-age robo-funk, his futuristic, rubbery rhythms the ideal canvas for Elliott's singular style. She rapped and sang about men (**Don't Be Comin' [In My Face]**), relationships (**Why You Hurt Me**), and her own flyness (**Izzy Izzy Ahh** and **I'm Talkin'**), spitting bars with confidence and clarity. She was sexy and strong, equally adept at riding Timba's rumbling beats (**Sock It 2 Me**) and creating moods inside his slinky slow jams (**Friendly Skies**, featuring Ginuwine).

Elliott and Timbaland would continue to reinvent rap's soundscapes for years, and in 2023, she became the first female rapper inducted into the Rock & Roll Hall of Fame. Supa Dupa Fly, indeed. *—AG*

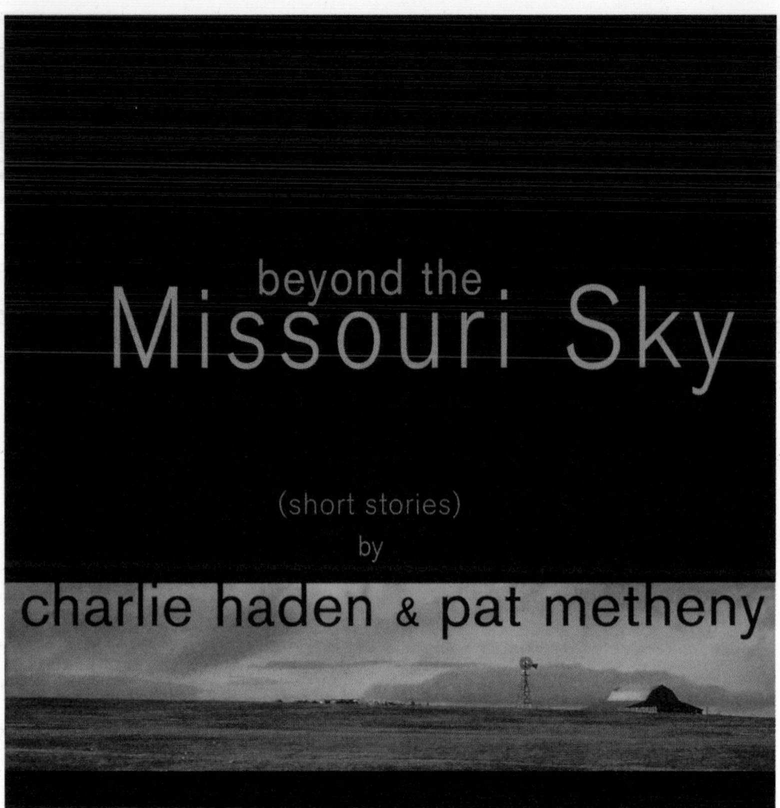

Charlie Haden & Pat Metheny

BEYOND THE MISSOURI SKY (SHORT STORIES)

POLYGRAM | Producers: Charlie Haden, Pat Metheny

RELEASED: FEBRUARY 27, 1997

1997

● Consider it inevitable that close friends and jazz soulmates of twenty-five years, bassist Charlie Haden and guitarist Pat Metheny—born half a generation apart, in 1937 and 1954, respectively, in small prairie towns in Iowa and Missouri—would collaborate on a timeless duet album. Early on, Metheny was a passionate follower of free-jazz alto saxophonist Ornette Coleman; Haden was his bassist. Metheny's admiration for Coleman led to his friendship with Haden, who became a central figure in Metheny's jazz evolution.

For *Beyond the Missouri Skies*, Haden and Metheny turned to tranquil, peaceful folk songs, lesser-known jazz tunes, and compassionate originals to render an impressionistic salute to America's heartland that earned the Grammy Award for Best Jazz Instrumental Performance. Haden contributed the lovely opener, **Waltz for Ruth**, written for his wife; Metheny was best man in their 1984 wedding, in fact. Metheny's articulate strumming and hand-picked notes on the track brought out the radiance of its homespun melody. On **First Song**, meanwhile, the duo's unified approach was resolute, steered by Haden's deep and tuneful bass.

Aptly, Metheny wrote **Message to a Friend** for Haden, copying the first three chords from Haden's standard "Silence" before veering into lustrous pastoral terrain. On **Tears of Rain**, Metheny unveiled an enigmatic sound palette with a new sitar-guitar. He and Haden reinvented Ennio Morricone's main theme and love song from their shared favorite film, *Cinema Paradiso*; Metheny shaped the melody with shimmery harmonics, while Haden bowed his bass to create a deep drone underlay. On the delicate closing track, **Spiritual**, Haden plucked the rustic and comforting melodic line while Metheny supplied contrast by playing multiple guitars, adding drums, synthesizer, and light orchestration. His guitar playing evoked a long-haul Missouri Pacific Railroad freight train, reminiscent of their boyhood days. To them, what lay beyond the Missouri sky was all heavenly music. *–CH*

David Bowie

EARTHLING

VIRGIN | Producers: David Bowie, Reeves Gabrels, Mark Plati

RELEASED: FEBRUARY 3, 1997

● David Bowie's early-'90s return to solo work stumbled with 1995's *Outside*, a lumbering concept album that divided fans with its mix of electronica, industrial, and avant-garde jazz. A subsequent US tour with Nine Inch Nails inspired him to ditch the art-rock schtick and dig deeper into the grooves of industrial and drum-and-bass on his follow-up, *Earthling*. The immersion served him well; Bowie sounded revitalized as he tapped the raw beats of the underground scene and channeled the sensory overstimulation of the newly arrived commercial internet.

Fortunately, his aural hyperactivity was backed up with some of the most solid songcraft in his late canon. Beneath its rapid-fire breakbeats and skittering noises, **Little Wonder** was a pop gem that, with a stripped-down arrangement, might have turned up on 1972's *Hunky Dory*. The IDM-inspired **Dead Man Walking** had an infectious chorus and shuffling groove that recalled Bowie's 1976 disco workout "Station to Station," while **Seven Years in Tibet** merged *Young Americans'* early-'70s blue-eyed soul with industrial rock. But far from rehashing his past, *Earthling* reasserted Bowie's genius as a pop magpie and made an inspired launch to a wildly creative, if sadly final, era in his remarkable career. *–CS*

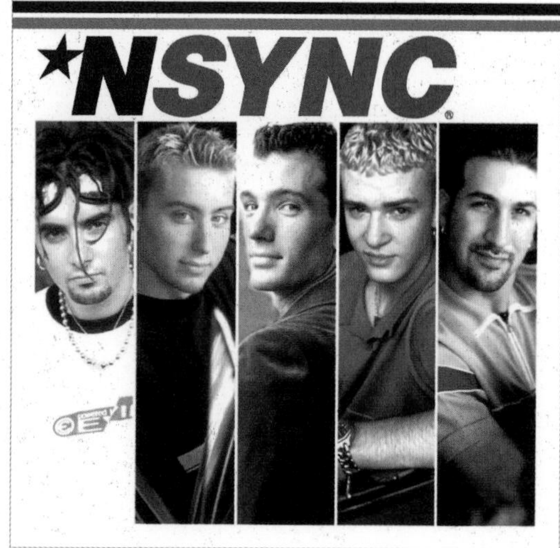

*NSYNC

*NSYNC

TRANS CONTINENTAL/RCA | Producers: Johnny Wright, Andreas von Oertzen

RELEASED: MAY 26, 1997

● *NSYNC's self-titled debut earned the quartet a spot as one of the most successful boy bands in music history, selling more than fifteen million copies worldwide and certified diamond in the US. Part of Lou Pearlman's notorious Trans Continental stable, the fivesome included a pair of cast members from Disney's *The New Mickey Mouse Club* (lead vocalists Justin Timberlake and JC Chasez), along with Joey Fatone, Chris Kirkpatrick, and Lance Bass.

NSYNC* spawned two big Pop Airplay hits in **I Want You Back (No. 7) and **Tearin' Up My Heart** (No. 6); the former was also the group's first entry on the Billboard Hot 100, peaking at No. 13, beaten out the following year at No. 8 by **(God Must Have Spent) A Little More Time on You** (which Alabama turned into a country hit in 1999). *NSYNC was credited, as a band, with co-writing one track (**Giddy Up**), while the album also included covers of Boston's **More Than a Feeling** and Christopher Cross's **Sailing**. A global campaign kept different singles popping in markets around the world, and a 1998 *Disney Channel in Concert* special really put some jet fuel behind the album and made sure *NSYNC was set up for something even greater next time out. *–MH2/GG*

Daft Punk

HOMEWORK

VIRGIN | Producers: Thomas Bangalter, Guy-Manuel de Homem Christo

RELEASED: JANUARY 20, 1997

1997

● The French have always been known for their superior quality when it comes to cuisine, and Daft Punk applied the same skillful craft to its debut album, *Homework*, feeding the world an electronic music masterpiece crafted in the bedroom of the duo's small flat (Daft House) in Paris.

Blending musical ingredients from house, techno, funk, disco, and rock, Thomas Bangalter and Guy-Manuel de Homem Christo stretched the boundaries of electronic music, giving birth to what was dubbed "robot rock." The duo had no intention of making an album; rather, they wanted to record a batch of singles using the basic equipment they had accumulated at home. Five months later, there were plenty of songs, and *Homework* was born.

Although all sixteen tracks were solid, four singles came off the album. The first, **Alive**, was a 1994 B-side that only received marginal attention at the time. But it was the second, **Da Funk**—with its catchy disco riff, acid melodies, and driving beat—that caught the world's attention, hitting the Top 10 in France, the UK, and other countries and No. 1 on many dance charts. **Around the World**, an infectious techno-house track with a repetitive and catchy vocoder chorus, did much the same, while the video for the smooth **Revolution 909** protested the French government's campaign against rave parties.

Homework was in a category of its own, proving that an electronic album so pure and filled with catchy, well-crafted songs, and just enough underground feel at its foundation, could be enjoyed by the masses as well. It was a true classic for any palate. *–MH*

1997

The Verve
URBAN HYMNS

HUT/VIRGIN | Producers: The Verve, Chris Potter, Youth

RELEASED: SEPTEMBER 29, 1997

● The Verve's third studio album catapulted the British quintet to fame, driven by the hit **Bitter Sweet Symphony**. The song was built on an uncredited sample of an orchestral version of The Rolling Stones' "The Last Time," creating a pop masterpiece—and legal woes. The band did not get proper clearance from the Stones, whose former management was successful in claiming all royalties (they were restored to frontman Richard Ashcroft in 2019). Despite a Grammy nomination, that put a cloud over a magnificent album that sold more than four million copies worldwide and featured other singles, including the upbeat **Lucky Man** and the dark, melodic **The Drugs Don't Work**. *–MR*

Crystal Method
VEGAS

OUTPOST | Producers: Scott Kirkland, Ken Jordan

RELEASED: AUGUST 26, 1997

● Crystal Method, the duo of Scott Kirkland and Ken Jordan, proclaimed that *Vegas* was the gateway drug for people to be introduced to electronic music. From this collaboration, these two grocery store workers created one of the most iconic electronic records of the '90s. The result was pedal-to-the-metal, nonstop, thumping big-beat techno infused with a funky rock flair. It was the perfect sound for the movie and video game industries, which used the duo's infectious songs as excitement cues. The album caught on throughout the world, leading to first gold and then, a decade later, platinum certifications. *–MH*

Jimi Hendrix
FIRST RAYS OF THE NEW RISING SUN

EXPERIENCE HENDRIX/MCA | Producers: Jimi Hendrix, Eddie Kramer, Mitch Mitchell, John Jansen

RELEASED: APRIL 1997

● Jimi Hendrix's fourth studio album, which he was working on at the time of his death, has been a subject of great conjecture and debate—not to mention controversial attempts to finalize it shortly after he passed away in 1970. This guesstimate, however, came from his family as the first release on its Experience Hendrix imprint shortly after it gained control of his catalog. The seventeen tracks here were recreated from the original multitracks, showing an earthier, more relaxed Hendrix incorporating more R&B and funk and stripped of Alan Douglas's reviled overdubs from the previous posthumous releases. *–GG*

Wyclef Jean
WYCLEF JEAN PRESENTS THE CARNIVAL

COLUMBIA | Producers: Wyclef Jean, Jerry Wonda

RELEASED: JUNE 24, 1997

● Sixteen months after settling *The Score* with the Fugees, the trio's Wyclef Jean took us to *The Carnival*—a sprawling twenty-four-track adventure that reached even beyond *The Score*'s rap-redefining reach to present a pan-global party. His Haitian roots get an even fuller airing here (the last three songs are sung in Creole), along with hip-hop, R&B, Cuban, reggae, and other flavors. His Fugees mates make guest appearances, as do the Neville Brothers and Cuban singing great Celia Cruz. It's flabby in spots but moves fast enough to keep us hanging on to hear the next cool idea. *–GG*

Carl Craig
MORE SONGS ABOUT FOOD AND REVOLUTIONARY ART

PLANET E COMMUNICATIONS | Producer: Carl Craig

RELEASED: 1997

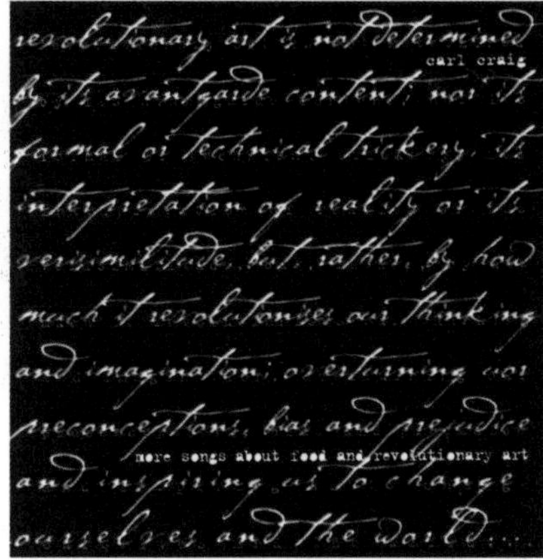

● If you have ever wondered what an electronic record from Miles Davis might sound like, this could easily be the answer—free, filling, boundary pushing, and truly innovative. Carl Craig delivered a masterpiece of "intelligent techno" here and, in doing so, proved that there could be an infusion of soul in the machine. Be it the beautiful **At Les** or the dreamy **As Time Goes By (Sitting under a Tree)** or the funky **Frustration**, Craig created a sublime mosaic of electronic bliss, all with his signature Detroit sound at the foundation, making it one of *the* essential electronic records of its time. *–MH*

Patty Loveless
LONG STRETCH OF LONESOME

EPIC | Producer: Emory Gordy Jr.

RELEASED: SEPTEMBER 30, 1997

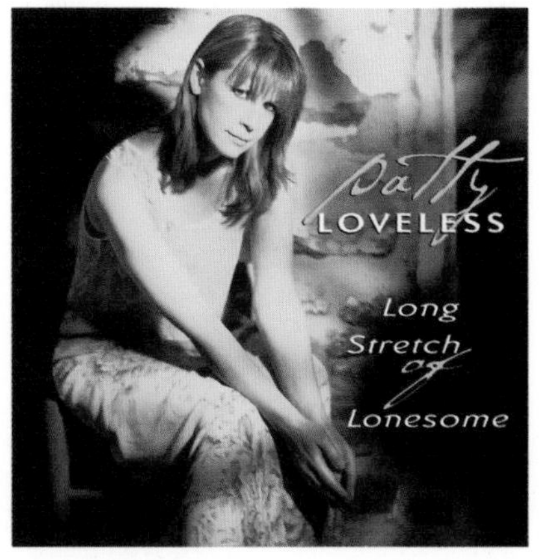

● Country music's late-'90s pop transformation didn't persuade Patty Loveless to abandon her new traditionalist style. In fact, she just dug in deeper. An actual coal miner's daughter and distant kin to Loretta Lynn, Loveless kicked off this set with the defiant **The Party Ain't Over Yet**. Three tracks—including the sublime Loveless/George Jones duet on Jim Lauderdale's **You Don't Seem to Miss Me**—made it to Billboard's Hot Country Songs Top 20. Thanks to it and songs by Kim Richey, Kostas Lazarides and Jeff Hanna, and Gretchen Peters, among others, and pitch-perfect production by husband Emory Gordy Jr., the album still sounds classic while others' hits of the day have faded. *–DD*

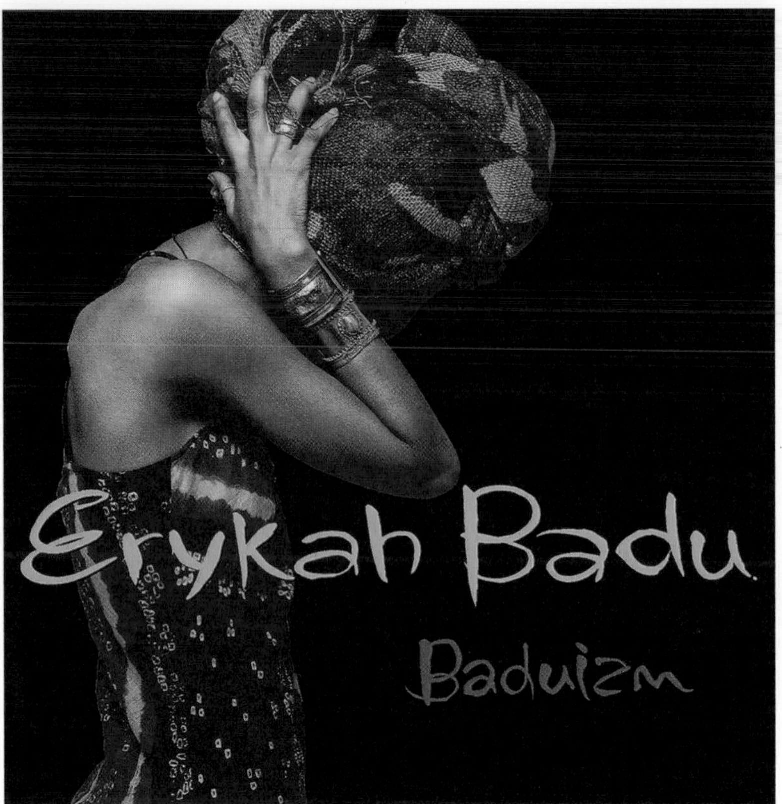

Erykah Badu

BADUIZM

KEDAR/UNIVERSAL | Producers: Madukwu Chinwah, Bob Power, JaBorn Jamal, Ike Lee III, Erykah Badu, the Roots, Richard Nichols, James Poyser, Tone the Backbone, Jaífar Barron, Robert Bradford

RELEASED: FEBRUARY 11, 1997

● With the arrival of her debut album, Dallas-born Erykah Badu was touted as a neo-soul Billie Holiday, a singer capable of channeling decades of grief and pain within a single note. But *Baduizm* wasn't such a gloomy record and can't be so easily defined with a quick comparison. True, her scarred voice recalled Lady Day in both tone and phrasing, but Badu delivered so much more than merely a copy of one of the twentieth century's all-time greatest vocalists.

Her recording contract was snagged by the demo *Country Cousins* and a duet with D'Angelo on Marvin Gaye and Tammy Terrell's "Your Precious Love." On her own album, Badu was aided by a long list of songwriters and producers who helped shape *Baduizm* into a multilevel listen. Its organic mix of live instruments along with the occasional studio boost gave the album a layer of vintage dust that complemented the songs and Badu's voice. On *Baduizm*'s best tracks—the Grammy-winning **On & On**, **Appletree**, **Otherside of the Game**, and **Next Lifetime**—Badu, who turned twenty-six two weeks after the album's release—bridged eras and genres. Forties jazz nudged against '90s hip-hop, with stops at '70s deep soul along the way.

There was a dark heart beating at the center of the record, linking it to other acclaimed records of the era such as D'Angelo's *Brown Sugar* and *Things Fall Apart* by *Baduizm* guests the Roots. Badu would go even deeper and darker on subsequent releases, but her first step—which won the Grammy Award for Best R&B Album—was accomplished and confident and a cornerstone of a genre she helped define. *–MG*

The Chemical Brothers

DIG YOUR OWN HOLE

FREESTYLE DUST/VIRGIN/ASTRALWERKS
Producers: The Chemical Brothers, Tom Rowlands/Ed Simons

RELEASED: APRIL 7, 1997

● The Chemical Brothers—Tom Rowlands and Ed Simons—honed their big-beat sensibilities as club DJs in their native Manchester, England, witnessing how the dancefloor reacted to the music in real time. They started out in the backroom of a pub in 1992, then worked their way up to bigger venues and ultimately recordings (first as the Dust Brothers before changing their name).

Dig Your Own Hole followed the duo's 1995 debut, *Exit Planet Dust*, which had sold more than a million copies and led to production work and remixes for other artists such as Oasis and Kylie Minogue. It was at the Glastonbury Festival in 1995 that Oasis's Noel Gallagher told the Chemical Brothers he would be interested in singing on a future track, which led to his guest vocals on **Setting Sun**. With its bombastic sound loops reminiscent of air raid sirens, **Setting Sun** entered the UK singles chart at No. 1; it also attracted the attention of lawyers for The Beatles, mistakenly claiming the duo sampled that group's "Tomorrow Never Knows" on the track. Though found innocent, you really have to believe once the dust settled, Rowlands and Simons took the comparison to the Fab Four as a compliment.

Dig Your Own Hole was the first Chemical Brothers album to reach No. 1 on the UK charts and sold more than two million copies worldwide. The breakout album earned a Grammy Award nomination for Best Alternative Music Album in 1998 and produced four additional singles, including **Where Do I Begin** with Beth Orton on guest vocals and **The Private Psychedelic Reel**, a trippy seven-minute instrumental that closed out the album. *—MR*

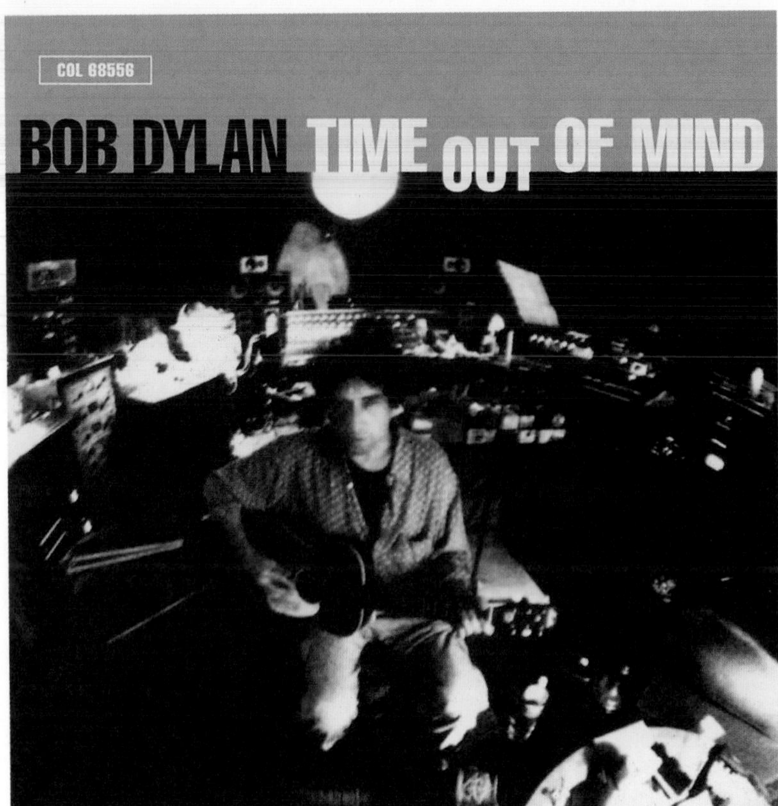

COL 68556
BOB DYLAN TIME OUT OF MIND

Bob Dylan

TIME OUT OF MIND

COLUMBIA | Producer: Daniel Lanois

RELEASED: SEPTEMBER 30, 1997

● After *Time Out of Mind* was recorded but before it was released, Bob Dylan was laid low by a case of histoplasmosis, a potentially fatal lung infection. On the record itself, Dylan sounded like a grizzled ghost ready to depart this world. But first there were some things he needed to get off his chest. Despite that grim premise, the album pulled Dylan out of a state of creative stasis that had lasted for years. He admitted to chasing hits that never materialized during the '80s, and in the '90s he had only released two albums of folk and blues covers, plus an *Unplugged* effort.

But in 1996, inspiration struck while he was snowed in on his Minnesota farm. The songs were as fantastic as they were fatalistic: **Love Sick**, **Standing in the Doorway**, **Trying to Get to Heaven**, **Not Dark Yet**, **Cold Irons Bound**, **Can't Wait**, and others turned out lovelorn and world-weary in the extreme. When a record begins with a spectral voice intoning, "I'm walking through streets that are dead," you know there's a rough ride ahead.

To produce the album, Dylan reconvened with Daniel Lanois, who had helmed 1989's *Oh Mercy*. Dylan told Lanois he was looking for a sound reminiscent of old blues and early rock 'n' roll records. He wanted it "greasy and dripping in sweat." Lanois delivered, bringing in a cadre of ace musicians, including Lanois himself on guitar. He altered Dylan's voice electronically, making it sound even more forlorn and forbidding than it already did. The result was one of Dylan's best albums, nearly perfect from conception to execution. Its one anomaly is the sentimental, even mawkish, **To Make You Feel My Love**, yet somehow that song has been recorded hundreds of times, including versions by Garth Brooks, Adele, Billy Joel, Neil Diamond, and Ed Sheeran.

Time Out of Mind won Dylan three Grammy Awards, including Album of the Year. —***DD***

Karen Clark Sheard

FINALLY KAREN

BLACK ISLAND MUSIC | Producers: Stanley Brown, Donald Lawrence, Cedric Thompson, J. Moss, Paul D. Allen, Kowan Paul, Milton Thornton

RELEASED: NOVEMBER 4, 1997

● After eleven albums with the Clark Sisters, vocalist Karen Clark Sheard stepped out with this debut solo album. *Finally Karen* mixed studio and live tracks, the latter recorded with Donald Lawrence's Tri-City Singers choir at Bailey Cathedral in Clark's native Detroit. The other Clark Sisters joined her for **Jesus Is a Love Song**, while her daughter Kierra Sheard dueted on **The Will of God** and Tri-City director Lawrence guested for **Heaven**. *Finally Karen* reached No. 2 on Billboard's Top Gospel Albums chart and even cracked the Top 30 (No. 28) of the Top R&B/Hip-Hop Albums. It also was nominated for a Grammy for Best Contemporary Gospel Album. *–CP*

Cornershop

WHEN I WAS BORN FOR THE 7TH TIME

WIIIJA | Producers: Tjinder Singh, Dan the Automator, Daddy Rappaport

RELEASED: SEPTEMBER 8, 1997

● Who is Asha Bhosle? If you didn't know Indian cinema, you had no idea. But in 1997, Kula Shaker gave us a **Brimful of Asha**, and we were grooving to this infectious, name-checking song on the third album from the British indie band. Tjinder Singh and company gave us catchy hooks, funk grooves, and cut-and-paste electronics, exotically spiced with trancey Punjabi on an album that topped the *Spin* year-end list and landed third on *The Village Voice*'s Pazz & Jop writers' poll. As Singh joyously sang, "Seems like the funky days, they're back again." *–SM*

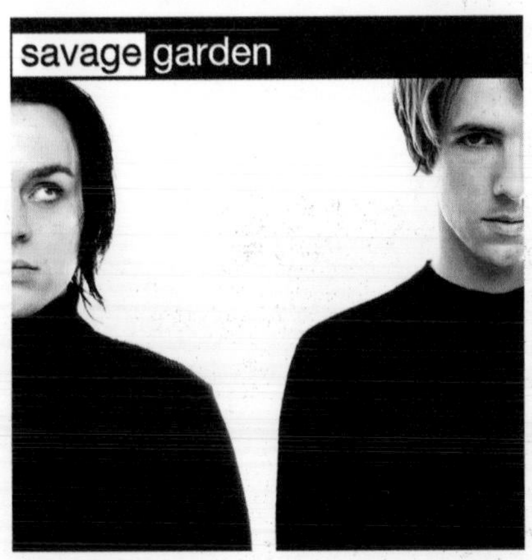

Savage Garden

SAVAGE GARDEN

ROADSHOW/COLUMBIA | Producer: Charles Fisher

RELEASED: MARCH 4, 1997

● Savage Garden's Darren Hayes and Daniel Jones said g'day to the world with their self-titled debut. The duo teamed up with producer Charles Fisher, who helped make hits for the likes of Air Supply and Olivia Newton-John. The first single, **I Want You**, was a No. 4 hit Down Under and on the Billboard Hot 100; the subsequent **Truly Madly Deeply** went to No. 1 in the US, where the album was certified seven-times platinum. Savage Garden only released one more studio album, *Affirmation*, in 1999. With their strong voices and writing skills, who knows what might have been if Hayes and Jones had stayed together? *–EP*

Deftones
AROUND THE FUR

MAVERICK | Producer: Terry Date

RELEASED: OCTOBER 28, 1997

● Deftones skated the line between alt-rock and nü metal, which allowed the group to join both the Vans Warped Tour and OZZFest during the late '90s. Their second album, *Around the Fur*, found the four-piece exploring the edges of its sound. There was plenty of aggression on display, but the key was the band's ear for melody and its embrace of both heavy and light elements. That balance made the opening **My Own Summer (Shove It)** and the follow-up single **Be Quiet and Drive (Far Away)** so dynamic. Frontman Chino Moreno wasn't just a shredder, either; he was a true singer—part metal, part Morrissey. *–AG*

Dr. Octagon
DR. OCTAGONECOLOGYST

DREAMWORKS | Producer: Dan the Automator

RELEASED: APRIL 29, 1997

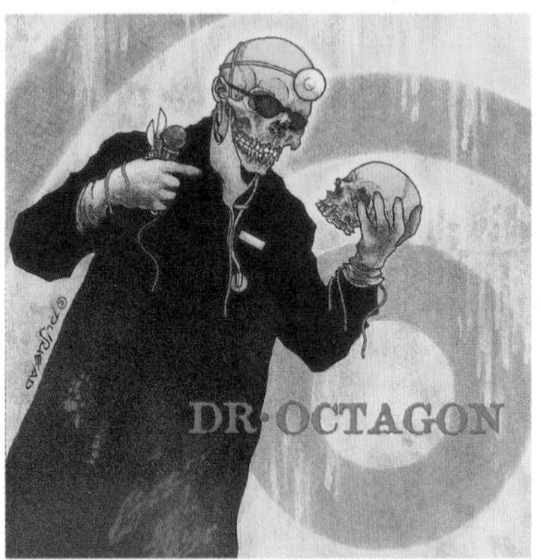

● There's experimental, there's out there, and then there's Kool Keith. The New York rapper, a member of the Bronx hip-hop collective Ultramagnetic MCs, took the alias Dr. Octagon for his first solo project, a demented interplanetary journey through sci-fi sex raps that sounded like it was recorded on Jupiter in the year 3000. With producer Dan "The Automator" Nakamura behind him, Keith sketched out a world of strange elective surgeries, animal crossbreeding and kinky pornocore eroticism. The soundscapes were so noteworthy that a companion album, *Instrumentalyst*, was issued. But stick with the good Doctor's primary release for a visit that's completely not of this Earth. *–AG*

John Fogerty
BLUE MOON SWAMP

WARNER BROS. | Producer: John Fogerty

RELEASED: MAY 20, 1997

● A dozen years after his mid-'80s comeback, during which he was still eschewing his Creedence Clearwater Revival (CCR) legacy, John Fogerty was in a better place. He began playing CCR songs live again, and, unlike 1986's *Eye of the Zombie*, *Blue Moon Swamp* tapped into his old band's spirit throughout the twelve tracks here, starting with the honky tonk twang of the opening **Southern Streamline**, the rockabilly groove of **Hot Rod Heart**, and the bayou-born swamp of **Blueboy**. His spirit revived, Fogerty reclaimed his niche status as a genuine rock 'n' roll icon *and* won a Grammy Award for Best Rock Album. *–GG*

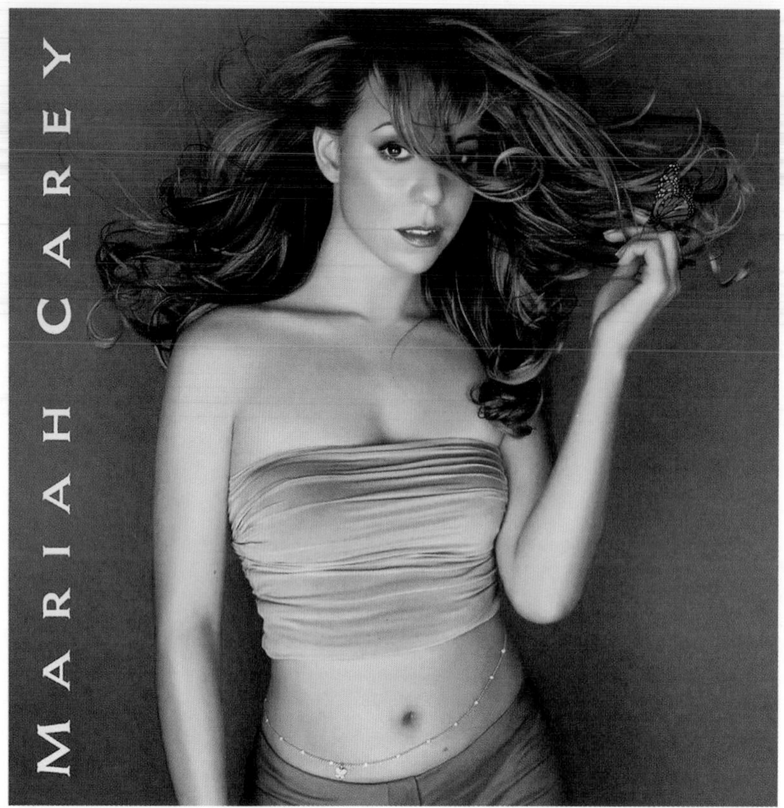

Mariah Carey

BUTTERFLY

COLUMBIA | Producers: Walter Afanasieff, Mariah Carey, Sean "Puffy" Combs

RELEASED: SEPTEMBER 10, 1997

● The metamorphosis began with "Fantasy." On the remix to her 1995 single, Mariah Carey enlisted Wu-Tang Clan's Ol' Dirty Bastard, a collaboration that was unthinkable at the time, given the pop/R&B hitmaker's squeaky-clean image. What was she doing with ODB? Was she okay?

As *Butterfly* came around, there were answers. This was Carey, twenty-eight at the time (though she famously does not acknowledge aging or the linear passage of time), breaking out of her cocoon and spreading her wings following the dissolution of her five-year marriage to Sony Music CEO Tommy Mottola, which was announced three months prior to the album's release. *Butterfly* leaned even further into hip-hop, and Carey flaunted a bikini in the video for first single, **Honey**—far from the conservative clothing in which she'd usually been seen. This was an all-new Carey, free for the first time, spearheading her own musical evolution.

Honey, which borrowed from World's Famous Supreme Team's "Hey DJ" and was produced by Sean "Puffy" Combs (Mase and The LOX are featured on the remix), went to No. 1 on Billboard's Hot 100, where it spent three weeks. (**My All**, a Spanish guitar ballad from the album, also went to No. 1). Just as important to *Butterfly*'s direction were **Breakdown** (featuring Bone Thugs-N-Harmony's Krayzie Bone and Wish Bone, which found Carey adopting Bone's signature sped-up flow) and **The Roof**, detailing a rooftop tryst between two lovers (later revealed to be an encounter between Carey and New York Yankee Derek Jeter), which interpolated Mobb Deep's "Shook Ones Pt. II." The album's title track, meanwhile, was a stirring gospel-tinged ballad detailing Carey's journey of self-discovery.

It would not have worked if her stylistic makeover was a cash grab, but Carey was completely at home with the modern sound—and it was the direction she'd follow going forward. Consider her metamorphosis complete. ***–AG***

Master P

GHETTO D

NO LIMIT/PRIORITY | Producers: Beats by the Pound

RELEASED: SEPTEMBER 2, 1997

● New Orleans hustler-turned-entrepreneur Percy "Master P" Miller built a Southern rap empire from mom-and-pop beginnings. No Limit started as a record store and became a label, specializing in gritty tales of street life told over funky, hard-hitting, lo-fi beats. After several years in the trenches, No Limit crashed the charts during the summer of 1997 with the soundtrack to the straight-to-video smash *(I'm Bout It*—written, directed, produced by, and starring P), which reached No. 4 on the Billboard 200. That teed up the release of *Ghetto D*, P's sixth studio album, which arrived at No. 1 (replacing Puff Daddy's *No Way Out*) and had everybody saying "uhhhhhh."

Make 'Em Say Uhh! came about two-thirds of the way into *Ghetto D*'s seventy-nine-minute runtime, the most music you could cram onto a single CD. It was a boisterous, horns-blasting posse cut led by P and featuring No Limit's heaviest hitters (Fiend, Silkk the Shocker, and Mia X), with a closing verse by Mystikal, the speed-rap whirlwind who tore apart the scenery like a hip-hop Tasmanian Devil. P is rarely alone on *Ghetto D*, surrounded by his stable of No Limit Soldiers (Silkk, P's little brother, appears on eleven of the nineteen tracks), and the album's production featured interpolations of Marvin Gaye (**Bourbons and Lacs**), Diana Ross (**Gangstas Need Love**), Timex Social Club (**Stop Hatin'**), and more familiar grooves tucked inside wall-to-wall crack raps and crime rhymes. The mournful **I Miss My Homies** recalled other rap tributes to fallen comrades (Ice Cube's "Dead Homiez" and Geto Boys' "Six Feet Deep") and stripped away the tough-guy bravado that marks much of the album.

P's label proved its might by adding Snoop Dogg to its roster and releasing a colossal forty albums between 1998 and 1999. No Limit was more than a name; it was P's philosophy—and *Ghetto D* showed the strength of his convictions. *—AG*

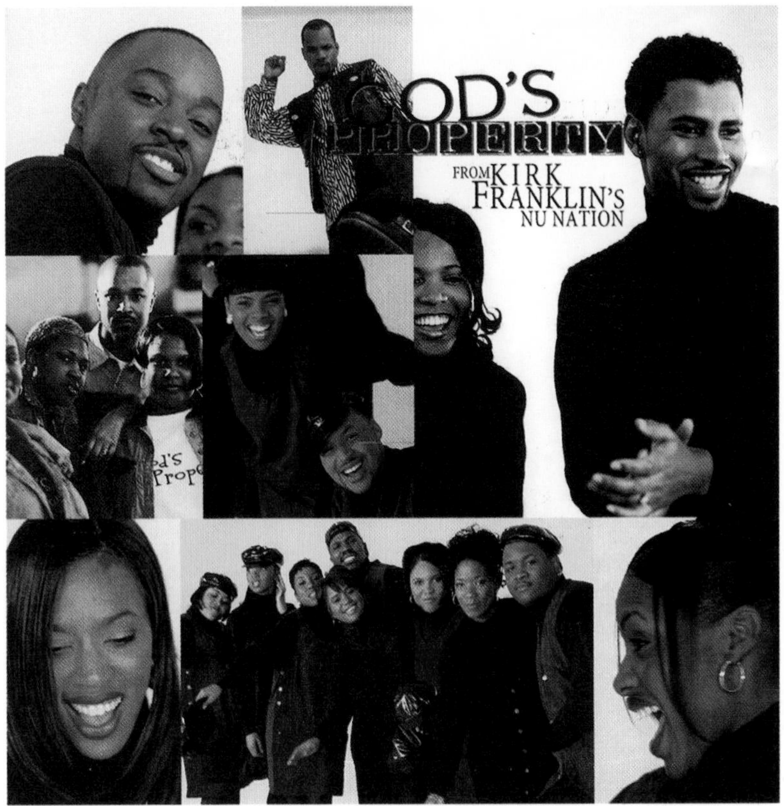

Kirk Franklin and God's Property

GOD'S PROPERTY FROM KIRK FRANKLIN'S NU NATION

B-RITE/INTERSCOPE | Producers: Kirk Franklin, Kevin Bond, Buster & Shavoni, Big Yardn, Victor Merritt

RELEASED: MAY 27, 1997

● God's Property was founded by Linder Ray Hall-Searight, a public-school music teacher. The group began working with Kirk Franklin on his 1995 album *Watcha Lookin' 4* and became a full-blown collaboration on this thirteen-song set, written mostly by Franklin but with significant arrangement contributions by Hall-Searight and her team. The idea, according to Franklin, was to push the boundaries of gospel music even further into the new dimensions he'd already charted; as he noted on the album-opening **Stomp (Remix)**, "For those of you that think gospel music has gone too far, you think we've gotten radical with our message, well I got news for you—you ain't heard nothing yet."

The album showcased heart-wrenching ballads composed by Franklin, including **My Life Is in Your Hands** (featured in the movie *Get on the Bus*), **More Than I Can Bear**, **Love**, and **The Storm Is Over**. The project also introduced future gospel music hitmaker Myron Butler on his composition **Up above My Head**. The lead single **Stomp** crossed several musical lines, featuring a rap by Cheryl "Salt" James from Salt 'N' Pepa along with an interpolation of Funkadelic's "One Nation under a Groove"; it spent two weeks at No. 1 on the R&B/Hip-Hop Airplay Charts and was bolstered by a hit video directed by Darren Grant.

The album spent forty-three weeks at No. 1 on Billboard's Top Gospel Album chart and five weeks atop the Top R&B/Hip-Hop Album survey. Its debut at No. 3 on the Billboard 200 was the highest position for a gospel album at the time. It won a Grammy Award for Best Gospel Choir or Chorus Album and a *Soul Train* Music Award for Best Gospel Album, and it brought the troupe NAACP Image Awards for Outstanding Gospel Artist and Outstanding Music Video. Certified triple-platinum, it's one of the top-selling gospel albums of all-time. *—CP*

Radiohead

OK COMPUTER

CAPITOL | Producers: Nigel Godrich, Radiohead

RELEASED: MAY 21, 1997

● Simply put, few '90s albums had the impact of Radiohead's *OK Computer*. The British quintet made huge creative leaps between its first and second releases; with its third, Radiohead reshaped the landscape of rock music moving forward. By mid-1996, when Radiohead began recording *OK Computer*, it had outgrown the guitar-based and self-probing songs of the previous year's *The Bends*. Piecing together random lyrics from singer Thom Yorke and constructing music based on jazz great Miles Davis's most experimental work and krautrock band Can's cut-and-paste techniques, Radiohead and producer Nigel Godrich forged an abstract masterpiece, a harbinger sound for the approaching new millennium.

Deliberate or not, the themes running through *OK Computer* coincided with the dawn of the internet age. Isolation, emotional withdrawal, cyber love/hate, technological fear, and social estrangement thread together now-classic songs such as **Paranoid Android**, **Subterranean Homesick Alien**, **Karma Police**, and **No Surprises**. Stitched-together instruments from electric piano and acoustic guitar to glockenspiel and cowbell—along with ambient noises, distorted and delayed effects, samplers, synths, and layered strings—emphasized the forward-thinking and avant-garde influences that went into the album's creation.

Despite the record company's fear that the intangible *OK Computer* wasn't marketable in the era of straightforward Britpop, the album debuted at No. 1 in the band's native UK, quickly sold more than two million copies in the US, and made Radiohead the most important act of its generation. For the next couple of decades the group's influence could be heard across the modern music spectrum, from indie to pop to electronic artists. And it was just getting started; when Radiohead returned three years later with the equally monumental *Kid A*, it shifted gears again, this time abandoning most traditional rock instruments altogether. *OK Computer* opened the gates. *–MG*

Björk

HOMOGENIC

ONE LITTLE INDIAN/ELEKTRA | Producers: Björk, Mark Bell, Guy Sigsworth, Howie B, Markus Dravs

RELEASED: SEPTEMBER 20, 1997

● The old adage says you can't go home again, but on her third solo album, Björk Guðmundsdóttir did—even if she wasn't actually *in* her native Iceland.

Homogenic was recorded primarily in Spain, where Björk had fled from London to escape the media storm caused by the suicide of a stalker there. But her heart (and her ears) was back in the land of ice and fire, channeled through an array of arrangements played by the Icelandic String Octet and indigenous singing techniques. Björk also wrote a pair of songs (**Joga** and **Bachelorette**) with the Icelandic poet Sigurjón Birgir "Sjón" Sigurðsson, who had ties to Björk's previous band, the Sugarcubes.

Homogenic was also the product of some fresh input on Björk's team. Nelle Hooper was gone, and Mark Bell of the techno group LFO stepped in as Björk's primary collaborator, co-producing six of the ten tracks with her. The effect was different than *Homogenic*'s predecessors, more elegiac and muted and missing the pop spirit of 1995's *Post*. But that was in keeping with Björk's shiftless muse, and that made it impossible to consign *Homogenic* to a particular genre. She was still mining the worlds of trip-hop and electronica, with more of a focus on chill ambience this time out. That gave the album a sense of grandeur, too; even in more spacious moments such as **All Neon Like**, there's an implied orchestration to the sonic air pockets that made it sound like more with less.

Homogenic gave Björk her second straight No. 1 album in Iceland and a then-career-high No. 28 on the Billboard 200 in the US, where it would also be certified gold. The album also netted three consecutive years of Grammy Award nominations for the singer—two for music videos—though none yielded trophies. ***—GG***

Hanson

MIDDLE OF NOWHERE

MERCURY/POLYGRAM | Producers: The Dust Brothers, Stephen Lironi

RELEASED: MAY 6, 1997

● After Dave Matthews's lawyer heard Hanson busking at South by Southwest and became their manager, he was turned down by fourteen pre-social-media-era labels unwilling to believe that the trio's self-recorded demo (especially the oh-so-infectious, just-try-getting-it-out-of-your-head hook of **MMMbop**) was the work of tween-teens singing and playing their own tunes, much less with such skill and charisma. Mercury A&R chief Steve Greenberg told *Billboard Book of No. 1 Hits* author Fred Bronson that he even went to a county fair to catch Hanson live "so I could sleep at night after I passed on them." Instead, he gave the group a contract.

Greenberg hired producers the Dust Brothers and Stephen Lironi to goose the original, slower version of **MMMbop**; the result sounded both bubble-gum retro and just modern enough, with dollops of turntable-scratching and funky cowbell. It dropped three weeks before *Middle of Nowhere*, and both became worldwide hits and made Hanson teen idols. But critics loved the trio's early R&B-influenced pop, too; **MMMbop** topped several prestigious year-end polls and scored two Grammy Award nominations. The album reached the Top 5 in seventeen countries and No. 1 in four of those. The Spice Girls blocked it from topping the Billboard 200 in the US, but *Middle of Nowhere* still spent fifty-eight weeks on the chart, going four-times platinum.

Four more singles followed, none as big as **MMMbop** but still displaying exceptional harmonies, instrumental chops, and lyrical depth. Isaac, Taylor, and Zac Hanson have since bopped their way into a respectable independent career. As for **MMMBop**, MTV counted ninety-three thousand cover versions, not including "MMMbop 2.0," Hanson's 2023 remake with the UK band Busted. *–LM*

19
1998

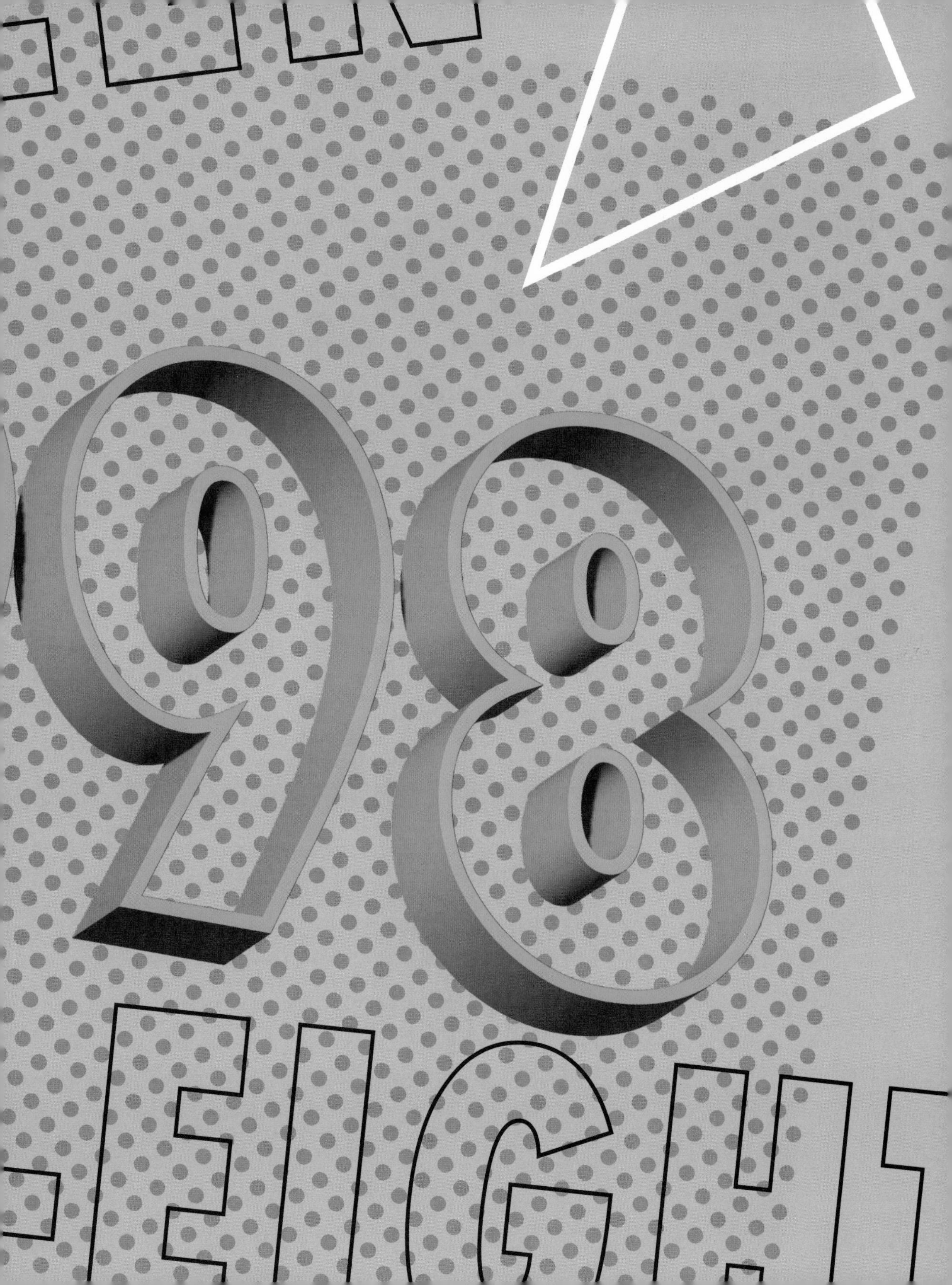
98

Elliott Smith

XO

DREAMWORKS | Producers: Elliott Smith, Rob Schnapf, Tom Rothrock

RELEASED: AUGUST 25, 1998

● Can something dark and disturbing also be beautiful? Elliott Smith's *XO* masterfully manages those contradictory ambitions.

No discussion of Smith's work can begin without referencing the tragic details of the Nebraska-born troubadour's too-short life and career. Throughout his adult life, Smith battled addictions to drugs and alcohol, bouts of extreme paranoia, and attempted and threatened suicides. On October 21, 2003, at the age of thirty-four, Smith was found dead from what was ruled two self-inflicted stab wounds. Like Kurt Cobain and Chris Cornell, Smith's work must forever be viewed through this sad prism.

That said, a casual listen to *XO* can find one entranced by Smith's trademark wispy, double-tracked vocals and sweet harmonies. The melodies and instrumental licks clearly showed the influence of pop icons such as The Beatles and the Hollies. From **Waltz #2**, a ballad of unrequited love, to **Oh Well, OK**, with a guitar riff that could seamlessly be dropped into The Beatles' *The White Album*, there were plenty of sonic confections to keep your ears happy. But dig into the lyrics and there was plenty of hostility and numerous lines that foreshadowed the tragedy to come.

In the opening track, **Sweet Adeline**, Smith claimed to be "waiting for sedation to disconnect my head or any situation where I'm better off than dead." **Baby Britain** referenced a "death that's not worth cheating." **Everybody Cares, Everybody Understands** told the story of an actual intervention held by Smith's friends. Songs like **Pitseleh**, **Bled White**, and **I Didn't Understand** were just a few of the acrimonious salutes to lost love. All that pretty music was covering a whole lot of anger and despair.

Ultimately, *XO* stands on its own as a brilliant piece of pop craftsmanship. But be aware that you will be taking a journey into the inner workings of a talented but deeply troubled artist. *–GP*

1998

Fatboy Slim

YOU'VE COME A LONG WAY, BABY

SKINT/ASTRALWERKS | Producer: Norman Cook

RELEASED: OCTOBER 19, 1998

● Norman Cook seemed like one of the most unlikely musicians to find fame in the United States. But thanks to *You've Come a Long Way, Baby*, his second album under the alias Fatboy Slim, the British musician shot to worldwide fame. Though Cook played in British bands the Housemartins and The Beautiful South during the '80s, he began moving to his own beat with the Beats International collective by the end of the decade. He became Fatboy Slim in 1996, releasing an album (*Better Living Through Chemistry*) but really finding his voice with the hypnotizing **Right Here, Right Now** and **The Rocafeller Skank**, the one-two punch that opened *You've Come a Long Way, Baby*.

1998

What really propelled . . . *Baby*, however, was its third single, **Praise You**. The multi-sampled masterpiece was marked by a twenty-five-year-old vocal borrow from "Take Yo' Praise" by relatively unknown artist Camille Yarbrough. It hit the Top 5 on the Billboard Alternative Airplay and Dance Singles Sales charts and No. 1 on several UK surveys and was nominated for a Grammy for Best Dance Recording.

Videos for **Praise You** and **Right Here, Right Now** became classics—the former, in particular. Directed by the legendary Spike Jonze with Roman Coppola (Francis Ford's son), it featured Jonze leading a flash mob–style dance troupe unannounced through a California mall with a boom box, dancing to the song, and took home three MTV Video Music Awards. The clip for **Right Here, Right Now**, meanwhile, was a bizarre romp through 350 billion years of evolutionary history.

While Cook was criticized for being unoriginal because of the heavy sampling throughout . . . *Baby*, it nevertheless showcased his studio acumen and fully cemented his transition to star producer and remixer, showing what a long way he had come, baby, from his modest beginnings as a bass player. *–ZC*

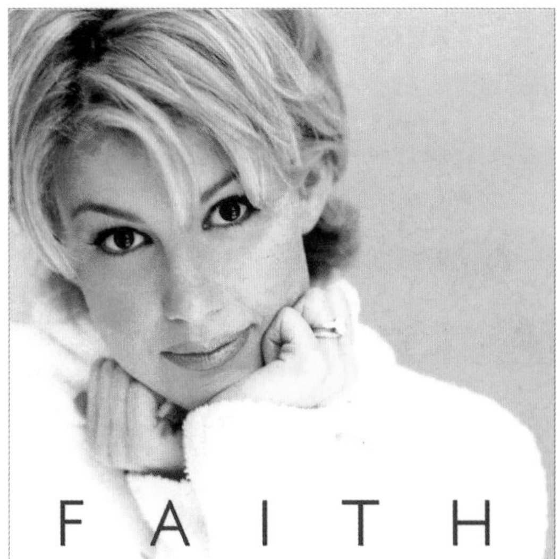

Faith Hill
FAITH

WARNER BROS. NASHVILLE | Producers: Byron Gallimore, Faith Hill, Dan Huff

RELEASED: APRIL 21, 1998

● Faith Hill's third studio album gave the country singer from Mississippi her first taste of international and crossover success. The twelve-song project produced a massive hit both in the US and overseas with the opening track **This Kiss**; the buoyant single—written by Beth Nielsen Chapman with Robin Lerner and Anne Roboff—not only hit No. 1 on Billboard's Top Country Songs chart but also was Top 10 on the Hot 100 and the Adult Contemporary survey. **This Kiss** was a hit in the UK, Europe, and Australia as well. It was the first of five singles released from the album, including another No. 1 country hit, **Let Me Let Go**, that featured background vocals by Vince Gill. Hill's husband, Tim McGraw, joined her for **Just to Hear You Say That You Love Me**, a Diane Warren–written track that took home prizes from the Academy of Country Music Awards and the TNN/Music City News Country Awards. *Faith* also featured writing contributions from Matraca Berg, Bekka Bramlett, Billy Burnette, Gretchen Peters, Aldo Nova, and Sheryl Crow, some of whom also performed on the recordings. *Faith* was certified six-times platinum and was nominated for a Grammy Award for Best Country Album. *–MH2*

Hole
CELEBRITY SKIN

DGC | Producer: Michael Beinhorn

RELEASED: SEPTEMBER 8, 1998

● The first sound on *Celebrity Skin* was a series of lacerating guitar riffs, followed by a mission statement from Courtney Love. "Oh, make me over," the grunge heroine politely demanded. It was time for Hole's glow-up.

Hole had ridden out the boys club of mid-'90s alt-rock with *Live Through This*, released just days after Love's husband Kurt Cobain committed suicide in 1994. For *Celebrity Skin*, Love repackaged Hole under an LA gloss so polished you could eat off it—twelve tracks of reckoning with the past and moving on, living as the best revenge.

With her co-writers (including Hole bandmates and The Smashing Pumpkins leader Billy Corgan), Love worked out her demons. The closing minute of **Reasons to Be Beautiful** was a naked plea to Cobain. The album moved forward with **Heaven Tonight**, **Boys on the Radio**, and **Awful**, landing between the pure FM pleasures of Cheap Trick and Fleetwood Mac's California confessionals. **Malibu** was the sound of Love cleansing herself in the Pacific Ocean and emerging anew.

The album's most poignant moment came as Love flipped a Neil Young quote from Cobain's suicide note, "It's better to burn out than to fade away," into a message of resilience: "It's better to rise," she sang, "than fade away." *–AG*

Madonna

RAY OF LIGHT

MAVERICK/WARNER BROS. | Producers: Madonna, William Orbit

RELEASED: FEBRUARY 22, 1998

● On her seventh studio album, the Mother of Reinvention faced her biggest change yet: motherhood. *Ray of Light* was Madonna's first album since the birth of her daughter, Lourdes, in 1996. It also dovetailed with the rise of electronica, a movement Madonna had a role in popularizing since her record label, Maverick, released Prodigy's breakthrough album, *The Fat of the Land*, during the summer of 1997. *Ray of Light* found the thirty-nine-year-old amid a spiritual and musical rebirth, and it signaled the beginning of the second half of her career, although Madonna righteously defied simple categorization.

Madonna's songwriting here was confessional, as the opener **Drowned World/Substitute for Love** detailed her relationship with success over producer William Orbit's ambient instrumental. "I traded fame for love without a second thought/And now I find I've changed my mind," she sang, her voice shaking with intimacy as Orbit's beat bubbled up underneath. Her quest for love and enlightenment unfolded over thirteen throbbing tracks, with the icy stabs of the single **Frozen** rejecting mainstream pop for a more forward-thinking sound (it still rose to No. 2 on the Billboard Hot 100) and **Shanti/Ashtangi** exploring Eastern Asian mysticism over pulsating dancefloor rhythms. The quiet, ethereal **Little Star** was the album's most direct dedication to her daughter, and **The Power of Good-Bye** was a plea for strength and an ode to making peace with moving on, which summed up Madonna's general mindset.

Everything coalesced on *Ray of Light's* title track, a vibrant techno-rock celebration that exploded into a burst of a million colors as Madonna literally screamed with joy. "And I feel like I just got home," shouted the singer, who had always been on the move. She found her ray of light, and on this four-times platinum release, she shared it with the world. *—AG*

Neutral Milk Hotel

IN THE AEROPLANE OVER THE SEA

MERGE | Producer: Robert Schneider

RELEASED: FEBRUARY 10, 1998

● Although many considered him late on the scene among the pioneers of indie and lo-fi rock, for some Jeff Mangum was *the* voice of the late-'90s post-grunge generation. His Louisiana band's second and final album began with **King of Carrot Flowers, Pt. 1**, an exquisite piece of proto-freak folk, setting the tone for a record that became progressively more weird, wonderful, confessional, and mind-altering as each song flowed seamlessly into the next. Inspired by Anne Frank's diary, there's a staggering beauty and energy to the whole messy affair. *–SM*

Various Artists

HOPE FLOATS (MUSIC FROM THE MOTION PICTURE)

CAPITOL | Producers: Don Was, Forest Whitaker

RELEASED: APRIL 7, 1998

● This thirteen-track collection of contemporary country with hints of mainstream pop was a perfect complement to the Sandra Bullock romantic drama. Co-produced by the film's director Forest Whitaker and Grammy winner Don Was, *Hope Floats* boasted several original songs composed for the film, including **In Need** by Sheryl Crow and **Chances Are**, a Bob Seger–penned duet with Martina McBride. The album also featured covers of well-known tracks, notably Garth Brooks's rendition of Bob Dylan's **To Make You Feel My Love**, which hit No. 1 on the Billboard Hot Country Songs chart. The soundtrack subtly nudged the film's story along to a predictable ending, with a smile. *–SS*

Bruce Hornsby

SPIRIT TRAIL

RCA | Producers: Bruce Hornsby, Michael Mangini

RELEASED: OCTOBER 13, 1998

● After utilizing more of the jazz language on his two preceding albums, Bruce Hornsby took a new approach with his piano playing for *Spirit Trail*, building his left-hand vocabulary and incorporating two-handed techniques for what he called "a newfound attempt at virtuosity in the pop song context." It worked like a charm on this thematic two-disc set, with contributions from Jerry Garcia, star violinists Ashley MacIsaac and David Mansfield, and John Leventhal, among others. The cover photo featuring his late uncle, Charles, meanwhile, has become an iconic hoot in its own right. *–GG*

Herbie Hancock
GERSHWIN'S WORLD

VERVE | Producers: Robert Sadin, Herbie Hancock, David Passick

RELEASED: OCTOBER 20, 1998

● Only a fellow musical genius could present George Gershwin in a way that expanded understanding of the composer's breadth and importance. Herbie Hancock achieved that by incorporating Gershwin's influences (Maurice Ravel, W. C. Handy, Duke Ellington, James P. Johnson) along with African percussion, jazz, and classical arrangements, with guests including Wayne Shorter, Chick Corea, Stevie Wonder, Kathleen Battle, and Joni Mitchell, whose performances of **Summertime** and **The Man I Loved** were sublime. Across fourteen tracks, Hancock and producer Robert Sadin connected the dots between St. Louis blues, Harlem jazz, *Porgy and Bess*, and gorgeous orchestral work. Hancock's piano playing was flawless, and the entire album was simply magnificent. *–LM*

Gang Starr
MOMENT OF TRUTH

NOO TRYBE/VIRGIN | Producers: DJ Premier, Guru

RELEASED: MARCH 31, 1998

● They weren't new to this; they were true to this. Gang Starr's fifth album, *Moment of Truth*, didn't differ from the Brooklyn duo's classic formula of slick rhymes over boom bap beats, courtesy of Keith "Guru" Elam and Chris "DJ Premier" Martin, respectively. Rather, it's the album's adherence to style that made it so reliable: "The rhyme style is elevated, the styles of beats is elevated, but it's still Guru and Premier," Guru says at the top of **You Know My Steez**, which kicks off twenty hard-hitting tracks that reaffirmed the Gang Starr's status as torchbearer of real-deal New York hip-hop. *–AG*

Kim Burrell
EVERLASTING LIFE

TOMMY BOY GOSPEL | Producer: Alex Asaph Ward

RELEASED: NOVEMBER 24, 1998

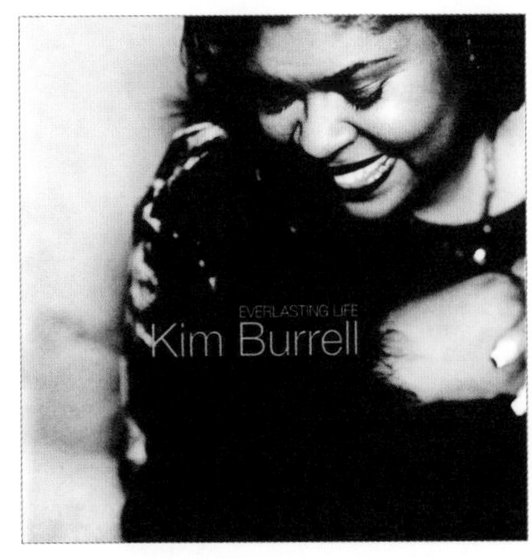

● With one of the most distinctive voices in gospel music, Kim Burrell incorporated jazz and R&B on her second album and debut for the gospel imprint of the revered hip-hop label Tommy Boy. Peaking at No. 10 on the Billboard Gospel Album charts, *Everlasting Life* was produced by Alex Asaph Ward (Dorinda Clark Cole, Smokie Norful) and highlighted Burrell's writing skills on songs such as **Holy Ghost**, **I Come to You More Than I Give**, and the title track. Other outstanding tracks included **Prodigal Son**, **It's Not Supposed to Be This Way**, and **I Keep Holding On**. *–CP*

Beck

MUTATIONS

DGC/BONG LOAD | Producers: Beck Hanson, Nigel Godrich

RELEASED: NOVEMBER 3, 1998

● Beck never hid his love of folk music. Although casual fans who only knew of him through upbeat, hip-hop-influenced hit singles such as "Loser" and "Where It's At" were caught off guard by the largely acoustic *Mutations*, the album simply found him bringing an already-important aspect of his work to the forefront. The independently released *One Foot in the Grave* mined similar territory in 1994, albeit in a much more ramshackle fashion; the woozy "Pay No Mind (Snoozer)," the track that followed "Loser" on Beck's commercial breakthrough album *Mellow Gold*, would have fit quite comfortably on *Mutations*. What's more, he reportedly first planned for 1996's *Odelay* to be an acoustic album before abandoning that direction in favor of teaming up with the Dust Brothers.

The bigger shock to fans who had been paying close attention throughout Beck's career may have been how somber and elegantly polished *Mutations* was. Working with Radiohead producer Nigel Godrich, Beck abandoned the everything-including-the-kitchen-sink pastiche approach of *Mellow Gold* and *Odelay* and, instead, stuck to a much more focused sonic palette. Luckily, his songwriting was more than strong and diverse enough to hold listeners' attention—although focus is a relative term, as Beck touched on folk, country, pop, and even bossa nova on *Mutations*, with highlights including the droning **Nobody's Fault But My Own** and the softly psychedelic **We Live Again**. He broke the mood just once, cutting loose with a blend of fuzz rock and shimmering pop on the album-closing **Diamond Bollocks**. Beck would revisit *Mutations'* modus operandi again, with similarly impressive results, on 2002's *Sea Change* and 2014's *Morning Phase*. *–MW*

Willie Nelson
TEATRO

ISLAND | Producer: Daniel Lanois

RELEASED: SEPTEMBER 1, 1998

● When Daniel Lanois decided to marry Willie Nelson's flamenco and gypsy jazz influences with Southwest-seasoned Spanish and Latin rhythms, he gave new life to several old Nelson compositions, plus a few new ones. Nelson set the tone with Django Reinhardt's **Ou Es-Tu, Mon Amour? (Where Are You, My Love?)** before segueing into his own **I Never Cared for You**, one of ten mostly sublime duets with Emmylou Harris. Though *Teatro* didn't do as well commercially as another Lanois-helmed project recorded in its namesake Oxnard, California, theater (namely Bob Dylan's Grammy-winning *Time Out of Mind*), the Lanois-composed track **The Maker** did get some airplay. *–LM*

B. B. King
BLUES ON THE BAYOU

MCA | Producer: B. B. King

RELEASED: OCTOBER 20, 1998

● By 1998, B. B. King was heading into the twilight of his illustrious career. He was also at a point where he was calling the shots on what sort of records he wanted to make. The tunes on this album were a bit more laid back, with his tight band and his super-clean guitar tone standing out front and center and, he claimed, no overdubs or "high-tech tricks." The addition of strings and a horn section helped make *Blues on the Bayou* one of his most accessible records, well received by fans and critics alike and winner of a Grammy for the Best Traditional Blues Album. *–WW*

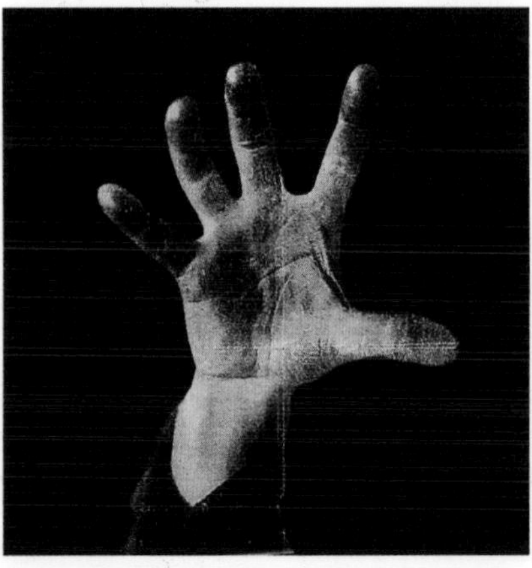

System of a Down
SYSTEM OF A DOWN

AMERICAN RECORDINGS/COLUMBIA | Producers: Rick Rubin, System of a Down

RELEASED: JUNE 30, 1998

● We'd never heard anything quite like System of a Down (SOAD) when the Los Angeles quartet's self-titled debut came blasting out the speakers—and from the second stage on that year's OZZFest. Though metal at its core, there was a skewed, adventurous, avant-garde aspect at work here, as akin to, say, Frank Zappa as to any of SOAD's nü metal peers. "Loud and noisy . . . gaining independence" was how Serj Tankian put it in **DDevil**, and SOAD followed no rules on these thirteen dynamically roiling tracks—many of them pointedly political—but still kept us rocking. *–GG*

Manu Chao

CLANDESTINO

VIRGIN/ARK 21 | Producers: Manu Chao, Renaud Letang

RELEASED: OCTOBER 6, 1998

● After parting ways with the French punk-rock troupe Mano Negro—Manu Chao's first prominent musical endeavor—he embarked on a three-year journey around the world that opened his eyes to the plight of the disenfranchised. *Clandestino* was born out of that experience, filled with eclectic, multilingual tracks that embodied Chao's vagabond lifestyle while exploring anti-capitalist and anti-globalist themes. A Parisian native of Spanish descent, Chao's solo debut effortlessly blended musical styles from reggae and flamenco to Afro-Cuban, world beat, and French chanson. Though the album struggled commercially in the US, *Clandestino* was widely praised globally, charting in ten countries and selling more than three million albums worldwide. *–JS*

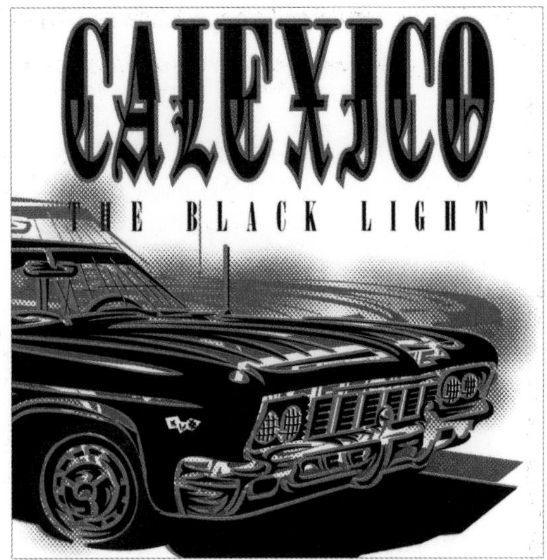

Calexico

THE BLACK LIGHT

QUARTERSTICK | Producers: Joey Burns, John Convertino

RELEASED: MAY 19, 1998

● When multi-instrumentalists Joey Burns and John Convertino moved from Los Angeles (where they'd met) to Tucson, Arizona, they became entranced by the sounds of mariachi, conjunto/norteño, cumbia, and other Latin/Hispanic styles permeating the border. *The Black Light*, their first release as Calexico (taken from a town named for California and Mexico), merged those influences with Morphine-like minimalist jazz, country, and rock, filtered through Ennio Morricone spaghetti Western scores, Cormac McCarthy novels, and beat poetry. Layering accordion, horns, vibraphone, strings, guitars, drums, percussion, and Burns's half-spoken vocals into a storyboarded concept album—complete with a bloody climax—they created a magnificently cinematic, intoxicatingly sensual sound aptly labeled "desert noir." *–LM*

Lauryn Hill

THE MISEDUCATION OF LAURYN HILL

RUFFHOUSE/COLUMBIA | Producers: Lauryn Hill, Che Pope, Vada Nobles

RELEASED: AUGUST 25, 1998

● How can something so multidimensional as love truly be defined when one definition can contrast and contravene another? The interstitial material between the tracks on *The Miseducation of Lauryn Hill* built the album's foundational philosophy while mining an answer to that question. The ongoing dialogue sounds like any urban high school in the US, where a knowing teacher asks teenage students to define love. No one wants to embarrass themselves in front of their classmates, but the fly-on-the-wall recording captures young people baring their thoughts on the most elusive, precious, and vital emotion.

It should be noted that Lauryn Hill was only twenty-three when this record came out and not far removed from high school herself. The vignettes of schoolkids are her internal voice made public. Hill's insights on the facets of love, her life experiences, and external voice burst from the grooves with purpose, power, and desire to find answers. Hill, just out of Fugees, brims with the love a mother has for her child ("I've never been in love like this before") in **To Zion**, the pain of love and breakups in **When It Hurt So Bad** ("So how could this be love and make me feel so bad?"), the misguided nature of lust in **Doo Wop (That Thing)**, and the compassion for those who have betrayed her in **Forgive Them Father**.

The Miseducation . . . was on par with Marvin Gaye's *What's Going On*, his own landmark paean to love and spirit. And like that album, *The Miseducation . . .* was a singular, timeless work by a singular artist. Its seamless melding of rap, reggae, dancehall, and old-school R&B never missed the mark. As of this writing, Hill has not released another studio album, but she doesn't necessarily need to. This one says everything. *–HK*

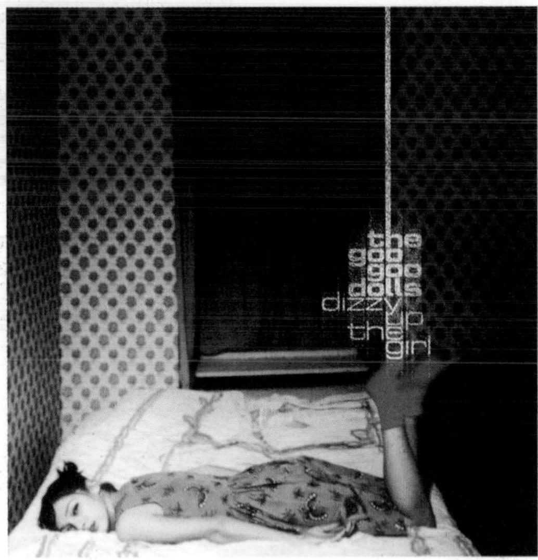

Goo Goo Dolls

DIZZY UP THE GIRL

WARNER BROS. | Producers: Rob Cavallo, Goo Goo Dolls

RELEASED: SEPTEMBER 22, 1998

● Unlike many '90s alt-rockers who disdained mainstream commercial music, Goo Goo Dolls channeled its creative energy into catchy, radio-friendly hits. It may have taken more than a decade for people to know the band's name, but the Buffalo, New York, trio finally reached global star status with its sixth studio album, *Dizzy Up the Girl*. The more upbeat, pop-oriented songs composed mainly by John Rzeznik and Robby Takac (with drummer Mike Malinin making his debut) were a stark departure from the Goos' punk-rock beginnings, and the polish contributed significantly to the record's commercial success.

The album spawned five singles, the first of which, **Iris** (originally released as part of the *City of Angels* movie soundtrack), stayed at the top of the Billboard Hot 100 for eighteen weeks and was nominated for three Grammy Awards. **Slide** and **Black Balloon** showcased Rzeznik's earnest, melodic style, while **Dizzy** was a nod to the gritty electric guitar fuzz of the band's earlier years. The Goos' blue-collar upbringing and early struggles were woven into **Broadway**, an ode to the rough neighborhood where Rzeznik and Takac grew up. With its five-times platinum sales, *Dizzy Up the Girl* proved to be a turning point for the Goos. *–SS*

Kid Rock

DEVIL WITHOUT A CAUSE

TOP DOG/LAVA/ATLANTIC | Producers: Kid Rock, John Travis

RELEASED: AUGUST 18, 1998

● Chuck Berry and rock 'n' roll. DJ Kool Herc and rap. The Ramones and punk. Those musical pioneers helped introduce new genres to the masses. The same can be said for Kid Rock and his fusion of rock, funk, country, and rap, culminating on his major label debut, *Devil Without a Cause*, specifically on the track **Cowboy**, an imagined story of the Detroit artist's hell-raising move to California.

Rock was not one to be pigeonholed, and *Devil . . .* was wildly flexible. The title track slams metal and funk together, while the late-'90s sound of nü metal screams through **Bawitdaba** (thanks to the rock backing of his Twisted Brown Trucker Band). *Devil . . .* does an emotional 180 on tracks such as **Only God Knows Why**, a ballad on which Rock grapples with the fame he hopes to achieve. *Devil Without a Cause* sold more than fourteen million copies, putting Rock on the map. His hip-hop roots, meanwhile, are still part of *Devil . . .* on **Welcome 2 the Party** and other tracks. He put a lot in the blender here, and one can wonder if Kid Rock was the pioneer of country-rap—or maybe it was just Southern rock with a Motor City backbone. *–ZC*

Queens of the Stone Age

QUEENS OF THE STONE AGE

LOOSEGROOVE/ROADRUNNER/MAN'S RUIN

Producers: Joe Barresi, Josh Homme

RELEASED: SEPTEMBER 22, 1998

● After serving as the primary songwriter and guitarist for the pioneering and now-legendary early-'90s stoner-rock band Kyuss, Josh Homme took full control and drastically sharpened his focus for his new group, Queens of the Stone Age (QOTSA). Homme handled all instruments except drums on the band's self-titled debut, replacing the expansive epics of his former group with much more compact, hook-filled songwriting.

At this early stage in QOTSA's evolution, things weren't nearly as buttoned-up and precise as they would come to be on albums such as *Songs for the Deaf.* There was still plenty of unhinged, fuzzy riffing to be had here, most spectacularly on the entirely instrumental second half of **Walking on the Sidewalks**. Homme's vocal powers weren't nearly as fully formed as they would be in later years, but he already exuded the charisma and sexuality that would quickly become such a big part of his band's sound and success. *Queens of the Stone Age* is the rare transitional album that successfully blends old and new styles to create something that's already new and exciting while clearly pointing to even bigger things in the future. *–MW*

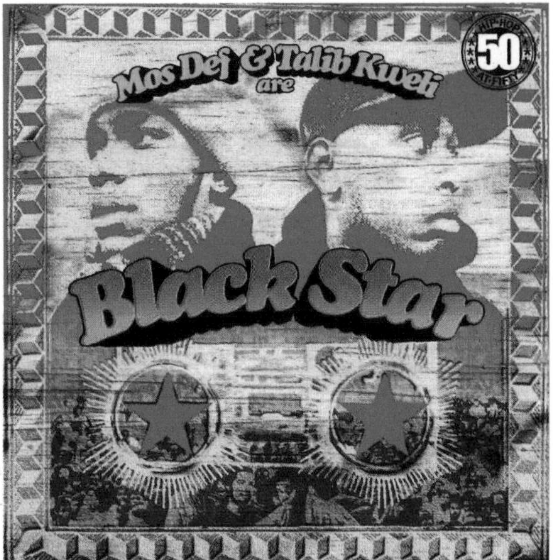

Black Star

MOS DEF & TALIB KWELI ARE BLACK STAR

RAWKUS/PRIORITY/EMI/MCA/UNIVERSAL MUSIC

Producers: Hi-Tek, Shawn J. Period, Ge-ology, 88-Keys, J. Rawls, Da Beatminerz

RELEASED: SEPTEMBER 29, 1998

● "We came to rock it on to the tip top/Best alliance in hip-hop," Mos Def and Talib Kweli proclaimed on **Definition**, the first single from their first album as the duo Black Star. That's quite a brag, but the two backed it up consistently on this thirteen-track set, one of just two full-lengths, fourteen years apart, from the ostensibly still-united pair. A pointed and progressive counter to gangsta rap on one hand and the overstuffed productions of the poppier side of the genre, *Mos Def & Talib Kweli Are Black Star* struck a positive and intellectually enlightened note, celebrating Black culture on tracks such as **Astronomy (8th Light)** and **Brown Skin Lady**, smacking down **Hater Players** and even drawing inspiration from the Toni Morrison novel *The Bluest Eye* for the track **Thieves in the Night**. The rhyming was clever but natural, spotlighting Def and Kweli's deft chemistry as they traded lines. And in unison moments, they were a genuine force to be reckoned with. Tony "Hi-Tek" Cottrell was the album's primary producer, while guests included Weldon Irvine, Vinia Mojica, and, on the second single **Respiration**, kindred spirit Common. Rap is a big umbrella, but . . . *Are Black Star* is a testament to the form at its best. *–GG*

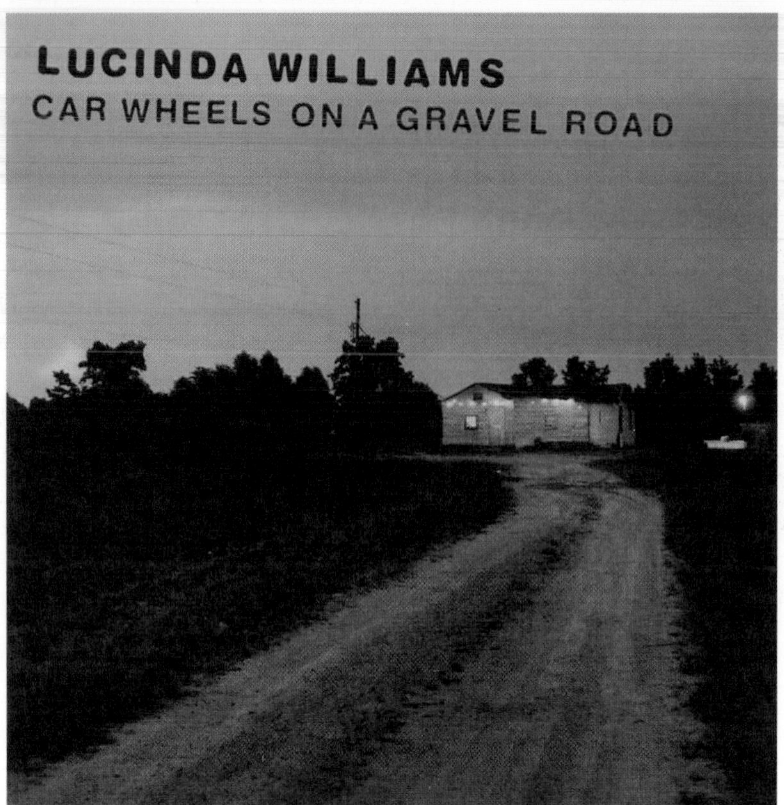

Lucinda Williams

CAR WHEELS ON A GRAVEL ROAD

MERCURY | Producers: Steve Earle, Ray Kennedy, Lucinda Williams, Roy Bittan

RELEASED: JUNE 30, 1998

● Much was made about the multiple producers Lucinda Williams worked with and the lengthy time spent recording her fifth studio album. It was all worth the wait—to the tune of a Grammy for Best Contemporary Folk Album and a top position on *The Village Voice*'s prestigious Pazz & Jop poll.

Locking us into a masterpiece of Americana from the opening drum fill and guitar chord of **Right in Time**, *Car Wheels On a Gravel Road* was Williams's artistic and commercial breakthrough. Nevertheless, the successor to her 1992 album *Sweet Old World* was a protracted process that began during early 1994 in Austin, Texas, for sessions with Gurf Morlix that were ultimately scrapped. Good pal Steve Earle and his longtime studio partner Ray Kennedy handled the bulk of the work—with guests such as Emmylou Harris, Jim Lauderdale, Buddy Miller, and others, including Roy Bittan from Bruce Springsteen's E Street Band, shepherding it over the finish line.

All those efforts paid off. Williams's unmistakable voice and sound were powerful, direct, and filled with longing and passion. Each of the thirteen tracks represented her reflections and observational storytelling at their very peak. The infectious singles **Right in Time** and the Grammy-nominated **Can't Let Go** became Williams's greatest commercial successes to date, but the title track and deeper cuts such as **Metal Firecracker** and **Greenville** took us into the rich emotional territory of childhood memories, complicated relationships, love, and hurt—but were mostly about trying to get home. **Drunken Angel**, meanwhile, was a song about the life and death of fellow songwriter Blaze Foley, while **Lake Charles** eulogized a former boyfriend who died long after they split up but who left a deep emotional mark on an album full of those. *—HH/GG*

Boards of Canada
MUSIC HAS THE RIGHT TO CHILDREN

SKAM/WARP RECORDS | Producers: Michael Sandison, Marcus Eoin

RELEASED: APRIL 20, 1998

● If one record helped electronic music creep closer to the global indie-rock sound, scene, and industry, it was *Music Has the Right to Children*. Composed and conjured by the Scottish duo Michael Sandison and Marcus Eoin, the seventeen-song album defined a sound rich in colors, textures, and sonic staying power. Preceding the prevalence of abstract beats and analog synths widely used in gaming and sync licensing, Boards of Canada imagined a broad palette of soundtrack possibilities, masterfully exploring a truly original cosmic funk. Elusive and reclusive, Board of Canada's low profile fueled the myth of its alternate playful way of approaching music itself. *–CW*

Korn
FOLLOW THE LEADER

IMMORTAL/EPIC | Producers: Steve Thompson, Toby Wright, Korn

RELEASED: AUGUST 18, 1998

● With its first two albums, Korn had done its part to help define nü metal's mélange of heavy and hip-hop but with a touch of alternative that gave the quintet its own identity within the rapidly crowding field. The group really hit its stride on *Follow the Leader*, however, combining its strongest compositions with its most adventurous playing and ambitious arrangements—hitting No. 1 on the Billboard 200 on its way to five-times platinum sales. **All in the Family** and **Freak On a Leash** became genre staples, and a hidden cover of Cheech & Chong's **Earache My Eye**, with Cheech Marin, was well worth finding. *–GG*

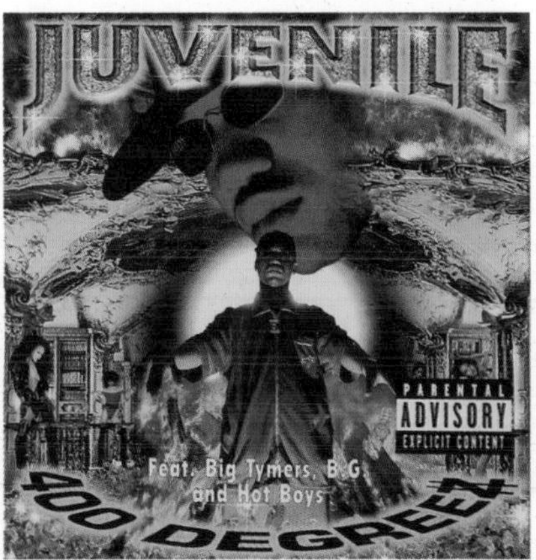

Juvenile
400 DEGREEZ

CASH MONEY/UNIVERSAL | Producers: Bryan "Baby" Williams, Ronald "Slim" Williams, Mannie Fresh

RELEASED: NOVEMBER 3, 1998

● Strings might seem anathema to rap, but New Orleans MC Juvenile brought them together on his third album, *400 Degreez*, specifically on the iconic **Back That Thang Up**. Violin drops provided an unexpected complement to his gritty, Crescent City rhymes. *400 Degreez* may be Juvenile's joint, but co-producer Mannie Fresh played an equal part in crafting its sound, popping up on tracks such as **Back That Azz Up** with Lil Wayne and on the set's opening **Intro (Big Tymers)**. Four million or so albums later, *400 Degreez* not only helped put Cash Money Records on the map but also added new flavor to the Southern rap game. *–ZC*

Jo Dee Messina
I'M ALRIGHT

CURB | Producers: Byron Gallimore, Tim McGraw

RELEASED: MARCH 17, 1998

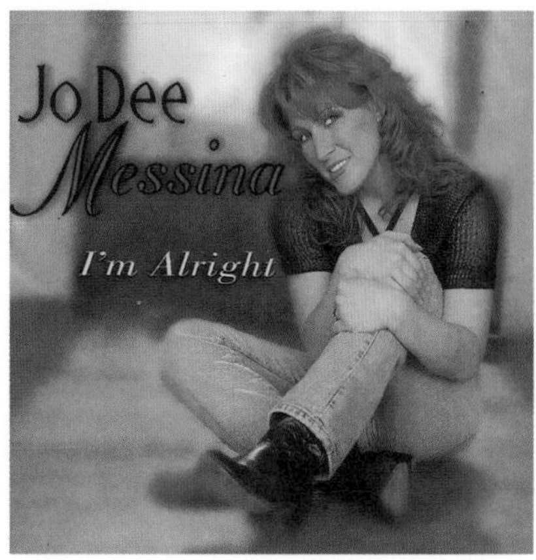

● One could say Jo Dee Messina really put her foot on the accelerator with her sophomore effort, *I'm Alright*. The record produced three No. 1 singles on the Billboard Hot Country Songs chart: the title track, **Bye, Bye**, and **Stand Beside Me**. It was a prime example of '90s country and its radio-friendly mentality, and there was plenty of twang in her voice and pedal steel on her songs to make Messina a staple on the airwaves. With a toss of her signature red locks and a jaunty wave, Messina belted out carefree, up-tempo earworms that have stuck with listeners for the long haul. *–SS*

Los Super Seven
LOS SUPER SEVEN

RCA NASHVILLE | Producer: Steve Berlin

RELEASED: SEPTEMBER 15, 1998

● This all-star septet covered a range of musical worlds with the likes of Freddy Fender, Flaco Jimenez, Los Lobos' David Hidalgo and Cesar Rosas, country singer Rick Trevino, Sir Douglas Sahm (in a guest role), and, best of all, Tejano titan Ruben Ramos, who featured on three of the album's thirteen tracks. Produced by Los Lobos' Steve Berlin, the troupe's Grammy-winning debut (Best Mexican/Mexican-American Album) was a sublime showcase of south-of-the-border delights, reinventing traditional Tejano by creating a few originals and offering a fresh take on Woody Guthrie's **Plane Wreck at Los Gatos (Deportee)**, sung by guest Joe Ely. *–GG*

Monster Magnet
POWERTRIP

A & M | Producers: Dave Wyndorf, Matt Hyde

RELEASED: JUNE 16, 1998

● *Powertrip*, the fourth album by stoner-rock pioneers Monster Magnet, proved to be its commercial breakthrough, hitting No. 1 on Billboard's Heatseekers chart and earning a gold record. Tired of the grunge music playbook, frontman/guitarist Dave Wyndorf wrote songs based on his observations of the chaos around him and people's everyday lives in Las Vegas. The themes made the music and lyrics relatable on heavy-grooving songs such as **Temple of Your Dreams**, **See You in Hell**, and the title track, all of which pushed Monster Magnet onto rock radio playlists, as well as in movies such as *Talladega Nights: The Ballad of Ricky Bobby*. *–WW*

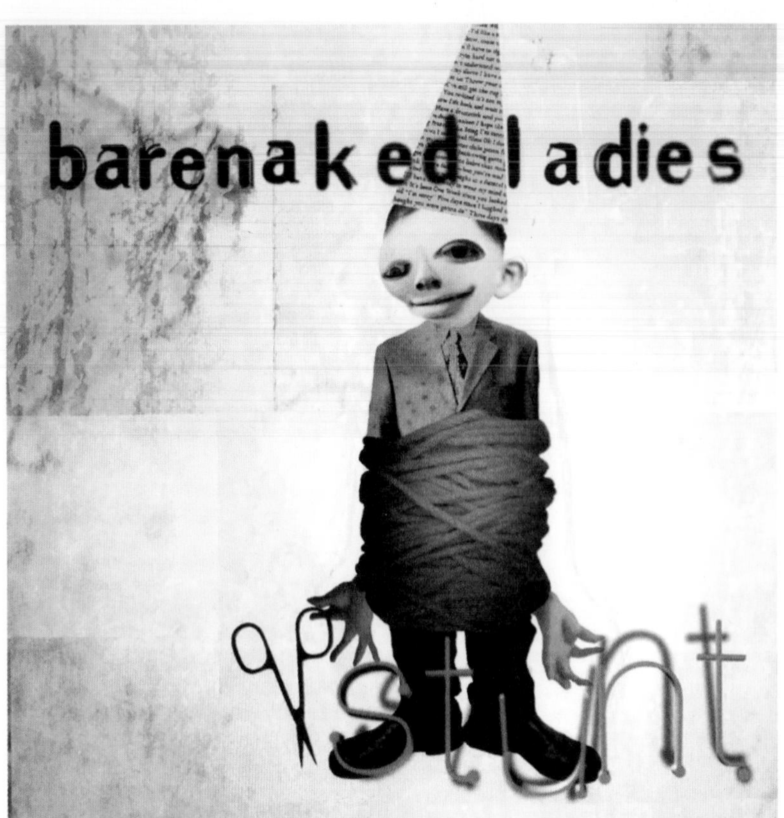

Barenaked Ladies

STUNT

REPRISE | Producers: Barenaked Ladies, Davide Leonard, Susan Rogers

RELEASED: JULY 7, 1998

● Barenaked Ladies' (BNL) Steven Page and Ed Robertson wrote an entire song about what they'd do if they ever had $1,000,000. *Stunt* made those wishes a reality.

After success in its homeland and in pockets of the US, the Canadian quintet's fifth studio album was a worldwide breakthrough. Witty and well crafted like its predecessors, *Stunt* benefitted from the band's incessant touring (including a stint with the H.O.R.D.E. package) as well as some radio airplay for a live version of "Brian Wilson"—previously a single from BNL's 1992 debut album, *Gordon*—off the 1997 live album *Rock Spectacle*.

"What worked (on *Stunt*) was changing and growing and trying to write the best songs we could," Robertson explained, and that was indeed the case for the four-times platinum album. BNL again displayed its trademark ability to weave together humor and pathos, sometimes in the same song; the breakout hit **One Week**, for instance, wrapped dark details about a couple's argument into a surging pop song marked by Robertson's rapid-fire raps with seemingly random references that, when examined, further fleshed out the song's characters. The killer tunes kept coming, too—among them the buoyant **It's All Been Done**, the fiery **Alcohol**, the gentle **Call and Answer**, the peppy **Never Is Enough**, the lusciously constructed **Some Fantastic (Ivory and Ivory)**.

Stunt gave BNL its highest spot on the Billboard 200 at No. 3—eighty-three points higher than *Rock Spectacle*. **One Week** topped the Billboard Hot 100 and scored Grammy Award and MTV Video Music Award nominations. **It's All Been Done** hit No. 15, and No. 1 in Canada, where BNL took home three Juno Awards, including Best Pop Album and Best Group. In one fell swoop, there were millions of new members in the Barenaked nation—and a bunch of early adaptors gloating, "Told ya so." *—GG*

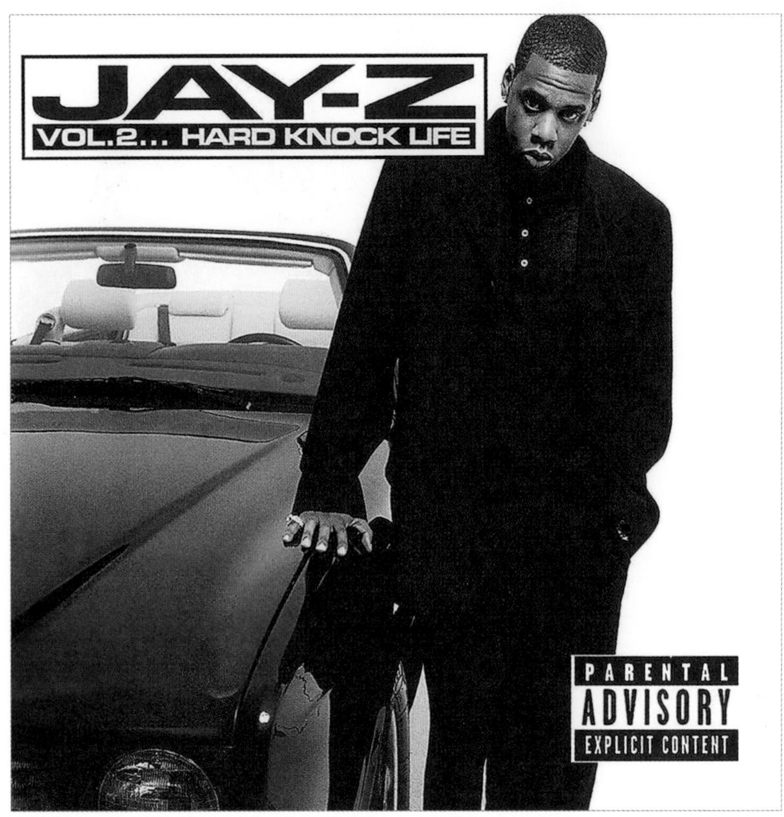

Jay-Z

VOL. 2 . . . HARD KNOCK LIFE

ROC-A-FELLA/DEF JAM | Producers: Shawn Carter, Damon Dash, Kareem "Biggs" Burke, Irv Gotti, Kid Capri, J-Runnah, Jermaine Dupri, Rockwilder, Lil Rob, Mahogany, The 45 King, DJ Premier, Erick Sermon, Stevie J, Swizz Beatz, Timbaland, Darold "POP" Trotter

RELEASED: SEPTEMBER 29, 1998

● It was an *Annie* sample that put Jay-Z over the top. The Brooklyn rapper had established himself with his 1996 debut *Reasonable Doubt*, which made a modest mark commercially, while its follow-up, 1997's *In My Lifetime, Vol. 1*, sold better but lost a bit of the first album's artistic spark. Both sides of Jay's appeal—his street smarts and his pop instincts—melded on *Vol. 2*, which spent five weeks at No. 1 on the Billboard 200 and came alive thanks particularly to producer The 45 King's playful, bouncy sample of "It's the Hard-Knock Life" from the 1977 Broadway musical *Annie* on the single **Hard Knock Life (Ghetto Anthem)**. It was a genius pairing: Jay-Z's relaxed, aspirational rhymes over Little Orphan Annie's chirpy tale of getting kicks instead of kisses. And it took the rapper, in his own words, "from lukewarm to hot."

That heat was scorching on *Vol. 2*, which produced another Top 20 hit in **Can I Get A . . .** , a classic battle-of-the-sexes rap featuring Amil and a star-making verse from Ja Rule. There were stellar cameos throughout the album: DMX and Jay-Z traded verses over Swizz Beatz's looped-up video game beats on **Money, Cash, Hoes**; Too $hort aired out snitches on **A Week Ago**; Foxy Brown made a Bonnie and Clyde reference on the Timbaland-produced **Paper Chase** (Beyoncé, notably, had not yet entered the picture); and Jermaine Dupri and Jay-Z went for a joyride on the flashy **Money Ain't a Thang**.

Throughout, however, it was Jay-Z's confidence that held the project together. The *Annie* sample could be seen as a crass commercial play, but he leveraged it for all it was worth and made it work, like the businessman that he became. *Vol. 2* was a key step in Jay-Z's artistic *and* entrepreneurial evolution. *—AG*

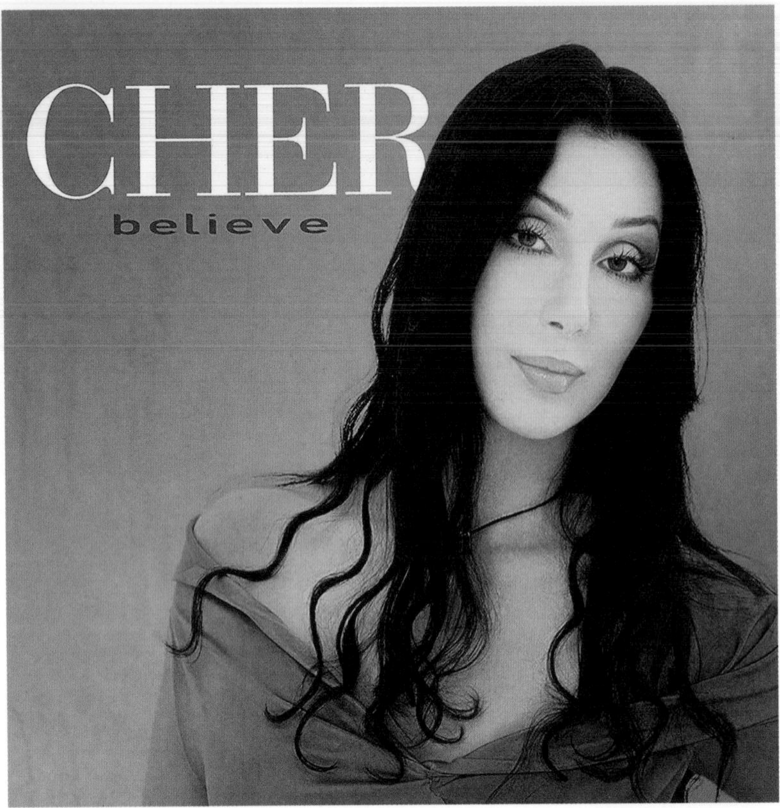

Cher

BELIEVE

WARNER BROS/WEA | Producers: Mark Taylor, Brian Rawling, Junior Vasquez, Todd Terry

RELEASED: OCTOBER 22, 1998

● Few artists have managed to reinvent themselves time and again, but you better *Believe* one of them has been Cher. With a dance beat and a now-infamous vocal effect, the American singer and actress resurrected her music career for her twenty-second studio album. The title track from the Euro-pop-oriented record became a dance club anthem, and the almost-robotic vocal sound echoed from radio station playlists for month after month after month.

Producers Mark Taylor and Brian Rawling utilized Auto-Tune in a specific way on *Believe*, and their technique essentially layered Cher's voice over itself by allowing the vocal to jump from pitch to pitch. The effect was later dubbed the "Cher Effect" and became commonplace in the recording world. At the time, however, it was considered a revolutionary move and changed the face of pop music forever.

Cher worked with the producers to remix some of her previously released tracks—notably the Desmond Child/Jon Bon Jovi/Richie Sambora–penned **We All Sleep Alone**—to fit *Believe*'s sonic approach. However, the most successful single releases were written by the team of Paul Barry and producer Mark Taylor; the pair was responsible for **Strong Enough**, **All or Nothing,** and *Believe*'s ubiquitous title track. That single led to numerous accolades, including three Grammy Award nominations and Cher's only win to date, for Best Dance Recording. When **Believe** topped the Billboard Hot 100, it closed the longest-ever gap between No. 1s—thirty-three years and seven months, to be exact, after "I Got You Babe," her 1965 duet with ex-husband and former musical partner Sonny Bono.

Thanks to all that, *Believe* provided yet another feather in the Bob Mackie headdress of Cher's long career. *–SS*

Dixie Chicks

WIDE OPEN SPACES

MONUMENT | Producers: Blake Chancey, Paul Worley

RELEASED: JANUARY 27, 1998

● Dixie Chicks (which became simply the Chicks in 2020) earned a spot in country music history as one of the genre's best-selling female acts ever with the Texas group's first major label release. After three independent albums and the addition of a new lead singer in Natalie Maines, the trio—co-founded in Dallas by multi-instrumentalist sisters Emily Strayer and Martie Maguire—grew considerably on *Wide Open Spaces*. Though the group was responsible for writing just one of the album's twelve tracks (**You Were Mine**), it offered a fresh, bluegrass-influenced sound that had plenty of undeniable hooks and vocal harmonies to let the songs soar.

With songs contributed by Bonnie Raitt, Maria McKee, J. D. Souther, and Radney Foster, a total of five singles were released from *Wide Open Spaces*. Three of those—**There's Your Trouble**, **You Were Mine**, and the double-platinum title track—hit No. 1 on the Billboard Hot Country Songs and Country Airplay charts, while the other two, **I Can Love You Better** and **Tonight the Heartache's on Me**, went Top 10. *Wide Open Spaces* debuted at No. 1 on the Top Country Albums chart and reached No. 4 on the Billboard 200, with diamond-certified sales of more than thirteen million copies.

The album gave the Chicks its first Grammy Awards, for Best Country Album and Best Country Performance by a Duo or Group with Vocals for **There's Your Trouble**. *Wide Open Spaces* was also Album of the Year at the Academy of Country Music Awards and CMT Music Awards, while the Country Music Association gave **Wide Open Spaces** Single of the Year and Music Video of the Year honors. And, hard as it was to believe, even greater success was waiting for the Chicks' next flight. *—MH2*

Air

MOON SAFARI

SOURCE/VIRGIN | Producer: Air

RELEASED: JANUARY 16, 1998

● Every trip to outer space needs its soundtrack. On its pristine debut album, the French duo Air—studio junkie perfectionists Nicolas Godin and Jean-Benoît Dunckel—crafted a luxe journey to the cosmos, mood music for sipping cocktails while orbiting Earth. And the view from above sure was nice.

The pair met at college in Versailles and played with another outfit, Orange, before breaking off on their own and synthesizing their love for '60s French pop, Italian movie soundtracks, prog rock, lounge themes, ambient instrumentals, sci-fi soundscapes, and good old-fashioned make-out music. It all came together on *Moon Safari*, a ten-track odyssey that was like elevator music for a ride to the big rock in the sky. Layers of keyboards are stacked on top of one another on *Moon Safari*; strip any two away and there were another three lying underneath. In addition, the boys added strings, shakers, glockenspiels, guitars, pan flutes, drum machines, and anything else within reach to add to their celestial daydream.

Album opener **La femme d'argent** was the blastoff, the signal we're leaving Earth's atmosphere behind as its groovy bass line wove around twinkles of dancing light beams, trails of space dust, and shooting stars. Like much of *Moon Safari*, it's an instrumental piece; elsewhere Dunckel and Godin lend heavily vocoder-assisted vocal touches to **Sexy Boy**, **Kelly Watch the Stars**, and **Remember**, while singer Beth Hirsch adds a human touch to **All I Need** and **You Make It Easy**. The closing track, **Le voyage de Pénélope**, never touches back down, leaving the listener drifting off into the nighttime sky.

Air made another handful of studio albums, including the soundtrack for Sofia Coppola's debut film, *The Virgin Suicides*, although none matched the evocative, rich, escapist *Moon Safari*. There was chillout and down-tempo music before *Moon Safari*, but Air took it to a whole new level. *–AG*

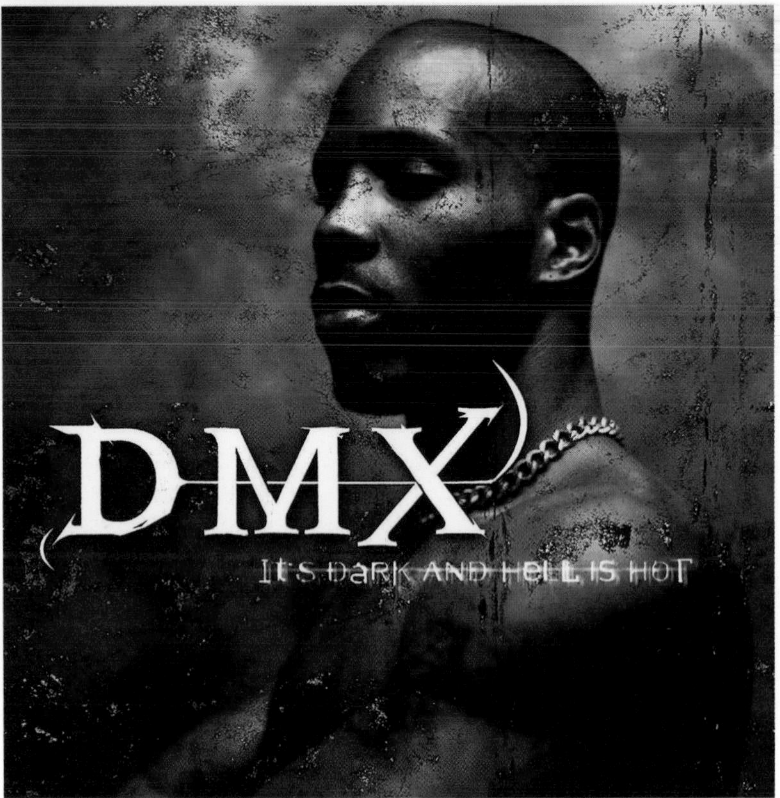

DMX

IT'S DARK AND HELL IS HOT

DEF JAM/RUFF RYDERS | Producers: Irv Gotti, Dee, Waah, Dame Grease, P. K., Lil Rob, Swizz Beatz

RELEASED: MAY 19, 1998

● The story goes that Sean "Puff Daddy" Combs decided against signing DMX because his voice was too rough—a sound that, of course, became the New York MC's trademark. DMX (né Earl Simmons) was not happy, and *It's Dark and Hell Is Hot* makes that abundantly clear.

The guest-filled nineteen-track album sounded like DMX might break through the fourth wall and come out of the speakers to beat your ass at any moment. In **The Convo**, DMX spoke directly with Satan. In **Damien**, he hobnobbed with the main character from *The Omen* film series. As he would throughout his career, the Ruff Ryders collective's marquee man used tracks such as **Anthem** and **Stop Being Greedy** to pledge allegiance to the streets. It was hard to find a track *not* laced with violence. If DMX's songs weren't vivid enough, the album also featured skits that depicted a life where acts of brutality were expected—and required.

It's Dark and Hell Is Hot wasn't just a launch pad for DMX. The unknown-at-the-time Ja Rule, Irv Gotti, Eve, and Drag-On appear in the video for **How It's Goin' Down**; Gotti also helped pilot the album as its co-executive producer. The LOX and Mase, meanwhile, popped up on the album-closing **Niggaz Done Started Something**.

DMX's debut debuted at No. 1 on the Billboard 200 and Top R&B/Hip-Hop Albums charts on its way to quadruple-platinum sales. **Get at Me Dog**, **Stop Being Greedy**, and the double-platinum **Ruff Ryders Anthem** were Top 10 rap hits, the latter even making it to No. 16 on the Billboard Hot 100. *It's Dark and Hell is Hot* was the culmination of a journey that sprawled out for more than a decade, an opportunity he'd ride until his 2021 death at the age of fifty from a cocaine-induced heart attack. *–ZC*

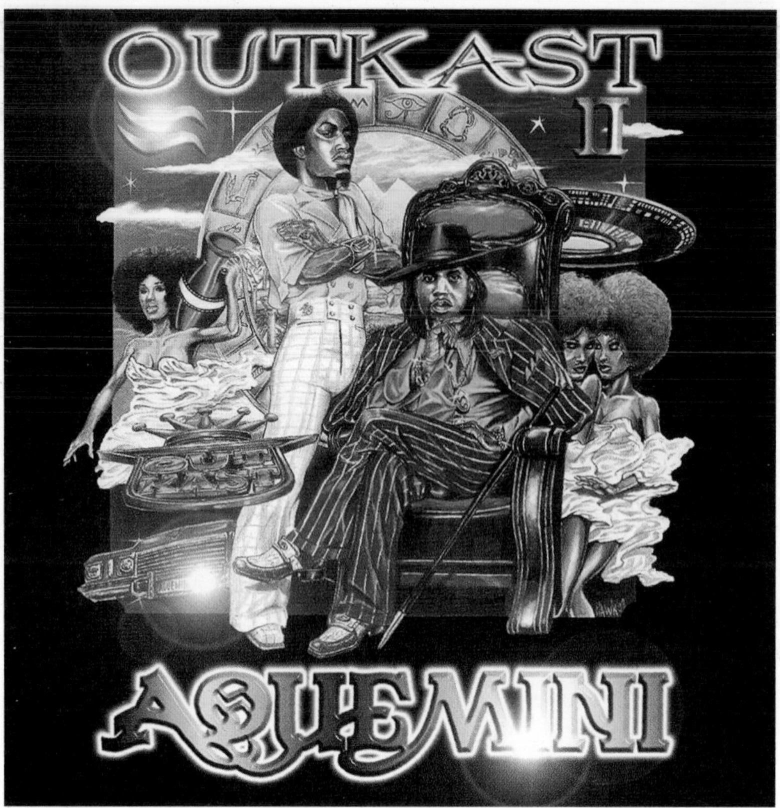

OutKast

AQUEMINI

LAFACE/ARISTA | Producers: Organized Noize, OutKast, Mr. DJ

RELEASED: SEPTEMBER 29, 1998

● OutKast's third album, *Aquemini*, was a transitional record for the Atlanta hip-hop duo of Big Boi and Andre 3000. Predecessor *ATLiens* (1996) was where they began to find their voice; on *Stankonia* (2000), that voice would become one of the most distinctive at the turn of the century. But *Aquemini* is where it all came together, brilliantly, for the first time. Employing a cadre of live musicians that gave the album an organic, lived-in warmth, Big Boi and Andre 3000—close friends whose tastes and styles were miles apart—rapped about space aliens, Civil Rights heroes, hip-hop culture, and the state of the world in seventy-five sprawling and way-out-there minutes.

The commercial success of *ATLiens* gave OutKast the creative freedom to dive deeper into the '70s-era funk and soul the duo loved; it also allowed the pair to further explore the fringes of their respective influences, presenting in some ways two sides of the same story. (The album's title is a play on their astrological signs.) OutKast would take this concept to its extreme on 2003's *Speakerboxxx/The Love Below*, the Grammy-winning double album that gave the two a disc each to roam at will.

Much of the music on *Aquemini* was written on the spot between 1996 and 1998 in two Atlanta studios, with the rappers and guests experimenting until something felt right. Like most OutKast albums, *Aquemini* flowed as a conceptual whole, with key tracks **Rosa Parks**, **Skew It On the Bar-B**, and **Da Art of Storytellin' (Pt. 1)** arriving at strategically placed intervals. Political, funny, and funky, the album was a cornerstone work of the era and genre and, in many ways, remains the group's most seamless LP. Nobody sounded like OutKast—nobody could. *Aquemini* was the moment where the duo became untouchable. ***–MG***

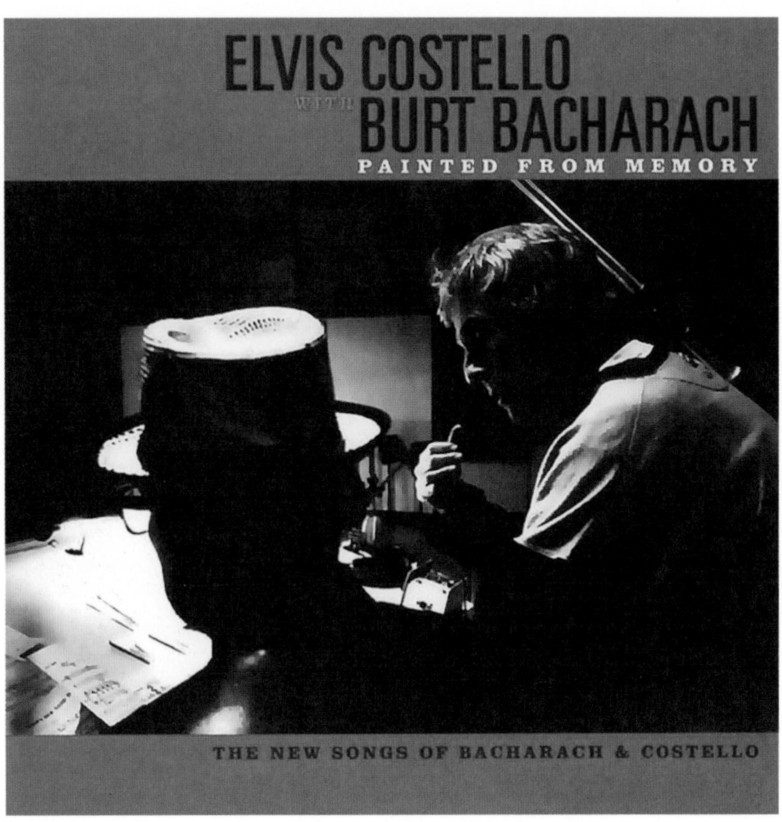

Elvis Costello with Burt Bacharach

PAINTED FROM MEMORY

MERCURY | Producers: Burt Bacharach, Elvis Costello

RELEASED: SEPTEMBER 29, 1998

● In 1977, in the throes of the punk explosion, Elvis Costello and the Attractions were part of a tour of the UK featuring artists from Stiff Records and a notable lack of the aggressive gnashing associated with punk. Costello's set included songs from his acclaimed debut, *My Aim Is True*; several new unrecorded tracks; and a few select covers. Among the latter was a song made popular by Dusty Springfield in 1964, the Burt Bacharach and Hal David composition "I Just Don't Know What to Do with Myself." In the moment, it might have seemed ironic; time proved it anything but.

Costello and Bacharach first collaborated on "God Give Me Strength," a song for the 1996 film *Grace of My Heart*. Both felt one song together wasn't enough, and two years later they reconvened. Bacharach hadn't released a record of his own in twenty-one years and had nothing to prove to anybody but himself. In Costello, he found a younger co-writer who shared his sensibilities, points of reference, and skill set. The hallmarks of Bacharach's best-known songs were all reflected anew here; in fact, Costello and Bacharach leaned in hard—the haunting flute on **In the Darkest Place**, the sweeping strings in **My Thief**, and the muted horn in **Toledo**. **This House Is Empty Now** would have sounded perfectly in place if sung by Dionne Warwick, though Costello's vocal style fits it hand in glove.

The songs on *Painted from Memory* were immediately accepted as if they were missing pages from the Great American Songbook; they were covered and explored by vocalists such as Jenni Muldaur and Cassandra Wilson. Jazz guitarist Bill Frisell took on the record in its entirety in a version entitled *The Sweetest Punch*. Looking back, *Painted from Memory* represented an era when the application of craft still applied to songwriting, and the results could be moving. *—HK*

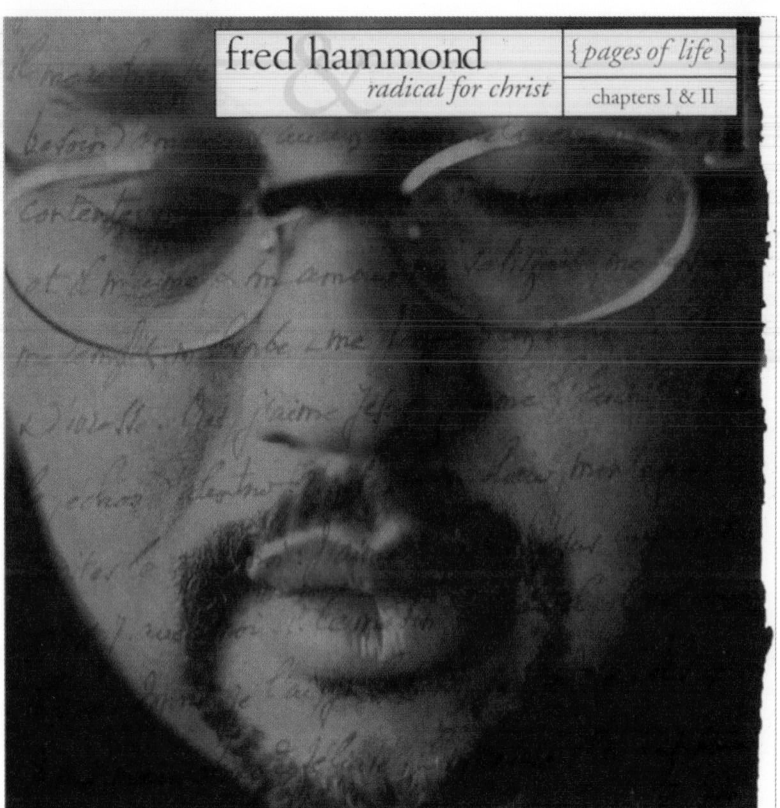

Fred Hammond & Radical for Christ

PAGES OF LIFE—CHAPTERS I & II

VERITY | Producers: Fred Hammond, Paul Wright III

RELEASED: APRIL 28, 1998

● *Pages of Life—Chapters I & II* was the fifth solo release by Fred Hammond and the third with his choir, Radical for Christ. One of the founding members of the groundbreaking urban gospel group Commissioned, Hammond is considered by many to be the architect of the contemporary Urban Praise and Worship movement, and for this release, he created a two-disc set featuring sixteen original studio recordings on the first (*Chapter I*) and another thirteen songs recorded live at Straight Gate Church in Hammond's native Detroit (*Chapter II*). *Pages of Life* topped Billboard's Top Gospel Albums chart for fifteen weeks, was certified double-platinum, and was nominated for a Grammy for Best Contemporary Soul Gospel Album and a *Soul Train* Award for Best Gospel album.

The Hammond-written single **Let the Praise Begin**, from *Chapter I*, featured him on bass, along with keyboardist Noel Hall and lead guitarist Darryl Dixon. The up-tempo track showcased Hammond's driving vocals and earned a Dove Award for Contemporary Gospel Song. **Just to Be Close to You**, by Hammond and music director Noel Hall, employs just one line of dedication for the entirety of its nearly three minutes and went on to become a popular hymn at church services.

Hammond and rising gospel artist Kim Rutherford, meanwhile, partnered to write two of the most moving tracks on the album, **Your Steps Are Ordered** and **No Way, No Way (You Won't Lose)**. *Chapter II* captured the power of Hammond on the pulpit, with full choir renditions of four songs from *Chapter I* and favorites from his previous projects, including **No Weapon**, **Glory to Glory to Glory**, and **We're Blessed**. *—CP*

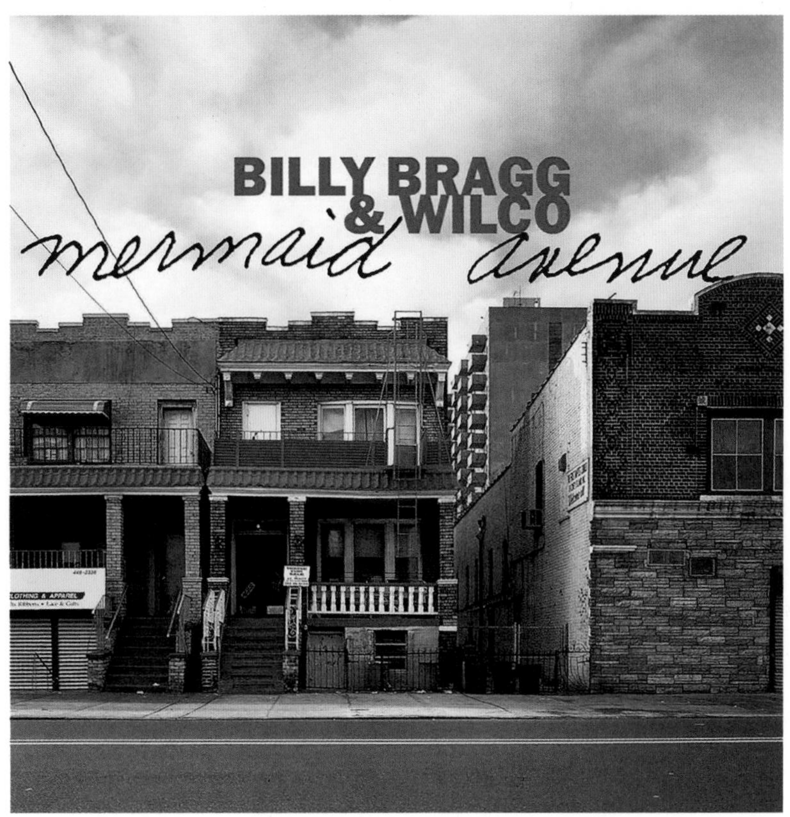

Billy Bragg & Wilco

MERMAID AVENUE

ELEKTRA | Producers: Wilco, Billy Bragg, Grant Showbiz

RELEASED: JUNE 23, 1998

● Nearly thirty years after his death, the name Woody Guthrie still resonated with many (though maybe not most) Americans. What was remembered about him, though, had shrunk to a near caricature: he wrote "This Land Is Your Land," yes, and was also—how to put it?—a kind of lefty hobo troubadour. Right? His daughter Nora Guthrie was the keeper of his legacy via the Woody Guthrie Archive and sought to change that portrayal. She had in her possession hundreds of sets of lyrics that her father composed, sans music, as his health deteriorated due to Huntington's disease.

Nora invited English folk-rocker Billy Bragg, a latter-day Guthrie kindred spirit, to comb through the archive and find lyrics for which to compose music and freshen up Woody's reputation. Bragg agreed, then asked Wilco—at the time, a nascent alt-country Uncle Tupelo offshoot—to join the project. Wilco frontman Jeff Tweedy and multi-instrumentalist Jay Bennett also chose lyrics and wrote music. Natalie Merchant, Corey Harris, and Eliza Carthy joined in on the proceedings here and there, contributing vocals, guitar, and fiddle, respectively.

Mermaid Avenue's fifteen songs hit the target that Nora was shooting for, offering a fuller picture of Woody's oeuvre—politically strident, perhaps, but also introspective, funny, richly poetic, and (in spots) horny. Bragg offered **She Came Along to Me**, an ahead-of-its-time song about racial and gender equality; the funny singalong **Walt Whitman's Niece**; and the movie-star mash note **Ingrid Bergman**. Wilco added the yearning **California Stars**, to this day a fan favorite; the goofy word salad **Hoodoo Voodoo**; and a pair of beautiful, plaintive tunes, **At My Window Sad and Lonely** and **Another Man Done Gone**.

The *Mermaid Avenue* sessions yielded enough material for a second volume, released in 2000, followed by a three-disc box set in 2012. *–DD*

19
INETY

EEN
99
1999
NINE

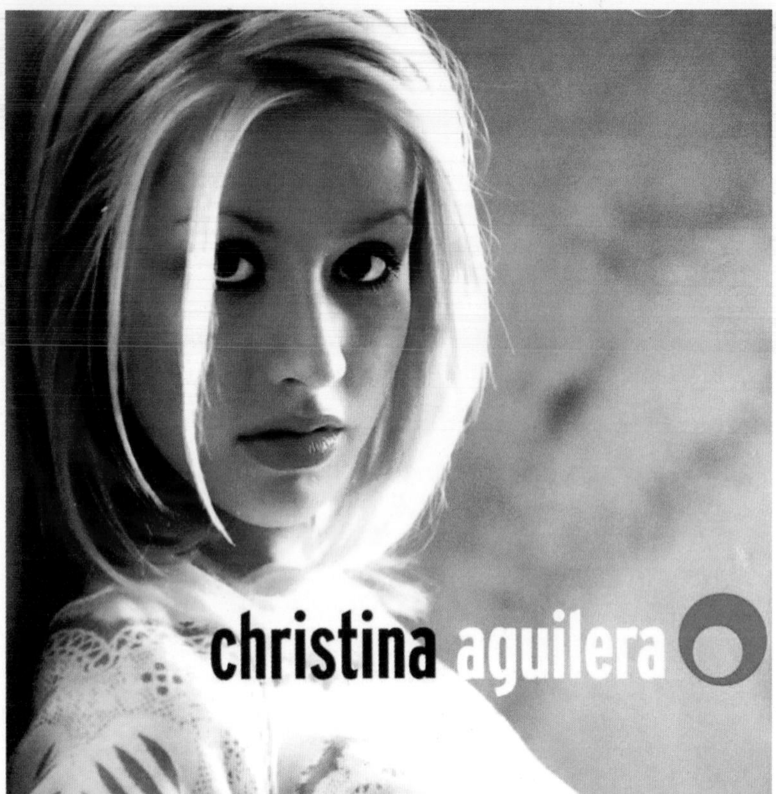

Christina Aguilera

CHRISTINA AGUILERA

RCA | Producer: Ron Fair

RELEASED: AUGUST 24, 1999

● Britney Spears kicked down the door, and by the end of 1999, music stores were filled with a wave of teen-pop starlets following in her wake. The most promising member of the new class was Christina Aguilera, a powerhouse vocalist raised in the suburbs of Pittsburgh who had a direct tie to Spears: the two came up together as castmates on The Disney Channel's *The All-New Mickey Mouse Club*, alongside a pair of *NSYNCers (Justin Timberlake, JC Chasez) and future movie (Ryan Gosling) and TV (Keri Russell) stars.

Disney gave Aguilera another break when she landed a song on the soundtrack to 1998's *Mulan*, and the success of "Reflection," a self-empowerment ballad in the classic Disney mold, laid the groundwork for her debut album. Aguilera worked with an army of songwriters and producers, and the slinky lead single **Genie in a Bottle** took off like a master's wish, spending five weeks atop Billboard's Hot 100 chart during the summer of 1999. Aguilera's self-titled debut album was released during that run and debuted at No. 1 on the Billboard 200, selling a quarter million copies its first week out.

While it was marketed to a teen-pop, *TRL*-leaning audience, much of the album slanted in a pop-R&B direction, more Whitney than Britney. (Early on, Aguilera sought a record deal by shopping a cover of Houston's "Run to You" to labels.) **Genie in a Bottle** showed off Aguilera's bombastic pipes over a bed of digital dancefloor pop-soul, and she turned in a cover of All-4-One's Diane Warren–penned ballad **I Turn to You** that recalled Celine Dion's "Because You Loved Me." **What a Girl Wants** and **Come on Over (All I Want Is You)** also went to No. 1 after being remixed for radio, and by then, the genie was out of the bottle. Aguilera was a megastar. *–AG*

Lonestar
LONELY GRILL

BNA | Producers: Dan Huff, Sam Ramage, Bob Wright

RELEASED: JUNE 1, 1999

● Lonestar captured a truly unique country-pop vibe on its third studio album. More polished than the neotraditional sound of its predecessors, it was a three-times platinum success that gave the Nashville group (of Texas natives) its highest-charting release to date: No. 3 on the country charts and No. 28 on the Billboard 200. It also featured four No. 1 country hits: **Amazed** (which also topped the Billboard Hot 100 thanks to vocalist Richie McDonald's powerful performance), **Smile**, **What About Now**, and **Tell Her**. **Amazed** was nominated for a Country Music Association Award, with Lonestar getting a nod for Group of the Year. *–TR/GG*

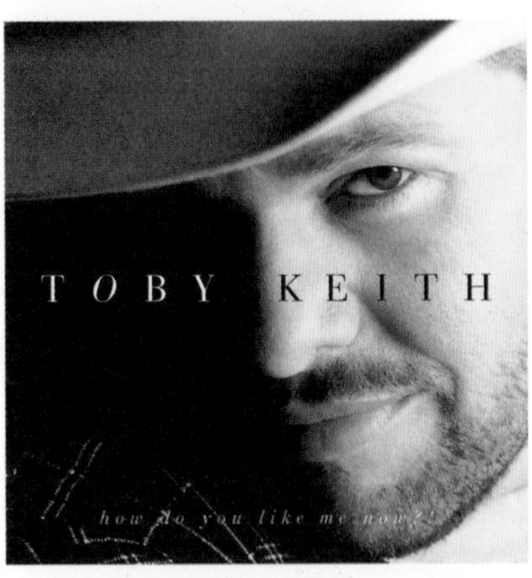

Toby Keith
HOW DO YOU LIKE ME NOW?!

DREAMWORKS | Producers: James Stroud, Toby Keith

RELEASED: NOVEMBER 2, 1999

● Toby Keith's first album with his new label made DreamWorks a serious contender on the country scene. The title track spent five weeks at No. 1 on Billboard's Hot Country Songs chart and was Keith's first Top 40 hit on the Billboard Hot 100. *How Do You Like Me Now?!* launched another No. 1, **You Shouldn't Kiss Me Like This**, as well as a Top 5 hit in **Country Comes to Town**. It was the Academy of Country Music's Album of the Year, and Keith was named the ACM's Top Male Vocalist. The album also began a songwriting partnership with Scotty Emerick, Keith's primary collaborator for another six albums. *–MH2*

Wilco
SUMMERTEETH

REPRISE | Producer: Wilco

RELEASED: MARCH 9, 1999

● If 1996's *Being There* attempted to alter the perception that Wilco was strictly an alt-country act, *Summerteeth* jettisoned the notion once and for all. With the partnership of frontman Jeff Tweedy and multi-instrumentalist Jay Bennett coming to full flower, Wilco got willfully weird. Wracked with personal issues, depression, and substance abuse, Tweedy's lyrics were dense, inscrutable, and sometimes disturbing; Bennett's ornate, layered instrumental fripperies opened new sonic vistas for the band. Though a difficult listen for longtime fans of the band and its predecessor, Uncle Tupelo, *Summerteeth* yielded some of Wilco's most enduring songs, including **She's a Jar**, **A Shot in the Arm**, and **Via Chicago**. It also flopped commercially and nearly destroyed the band. *–DD*

Tom Waits
MULE VARIATIONS

ANTI- | Producers: Kathleen Brennan, Tom Waits

RELEASED: APRIL 16, 1999

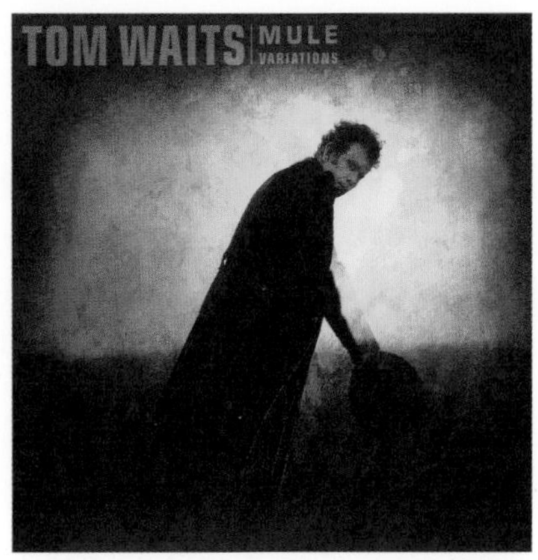

● Tom Waits's recording career fits neatly into three phases: the Asylum Record years, the Island Records years, and, beginning with this album, the ANTI- Records years. On *Mule Variations*, the bedrock was the blues, as exhibited in tracks such as **Get Behind the Mule**, **Chocolate Jesus**, and **Cold Water**. Waits and Kathleen Brennan, his wife and collaborator, refined the spaces in their self-declared grim reapers and grand weepers with sublime pop (**Hold On**) and trademark weirdness (**What's He Building in There?**). Some consider Waits an acquired taste, but a straight shot of this album goes down easy. *–HK*

Asleep at the Wheel
RIDE WITH BOB: A TRIBUTE TO BOB WILLS AND THE TEXAS PLAYBOYS

DREAMWORKS | Producer: Ray Benson

RELEASED: AUGUST 10, 1999

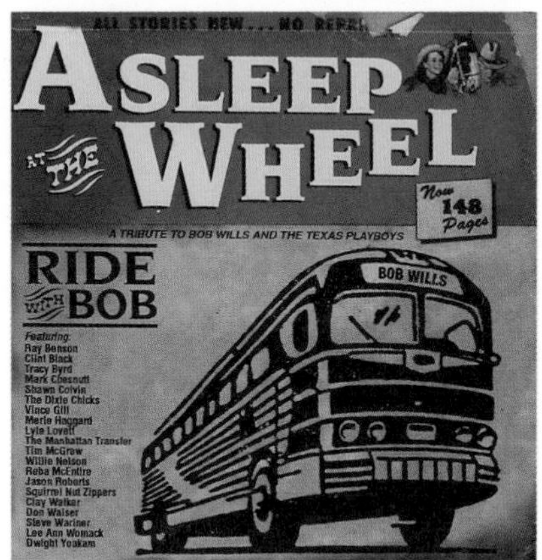

● *Ride With Bob* accomplished two goals: it paid perfect tribute to its subject, Western swing master Bob Wills and his Texas Playboys, and showed just how good Ray Benson and his Asleep at the Wheel crew played that music, with help from guests including Merle Haggard, Willie Nelson and the Manhattan Transfer, Reba McEntire, Dixie Chicks, Lyle Lovett and Shawn Colvin, Tim McGraw, Clint Black, Johnny Gimble, and more. The follow-up to an initial Wills tribute in 1993, it was a critical and commercial success, winning three Grammy Awards from seven nominations and giving *Asleep . . .* its highest position on the Country charts (No. 24) in twelve years. *–TR*

Sugar Ray
14:59

ATLANTIC | Producers: David Kahne, Ralph Sall

RELEASED: JANUARY 12, 1999

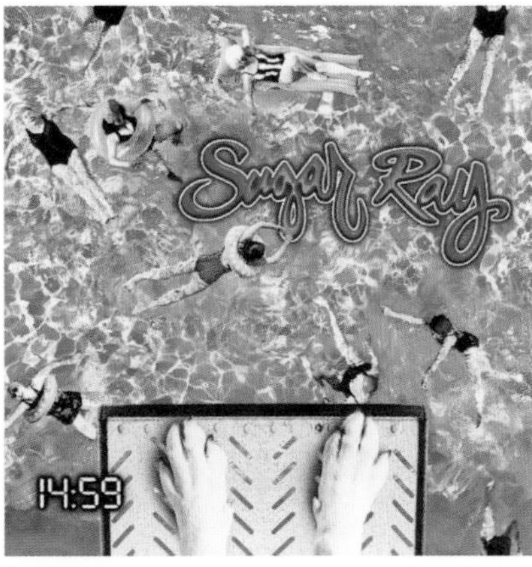

● After Sugar Ray hit with "Fly" from its 1997 album *Floored*, snarky critics posited that Sugar Ray was in its "fifteen minutes of fame moment," thus inspiring the title of its third full-length release. On *14:59*, Sugar Ray proved the naysayers wrong, of course, with breezy and melodic (albeit alternative-flavored) hits such as **Every Morning** and **Someday**. The album was a triple-platinum success, but those worried about Sugar Ray turning "soft" and going mainstream were reassured by the punk tracks **Aim for Me** and **Burning Dog**, while KRS-One fired up **Live & Direct**. *–GG*

Santana

SUPERNATURAL

ARISTA | Executive Producer: Clive Davis

RELEASED: JUNE 15, 1999

● It's fair to say that the world was not clamoring for a new Santana album in 1999.

The band's legend and legacy were well established by then, from the fields of Woodstock to hit singles from the '60s, '70s, and '80s. Santana was still a potent brand at the box office, but album sales were flagging, and it hadn't had a Top 20 pop hit in sixteen years. Nevertheless, Carlos Santana was receiving cosmic messages that those fortunes were about to change.

"They told me, 'We're going to open the door for you,'" Santana said at the time. "They said, 'We're going to hook you up . . . we're going to get you back onto the radio. All you have to do is be patient, gracious, and grateful.'"

Those voices did not lie.

Supernatural, Santana's eighteenth album, was a generational phenomenon—a comeback that more than accomplished its stated mission "to assault the radio airwaves with the Santana vibration." The thirteen-song set hit No. 1 on the Billboard 200 and beyond, ultimately selling more than thirty million copies worldwide and winning a record-breaking nine Grammy Awards, including the first Album of the Year for a Hispanic artist. It also produced a pair of No. 1 singles: **Smooth**, featuring Rob Thomas of Matchbox Twenty, and **Maria Maria** with the Product G&B and Wyclef Jean.

Beyond its commercial achievements, *Supernatural* was also one of the group's finest creative moments. Executive-produced by Clive Davis, who'd signed Santana to Columbia Records back in 1968, it teamed the guitarist with the additional likes of the Dave Matthews Band, Lauryn Hill and Cee Lo Green, Everlast, Eagle-Eye Cherry, and Mana. It also housed the first-ever recorded meeting between Santana and Eric Clapton, a twelve-minute-plus guitar summit on **The Calling**, which Santana aptly described as "like having two Apaches in the Grand Canyon, evoking the spirits." *–GG*

1999

Magnetic Fields

69 LOVE SONGS

MERGE | Producer: Stephin Merritt

RELEASED: SEPTEMBER 7, 1999

● The title indicated exactly what you were getting—but it didn't tell you that every note would be worth hearing. That's certainly something to say about three CDs and nearly three hours of music, but *69 Love Songs* was, well, whatever you want to call it—magnum opus, tour de force, masterpiece. . . . Composed primarily by Stephin Merritt, *69 Love Songs* was an oeuvre unto itself. Conceived as a stage revue (of one hundred songs before Merritt truncated his ambitions), it boasted a Sondheim-esque grandeur and variety that kept things interesting from start to finish. There was nothing in the way of hip-hop here, perhaps, but there were plenty of shades of pop, jazz, country, blues, soul, and . . . name a genre. Banjos popped up here, synthesizers over there. Merritt was credited with playing nearly sixty instruments, from jugs to musical saw, recorder to vocal effect devices. The group's Claudia Gonson, meanwhile, sang lead on six tracks and dueted with Merritt on **Yeah! Oh, Yeah!** to fortify the theatrical premise. That you can needle-drop anywhere and land on a gem was a testament to what a fabulously rare and accomplished work this was—and is. *–GG*

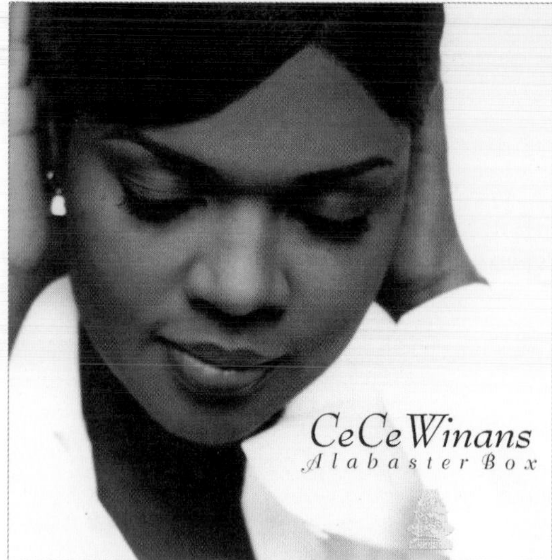

CeCe Winans

ALABASTER BOX

WELLSPRING GOSPEL | Producers: CeCe Winans, Alvin Love

RELEASED: OCTOBER 19, 1999

● To launch her new label, Wellspring Gospel, Grammy-winning CeCe Winans returned to her church roots for her fourth solo release. *Alabaster Box* presented a departure from the more secular Urban Contemporary sounds on her previous solo albums and her duo recordings with her brother BeBe Winans. The title track, written by Dr. Janice Lyn Sjostrand, told the biblical story about the woman who washed Jesus's feet with oil; the song won the 2001 Dove Award for Contemporary Gospel Recorded Song. Winans partnered with fellow Detroit native and gospel sensation Fred Hammond to write and produce four of the tracks on this project, including **King of Kings (He's a Wonder)**, **Love of My Heart**, **Without Love**, and **Higher Place of Praise**. Also featured on the project was the vocal group Take 6, which joined Winans on the track **One and the Same**. Winans's change was welcomed by fans; the collection of spiritually motivated songs hit No. 1 on Billboard's Top Gospel Albums chart as well as No. 5 on the Top Christian Albums. It also earned Winans a gold album as well as a Grammy Award nomination for Best Contemporary Soul Gospel Album. *–CP*

Jason Moran
SOUNDTRACK TO HUMAN MOTION

BLUE NOTE | Producer: Greg Osby

RELEASED: AUGUST 6, 1999

● Pianist Jason Moran emerged on the modern jazz scene with this absorbing debut brimming with spry improvisation and enterprising compositional ideas. Veteran saxophonist Greg Osby was pivotal in the quintet's mix, as a mentor and by adding his textured and wizardly improvisations, while vibraphonist Stefon Harris brightened the overall ensemble sound. Moran's classical influence was evident throughout. The medley **Le Tombeau de Couperin/States of Art** was a virtuoso centerpiece integrating French composer Maurice Ravel's difficult piano suite with Moran's advanced jazz vision. **Root Progression** closed the set with a charismatic duet, playing off Moran's fleet pianism against Osby's ruminating and serpentine soprano sax. *—CH*

Drexciya
NEPTUNE'S LAIR

TRESOR | Producers: James Stinson, Gerald Donald

RELEASED: NOVEMBER 1, 1999

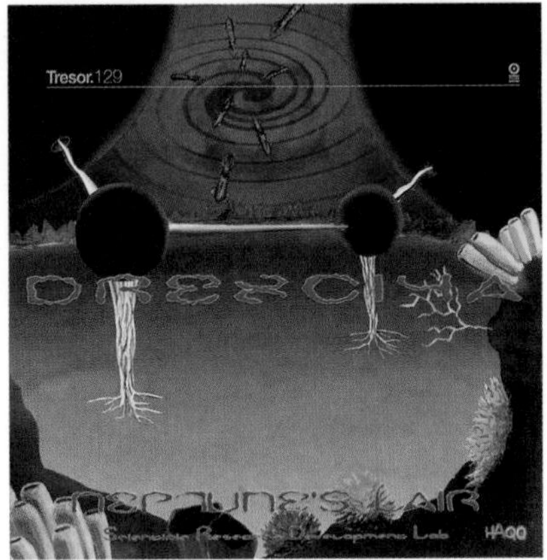

● The Detroit duo of James Stinson and Gerald Donald changed the landscape of electronic music with *Neptune's Lair*, considered one of the most influential and important techno records of all time. The catalyst for the album was to musically tell a fictional story the duo had created about the Drexciyans, a society of underwater sea dwellers. Thick bass lines and dark pulsating rhythms with the infusion of Detroit electro grooves told the tale. Influenced by Cybotron, Kraftwerk, and George Clinton, this has been called *The Matrix* of albums due to the fact that it transported the listener into a mind-altering sonic dimension. *—MH*

Nine Inch Nails
THE FRAGILE

NOTHING/INTERSCOPE | Producers: Trent Reznor, Alan Moulder

RELEASED: SEPTEMBER 21, 1999

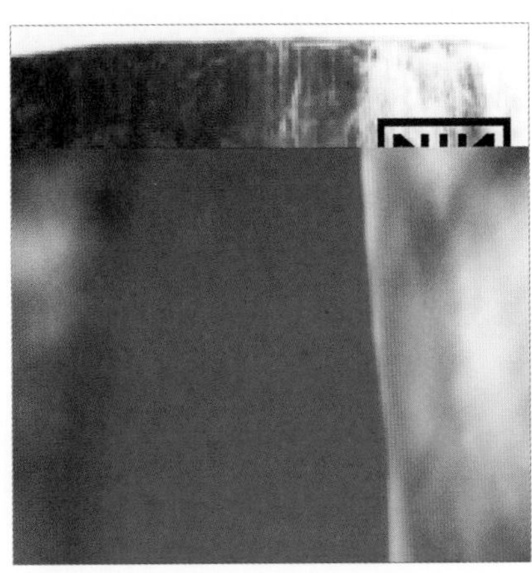

● A full half-decade passed between *The Downward Spiral* and its follow-up, but when industrial rock techno-goth prince Trent Reznor declared he'd "lost my faith in everything" about a minute into *The Fragile*, it was like he'd never left. The sprawling double album clocked in at twenty-three tracks, oscillating between rock-driven epics (**The Day the Whole World Went Away** and **We're in This Together**) and reflective, moody instrumentals (**La Mer** and **Just Like You Imagined**). It offered a deep, foreboding dive into Reznor's tortured psyche, *The Wall* for the Gen-X set, where isolation, paranoia, and fear were matched only by Reznor's sense of beauty in the darkness. *—AG*

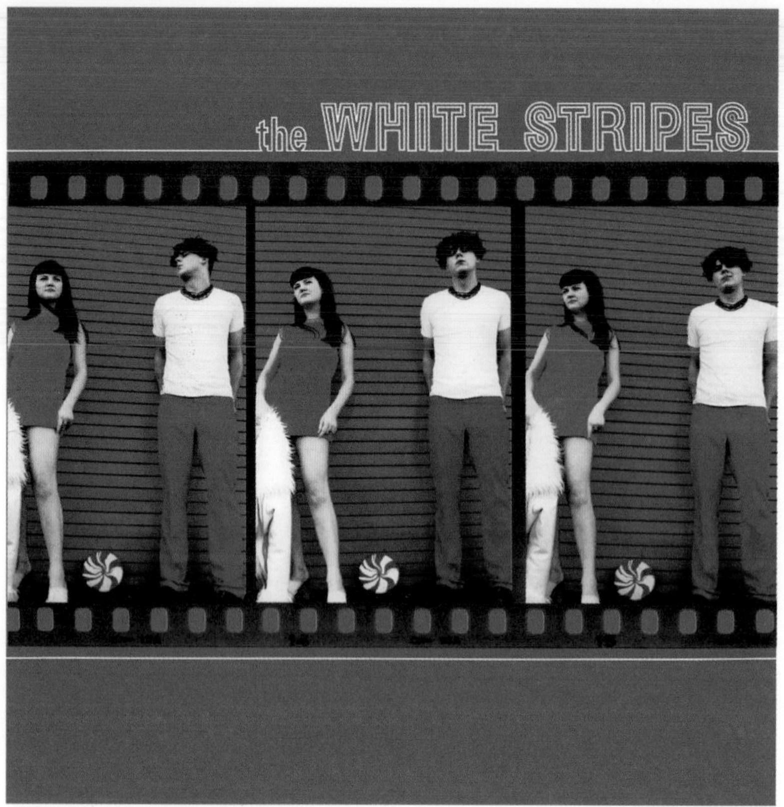

The White Stripes

THE WHITE STRIPES

SYMPATHY FOR THE RECORD INDUSTRY
Producers: Jack White, Jim Diamond

RELEASED: JUNE 15, 1999

● As an upholsterer, Jack White learned a solid frame was key to rehabbing old furniture. At the time, post-grunge rock was becoming like a lifeless, overstuffed couch—so White stripped it all back. Copping it down to a two-seater, cladding it in the visual scheme of peppermint candies, the White Stripes' self-titled debut was built on rock 'n' roll's most functional and sturdy frame—the blues.

The lo-fi intensity of *The White Stripes* created an urgent path forward by recontextualizing the past in a manner that the album's various covers make clear. Be it the noisy, garage-y take on Delta legend Robert Johnson's **Stop Breakin' Down** or **Cannon**, a reinterpretation of Son House's "John the Revelator," White appeared to be saying blues *is* the canon, the yardstick by which rock 'n' roll should be measured. The White Stripes' take was sonically different than earlier groups due in part to the duo's primal minimalism. Meg White's swing, stop-start, and stomp dynamics simplified while elevating tracks such as **Sugar Never Tasted So Good** and **Do** into something bigger than the sums of their parts. Jack's "sister" (actually his then-first wife) held down the beat in the most primitive yet effective way this side of the Velvet Underground's Mo Tucker.

The plaudits for White's guitar playing often gave his vocals short shrift. White's lyrical urgency on this first outing allowed him to cut through and grab listeners by their collars, similar to what made Nirvana's Kurt Cobain so effective but with a tone closer to Led Zeppelin's Robert Plant, minus the operatics. No matter where the White Stripes or Jack White have gone since, this first album truly set the framework for all that would follow. *—RSM*

1999

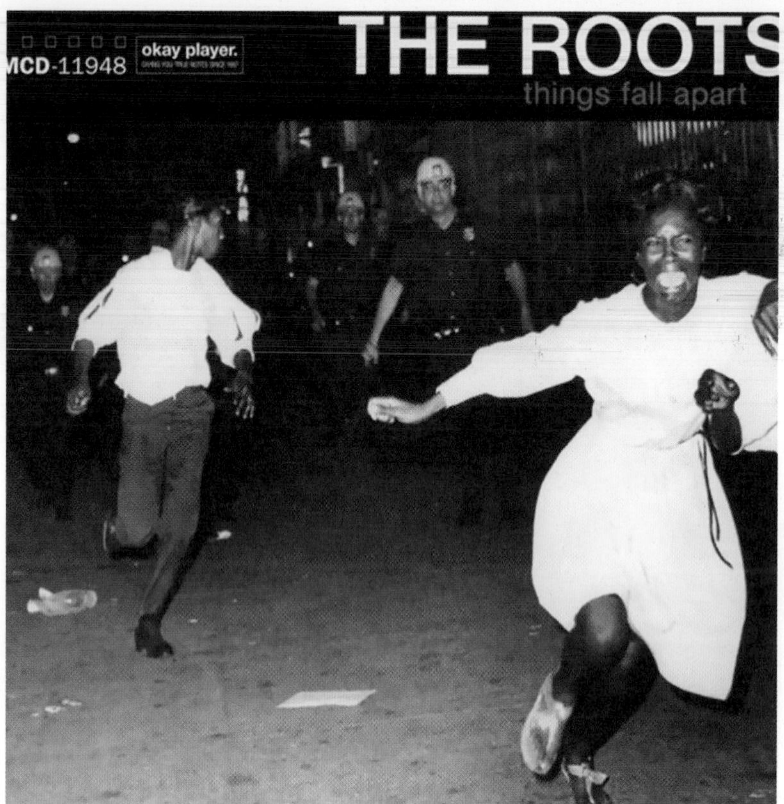

The Roots

THINGS FALL APART

M C A | Producers: The Grand Wizzards, Scott Storch, Jay Dee

RELEASED: FEBRUARY 23, 1999

● The Philadelphia hip-hop troupe's fourth studio album was a landmark for the Soulquarians, the troupe of writers, rappers, musicians, and producers who collaborated on several key works. It came from sessions that also produced D'Angelo's *Voodoo*, Common's *Like Water for Chocolate*, and Erykah Badu's *Mama's Gun*, which all released the following year. Questlove said the Roots worked on more than twelve dozen songs itself. Clearly there was something in the air, and maybe even the water, at Electric Lady Studios in New York City.

Things Fall Apart found the Roots perfecting the lane it had started six years earlier. Black Thought was at his new peak as a lyricist and vocalist, flowing with smooth assurance, high-minded urgency, and a dynamic potency. "From this worthy life you'll soon depart," he promised in **Step Into the Realm**, and throughout the album he made it clear that there's a great deal of work to be done before that happens. Instrumentally the band was even more on point than ever, blending live playing and samples in a rich but spacious sonic tapestry that made sure we felt the songs' impact as they rolled by.

The album's various producers—band members (aka the Grand Wizzards), Scott Storch, and Jay Dee (aka J Dilla)—wove everything together with one mind, and the guests (Common, Mos Def, Eve, Dice Raw, Beanie Segal, DJ Jazzy Jeff, and more) were impactful. *Things Fall Apart* was nominated for a Grammy for Best Rap Album, while the single **You Got Me**, with Badu and Eve, took home the Best Rap Performance by a Duo or Group trophy. It was—without a doubt, as the song said—a moment of perfection, for the Roots and the school of hip-hop the group continues to represent. *—GG*

Rage Against the Machine

THE BATTLE OF LOS ANGELES

EPIC | Producer: Brendan O'Brien

RELEASED: NOVEMBER 2, 1999

● In a decade thick with muddled, unfocused rage, the band with that word right in its name was laser-focused on legitimate left-wing activism. The Los Angeles–based group came out hot with **Testify** and kept the flame high for the majority of its third and final album of original material. Frontman Zack de la Rocha sounded like he'd been off planning the revolution and had come to warn us, while guitarist Tom Morello and the crew backed him with monster riffs and sledgehammer beats. It was so good that the music industry machine gave Rage a Grammy for **Guerilla Radio**. Turn that shhh up! *–SM*

Dido

NO ANGEL

ARISTA | Producers: Dido, Rollo, Rick Nowels

RELEASED: JUNE 1, 1999

● On her debut album, British singer Dido Armstrong married folky pop with electronica-lite touches, like a chillout tent at the Lilith Fair. She sang of love's ups and downs, and **Here With Me** placed her clean, gorgeous vocal delivery underneath a bed of acoustic guitars and stormy hip-hop beats. Dido's brother Rollo Armstrong produced a good chunk of the album, including **Thank You**, a soft, touching ballad about seeing the good through the bad; it became something much darker when it was sampled a year later by Eminem, who built his stalker anthem "Stan" around it, highlighting the haunting qualities of Dido's angelic voice. *–AG*

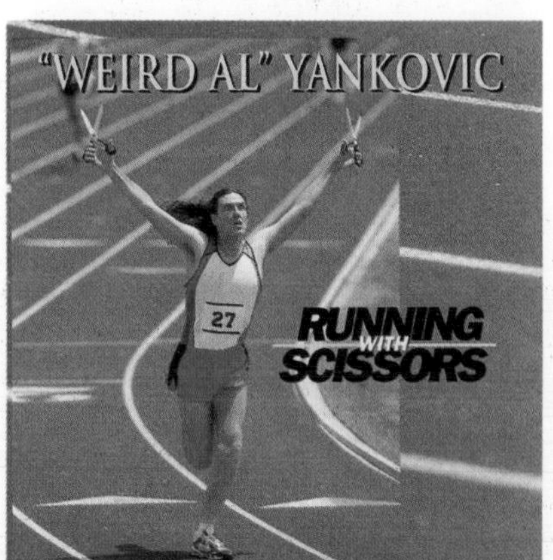

"Weird Al" Yankovic

RUNNING WITH SCISSORS

VOLCANO | Producer: Al Yankovic

RELEASED: JUNE 29, 1999

● "Weird Al" Yankovic was firmly established as the preeminent parody and comedy musician by the time his tenth studio album, *Running With Scissors*, was released. Though it unveiled a new look, sans glasses and moustache, this set provided his loyal fanbase more of the same, leaving no music genre unspoofed as he recast hits by The Offspring, Barenaked Ladies, Puff Daddy, and Cherry Poppin' Daddies, along with originals in the style of Nine Inch Nails and others. But it was **The Saga Begins**, a timely blending of *Star Wars: Episode I* plot points with Don McLean's "American Pie," that pushed *Running With Scissors* to platinum sales. *–JC*

Guster
LOST AND GONE FOREVER

SIRE | Producer: Steve Lillywhite

RELEASED: SEPTEMBER 28, 1999

● When Guster showed up to record its third album, producer Steve Lillywhite quipped the trio had "two rubber bands and a box of soap" in tow, referring to the acoustic guitars and bongos the New England trio typically utilized. In truth, *Lost and Gone Forever* welcomed a wider array of instruments, including strings, horns, and an actual drum kit. The group even incorporated the tapping of a typewriter for **Barrel of a Gun**. The album peaked at No. 169 on the Billboard Top 200, but what it lacked in radio hits the band made up for with a relentlessly loyal fanbase that treated this as a definitive statement. *–JS*

Various Artists
MAGNOLIA (MUSIC FROM THE MOTION PICTURE)

REPRISE | Producers: Jon Brion, Buddy Judge, Aimee Mann, Brendan O'Brien, Michael Penn

RELEASED: DECEMBER 7, 1999

● The soundtrack to Paul Thomas Anderson's sprawling three-hour drama about intertwined lives dealing with regret, forgiveness, and existential angst in suburban Los Angeles made judicious use of limited elements, chiefly Jon Brion's subdued score, a couple of Supertramp needle drops, and nine tracks by Aimee Mann. The soundtrack made a great introduction to the singer/songwriter, who listeners knew mostly via "Voices Carry," a 1985 Top 10 hit for her former band 'Til Tuesday. Mann's haunting cover of Harry Nilsson's **One** was a potent opening track, while her closing number, **Save Me**, was nominated for an Academy Award for Best Original Song. *–RSM*

Linda Ronstadt & Emmylou Harris
WESTERN WALL: THE TUCSON SESSIONS

ASYLUM RECORDS | Producer: Glyn Johns

RELEASED: AUGUST 24, 1999

● Quirkier and more engaging than their *Trio* albums with Dolly Parton, *Western Wall* offered a concise look at the contrasting but complementary vocal styles of its two principals. Linda Ronstadt was a belter whose range at that stage of her career was still astounding. Emmylou Harris, as ever, was an angel flying too close to the ground. The pair brought the heat to compositions by Jackson Browne, Rosanne Cash, Leonard Cohen, Sinéad O'Connor, and Bruce Springsteen, as well as Harris writing on her own and collaborating with Kate and Anna McGarrigle and Luscious Jackson's Jill Cuniff. The only negative here is that the pair didn't make a dozen more albums in the same vein. *–DD*

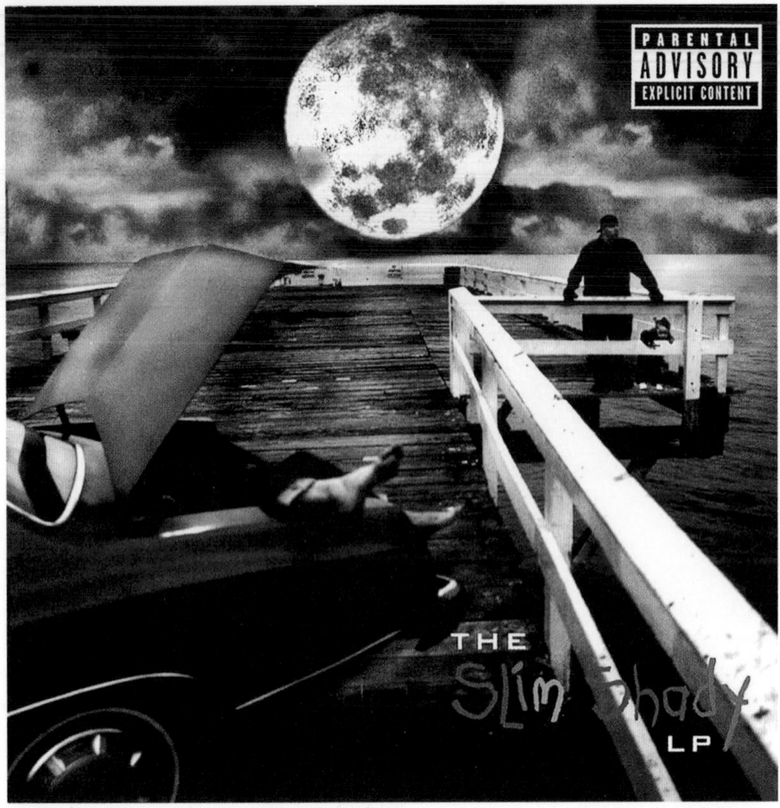

Eminem

THE SLIM SHADY LP

AFTERMATH/INTERSCOPE | Producers: Dr. Dre, Eminem, Mark and Jeff Bass

RELEASED: FEBRUARY 23, 1999

● It took just six words—"Hi kids, do you like violence?"—for Eminem to become pop's new favorite villain. The wholesomely named Marshall Mathers III appeared out of nowhere on *Total Request Live* during the winter of 1999 with ready-made good looks and a goofy, satirical demeanor. It was immediately clear he was ready to cause havoc.

My Name Is was the colorful introduction into Eminem's dark world. He grew up poor, bullied, and abused in a trailer park near Eight Mile Road in Detroit, and hip-hop was not only his only solace—it was his only hope. After nearly flunking out of music with his independently released 1996 album *Infinite*, his songs eventually found the ear of Interscope's Jimmy Iovine, who passed them on to Dr. Dre. The super-producer knew he'd heard something special, and in Dre, Eminem found a kindred spirit whose co-sign gave him instant credibility in the rap world, where white MCs still faced questions of legitimacy.

Eminem had the skills to back everything up, which fans discovered as they dove into *The Slim Shady LP*'s twenty tracks. It's a demented world of drug abuse, family drama, and upside-down pop culture references, delivered with a sinister sense of humor and a dizzying rhyme style that compounded syllables and internal rhyme schemes on top of each other until they folded into themselves.

Dre handled production on three tracks, including **My Name Is** and **Guilty Conscience**, in which he and Em played the angel and devil on a series of characters' shoulders. But it wasn't all fun and games: **'97 Bonnie & Clyde** was a pitch-black murder fantasy that showed off Em's storytelling skills and introduced his own angel and devil, his daughter Hailie and his on-again, off-again love interest Kim, subjects who would be long-running figures in his history-making career. *–AG*

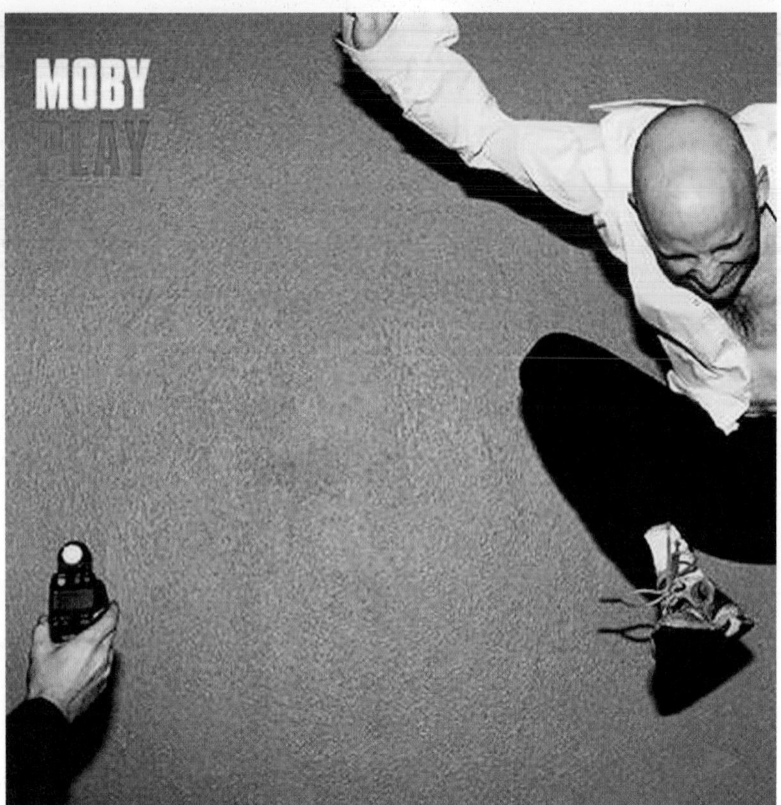

Moby

PLAY

MUTE/V2 | Producer: Moby

RELEASED: MAY 17, 1999

● Moby's commercial breakthrough came with his fifth studio set, which found him layering old soul and gospel samples over dancefloor beats. The album expanded electronic music's reach and commercial viability and elevated Moby, previously praised in critical and dance music circles, to worldwide star.

Moby had little hope the set would rescue him from his career doldrums. He was coming off 1996's commercially and critically underperforming *Animal Rights* and planned *Play* to be his final album before leaving music for greener pastures. But there was magic in those samples of folk singers Bessie Jones (opener **Honey**), Boy Blue (**Find My Baby**), Vera Hall (**Natural Blues**), and Bill Landford (**Run On**). And while it didn't initially catch fire, *Play* charted for the next two years and produced a whopping eight singles, which allowed for the release of 2000's companion album *Play: The B Sides*.

Recorded in Moby's Manhattan home studio, *Play* didn't always find Moby ceding the spotlight to his crate of samples. He fronted **South Side**, a galvanizing rocker with a pumped-up chorus that became a hit when Gwen Stefani jumped on its remix. He also provided vocals on **Porcelain**, a rush of lovelorn lyrics and down-tempo vibes which caught on when it was featured in *The Beach*, starring Leonardo DiCaprio.

Play helped mark the end of the '90s in more ways than one. Throughout the decade, there was a wariness of "selling out," and mainstream success was perceived to run in opposition to an artist's credibility. Moby blew that paradigm out of the water by licensing every song on *Play* for commercial use, placing its songs in television ads, movies, and TV shows. It helped bring *Play* to the masses, and future generations would adopt Moby's mentality toward licensing, while any stigma associated with that stayed mostly relegated to the '90s. *–AG*

DIESEL

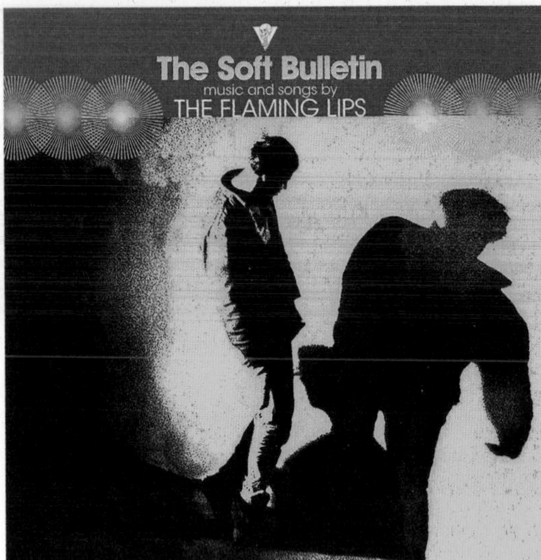

The Flaming Lips

THE SOFT BULLETIN

WARNER BROS. | Producers: The Flaming Lips, Dave Fridmann, Scott Booker

RELEASED: JUNE 22, 1999

● The ninth studio album by the Flaming Lips was a departure from its previous work—and all for the better. It's an album that was best listened to in its entirety rather than picking out individual tracks; it takes you for a ride through luminous soundscapes and lushly arranged melodies that feel like a cohesive, enveloping organism. Introspective and emotional, *The Soft Bulletin* was inspired by what was going on in the band members' lives at the time: frontman Wayne Coyne's father was fighting a losing battle with cancer, reflected in **Waiting for Superman**, while drummer Steven Drozd was dealing with a heroin addiction (he used to tell people the needle tracks were spider bites), and bassist Michael Ivins was in a bizarre car accident, both referenced in **The Spider Bite Song**. The rest of the tracks revolved around the love and loss being experienced at the time, but *The Soft Bulletin* was more inspirational and uplifting than melancholy, and its layered, trippy, orchestral sound broke new ground for the band most people knew for its 1993 hit "She Don't Use Jelly." Britain's *New Musical Express* named *The Soft Bulletin* its album of the year, while *Pitchfork* gave it a rare perfect score. *–MR*

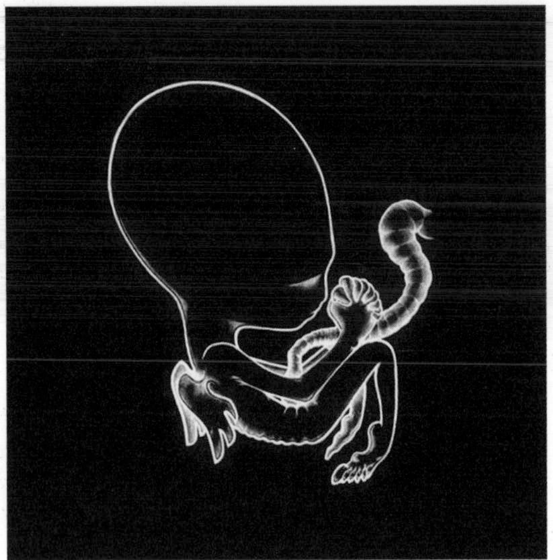

Sigur Rós

ÁGÆTIS BYRJUN

FAT CAT/SMEKKLEYSA | Producer: Ken Thomas

RELEASED: JUNE 12, 1999

● Despite its title, *Ágætis byrjun* (Icelandic for "a good beginning") wasn't post-rock act Sigur Rós's first album but its second. Particularly striking were the soaring vocals of Jón Þór Birgisson (aka Jónsi), who also played guitar, albeit with a cello bow. He sometimes sang in Icelandic, sometimes in the made-up language Vonlenska (Hopelandic). Thus, for most listeners, the songs' meanings were not conveyed by the lyrics but by the music: hushed ambient soundscapes that could suddenly turn explosive, mirroring the band's homeland, an island of volcanos and glaciers.

The band—at the time a quartet comprising Jónsi, keyboardist Kjartan Sveinsson, bassist Georg Hólm, and drummer Ágúst Ævar Gunnarsson—was abetted by occasional brass and a double string octet, making rich orchestrations a part of the distinctive sound. Also evident were experimental and improvised studio techniques: Jónsi singing through his guitar's pickup, various tape manipulations, sampling, and so on. Among the highlight tracks were the meditative, slow-as-molasses **Svefn-g-englar**; the bright, melodic **Starálfur**, perhaps best known for its use in the Wes Anderson film *The Life Aquatic with Steve Zissou*; and the gorgeous, string-laden **Viðrar vel til loftárása**. *Ágætis byrjun* won the US's Shortlist Music Prize in 2001, the first time that award was given. *–DD*

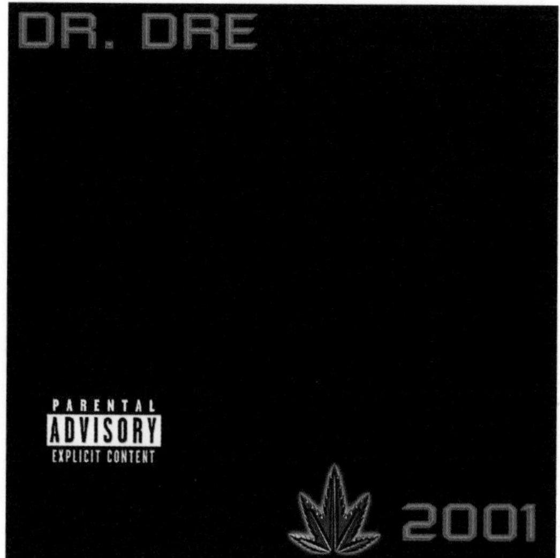

Dr. Dre
2001

AFTERMATH/INTERSCOPE | Producers: Dr. Dre, Mel-Man, Lord Finesse

RELEASED: NOVEMBER 16, 1999

● It's hard to remember a time when Dr. Dre had something to prove. But in countless interviews during the mid- to late '90s, the rapper and super-producer spoke of feeling forced to answer critics—which is exactly how *2001* came about eight years after his groundbreaking solo debut *The Chronic*. As Dre noted in **Still D.R.E.**, he was still "ahead of my game . . . still doing my thang."

An up-and-coming Eminem exploded on **Forgot About Dre**, a violent track about the peril of underestimating the man also known as Andrew Young. Snoop Dogg returned on **The Next Episode**, a gangsta rap masterpiece with a simple beat that drew in the listener with an orchestral arrangement and an iconic drop at the end that encouraged us to "smoke weed every day." In **The Watcher**, Dre pondered the challenges of maturating while staying true to oneself.

Dre shines as a rapper throughout, but he cemented himself as a legendary producer in the process—and the sound was a matured edition of the West Coast G-funk that he pioneered years earlier. With *2001*, Dre accomplished what he was out to prove: that he hadn't lost a step and that he was even more dominant than before. *–ZC*

Ricky Martin
RICKY MARTIN

COLUMBIA | Producers: Desmond Child, Draco Rosa, Emilio Estefan, Jon Secada, George Noriega, Madonna, William Orbit, Randall Barlow, Walter Afanasieff, Juan Vicente Zambrano

RELEASED: MAY 11, 1999

● Ricky Martin lit a fire—literally—with his dynamic performance at the 41st Annual Grammy Awards in February 1999. The Anglo pop audience, under- and mostly unexposed to the Puerto Rican native's four Spanish-language albums (and Martin's tenure with the boy band Menudo), was united in a collective wonderment of "Who *is* this guy?" They learned soon enough as *Ricky Martin* followed three months later, its crossover success guaranteed by proven writer/producer hitmakers such as Diane Warren, Desmond Child, Walter Afanasieff, Jon Secada, Eric Bazilian and Robert Hyman of the Hooters, and even Madonna, who dueted with Martin on **Be Careful (Cuidado Con Mi Corazón)**.

It was the arrival moment for the Latin pop movement; the album debuted at No. 1 on the Billboard 200 with the largest first-week sales for any pop or Latin artist ever and ultimately went seven-times platinum. The banging, brassy **Livin' La Vida Loca** topped the Billboard Hot 100 and Latin charts, and the lush ballad **She's All I Ever Had** was also a massive hit. By the time the dust settled, Martin had every reason to be shaking his bon-bon, just like those listening to him. *–GG*

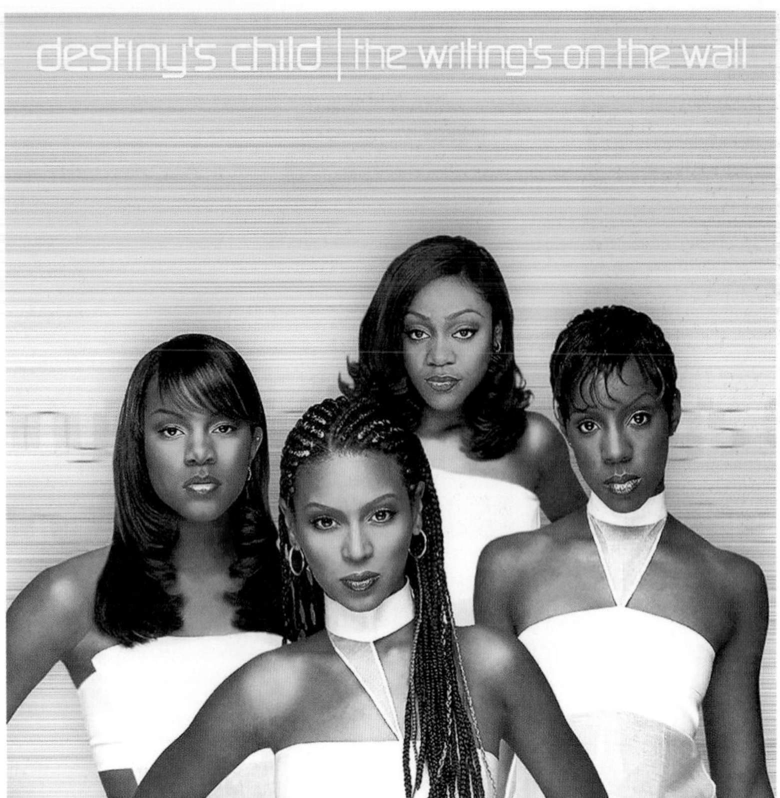

Destiny's Child

THE WRITING'S ON THE WALL

COLUMBIA | Producers: Jovonn Alexander, Kevin "She'kspere" Briggs, Donnie "D-Major" Boynton, Chad "Dr. Ceuss" Elliott, Missy Elliott, Ken "K-Fam" Fambro, Anthony Hardy, Donald Holmes, Oshea Hunter, Rodney Jerkins, Beyoncé Knowles, Platinum Status, Daryl Simmons, Chris Stokes, Terry T, Gerard Thomas, D'wayne Wiggins

RELEASED: JULY 14, 1999

● This is the album that made Beyoncé a star. Following the collective shrug that greeted Destiny's Child's self-titled debut in 1998, the Houston R&B quartet—led by Beyoncé Knowles and managed by her father, Mathew—went all in for the follow-up. Enlisting an army of the best and biggest songwriters and producers of the time, the group spared no time or expense. Recorded over a six-month period at more than a dozen studios across the country, the album became a beacon for R&B-based pop music moving into the twenty-first century. More importantly, it showcased the growing talents of the then-seventeen-year-old Beyoncé.

The album was preceded by the single **Bills, Bills, Bills**, which became the first of four chart-toppers just days after the LP's release in mid-July. A second song, **Bug a Boo**, came out a week before the album and stalled outside the Top 30, but the next two singles—**Say My Name** and **Jumpin', Jumpin'**—reached No. 1 and 3, respectively. By the end of summer, *The Writing's on the Wall* had peaked at No. 5 on its way to more than eight million copies sold.

Although behind-the-scenes turmoil threatened to derail the group—two members were replaced by Mathew Knowles months after the album's release, and one of those lasted less than half a year, whittling down the group to a trio—Destiny's Child continued to thrive into the 2000s, until Beyoncé's solo career, launched with *Dangerously in Love* in 2003, took precedence. *The Writing's on the Wall* remains the group's most pivotal work, a state-of-the-art semi-concept album whose pop/R&B hybrid provided a template for the coming new century. *–MG*

Mos Def

BLACK ON BOTH SIDES

RAWKUS | Producers: Mos Def, Diamond D, Ge-ology, 88-Keys, DJ Premier, Ayatollah, D Prosper, Ali Shaheed Muhammad, Psycho Les, DJ Etch-A-Sketch, David Kennedy

RELEASED: OCTOBER 12, 1999

● Mos Def's breakthrough came in 1998 with the release of *Mos Def & Talib Kweli Are Black Star*, but the Brooklyn rapper's masterpiece arrived the following year with his solo debut. *Black on Both Sides* blended social consciousness, live instruments, and some well-placed samples (from Aretha Franklin to Kraftwerk to KC & the Sunshine Band), resulting in a record that helped hip-hop swing back from the increasingly tiresome gangsta rap that dominated much of the decade. An old-school throwback for a new generation. *–MG*

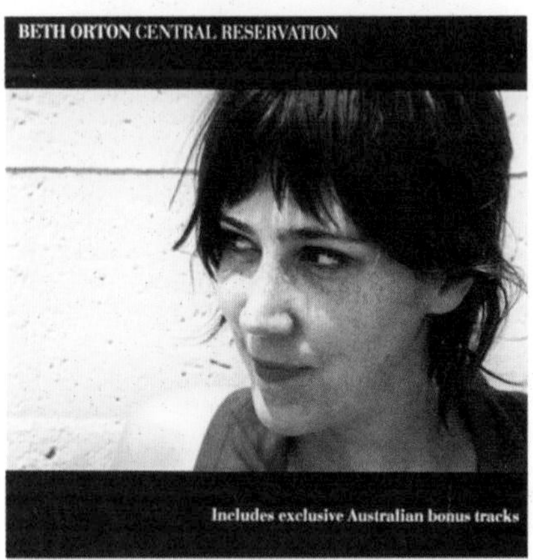

Beth Orton

CENTRAL RESERVATION

HEAVENLY | Producers: Victor Van Vugt, Ben Watt, Mark Stent, Beth Orton, Dr. Robert, David Roback

RELEASED: MARCH 9, 1999

● Bizarrely labeled "folktronica" in some camps, *Central Reservation* was a genre-defying showcase for Beth Orton's exquisite soprano and deep explorations of love, loss, and endurance. Gliding on plump clouds of strings, percussion, vibraphone, keyboards, and guitar, the British singer/songwriter's moody vocals and gently unwinding melodies owed far more to jazz than folk or electronica. These organic arrangements created textures, not styles, and some of the strongest were quite stripped down. Employing only Orton's voice and guitar, **Feel to Believe** gained tsunami-like force before pulling back like a low tide. **Pass in Time** ebbed and flowed like the grief it addresses. End to end, it's gorgeous work. *–LM*

John Prine

IN SPITE OF OURSELVES

OH BOY | Producers: Jim Rooney, John Prine

RELEASED: SEPTEMBER 1999

● For this album of classic country duets, John Prine made a list of his favorite "girl singers" (his words)—including Lucinda Williams, Emmylou Harris, Delores Keane, Patty Loveless, and Iris DeMent—and was delighted when they all signed on. Prine selected songs by several of country music's finest writers, some of whom, no doubt, informed his own smart/sweet/poignant/funny/sad style. The one Prine-penned song (the title track, one of four duets with DeMent) was an absolute hoot. *In Spite of Ourselves* was a triumph, too, in that it was Prine's first album following major surgery for neck cancer. His voice was changed somewhat but lost none of its everyman character. *–DD*

Dan Penn and Spooner Oldham
MOMENTS FROM THIS THEATRE

PROPER | Producer: Bobby Irwin

RELEASED: SEPTEMBER 14, 1999

● The list of artists whom Dan Penn and Spooner Oldham have produced, played behind, and written for is significant. On this album, recorded live in the UK while supporting Nick Lowe, they dished out songs that practically defined soul music. Penn and Oldham, on only acoustic guitar and electric piano, respectively, brought delicate new dimensions to chestnuts such as **Do Right Woman, Do Right Man**, **It Tears Me Up**, and **I'm Your Puppet**, all of which they had a hand in composing. The universal beauty of soul music was on full display here in the hands of masters. *–HK*

Various Artists
RUSHMORE (ORIGINAL MOTION PICTURE SOUNDTRACK)

POLYGRAM | Producer: Mark Mothersbaugh

RELEASED: FEBRUARY 2, 1999

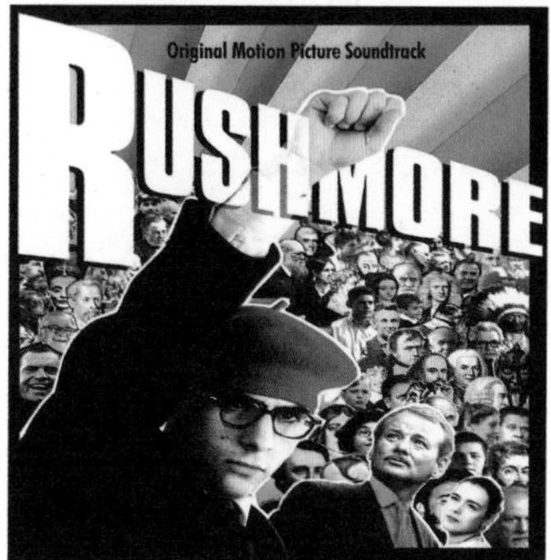

● Part of the allure of Wes Anderson's films—other than his quintessential hyperreal cinematographic style—is his deliberately curated soundtracks, each perfectly complementing the tone of his eccentric films. *Rushmore* was no different. Tracks from The Who, the Kinks, the Faces, and other British "Mod" artists of the '60s created an entirely different mood than your typical '90s coming-of-age story—which this film is not. Composer (and Devo mainstay) Mark Mothersbaugh's original score, featuring almost Baroque-sounding glockenspiel and harpsichord, rounded things out and helped capture the high-society essence of Rushmore Academy and the school's "worst" and most overzealous student, Max Fischer (Jason Schwartzman). *–JS*

Paul McCartney
RUN DEVIL RUN

CAPITOL | Producers: Paul McCartney, Chris Thomas

RELEASED: OCTOBER 4, 1999

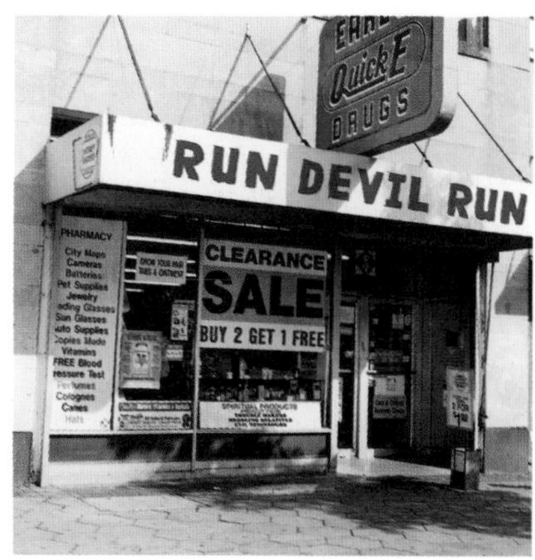

● Paul McCartney ushered out the '90s by returning to his '50s roots. Recorded and released one year after the death of his wife Linda, it was as if McCartney was purging his grief with the album's fifteen tracks, including covers of classics well known (Elvis Presley's **All Shook Up**) and obscure (Dickie Bishop's **No Other Baby**). Three originals reflected the raucous spirit of the music that first enchanted McCartney. *Run Devil Run* was more ferociously focused than McCartney's previous oldies release, 1988's *Choba B CCCP (Back in the USSR)*, thanks, in part, to the contributions of A-list sidemen like Pink Floyd guitarist David Gilmour and Deep Purple drummer Ian Paice. *–BH*

Red Hot Chili Peppers

CALIFORNICATION

WARNER BROS. | Producer: Rick Rubin

RELEASED: JUNE 8, 1999

● On its seventh album, Red Hot Chili Peppers expanded its trademark punk-funk sound and exuberant lyricism to explore themes such as death, suicide, drugs, globalization, and travel—as well as the dichotomy of California, which the quartet called home even though none of its members were natives. The result was a perfect blend of energetic funk-rock jams and softer melodies among its fifteen songs as it became one of the group's best-selling releases.

Much of *Californication*'s success has been attributed to the return of guitarist John Frusciante after a six-year absence and overcoming a drug addiction. Along with his atmospheric playing, Frusciante's reemergence brought the Chili Peppers a rejuvenated sense of passion, enthusiasm, and chemistry. The instrumentalists' interplay was at an all-time high, frontman Anthony Kiedis's singing and rapping at its peak, and the rhythm section of bassist Flea and drummer Chad Smith locked in at its instinctive, powerhouse best. All of that gave the group a No. 3 debut on the Billboard 200 and seven-times platinum sales, equaling 1991's breakthrough *BloodSugarSexMagic*.

Californication also spawned three No. 1 hits on the Alternative Airplay chart. With its mellow intro guitar riff and solo breaks, **Scar Tissue** spent sixteen straight weeks atop Billboard's Modern Rock chart and also won a Grammy for Best Rock Song in 2000. The reflective ballad was based on the band members' experiences with the toll taken by substance abuse. **Otherside**, a thirteen-week chart-topper, also confronted addiction as it paid tribute to original guitarist Hillel Slovak, who died from an overdose in 1980.

The title track, meanwhile, hit No. 1 on both the Mainstream and Modern Rock charts. Its relaxed, infectious tone belied the deeper, darker lyrics striking at the extreme contrasts of the rich, celebrity lifestyle and the dark, desperate underbelly just beneath the surface of the band's home state. *–JC*

Britney Spears

. . . BABY ONE MORE TIME

JIVE | Producers: Max Martin, Eric Foster White

RELEASED: JANUARY 12, 1999

● By the late '90s, teen pop was already infecting the airwaves, thanks to acts such as the Spice Girls, Hanson, and Backstreet Boys. But a former Mickey Mouse Club member from Kentwood, Louisiana, sent the movement into hyperdrive when her debut single and its commanding three-note opening salvo—dun-DUN-DUN—arrived during the fall of 1998.

That single, **. . . Baby One More Time**, introduced the world to Britney Spears, and it would bridge the gap between the sound of the '90s and the decade to come. "Oh bay-buh, bay-buh," Spears cooed over producer Max Martin's peremptory synths, and before you knew it, boy bands and bare-midriffed girls were flooding the charts and blasting out of middle-school hallways everywhere, while MTV's *TRL* became the pop world's favorite after-school hangout.

Spears, doe-eyed and full of Southern charm, was just seventeen when the . . . *Baby One More Time* album was released the following January. It started out at the top of the Billboard 200 and ultimately spent six weeks at No. 1, producing four more singles, including the sugary-sweet mid-tempo love song **Sometimes** and the propulsive dance track **(You Drive Me) Crazy**. Elsewhere there's a handful of syrupy ballads (**Born to Make You Happy**, **From the Bottom of My Broken Heart**), a Sonny & Cher cover (**The Beat Goes On**), a duet with the never-to-be-heard-from-again Don Philip (**I Will Still Love You**), a fizzy reggae-lite beachside bop (**Soda Pop**), and an adorably goofy ode to emerging technology (**E-Mail My Heart**). Mostly it's a young artist trying on a lot of styles to see what works best and discovering her voice in the process.

Spears went on to become a generation-defining star, for reasons right and wrong. But her journey—"Miss American Dream since I was seventeen," she'd later sing—started here. *–AG*

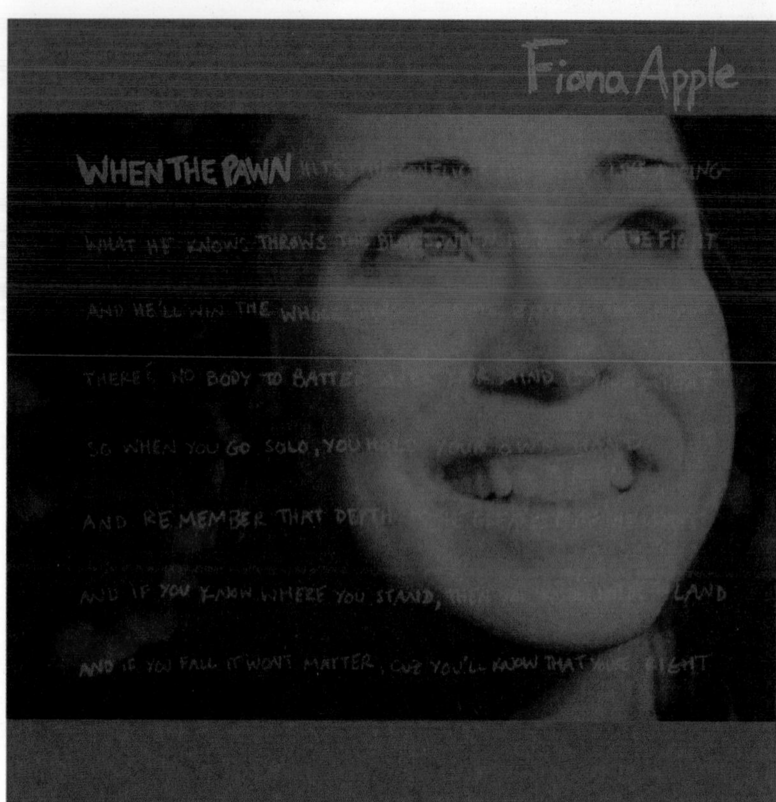

Fiona Apple

WHEN THE PAWN . . .

EPIC | Producer: Jon Brion

RELEASED: NOVEMBER 9, 1999

● Fiona Apple's 1996 debut album *Tidal* merely hinted at what the New York City singer/songwriter was capable of. The surprise chart hit "Criminal" gave her the bargaining muscle to make her next LP with less label interference, and Apple took full advantage of her growing creative control, from the second album's full ninety-word title (Google it) to more deliberately arty songs with elaborate string arrangements and oddball percussion backing.

More confident in her songwriting three years removed from *Tidal*, the twenty-two-year-old Apple balanced sexual fearlessness with relationship insecurities on *When the Pawn . . .*, following the line "When I think of it, my fingers turn to fists" with a defiant "It won't be long till you'll be lying limp in your own hands" (in **Limp**). She sounded both anguished and angry throughout *When the Pawn . . .*, exasperated and exhilarated in her new freedom. From the opening **On the Bound**, with its skipping piano and ghostly synthesizers, the album sounds like a makeover and reinvention for one of the most restless artists of the twentieth century.

Producer Jon Brion had no small part in sculpting the sound of *When the Pawn . . .*, applying intricate grace notes to all ten songs. Apple would later co-produce her albums, but Brion's influence runs through her catalog—she's never had a more compatible collaborator. But make no mistake: *When the Pawn . . .* was Apple's show. Her singing was stronger, as were her compositions. **Paper Bag** and **Fast As You Can**, both extensions of her early-twenties neuroses, were among her best songs and helped sketch out her future songwriting. Bolder, more accomplished records were to come. *When the Pawn . . .* planted the seeds. *–MG*

Shelby Lynne

I AM SHELBY LYNNE

ISLAND | Producer: Bill Bottrell

RELEASED: APRIL 1999

● Among the absurdities the Grammy Awards have produced over the years, the honor accorded Shelby Lynne for *I Am Shelby Lynne* was a doozie. Not that she didn't deserve recognition, but Lynne won in the category of Best New Artist—never mind that *I Am . . .* was her sixth album in a career that dated back more than a decade. But let's give the Grammy apparatus a break; the album was such a departure for the Alabama-raised singer that it's not hard to imagine that this was perhaps an entirely different person.

Lynne spent most of the late '80s and early '90s as a Music Row country aspirant interpreting contributed songs. An early sign of rebellion came when Lynne left Epic Records to record the 1993 Western swing–influenced *Temptation* and 1995's *Restless*. But the real change was when Lynne stepped out of Nashville, making camp at studios in Alabama and California with a new producer, Bill Bottrell, a veteran of Michael Jackson, ELO, and Tom Petty albums who was better recognized for Sheryl Crow's career-making *Tuesday Night Music Club*.

Lynne's sixth album opened with the bold **Your Lies**, perhaps best described as (Phil) Spectorian Americana, channeled the Delta rasp of Bobbie Gentry in **Leavin'** and **Why Can't You Be**, and evoked Dusty Springfield in **Thought It Would Be Easier** and **Gotta Get Back**. Buoyed by Bottrell on keyboards and spare, effective guitar from Roger Fritz, the songs struck a soulful, jazz-tinged groove all their own.

Lynne said of *I Am Shelby Lynne*, "Every song is about true feelings. Pain, loneliness, and being cheated—a record of the acceptance of me." Sonically, it was one part Sheryl Crow, one part Bonnie Raitt but most importantly defined the newly resolute Shelby Lynne. *–DD/CB*

Dixie Chicks

FLY

MONUMENT | Producers: Blake Chancey, Paul Worley

RELEASED: AUGUST 31, 1999

● When the Chicks released *Fly*, its second album as a trio and fourth overall, the group was still whistling Dixie—not the tune or the fraught history with which the word is laden. It was just the trio's name.

Back then, Natalie Maines, Martie Seidel (now Maguire), and Emily Robison (now Strayer) were the toast of Nashville. Having broken through with 1997's *Wide Open Spaces*, the group was regularly flying high on the country charts, singlehandedly outselling all other country acts combined (seriously) and raking in awards. *Fly*, not surprisingly, debuted at No. 1 on the Billboard 200 as well as the Top Country Albums chart. It spun off eight singles, two of which—**Cowboy Take Me Away** and **Without You**—were country No. 1s, while four others went Top 10. It was a critical and commercial juggernaut, just like its predecessor.

Was that because of the songs? The band members wrote or co-wrote many of them, collaborating with or covering some of Nashville's ace tunesmiths. Or maybe the performances? Seidel and Robison especially are skilled instrumentalists, and Maines took the Chicks to another level vocally. Then, too, the album was musically adventurous, stepping outside the constraints of mainstream country—but not too far. The group courted some controversy with the empowering, reverse-gender murder ballad **Goodbye Earl** and with **Sin Wagon** and its reference to "mattress dancing." But those served to fuel interest rather than repel listeners.

More than anything, *Fly* was simply fun. You could sense the Chicks' joy throughout and feel how hard the group leaned into every last detail. Some darker days were around the corner, but during the last gasp of the twentieth century, the Chicks ruled the roost. ***–DD***

Blink-182

ENEMA OF THE STATE

MCA | Producer: Jerry Finn

RELEASED: JUNE 1, 1999

● Blink-182's third album marked a momentous breakthrough for the irreverently silly skate-punk trio and for pop-punk music in general, helping to spark a mainstream obsession with the genre that lasted well into the early '00s. The group had already established itself with the success of its energetic sophomore album *Dude Ranch* in 1997, which set Blink off on an extended global tour that brought the band to a breaking point—culminating in drummer Scott Raynor's firing.

Guitarist Tom DeLonge and bassist Mark Hoppus pressed on, replacing Raynor with skank beat superstar Travis Barker of the Aquabats to form what became the band's classic lineup for *Enema of the State*. It was also Blink's first release under a major label, a move the band was fiercely criticized for, in typical '90s contrarian hipster fashion. Armed with a larger budget and guidance from punk rock producer Jerry Finn, who worked on Green Day's pivotal 1994 album *Dookie*, a sharper version of Blink-182 emerged.

Though less raw than its previous records, *Enema . . .* retained all the elements that defined the SoCal trio, from tight, catchy hooks and palm-muted power chords to a melancholic air of suburban teenage aimlessness and cheeky lyrics. Blink never took itself too seriously, and we loved them for it. *Enema . . .*'s three singles—**What's My Age Again**, **All the Small Things**, and **Adam's Song**—were inescapable on alternative radio at the time and became permanent fixtures on MTV's *Total Request Live* for months.

The album peaked at No. 1 on the Billboard 200, selling more than fifteen million copies worldwide. While it was predictably chided by some purist punk fans and other critics, it's hard to deny the integral role *Enema . . .* played in recalibrating popular music and creating a template still heard decades later. *—JS*

Backstreet Boys

MILLENNIUM

JIVE | Producers: Max Martin, Kristin Lundin, Rami Yacoub, Robert John "Mutt" Lange, Patrik "The Hitmaker" Lindqvist, Stephen Lipson, Mattias Gustafsson, Timmy Allen, Edwin "Tony" Nicholas, Eric Foster White

RELEASED: MAY 18, 1999

● A boy-band battle was brewing during the mid-'90s. Both Backstreet Boys and *NSYNC had released introductory albums, but Backstreet's *Millennium* was the massive, multiplatinum salvo that took the war for teen-pop supremacy to a new level, selling more than 1.1 million copies in its first week (a new record that *NSYNC would better with *No Strings Attached* in 2000).

Millennium backed up its sales popularity, however. The first three tracks—**Larger Than Life**, **I Want It That Way**, and **Show Me the Meaning of Being Lonely**—packed as powerful a punch as any hit album in history. Billboard even deemed the melodic **I Want It That Way** the greatest boy-band single ever, putting it ahead of offerings from The Jackson 5 and The Beatles. The quintet's third album overall was wildly catchy throughout and dealt in typical subjects surrounding the many angles of young love. *Millennium* plays like a roller coaster, both sonically and stylistically; the ballad **I Need You Tonight** was a proposal of love, followed by the energetic **Don't Want You Back**, about moving on from a breakup. And another dip followed with the quintet crooning about the fear of separation in **Don't Wanna Lose You Now** before finding **The One** in the next track.

Millennium cannot be discussed without mentioning the group's earthshaking appearance on *Total Request Live* to promote it. Per tradition, fans lined up on the sidewalk outside of MTV's Times Square studio; for this episode, New York police had to shut down the intersection to accommodate the screaming thong for an appearance that ranks as an all-time '90s Moment.

Regardless of how one feels about teen pop or boy bands, there's no question that with *Millennium*, Backstreet Boys defined a generational sound that throttled the mainstream for years. *–ZC*

Acknowledgments

The best part of this enterprise was the opportunity to work with so many valued friends and respected colleagues—even if some of them may be cursing the editing changes made to their entries. (None practice voodoo . . . that I know of.) Everybody's skills, hard work, dedication, and enthusiasm were deeply appreciated throughout the project. Special nods go to Daniel Durchholz, Michael Gallucci, Adam Graham, Howard Kramer, and Stacey Sherman, who did extra-heavy lifting both at the beginning of and throughout the process, providing expertise, encouragement, and opinions that helped shape this book and those that will follow.

My thanks also to Dennis Pernu at Quarto. This is our fourth book together, and it's always a pleasure. The Quarto crew—project manager Brooke Pelletier, art director Anne Re, creative director Reg Grenier, and copy editor David Umla—did their usual job of making it look amazing; and marketing manager Steve Roth once again beat the drum tirelessly to get the word out.

I am genuinely blessed to work day to day with colleagues who make the hard work worthwhile and even more rewarding, including, in no particular order, Michael Norman, Joe Lynch, Matthew Wilkening, Michael Gallucci, Jason Alley, Steve Frye, Brian Johnston, Eric Jenson, Bob Madden, Brian Nelson, Borna Velic, Zach Clark, Howard Handler, Kim Klein, Bryant Fillmore, Carly Somers, Kelly Franz, Clare Baker, Jackie Headapohl, Alicyn Hanford, Shannon McCombs, Joseph Maltese, Drew Lane, Marc Fellhauer, Mark Nardone, Sian Llewellyn, and Ryan Borba. Regards, too, to my Detroit Music Awards family: Stacey Sherman, Jim Edelman, Joe Bellanca, Howard Hertz, Jim Reid, Kent Agee, and the rest of that crew.

And to my real family—Stacey, Hannah, Josh, Ben, Sean, Ari, Harvey, and Vicki—much love and appreciation for the support and encouragement that helps keep, as Queen would say, my rockin' world go 'round.

Photo Credits

Alamy Stock Photos: 15 (dpa), 19 (Pictorial Press), 23 (Pictorial Press), 39 (dpa), 45 (mark reinstein), 49 (dpa), 53 (ZIK Images), 55 (Kevin Estrada/MediaPunch), 59 (Kevin Estrada/MediaPunch), 67 (Trinity Mirror/Mirrorpix), 77 (Pat Johnson/MediaPunch), 85 (Barry King), 109 (Trinity Mirror/Mirrorpix), 111 (Barry King), 115 (John Atashian), 123 (dpa), 139 (MediaPunch), 163 (TBM/United Archives GmbH), 193 (Demed), 211 (Rob Watkins), 219 (©RTMcafee/MediaPunch), 239 (Pictorial Press), 265 (dpa), 269 (Simon Meaker), 277 (Fabio Diena), 281 (Scott Weiner/MediaPunch), 317 (Mel Longhurst/Performing Arts Images www.performingartsimages.com), 321 (Pictorial Press), 327 (Fabio Diena), 331 (Allstar Picture Library), 335 (jeremy sutton-hibbert), 355 (Fabio Diena), 363 (Rob Watkins), 369 (Rob Watkins), 373 (Sueddeutsche Zeitung Photo), 377 (Pictorial Press), 381 (© Globe Photos ZUMA Press), 391 (Scott Weiner/MediaPunch), 403 (© RTCanova/MediaPunch), 417 (Edd Westmacott), 419 (James Arnold), 423 (Robert Hoetink), 427 (Janerik Henriksson/TT News Agency).

AP Photos: 99 (Mark Humphrey), 129 (Ross Marino Archive/MediaPunch), 143 (©RTNVictor/MediaPunch/IPX), 179 (Chris Martinez), 243 (Bebeto Matthews), 247 (Robert F. Bukaty), 251 (Jim Cooper), 259 (Stefan Rousseau), 285 (*Houston Chronicle*/Paul Howell), 307 (Ron Frehm), 345 (Joe Fudge/*The Daily Press*), 359 (Eckehard Schulz), 395 (Kevork Djansezian), 433 (James Nielsen/*Houston Chronicle*).

Getty Images: 27 (Avalon/Hulton Archive), 31 (Al Pereira/Michael Ochs Archives), 63 (Kevin Mazur/WireImage), 69 (Gie Knaeps), 73 (MPIRock/MediaPunch), 83 (Niels van Iperen/Hulton Archive), 89 (Paul Natkin/WireImage), 93 (Al Pereira/Michael Ochs Archives), 103 (Al Pereira/Michael Ochs Archives), 105 (Chris Carroll/Corbis Entertainment), 119 (Steve Eichner/WireImage), 133 (Steve Rapport/Hulton Archive), 149 (David Corio/Redferns), 153 (David Corio/Redferns), 157 (Paul Natkin/WireImage), 169 (Jim Steinfeldt/Michael Ochs Archives), 175 (Brian Rasic/Hulton Archive), 183 (Gie Knaeps/Hulton Archive), 189 (Ebet Roberts/Redferns), 197 (Lindsay Brice/Michael Ochs Archives), 203 (Koh Hasebe/Shinko Music/Hulton Archive), 207 (KMazur/WireImage), 215 (Rick Diamond), 225 (Mick Hutson/Redferns), 229 (Larry Hulst/Michael Ochs Archives), 233 (L. Busacca/Michael Ochs Archives), 291 (Kevin Mazur/WireImage), 297 (Jeffrey Mayer/WireImage), 303 (Gary Reyes/*Oakland Tribune* Staff Archives/MediaNews Group/Bay Area News), 341 (Mark Peterman/WireImage), 349 (Mick Hutson/Redferns), 385 (Alex Wong/Hulton Archive), 407 (Victor Spinelli/WireImage), 411 (Gie Knaeps/Hulton Archive), 413 (Paul Natkin), 429 (Diena/Brengola/WireImage).

Index

A

B

C

D

E

F

G

H

I

J

K

N

O

P

Q

R

S

T

U

V

W

INDEX

X

Y

Z